INTERNATIONAL HUMAN RIGHTS LAW

Other books in the *Essentials of Canadian Law* Series

ESSENTIALS OF
CANADIAN LAW

INTERNATIONAL HUMAN RIGHTS LAW

MARK FREEMAN
GIBRAN VAN ERT

IRWIN
LAW

International Human Rights Law
© Irwin Law Inc., 2004

Published in 2004 by

Irwin Law
347 Bay Street
Suite 501
Toronto, Ontario
M5H 2R7
www.irwinlaw.com

ISBN: 1-55221-094-4

Library and Archives Canada Cataloguing in Publication

Freeman, Mark, 1968–
    International human rights law / Mark Freeman, Gibran van Ert.

Includes bibliographical references and index.

ISBN 1-55221-094-4

    1. Human rights. I. Van Ert, Gibran, 1973– II. Title.

K3240.F74 2004   341.4'8   C2004-903427-8

The publisher acknowledges the financial support of the Government of Canada through the Book Publishing Industry Development Program (BPIDP) for its publishing activities.

Printed and bound in Canada.

1 2 3 4 5   07 06 05 04 03

SUMMARY
TABLE OF CONTENTS

DETAILED
TABLE OF CONTENTS

RECEPTION OF SPECIFIC INTERNATIONAL HUMAN RIGHTS *215*

CHAPTER 13:
CANADIAN HUMAN RIGHTS MECHANISMS 348

CHAPTER 14:
UN HUMAN RIGHTS MECHANISMS 383

FOREWORD

This book deserves a very warm reception. It is timely and relevant, appearing as international human rights law itself is promoting and shaping the globalisation of a culture of rights. As the first comprehensive Canadian international human rights law text, this volume provides a particularly illuminating Canadian perspective and approach to the subject, including a very useful consideration of our domestic reception of international human rights law. In filling this lacuna in the literature, I expect this work to reduce the reliance previously placed by Canadian students and instructors on materials developed with American and British audiences in mind. As if this were not enough, compounding the value of the text's unique Canadian perspective, timeliness, and relevance, is the obvious care and exhaustiveness with which it has been researched and the accessible style in which it is written.

Although the roots of international human rights law can be traced back at least several centuries, as Freeman and van Ert ably explain, it only recently emerged as an independent field of law with developments in the aftermath of the Second World War. Prominent among these postwar developments were the formation of the United Nations in 1945 and the adoption and proclamation by the General Assembly of the Universal Declaration of Human Rights on 10 December 1948. The authors skilfully link the *Canadian Charter of Rights and Freedoms* to this parentage, while others, including the courts, have been more tentative, or "opaque," as the authors put it, in doing so.

Apart from the immense value of their work to a Canadian audience, Freeman and van Ert have provided a useful synthesis of the international dimensions of human rights law by describing in considerable detail the history, the content, and the application of the various extant United Nations and regional human rights instruments. In addition, the authors expertly outline the major mechanisms through which international human rights laws are promoted and protected, a topic that is of crucial importance as the field continues to develop and realize its potential for the widespread betterment of the human condition.

I will only add that the concluding chapter on Contemporary Trends and Issues invites a full companion volume, or an expanded second edition, to tackle more comprehensively the difficult related issues of terrorism, humanitarian intervention, and UN reform, to take just a few of the topics addressed in the conclusion. This is not meant as criticism. There is no greater compliment to an author than to regret that a book is inevitably coming to an end.

Ottawa, 24 March 2004

THE HONOURABLE MADAM JUSTICE LOUISE ARBOUR
SUPREME COURT OF CANADA

(Appointed United Nations High Commissioner for Human Rights)

PREFACE

The last fifty years have witnessed the development of a global system of human rights promotion and protection. Canada has played a significant role in its growth and there is every indication it will continue to do so. Canada has ratified and implemented most major international human rights treaties and actively participates in most multilateral human rights institutions. We might say that human rights have become part of the Canadian identity.

It is surprising, then, that a comprehensive, textbook-style account of international human rights law has never before been undertaken for a Canadian audience. This book is our attempt to meet this need and, in doing so, to encourage greater understanding and use of international human rights law by Canadian litigants, lawyers, and judges. We have not, however, written this book with the Canadian legal audience exclusively in mind. To the contrary, we have made a conscious effort to reach non-Canadian and non-legal audiences too.

International human rights law is a vast field whose borders are not always clear. In recognition of this, we have included brief but (we hope) helpful discussions of four areas of international law closely related to human rights: international labour, refugee, humanitarian, and criminal law. There are still more human rights-related topics we were forced to exclude. We have not, for instance, appraised the social or legal history of human rights in Canada. Nor have we examined such topics as conflict prevention, disarmament, global trade, and economic development. We hope the strengths of what we have included will outweigh the book's inevitable limitations.

We have organized the book into three parts. The first part introduces the international law of human rights — its history, its theoretical underpinnings, and its requirements. The second part describes the reception of international human rights law in Canada, including general reception rules and the reception of specific human rights norms into Canadian law. The third part examines the main Canadian and multilateral mechanisms responsible for promoting and protecting human rights. The book concludes with a series of short essays on contemporary trends and issues in the field. Readers may also wish to consult the companion volume to this book — *International Human Rights Law: Texts, Cases, and Materials* — which is also available from Irwin Law.

This work takes account of the law as it stood on 1 June 2004, except where otherwise noted. All website references are current as of 1 June 2004.

The authors welcome comments on the book. They can be reached by e-mail at markfreeman01@hotmail.com and gib@gibvanert.com.

MARK FREEMAN   GIBRAN VAN ERT
Toronto   Vancouver

ACKNOWLEDGMENTS

The authors gratefully acknowledge the assistance of Sharryn Aiken, Ben Berger, Federico Borello, Anthony di Caprio, Laila Demirdache, Claire and David Freeman, Nicos Fassler, Joanna Harrington, Andrew Matheson, Stefan Matiation, Hanny Megally, John Mihevc, Roger O'Keefe, Goro Onojima, Joanna Quinn, Ena Paul, Sacha Paul, Stéphanie Sirois, and Marieke Wierda. Mark Freeman is particularly grateful to Betty Feder, Sarah Hellmann, Adela Mall, and Norma Won for their extensive editorial assistance, and to Annamie Paul for her tremendous love and support throughout the writing of this book. Gib van Ert wishes to express his gratitude to Claude Beaulne, Leslie Hinds, Alicia Loo and the rest of the staff of the Library of the Supreme Court of Canada. He also wishes to acknowledge the support of the Lauterpacht Research Centre for International Law, University of Cambridge, and the Vancouver offices of Borden Ladner Gervais LLP. Finally, both authors are especially grateful to Stephen Toope for his comments on the final manuscript, and to William Kaplan, Jeffrey Miller, Catherine Hatt, and Heather Raven at Irwin Law.

ABBREVIATIONS

AfrCHPR	African Charter on Human and Peoples' Rights 1981
AfrCHPR Women's Protocol	Protocol to the African Charter on Human and Peoples' Rights on the Rights of Women in Africa 2003
ACHR	American Convention on Human Rights 1969
ACHR-OP1	Additional Protocol to the American Convention on Human Rights in the Area of Economic, Social and Cultural Rights 1988
ACHR-OP2	Protocol to the American Convention on Human Rights to Abolish the Death Penalty 1990
AJIL	American Journal of International Law
AmDR	American Declaration on the Rights and Duties of Man 1948
AU	African Union
Bill of Rights	*Canadian Bill of Rights*, SC 1960, c. 44
CanTS	Canada Treaty Series
CAT	Convention Against Torture and Other Cruel, Inhuman or Degrading Treatment or Punishment 1984
CAT-OP	Optional Protocol to the Convention Against Torture and Other Cruel, Inhuman or Degrading Treatment or Punishment 2002
CEDAW	Convention on the Elimination of All Forms of Discrimination Against Women 1979
CEDAW-OP	Optional Protocol to the Convention on the Elimination of All Forms of Discrimination Against Women 1999
CERD	International Convention on the Elimination of All Forms of Racial Discrimination 1966

Charter	*Canadian Charter of Rights and Freedoms*, Part I of the *Constitution Act 1982* being Schedule B to the *Canada Act 1982* (UK) 1982 c. 11, s. 33
Common Article 3	Article 3 common to each of the four Geneva Conventions of 1949
Constitution Act 1867	*Constitution Act 1867* (UK). 30 & 31 Vict. c. 3, reprinted in RSC 1985 App. II No. 5. Formerly the *British North America Act* 1867
Constitution Act 1982	*Constitution Act 1982*, being Schedule B to the *Canada Act 1982* (UK) 1982 c. 11, s. 33
CRC	Convention on the Rights of the Child 1989
CRC-OP-AC	Optional Protocol to the Convention on the Rights of the Child on the involvement of children in armed conflict 2000
CRC-OP-SC	Optional Protocol to the Convention on the Rights of the Child on the sale of children, child prostitution and child pornography 2000
Draft Articles	International Law Commission Draft Articles on Responsibility of States for Internationally Wrongful Acts 2001
ECHR	Convention for the Protection of Human Rights and Fundamental Freedoms 1950 (a.k.a. European Convention on Human Rights), as amended by Protocol nos. 3, 5, 8 and 11.
ECOSOC	UN Economic and Social Council
ECR	European Court Reports
ETS	European Treaty Series
EurSC	European Social Charter (revised) 1996
FC	Canada Federal Court Reports
FCA	Federal Court of Canada, Appeal Division
FCTD	Federal Court of Canada, Trial Division
GA res.	General Assembly resolution
GC1	Geneva Convention for the Amelioration of the Condition of the Wounded and Sick in Armed Forces in the Field 1949
GC2	Geneva Convention for the Amelioration of the Condition of Wounded, Sick and Shipwrecked Members of Armed Forces at Sea 1949
GC3	Geneva Convention relative to the Treatment of Prisoners of War 1949

GC4	Geneva Convention relative to the Protection of Civilian Persons in Time of War 1949
GC Protocol I	Protocol Additional to the Geneva Conventions of 12 August 1949, and relating to the Protection of Victims of International Armed Conflicts (Protocol I) 1977
GC Protocol II	Protocol Additional to the Geneva Conventions of 12 August 1949, and relating to the Protection of Victims of Non-International Armed Conflicts (Protocol II) 1977
Geneva Conventions	Collectively GC1, GC2, GC3, GC4
Genocide Convention	Convention on the Prevention and Punishment of the Crime of Genocide 1948
HL	House of Lords (UK)
ICC Elements of Crimes	Elements of Crimes of the International Criminal Court
ICC Rules	Rules of Procedure and Evidence of the International Criminal Court
ICCPR	International Covenant on Civil and Political Rights 1966
ICCPR-OP1	Optional Protocol to the International Covenant on Civil and Political Rights 1966
ICCPR-OP2	Second Optional Protocol to the International Covenant on Civil and Political Rights, aiming at the abolition of the death penalty 1989
ICESCR	International Covenant on Economic, Social and Cultural Rights 1966
ICJ Rep	International Court of Justice Law Reports
ICJ Statute	Statute of the International Court of Justice 1945
ICRC	International Committee of the Red Cross
ICTR	International Criminal Tribunal for Rwanda
ICTY	International Criminal Tribunal for the former Yugoslavia
IDP	Internally Displaced Person
ILM	International Legal Materials
ILO	International Labour Organization
ILR	International Law Reports (incorporating the Annual Digest and Reports of Public International Law Cases)

Martens Clause	The clause contained in the preamble to the Hague Regulations of 1907 concerning the Laws and Customs of War on Land, and later included in the Geneva Conventions (GC1 art. 63, GC2 art. 62, GC3 art. 142, and GC4 art. 158), GC Protocol I (art. 1) and GC Protocol II (preamble)
MWC	International Convention on the Protection of the Rights of All Migrant Workers and Members of Their Families 1990
NAALC	North American Agreement on Labour Cooperation 1993
NAFTA	North American Free Trade Agreement 1992
NGO	Non-governmental organization
OAS	Organization of American States
OAS TS	OAS Treaty Series
OHCHR	UN Office of the High Commissioner for Human Rights
OSCE	Organization for Security and Cooperation in Europe
Quebec Charter	*Quebec Charter of Human Rights and Freedoms*, RSQ c. C-12
Refugee Convention	Convention Relating to the Status of Refugees 1951
Rome Statute	Rome Statute of the International Criminal Court 1998
SCR	Canada Supreme Court Reports
SC res.	Security Council Resolution
UDHR	Universal Declaration of Human Rights 1948
UNESCO	United Nations Educational, Scientific and Cultural Organization
UNHCR	Office of the United Nations High Commissioner for Refugees
UNICEF	United Nations Children's Fund
UN Charter	Charter of the United Nations 1945
UNTS	United Nations Treaty Series
VCLT	Vienna Convention on the Law of Treaties 1969

PART ONE

THE INTERNATIONAL LAW OF HUMAN RIGHTS

CHAPTER 1

HISTORY OF HUMAN RIGHTS

The field of international human rights law has disparate historical origins. Among the most important early developments were the emergence of public international law and the idea of individual rights in the period following the Treaty of Westphalia 1648. Although historically international law did not embrace individual rights, there were some exceptions in the nineteenth and early twentieth centuries. The formal emergence of the field of international human rights law coincided with the adoption of the Universal Declaration of Human Rights 1948 (UDHR), but even it was preceded by other key events including the adoption of the Charter of the United Nations 1945 (UN Charter), the establishment of the UN, and the international trials of Nuremberg and Tokyo. All of these developments will be reviewed in this chapter, with the exception of the UDHR. It is examined in Chapter Four.

A. THE DEVELOPMENT OF PUBLIC INTERNATIONAL LAW

"Public international law" refers to the corpus of law governing relationships between states. It is to be distinguished from "domestic law" (also known as "municipal" or "national" law), which at its most general level refers to the laws applicable within a state and not between states. It is also to be distinguished from "private international law" (also known as "conflict of laws"), which at its most general level refers to rules of domestic law that govern the relationship between domestic and foreign law in the context of transactions or events that involve one or more foreign elements.

Although there have long been rules about the relationships between states, the advent of public international law is generally agreed to have occurred in Europe following the Peace of Westphalia in 1648. The Peace of Westphalia signalled the end of the Thirty Years' War and marked the creation of the modern independent state. Protestant states had fought the war largely in order to free themselves more fully from the control of the Catholic Church, while member states of the Holy Roman Empire had fought the war largely to free themselves more fully from the Empire. At the end of the war, many of these states became free from their respective sources of external control, acquiring powers to independently enter into and withdraw from treaties with other states, wage war and declare peace, and, most importantly, manage domestic affairs without external interference.[1] Accompanying these events was an emerging scholarship on the idea of international law, led by Hugo Grotius who is often described as the intellectual founder of public international law.[2] This early international law scholarship was focused exclusively on the rights of states. The notion of international human rights was still a long way off.

Over the following two centuries, the newly independent states of Europe increasingly asserted themselves, each centralizing its control over domestic affairs and entrenching its external independence. The interaction among states during this period produced the founding tenets and practices of international law. Three inter-related tenets attained broad acceptance: (i) states are free under international law (and thus only bound by it upon their consent),[3] (ii) states are sovereign under international law (and thus able to exercise exclusive juris-

---

1.   J. Currie, *Public International Law* (Toronto: Irwin Law, 2001) at 6–7.

2   Grotius' principal work on international law is *De Jure Belli ac Pacis Libri Tres* (Three Books on the Law of War and Peace), trans. by F. Kelsey (Oxford: Oxford University Press, 1925) [Grotius, *De Jure Belli ac Pacis Libri Tres*]. Other important scholars of the time (collectively known as the "primitives") included Francisco de Vitoria, Alberico Gentili, and Francisco Suarez.

3   A partial exception to this within contemporary international law is the principle of *jus cogens*, discussed in Chapter Three. For a more general challenge to the consent-based theory of international law, see B. Simma, "From Bilarteralism to Community Interest in International Law" (1994) 250 (VI) Recueil des Cours 221 at 257-27.

diction over their territory and population),[4] and (iii) states are equal as a matter of international law (and thus bound by the same underlying set of international legal principles, rights, and obligations).[5]

This conception of public international law accorded individuals no international legal rights. States were the only lawmakers as well as the only subjects of international law. International law was the "law of nations"; it was not the "law of humans." States could generally treat their own citizens however they wished.

B. THE DEVELOPMENT OF INDIVIDUAL RIGHTS

Concurrent with, but largely independent of the development of public international law, another idea began to take root in Western political thought in the seventeenth century: the idea of individual rights. The idea of rights had its earliest origins in the political, legal, and moral theories of scholars of various ancient civilizations, notably those of Greece and Rome, which drew upon those of Egypt and Sumeria.[6] It was, however, in Europe and America in the seventeenth and eighteenth centuries that the idea of individual rights found its most developed early expression.[7] In particular, philosophers such as John Locke, Baron de Montesquieu, Jean-Jacques Rousseau, and Thomas Paine developed a concept of individual rights based on theories of natural law. The classic expression of this concept is captured in the well-known phrase of Rousseau that "all men are born equal, and with equal natural right."[8]

---

4   This principle is expressly preserved in the Charter of the United Nations 1945 (UN Charter) CanTS no. 7, art. 2(7), which provides in part: "Nothing contained in the present Charter shall authorize the United Nations to intervene in matters which are essentially within the domestic jurisdiction of any state . . . ."

5   The UN Charter, ibid., preserved this principle in art. 2(1). It provides: "The [UN] is based on the principle of the sovereign equality of all its Members."

6   L. Henkin et al., Human Rights (New York: Foundation Press, 1999) at 16.

7   While various other religions and civilizations from Asia and Africa espoused related ideas and values such as equality, justice, and human dignity, none appears to have expressed a modern conception of individual rights (that is, the notion of individual claims upon or against society). See the discussion "Human Rights, History, and Culture" in Chapter Two.

8   The above quote notwithstanding, Rousseau is more often associated with those who partly reject rather than support the idea of individual rights. Rousseau is famous for having argued that after an individual leaves the state of nature and enters into the "social contract," he relinquishes individual entitlements and

This nature-based conception of individual rights was later codified in legal texts such as the American *Declaration of Independence* 1776[9] and the French *Declaration of the Rights of Man and of the Citizen* 1789.[10] Although these declarations were inspired by earlier constitutional documents from England such as the *Magna Carta* 1215,[11] the *Petition of Right* 1627,[12] and the *Bill of Rights 1689*,[13] English law came to affirm the doctrine of parliamentary supremacy and reject limits on state action.[14] There was no equivalent in England to the US *Bill of Rights* 1791, which prohibits the US Congress from enacting any law that would, for example, abridge freedom of speech.[15]

Both in its early and modern expressions, the concept of individual rights remains closely linked to notions of social contract, democracy, limited government, liberty, equality, liberalism, and constitutionalism — and later, in the writings of Immanuel Kant, human dignity.[16] Rights are a kind of legal proposition about the relationship between the state and its subjects, the proposition being that the state's powers in respect

---

becomes subject to the "general will" of society. See generally *The Social Contract* (1762), trans. by G.D.H. Cole (London: J.M. Dent, 1913).

9   The preamble to the *Declaration* famously provides: "We hold these truths to be self-evident, that all men are created equal, that they are endowed by their Creator with certain unalienable Rights, that among these are Life, Liberty and the pursuit of Happiness." This phrase derives in part from the writings of John Locke, who spoke of the "natural right" to preserve one's property, which he defined as "his life, liberty, and estate." A similar instrument, the *Virginia Bill of Rights* 1776, preceded and partly inspired the American *Declaration of Independence*.

10   For example, art. 2 of the *Declaration* provides: "The aim of every political association is the preservation of the natural and inalienable rights of man; these rights are liberty, property, security and resistance to oppression." The *Declaration*, proclaimed by the French National Assembly, was appended to the French *Constitution* of 1791.

11   17 Joh.

12   3 Car. I c.1.

13   1 Wm. & Mary, sess. 2 (1689) c.2.

14   Some consider the *Magna Carta* to be the first human rights charter. Although it was limited in its application primarily to nobles, in it can be found the earliest known expressions of some core human rights ideas including the right to *habeas corpus* and the right to due process of law. The *Magna Carta* was confirmed and reissued more than three dozen times by later sovereigns. A. Robertson (revised by J. Merrills), *Human Rights in the World*, 3d ed. (Manchester: Manchester University Press, 1992) at 4 [Robertson, *Human Rights*].

15   See the judgment of the US Supreme Court in *Marbury v. Madison*, 5 US 137 (1803). The judgment established the supremacy of the *Constitution* and the power of judicial review.

16   See I. Kant, *The Metaphysics of Morals* (1785), trans. by M. Gregor (Cambridge: Cambridge University Press, 1991).

of the subject are limited. Underpinning this proposition is the notion that individuals, in joining together to form societies and governments, voluntarily forfeit their natural state of autonomy and liberty in favour of a state that will protect and advance their interests.

The early notion of individual rights was strictly liberal. That is, the state was not required to take affirmative steps to ensure individual rights, but only to refrain from interfering with those rights. It was not until much later, and following significant social upheaval, that governments began to create and enforce laws of general welfare in areas such as public education, public health, and social security.[17] The early notion of individual rights was also limited in conception and in practice to (mostly white) Christian male property holders. It was not a notion of "human" rights.

C. FORERUNNERS OF INTERNATIONAL HUMAN RIGHTS LAW

By and large, the development of public international law was not directly touched by the notion of individual rights until the end of the Second World War. To the extent that individual rights thrived at all, it was within domestic constitutions and laws and not within international law. Gradually, however, the view emerged that public international law should provide normative and institutional restraints on the governance by states of their internal affairs. Discussed below are some of the early examples of such restraints, some of which remain very much part of contemporary international human rights law.

1) Just War Theory and Humanitarian Intervention

The concept of a "just war" can be traced back at least as far as St. Augustine in the fourth century and probably earlier. Just war theory seeks to explain and control why and how wars may be fought.[18] Just war theory served in many ways as the foundation for the doctrine of humanitarian intervention, whose most prominent early exponent was

---

17 The notion of the welfare state only really began to take form in the twentieth century, notably in the UK (the Beveridge Plan) and in the US (the New Deal).

18 On just war theory generally, see M. Walzer, *Just and Unjust Wars: A Moral Argument with Historical Illustrations* (New York: Basic Books, 1977) and J. T. Johnson, *Just War Tradition and the Restraint of War: A Moral and Historical Inquiry* (Princeton: Princeton University Press, 1981).

Hugo Grotius. His view was that it would be lawful for one state to use force against another if the mistreatment by that state of its nationals was particularly widespread and severe.[19] The following have generally been considered by Grotius and others as preconditions to any proper invocation of the doctrine of humanitarian intervention:

- peaceful means of resolving the issue have been exhausted;
- the intervention aims to redress a genuine situation of suffering and not a hypothetical or trumped-up situation;
- there is a reasonable chance of success;
- the ultimate goal is to end suffering and restore peace and order;
- the violence employed to achieve the purpose is proportional to the injury suffered; and
- the intervenor's use of force is directed at combatants, not at civilians.[20]

The doctrine of humanitarian intervention enjoyed fairly broad support before 1945 among international jurists.[21] It was, however, rarely invoked in practice. There were but a few instances of its invocation by the US and European states in the nineteenth and early twentieth centuries, usually in the context of interventions to protect fellow nationals or co-religionists resident in other states.[22] Such instances might be better characterized as acts of self-help or self-defence than humanitarian intervention.[23]

With the advent of the UN Charter,[24] the threat or use of force by one state against another was outlawed (article 2(4)), except in cases of self-defence (article 51) or pursuant to Security Council authoriza-

---

19 Grotius, *De Jure Belli ac Pacis Libri Tres*, above note 2. See also E. de Vattel, *The Law of Nations*, trans. by J. Chitty (Philadelphia: T. & J.W. Johnson, 1883) at 155: "[I]f the prince, by violating the fundamental laws, gives his subjects a legal right to resist him — if tyranny, becoming insupportable, obliges the nation to rise in their own defence — every foreign power has a right to succor an oppressed people who implore their assistance."

20 Another criterion that would be added today, in the era of the UN Security Council, is that the intervention be ordered by a proper authority. On the criteria for humanitarian intervention generally see, for example, J. Charney, "Anticipatory Humanitarian Intervention" (1999) 93 AJIL 834 at 838–40.

21 I. Brownlie, *International Law and the Use of Force by States* (Oxford: Oxford University Press, 1963) at 338.

22 *Ibid.* at 338–42.

23 See S. Murphy, *Humanitarian Intervention: The United Nations in an Evolving World Order* (Philadelphia: University of Pennsylvania Press, 1996) at 49–64.

24 Above note 4.

tion (article 42). Still, the concept of humanitarian intervention continues to be invoked and debated notwithstanding its non-recognition in the UN Charter.[25]

2) Law of State Responsibility for Injuries to Aliens

International law has almost always obliged states to treat aliens (foreign nationals in their territory) with a minimum of civility. The rules regarding state mistreatment of aliens and their property arose as a direct extension of the more general international rule prohibiting one state from causing harm to another. Causing harm to a national of another state was tantamount to harming the state itself. In this sense, the direct concern was not with the harm to the individual, or with any interference with his rights, but rather with the harm caused to the interests and rights of the state of which he was a national. The individual alien was merely a beneficiary of the obligations owed to his state. Thus, injured aliens did not have an independent cause of action against the host state that caused the injury. Instead, the alien's state of nationality had to espouse or adopt the claim on his behalf.[26] In this way, the law of state responsibility for injury to aliens was consistent with the prevailing notion that individuals were not subjects of international law.

Contentious cases involving injuries to aliens typically would be resolved through diplomatic means. Sometimes, however, they were resolved by international arbitration or adjudication, or, in extreme cases, by resort to force. The jurisprudence generated by reparations claims for injuries to aliens provides a fruitful, if indirect, source for remedying violations of human rights. In her seminal book *Remedies in International Human Rights Law*, Dinah Shelton observes:

> Of all the breaches of international law that give rise to state responsibility, those involving injury to aliens are the closest to modern international human rights violations.[27]

Shelton demonstrates that in the law of state responsibility for injury to aliens, as in international human rights law, the remedy of restitu-

---

25   See the discussion of humanitarian intervention in the Conclusion.

26   State injuries against stateless persons — who lack any state that might espouse their claim — would be unprotected by this rule.

27   D. Shelton, *Remedies in International Human Rights Law* (Oxford: Oxford University Press, 1999) at 103 [Shelton, *Remedies*]. Shelton's book was preceded by C. Gray's equally important book, *Judicial Remedies in International Law* (Oxford: Clarendon Press, 1996).

tion is generally inapplicable because of the irreparable nature of violations like wrongful death. Instead, in both areas of law, compensation for material and non-material injury constitutes the primary form of reparation.[28]

Today, injury to aliens — both individual and corporate — is generally covered by bilateral or multilateral investment treaties or by "friendship, commerce and navigation" treaties, which often provide for international arbitration or adjudication of claims.[29] There are also a number of specialized multilateral treaties covering certain categories of aliens,[30] as well as some innovative examples of compensation schemes for large-scale injury to aliens.[31]

3) Treaties to Protect Religious Minorities

Several historic international treaties included provisions to protect ethnic and religious minorities living in states dominated by different ethnic or religious groups. These provisions were typically found in peace treaties and considered essential to the maintenance of peace. Examples of such protections can be found, for example, in the Treaty of Westphalia 1648,[32] in various nineteenth-century treaties to protect Christian minorities living in the Ottoman empire,[33] and in the Treaty

---

28 Shelton, Remedies, ibid. at 132.
29 Such procedures tend to afford more expeditious resolution than supranational human rights mechanisms that might be simultaneously applicable.
30 See, for example, Vienna Convention on Diplomatic Relations 1961 [1966] CanTS no. 29.
31 For example, the Iran-United States Claims Tribunal was established to resolve claims related to the detention of fifty-two US nationals at the US Embassy in Tehran in 1979, and to the ensuing US freezing of Iranian assets. See http://www.iusct.org.
32 The treaty confirmed the Peace of Augsburg 1555, which had accorded Lutherans guarantees of religious tolerance. In addition, the peace settlement extended the Peace of Augsburg's provisions for religious toleration to the Reformed (Calvinist) church. States were required to permit private worship, liberty of conscience, and the right of emigration to all religious minorities and dissidents within their jurisdiction. See generally R. Bonney, The Thirty Years' War 1618–1648 (Great Britain: Osprey Publishing, 2002) at 82–90.
33 See, for example, the Treaty of Paris 1856 and the Treaty of Berlin 1878. These treaties provided a basis for member states of the Concert of Europe to intervene in defence of Christian populations living in the Ottoman empire. The Berlin treaty influenced the subsequent minorities system of the League of Nations, discussed below. See generally L. Sohn & T. Buergenthal, International Protection of Human Rights (Indianapolis: Bobbs Merrill, 1973) at 143–92.

of Versailles 1919 and other treaties adopted in Versailles after the First World War.[34]

4) Slavery and the Slave Trade

Perhaps the earliest recognized human right was the right not to be a slave — a right not dependent on one's nationality or religion. As early as 1794, the French National Convention emancipated all slaves in the French colonies.[35] In 1807, the British Parliament banned the slave trade, and in 1833 it banned the institution of slavery itself.[36] Slavery and the slave trade were banned by other governments in subsequent decades, and over time came to be viewed as violations of international law.[37] There was also an international accountability mechanism established, namely the Mixed Commissions for the Suppression of the Transatlantic Slave Trade.[38] These efforts notwithstanding, the practice of slavery continued in many parts of the colonized world and continues to this day, though on a diminished scale.[39]

While there have been dozens of historical treaties prohibiting slavery,[40] the most universal and comprehensive treaty remains the Slavery Convention 1926.[41] This convention was modified by the Protocol

---

34   See note 58 below.
35   The French emancipation was preceded by prohibitions on slavery in Upper Canada. See *An Act to Prevent the Further Introduction of Slaves and to Limit the Term of Contracts for Servitude within this Province* 1793 SUC (2nd sess.) c.7.
36   P. Sieghart, *The Lawful Rights of Mankind* (Oxford: Oxford University Press, 1985) at 34.
37   See, for example, General Act of the Berlin Conference on Central Africa 1885, which declared "trading in slaves is forbidden in conformity with the principles of international law" (chapter 2 art. IX).
38   The Commissions, one based in Cuba and one in Sierra Leone, were in operation *circa* 1819–1866. See generally L. Bethell, "The Mixed Commissions for the Suppression of the Transatlantic Slave Trade in the Nineteenth Century" (1966) 7 Journal of African History 79. Subsequently, an International Maritime Office was established in Zanzibar in 1890 to help eliminate the slave trade. Robertson, *Human Rights*, above note 14 at 15.
39   See the website of Anti-Slavery International: http://www.antislavery.org.
40   There were, for example, a number of treaties dealing with trafficking in women and children. See: International Agreement for the Suppression of the White Slave Traffic 1904 BTS 24 (1905); International Convention for the Suppression of the White Slave Traffic and Protocol 1910 BTS 20 (1912); International Convention for the Suppression of the Traffic in Women and Children 1921 BTS 26 (1923).
41   [1928] CanTS no. 5.

Amending the Slavery Convention 1953.[42] Thereafter the Supplementary Convention on the Abolition of Slavery, the Slave Trade, and Institutions and Practices Similar to Slavery 1956 was adopted.[43] These treaties are discussed in Chapter Seven.

5) International Humanitarian Law

The field of international humanitarian law overlaps significantly with human rights.[44] The rules of international humanitarian law trace their origins to the beginnings of Western civilization, and probably earlier, and elsewhere.[45] Rules on the humanitarian conduct of warfare were not thoroughly codified until after the mid-nineteenth century, although there are partial codes dating back to the medieval era.[46] The key breakthroughs were (i) the *Lieber Code* 1863, a code of army conduct promulgated by US President Abraham Lincoln, and (ii) Jean-Henri Dunant's founding of the International Committee for Relief of Wounded Soldiers, now the International Committee of the Red Cross, and its ensuing treaty-making efforts in the field of international humanitarian law.

The primary ambition of international humanitarian law is to "humanize" war by placing restraints on its legitimate conduct. It has no application in times of peace or in situations short of armed conflict. International humanitarian law deals with both *jus ad bellum* (the laws used to justify resort to war) and *jus in bello* (the laws applicable in

---

42   [1953] CanTS no. 26. The purpose of the Protocol was to formally transfer administrative responsibility regarding the Slavery Convention 1926 from the League of Nations (by then defunct) to the UN.

43   [1963] CanTS no. 7. On the history of international law on slavery see Y. Rassam, "Contemporary Forms of Slavery and the Evolution of the Prohibition of Slavery and the Slave Trade Under Customary International Law" (1999) 39 Virginia Journal of International Law 303 at 329–42.

44   On the relation between international humanitarian and human rights law, see Chapter Seven.

45   See generally M. Howard *et al.*, eds., *The Laws of War: Constraints on Warfare in the Western World* (New Haven: Yale University Press, 1997). Regarding the writing of, for example, Sun Tzu in the sixth century BCE, see T. McCormack, "From Sun Tzu to the Sixth Committee: The Evolution of an International Criminal Law Regime," in T. McCormack & G. Simpson, eds., *The Law of War Crimes: National and International Approaches* (London: Kluwer Law International, 1997) at 32–43.

46   For example, in 1439 Charles VII of Orleans enacted a law that made officers liable for "the abuses, ills, and offences" committed by the men they commanded. Officers who failed to take action promptly or allowed offenders to escape punishment would be punished as if they were the original offenders.

war). Prior to the adoption of the Geneva Conventions,[47] the field of international humanitarian law applied exclusively in contexts of international armed conflict. The only exception was the so-called Martens Clause, which has been part of the laws of armed conflict since it first appeared in the preamble to the Hague Convention (II) with Respect to the Laws and Customs of War on Land 1899.[48] It simply provides that

> Until a more complete code of the laws of war is issued, the High Contracting Parties think it right to declare that in cases not included in the Regulations adopted by them, populations and belligerents remain under the protection and empire of the principles of international law, as they result from the usages established between civilized nations, from the laws of humanity and the requirements of the public conscience.[49]

Like slavery, humanitarian law represents an exception to the former conception of public international law that afforded no protection to individuals. Early and noteworthy international humanitarian law treaties include: the Geneva Convention for the Amelioration of the Condition of the Wounded in Armies in the Field 1864,[50] the Hague Convention (II) with Respect to the Laws and Customs of War on Land 1899,[51] the Hague Convention for the Amelioration of the Condition of the Wounded and Sick in Armies in the Field 1906,[52] the Hague Convention (IV) respecting the Laws and Customs of War on Land 1907,[53] the Geneva Convention for the Amelioration of the Condition of the

---

47   Geneva Convention for the Amelioration of the Condition of the Wounded and Sick in Armed Forces in the Field 1949 [1965] CanTS no. 20; Geneva Convention for the Amelioration of the Condition of Wounded, Sick, and Shipwrecked Members of Armed Forces at Sea 1949 [1965] CanTS no. 20; Geneva Convention relative to the Treatment of Prisoners of War 1949 [1965] CanTS no. 20; Geneva Convention relative to the Protection of Civilian Persons in Time of War 1949 [1965] CanTS no. 20.

48   [1942] CanTS no. 6.

49   The Martens Clause is also referred to in art. 1(2) of the Protocol Additional to the Geneva Conventions of 12 August 1949, and relating to the Protection of Victims of Non-International Armed Conflicts (Protocol II) 1977. The Martens Clause has arguably acquired customary status. See *Corfu Channel Case (UK v. Albania)*, [1949] ICJ Rep 4; *Case Concerning Military and Paramilitary Activities in and against Nicaragua (Nicaragua v. USA)*, [1986] ICJ Rep 14 [*Military*].

50   [1942] CanTS no. 6.

51   Above note 48.

52   BTS 15 (1907).

53   BTS 9 (1910). The various 1899, 1906, and 1907 international humanitarian law treaties — only some of which have been noted here — are collectively referred to as the "Law of the Hague" (in contrast to the more contemporary "Law of Geneva").

Wounded and Sick in Armies in the Field 1929,[54] and the Geneva Convention relative to the Treatment of Prisoners of War 1929.[55]

Contemporary international humanitarian law treaties are discussed in Chapter Seven.

6) International Criminal Justice

Following the First World War, the victorious Allied Powers created the Commission on the Responsibility of the Authors of the War and on Enforcement of Penalties, an *ad hoc* commission mandated to examine the question of responsibility for wartime atrocities. In its final report,[56] the Commission found that the Central Powers had committed numerous violations of the laws of war and of "elementary laws of humanity," and called for the holding of international trials.[57] Subsequently, the Allied Powers incorporated provisions into the Treaty of Versailles 1919[58] providing for the prosecution of those responsible for such crimes before Allied military tribunals.[59] In the end, however, international trials were never held due primarily to the refusal by the Netherlands to extradite Kaiser Wilhelm II. Instead, the German government was permitted to hold a small number of trials in Leipzig. Those trials were conducted by the so-called "Leipzig Tribunal," which was in fact the German supreme court sitting at Leipzig.[60] In total only twenty-two persons were prosecuted, of whom ten were acquitted.[61]

---

54   [1933] CanTS no. 5, [1942] CanTS no. 6.

55   [1933] CanTS no. 5, [1942] CanTS no. 6.

56   Report Presented to the Preliminary Peace Conference, 29 March 1919, reprinted in (1920) 14 AJIL 95.

57   The Commission found evidence sufficient for prosecution in respect of some 20,000 war criminals.

58   [1919] CanTS no. 4. Canada signed the Treaty of Versailles on 28 June 1919. It came into force for Canada on the same day by virtue of ratification by the UK on Canada's behalf. The Treaty of Versailles and various other post-war treaties were incorporated into Canadian law by the *Treaties of Peace Act* 1919, SC 1919 (2nd sess.), c.30.

59   Article 227 of the Treaty of Versailles, *ibid.*, authorized the prosecution of Kaiser Wilhelm II, the former German Emperor, for "a supreme offence against international morality and the sanctity of treaties." Arts. 228 and 229 provided for the establishment of tribunals to try "persons accused of having committed acts in violations of the laws and customs of war."

60   S. Ratner & J. Abrams, *Accountability for Human Rights Atrocities in International Law*, 2d ed. (Oxford: Oxford University Press, 2001) at 6. Some of the judgments of the Tribunal were cited by the Supreme Court of Canada in *R. v. Finta*, [1994] 1 SCR 701 at 831–834.

61   See generally C. Mullins, *The Leipzig Trials: An Account of the War Criminals' Tri-

Another early effort in the area of international criminal justice was made by the League of Nations, which adopted the Convention for the Prevention and Punishment of Terrorism 1937.[62] The Convention contained a protocol for the creation of an international criminal court to try acts of terrorism. India was the only country ever to ratify the Convention, and as a consequence neither the Convention nor its protocol came into force.

Although these early efforts in the area of international criminal justice failed, they helped inspire and influence subsequent developments in international criminal law and international human rights law.

7) The League of Nations: the Mandates System, the ILO, and the Protection of Minorities

The League of Nations was established pursuant to the Covenant of the League of Nations 1919,[63] a treaty adopted at the Paris Peace Conference at the end of the First World War. The Covenant did not deal with human rights as such, but it contained two important provisions that inspired later developments in human rights: one dealing with the protection of former colonies of the states that had lost the First World War (article 22), and one dealing with international labour rights and protections (article 23). The mandate of the League also included an important oversight role in relation to various treaties established after the war for the protection of minority groups. The Permanent Court of International Justice, the League's chief judicial organ and the direct predecessor to the International Court of Justice, also played a key role in relation to minority protection.

The Mandates System. Article 22 of the Covenant of the League of Nations established the League's Mandates System. Colonies of countries that had lost the First World War were held in "sacred trust" by the League, and passed under the administration of the victorious states or "Mandatory Powers." The Mandatory Powers were required to administer the colonies under conditions "which will guarantee freedom of conscience and religion . . . and the prohibition of abuses such as the slave trade." They were also required to give the League's Man-

---

als and a Study of German Mentality (London: H.F. & G. Witherby, 1921) at 98–112.
62   94 LNTS 65.
63   BTS 4 (1919), Cmd. 159 p. 9; BTS 37 (1924), Cmd. 2300 (as amended).

dates Commission annual performance reports on their trusteeship. With the collapse of the League of Nations the remaining Mandates were conferred upon the UN Trusteeship Council, which looked after them and other "non-self-governing territories." By 1994, all "Trust Territories" had become self-governing either as independent states or as parts of other states.[64]

The ILO. Article 23 of the Covenant of the League of Nations addressed "fair and humane conditions of labour for men, women, and children" and led to the establishment of the International Labour Organization (ILO).[65] The ILO operated autonomously from the League but had the status of an official intergovernmental organization. It remains best known for its unique tripartite oversight structure consisting of government, employer, and worker representatives. The ILO is the only body that survived the dissolution of the League. Today it is a "specialized agency" of the UN.

In its early years, the ILO set international standards in the area of labour rights via a range of important treaties including, *inter alia*, the Hours of Work (Industry) Convention (No. 1) 1919,[66] the Forced Labour Convention (No. 29) 1930,[67] and the Migration for Employment Convention (No. 66) 1939.[68] Canada ratified many ILO treaties and enacted extensive implementing legislation in the 1930s, but its enthusiasm was quickly tamed by the Privy Council in its watershed decision in *Attorney General for Canada v. Attorney General for Ontario (Labour Conventions).*[69]

The modern ILO regime is discussed in detail in Chapters Seven and Sixteen.

---

64 Some have suggested that the UN Trusteeship Council be reconstituted to supervise modern *de facto* UN protectorates such as Kosovo. Speech by G. Evans, 8 October 2003, Canadian Institute of International Affairs Distinguished Lecture Series, Toronto.

65 The ILO was established pursuant to several treaties: the Treaty of Versailles 1919, the Treaty of Saint Germain 1919, the Treaty of Neuilly 1919, and the Treaty of Trianon 1920. Article 427 of the Treaty of Versailles, above note 58, declared various "principles for regulating labour conditions which all industrial communities should endeavour to apply," including the right of association, the payment of an adequate wage, the abolition of child labour, and the principle of equal pay for men and women for work of equal value.

66 38 UNTS 119. The convention entered into force for Canada on 21 March 1935.

67 39 UNTS 55. Canada is not a state party.

68 Canada is not a party to the treaty. Although not discussed here, it should be noted that there were at least a few multilateral treaties on labour rights which preceded the ILO. See, for example, the Berne Convention on Night Work for Women in Industrial Employment 1906.

69 [1937] AC 326 (PC). See generally Chapter Eight.

Protection of Minorities. The League of Nations played an important role in protecting a number of minority groups pursuant to post-
war peace treaties. These treaties sought to protect ethnic, linguistic,
and religious minorities living in Central and Eastern Europe. The
Allied Powers had insisted on their protection from discrimination or
persecution within their countries of residence, and also on their
receiving affirmative entitlements such as rights to teach in their own
language at their own schools.[70] In furtherance of its mandate to guarantee these rights, the League permitted members of protected minority groups to submit complaints of violations. The League's Council
would appoint an ad hoc Minorities Committee to handle admissible
cases. The Committee would then review the complaint, permitting
implicated states an opportunity to reply. Contentious questions of law
could be referred to the Permanent Court of International Justice.[71]

During its brief lifetime (1919–40),[72] the Court rendered a number
of important judgments, several of which dealt with minority rights.
For example, in *Rights of Minorities in Upper Silesia (Minority
Schools)*,[73] a case brought by Germany against Poland in challenge to
individuals' claims to membership in a particular linguistic group, the
Court sided with Poland, finding that the question of whether a person
belongs to a minority group is "a question of fact and not solely one of
intention."[74] Since then, international jurisprudence has tended to follow the same approach, relying on a combination of subjective criteria
(claims of the individual and counter-claims of the community) and

---

70   See, for example, Treaty between the Allied and Associated Powers and Poland
     on the Protection of Minorities 1919 BFSP 112: 232. The treaty provided for
     freedom of religion, a ban on anti-semitism, equality before the law, and lan-
     guage and education rights. Other equivalent treaties were signed with Romania,
     Greece, Czechoslovakia, and Yugoslavia. There were also chapters on minority
     rights in post-war peace treaties with Austria, Bulgaria, Hungary, and later
     Turkey. See generally P. de Azcarate, *League of Nations and National Minorities*
     (Washington: Carnegie Endowment for International Peace, 1945).
71   Canada accepted the jurisdiction of the Permanent Court of International Jus-
     tice. See *Declaration of Acceptance of the Optional Clause of Article 36 of the
     Statute of the Permanent Court of International Justice* 1929 [1930] CanTS no. 9.
72   Although the Permanent Court of International Justice was not formally dis-
     banded until 1945, it stopped functioning in 1940 after Germany occupied The
     Netherlands.
73   (1928) PCIJ ser. A no. 12.
74   A similar finding was made in *Minority Schools in Albania* (1935) PCIJ ser. A/B
     no. 64.

objective criteria (facts about the individual, facts about the community, and facts about the law).[75]

During the inter-war period, the League of Nations also supervised a unique arrangement concerning Upper Silesia, a region divided into two parts, one on each side of the German and Polish borders. To protect minorities in Upper Silesia, there was a Minorities Office in each part of the region, a Mixed Commission, and an Arbitral Tribunal that rendered decisions binding on Germany and Poland. The League Council appointed the president of the Commission and the Tribunal. The Commission handled more than 2,000 cases during its existence from 1922 to 1937.[76]

The League's mechanisms for minority protection disappeared together with the League, having failed to halt the rise of anti-semitism and Nazism. Aspects of its mechanisms have, however, been incorporated into some modern-day bodies such as the OSCE High Commissioner for National Minorities, discussed in Chapter Fifteen.

8) The Inter-American System

The world's first regional intergovernmental organization was the International Union of American Republics. It was formed in 1890 at the first Pan-American conference with the aim of promoting economic, social and cultural agreement among the states comprising the Americas. Canada was not invited to participate at the conference, as it was still dependent on Great Britain for its international relations.[77] In 1910, the organization changed its name to the Pan American Union, and in 1948 it was reconstituted by its twenty-one member states as the Organization of American States (OAS).

In its early years, the Pan American Union adopted a number of important treaties that influenced the development of human rights following the Second World War. These included the Convention relative to the Rights of Aliens 1902,[78] the Convention on Asylum 1928,[79] the Convention on the Status of Aliens 1928,[80] the Convention on

---

75   See, for example, *Lovelace v. Canada* (1981), Comm. No. R.6/24 (UN Human Rights Committee).

76   Robertson, *Human Rights*, above note 14 at 20–21.

77   P. McKenna, "Canada and the Inter-American System, 1890–1968" (1995) 41 Australian Journal of Politics and History 253 at 254.

78   OAS TS no. 32. Canada is not a state party.

79   International Conferences of American States, 1889–1928 at 434. Canada is not a state party.

80   OAS TS no. 34. Canada is not a state party.

Political Asylum 1933,[81] and the Convention on the Nationality of Women 1933.[82]

D. THE BIRTH OF INTERNATIONAL HUMAN RIGHTS LAW

As the previous discussion reveals, the establishment of the modern era of human rights was preceded by a number of norms and mechanisms that to some extent linked international law with individual rights. It was the events of the Holocaust, however, that crystallized international will in favour of an international law of human rights.[83] If there was ever any doubt that some of the worst atrocities are committed by governments against their own citizens, that doubt disappeared after the Holocaust. After the Second World War, a link between international law and individual rights became unavoidable.

1) The UN Charter and the Establishment of the UN

Even before the end of the Second World War, there was a widespread desire to create a new permanent international organization to replace the defunct League of Nations. The new organization was to be called the United Nations. The UN Charter was finalized at a conference in San Francisco held from April to June 1945, and then signed on 26 June 1945 by fifty states, including Canada. Unlike the League of Nations, which was overwhelmingly composed of European states, the UN was truly global. The UN's original members included states from every continent. Since the founding of the UN, Canada has been one of its strongest supporters and most active member states.[84]

---

81 International Conferences of American States, 1st Supplement, 1933–1940 at 116. Canada is not a party.

82 [1991] CanTS no. 28.

83 As early as 1941, the Allied Powers adopted human rights proclamations. See, e.g., the Atlantic Charter 1941 [1942] CanTS no. 1, which called for "freedom from fear and want" and proclaimed the right to self-determination.

84 According to the Department of Foreign Affairs and International Trade's website, Canada presently ranks as the seventh largest financial contributor to the UN. For 2003, Canada's assessed contribution to the UN regular budget was 2.5% or US$34.5 million. Canada's present assessment rate under the UN peacekeeping scale is also 2.5%. See http://www.dfait-maeci.gc.ca/canada_un/cdn_un-en.asp.

The UN Charter established six principal organs: the General Assembly, the Security Council, the Economic and Social Council (ECOSOC), the Trusteeship Council, the International Court of Justice, and the UN Secretariat (which consists of various departments — political affairs, legal affairs, etc. — that provide technical assistance to the other principal organs and to UN member states). Most of these are discussed in Chapter Fourteen, with a focus on their role in the promotion and protection of human rights.

Although some of its provisions may now be peremptory norms of international law,[85] the UN Charter is not a world constitution but merely a treaty binding on its states parties. Indeed, to this day international law continues to exist in a highly decentralized form. There is still no "world government": the UN General Assembly does not serve as the world's legislature; the International Court of Justice does not serve as the world's court, but only has jurisdiction over states that have voluntarily recognized its jurisdiction;[86] and even the Security Council is ultimately only a treaty body, limited to enforcement of the UN Charter. Still, the UN is the closest thing we have to a world government, and unquestionably represents the most universal vehicle for the promotion and protection of human rights.

The UN Charter is the most widely ratified of all international treaties.[87] It treats human rights as a core value of the UN, although it does not define the term human rights. UN Charter article 1(2) includes as one of the purposes of the UN "[t]o develop friendly relations among nations based on respect for the principle of equal rights and self-determination of peoples, and to take other appropriate measures to strengthen universal peace."[88] Article 1(3) includes "promoting and encouraging respect for human rights and for fundamental free-

---

85   The UN Charter, above note 4, art. 2(4) prohibition on the use of force, for example, is often considered a peremptory norm. See, for example, *Military*, above note 49 at para. 190.

86   What's more, the decisions of the Court in contentious cases — no matter how influential — are binding only on the parties to the particular dispute. UN Charter, *ibid.*, art. 59 provides "The decision of the Court has no binding force except between the parties and in respect of that particular case." This language also clearly indicates the non-applicability of the principle of *stare decisis* (binding precedent).

87   Today, largely due to the demise of most colonial arrangements around the world, there are 191 states parties to the UN Charter and thus 191 UN member states. Only Taiwan and Vatican City are not members of the UN.

88   Note that this article draws a direct connection between respect for human rights and the attainment of peace.

doms for all without distinction as to race, sex, language, or religion" as a purpose of the UN. Also, UN Charter article 55 provides that the UN shall promote "universal respect for, and observance of, human rights and fundamental freedoms for all without distinction as to race, sex, language, or religion." Article 56 requires UN member states to "take joint and separate action in co-operation with" the UN to achieve that purpose.

2) The Nuremberg and Tokyo Tribunals

Following the conclusion of the Second World War, the Allied Powers were determined not to repeat the mistake they made after the First World War when they opted against the creation of an international war crimes tribunal to try leaders of the Central Powers. In August 1945, the American, British, Soviet, and French governments reached an agreement for the establishment of an International Military Tribunal to be located in Nuremberg, Germany for purposes of prosecuting the Nazi leadership. The agreement was known as the London Agreement 1945,[89] and it was ultimately acceded to by nineteen other states including Canada. The charter for the Tribunal (IMT Charter) was annexed to the London Agreement. While the London Agreement and the IMT Charter focused on Nazi leaders, the Moscow Declaration 1943 (declared jointly by the American, British, Soviet, and Chinese governments) provided that minor Nazi war criminals would be tried in the states where the crimes were carried out.

The International Military Tribunal was composed of judges from each of the four states that established it. Article 6 of the IMT Charter enumerated three crimes within the jurisdiction of the Tribunal: crimes against peace (also known as crimes of aggression), war crimes, and crimes against humanity. The IMT Charter ousted any claims of state or sovereign immunity (article 7), and prohibited the defence of obedience to superior orders (article 8). Trials in abstentia were permitted (article 12). One of the most controversial issues was the question of retroactive criminalization, also known as the principle of nullem crimen sine lege. Several defendants argued that the crimes listed in the IMT Charter — in particular, the categories of crimes against peace and crimes against humanity — were not criminal under international law

---

89   Its full name was the Agreement for the Prosecution and Punishment of the Major War Criminals of the European Axis 1945, 82 UNTS 280.

as of 1939, and hence could not be used as a basis for conviction. The Tribunal rejected these arguments, although debate persisted.[90]

The most famous trial held at Nuremberg — and the only one that was actually conducted by an international tribunal — was a single group trial that took place between November 1945 and September 1946. Twenty-two defendants were prosecuted, one of whom was tried *in abstentia*; nineteen of these were convicted, of whom twelve were sentenced to death and seven to prison terms. Other "Nuremberg trials" were conducted by American military tribunals authorized by *Control Law No. 10* (issued by the Allied Control Council) and established under *Ordinance 7* (issued by the Military Governor of the American Zone).[91] These American tribunals tried 185 persons in twelve cases between 1946 and 1949, including doctors, lawyers, bankers, and the heads of a number of private companies. The vast majority of those tried were convicted to long prison terms, but many convicts were quietly paroled in the early 1950s.[92]

In addition to the tribunals of Nuremberg, an international tribunal was established in Tokyo to prosecute Japanese military and other leaders. Their prosecution was authorized under the Charter of the International Military Tribunal for the Far East 1946, which was based upon, but different from, the IMT Charter. It was proclaimed by executive order of US General Douglas MacArthur while he was the Supreme Allied Commander for Japan.[93] MacArthur also selected the eleven international judges and the prosecutor. The Tokyo tribunal held only one trial, which lasted from May 1946 through November 1948. Twenty-eight Japanese leaders were tried,[94] all but three of whom

---

90   See *Nazi Conspiracy and Aggression, Opinion and Judgment*, Nuremberg Tribunal, 1946, reprinted in (1947) 41 AJIL 172. See more generally T. Taylor, *The Anatomy of the Nuremberg Trials* (New York: Alfred A. Knopf, 1992). Arguments about violations of the principle of *nullem crimen sine lege* became less compelling when the UN General Assembly formally endorsed the IMT Charter in 1946.

91   *Control Law No. 10*, issued on 20 December 1945, authorized each of the occupying powers in its occupation zone to try persons suspected of war crimes. Acting under the Law, the Military Governor of the American Zone issued *Ordinance No. 7*, establishing American military tribunals comprised of three American lawyers, usually past or present members of state judiciaries, all recruited by the War Department.

92   P. Maguire, *Law and War: An American Story* (New York: Columbia University Press, 2000) at c. 6.

93   Special Proclamation by the Supreme Commander for the Allied Powers at Tokyo, dated 19 January 1946, amended Charter dated 26 April 1946, TIAS 1589, 4 Bevans 20.

94   The Japanese emperor was not among those tried.

were convicted; of these, seven were sentenced to death, sixteen to life in prison, and two to lesser prison terms. The trial made no reference to sexual slavery and the use of "comfort women" by Japanese forces. Other Allied tribunals also conducted war crimes trials of more than 5,000 Japanese defendants.[95]

The Nuremberg and Tokyo trials were controversial. Some regarded both sets of trials, but particularly the Tokyo trials, as deplorable examples of "victor's justice," given that no Allied soldier was tried for war crimes by any of the tribunals.[96] There were also criticisms about the absence of impartiality on the part of the judges, all of whom were nationals of Allied Power states. Nevertheless, these trials stand as important examples of the proposition that individuals have fundamental obligations under international law for which they can be held criminally responsible. The trials also directly presaged subsequent developments in international criminal and human rights law, as well as inspiring the Convention on the Prevention and Punishment of the Crime of Genocide 1948 (Genocide Convention) and the Geneva Conventions, both discussed in Chapter Seven.

E. CONCLUSION

The historical origins of international human rights law are too many to name. We have tried to identify and describe only the most prominent among them. The history of human rights is not, however, of mere academic interest. The intellectual traditions and historical events that preceded and influenced the development of human rights continue to be relevant in the present. Thus, contemporary users of international human rights law continue to make use of sources as disparate as the works of Hugo Grotius and Immanuel Kant, the US *Bill of Rights* and its jurisprudence, and the Hague Conventions governing the conduct of international armed conflict. Likewise, concepts such as state sovereignty, just war, and minority rights remain as relevant today as in the past.

---

95 See R. Pritchard, "The International Military Tribunal for the Far East and the Allied National War Crimes Trials in Asia," in M. C. Bassiouni, ed., *International Criminal Law*, 2d ed. (New York: Transnational Publishers, 1999) at 135–36.

96 R. Minear, *Victor's Justice: The Tokyo War Crimes Trial* (Princeton: Princeton University Press, 1971) at 75–86.

CHAPTER 2

THE CONCEPT OF HUMAN RIGHTS: THEORY AND CONTESTATION

This chapter reviews the principal characteristics of the concept of human rights as it is expressed in contemporary international law. The aim is to provide the reader with a basic conceptual framework to undergird the more detailed treatments of individual treaties and norms in subsequent chapters.

There is a general consensus that human rights are useful and important, but criticisms of the theory and practice of human rights persist. There remains disagreement about, for example, the relative priority of different human rights, how they are best protected, whether there is an underlying historical or cultural bias in their formulation, and whether they are the best way of conceptualizing the relationship between the individual and the state. This chapter will survey some of these criticisms or challenges, and offer some tentative responses.

A. DEFINING CHARACTERISTICS OF THE CONCEPT OF HUMAN RIGHTS

1) Founded on Human Dignity

As Chapter One demonstrates, the law of human rights was preceded and influenced by a mixture of natural law theory and domestic constitutional law. While most early rights theorists asserted that the source of rights was divine or natural, by the twentieth century the concept of "natural rights," in the divine sense, had been largely discredited.[1] Contemporary justifications for human rights are based instead on notions of human dignity and the inherent worth of human beings. For example, the preamble of the Universal Declaration of Human Rights 1948 (UDHR)[2] declares "recognition of the inherent dignity . . . of all members of the human family" to be "the foundation of freedom, justice and peace in the world . . . ." Similarly, the preamble to the International Covenant on Civil and Political Rights 1966 (ICCPR)[3] and the International Covenant on Economic, Social and Cultural Rights 1966 (ICESCR)[4] proclaim that human rights "derive from the inherent dignity of the human person." None of these instruments posits a foundational theory, natural or divine, as to why humans possess human rights; each simply declares that they do.

While competing foundational theories for human rights abound,[5] none has achieved significant consensus. Although this may leave the theory of human rights, like many moral and legal theories, somewhat unmoored, it may be enough to show that human rights are necessary or useful or advantageous to individuals and to human society as a whole.[6]

2) Prescribed by International Law

International human rights law and its regional equivalents form a branch of public international law. Human rights are principally established by way of treaties created at the international level by the international community. International human rights law is like most law in that its central purpose is to regulate behaviour, but in this case the primary focus of regulation is state behaviour and not individual behaviour. Human rights law is also like other forms of law in that it expresses not only substantive norms, but also procedural norms and remedies.

---

1   L. Henkin *et al.*, *Human Rights* (New York: Foundation Press, 1999) at 79.
2   GA res. 217(III) (1948).
3   [1976] CanTS no. 47.
4   [1976] CanTS no. 46.
5   For a summary of most of the leading theories, see J. Donnelly, *Universal Human Rights in Theory and Practice*, 2d ed. (Ithaca: Cornell University Press, 2003) [Donnelly, *Universal*] at 13–21.
6   Michael Ignatieff properly queries whether human rights would be worth having if we could prove a natural law basis for having them, but not establish their utility. M. Ignatieff, "Human Rights as Politics and Idolatry," in A. Gutman, ed., *Human Rights as Politics and Idolatry* (Princeton: Princeton University Press, 2001) at 55 [Ignatieff, "Human Rights"].

3) Universal and Human

The human rights concept is a universal one: all human beings have human rights. As UDHR article 1 declares, "All human beings are born free and equal in dignity and rights." The universal character of human rights is to be contrasted with "particularist" notions of rights that would apply only to some groups or classes of people, or would apply differently to some groups or classes than others.[7]

The universality of human rights does not mean that their content is universally agreed upon. As discussed below, some Asian countries have asserted that human rights are not universal, but instead represent a specific cultural, historical, and religious tradition, namely the "Western" tradition.[8] Nor does the universality of human rights imply that the content of human rights cannot change over time. Indeed, new human rights continue to be recognized.[9]

Human rights are "human" in the sense that they apply to sentient and living human beings. Legal persons (for example, corporations),[10]

---

7 While some human rights do create conditions of eligibility beyond the mere fact of being human (for example, ICCPR, above note 3, art. 12(1) limits freedom of movement and residence to persons "lawfully within the territory of a state"; ICCPR art. 25 limits the right to vote to "citizens"), the rights are still universal. The rights inure by virtue of being human not by virtue of being a citizen or lawful resident of any particular country.

8 Although references to "the West" are common, it may ultimately be impossible to define a term that includes so many traditions. Donnelly makes the point well: "Politically, 'the West' has been classically embodied in Sparta, Athens, and Rome (both the Republic and the Empire); the France of Louis IX . . . and de Gaulle; the Germany of . . . Adolf Hitler, Willy Brandt and Helmut Kohl; the England of Henry VIII . . . Thatcher, and Lady/Princess Diana; and the United States of Washington, Jefferson . . . and various Bushes. . . . And the cultural variation — Strauss and the Sex Pistols, the Arc de Triomphe and the Golden Arches, Don Quixote and Donald Duck — is, if anything, even greater." Donnelly, *Universal*, above note 5 at 62.

9 See, for example, the Additional Protocol to the Convention for the Protection of Human Rights and Dignity of the Human Being with regard to the Application of Biology and Medicine, on the Prohibition of Cloning Human Beings 1998, ETS no. 168. While many have argued that the list of human rights is incomplete, or that some human rights are not given sufficiently serious treatment, few if any have argued that any existing human rights should be removed.

10 Article 1 of the European Convention on Human Rights 1950 (ECHR), Protocol No. 1 (1952) ETS no. 9 contains the only explicit recognition of human rights for legal persons. It provides "every natural or legal person is entitled to the peaceful enjoyment of his possessions." Even in the Council of Europe system, however, corporations enjoy only some human rights. See F. Jacobs & R. White, *The European Convention on Human Rights*, 2d ed. (Oxford: Oxford University Press, 1996) at 350.

fetuses,[11] and the dead[12] do not generally enjoy human rights. Human rights are also "human" in the sense that they have humans as their source just as contractual rights have contracts as their source.[13] The fact of being human is the foundation of the right.

4) Focused on Rights Not Duties

International human rights law does not confer mere privileges to individuals that can be easily removed at the discretion of a public authority. Nor with some exceptions does it create duties owed by individuals to each other, to community, or to states.[14] Instead, as its name suggests, international human rights law declares rights.[15] Rights are legal entitlements and not merely political promises or aspirations. As such, they are less amenable to trade offs in the face of competing claims and interests.[16]

The rights proclaimed in human rights instruments create claims against government or, as Louis Henkin asserts, "upon society."[17] This flows from the nature of all rights, the recognition and implementation

---

11 Unique among human rights treaties, the American Convention on Human Rights 1969 (ACHR), OAS TS no. 36 art. 4(1) provides: "Every person has the right to have his life respected. This right shall be protected by law and, in general, from the moment of conception."

12 For example, there is no internationally recognized human right to have one's reputation protected after death. The human right against injury to reputation only covers living human beings. On the other hand, relatives of a deceased torture victim may be able to rely on the victim's right to life as a basis for posthumously commencing a legal action.

13 Donnelly, *Universal*, above note 5 at 13.

14 Human duties can be found in some human rights instruments including, *inter alia*, UDHR, above note 2, art. 29, the American Delcatation on the Rights and Duties of Man 1948 (AmDR), OAS res. XXX arts. 29–38 and the African Charter on Himan and Peoples' Rights 1981 (AfrCHPR) OAU doc. CAB/LEG/67/3 rev. 5 arts. 27–29. These duties are not, however, a precondition to holding or exercising any human rights; one does not lose one's human rights by failing to carry out any particular duty. Donnelly, *Universal, ibid.* at 25.

15 International human rights law also confers freedoms, but these are expressed directly or indirectly as rights (for example, the right to freedom of association).

16 The idea is that the benefit or importance of upholding a right is essential even if it produces a cost in terms of efficiency or social policy. See R. Dworkin, *Taking Rights Seriously* (Cambridge: Harvard University Press, 1977) at xi, 90. On judicial concepts of rights, see W. Hohfeld, *Fundamental Legal Conceptions as Applied in Judicial Reasoning* (New Haven: Yale University Press, 1964).

17 L. Henkin, *The Rights of Man Today* (Boulder: Westview Press, 1978) at 10 ("[E]very individual has claims upon . . . society — both claims to freedom from undue governmental intrusion and claims for governmental support for economic and social welfare").

of which are premised on the existence of a state or at least some form of government. But human rights may not be invoked by any individual against any government; states only have obligations to their own nationals and to foreign nationals within their territory or otherwise subject to their jurisdiction.[18]

Implicit in the idea of a right is the availability of a remedy. In most legal traditions a right without a corresponding enforceable remedy is not properly called a right.[19] Violations of most human rights require a remedy, which can usually be effected by executive, legislative, or judicial action.[20] However, some human rights treaties do not establish a right to a remedy,[21] and some human rights are not justiciable, at least not by international bodies.[22]

5) Focused on Individuals Not Groups

International human rights law overwhelmingly accords rights to individuals as opposed to groups or peoples. In the International Bill of Human Rights,[23] for example, all of the enumerated rights are individual rights, with the exception of the right to self-determination.[24] This approach is consistent with the liberal origins of the human rights concept. It is also consistent with the notion that a human right belongs to a human. By biology a human is an individual not a collective. This is not to deny that an individual may choose to define herself within a

---

18   See, for example, ICCPR, above note 3, art. 2(1): "Each State Party to the present Covenant undertakes to respect and to ensure to all individuals within its territory and subject to its jurisdiction the rights recognized in the present Covenant, without distinction of any kind, such as race, colour, sex, language, religion, political or other opinion, national or social origin, property, birth or other status."

19   The famous Latin maxim, *ubi jus ibi remedium* (for every violation of the law there must be a remedy) has long been considered a principle of the common law. See D. Shelton, *Remedies in International Human Rights Law* (Oxford: Oxford University Press, 1999) at 292. See also Chapter Thirteen.

20   See, for example, ICCPR, above note 3, art. 2(3)(b).

21   For example, the ICESCR does not explicitly guarantee a right to remedy. This does not, however, imply that economic, social and cultural rights are not human rights. See the discussion of negative and positive rights, below.

22   Note, for example, that the right of "peoples" to self-determination is considered non-justiciable by the UN Human Rights Committee. See *Lubicon Lake Band v. Canada* (1990), Comm. no. 167/1984 at para. 32.1 [*Lubicon*].

23   See Chapter Four.

24   The International Bill of Rights, which comprises the UDHR, the ICCPR and its optional protocols, and the ICESCR, is examined in detail in Chapter Four.

group rather than as an individual. Indeed, all humans define their identities within the context of some form of group association, whether family, community, country, gender, religion, language, profession, etc. Yet biologically and physically a human is an individual, even if socially and spiritually she defines herself within the larger group.

Some human rights are accorded to individuals *qua* individuals (for example, the right to life), while other rights are accorded to individuals *qua* members of groups (for example, the right to practice one's religion or speak one's language). Underlying the idea of individual human rights is the notion that an individual has inherent value separate and apart from the group; that is, she is valued as such, irrespective of any additional value she possesses within or contributes to a particular group or society. Still, many (indeed most) individual rights only have meaning or utility when they are exercised collectively, including minority rights, freedom of association, freedom of speech, the right to vote in periodic elections, the right to marry, and the right to favourable working conditions. Human rights are not premised on the protection of an atomistic individual. They are premised on the protection and development of an individual situated within the context of a wider society.

Despite its emphasis on individual rights, international human rights law does accord some rights to groups or collective entities *qua* groups, albeit on a limited basis. These are sometimes referred to as third generation human rights (individual civil and political human rights being the first generation and individual economic, social and cultural human rights being the second). For example, "peoples" are entitled to the right of self-determination under certain human rights treaties,[25] and to the free and full use and enjoyment of their natural wealth and resources.[26] National, ethnic, racial, and religious groups are also entitled to protection against genocide (though protection from genocide is not typically considered a third generation right).[27] The AfrCHPR recognizes a whole series of peoples' rights ranging from the right to economic, social and cultural development (article 22(1))

---

25   See ICCPR, above note 3, art. 1; ICESCR, above note 4, art. 1; AfrCHPR, above note 14, art. 20.

26   See ICCPR, *ibid.*, art. 47, ICESCR, *ibid.*, art. 25, AfrCHPR, *ibid.*, art. 21.

27   Article 2 of the Convention on the Prevention and Punishment of Genocide 1948 (Genocide Convention), [1949] CanTS no. 27 prohibits certain acts committed "with intent to destroy, in whole or in part, a national, ethnical, racial or religious group, as such . . . ." The term genocide derives from the ancient Greek terms *genos* (people) and *cide* (to kill).

to the right to peace (article 23(1))[28] to the right to a clean environment (article 24).

Overall, collective rights of this sort still rest on less solid ground at international law and are much fewer in number. For example, with the exception of article 24 of the AfrCHPR and article 11 of the Additional Protocol to the ACHR (ACHPR-OP1),[29] there is no right to a clean environment. There is only a provision in the ICESCR requiring states parties to take steps to improve "all aspects of environmental and industrial hygiene" (article 12(2)(b)), and a non-binding Draft UN Declaration of Principles on Human Rights and the Environment 1994.[30] It may also be unclear in some cases what advantage there is to group human rights as compared to collective exercises of individual human rights by groups with a common bond or objective — with the possible exception of indigenous peoples.[31] Similarly, it is not obvious that a state that systematically violates the individual human rights of the members of a particular group would be any less likely to violate collective human rights.[32]

Still, the rights of a group may often need to be protected in order to ensure the enjoyment of certain individual rights. Thus, to enjoy the right to practice one's own culture, the culture of the group may often require protection by means of affirmative state interventions. In its General Comment 23,[33] the UN Human Rights Committee states:

> Although the [minority] rights protected under article 27 are individual rights, they depend in turn on the ability of the minority group to maintain its culture, language or religion. Accordingly, positive meas-

---

28   See also the UN Declaration on the Right of Peoples to Peace, approved by GA res. 39/11 (1984).

29   OAS TS no. 69.

30   There may be ways, nevertheless, to vindicate environmental issues as individual human rights claims. For example, the European Court of Human Rights has declared that environmental contamination might in some cases constitute a violation of the right to privacy under European Convention on Human Rights 1950 (ECHR), ETS no. 5 art. 8. See *López-Ostra v. Spain* (1994), 20 EHRR 277. Query too whether deliberate and massive destruction of the environment could violate the right to life.

31   Indigenous peoples in countries around the world have refused, so far unsuccessfully, to be treated as minority groups under international law. On the claims of indigenous peoples under international law generally, see B. Kingsbury, "Reconciling Five Competing Conceptual Structures of Indigenous Peoples' Claims in International and Comparative Law" (2001) 34 New York University Journal of International Law and Politics 189. See also Chapter Four.

32   Donnelly, *Universal*, above note 5 at 210, 212.

33   ICCPR General Comment 23 (1994).

ures by States may also be necessary to protect the identity of a minority and the rights of its members to enjoy and develop their culture and language and to practice their religion, in community with the other members of the group.

To be consistent with human rights principles, however, neither the state nor the protected group should be entitled to prevent or punish an individual member for voluntarily exiting the group or making an unpopular choice in her capacity as a member of the group, such as to be educated or married outside of the group.[34] As Michael Ignatieff writes, "Individual rights without collective rights may be difficult to exercise, but collective rights without individual ones end up in tyranny."[35]

6) Negative (Civil/Political) and Positive (Economic/Social/Cultural) Rights

A basic distinction is often made between negative rights and liberties (and the corresponding negative obligations of the state) and positive rights and liberties (and the corresponding positive obligations of the state).[36] The distinction partly reflects the difference between the classic notion of a liberal democracy, which is minimalist and *laissez faire*, and the notion of a social democracy, which is more activist and interventionist. The distinction is also a vestige of the old dispute between Western capitalist states, which were seen to emphasize civil and political rights (including the right to property), and communist and developing world states, which were seen to champion economic and social (and group) rights.

Conceptually, negative rights are rights that exist independent of state action. The state simply has to respect them or not interfere with them; it has to desist from action. Negative rights tend to correspond with civil and political rights. Examples include freedom of expression, freedom of association and assembly, and the right to privacy.

---

34   The classic case on this point is *Lovelace v. Canada* (1981), Comm. no. R.6/24, in which the complainant — born and registered as a Maliseet Indian — lost her rights and status as an Indian in accordance with section 12(1)(b) of the *Indian Act* after marrying a non-Indian. The UN Human Rights Committee found in favour of the complainant, finding that a denial of her right to reside on the reserve was unreasonable and unnecessary to preserve the identity of the tribe (para. 17).

35   Ignatieff, "Human Rights," above note 6 at 89–90.

36   See I. Berlin, *Four Essays on Liberty* (Oxford: Oxford University Press, 1969) at 118–72.

By way of contrast, positive rights are rights that, in order to be realized, require not state restraint but state action or assistance. Positive rights usually correspond to economic, social and cultural rights. Economic rights directly concern the need for material well-being. Examples include the right to social security and insurance and the right to favourable working conditions. Social rights aim to advance various values and goals of broader society. Examples include the right to education and the right to the highest attainable standards of physical and mental health. Cultural rights seek to preserve similar goals to social rights including, for example, the right to enjoyment of the benefits of cultural freedom and scientific progress.

The categories of civil, political, economic, social and cultural rights all form part of the corpus of international human rights law, but the categories can be artificial and misleading. For example, the right to property can be described as a civil right and an economic right. The right against injury to reputation can be described as a civil, economic, and social right. The right to life can be described as just about every kind of right. Thus, these categories ought to be approached with some scepticism even if, on balance, they are useful descriptors.

The negative/positive distinction may be equally misleading. Generally it is fair to say that the fulfillment of civil and political rights tends to involve little in the way of state action. The main commitment is to enact protective legislation and to ensure that certain illegal forms of conduct are prevented and punished. By contrast, many economic and social rights present direct and substantial resource burdens that render realization of the right more difficult. For example, it will generally be easier (that is, less costly) for a post-conflict democratic government in an economically ravaged state to restore freedom of expression than to ensure a right to social insurance. Yet the fulfilment of some civil and political rights requires significant state action. For example, ensuring the right to a fair trial requires affirmative legislative, institutional, and financial acts on the part of the state.[37] The right of prisoners to humane treatment requires the state to afford minimally adequate conditions in detention facilities.[38] The right to counsel

---

37 See, for example, ICCPR, above note 3, art. 2(2)–(3).

38 See, for example, the judgment of the European Court of Human Rights in *Valasinas v. Lithuania*, Application no. 44558/98, [2001] ECHR 479, Judgment of 24 July 2001. See also art. 11 of the Convention Against Torture and Other Cruel, Inhuman or Degrading Treatment or Punishment 1984 (CAT), [1987] CanTS no. 36, which obligates states parties to systematically review "rules, instructions, methods and practices . . . with a view to preventing any cases of torture."

requires a state to provide free counsel to indigent accused.[39] Similarly, some economic and social rights require state abstention rather than action. For example, realizing the right to freedom of contract and free allocation of one's labour and the right to participate in the cultural life of one's community may require significant abstention on the part of the state.[40] These examples illustrate that some "negative" rights may have "positive" aspects, and vice versa.

The fact is that all categories of human rights require the state to be active to some degree and to stand aside to some degree. Whichever the case, the relative ease or difficulty of implementation of any right or category of right has no bearing on the moral, legal, or political value of that right. A right is not accorded any greater or lesser priority based on the degree of intervention or restraint required.

Finally, it is important to note that while the degree of intervention or restraint will depend to some extent on the nature of the right, it will also be contingent on context. The right to counsel will require less intervention in a state in which there are 50,000 lawyers than in an equally populous state in which there are 500 lawyers.

7) Limited Not Absolute

Human rights claims are sometimes depicted in absolute, zero-sum terms that suggest they are subject to no limitations or restrictions. This is not the case.

First, under a variety of treaties, certain human rights are subject to specific limitations or restrictions. These may be explicit and broad. ICCPR article 14(1), for example, permits states to allow *in camera* trials

> for reasons of morals, public order (*ordre public*) or national security in a democratic society, or when the interest of the private lives of the parties so requires, or to the extent strictly necessary in the opinion of the court in special circumstances where publicity would prejudice the interests of justice [or] for the protection of national security or of public order (*ordre public*), or of public health or morals.

---

39 See, for example, ICCPR, above note 3, art. 14(3).

40 See A. Eide, "Economic, Social and Cultural Rights as Human Rights," in A. Eide *et al.*, eds., *Economic, Social and Cultural Rights: A Textbook* (The Hague: Kluwer, 1995) at 36–39, in which the author describe various examples of economic and social rights that a state should implement by minimal intervention (that is, without expending significant resources).

Similarly, ICCPR article 12(3) allows states to limit freedom of movement and residence and the right to leave and return to a country of one's own when "necessary to protect national security, public order, public health or morals or the rights and freedoms of others" provided that the limitations are consistent with the other rights recognized in the ICCPR.[41] Other limitations are narrower. ICCPR article 17(1), for example, prohibits "arbitrary or unlawful" interference with privacy, family, home, or correspondence, meaning that interference is valid provided it is neither arbitrary nor unlawful.

Other human rights treaties contain similar limitations to those found in the ICCPR.[42] It is generally understood that such limitations must respond to a "pressing public or social need," pursue a legitimate and authorized purpose, be proportionate to that purpose, and be applied in a non-discriminatory manner.[43] States are also prohibited from restricting human rights that are found in existing domestic law on the pretext that the human rights treaty in question does not recognize them.[44]

In addition to these permitted limitations on human rights, some of the core treaties permit derogations from, or suspensions of, some of the human rights they proclaim.[45] Derogations, unlike limitations, are not permitted at all times but only in times of national emergency.[46] In addition, derogations may only remain in place temporarily.[47] Deroga-

---

41   Thus, for example, a government may legitimately impose restrictions on freedom of movement in a location in which riots are disturbing public order without actually violating the right to freedom of movement. For similar limitations, see ICCPR, above note 3, arts. 21 (limits on the right of peaceful assembly) and 22(2) (limits on freedom of association).

42   See, for example, ICESCR, above note 4, art. 4; ACHR, above note 11, arts. 12, 13, 15, 16, and 22; ECHR, above note 30, arts. 8–11; and CRC, above note 38, arts. 10, 14, and 15.

43   See the Siracusa Principles on the Limitations and Derogations Provisions in the International Covenant on Civil and Political Rights (1985) 7 Human Rights Quarterly 237 at para. 10.

44   Most human rights treaties include such "savings clauses." See, for example, art. 5(2) common to the ICCPR, above note 3 and the ICESCR, above note 4.

45   See, for example, ICCPR, ibid., art. 4(1); ECHR, above note 30, art. 15; and ACHR, above note 11 art. 27(2). Derogations are not permitted under any of the ICESCR, the CRC, the CAT, the CERD, the CEDAW, or the AfrCHPR.

46   On derogation in public emergency generally, see J. Fitzpatrick, Human Rights in Crisis: The International System for Protecting Rights During States of Emergency (Philadelphia: University of Pennsylvania Press, 1994).

47   For example, in ICCPR General Comment 5 (1981), the UN Human Rights Committee asserts that measures taken under ICCPR, above note 43, art. 4 must be of an "exceptional and temporary nature and may only last as long as the life of the nation is threatened."

tions are, however, generally permitted only to the extent strictly required in the situation, and provided that the derogation is non-discriminatory as well as consistent with the state's other international obligations.[48] Also, derogations may be made only in respect of a limited set of human rights. Under the ICCPR, states may not derogate from the following: the prohibition on genocide (article 6), limitations on capital punishment (article 6), freedom from torture and cruel, inhuman, or degrading treatment or punishment (article 7), freedom from slavery (article 8), the right not to be imprisoned for debt (article 11), the prohibition on *ex post facto* laws (article 15), the right to personhood (article 16), and the right to freedom of thought (article 18).[49] The ECHR contains a shorter list of non-derogable rights than the ICCPR, whereas the ACHR contains a longer list. The ACHR also uniquely declares as non-derogable "the judicial guarantees established for the protection" of such non-derogable rights.[50]

Human rights, like all rights, are also limited between themselves. One person's exercise of her human rights may conflict with the rights of another. Rights to free speech and freedom of the press can, for example, conflict with the right to privacy and the right against injury to reputation.[51]

8) Internally Hierarchical Not Equal

It is commonly asserted that human rights are "equal." In at least one sense this is certainly true: all humans have equal human rights.[52] Were it otherwise, the predicate "human" in human rights would be misplaced. Yet the equality of human rights among humans neither expresses nor implies the equality of human rights between themselves.

---

48   See, for example, ICCPR, *ibid.*, art. 4(1); ECHR, above note 30, art. 1; and ACHR, above note 11, art. 27(2).

49   In ICCPR General Comment 29 (2001), the UN Human Rights Committee asserted that fair trial rights are also non-derogable even though they are not so described in the ICCPR.

50   For an interpretation of the meaning and scope of this phrase, see *Advisory Opinion OC-8/87* (1987) I/A Court HR Series A no. 9. On derogation in Canadian law, see Chapter Ten.

51   For example, ICCPR, above note 3, art. 19(3)(a) permits states to limit freedom of expression by law where necessary to ensure "respect of the rights or reputation of others."

52   See, for example, the UDHR preamble, above note 2, which refers to the "equal . . . rights of all members of the human family."

For example, the UN Human Rights Committee hears individual petitions on all rights other than the right to self-determination, which it considers non-justiciable under the Optional Protocol to the ICCPR 1966 (ICCPR-OP1).[53] Some human rights (for example, most of the rights proclaimed in the ICESCR) may be progressively implemented, whereas others (for example, the rights proclaimed in the ICCPR) must be immediately implemented or "ensured."[54] Also, as demonstrated immediately above, an internal hierarchy exists among recognized human rights in which some rights are subject to specific limitations, other rights are subject to derogation, and still others are subject neither to limitation nor derogation. Some human rights, therefore, enjoy preferred status over others.[55]

9) Inalienable and Non-Extinguishable

Because human rights inhere in human beings, an individual human cannot voluntarily alienate or dispossess himself of such rights (that is, he cannot transfer a human right like he could a property right).[56] That human rights are inalienable does not, however, mean they cannot be waived. While alienation involves an act of dispossession, waiver of a right merely involves a decision not to exercise a possessed right, inalienable or otherwise, in a particular instance.

Human rights are also non-extinguishable, meaning that they cannot be permanently removed at the discretion or pleasure of the state even if a person chooses not to exercise them or chooses to exercise them in a harmful or reckless manner. Thus, if a person commits voting fraud, she does not lose her human right to vote although she could be fined or put in jail and have reasonable limitations placed on her exercise of the right. The human right inheres in the human being and

---

53 [1976] CanTS no. 47. See ICCPR General Comment 23 (1994) at para 3.1. See also *Lubicon*, above note 22.
54 See the discussion in Chapter Four.
55 Analogous rights hierarchies can be found in domestic constitutional jurisprudence in many countries. For example, in relation to the US equal protection clause, the US Supreme Court subjects certain distinctions or classifications to higher levels of judicial scrutiny than other distinctions (for example, race-based distinctions are treated as "immediately suspect," whereas gender-based distinctions are not). See generally M. Tushnet, *Making Constitutional Law: Thurgood Marshall and the Supreme Court, 1961–1991* (New York: Oxford University Press, 1997) at c. 5.
56 Human rights are described as "inalienable" in the preamble to each of the UDHR, the ICCPR, and the ICESCR.

thus cannot be extinguished so long as she remains alive. But as noted above, states are permitted to derogate from certain human rights in emergency circumstances. The practical effect of such derogations is to extinguish rights, albeit only for the duration of a properly applied and enforced derogation period.

10) Indivisible, Interdependent, and Interrelated

Human rights have often been described as indivisible, interdependent, and interrelated. For example, paragraph 5 of the Vienna Declaration and Programme of Action 1993 adopted at the last World Conference on Human Rights declares, "All human rights are universal, indivisible and interdependent and interrelated."[57]

The indivisibility of human rights implies that a state generally cannot pick and choose, as from a menu, which rights it will uphold and which it will not. This characteristic of human rights is most frequently invoked to assert that civil and political rights cannot be "divided from" or treated as separate or less important than economic, social and cultural rights.[58]

The interdependence and interrelatedness of human rights constitute two sides of the same coin. The adjective "interdependent" is simply a subset of the broader category of "interrelated"; being interdependent is one way of being interrelated. The point is that all human rights are necessary to a life of human dignity, and all human rights interact with each other in direct and indirect ways with the net effect that the breach of one will affect the realization of another. US President F.D. Roosevelt captured this notion well when he famously observed that "Necessitous men are not free men."[59]

---

57   UN doc. A/CONF. 157/23 (1993).

58   See, for example, art. 6 of the UN Declaration on the Right to Development 1986 GA res. 41/128: "All human rights and fundamental freedoms are indivisible and interdependent; equal attention and urgent consideration should be given to the implementation, promotion and protection of civil, political, economic, social and cultural rights."

59   "The Economic Bill of Rights," President Roosevelt's 11 January 1944 message to the US Congress on the State of the Union. More recently, Amartya Sen has argued that no substantial famine in the past fifty years has occurred in any state with a democratic form of government and a relatively free press. See generally A. Sen, *Poverty and Famines: An Essay on Entitlement and Deprivation* (Oxford: Clarendon Press, 1981).

11) Complementary to Domestic Laws and Institutions

An inherent challenge in applying international human rights law is to balance the universality of international norms with the particularity of the contexts in which their application arises. By design, the purpose of human rights is to complement, supplement, and in some cases encourage domestic efforts. International human rights law and international supervisory mechanisms are not intended or designed to replace domestic laws and institutions. States remain, and are intended to remain, primarily responsible for the protection of human rights within their jurisdiction. The limited purpose of international institutions is to serve as a safety net in circumstances where domestic mechanisms are exhausted, ineffective, or otherwise unavailable.

The specific relationship between domestic and international laws and institutions is demonstrated and reinforced by a number of features of contemporary human rights practice. For example, the general requirement of exhaustion of domestic remedies — a precondition of admissibility in individual petitions before UN treaty bodies and their regional equivalents — helps ensure that victims focus on available and sufficient domestic remedies first before turning to supranational mechanisms. Another example is the allowance of treaty reservations. By permitting reservations to human rights treaties, states are able to take on international obligations in a way that accords with their local context, provided the reservation is compatible with the object and purpose of the treaty.[60]

Other examples of domestic-international complementarity include the European concepts of "margin of appreciation" and "subsidiarity." The margin of appreciation concept is an original and defining feature of the jurisprudence of the European Court of Human Rights. It seeks to balance the primacy of domestic implementation and enforcement with the need for supranational supervision. The concept refers to the "room of manoeuvre" (or degree of deference) the Court will permit national authorities in fulfilling their obligations under the ECHR. It helps ensure respect for the state's greater knowledge of local conditions, and accommodation of diverse forms of rights adherence. In deciding on the applicable margin of appreciation in any one case, the Court looks to the degree of consensus or divergence among member states on the issue.[61]

---

60   See the discussion of treaties in Chapter Three.
61   See generally C. Yourow, *The Margin of Appreciation Doctrine in the Dynamics of European Human Rights Jurisprudence* (The Hague: Martinus Nijhoff, 1996).

Subsidiarity, a similar principle, has emerged most prominently within the EU. It consists of a preference for taking decisions as near as possible to the local or individual level. Within the EU it means, among other things, that action at the Union (that is, supranational) level in non-exclusive areas of competence is only justified where it is more effectively done there than at the domestic or local level. Through the adoption of the EU Charter of Fundamental Rights 2000, the principle of subsidiarity was directly linked to human rights.[62]

A final and notable example is the (domestic-international) "complementarity" principle established under the Rome Statute of the International Criminal Court 1998 (Rome Statute).[63] By operation of this principle, the Court will only have power to act in cases where states parties are unable or unwilling genuinely to investigate or prosecute cases at the national level (Rome Statute article 17). This is in direct contrast to the jurisdiction of the International Criminal Tribunal for the former Yugoslavia (ICTY) and the International Criminal Tribunal for Rwanda (ICTR), both of which enjoy primacy over domestic courts.[64]

12) Based on Minimum Standards

Although in some states the provisions of international human rights law may exceed domestic standards, the purpose of human rights is to set a minimum standard regarding state conduct. In this respect, human rights are akin to constitutional rights. They serve as a last resort to be invoked in the absence or following the failure of other legal rights or claims under ordinary statutes or general law. There is no right more basic than a "human" right. (In any case the minimalist character of human rights is inescapable since, for the most part, human rights norms are established by means of multilateral negotiation between states in which a low common denominator is often necessary to attract consensus.)

Because human rights standards are minimal, their precise scope and reach can only emerge through interpretation and application. The interpretation of any individual human right is not, however, infinitely elastic; certain interpretations of a human right will inevitably fall

---

62 Article 51 provides that the Charter (OJ no. C 364/1) is "addressed to the institutions and bodies of the Union with due regard for the principle of subsidiarity."

63 [2002] CanTS no. 13.

64 Even in respect of the ICTY and the ICTR, however, domestic courts retain concurrent personal and subject matter jurisdiction. See generally Chapter Seventeen.

afoul of the ordinary or plausible meaning of the right. For example, a state that required all citizens to keep state surveillance cameras in their homes would unavoidably violate the human right to privacy. As the Committee on Economic, Social and Cultural Rights has said:

> [While] the precise method by which Covenant rights are given effect in national law is a matter for each State party to decide, the means used should be appropriate in the sense of producing results which are consistent with the full discharge of its obligations by the State party.[65]

13) Obligations Owed to the International Community as a Whole

International human rights law creates obligations for states vis-à-vis persons within their territory or subject to their jurisdiction. But human rights law obligations also apply *erga omnes*; that is, they are owed to the international community as a whole.[66] The International Court of Justice first made famous this notion in *Case Concerning the Barcelona Traction Light and Power Company, Ltd. (Belgium v. Spain)*, in which it held that human rights obligations are *erga omnes* obligations.[67]

Recently the International Law Commission has also endorsed the idea. Article 48(1)(b) of the Commission's Draft Articles on the Responsibility of States for Internationally Wrongful Acts 2001 (Draft Articles)[68] permits "states other than the injured state" to invoke the responsibility of another state if the obligation breached is owed to the international community as a whole. In its Commentaries to the Draft Articles, the Commission noted "substantial overlap" between the cat-

---

65   ICESCR General Comment 9 (1998) at para. 5.

66   On *erga omnes* obligations generally, see A. de Hoogh, *Obligations Erga Omnes and International Crimes: A Theoretical Inquiry into the Implementation and Enforcement of the International Responsibility of States* (The Hague: Kluwer, 1996); M. Ragazzi, *The Concept Of International Obligations Erga Omnes* (Oxford: Oxford University Press, 1997).

67   [1970] ICJ Rep 3 at 32. Specifically, the Court noted "such obligations derive, for example, in contemporary international law, from the outlawing of acts of aggression and of genocide, and also from the principles and rules concerning the basic rights of the human person, including protection from slavery and racial discrimination." In later cases the Court reaffirmed the concept. See, for example, *Application of the Convention on the Prevention and Punishment of the Crime of Genocide (Preliminary Objections)* [1996] ICJ Rep 4 at paras. 31–32, in which the Court held that the rights and obligations contained in the Genocide Convention apply *erga omnes*.

68   UN doc. A/56/10.

egories of *jus cogens* (peremptory norms) and *erga omnes* obligations.[69] It notes, however, that there is a difference in emphasis:

> While peremptory norms of general international law focus on the scope and priority to be given to a certain number of fundamental obligations, the focus of obligations to the international community as a whole is essentially on the legal interests of all States in compliance — i.e., in terms of the present Articles, in being entitled to invoke the responsibility of any State in breach.[70]

B. CHALLENGES TO THE MODEL

This section will briefly review some of the more prominent challenges to the human rights concept, in order to provide the reader with a sense of the continuing tensions in the theory and practice of human rights. The criticisms discussed in this section have been clustered under headings for purposes of explanation, but many of the arguments overlap.[71]

1) Human Rights and Communism

With only a few remaining communist countries in the world today, the challenge that communism once presented to the human rights agenda has greatly diminished, if not vanished. After 1989, when democratic elections were finally held in the states of the former Soviet empire, communist parties were generally ousted from power and replaced by parties that espoused human rights agendas. Since then, communist parties have generally had to embrace democracy and human rights to remain credible.

A cornerstone idea of early communist theory and practice was that the interests of society (as embodied in the state) should always take precedence over those of the individual. This is a theory that is fundamentally at odds with the human rights idea, which is based on the protection of individual rights and freedoms from state encroachment or neglect. For this reason, during much of the Cold War — particularly prior to the Helsinki process of the 1970s when the Soviet

---

69   See Chapter Three on *jus cogens* norms.
70   Commentaries at 281.
71   The challenge that terrorism presents to human rights is discussed in the book's Conclusion.

Union accepted the universality of human rights[72] — the idea of human rights was considered anathema to communist thinking.

Much of communism's opposition to human rights, both before and after the Helsinki process, was misplaced. First, it is not the purpose of human rights to eviscerate the state; indeed, many if not all human rights require a strong state prepared actively to assist in the realization of human rights. Second, international human rights law permits deep inroads in favour of the interests of society by allowing states to limit and in some cases even derogate from their human rights obligations. Third, while human rights do not require individuals to put state above self, neither do human rights preclude an individual from making that choice.

But that is perhaps where the harmony between human rights and communism ends. Certainly in its extreme form (where individuals exist to serve the state), communism is inherently incompatible with the human rights idea.[73] Where the communist challenge remains relevant is in relation to the longstanding debate over international law's alleged under-emphasis of economic, social and cultural rights in comparison to civil and political rights. While few states continue to insist that capitalism is the source of most violations of economic, social and cultural rights, and while it is unlikely that communism will again present a competing worldview to the human rights idea any time soon, the insistence of communist states on the relative importance of economic, social and cultural rights ("human rights begin after breakfast") continues to find broad support in many corners of the world.

2) Human Rights and Religion

There is no inherent conflict between religion and human rights. To the contrary, freedom of religion is one of the core human rights found in most major human rights treaties, albeit subject to reasonable limitations in the public interest.[74] There are also provisions in human rights

---

72   Helsinki Final Act 1975 (1975) 14 ILM 1292.

73   Likewise, the idea espoused by some communist states (prominently the former USSR) that they had a right to "assist" the working class in other states in achieving revolution is wholly at odds with the right to self-determination and the rule of non-interference in the affairs of other states. See J. Currie, *Public International Law* (Toronto: Irwin Law, 2001) at 10.

74   See, for example, UDHR, above note 2, art. 18: ICCPR, above note 3, art. 18(3); International Convention on the Elimination of All Forms of Racial Discrimination 1966 (CERD), [1970] CanTS no. 28, art. 5(d)(vii); Convention on the Rights of the Child 1989 (CRC), [1992] Can TS no. 3, art. 14(1); AmDR, above

treaties that protect, *inter alia*, the freedom to adopt a religion or belief,[75] and the freedom of parents and guardians to ensure the religious and moral education of their children consistent with their own convictions.[76] Also, many domestic human rights charters and constitutions — including the Canadian *Charter* — are explicitly premised on a belief in God.[77] There are also examples of states that are based on a particular religious identity but which nonetheless incorporate and work within an explicit human rights framework.[78] Even theocracies like Iran participate in the international human rights system, albeit with many reservations aimed at protecting the Islamic character of the state and its fundamental laws.[79] While lack of separation of "church" and state will generally complicate or strain the application of human rights,[80] religion and human rights can co-exist in relative harmony.

---

note 14, art. 3; ACHR, above note 11, art. 12; ECHR, above note 30, art. 9(1); AfrCHPR, above note 14, art. 8.

75 See, for example, ICCPR, *ibid.*, art. 18(2). This includes the right to hold non-theistic and atheistic beliefs, the right not to subscribe to any religion or belief, and the right to replace one's religion or belief with another. See the Human Rights Committee's General Comment no. 22 (1993) at paras. 2 and 5 regarding the right to freedom of thought, conscience, and religion (art. 18).

76 See, for example, ICCPR, *ibid.*, art. 18(4).

77 The preamble to the Canadian *Charter* proclaims "Canada is founded upon principles that recognize the supremacy of God and the rule of law."

78 Israel is perhaps the most obvious example (in law, if not always in practice).

79 See, for example, Committee on Economic, Social and Cultural Rights, *Concluding Observations: Iran* (1993) at para. 4:

> [V]arious articles of the *Constitution* of Iran subject the enjoyment of universally recognized human rights, including economic, social and cultural rights, to such restrictions as: 'provided it is not against Islam' (article 28); 'with due regard to Islamic standards' (article 20); 'in conformity with the Islamic criteria' (article 20); and 'except when it is detrimental to the fundamental principles of Islam' (article 24). In that connection the Committee considers, in the light of the Covenant provisions and of all the information available to it, that such restrictive clauses negatively affect the application of the Covenant. . . . It is apparent that the authorities in Iran are using the religion as a pretext in order to abuse these rights.

80 See, for example, the UN Human Rights Committee's interpretation of ICCPR, above note 3, art. 18 in General Comment no. 22 (1993) at para. 9:

> The fact that a religion is recognized as a state religion or that it is established as official or traditional or that its followers comprise the majority of the population, shall not result in any impairment of the enjoyment of any of the rights under the Covenant, including articles 18 and 27, nor in any discrimination against adherents to other religions or non-believers. In particular, certain measures discriminating against the latter, such as measures restricting eligibility for government service to members of the predominant religion or giving

Nevertheless, a spirited debate has emerged in recent years about the purportedly antagonistic relationship between religion — and in particular certain interpretations of Islam — and human rights. Conservative religious critics have claimed that human rights are incompatible with religious values because they are founded on a secular and hedonist vision of human life and the state, that human rights focus on rights to the exclusion of religious duties toward family and community, and that human rights impose Western values which upset, among other things, the proper roles of women and men.[81] All of these criticisms, to varying degrees, misconceive the content of human rights and the limited role it purports to play in advancing human dignity and freedom.

First, human rights are founded on a concept of a human being living in a society, not in a social vacuum, and they presuppose neither a secular nor a pleasure-seeking society. Instead, human rights seek to provide a universal minimum standard below which no society — secular, religious, or otherwise — could fall without undermining the concept of the "good society." Furthermore, international human rights law seeks neither to replace nor to undermine the duties, religious or otherwise, that people may bear toward family, community, or state. Instead, it aims to preserve the rights of individual members of those groups to make different choices including, for example, to reject a religious duty imposed by the state.[82] But if family, religion, and community are positive forces in an individual's life, that individual will in all likelihood choose to exercise her rights and duties in a way that supports rather than hurts the group's interests.

Where perhaps conservative religion and human rights most come into conflict is on issues of gender and sexual orientation. Conservative religious objections to human rights often reflect retrograde ideas

---

economic privileges to them or imposing special restrictions on the practice of other faiths, are not in accordance with the prohibition of discrimination based on religion or belief and the guarantee of equal protection under article 26.

81   For a more detailed discussion of these claims, see K. Dalacoura, *Islam, Liberalism and Human Rights* (London: I.B. Tauris, 1998); A. An Na'im, ed., *Human Rights in Cross-Cultural Perspectives* (Philadelphia: University of Pennsylvania Press, 1992) at c. 1; C. Gustafson & P. Juviler, eds., *Religion and Human Rights: Competing Claims?* (Armonk, NY: M.E. Sharpe, 1998).

82   See the Human Rights Committee's General Comment no. 22 (1993) at para. 10:

If a set of beliefs is treated as official ideology in constitutions, statutes, proclamations of ruling parties, etc., or in actual practice, this shall not result in any impairment of the freedoms under article 18 or any other rights recognized under the Covenant nor in any discrimination against persons who do not accept the official ideology or who oppose it.

about the place and roles of women and men in society. Even on this issue, however, international human rights law allows a measure of differential treatment between men and women — provided that the intent or effect of the treatment does not vitiate fundamental human rights. Thus, for example, it may be permissible as a matter of international human rights law for a religious group in a secular state to forbid its female members from becoming clerics. Freedom of religion likely tolerates that practice, at least for now. On the other hand, international human rights law would not protect any exclusion of women from access to public education on the basis of religion.

Finally, it is true that in contrast to religion, human rights do not address many of the most important aspects of peoples' lives. There is, for example, no human right to be loved or respected by our friends. However, this is not a flaw in the human rights concept. It is not the "job" of human rights to produce love, charity, and friendship. The limited purpose of human rights is to help create the minimum conditions necessary to make the realization of those ideals possible.

3) Human Rights, Democracy, and Community

Human rights posit the state as the primary threat to human dignity. That is, human rights protections are aimed primarily at the state rather than at private abuses. Some question this approach, arguing that the state is more often the friend than the enemy of human rights, and that many of the worst affronts occur in the private sphere.[83] In some contexts this is undeniable. In modern-day "failed states," where life resembles nothing so much as Hobbes' depiction of the state of nature — "solitary, poor, nasty, brutish, and short"[84] — often the chief threat to human rights is not an excess of state power but rather its absence.[85] In such situations, the consolidation and not the curtailment of state power should be the primary objective of human rights supporters. While the international community, via the UN, can do much to protect human rights in some of these extreme situations, it is no substitute for a functioning state.

---

83   See generally A. Clapham, *Human Rights in the Private Sphere* (Oxford: Oxford University Press, 1996).

84   T. Hobbes, *Leviathan* (1651).

85   See Donnelly, *Universal*, above note 5 at 36, where the author asserts: "'Failed states' such as Somalia suggest that one of the few things as frightening in the contemporary world as an efficiently repressive states is no state at all."

But obviously more than a functioning state is required to ensure adequate human rights protection. Democratic states are widely viewed as the preferred model of protection. Certainly most of the evidence of human rights practices in democratic states, as compared to non-democratic ones, bears this out. There is, however, an inherent tension between democracy and human rights. Whereas a primary objective of democracy is to reflect the voice of the majority within the state, a primary objective of human rights is to help protect the individual from the majority and the state. In short, democracy alone is insufficient to ensure human rights; constitutionalism, or the limitation of state power, is the necessary companion of democracy. In the absence of constitutionalism, tyranny of the majority is a constant threat. In any case, we have seen that the response of international human rights law is to balance democracy with human rights by permitting public interest limitations and derogations in a narrow set of circumstances. One might say that these limitations on the exercise of human rights are the tribute that human rights pay to democracy.

A related issue is the perceived tension between human rights and the quality of community life. Some complain that rights regimes produce litigious societies, shift focus away from collective action and toward individual action, and undermine a sense of civic duty or social responsibility.[86] The evidence for the first claim is far from clear. It may also be beside the point. The advantage of human rights is that they create and reinforce expectations among humans regarding a baseline of dignity and fair treatment. Indeed, the promise of rights in many cases appears to be positively motivational.[87] If one of the secondary consequences of their conferral is the generation of litigation, this may as easily be something to celebrate as to lament. It may simply represent the political awakening of classes of persons that hitherto saw themselves as excluded from legal protection.

As to the concern about the effect of human rights on collective action and civic duty, it must be emphasized that rights are not a substitute for duties. As already noted, human rights perform an entirely different function, namely to protect individuals who choose to deviate from what society or community demands. The very essence of the

---

86   See, for example, M. Tushnet, "An Essay on Rights" (1984) 62 Texas Law Review 1363. See also M. Glendon, *Rights Talk: The Impoverishment of Political Discourse* (New York: The Free Press, 1991).

87   See, for example, P. Williams, "Alchemical Notes: Reconstructed Ideals from Deconstructed Rights" (1987) 22 Harv. C.R.-C.L.L. Rev. 401 at 404–17, where the author argues that rights help disadvantaged groups and provide a source of hope and inspiration.

human rights concept is that humans do not exist to serve state or community but are valued for their own sake, no matter what their choices or preferences.

4) Human Rights, History, and Culture

It is largely uncontroversial that the origins of the human rights concept (its legal expression, not its moral inspiration) are "Western."[88] This does not indicate the superiority of Western civilizations. Many of the worst human rights atrocities of the last five centuries — slavery and the slave trade, colonialism, genocide, fascism — are attributable to the West.

The Western origins of the human rights concept have provided fertile ground for some non-Western states to justify their opposition to human rights. Perhaps the biggest clash on the issue in recent years occurred at the Vienna World Conference on Human Rights in 1993, when a group of Asian states (opposed by Asian human rights NGOs) questioned the universality of human rights on the basis of their origins as well as their appropriateness in the Asian context.[89] Various declarations were made, including that human rights must be understood differently in different cultural contexts, and that religious, cultural, and historical differences require greater recognition.[90] Yet the expressed opposition was not so much to the concept of human rights

---

88 But see, for example, K. Mahbubani, *Can Asians Think? Understanding the Divide Between East and West* (Hanover, NH: Steerforth Press, 2002); I. Al-Marzouqi, *Human Rights in Islamic Law* (Abu Dhabi: International Specialized Book Service Inc., 2000); S. Angle, *Human Rights and Chinese Thought: A Cross-Cultural Inquiry* (Cambridge: Cambridge University Press, 2002); D. Wai, "Human Rights in Sub-Saharan Africa," in *Human Rights: Cultural and Ideological Perspectives*, A. Pollis & P. Schwab, eds. (New York: Praeger, 1980); Y. Khushalani, "Human Rights in Asia and Africa" (1983) 4 Human Rights Law Journal 403.

89 See F. van Hoof, "Asian Challenges to the Concept of Universality: Afterthoughts on the Vienna Conference on Human Rights," in *Human Rights: Chinese and Dutch Perspectives*, P. Baehr *et al.*, eds. (The Hague: Martinus Nijhoff, 1996). On the "Asian values" debate more generally, see J. Bauer & D. Bell, eds., *The East Asian Challenge for Human Rights* (Cambridge: Cambridge University Press, 1999); D. Bell, "The East Asian Challenge to Human Rights: Reflections on an East-West Dialogue" (1996) 18 Human Rights Quarterly 641; J. Hsiung, "Human Rights in an East Asian Perspective," in J. Hsiung, ed., *Human Rights in East Asia: A Cultural Perspective* (New York: Paragon House Publishers, 1985).

90 The formal position was expressed in the Final Declaration of the Regional Meeting for Asia of the World Conference on Human Rights 1993 (better known as the Bangkok Declaration), UN docs. A/CONF.157/ASRM/8 and A/CONF.157/PC/59. Among other things, the Bangkok Declaration reaffirmed a commitment

as to specific aspects of its practice. Indeed, at the end of the Vienna Conference, the universality of human rights was upheld in a final resolution with the full backing of Asian states.[91]

From a human rights perspective, it is desirable to allow a state to interpret and apply human rights norms in line with its particular history, culture, or values. Human rights are not intended as a device to force Western values onto other societies. At the same time, certain social or cultural practices (for example, slavery, the caste system, male-only suffrage) are inherently incompatible with human rights and are not saved by recourse to cultural relativist arguments. Where cultural diversity is no more than a pretext for abuse or diverting attention from a state's human rights record, it should not be tolerated. For this reason, it is important to challenge assertions of cultural relativism where the sources of the assertions are states that suppress the voice of their own nationals.

5) Human Rights and Economic Development

It has been asserted by a wide variety of actors, but especially states from the developing world, that human rights obligations present an impediment to economic development. The common claim is that states managing emerging economies must be very strict and aggressive in their economic planning, and that this requires the temporary suppression of certain human rights such as, for example, freedom of association, freedom of expression, or democratic rights.[92] There may be a basis for this argument in the experiences of such East Asian countries

---

to the principles contained in the UN Charter and the UDHR (para. 1). It also recognized that "while human rights are universal in nature, they must be considered in the context of a dynamic and evolving process of international norm-setting, bearing in mind the significance of national and regional particularities and various historical, cultural and religious backgrounds" (para. 8).

91   Para. 5 of the Vienna Declaration and Programme of Action, above note 57, reads:

All human rights are universal, indivisible and interdependent and interrelated. The international community must treat human rights globally in a fair and equal manner, on the same footing, and with the same emphasis. While the significance of national and regional particularities and various historical, cultural and religious backgrounds must be borne in mind, it is the duty of States, regardless of their political, economic and cultural systems, to promote and protect all human rights and fundamental freedoms.

92   This view of the relation between human rights and economic development is also implicit in many international lending policies, which often place states in the invidious position of cutting important social programs in order to obtain loans.

as China and Singapore, although it is unknown how these countries' economic development might have differed in the absence of repression. It appears, however, that most autocratic states become impoverished kleptocracies rather than rights-respecting democracies.[93]

Economic development is not and cannot be an end in itself.[94] If we are to take the claims of many developing world states seriously (and local human rights NGOs generally do not), the ostensible purpose of sacrificing some rights in the short term is to generate the economic development necessary to guarantee all human rights in the long term, but particularly economic and social rights, which some of these states dubiously claim to value more than developed states. Yet the notion of rights sacrifice contradicts the "right to development" that such states claim to prize. The preamble to the UN Declaration on the Right to Development 1986 is clear on this. It reads:

> Concerned at the existence of serious obstacles to development, as well as to the complete fulfilment of human beings and of peoples, constituted, inter alia, by the denial of civil, political, economic, social and cultural rights, and considering that all human rights and fundamental freedoms are indivisible and interdependent and that, in order to promote development, equal attention and urgent consideration should be given to the implementation, promotion and protection of civil, political, economic, social and cultural rights and that, accordingly, the promotion of, respect for and enjoyment of certain human rights and fundamental freedoms cannot justify the denial of other human rights and fundamental freedoms. . . .

The better, and more contemporary, view is that human rights and development are interdependent. We note in this regard that at least two bridging concepts — "human development"[95] (or "sustainable

---

93   Some examples include North Korea under the KWP, Burma under the SLORC, and Zimbabwe under ZANU-PF.

94   As art. 2 of the UN Declaration on the Right to Development, above note 58, provides: "The human person is the central subject of development and should be the active participant and beneficiary of the right to development."

95   The UN Development Programme (UNDP) is the most prominent exponent and user of the concept of human development. For more than a decade, it has produced a global Human Development Report, which ranks every state in areas such as per capita income, literacy, life expectancy, and respect for women's human rights. The UNDP defines human development as a process of enlarging human choices. Its website (http://www.undp.org) states: "In the ultimate analysis, human development is development of the people, development for the people, and development by the people."

human development")[96] and "human security"[97] — have acquired significant currency in recent years. While it is true that both concepts reflect a "contemporary tendency to conflate all good things,"[98] they also help to close out analyses premised on the opposition of human rights and development — analyses which at the end of the day serve neither cause especially well.

C. CONCLUSION

Human rights will likely remain a contested concept. It strikes at the core of many central features of human existence including how we interact with each other and the state, how we punish criminal behaviour, and how we protect the vulnerable among us. Its breadth as a concept is both its virtue and its vice. It contains elements that are bound to appeal to many, but also elements that are bound to offend some. Were it less ambitious or comprehensive, though, it is unlikely that the human rights concept would hold such widespread popularity and moral currency in international affairs. A suitable replacement for it is nowhere in sight.

This is not to say that the human rights concept cannot be improved. As later chapters will demonstrate, new human rights continue to be added and existing human rights continue to be refined through interpretation. In addition, new international and domestic mechanisms for the promotion and protection of human rights are being created all the time, mechanisms which in some cases vastly enhance human rights outcomes. But whether any expansions in coverage or improvements in enforcement will prove the worth of human rights to its toughest critics is uncertain. What is certain is that the criticisms of human rights, fewer with each passing year, have always served to improve them.

---

96   See S. Anand & A. Sen, *Sustainable Human Development: Concepts and Priorities* (New York: UNDP Office of Development Studies, 1996); and UNDP, *Integrating Human Rights with Sustainable Human Development: A UNDP Policy Document* (1998).

97   The concept of human security — ostensibly focused on "freedom from fear" — appears to include a motley assortment of subjects including protection of civilians, peace support operations, conflict prevention, public safety, corporate social responsibility, corruption and transparency, and human rights. See, for example, the Canadian government's human security website: http://www.humansecurity.gc.ca.

98   Donnelly, *Universal*, above note 5 at 196.

CHAPTER 3

SUBJECTS AND SOURCES OF INTERNATIONAL HUMAN RIGHTS LAW

Before turning to the substance of international human rights law, one must understand who it applies to and where it comes from. This chapter introduces the subjects and sources of international human rights law, and indeed of international law in general.

As this chapter and later chapters demonstrate, states are the central actors in the creation and application of international human rights law. For better or worse, they are its authors and its main subjects. Although human rights serve to limit the power of states, the fact is that their recognition and realization largely depends on state action. A basic appreciation of the role of states is therefore essential to any proper account of human rights.

A. SUBJECTS OF INTERNATIONAL HUMAN RIGHTS LAW

The classic definition of a subject of international law is an entity possessing (i) international legal rights upon which it can rely for purposes of bringing international claims in its own name, and (ii) international legal obligations.[1] Among the rights enjoyed by international legal subjects are the right to enter into treaties with other international legal sub-

---

1   *Reparations for Injuries Suffered in the Service of the United Nations*, Advisory Opinion [1949] ICJ Rep 174 at 179.

jects and the right to assert certain legal privileges and immunities on their own behalf. Among the types of obligations possessed by international legal subjects are, of course, human rights obligations.

States are the primary subjects of the international legal system. They have plenary treaty-making power. They have standing before international judicial and quasi-judicial bodies. They enjoy the broadest set of privileges and immunities under international law. And most significantly for our purposes, states have treaty and customary law obligations, not least in the field of human rights.

All other international legal subjects derive their status as subjects from recognition by states. In other words, to the extent that there are other international legal subjects at all, it is because states have chosen to confer that status upon them. It follows that other international legal subjects have a narrower set of rights and obligations.

The most widely acknowledged international legal subjects other than states are **international organizations** (also known as intergovernmental organizations). As early as 1949, the International Court of Justice recognized the UN as an international legal subject.[2] Today the assertion that the UN is a subject in international law is unassailable; likewise the Council of Europe, the Organization of American States (OAS), and the African Union (AU). Many of the principal organs of these international organizations have independent treaty-making power,[3] and many of their key officers have immunities and privileges roughly equivalent to those of state diplomats.[4] However, not all organs of the UN and not all international organizations are necessarily international legal subjects.[5] Among the qualifying criteria are: whether the organization represents a permanent association of states, whether there is a distinction between the legal powers of the organization and those of its member states, and whether it has rights and duties that can be exercised within the international legal system.[6]

---

2   *Ibid.* at 185.

3   See, for example, the Vienna Convention on the Law of Treaties between States and International Organizations or between International Organizations 1986, reproduced at (1986) 25 ILM 543.

4   See, for example, the Convention on the Privileges and Immunities of the United Nations 1946 [1948] CanTS no. 2.

5   See generally J. Currie, *Public International Law* (Toronto: Irwin Law, 2001) [Currie, *International Law*] at 60.

6   See the *Yearbook of International Organizations*, published annually by the Union of International Associations, which aims to identify and list all international organizations. It defines international organizations as: being based on a formal instrument of agreement between the governments of states; including three or

Individuals (that is, humans) may also be international legal subjects, albeit with a far narrower set of rights and obligations. International human rights law, as well as international humanitarian and criminal law, create rights and obligations for individuals. Human rights law creates a wide array of individual rights and a much lesser number of individual duties. Humanitarian law and international criminal law impose significant obligations upon individuals, while also granting them rights in situations of armed conflict.[7] Yet the legal personality of individuals, when compared with states, is quite limited. Individuals lack treaty-making power. They enjoy no significant privileges or immunities as individuals.[8] And they have only limited standing before international bodies, whether judicial, quasi-judicial, or political.

Other actors possibly (but generally not) constituting international legal subjects are: peoples,[9] non-governmental organizations (NGOs),[10] the International Committee of the Red Cross (ICRC),[11] private corporations,[12] employer and worker organizations,[13] and organized armed movements.[14]

---

more states as parties to the agreement; and possessing a permanent secretariat that performs ongoing tasks.

7   See the discussion in Chapter Seven.

8   Individuals who serve as diplomats, by contrast, have many privileges and immunities.

9   Peoples enjoy a right to self-determination but have limited, if any, standing before international bodies and no recognized treaty-making power, privileges, or immunities under international law.

10   NGOs have standing before various judicial and quasi-judicial human rights bodies (including the UN Human Rights Committee, the European Court of Human Rights, and the Inter-American Commission on Human Rights) but lack all other attributes of international legal personality.

11   The ICRC has a *sui generis* status and role. See the discussion in Chapter Sixteen.

12   Private corporations only have standing within the Council of Europe human rights system, and even there it is limited in comparison to individuals. See the discussion in Chapter Fifteen. As for public corporations, they are — as their name suggests — state actors.

13   The unique tripartite oversight system of the ILO gives employer and worker organizations a near-equal seat with governments, and a variety of important rights and obligations. Still, employer and worker organizations lack treaty-making power or any distinctive privileges and immunities under the ILO system or international law generally. See the discussion in Chapter Sixteen.

14   "National liberation" movements enjoy various protections under the Protocol Additional to the Geneva Conventions of 12 August 1949, and relating to the Protection of Victims of International Armed Conflicts 1977 (GC Protocol I), [1991] CanTS no. 2 — most importantly, prisoner-of-war status. Such movements can even take on the equivalent rights and obligations of states by making a unilateral declaration under art. 96(3) of GC Protocol I. That article provides:

B. SOURCES OF INTERNATIONAL HUMAN RIGHTS LAW

1) Overview

The origins of most public international law can be traced to customary law. International human rights law is an exception: its content has been established primarily through multilateral treaties which, over time, have helped to shape the content of custom.

Article 38(1) of the Statute of the International Court of Justice 1945 (ICJ Statute)[15] is the most widely cited statement of the sources of international law, including international human rights law. It lists the following sources:

> *a.* international conventions, whether general or particular, establishing rules expressly recognized by the contesting states; *b.* international custom, as evidence of a general practice accepted as law; *c.* the general principles of law recognized by civilized nations; and *d.* subject to the provisions of article 59, judicial decisions and the teachings of the most highly qualified publicists of the various nations, as subsidiary means for the determination of rules of law.[16]

Each of these sources will be analyzed in turn with specific reference to international human rights law.

While authoritative, the article 38(1) list of sources may not be comprehensive. For example, UN member states are required to "accept

---

Such declaration shall, upon its receipt by the depositary, have in relation to that conflict the following effects: (a) the [Geneva] Conventions and this Protocol are brought into force for the said authority as a Party to the conflict with immediate effect; (b) the said authority assumes the same rights and obligations as those which have been assumed by a High Contracting Party to the Conventions and this Protocol; and (c) the Conventions and this Protocol are equally binding upon all Parties to the conflict.

Other organized armed movements (that is, non-liberation movements) engaged in internal armed conflicts enjoy more limited protection, whether under art. 3 common to the Geneva Conventions of 1949 (Common Article 3), [1965] CanTS no. 20, or under the Protocol Additional to the Geneva Conventions of 12 August 1949, and relating to the Protection of Victims of Non-International Armed Conflicts 1977 (GC Protocol II), [1991] CanTS no. 2. No armed movement, however, possesses standing before any international judicial or quasi-judicial body, nor do they possess any special privileges and immunities under international law.

15   [1945] CanTS no. 7.

16   Article 59, referred to in art. 38(1)(d), provides: "The decision of the Court has no binding force except between the parties and in respect of that particular case."

and carry out" decisions of the Security Council.[17] Thus, resolutions of the Security Council are a binding source of international law for UN member states like Canada. Also, as discussed at the end of this chapter, international judicial and quasi-judicial bodies occasionally (and controversially) make use of "soft law" sources.

2) Treaties

a) Definition

The Vienna Convention on the Law of Treaties 1969 (VCLT),[18] itself a treaty, sets out the law of treaties.[19] It is the chief source for understanding and interpreting treaties between states.[20] It was conceived, and is still generally viewed, as declaratory of customary international law — despite only having ninety-three states parties.[21]

Article 2 of the VCLT defines a treaty as "an international agreement concluded between States in written form and governed by international law, whether embodied in a single instrument or in two or more related instruments and whatever its particular designation." There are thus four elements to a treaty. It is (1) an international agreement, (2) made between states, (3) in written form, and (4) governed by international law.

There are many synonyms for the term "treaty" including pact, covenant, charter, agreement, convention, and protocol. None of these designations has any substantive impact on the bindingness of the instrument provided the elements of VCLT article 2 are present. The term "protocol" is distinguishable from the other terms in that it tends to be used to describe a particular kind of treaty, namely one that amends and/or adds to another treaty. Because of the difficulty of amending treaties — a process that usually requires the consent of all or a supermajority of states

---

17   Charter of the United Nations 1945 (UN Charter), [1945] CanTS no. 7 art. 25.

18   [1980] CanTS no. 37.

19   Canada tends to view the VCLT as second in importance only to the UN Charter in the field of international law. See M. Copithorne, "National Treaty Law and Practice: Canada" in M. Leigh et al., eds., National Treaty Law and Practice (Baltimore: American Society of International Law, 2003) at 2 [Copithorne, "National Treaty Law"].

20   Article 1 of the Convention declares that it applies only to treaties between states.

21   The International Law Commission's Draft Articles on the Responsibility of States for Internationally Wrongful Acts 2001 (Draft Articles), UN doc. A/56/10, partly overlap with the VCLT. But the Draft Articles relate to all sources of binding international law and not just to treaties, and have yet to be formally adopted outside the International Law Commission. On the other hand, the Draft Articles fill in some gaps left by the VCLT on certain issues, such as the nature of a state's international liability for breach of a treaty.

parties — most treaties are amended by way of optional protocols which individual states parties to the original treaty are free to ratify or reject.

b) Types of Treaty

There are two main types of treaty: bilateral (that is, between two states) and multilateral (that is, between three or more states). As of 1998, Canada had obligations under approximately 500 multilateral treaties and 2,500 bilateral treaties.[22] Bilateral treaties may be quite limited in scope, such as the Canada-South Africa Extradition Treaty 2001,[23] or very broad, such as the Canada-United States Free Trade Agreement 1988.[24] Multilateral treaties also vary in their reach. Some are intended for universal ratification, such as UN human rights treaties, ILO treaties, and international humanitarian law treaties. Others are regional or local in their reach, such as OAS human rights treaties and the North American Free Trade Agreement 1992.[25]

Human rights treaties are almost always multilateral, but they are distinguishable from other multilateral treaties in two respects. First, rather than simply creating an obligation to respect and ensure the rights of other states parties, human rights treaties create a state obligation to respect and ensure the rights of individuals within the territory or subject to the jurisdiction of the state. This makes individuals third party beneficiaries of an agreement to which they are not parties. The Inter-American Court of Human Rights has explained:

> [M]odern human rights treaties in general . . . are not multilateral treaties of the traditional type concluded to accomplish the reciprocal exchange of rights for the mutual benefit of the contracting States. . . . In concluding these human rights treaties, the States can be deemed to submit themselves to a legal order within which they, for the common good, assume various obligations, not in relation to other States, but towards all individuals within their jurisdiction.[26]

Second, human rights and human rights-related treaties are among the most widely ratified of all multilateral treaties. For example, there are 191 states parties to the Convention on the Rights of the Child 1989 (CRC)[27] and the Geneva Conventions.[28]

---

22   Copithorne, "National Treaty Law," above note 19 at 13.
23   [2001] CanTS no. 20.
24   [1989] CanTS no. 3.
25   [1994] CanTS no. 2.
26   *Advisory Opinion OC-2/82* (1982) I/A Court HR Series A no. 2 at para. 29.
27   [1992] CanTS no. 3.
28   Geneva Convention for the Amelioration of the Condition of the Wounded and Sick in Armed Forces in the Field 1949 [1965] CanTS no. 20; Geneva Conven-

c) Drafting and Negotiation of Treaties

In international law there is no central legislative body that votes on or approves laws or treaties. The whole system is decentralized; each state decides for itself whether it wants to adopt or become party to a treaty.

In the case of human rights treaties intended for universal application, the UN has been the focal point for their drafting and negotiation. Often draft articles for a treaty are produced by the UN Commission on Human Rights and its Sub-Commission. But they are also produced by the International Law Commission, a body established by the UN General Assembly in 1947 and composed of thirty-four of the world's foremost international law jurists.[29] Its mandate is "the promotion of the progressive development of international law and its codification."[30] After draft articles for a treaty have been finalized, the UN General Assembly generally convenes an international conference. A period of debate and negotiation ensues. Increasingly, the trend in international lawmaking is to reach agreement by consensus rather than by vote. Although this necessarily produces a lowest common denominator effect that reduces the normative potency of a treaty, it also increases universality.

In comparison to the lawmaking process in most democratic states, international lawmaking is markedly less public and participatory. While intergovernmental and non-governmental organizations often contribute to the preparation of draft human rights treaties and exert influence in the negotiation phase, states — the only true "lawmakers" under international law — have the final word.

d) Signature, Ratification, Accession, Succession, Entry into Force

At the conclusion of a treaty negotiation, each state will be presented with the option of signature. A state's signature of a treaty may represent different things. Under some treaties, the act of signature denotes consent to become a party to the treaty (that is, to be bound by its terms). For most if not all human rights treaties, however, signature

---

tion for the Amelioration of the Condition of Wounded, Sick, and Shipwrecked Members of Armed Forces at Sea 1949 [1965] CanTS no. 20; Geneva Convention relative to the Treatment of Prisoners of War 1949 [1965] CanTS no. 20; Geneva Convention relative to the Protection of Civilian Persons in Time of War 1949 [1965] CanTS no. 20.

29 Commission members serve in their individual capacity and are elected by the UN General Assembly for terms of five years.There are currently no Canadian members of the Commission but there are two past Canadian members: Marcel Cadieux (1962–66) and John Alan Beesley (1987–91). There are regional equivalents to the International Law Commission too such as the Inter-American Juridical Committee. A Canadian, Jonathan Fried, is a member of that Committee.

30 Statute of the International Law Commission, art. 1, para. 1.

merely denotes agreement with the text of the treaty and the intention, but not the obligation, to ratify at a later date. A state that signs but does not ratify a human rights treaty becomes what is known as a "signatory," as distinct from a "party." Signatories have an obligation to "refrain from acts that would defeat the object of purpose" of the treaty in question,[31] but do not yet have obligations under the treaty itself.

Between signature and ratification, signatory states undertake the necessary steps within domestic law and procedure to enable ratification. In many states, including Canada, these steps may include legislative implementation of some or all of the treaty's provisions. Not infrequently, states remain signatories for several years. Much may depend on changes in domestic government, constitutional obstacles to ratification, and shifts in public opinion.[32]

The act of ratification constitutes a state's formal expression of consent to be bound by the terms of a treaty. For states that did not participate in the negotiation of a treaty but who subsequently express their consent to be bound, the term used is "accession." Accession does not require prior signature. For purposes of international law the effects of ratification and accession are identical: the state becomes bound by the treaty.

In rare cases, states become bound under treaties by way of succession. Succession occurs when there is a change in the identity of a state under international law. The general rule is that the new state does not succeed to the treaty rights and obligations of the antecedent state.[33] However, this rule can vary depending on whether succession occurs by way of separation, secession, decolonization, merger, absorption, or annexation.[34] Changes of government do not trigger the rules of succession or affect the state's treaty rights and obligations, even where those changes have occurred in a manner that is unconstitutional.[35] The new

---

31   VCLT, above note 18, art. 18.

32   The US, for example, has remained a signatory to the International Covenant on Economic, Social and Cultural Rights 1966 (ICESCR), [1976] CanTS no. 46, since 1977. The US is also the first state to attempt to "unsign" a human rights-related treaty, namely the Rome Statute of the International Criminal Court 1998 (Rome Statute), [2002] CanTS no. 13. See "US Renounces World Court Treaty," BBC News (http://news.bbc.co.uk), 6 May 2002.

33   Prior to the Second World War, the rule was the opposite. Canada, for example, inherited the obligations assumed on its behalf by the UK prior to the *Statute of Westminster 1931*.

34   See generally Currie, *International Law*, above note 5 at 39–42.

35   Economists such as Michael Kremer have suggested that successor governments should not inherit the obligations of repressive predecessors in order to discourage lending to the latter, thus precipitating their overthrow. See, for example, "Who Can Sell Iraq's Oil," BBC News (http://news.bbc.co.uk), 17 April 2003, in

government simply takes on the predecessor government's rights and obligations. However, this rule does not apply to changes of government that are externally imposed in violation of international law, such as by armed invasion and occupation. In such cases, the state continues to possess the same international legal rights, while the occupying power assumes its international legal obligations.[36]

Treaties do not necessarily come into force for a state upon ratification or accession. Typically, a human rights treaty only comes into force upon the occurrence of a particular triggering event such as the passage of a specific date or ratification of the treaty by a specified number of states. The treaty itself will dictate the conditions of its entry into force.

e) Reservations and Objections, Statements of Understanding, Declarations

A reservation is defined in VCLT article 2 as "a unilateral statement, however phrased or named, made by a State, when signing, ratifying, accepting, approving or acceding to a treaty, whereby it purports to exclude or to modify the legal effect of certain provisions of the treaty in their application to that State." Reservations, when not prohibited by the VCLT or the treaty itself, and when not objected to by other parties, modify the provisions of the treaty as between the reserving party and the other parties. So if states A, B and C conclude a treaty to which A enters a valid reservation, the reservation modifies the provisions of the treaty between A and B and A and C, but not between B and C.[37]

Although not all human rights treaties or treaty provisions permit reservations,[38] they are a standard feature of treaty practice.[39] As a rule, states tacitly accept most reservations made by other states parties. Reservations must, however, be compatible with the object and purpose

---

which Kremer calls for a new institution empowered to declare certain regimes "odious"; the designation would mean that after the fall of the regime, the debts would be annulled. This would discourage bank lending to such countries because lenders would know in advance that the loans would not be repaid following a change in regime.

36 See Currie, *International Law*, above note 5 at 35–37.

37 *Ibid.* at 122.

38 The ILO, for example, bars reservations to its treaties. Other treaties, such as the Second Optional Protocol to the International Covenant on Civil and Political Rights, Aiming at the Abolition of the Death Penalty 1989 (ICCPR-OP2), 999 UNTS 302, prohibit reservations only in respect of certain provisions. See also the Human Rights Committee's General Comment no. 24 (1994), in which the Committee purports to prohibit reservations to all non-derogable rights.

39 Reservations to bilateral treaties generally do not arise since they would imply an absence of agreement between the two contracting parties.

of the treaty. Reservations that are prohibited by the terms of a treaty, or that are incompatible with its object and purpose, are impermissible.[40]

In their most innocuous form, reservations allow for an accommodation of domestic barriers to ratification. Federalism is one such barrier for many states, including Canada. Some human rights treaties therefore include "federal clauses." For example, under the American Convention on Human Rights 1969 (ACHR) article 28, states may accept as binding only those obligations over which they exercise "legislative and judicial jurisdiction."[41] A very different approach is taken in the International Covenant on Civil and Political Rights 1966 (ICCPR)[42] and the International Covenant on Economic, Social and Cultural Rights 1966 (ICESCR).[43] Both treaties "extend to all parts of federal States without any limitations or exceptions."[44]

Reservations highlight the tension inherent in human rights treaty-making between the desire for universal ratification (which militates in favour of permitting reservations) and the desire to preserve the moral and humanitarian principles that are the treaty's basis (which militates against).[45] International practice generally falls somewhere in the middle. The International Law Commission once urged that, for legal certainty, clauses on reservations be included in all future treaties.[46] The idea has not yet taken hold.[47]

---

40   VCLT, above note 18, art. 19. On the legal consequences that follow a determination of invalidity of a reservation to a human rights treaty, see R. Goodman, "Human Rights Treaties, Invalid Reservations, and State Consent" (2002) 96 ASIL 531. Goodman argues that invalid reservations to human rights treaties should be presumed to be severable, meaning that the ratifying state should remain bound to the treaty — including to the article in respect of which the invalid reservation was placed.

41   OAS TS no. 36. The provision was included at US insistence, allegedly because it was the only way it could become party to the ACHR.

42   [1976] CanTS no. 47.

43   ICESCR, above note 32.

44   ICCPR, above note 43, art. 50; ICESCR, ibid., art. 28.

45   See *Advisory Opinion on Reservations to the Convention on the Prevention and Punishment of the Crime of Genocide* [1951] ICJ Rep 15.

46   See *Report of the International Law Commission*, UN doc. A/1858, c. II, paras. 12–34 (1951).

47   For an alternative approach, note the flexible and unique system used in Europe, especially regarding the European Social Charter (revised) 1996 (EurSC), ETS no. 163 discussed in Chapter Six. The system avoids messy and detailed reservations by allowing states to accept as binding only a sub-set of the total set of treaty rights.

When a state places a reservation to a treaty, other parties may respond with an objection to the reservation.[48] The admission of objections is the *quid pro quo* for the admission of reservations. The legal consequences of placing an objection are established by VCLT article 20(b), which provides

> an objection by another contracting State to a reservation does not preclude the entry into force of the treaty as between the objecting and reserving States unless a contrary intention is definitely expressed by the objecting State.

Some human rights treaties provide that where there are enough objections to a reservation, the reservation will be deemed invalid.[49]

In addition to or in lieu of reservations, states may also place "statements of understanding" (also known as "interpretive declarations"). A statement of understanding affirms a state's understanding of the nature or scope of a particular treaty provision, whether in relation to itself or generally.[50] The line between a reservation and a statement of under-

---

48   For example, on 1 July 1993, Maldives placed the following reservation to the Convention on the Elimination of All Forms of Discrimination Against Women 1979 (CEDAW), [1982] CanTS no. 31:

> The Government of the Republic of Maldives will comply with the provisions of the Convention, except those which the Government may consider contradictory to the principles of the Islamic Shariah, upon which the laws and traditions of the Maldives are founded. Furthermore, the Republic of Maldives does not see itself bound by any provision of the Convention which obliges it to change its Constitution and laws in any manner.

Canada placed the following objection to Maldives' reservation:

> In the view of the Government of Canada, this reservation is incompatible with the object and purpose of the Convention (article 28, paragraph 2). The Government of Canada therefore enters its formal objection to this reservation. This objection shall not preclude the entry into force of the Convention as between Canada and the Republic of Maldives.

49   See, for example, art. 20(2) of the International Convention on the Elimination of All Forms of Racial Discrimination 1966 (CERD), [1970] CanTS no. 28, which deems reservations incompatible reservations where two-thirds of the contracting states object.

50   See, for example, Canada's statement of understanding regarding CRC, above note 27, art. 30:

> It is the understanding of the Government of Canada that, in matters relating to aboriginal peoples of Canada, the fulfilment of its responsibilities under article 4 of the Convention must take into account the provisions of article 30. In particular, in assessing what measures are appropriate to implement the rights recognized in the Convention for aboriginal children, due regard

standing is not always clear. The term "statement of understanding" is not referred to anywhere in the VCLT; it appears to be an invention of state practice. Canadian treaty practice is to become party only to treaties that do not require it to place a large number of reservations and/or statements of understanding.

Some treaties permit the making of "declarations." Declarations are generally directed at acceptance of optional aspects of a treaty and not at the exclusion or limitation of otherwise binding provisions. For example, articles 21, 22, and 30 of the Convention Against Torture and Other Cruel, Inhuman or Degrading Treatment or Punishment 1984 (CAT)[51] permit a state to make a declaration to accept the treaty's interstate complaint mechanism, to accept its individual complaint mechanism, and to decline referral to the International Court of Justice of interpretive disputes under the treaty.

Unless a treaty provides otherwise, state parties may withdraw or amend reservations, objections, statements of understanding, and declarations at any time.

f) Treaty Observance

There are many general rules about treaty observance under international law. For present purposes, two are relevant. The first is *pacta sunt servanda*. Perhaps the most fundamental rule of treaty law, this rule holds that legal undertakings assumed by international legal subjects must be performed by them in good faith.[52] The second rule is that a state may not invoke the provisions of its internal law as justification for its failure to perform a treaty.[53]

g) Suspension or Termination of Treaties

A state may be entitled to suspend its obligations under a treaty to which it is party. Suspension is the temporary withdrawal from a treaty. Suspension is different from derogation. Derogation involves reliance on a treaty's provisions to disapply certain rights in times of national emergency. In this sense derogation involves an affirmation of the applicability of the treaty to the state.

---

must be paid to not denying their right, in community with other members of their group, to enjoy their own culture, to profess and practice their own religion and to use their own language.

51 [1987] CanTS no. 36.
52 VCLT, above note 18, art. 26.
53 *Ibid.*, art. 27.

A state may also be entitled to terminate its obligations under a treaty to which it is party. Termination is the denunciation or permanent withdrawal from a treaty.

Some treaties provide rules about suspension or termination.[54] In other cases, suspension or termination may occur only on the following grounds: consent,[55] material breach,[56] "supervening impossibility of performance,"[57] or "fundamental change of circumstances."[58] In practice, states parties rarely accept claims for suspension or termination on these grounds.

3) Custom

a) Definition

Not all international laws arise from express agreements formed through deliberation and negotiation. International norms may also develop through the evolution of state behaviour and attitude, or what is known as custom. Consistent with ICJ Statute article 38(1)(b), two elements must be demonstrated to establish an obligation as a customary norm: (i) there must be widespread and consistent state practice, often called "general practice," and (ii) that practice must be accompanied by *opinio juris*, meaning the belief that it is required as a matter of international law.[59] General practice need not be universal or long-

---

54 For example, art. 33 of the Optional Protocol to the Convention Against Torture and Other Cruel, Inhuman or Degrading Treatment or Punishment 2002 (CAT-OP), GA res. A/RES.57/199, permits states parties to denounce the protocol at any time. The denunciation takes effect one year thereafter. The denunciation does not release the state from its obligations in relation to any act or situation which occurred prior to the date when the denunciation became effective, whether or not it was under consideration by the Sub-Committee on Prevention (the body established by the CAT-OP). But the Sub-Committee may not commence consideration of any new matter affecting the state after the effective date of the denunciation.

55 See VCLT, above note 18, arts. 54–59, and Draft Articles, above note 21, art. 20.

56 VCLT, *ibid.*, art. 60.

57 *Ibid.*, art. 61. The impossibility must be physical ("disappearance or destruction of an object indispensable for the execution of the treaty").

58 *Ibid.*, art. 62 provides that a fundamental change of circumstances must have been unforeseen by the parties at the time the treaty was ratified, and may not be invoked as a ground for terminating or withdrawing from a treaty "unless the existence of those circumstances constituted an essential basis of the consent of the parties to be bound by the treaty . . . and the effect of the change is radically to transform the extent of obligations still to be performed under the treaty."

59 *Opinio juris* is in fact an abbreviated term; the full term is *opinio juris sive necessitatis*, meaning "opinion that an act is necessary by rule of law."

standing. Inaction may constitute state practice where it amounts to acquiescence to the general practice.

All states are bound by rules of customary law except for those that actively dissociate themselves from the rule during its formation. Such states are known as "persistent objectors." Those states that do not persistently object to the rule are deemed to consent to it.

Customary international law permits the establishment of competing customary norms of a regional or special character created by a group of states.[60] Such "local custom" only binds, and is only opposable against, those states that participated in its creation.

Customary international law can be further divided into those norms from which derogation by treaty is permitted, and those from which no such derogation is permitted. The latter are known as *jus cogens* norms. Article 53 of the VCLT defines a *jus cogens* norm as one

> accepted and recognized by the international community of States as a whole as a norm from which no derogation is permitted and which can be modified only by a subsequent norm of general international law having the same character.

Thus, the chief distinguishing factors of *jus cogens* norms are

- their universality ("accepted and recognized by the international community of States as a whole"),
- their insusceptibility to any form of derogation, whether by treaty or by subsequent persistent objection ("norm from which no derogation is permitted"), and
- their immunity to change except by the development of a replacement norm of *jus cogens* ("modified only by a subsequent norm of general international law having the same character").[61]

Uncontroversial examples of *jus cogens* norms include the prohibitions on international crimes such as genocide, crimes against humanity, slave-trading, and piracy.[62]

---

60   See generally Currie, *International Law*, above note 5 at 177–81.
61   See VCLT, above note 18 art. 64: "If a new peremptory norm of general international law emerges, any existing treaty which is in conflict with that norm becomes void and terminates."
62   See I. Brownlie, *Principles of Public International Law*, 5th ed. (Oxford: Oxford University Press, 1998) at 514–17.

b) Advantages of Custom

In a world where all multilateral treaties enjoyed universal adherence, the concept of customary international law would be almost superfluous — one could simply cite the treaty without any need to prove custom. But treaty adherence is not universal, even if overall levels of adherence to human rights treaties are encouraging. In addition, while many fundamental human rights are recognized in existing treaties, the existing list of human rights is not necessarily exhaustive.

Thus, customary international law helps to circumvent gaps in treaty participation and in positive law. For example, a victim who might be precluded from invoking a treaty-based right can potentially rely on its customary equivalent, provided that such an equivalent exists and that the concerned state was neither a persistent objector nor bound by a different rule of local custom.[63] But given their consensual nature, customary norms will provide minimal protection in most cases. For that reason they may often be of limited practical application or relevance.

c) How the Content of Custom is Determined

We have noted the requirements of state practice and *opinio juris* to prove custom. In practice, evidence of a customary norm is usually established by reference to multilateral treaties, subsidiary sources such as judicial decisions and scholarly work, and "soft law" sources such as non-binding UN declarations and resolutions, and diplomatic actions and statements.[64] This disparate list of bases for determining the content of custom accounts for its imprecision and ambiguity — but also its flexibility.

Despite centuries of development, there is still no authoritative methodology for determining the content of international customary law, not least because of the vague elements of its definition. Debate persists as to the requisite degree of consistency to prove state practice,

---

63   In cases of conflict between an applicable treaty and customary norm, the general rule is that the treaty norm will supersede the customary norm as beween the parties to that treaty; however, if the customary norm has attained *jus cogens* status, it will trump a conflicting treaty norm. VCLT, above note 18, art. 53.

64   The propriety of using these sources to establish customary norms is not uncontroversial. One may argue, for example, that state treaty actions tend to undermine, rather than support, the claim that a given norm is customary. For if the state is already bound by a customary rule, why would it conclude a treaty providing for the same rule?

as well as the requirement or even necessity to prove *opinio juris*, particularly in relation to human rights norms.[65]

For example, it is not clear what weight should be given to what states say (and do not say) about their own conduct and that of others, what states do (and fail to do) in domestic practice and foreign policy, and which norms states do (or do not) codify in domestic constitutions and laws. It is tempting for human rights supporters to focus on the facts that favour the existence of custom. These include: the widespread codification of human rights in most state constitutions, state condemnations of gross and systematic human rights violations by other states, and the fact that today no states seriously claim not to have human rights obligations. But actual state violations of human rights are at least as relevant in determining custom and any assessment of the state of human rights compels recognition of the immense gap between the law on the books and the law in action. At the same time, one must acknowledge that there is a truly massive amount of data that is potentially legally relevant, whatever one's methodology. The result is that any conclusion about the content of custom will be largely determined by the kinds of state behaviour that one considers legally relevant.

Of the diverse attempts to enumerate the content of customary human rights law, two stand out. First, the US *Restatement (Third) of the Foreign Relations Law of the United States* 1987 provides at section 702 that as a matter of customary international law it is unlawful for a state to "practice, encourage or condone" torture, genocide, slavery, murder or disappearance of individuals, prolonged arbitrary detention, or systematic racial discrimination. Second, the UN Human Rights Committee has developed a list of customary human rights norms, albeit without adducing any evidence of state practice or *opinio juris*:

> [P]rovisions in the Covenant that represent customary international law (and *a fortiori* when they have the character of peremptory norms) may not be the subject of reservations. Accordingly, a State may not reserve the right to engage in slavery, to torture, to subject persons to cruel, inhuman or degrading treatment or punishment, to arbitrarily deprive persons of their lives, to arbitrarily arrest and detain persons, to deny freedom of thought, conscience and religion, to presume a person guilty unless he proves his innocence, to execute

---

65   See generally, B. Simma & P. Alston, "The Sources of Human Rights Law: Custom, Jus Cogens, and General Principles" (1992) 12 Australian Yearbook of International Law 82; and J. Paust, "The Complex Nature, Sources and Evidence of Customary Human Rights" (1995/6) 25 Georgia Journal of International and Comparative Law 147.

pregnant women or children, to permit the advocacy of national, racial or religious hatred, to deny to persons of marriageable age the right to marry, or to deny to minorities the right to enjoy their own culture, profess their own religion, or use their own language.[66]

4) General Principles of Law

Article 38(1)(c) of the ICJ Statute describes "general principles of law recognized by civilized nations" as a primary source of international law. In practice, general principles are invoked only in those rare cases when applicable norms cannot readily be found in treaty or customary law.[67] The phrase "civilized nations" is not defined in the ICJ Statute, but in practice no significance is attached to it. General principles of law recognized within the domestic legal systems of all states may be considered.

As with customary international law, there is no universally-accepted methodology for deducing the content of general principles of law. At the same time, there is unlikely to be any dispute about the inclusion of general principles such as the following: the requirement of good faith and the related prohibition on the abuse of rights, the principle that every violation of an engagement generates an obligation to make reparation, the rule that a wrongdoer cannot plead his own wrong, the principle that no benefit can be obtained from an illegal act, the rule of *res judicata* (namely, that a matter is settled once a final judgment has been made), and considerations of equity.[68] All of these principles are undoutedly part of most legal systems, and certainly part of Canadian law.[69]

5) Judicial Decisions and Scholarly Writings

Article 38(1)(d) of the ICJ Statute lists "judicial decisions and the teachings of the most highly qualified publicists of the various nations" as subsidiary sources for determining rules of international law. In

---

66   ICCPR General Comment no. 24 (1994) at para. 8.

67   The leading decision on the interpretation of art. 38(1)(c) is the separate opinion of Judge McNair in *International Status of South-West Africa*, Advisory Opinion [1950] ICJ Rep 128.

68   G. van Ert, *Using International Law in Canadian Courts* (The Hague: Kluwer Law International, 2002) at 23.

69   William Schabas has aptly observed: "Because, by definition, [general principles] are derived from domestic law, most if not all of them are already recognized by Canadian courts." W. Schabas, *International Human Rights Law and the Canadian Charter*, 2d ed. (Toronto: Carswell, 1996) at 20.

other words, judicial decisions and scholarly writings are not primary or independent sources of international law in the same way as treaties, custom, and general principles. They are only subsidiary or evidentiary sources used to help find the law.

The language of article 38(1)(d) permits reliance on relevant judicial decisions of any court, whether international, regional, or even domestic. The question arises whether the "general comments," "concluding observations," and "views" expressed by UN treaty bodies and their regional equivalents may be considered judicial decisions within the meaning of article 38(1). Given the non-judicial character of such bodies, this seems doubtful, although the decisions of arbitral tribunals are an accepted subsidiary source of international law.

As to the writings of highly qualified publicists, great significance is attached to the work of the International Law Commission. The legal treatises of leading experts also serve as important subsidiary sources of international law.[70]

C. SOFT LAW

So-called "soft law" is more soft than it is law. The term has come to describe the great variety of international instruments, declarations, observations, guidelines, etc., which, though non-binding as a matter of current international law (*lex lata*), may nevertheless indicate what international law may or should become (*lex ferenda*). Soft law is therefore not law at all, and must not be looked to as a source of international law unless it can be shown to meet the requirements of state practice and *opinio juris* necessary to become customary international law. Such transformations are rare in international law, but they do occur. A leading example in international human rights law is the UDHR, which began life as a non-binding declaration of the UN General Assembly, but has now been recognized as mostly declaratory of customary international law. Other soft law sources include, for example, unilateral state declarations, and draft codes and treaties produced by the International Law Commission.[71]

---

70   *Ibid.* at 25.
71   On soft law generally, see Currie, *International Law*, above note 5 at 94–101.

CHAPTER 4

THE INTERNATIONAL BILL OF HUMAN RIGHTS

The primary source of international human rights law is the corpus of human rights instruments known as the International Bill of Human Rights. The Bill encompasses the Universal Declaration of Human Rights 1948 (UDHR),[1] the International Covenant on Civil and Political Rights 1966 (ICCPR),[2] the International Covenant on Economic, Social and Cultural Rights 1966 (ICESCR),[3] and the Optional Protocol to the ICCPR 1966 (ICCPR-OP1).[4] All but the latter will be addressed in this chapter. The ICCPR-OP1 will be discussed in Chapter Fourteen. Although it is formally part of the International Bill of Human Rights, the ICCPR-OP1 establishes no new rights; instead, it establishes procedures for the vindication of rights proclaimed in the ICCPR.

While dozens of human rights instruments exist today on a wide range of themes, users of international human rights law continue to be most familiar with and have greatest recourse to the instruments comprising the International Bill of Human Rights. Other human rights instruments examined in later chapters often only elaborate what is already present in or implied by them. Any proper understanding of human rights, therefore, requires an appreciation of the Bill.

---

1   GA res. 217(III) (1948).
2   [1976] CanTS no. 47.
3   [1976] CanTS no. 46.
4   [1976] CanTS no. 47. Now there is also the Second Optional Protocol to the ICCPR Aiming at the Abolition of the Death Penalty 1989 (ICCPR-OP2) 999 UNTS 302. It is discussed later in this chapter.

A. THE UNIVERSAL DECLARATION OF HUMAN RIGHTS

The UDHR was adopted by the UN General Assembly primarily in response to the horrors of the Holocaust.[5] It was adopted without dissent and with only a few abstentions. The draft text was prepared by the UN Commission on Human Rights and drew upon the articulation of civil and political rights in various domestic constitutions, particularly those of the US and Western Europe. John Peters Humphrey, a Canadian who at the time headed the secretariat of the Commission on Human Rights, played a lead role in drafting it.[6] Canada abstained from the vote to adopt the draft UDHR in the Third Committee of the UN General Assembly. Apparently, the Canadian government was concerned that Jehovah's Witness adherents might take advantage of the freedom of religion provision, and that "communists" working within the public service might seek to exploit the UDHR's right to freedom of association.[7] Ultimately, however, Canada voted in favour of adopting the UDHR on 10 December 1948.

The avowed purpose of the UDHR is to provide a comprehensive statement of basic human rights and freedoms to serve as a "common standard of achievement for all peoples and all nations."[8] The lesson from the Second World War, and in particular from the Holocaust, was that international law had to do more than simply protect the sovereignty of states; it also had to protect individuals living within those states. The UDHR was not a binding treaty but only a declaration of the UN General Assembly. At the time of its adoption, most human rights supporters — in particular NGOs and a number of smaller countries — saw the UDHR as a major compromise. They had wanted a legally binding Bill of Rights.[9]

---

5   On the UDHR generally, see J. Morsink, *The Universal Declaration of Human Rights: Origins, Drafting, and Intent* (Philadelphia: University of Pennsylvania Press, 1999) and A. Eide & T. Swinehart, eds., *The Universal Declaration of Human Rights: A Commentary* (New York: Oxford University Press, 1992).

6   See J. Humphrey, *Human Rights and the United Nations: A Great Adventure* (New York: Transnational Publishers, 1984) at 31–33, 42–43. More generally see A.J. Hobbins, ed., *On the Edge of Greatness: The Diaries of John Humphrey* (Montreal and Kingston: McGill-Queen's University Press, 1994–2000).

7   W. Schabas, *International Human Rights Law and the Canadian Courts* (Scarborough: Carswell, 1996) at 64–65.

8   UDHR preamble, above note 1.

9   L. Henkin *et al.*, *Human Rights* (New York: Foundation Press, 1999) at 286.

Despite its non-binding character, for the next twenty-eight years the UDHR remained the only comprehensive human rights instrument and a major influence on the content of domestic constitutions around the world.[10] Today no-one would seriously suggest re-examination of the UDHR, and parts of it have certainly attained customary status.[11] It remains the most widely accepted statement of human rights; indeed, there has never really been any challenge made to it by the international community.

One of the reasons for the appeal of the UDHR is the fact that it includes all of the major categories of rights: civil, political, economic, social, and cultural.[12] Although it does not classify rights as such, articles 1–21 are generally understood as civil and political rights, and articles 22–28 are generally understood as economic, social and cultural rights.

The clear emphasis of the UDHR is on civil and political rights. Most of the civil and political rights and freedoms contained in the UDHR will be familiar. They include:

- the right to life, liberty and security of the person (article 3);
- freedom from slavery and servitude (article 4);
- freedom from torture (article 5);
- equal protection of the law (article 7);
- the right to an effective remedy (article 8);
- freedom from arbitrary arrest, detention, or exile (article 9);
- fair trial rights (articles 10 and 11);
- freedom of thought, conscience and religion (article 18);
- freedom of opinion and expression (article 19);
- freedom of peaceful assembly and association (article 20); and
- the right of participation in the government of one's country (article 21(1)).

Other important civil and political rights include:

- freedom from arbitrary interference with privacy, family, home or correspondence (article 12);

---

10 *Ibid.* at 322 ("Its greatest importance may be its influence on the development of constitutionalism and the establishment of human rights in the one hundred (and more) constitutions that have been ordained in the second half of the [twentieth] century.").

11 On the question of the customary status of the UDHR see, for example, *Advisory Opinion on the continued presence of South Africa in Namibia (S.W. Africa)* [1971] ICJ Rep 16 at 76 [*South Africa*], per Judge Ammoun; see also the dissent of Judge Tanaka in *South West Africa Cases, Second Phase* [1966] ICJ Rep 4 at 288–93.

12 This approach was a necessity: the UDHR had to be crafted in a way that would appeal to societies based on communist as well as capitalist ideologies.

- freedom of movement and residence, including the right to leave and return from one's country (article 13);
- the right to asylum (article 14);
- the right to a nationality (article 15);
- the right to contract a marriage and found a family (article 16(1));
- the right to own property and not to be arbitrarily deprived of it (article 17); and
- the right of equal access to public services in one's country (article 21(2)).

The economic, social and cultural rights contained in the UDHR may be less familiar, since they are less frequently included in domestic constitutions. Declared rights include:

- the right to social security, including social insurance (article 22);
- the right to equal pay for equal work (article 23(2));
- the right to free choice of employment (article 23(1));
- the right to just and favourable remuneration ensuring an existence worthy of human dignity (article 23(3));
- the right to rest and leisure (article 24);
- the right to a standard of living adequate for health and well-being (article 25(1));
- the protection of motherhood and childhood (article 25(2));
- the right to education, with parental right of choice (article 26);
- the right of participation in the cultural life of one's community (article 27(1)); and
- the protection of moral and material interests resulting from one's authorship of scientific, literary, or artistic productions (article 27(2)).

The final three articles of the UDHR stand apart from the rest. Article 28 provides that everyone is entitled to a social and international order in which the rights declared in the UDHR can be fully realized — an admirable but hardly justiciable norm. Article 29 ascribes to every individual a generic duty "to the community."[13] It also sets out the basis and scope for a state to place limitations on the exercise of the rights and freedoms established under the UDHR. Specifically, article 29(2) provides:

---

13   Note that the UDHR did not include any of the duties found at arts. 29–38 of the American Declaration on the Rights and Duties of Man 1948 (AmDR), OAS res. XXX, which preceded it. Instead, UDHR, above note 1, art. 1 simply provides that all human beings "should act towards one another in a spirit of brotherhood."

> In the exercise of his rights and freedoms, everyone shall be subject
> only to such limitations as are determined by law solely for the pur-
> pose of securing due recognition and respect for the rights and free-
> doms of others and of meeting the just requirements of morality,
> public order and the general welfare in a democratic society.[14]

Lastly, article 30 provides a sort of good faith clause precluding any
state, group, or person from invoking the UDHR as a basis for the
"destruction" of any of its declared rights and freedoms.[15]

Despite its broad coverage, a number of important human rights
did not make it into the UDHR. These include:

- the right to self-determination,[16]
- the right to a clean environment,[17]
- the right to be informed of one's rights and the reasons for any
  detention,[18]
- the right to a name and the right to have it registered,[19]
- protection from expulsion,[20]
- the right against self-incrimination,[21]
- the right to submit petitions to government and to obtain a prompt
  response thereto,[22] and
- the right of reply for purposes of protecting one's reputation.[23]

For a more comprehensive comparison of the UDHR norms with those
of other major human rights treaties, see the concordance of Canadian
and international human rights instruments in Appendix 1.

---

14 Thus, in contrast to the ICCPR (discussed below), limitations can be applied to
    all of the rights in the UDHR. The ICCPR only allows limitations and deroga-
    tions in respect of some rights.
15 An identical provision was included in art. 5(1) common to the ICCPR, above
    note 2, and the ICESCR, above note 3.
16 See, for example, the Charter of the United Nations 1945 (UN Charter), [1945]
    Can TS no. 7 art. 1(2); ICCPR, ibid., art. 1; and ICESCR, ibid., art. 1.
17 See, for example, ICESCR, ibid., art. 12(2)(b) and the African Charter on
    Human and Peoples' Rights 1981 (AfrCHPR), OAU doc. CAB/LEG/67/3 rev. 5
    art. 24.
18 See, for example, ICCPR, above note 2, arts. 9(2) and 14(3).
19 See, for example, ibid., art. 24.
20 See, for example, ibid., art. 13.
21 See, for example, ibid., art. 14(3)(g) and the American Convention on Human
    Rights 1969 (ACHR), OAS TS no. 36 art. 8(3)(g).
22 See, for example, AmDR, above note 13, art. 24.
23 See, for example, ACHR, above note 21, art. 14.

B. THE INTERNATIONAL COVENANT ON CIVIL AND POLITICAL RIGHTS AND THE INTERNATIONAL COVENANT ON ECONOMIC, SOCIAL AND CULTURAL RIGHTS

Despite its global influence, the UDHR was only a non-binding declaration. Converting the UDHR's provisions into treaty form proved a controversial project, due largely to Cold War-related disagreements over the content and relative importance of civil and political rights on the one hand, and economic, social and cultural rights on the other. As Cold War rivalries intensified, the momentum that had generated the UDHR (and the UN Charter) was largely arrested.

It was only in 1966, eighteen years after the adoption of the UDHR, that the log jam between Western and Eastern bloc states was broken. The solution was to create two separate treaties: a treaty on civil and political rights favoured above all by Western bloc states (namely, the ICCPR) and a treaty on economic, social and cultural rights favoured above all by Eastern bloc states (namely, the ICESCR). Although separate treaties, at the time of their adoption the UN General Assembly declared them to be "interconnected and interdependent."[24]

1) The International Covenant on Civil and Political Rights

a) Relation to the Universal Declaration of Human Rights

With the exception of the right to property and the right to asylum — both of which are omitted from the ICCPR — the ICCPR incorporates and generally expands upon the civil and political rights contained in the UDHR. For example, where the UDHR provides for the right not be arbitrarily detained (article 9), the ICCPR adds a right against arbitrary imprisonment (article 14(1)), a right not to be imprisoned for debt (article 11), a right to be informed of the reason for arrest or detention (article 9(2)), a right to counsel (article 14(3)), a right of habeus corpus (article 9(4)), and a right to be informed of an offence upon being criminally charged (article 9(2)). But the ICCPR does not always expand on the UDHR. For example, ICCPR article 6 permits certain instances of capital punishment as an exception to the right to life, whereas UDHR article 3 simply provides for a right to life.

---

24   GA res.2200 A (XXI) (1966).

Unlike the UDHR, the ICCPR does not declare any individual duties. The preamble, however, recognizes that "the individual, having duties to other individuals and to the community to which he belongs, is under a responsibility to strive for the promotion and observance of the rights recognized in the [ICCPR]."

b) Minority Rights

One of the provisions of especial significance in the ICCPR is article 27. It declares that individuals belonging to ethnic, religious, or linguistic minorities "shall not be denied the right" to enjoy their culture, practise their religion, or use their own language.[25] There is no equivalent provision in the UDHR,[26] and there are only a few other UN human rights instruments that deal with minority rights at all.[27] Article 27 remains the broadest provision on the rights of minorities to be found in a UN human rights treaty.[28] Still, on its face the provision offers little protection to minorities. It is framed as an individual right that gives rise only to a negative state obligation (persons "shall not be denied the right"). The UN Human Rights Committee has, however, observed that the exercise of the right turns on the ability of the minority group to maintain its language, religion, or culture, as the case may be, and that this implies affirmative obligations for the state to promote and protect the group as a means to protect the individual's right.[29]

---

25 Note that racial minorities are excluded from the list of protected minorities. Unlike ethnic, religious, and cultural minority groups, however, racial minorities have the benefit of extensive protections under the International Convention on the Elimination of All Forms of Racial Discrimination 1966 (CERD), [1970] CanTS no. 28.

26 The closest the UDHR, above note 1, comes to minority protection is art. 27: "Everyone has the right freely to participate in the cultural life of the community." See also art. 18, which provides for "freedom to change [one's] religion or belief, and freedom, either alone or in community with others and in public or private, to manifest [one's] religion or belief in teaching, practice, worship and observance."

27 The key exceptions are: (i) the CERD, which concerns only discrimination against racial minorities; (ii) the minority rights provisions for children in arts. 17 (minority linguistic needs) and 30 (rights of indigenous children) of the Convention on the Rights of the Child 1989 (CRC), [1992] CanTS no. 3; and (iii) the UN General Assembly's non-binding Declaration on the Rights of Persons belonging to National or Ethnic, Religious or Linguistic Minorities 1992, GA res. 47/135 (1992).

28 In the European human rights system, by contrast, minority rights garner more sustained interest. See, for example, the Framework Convention for the Protection of National Minorities 1995, ETS no. 157.

29 ICCPR General Comment 23 (1994) at paras. 6.1 and 6.2. On the limitations of minority protections under international human rights law, see J. Rehman, *The Weakness in the International Protection of Minority Rights* (The Hague: Kluwer Law International, 2000).

For many years after the formation of the UN, the general view of minority rights was that they were best kept a thing of the past. This had much to do with the experience of the Second World War when Germany invoked minority rights as a pretext for invading neighbouring countries like Czechoslovakia, Poland, and Hungary. Today, the resistance has more to do with many states' self-interest in preserving the dominance of particular ethnic, religious, or linguistic majority groups. Yet it seems reasonable to suppose that minorities whose rights are promoted and protected within a state will be less likely to resort to separatist claims or violence and more likely to pursue internal forms of self-determination and civic participation. Promotion and protection of minority rights can be effected by constitutional arrangements based on intra-state autonomy, federalism, self-government, or devolution, and by affirmative law and policy measures such as minority judicial and political appointments.[30]

c) Democratic Rights

ICCPR article 25 sets out core democratic rights, though without recognizing a right to democracy as such.[31] Article 25 provides:

> Every citizen shall have the right and the opportunity, without any of the distinctions mentioned in article 2 and without unreasonable restrictions: (a) To take part in the conduct of public affairs, directly or through freely chosen representatives; (b) To vote and to be elected at genuine periodic elections which shall be by universal and equal suffrage and shall be held by secret ballot, guaranteeing the free expression of the will of the electors; (c) To have access, on general terms of equality, to public service in his country.

The democratic rights of article 25 are not enjoyed by all individuals within the territory or subject to the jurisdiction of a state party. They

---

30   On minority rights generally, see W. Kymlicka, ed., *The Rights of Minority Cultures* (Oxford: Oxford University Press, 1995) and W. Kymlicka & W. Norman, eds., *Citizenship in Diverse Societies* (New York: Oxford University Press, 2000). See also the report prepared by Mr. Justice Jules Deschênes, a Canadian, undertaken at the request of the UN Sub-Commission on the Prevention of Discrimination and Protection of Minorities. "Promotion, Protection and Restoration of Human Rights at the National, Regional and International Level, Proposal concerning a definition of the term 'minority,'" UN Doc. E/CN.4/Sub.2/1985/31 and Corr. 1.

31   The only ICCPR provisions that mention democracy by name are arts. 14, 21, and 22. But in each case democracy is listed as a basis for placing limitations on rights.

are limited to "citizens."[32] In its General Comment on article 25, the UN Human Rights Committee has stressed that no distinctions are permitted between citizens on any prohibited or discriminatory ground, and that the conditions for exercising democratic rights should be based on objective and reasonable criteria.[33]

Since the end of the Cold War, there has been increased interest in establishing a right to democracy. In one particularly influential article, it was asserted that a customary norm is emerging by which democracy is being transformed from a moral prescription to a binding obligation under international law.[34] There is also a significant body of research on the so-called "democractic peace," a theory which holds that major armed conflicts will rarely if ever occur between democratic states.[35] If the theory of democratic peace is valid, and if it is true that human rights violations are at their most common in times of armed conflict, then democracy should be one of the most important rights deserving international nurturing and protection. In the OAS, at least, some early steps have been taken to that end.[36]

---

32 Compare with art. 23 of the ACHR, above note 21, and art. 13 of the AfrCHPR, above note 17, both of which provide democratic rights only to "citizens." Compare with the more ambiguous wording of UDHR, above note 1, art. 21 (everyone has rights to participate in the government "of his country," and the will of "the people" is the basis of the authority of government).

33 ICCPR General Comment no. 25 (1996) at paras. 3–4. Compare with CERD, above note 25, art. 1(2): "This Convention shall not apply to distinctions, exclusions, restrictions or preferences made by a State Party to this Convention between citizens and non-citizens."

34 T. Franck, "The Emerging Right to Democratic Governance" (1992) 86 AJIL 46. Franck asserts that "democracy is beginning to be seen as the *sine qua non* for validating governance."

35 See, for example, M. Brown *et al.*, *Debating the Democratic Peace* (Cambridge: MIT Press, 1996).

36 See the Inter-American Democratic Charter 2001 adopted on 11 September 2001 by the OAS General Assembly. Article 1 provides: "The peoples of the Americas have a right to democracy and their governments have an obligation to promote and defend it. Democracy is essential for the social, political, and economic development of the peoples of the Americas." Article 3 provides:

> Essential elements of representative democracy include, *inter alia*, respect for human rights and fundamental freedoms, access to and the exercise of power in accordance with the rule of law, the holding of periodic, free, and fair elections based on secret balloting and universal suffrage as an expression of the sovereignty of the people, the pluralistic system of political parties and organizations, and the separation of powers and independence of the branches of government.

d) The Death Penalty

The ICCPR was recently supplemented by a second protocol, the ICCPR-OP2, which bans the death penalty.[37] The ICCPR already bans most applications of the death penalty. Article 6(2) of the ICCPR provides that the death penalty can be applied "only for the most serious crimes." Also, ICCPR article 6(5) declares that no death sentences may be carried out against pregnant women or persons under eighteen years of age. The ICCPR-OP2 limits the death penalty further. Article 1 of the ICCPR-OP2 bans all resort to the death penalty. The only exception is provided in article 2, which allows states to make a reservation providing for the use of the death penalty "in time of war pursuant to a conviction for a most serious crime of a military nature committed during wartime."[38]

To date, Canada has not ratified the ICCPR-OP2. However, Canada remains subject to rulings of the UN Human Rights Committee pertaining to ICCPR article 6, of which there have been four to date, each case arising from extraditions by the Canadian government of US convicts or accused persons.[39] The general practice now in Canada for such cases is to obtain prior assurances that an extraditable person will not be subjected to capital punishment.[40]

2) The International Covenant on Economic, Social and Cultural Rights

As noted above, the ICESCR was adopted in 1966 and came into force in 1976. There are no additional protocols to the treaty. The ICESCR incorporates and generally expands upon the economic, social and cul-

---

37   On the death penalty generally, see W. Schabas, *The Abolition of the Death Penalty in International Law*, 3d ed. (Cambridge: Cambridge University Press, 2002).

38   Article 2(3) of the Protocol to the ACHR to Abolish the Death Penalty 1990 (ACHR-OP2), OAS TS no. 73, similarly allows the death penalty only for "extremely serious crimes of a military nature." In the opinion of the European Court of Human Rights, the human suffering attendant on simply being placed on death row (the "death row phenomenon") may itself violate human rights. See *Soering v. UK*, (1989) 11 EHRR 439.

39   See *Kindler v. Canada* (1993), Comm. no. 470/1991 [finding: no violation]; *Ng v. Canada* (1993), Comm. no. 469/1991 [finding: violation of ICCPR arts. 6 and 10]; *Cox v. Canada* (1994), Comm. no. 539/1993 [finding: no violation]; and most recently, *Judge v. Canada* (2003), Comm. no. 829/1998 [finding: violation of ICCPR art. 6(1)]. See the discussion of these cases in Chapter Ten.

40   See the discussion of life, liberty and security of the person in Chapter Ten.

tural rights contained in the UDHR, much as the ICCPR does in respect of the UDHR's civil and political rights.

In contrast to the ICCPR, states parties to the ICESCR do not have an obligation "to respect and to ensure" the rights it proclaims. Instead, under ICESCR article 2(1), a state party is required

> to take steps, individually and through international assistance and co-operation, especially economic and technical, to the maximum of its available resources, with a view to achieving progressively the full realization of the rights recognized in the present Covenant by all appropriate means, including particularly the adoption of legislative measures.

To use a distinction that is commonly invoked in international law, the ICESCR creates "obligations of conduct" rather than "obligations of result." As article 2(1) states, the rights are to be "progressively" (as opposed to immediately) achieved and the obligation is merely to "take steps" toward (as opposed to ensure) the realization of the rights in question. Concerning the obligation to "take steps," the Committee on Economic, Social and Cultural Rights has asserted that states must take steps within a "reasonably short time" of ratification or accession.[41] Also, at least one right in the ICESCR declares a specific time limit. ICESCR article 14 provides that states parties must undertake

> within two years, to work out and adopt a detailed plan of action for the progressive implementation, within a reasonable number of years, to be fixed in the plan, of the principle of compulsory education free of charge for all.

The progressive nature of the rights proclaimed under the ICESCR does not mean that all of them are non-justiciable. For example, the Committee on Economic, Social and Cultural Rights has stated that articles 3 (prohibition of gender-based discrimination), 7(a)(i) (a further guarantee of non-discrimination on the basis of gender), 8 (trade union rights), 10(3) (special protections for children and young persons), 13(2)(a) (compulsory and free primary education), 13(3) (parental free choice in educating children), 13(4) (the right to set up private educational institutions), and 15(3) (rights to scientific and creative freedom) are all likely justiciable.[42] Yet the justiciability of economic, social and cultural rights is clearly something less than for civil and political rights. The noncommittal phrasing of ICESCR article

---

41   See ICESCR General Comment no. 3 (1990) at para. 2.
42   *Ibid.* at para. 5.

2(1), the absence of any equivalent in the ICESCR to the ICCPR's right to an "effective remedy," and the lack of any individual or inter-state complaint mechanism under the ICESCR, all substantiate the point.[43] In addition, evidence of the justiciability of economic, social and cultural rights within domestic jurisdictions is much harder to find, although there are signs of change on the horizon.[44]

States parties to the ICESCR are required only to take steps to the maximum of their "available resources" (article 2(1)). This standard is at once pragmatic and problematic. On the one hand, it serves a function similar to the European "margin of appreciation" test for civil and political rights: it avoids applying uniform results-based criteria to assess compliance. This is particularly important for economic rights because economic development depends heavily upon factors beyond the control of any one state. On the other hand, article 2(1)'s standard also furnishes a convenient pretext with which states may justify non-compliance. It is perhaps for this reason that the Committee on Economic, Social and Cultural Rights has stressed that all states parties "must ensure the satisfaction of, at the very least, minimum essential levels of each of the rights."[45] The Committee has observed that:

> [a] State party in which any significant number of individuals is deprived of essential foodstuffs, of essential primary health care, of basic shelter and housing, or of the most basic forms of education is, prima facie, failing to discharge its obligations under the Covenant.[46]

States parties are also expected to protect the "most vulnerable members of society," even in times of severe constraints on resources.[47] In addition, states parties are expected to ensure certain rights to individuals who "for reasons beyond their control" are unable to exercise the right themselves.[48]

The ICESCR draws an express distinction between the obligations owed by developed states and developing states. Article 2(3) of the ICESCR provides: "Developing countries, with due regard to human

---

43 At the 2002 session of the UN Commission on Human Rights, a working group on the justiciability of economic, social, and cultural rights was established.
44 See, for example, J. Fitzpatrick & R. Slye, "Republic of South Africa v. Grootboom and Minister of Health v. Treatment Action Campaign" (2003) 97 AJIL 669. See also *Gosselin v. Quebec (Attorney General)* (2002), SCC 84, discussed in Chapter Ten.
45 ICESCR General Comment 3, above note 41 at para. 10.
46 *Ibid.*
47 *Ibid.* at para. 12.
48 See, for example, the Committee on Economic, Social and Cultural Rights' General Comment no. 12 (1999) at para. 15.

rights and their national economy, may determine to what extent they would guarantee the economic rights recognized in the present Covenant to non-nationals." Thus, developing countries have discretion to accord differential treatment to non-nationals; and, by implication, developed states do not have the same discretion. This distinction is further underscored by the article 2(1) obligation to take steps "individually and through international assistance and cooperation." This compromise phrase reflected the expectation of a number of developing states that developed states would provide them with the economic assistance necessary to fulfil their obligations under the ICESCR.[49]

Of final note, the ICESCR contains a general limitations clause similar to UDHR article 29 that is applicable to all of the rights listed in the treaty. ICESCR article 4 provides

> in the enjoyment of those rights provided by the State in conformity with the present Covenant, the State may subject such rights only to such limitations as are determined by law only in so far as this may be compatible with the nature of these rights and solely for the purpose of promoting the general welfare in a democratic society.

Although the provision is not open-ended, it nevertheless enables further limitations on the enjoyment of economic, social and cultural rights. The ICESCR contains no derogation clause.[50]

3) The Question of Self-Determination

Self-determination was included as a purpose of the UN in the UN Charter (article 1(2)), and as a recognized right in the ICCPR (articles 1 and 47) and the ICESCR (articles 1 and 25).[51] ICCPR article 1 and ICESCR article 1 both provide:

---

49   The idea of "differentiated responsibilities" between rich and poor states is not uncommon in international law. See generally C. Stone, "Common but Differentiated Responsibilities in International Law" (2004) 98 AJIL 277.

50   This fact results in an incongruity vis-à-vis the ICCPR. The right to form and join trade unions is recognized in both the ICCPR (art. 22(1)) and the ICESCR (art. 8(1)(a)). The right is derogable in a public emergency under the ICCPR, but non-derogable under the ICESCR.

51   On self-determination under international law generally, see H. Hannum, *Autonomy, Sovereignty, and Self-Determination: The Accommodation of Conflicting Rights* (Philadelphia: University of Pennsylvania Press, 1996) at c. 3, and K. Knop, *Diversity and Self-Determination in International Law* (Cambridge: Cambridge University Press, 2002).

1. All peoples have the right of self-determination. By virtue of that right they freely determine their political status and freely pursue their economic, social and cultural development.
2. All peoples may, for their own ends, freely dispose of their natural wealth and resources without prejudice to any obligations arising out of international economic co-operation, based upon the principle of mutual benefit, and international law. In no case may a people be deprived of its own means of subsistence.
3. The States Parties to the present Covenant, including those having responsibility for the administration of Non-Self-Governing and Trust Territories, shall promote the realization of the right of self-determination, and shall respect that right, in conformity with the provisions of the Charter of the United Nations.

ICCPR article 47 and ICESCR article 25 both provide:

> Nothing in the present Covenant shall be interpreted as impairing the inherent right of all peoples to enjoy and utilize fully and freely their natural wealth and resources.

Recently self-determination was declared by the International Court of Justice to be "one of the essential principles of contemporary international law."[52] Despite this, there is still no general consensus about the nature or scope of the right. It remains unclear how the right can be legitimately exercised, who bears what obligations, and to what extent it is a right subject to public interest limitations or derogation during a national emergency.[53]

Part of the difficulty stems from the uncertain meaning of the term "peoples." There is broad consensus that it includes colonized and other non-self-governing peoples, as well as peoples forcibly subjugated or occupied by a foreign state.[54] Such peoples are entitled to what is

---

52   *Case Concerning East Timor (Portugal v. Australia)*, [1995] ICJ Rep 90 at 102.

53   See, for example, *Re Secession of Quebec*, [1998] 2 SCR 217. Among other things, the case highlights how complex it is to decide who should be entitled to vote in a proposed secession referendum (just Quebec or all Canadian provinces) and how mixed results should be handled.

54   See, for example, *Western Sahara (Advisory Opinion)* [1975] ICJ Rep 12; and *South Africa*, above note 11. See also the Declaration on Principles of International Law Concerning Friendly Relations and Cooperation among States in Accordance with the Charter of the United Nations, GA res. 2625 (XXV) (1970) [Friendly Relations Declaration 1970]. The Declaration provides in part:

commonly described as a right to "external" self-determination, meaning the right to form an independent state. The right of external self-determination may also apply, in some cases, to a people that is severely persecuted or denied any meaningful right to to "internal" self-determination.[55] This, however, is controversial. To acknowledge such a right is to threaten the territorial sovereignty of states. A related area of uncertainty concerns minority groups. While it is clear that, unless they constitute "peoples," they do not possess a right to self-determination under international law. Distinguishing minorities from peoples is not easy.[56]

The classic limitation on the exercise of the right of self-determination is expressed in the UN General Assembly's Friendly Relations Declaration 1970. It declares that "all peoples have the right freely to determine, without external interference, their political status and to pursue their economic, social and cultural development," but precludes "any action which would dismember or impair, totally or in part the territorial integrity or political unity of sovereign and independent States conducting themselves in compliance with the principle of equal rights and self-determination of peoples." This widely accepted restriction on the exercise of the right to self-determination will at times adversely affect large minorities living within sovereign states, whether linguistic, ethnic, religious, racial, or indigenous. Indigenous peoples, for example, are particularly adversely affected by the limited notion of self-determination. They consistently describe themselves as "peoples" and in so doing seek to invoke a collective right to self-determination.

[S]ubjection of peoples to alien subjugation, domination and exploitation constitutes a violation of the principle [of self-determination], as well as a denial of fundamental human rights, and is contrary to the Charter.

55   See, for example, *The Aaland Islands Question: Report Submitted to the Council of the League of Nations by the Commission of Rapporteurs*, League of Nations doc. B7.21/68/106 (1921) at 28. See also *Re Secession of Quebec*, above note 53 at para. 154, in which the Supreme Court of Canada held:

[A] right to secession only arises under the principle of self-determination of people at international law where 'a people' is governed as part of a colonial empire; where 'a people' is subject to alien subjugation, domination or exploitation; and possibly where 'a people' is denied any meaningful exercise of its right to self-determination within the state of which it forms a part. In other circumstances, peoples are expected to achieve self-determination within the framework of their existing state.

56   Compare, for example, ICCPR, above note 2, art. 1 (right of peoples to self-determination) to art. 27 (rights of individuals belonging to certain minority groups).

States, however, prefer to treat them as "minorities" to forestall any claims to external self-determination.[57]

The limitation placed on the scope of the right to self-determination by the Friendly Relations Declaration 1970 continues to generate criticism. But the limitation is to some extent prudential: it would be dangerous to global, regional, and national order to permit an unlimited right to self-determination, regardless of the justness of the cause. As the Committee on the Elimination of Racial Discrimination has said, in affirming the report of a previous UN Secretary-General:

> [I]nternational law has not recognized a general right of peoples unilaterally to declare secession from a State. In this respect, the Committee follows the views expressed in *An Agenda for Peace* (paras. 17 and following), namely, that a fragmentation of States may be detrimental to the protection of human rights, as well as to the preservation of peace and security. This does not, however, exclude the possibility of arrangements reached by free agreements of all parties concerned.[58]

---

57   But see the Draft UN Declaration on the Rights of Indigenous Peoples 1993, UN doc. E/CN.4/Sub.2/1993/29/Annex I. Article 3 of the Declaration provides:

> Indigenous peoples have the right of self-determination. By virtue of that right they freely determine their political status and freely pursue their economic, social and cultural development.

Article 31 provides:

> Indigenous peoples, as a specific form of exercising their right to self-determination, have the right to autonomy or self-government in matters relating to their internal and local affairs, including culture, religion, education, information, media, health, housing, employment, social welfare, economic activities, land and resources management, environment and entry by non-members, as well as ways and means for financing these autonomous functions.

Since the completion of the Declaration in 1993, states have been singularly unwilling to adopt it.

58   CERD General Recommendation no. 21 (1996) at para 11.

CHAPTER 5

OTHER UN HUMAN RIGHTS INSTRUMENTS

A. INTRODUCTION

Since the adoption of the International Covenant on Civil and Political Rights 1966 (ICCPR)[1] and the International Covenant on Economic, Social and Cultural Rights 1966 (ICESCR),[2] several other important human rights treaties have come into force. Especially noteworthy are the International Convention on the Elimination of All Forms of Racial Discrimination 1966 (CERD),[3] the Convention on the Elimination of All Forms of Discrimination Against Women 1979 (CEDAW),[4] the Convention Against Torture and Other Cruel, Inhuman or Degrading Treatment or Punishment 1984 (CAT),[5] and the Convention on the

---

1   [1976] CanTS no. 47.
2   [1976] CanTS no. 46.
3   [1970] CanTS no. 28.
4   [1982] CanTS no. 31. Upon ratification, Canada made the following declaration:

> The Government of Canada states that the competent legislative authorities within Canada have addressed the concept of equal pay referred to in article 11(1)(d) by legislation which requires the establishment of rates of remuneration without discrimination on the basis of sex. The competent legislative authorities within Canada will continue to implement the object and purpose of article 11(1)(d) and to that end have developed, and where appropriate will continue to develop, additional legislative and other measures.

5   [1987] CanTS no. 36.

Rights of the Child 1989 (CRC).[6] Together with the ICCPR and the ICESCR these constitute the six most important human rights treaties within the UN system. More than 80 percent of all states have ratified at least four of these six treaties, although some (especially the CEDAW) have been limited by the extensive use of reservations.[7]

This chapter will review the most important features of the CERD, the CEDAW, the CAT, and the CRC (including its optional protocols). It will also briefly discuss the International Convention on the Protection of the Rights of All Migrant Workers and Members of Their Families 1990 (MWC),[8] a significant and broad-ranging treaty which came into force only recently. The chapter will conclude with a survey of some significant UN non-treaty sources of human rights. The operation of the treaty bodies established under the treaties discussed in this chapter is analyzed in Chapter Fourteen.

The content of the main UN human rights treaties often overlap. For example, the prohibition of torture (CAT), the protection of children's human rights (CRC), and the prohibitions of discrimination based on race (CERD) and gender (CEDAW) are already covered in the ICCPR, the ICESCR, or both. The advantage of these specialized treaties, however, is that they may appeal to states reluctant to take on the more comprehensive obligations of the ICCPR and the ICESCR. Often these more

---

6   [1992] CanTS no. 3. Canada placed two reservations and a statement of understanding upon ratification. The reservation to art. 21 provides:

> With a view to ensuring full respect for the purposes and intent of Article 20(3) and Article 30 of the Convention, the Government of Canada reserves the right not to apply the provisions of Article 21 to the extent that they may be inconsistent with customary forms of care among aboriginal peoples in Canada.

The reservation to art. 37(c) provides:

> The Government of Canada accepts the general principle of Article 37(c) of the Convention, but reserves the right not to detain children separately from adults where this is not appropriate or feasible.

The statement of understanding was referred to in Chapter Three at note 50. The Committee on the Rights of the Child has asked Canada to consider withdrawing its reservations to arts. 21 and 37(c): Committee on the Rights of the Child, *Concluding Observations: Canada* (1996) at paras. 559, 567.

7   The number of states parties to each of the treaties is as follows: ICCPR (150, with 8 remaining signatories), ICESCR (147, with 7 remaining signatories), CERD (169, with 7 remaining signatories), CEDAW (174, with 1 remaining signatory), CAT (133, with 12 remaining signatories) and CRC (191, with 2 remaining signatories). Those states which have not ratified the major human rights treaties tend to be small islands in the Caribbean and the South Pacific, or rogue states that have long been antipathetic to human rights.

8   GA res. 45/158 (1990).

limited treaties are, politically speaking, harder to spurn because their subjects are so universally condemned. States may join an anti-torture or anti-discrimination treaty for fear of being seen to condone either practice. In becoming party to such limited treaties, states often end up assuming more onerous obligations in relation to the treaty's theme or protected group than they would under the ICCPR or the ICESCR.[9]

B. THE INTERNATIONAL CONVENTION ON THE ELIMINATION OF ALL FORMS OF RACIAL DISCRIMINATION

Like the CEDAW (discussed below), the International Convention on the Elimination of All Forms of Racial Discrimination (CERD) is an anti-discrimination convention.[10] Like most other human rights treaties, it was preceded by a UN General Assembly Declaration.[11] Article 1(1) prohibits racial discrimination on the basis of "race, colour, descent or national or ethnic origin," thus extending protection beyond race in the sense of skin colour.[12] In addition, article 1(1) prohibits racial discrimination that has the purpose or effect of denying fundamental human rights, whether of a civil, political, economic, social, or cultural character. Thus, racial discrimination may occur even in the absence of any intention to discriminate; in other words, the concern is with equality in fact and not just in law. States parties to the CERD also have an obligation to "bring to an end" racial discrimination between private actors (article 2(1)(d)).

9   For example, in comparison to the ICCPR, which simply prohibits torture, the CAT, above note 5, creates a state obligation to prosecute or extradite those who commit torture (art. 8), to compensate victims (art. 14), and to refrain from expelling, returning, or extraditing individuals to a state where torture is likely to be committed (art. 3(1)).

10 On racial discrimination and human rights generally, see S. Fredman *et al.*, eds., *Discrimination and Human Rights: The Case of Racism* (Oxford: Oxford University Press, 2001) and M. Banton, *Combating Racial Discrimination: The UN and Its Member States* (London: Minority Rights Group, 2000).

11 UN Declaration on the Elimination of All Forms of Racial Discrimination, proclaimed by GA res. 1904 (XVIII) (1963). The CERD was also succeeded by a treaty banning systemic racism, namely the International Convention on the Suppression and Punishment of the Crime of Apartheid 1973, which is discussed in Chapter Seven.

12 But note CERD, above note 3, art. 1(3): "Nothing in this Convention may be interpreted as affecting in any way the legal provisions of States Parties concerning nationality, citizenship or naturalization, provided that such provisions do not discriminate against any particular nationality."

CERD article 5 requires state parties to guarantee the right of everyone to equality before the law generally and particularly in the enjoyment of certain rights. These include civil and polical rights, economic, social and cultural rights, the right of security of person and state protection from violence, and the right of access to public places.

The CERD contemplates both optional affirmative action measures (referred to as "special measures" in article 1(4)) and mandatory affirmative action measures (article 2(2)).[13] Those articles provide that such measures are valid only if their purpose is to attain equality in fact. The measures must also be temporary and they must not lead to the maintenance of separate rights.[14]

Where a person is a victim of racial discrimination, states parties must "assure" him the right to effective protection and remedies, including the right to seek just and adequate reparation (article 6). The CERD also affirmatively requires states parties to criminalize the dissemination or financing of race-based claims of superiority and to prohibit any such propaganda, organized or otherwise (article 4).

C. THE CONVENTION ON THE ELIMINATION OF ALL FORMS OF DISCRIMINATION AGAINST WOMEN

While both are anti-discrimination treaties, the Convention on the Elimination of All Forms of Discrimination Against Women (CEDAW) has proven to be far more controversial than the CERD.[15] This may be

---

13   While the ICCPR does not contain provisions on "special measures" to overcome discrimination, in ICCPR General Comment 18 (1989) at para. 10, the UN Human Rights Committee observed that such measures are allowed and may in some instances be required.

14   See, for example, art. 2(2):

> States Parties shall, when the circumstances so warrant, take, in the social, economic, cultural and other fields, special and concrete measures to ensure the adequate development and protection of certain racial groups or individuals belonging to them, for the purpose of guaranteeing them the full and equal enjoyment of human rights and fundamental freedoms. These measures shall in no case entail as a consequence the maintenance of unequal or separate rights for different racial groups after the objectives for which they were taken have been achieved.

15   On women's human rights generally, see P. Grimshaw et al., eds., Women's Rights and Human Rights: International Historical Perspectives (Basingstoke, New Hampshire: Palgrave, 2001).

due in part to the CEDAW being so elaborate, but continuing resistance to women's full equality is likely the real explanation. The CEDAW was preceded by a UN General Assembly declaration[16] and by two UN treaties.[17] There is now an optional protocol to the CEDAW, which is discussed in Chapter Fourteen.

The CEDAW protects against acts that have the intent or effect of discriminating on the basis of sex. Article 4 allows for — but does not expressly require — temporary affirmative action-like measures to speed up the realization of de facto equality. The CEDAW also contains a number of important positive obligations for states. States parties must:

- take affirmative measures to eliminate discrimination against women by any persons, organization, or enterprise (article 2(e));
- modify "social and cultural patterns" which are based on stereotypes or notions of inferiority of either gender (article 5);
- encourage coeducation and the revision of textbooks for purposes of eliminating stereotypes about men or women (article 10(c));[18] and
- ensure equal access to bank loans, mortgages, and other forms of credit (article 13).

The CEDAW also provides special protections for women prostitutes (article 6) and rural women (article 14). In addition there are protections for women in matters of education (article 10), employment (article 11), health care (article 12), and marriage and family life (article 16).[19] The CEDAW is silent on the question of violence against women.[20]

---

16 Declaration on the Elimination of Discrimination against Women, GA res. 2263(XXII) (1967).

17 The Convention on the Political Rights of Women 1952 [1957] CanTS no. 3, and the Convention on the Nationality of Married Women 1957 [1960] CanTS no. 2. On the former, Canada placed the following reservation:

   Inasmuch as under the Canadian constitutional system legislative jurisdiction in respect of political rights is divided between the provinces and the Federal Government, the Government of Canada is obliged, in acceding to this Convention, to make a reservation in respect of rights within the legislative jurisdiction of the provinces.

18 More generally, see the UNESCO Convention Against Discrimination in Education 1960, 429 UNTS 93. Canada is not a party to the treaty or its protocol.

19 Compare with the Convention on Consent to Marriage, Minimum Age for Marriage and Registration of Marriages 1962, 521 UNTS 231. Canada is not a party to the treaty.

20 But note that the Committee on the Elimination of Discrimination against Women has adopted General Recommendation no. 19 (1992) regarding violence against women. Note also the UN General Assembly's Declaration on the Elimination of Violence Against Women, GA res. 48/104 (1993).

Although sex or gender is an impermissible basis for adverse discrimination under all major human rights treaties,[21] the CEDAW has attracted by far the largest quantity and most questionable quality of reservations of any human rights treaty. Most reservations are justified on the basis of incompatibility with national law, tradition, religion, or culture.[22] These reservations have prompted many states, including Canada, to file objections asserting that the reservations are incompatible with the object and purpose of the treaty.[23] The Committee on the Elimination of Discrimination against Women has voiced repeated concern about CEDAW reservations, particularly before and after the 1993 Vienna World Conference on Human Rights where considerable pressure was placed on states to withdraw inappropriate reservations.[24] Many of these reservations highlight the tension between universality on the one hand, and cultural and religious autonomy on the other.

D. THE CONVENTION AGAINST TORTURE AND OTHER CRUEL, INHUMAN OR DEGRADING TREATMENT OR PUNISHMENT

The Convention Against Torture (CAT) is a treaty for the criminalization, prevention, repression, punishment, and compensation of acts of torture and cruel, inhuman or degrading treatment or punishment.[25] As

---

21   See, for example, Charter of the United Nations 1945 (UN Charter), [1945] CanTS no. 7 art. 1(3); ICCPR, above note 1, arts. 2 and 3; and ICESCR, above note 2, arts. 2 and 3. See also arts. 1 and 24 of the American Convention on Human Rights 1969 (ACHR), OAS TS no. 36; art. 14 of the European Convention on Human Rights 1950 (ECHR), ETS. no 5; and arts. 2 and 18(3) of the African Charter on Human and Peoples' Rights 1981 (AfrCHPR), OAU doc. CAB/LEG/67/3 rev. 5.

22   For example, Bahrain has placed reservations to CEDAW, above note 4, arts. 2 ("in order to ensure its implementation within the bounds of the provisions of the Islamic Shariah") and 16 ("in so far as it is incompatible with the provisions of the Islamic Shariah").

23   Note that CEDAW, ibid., art. 28(2) specifically adopts the international rule that a reservation incompatible with the "object and purpose" of the CEDAW is impermissible.

24   See generally W. Schabas, "Reservations to the Convention on the Elimination of All Forms of Discrimination Against Women and the Convention on the Rights of the Child" (1997) 3 William & Mary Journal of Women & the Law 79.

25   On the CAT generally, see A. Boulesbaa, The UN Convention on Torture and the Prospects for Enforcement (The Hague: Martinus Nijhoff, 1999).

with other UN human rights treaties, it was preceded by a General Assembly declaration.[26] It is complemented by parallel prohibitions on torture found in many other international instruments.[27] There is also an optional protocol to the CAT, which is discussed in Chapter Fourteen.

Under CAT article 1, torture is defined as

> any act by which severe pain or suffering, whether physical or mental, is intentionally inflicted on a person for such purposes as obtaining from him or a third person information or a confession, punishing him for an act he or a third person has committed or is suspected of having committed, or intimidating or coercing him or a third person, or for any reason based on discrimination of any kind, when such pain or suffering is inflicted by or at the instigation of or with the consent or acquiescence of a public official or other person acting in an official capacity.

Article 1 expressly excludes from the definition of torture "pain or suffering arising only from, inherent in or incidental to lawful sanctions." It is not clear what the scope of "lawful sanctions" are, so it is hard to know what is exempted from the definition.

Torture is absolutely prohibited under the CAT. Article 2(2) provides, "No exceptional circumstances whatsoever, whether a state of war or a threat of war, internal political instability or any other public emergency, may be invoked as a justification of torture."[28] Article 2(3) precludes justifications of torture based on assertions of due obedience to a superior officer or a public authority.

CAT article 3(1) provides that no state party shall "expel, return (*"refouler"*) or extradite a person to another State where there are substantial grounds for believing that he would be in danger of being subjected to torture." Article 4 requires states parties to make all acts of

---

26   Declaration on the Protection of All Persons from Being Subjected to Torture and other Cruel, Inhuman or Degrading Treatment or Punishment, GA res. 3452 (XXX) (1975).

27   See, for example, ICCPR, above note 1, art. 7; ECHR, above note 21, art. 3; ACHR, above note 21, art. 5(2); AfrCHPR, above note 21, art. 5. See also the Inter-American Convention to Prevent and Punish Torture 1985, OAS TS no. 67; and the European Convention for the Prevention of Torture and Inhuman or Degrading Treatment or Punishment 1987, ETS no. 126.

28   The prohibition on torture and cruel, inhuman or degrading treatment or punishment is expressly non-derogable under all human rights treaties. See generally T. van Boven, "Report of UN Special Rapporteur on the Question of Torture," UN doc. E/CN.4/2002/13 at paras. 8–15.

torture criminal offences, including attempts and complicity. States parties must also assert jurisdiction over torture offences when they are committed in their territory,[29] when the alleged offender is one of their nationals,[30] and when the alleged offender is within their territorial jurisdiction and not extradited.[31] A state party may also take jurisdiction over torture offences when the victim is its national.[32] Other CAT provisions govern the prosecution and extradition of alleged offenders,[33] the education of law enforcement personnel and others,[34] the rights of victims,[35] and the inadmissibility in court of statements gained through torture.[36]

The phrase "cruel, inhuman or degrading treatment or punishment" is not defined in the CAT. It is clearly a form of treatment or punishment less severe than torture.[37] State obligations in respect of such treatment or punishment are less onerous. For example, while there is a state obligation under the CAT to criminalize and compensate instances of torture, there are no equivalent obligations in respect of cruel, inhuman or degrading treatment or punishment. The UN Human Rights Committee asserts that it is not possible to draw sharp distinctions between the prohibited forms of treatment or punishment, since each instance must be judged according to its nature, purpose, and severity.[38]

E. THE CONVENTION ON THE RIGHTS OF THE CHILD AND ITS OPTIONAL PROTOCOLS

The Convention on the Rights of the Child (CRC) is the most widely ratified of all human rights treaties. It is neither a thematic nor an anti-discrimination treaty. It is a treaty focused on the protection of a par-

---

29 CAT, above note 5, art. 5(1)(a).
30 *Ibid.*, art. 5(1)(b).
31 *Ibid.*, art. 5(2).
32 *Ibid.*, art. 5(1)(c).
33 *Ibid.*, arts. 7–9.
34 *Ibid.*, art. 10.
35 *Ibid.*, arts. 13–14.
36 *Ibid.*, art. 15.
37 See, for example, art. 16(1): "Each State Party shall undertake to prevent in any territory under its jurisdiction other acts of cruel, inhuman or degrading treatment or punishment *which do not amount* to torture" [emphasis added].
38 ICCPR General Comment no. 20 (1992) at para. 4.

ticular group, namely children.[39] The CRC was preceded by a UN General Assembly Declaration,[40] and builds on the child-focused protections in other human rights instruments.[41] The CRC is also complemented by a number of important UN rules and guidelines to encourage appropriate standards of treatment for juvenile offenders.[42]

Article 3 of the CRC defines children as persons below the age of eighteen, unless the age of majority is attained earlier under the applicable law. The four "guiding principles" of the CRC are non-discrimination (article 2), the best interests of the child (article 3), maximum survival and development (article 6), and participation (article 12). The CRC covers the full range of civil, political, economic, social and cultural rights. The CRC also seeks to protect children from such practices as economic exploitation (article 32), illicit drug use (article 33), and sexual exploitation (article 34).

Most of the rights in the CRC are conferred to children as individuals, and as such may be exercised independently of parents or other family members.[43] But states must respect parents' primary responsibility for giving care and guidance to their children (article 5), and must prevent children from being separated from their families except where separation is in the child's best interests (article 10).

Recently, the CRC has been supplemented by two optional protocols. The Optional Protocol to the Convention on the Rights of the Child on the involvement of children in armed conflicts 2000 (CRC-OP-AC)[44] seeks to lift the minimum age of persons involved in armed conflicts to eighteen.[45] While the CRC-OP-AC establishes eighteen as

---

39   Only the US and Somalia are non-parties. Both have signed, but not ratified, the CRC. On the CRC generally, see S. Detrick, *A Commentary on the United Nations Convention on the Rights of the Child* (The Hague, Boston: M. Nijhoff Publishers, 1999).

40   Declaration on the Rights of the Child, GA res. 1386(XIV) (1959).

41   See, for example, the Universal Declaration of Human Rights 1948 (UDHR), GA res. 217 (III), art. 2(2); ICCPR, above note 1, art. 24; ICESCR, above note 2, art. 10(3).

42   See, for example, UN Rules for the Protection of Juveniles Deprived of their Liberty, GA res. 45/113 (1990); and UN Standard Minimum Rules for the Administration of Juvenile Justice ("The Beijing Rules"), GA res. 40/33 (1985). See also: UN Guidelines for the Prevention of Juvenile Delinquency ("The Riyadh Guidelines"), GA res. 45/112 (1990).

43   See, for example, arts. 13 (freedom of expression), 14 (freedom of thought, conscience, and religion) and 15 (freedom of association and peaceful assembly).

44   [2002] CanTS no. 5.

45   See also art. 77 of the Protocol Additional to the Geneva Conventions of 12 August 1949, and relating to the Protection of Victims of International Armed Conflicts (Protocol I) 1977 (GC Protocol I), which provides in its relevant part:

the minimum age for compulsory recruitment, it does not establish that age as a minimum for voluntary recruitment. Instead, CRC-OP-AC article 3(2) requires states parties to make a declaration upon becoming a party regarding the age at which national armed forces will permit voluntary recruitment, and provide a description of the measures it has taken to ensure that such recruitment is not coerced.[46] Article 4 of the CRC-OP-AC stipulates that private armed groups also should not recruit or use persons under the age of eighteen in armed hostilities.

> 2. The Parties to the conflict shall take all feasible measures in order that children who have not attained the age of fifteen years do not take a direct part in hostilities and, in particular, they shall refrain from recruiting them into their armed forces. In recruiting among those persons who have attained the age of fifteen years but who have not attained the age of eighteen years the Parties to the conflict shall endeavour to give priority to those who are oldest.
>
> 3. If, in exceptional cases, despite the provisions of paragraph 2, children who have not attained the age of fifteen years take a direct part in hostilities and fall into the power of an adverse Party, they shall continue to benefit from the special protection accorded by this Article, whether or not they are prisoners of war.
>
> 4. If arrested, detained or interned for reasons related to the armed conflict, children shall be held in quarters separate from the quarters of adults, except where families are accommodated as family units as provided in Article 75, paragraph 5.

46   Canada's declaration under art. 3(2) provides:

> 1. The Canadian Armed Forces permit voluntary recruitment at the minimum age of 16 years.
>
> 2. The Canadian Armed Forces have adopted the following safeguards to ensure that recruitment of personnel under the age of 18 years is not forced or coerced: (a) all recruitment of personnel in the Canadian Forces is voluntary. Canada does not practice conscription or any form of forced or obligatory service. In this regard, recruitment campaigns of the Canadian Forces are informational in nature. If an individual wishes to enter the Canadian Forces, he or she fills in an application. If the Canadian Forces offer a particular position to the candidate, the latter is not obliged to accept the position; (b) recruitment of personnel under the age of 18 is done with the informed and written consent of the person's parents or legal guardians. Article 20, paragraph 3, of the National Defence Act states that "a person under the age of eighteen years shall not be enrolled without the consent of one of the parents or the guardian of that person"; (c) personnel under the age of 18 are fully informed of the duties involved in military service. The Canadian Forces provide, among other things, a series of informational brochures and films on the duties involved in military service to those who wish to enter the Canadian Forces; and (d) personnel under the age of 18 must provide reliable proof of age prior to acceptance into national military service. An applicant must provide a

The Optional Protocol to the Convention on the Rights of the Child on the sale of children, child prostitution, and child pornography 2000 (CRC-OP-SC)[47] was adopted at the same time as the CRC-OP-AC. Canada has signed but not yet ratified the CRC-OP-SC.[48]

Article 2 of the CRC-OP-SC provides definitions for each of the prohibited acts:

(a) Sale of children means any act or transaction whereby a child is transferred by any person or group of persons to another for remuneration or any other consideration;

(b) Child prostitution means the use of a child in sexual activities for remuneration or any other form of consideration;

(c) Child pornography means any representation, by whatever means, of a child engaged in real or simulated explicit sexual activities or any representation of the sexual parts of a child for primarily sexual purposes.

Article 3(1) requires states parties to criminalize the following acts:

(a) In the context of sale of children as defined in article 2:
  (i) Offering, delivering or accepting, by whatever means, a child for the purpose of: a. Sexual exploitation of the child; b. Transfer of organs of the child for profit; c. Engagement of the child in forced labour;
  (ii) Improperly inducing consent, as an intermediary, for the adoption of a child in violation of applicable international legal instruments on adoption;

(b) Offering, obtaining, procuring or providing a child for child prostitution, as defined in article 2;

(c) Producing, distributing, disseminating, importing, exporting, offering, selling or possessing for the above purposes child pornography as defined in article 2.

These acts are to be criminalized irrespective of whether they are committed within or outside the territory of a state party (article 3(1)).

The CRC-OP-SC also requires the confiscation of crime-related material and assets (article 7) and the adoption of special measures to ensure the safety and well-being of children within the criminal justice process (article 8). States parties must also carry out public awareness,

---

legally recognized document, that is an original or a certified copy of their birth certificate or baptismal certificate, to prove his or her age.

47   GA res. 54/263 (2000).
48   Canada deposited its signature on 10 November 2001.

information, and education campaigns to enhance the protection of children at risk (article 9) and take "all necessary steps" to ensure international cooperation in combating not only the enumerated offences but also child sex tourism (article 10).

F. THE INTERNATIONAL CONVENTION ON THE PROTECTION OF THE RIGHTS OF ALL MIGRANT WORKERS AND MEMBERS OF THEIR FAMILIES

The other major UN human rights treaty, though one that has yet to attain the broad membership of the six major treaties, is the International Convention on the Protection of the Rights of All Migrant Workers and Members of Their Families (MWC).[49] It came into force on 1 July 2003. The MWC complements the efforts of the International Labour Organization (ILO), which has for decades led international efforts to protect the rights of migrant workers and their families.[50]

The MWC aims to protect against the exploitation of migrant workers at all stages of the migration process, and in particular to protect against the illegal recruitment and trafficking of migrant workers and their irregular or undocumented employment. The treaty accords a comprehensive set of civil, political, economic, social and cultural rights to migrant workers and their families.

Article 2(1) defines a migrant worker as "a person who is to be engaged, is engaged or has been engaged in a remunerated activity in a State of which he or she is not a national." Refugees and stateless persons are excluded from the definition of migrant worker.[51] The MWC estab-

---

49   There are currently twenty-two states parties and ten additional signatories to the MWC. Canada has not acceded to the treaty.

50   The preamble to the MWC lists the key ILO conventions and recommendations on the topic:

> Convention concerning Migration for Employment (No. 97), the Convention concerning Migrations in Abusive Conditions and the Promotion of Equality of Opportunity and Treatment of Migrant Workers (No. 143), the Recommendation concerning Migration for Employment (No. 86), the Recommendation concerning Migrant Workers (No. 151), the Convention concerning Forced or Compulsory Labour (No. 29), and the Convention concerning Abolition of Forced Labour (No. 105).

> See also the European Convention on the Legal Status of Migrant Workers 1977, ETS No. 93.

51   MWC, above note 8, art. 3.

lishes standards to address the human rights of migrant workers regardless of their legal status in the country of employment. It also particularizes worker entitlements based on the following categories of migrant:

- frontier worker (article 2(2)(a)),
- seasonal worker (article 2(2)(b)),
- seafarer (article 2(2)(c)),
- worker on offshore installations (article 2(2)(d)),
- itinerant worker (article 2(2)(e)),
- project-tied worker (article 2(2)(f)),
- specified-employment worker (article 2(2)(g)), and
- self-employed worker (article 2(2)(h)).

The MWC establishes obligations both for sending and receiving states. These include the giving of information to employers, workers, and their organizations on policies, laws, and regulations (article 33) and the exchange of information with other states parties (article 65).

G. SIGNIFICANT UN NON-TREATY SOURCES OF HUMAN RIGHTS

In addition to UN human rights treaties, there are many important non-binding UN human rights standards on such matters as the protection of human rights defenders,[52] the elimination of religious discrimination,[53] the treatment of prisoners,[54] law enforcement,[55] the rights of crime victims,[56] and the independence of the judiciary.[57] As noted above, UN declarations may sometimes lead to the establishment of binding treaties. But there is no guarantee of that. Important UN declarations

---

52   UN Declaration on the Right and Responsibility of Individuals, Groups and Organs of Society to Promote and Protect Universally Recognized Human Rights and Fundamental Freedoms, GA res. 53/144 (1999).

53   UN Declaration on the Elimination of All Forms of Intolerance and of Discrimination Based on Religion or Belief, GA res. 36/55 (1981).

54   Standard Minimum Rules for the Treatment of Prisoners, ECOSOC res. 663C (XXIV) (1957) and res. 2076 (LXII) (1977).

55   UN Code of Conduct for Law Enforcement Officials, GA res. 34/169 (1979).

56   Declaration of Basic Principles of Justice for Victims of Crime and Abuse of Power, GA res. 40/34 (1985).

57   Basic Principles on the Independence of the Judiciary, adopted by the Seventh UN Congress on the Prevention of Crime and the Treatment of Offenders held at Milan from 26 August to 6 September 1985 and endorsed by GA res. 40/32 (1985) and GA res. 40/146 (1985).

regarding the protection of minority groups,[58] the right to development,[59] the prohibition of forced disappearances,[60] and the rights of disabled persons,[61] have not yet been converted into treaty form within the UN system — although this may soon change.[62] However, even without conversion to treaty form, UN declarations — particularly those of the UN General Assembly — may represent important evidence of customary international law. This is especially the case when they are adopted unanimously or almost unanimously. Canadian courts have cited many UN non-treaty sources in their judgments.[63]

There have also been a number of particularly influential reports written by UN special rapporteurs and independent experts appointed by the Commission on Human Rights. Significant and oft-cited examples include past reports on internally displaced persons (IDPs),[64] reparation for human rights violations,[65] and amnesty laws.[66]

Despite the breadth of topics covered by UN instruments, some important human rights issues have not made it into any major treaty or declaration. Prominent among such issues is the protection of sexu-

---

58 Declaration on the Rights of Persons Belonging to National or Ethnic, Religious or Linguistic Minorities, GA res. 47/135, annex (1993).

59 Declaration on the Right to Development, GA res. 41/128 (1986).

60 Declaration on the Protection of All Persons from Enforced Disappearances, GA res. 47/133 (1992).

61 Declaration on the Rights of Mentally Retarded Persons, GA res. 2856 (XXVI) (1971); and Declaration on the Rights of Disabled Persons, GA res. 3447 (XXX) (1975).

62 In 2001 the UN Commission on Human Rights established an intersessional, open-ended working group to elaborate a draft treaty for the protection of all persons from enforced disappearance, taking into account a draft treaty that had previously been transmitted by the Sub-Commission on the Promotion and Protection of Human Rights in its resolution 1998/25 (1998). See the working group's most recent report at UN doc. E/CN.4/2003/71 (2003). Also, in 2002 the UN General Assembly established an Ad Hoc Committee on a Comprehensive and Integral International Convention on Protection and Promotion of the Rights and Dignity of Persons with Disabilities. See the Committee's most recent report at UN doc. A/58/118 (2003).

63 See W. Schabas, International Human Rights Law and the Charter, 2d ed. (Scarborough: Carswell, 1996) at 80–81 and G. van Ert, Using International Law in Canadian Courts (The Hague: Kluwer, 2002) at 29–30.

64 F. Deng, "Guiding Principles on Internal Displacement," UN doc. E.CN.4/1998/53/Add. 2.

65 M. C. Bassiouni, "The Right to Restitution, Compensation and Rehabilitation for Victims of Gross Violations of Human Rights and Fundamental Freedoms — Final Report," UN doc. E/CN.4/2000/62.

66 L. Joinet, "Study on Amnesty Laws and Their Role in the Safeguard and Promotion of Human Rights," UN doc. E/CN.4/Sub.2/1985/16.

al minorities (persons who identify themselves as gay, lesbian, bisexual, or transgendered). Members of sexual minorities continue to be viewed by most states as immoral or unnatural. Indeed, it was only in 1991 that the World Health Organization removed homosexuality from its International Classification of Diseases.[67]

The UN Human Rights Committee has occasionally grappled with the issue of discrimination against sexual minorities. In 1979, the Committee observed that legislation criminalizing sexual relations between consenting adults of the same sex violates the right to privacy in ICCPR article 17.[68] More recently, in *Toonen v. Australia*,[69] the Committee reiterated this view[70] and declared that the reference to "sex" in ICCPR article 2(1) includes sexual orientation.[71] The Committee declined to determine whether one could read the ICCPR article 2(1) reference to "other status" to include sexual orientation.

The European Court of Human Rights has also rendered a few important decisions on the rights of sexual minorities. In both *Goodwin v. United Kingdom*[72] and *I. v. United Kingdom*,[73] the Court held unanimously that the practice of limiting gender in domestic law to the gender registered at birth infringed the right to marry (ECHR article 12) and the right to respect for private life (ECHR article 8(1)). In both cases the applicants were transgendered persons.

Yet such cases are exceptional. There is clearly a need, if little present support, for international norms to address the particular challenges and mistreatment that members of sexual minorities face. The range of violations they endure is extremely broad, including everything from systemic discrimination to torture to denial of the right of asylum. In many countries, consensual sexual relations between adults of the same sex remain criminal acts that attract severe penalties.[74]

---

67 J. Dorf, "Sexual Orientation and Human Rights in the United Nations," in Y. Danieli *et al.*, eds., *The Universal Declaration of Human Rights: Fifty Years and Beyond* (Amityville, NY: Baywood Publishers, 1999) at 230.

68 Human Rights Committee, *Concluding Observations: Chile* (1979) at para. 216.

69 (1994) Comm. no. 488/1992.

70 *Ibid.* at para. 8.2.

71 *Ibid.* at para. 8.7.

72 (2002) App. no. 28957/95, Grand Chamber.

73 (2002) App. no. 25680/94, Grand Chamber.

74 On human rights violations committed against members of sexual minorities, see generally the website of the International Gay and Lesbian Human Rights Commission, a US-based NGO (http://www.iglhrc.org). See also relevant excerpts from Human Rights Watch's *2002 World Report* (http://www.hrw.org/wr2k2/lgbt.html).

CHAPTER 6

REGIONAL HUMAN RIGHTS INSTRUMENTS

The enthusiasm for human rights in the post-war era produced not only the UN instruments considered in the previous two chapters, but also regional human rights law in the Americas, Europe, and (somewhat later) Africa. This chapter will review the main regional treaties and declarations. Notably missing from this account are the Asian and Middle Eastern regions. To date there is no Asian human rights system. As for the Middle East, the League of Arab States has produced one human rights treaty, but has so far attracted only one ratification.[1] The Organization of the Islamic Conference has adopted the Cairo Declaration on Human Rights in Islam 1990,[2] but the Declaration bears little resemblance to any of the leading human rights treaties and appears to draw its primary inspiration from the Islamic Shari'ah.[3]

---

1 Arab Charter on Human Rights 1994, adopted by the League of Arab States, reprinted at (1997) 18 Human Rights Law Journal 151. Article 42(b) of the Charter provides that it will enter into effect two months after the date of deposit of the seventh instrument of ratification or accession with the Secretariat of the League of Arab States. As of this writing, the Charter is under review. A replacement treaty will likely be adopted in the near future.

2 Adopted 5 August 1990, at the Nineteenth Islamic Conference of Foreign Ministers (Session of Peace, Interdependence and Development), Cairo.

3 See, for example, art. 1(a), which provides that "All human beings form one family whose members are united by their subordination to Allah and descent from Adam. . . ." Article 1(b) provides that "no one has superiority over another except on the basis of piety and good deeds." All the rights and freedoms listed

Canada is a member of the Organization of American States (OAS) and the Organization for Security and Co-operation in Europe (OCSE), and has observer status in the Council of Europe. Canada is neither a member nor an official observer to the EU or the African Union, although there are longstanding areas of co-operation with the EU.[4] As a rule, these regional human rights systems have operated compatibly with the more universal UN system.

A. INSTRUMENTS OF THE ORGANIZATION OF AMERICAN STATES

The Organization of American States (OAS) has created an extensive legal framework for the protection of human rights. Its scope of coverage and its impact is second only to the Council of Europe, discussed below. Canada has been a member of the OAS since 1990.

1) The OAS Charter

Like the UN Charter, the Charter of the Organization of American States 1948 (OAS Charter),[5] as revised,[6] makes only a few explicit references to human rights. Article 3(l) of the revised OAS Charter provides that "the American States proclaim the fundamental rights of the individual without distinction as to race, nationality, creed, or sex." Also, article 17 of the revised OAS Charter provides: "Each State has the right to develop its cultural, political and economic life freely and naturally. In this free development the State shall respect the rights of the individual and the principles of universal morality." The most significant human rights provision is article 45, under which OAS mem-

---

in the Declaration are subject to the Islamic Shari'ah (art. 24), and the Islamic Shari'ah is the only valid source of reference for explaining or clarifying any of its articles (art. 25).

4   See, for example, the Framework Agreement for Commercial and Economic Cooperation between the European Communities and Canada 1976 [1976] CanTS no. 35.

5   1948 [1990] CanTS no. 23.

6   At the time of Canada's accession, the OAS Charter included prior amendments pursuant to the Protocol of Buenos Aires, signed on 27 February 1967 at the Third Special Inter-American Conference, and the Protocol of Cartagena de Indias, approved on 5 December 1985 at the Fourteenth Special Session of the General Assembly. The OAS Charter was subsequently amended by the Protocol of Managua 1993 and the Protocol of Washington 1992. Canada ratified both Protocols on 26 August 1993, but neither is listed in the CanTS.

ber states agree to dedicate "every effort" to ensuring, *inter alia*, a right to material well-being, a right to work, a right to free association, and access to legal aid.

2) The American Declaration on the Rights and Duties of Man

The American Declaration on the Rights and Duties of Man 1948 (AmDR),[7] adopted seven months prior to the UDHR, remains the OAS's most comprehensive declaration on the subject of human rights. The AmDR was adopted as an ordinary conference resolution in 1948 and understood by OAS member states at the time to have no legal effect. Yet in 1989, the Inter-American Court of Human Rights held in an advisory opinion that the AmDR constitutes an authoritative interpretation of the "fundamental rights of the individual" referred to in article 3(1) of the OAS Charter.[8] Today, as explained in Chapter Fifteen, the Inter-American Commission on Human Rights reviews OAS member states' compliance with the rights and duties set out in the AmDR and accepts individual petitions alleging violations of it by all OAS member states. Canada became subject to the procedures of the Inter-American Commission on Human Rights in respect of the AmDR upon becoming an OAS member state. It has never questioned the binding character of the AmDR for OAS purposes (though it may dispute the justiciability of particular AmDR provisions).

Like the UDHR, the AmDR covers a wide range of civil, political, economic, social and cultural rights. These include familiar civil and political rights such as the right to life, liberty and security of the person (article 1) and the right to participate in government (article 20), and economic, social and cultural rights such as the right to an education (article 12), the right to participate in the cultural life of the community (article 13), and the right to work (article 14). The AmDR also recognizes less familiar rights such as the right to "special protection, care and aid" for women during pregnancy and nursing (article 7), and the right to simple, brief court procedures for violations of fundamental constitutional rights (article 18). All of the AmDR's rights are "limited by the rights of others, by the security of all, and by the just demands of the general welfare and the advancement of democracy" (article 28).

---

7   OAS res. XXX. Reprinted in *Basic Documents Pertaining to Human Rights in the Inter-American System*, OEA/Ser.L.V/II.82 doc.6 rev. 1 at 17 (1992).

8   *Advisory Opinion OC-10/89* (1989) I/A Court HR Series A no. 10 at para. 45.

What most distinguishes the AmDR — other than its distinctive phrasing[9] — is Chapter Two which sets out ten specific duties owed by individuals to each other and to the state. These include duties toward society (article 29), toward children and parents (article 30), to acquire an elementary education (article 31), to vote (article 32), to obey the law (article 33), to serve the community and the nation (article 34), to contribute to social security and welfare (article 35), to pay taxes (article 36), to work (article 37), and to refrain from political activities in a country in which one is not a citizen (article 38). These duties are not justiciable before the Inter-American Commission on Human Rights.[10]

3) The American Convention on Human Rights and its Protocols

The majority of OAS member states are parties to the American Convention on Human Rights 1969 (ACHR).[11] Canada has yet to become a party.[12]

A central purpose of the ACHR was to convert the norms of the AmDR into treaty form, and in doing so expand their scope and reach — much like the ICCPR and ICESCR did in relation to the UDHR. The ACHR did not, however, carry forward all of the provisions of the AmDR. Duties were mostly omitted.[13] So too were economic, social and

---

9   The phrasing of several of the rights covered in the AmDR may strike many common law-trained readers as unusual. To some degree it simply reflects differences in the conception of certain rights within the civil law tradition, being the legal system of the majority of OAS member states.

10   This is partly because states and individuals cannot bring petitions against other individuals within the OAS human rights system.

11   OAS TS no. 36.

12   The Senate Standing Committee on Human Rights tabled in Parliament a report recommending that Canada take all necessary action to ratify the ACHR by 18 July 2008, the date of the treaty's thirtieth anniversary of entry into force. The Committee also recommended that Canada recognize the jurisdiction of the Inter-American Court of Human Rights upon ratification. See "Enhancing Canada's Role in the OAS: Canadian Adherence to the American Convention on Human Rights," Report of the Senate Standing Committee on Human Rights, May 2003 (http://www.gibvanert.com/using/pdfs/senate_achr.pdf).

13   Article 32(1) of the ACHR, above note 11, simply provides: "Every person has responsibilities to his family, his community, and mankind." Article 32(2) then provides a general, if implicit, duty: "The rights of each person are limited by the rights of others, by the security of all, and by the just demands of the general welfare, in a democratic society."

cultural rights.[14] The ACHR also added some new and controversial elements such as article 4(1), which provides that the right to life shall be protected "in general, from the moment of conception."[15]

In terms of its civil and political guarantees, the ACHR compares favourably with similar human rights treaties, though it, too, exhibits the AmDR's distinctive phrasing. Like the ICCPR and the European Convention on Human Rights 1950 (ECHR),[16] the ACHR guarantees such rights as freedom of opinion and expression (article 3(1)), privacy (article 11), the right to a remedy (article 25), and protection from discrimination (articles 1 and 24). Like the ECHR, but unlike the ICCPR, the ACHR provides a right to protection of property (article 21) and a prohibition on collective expulsion (article 22(9)). Unlike both the ECHR and the ICCPR, the ACHR contains a right of reply to false statements (article 14) and a right to seek and be granted asylum (article 22(7)). The ACHR, however, lacks provisions on the right to bail, the right to compensation for unlawful arrest, the right to form trade unions, the right of self-determination, and a minority rights clause — all of which are found in the ICCPR.

ACHR article 27 provides a unique derogation test. It sets a lower threshold for legitimate derogation (referred to as "suspension" in the ACHR) than does the ICCPR,[17] but it prescribes a longer list of non-derogable rights.[18] In addition, article 27(2) declares as non-derogable "the judicial guarantees established for the protection" of the specifically enumerated non-derogable rights.[19]

---

14   ACHR, *ibid.*, art. 26 only provides that states should seek to achieve progressively the rights "implicit in the economic, social, educational, scientific, and cultural standards" outlined in the OAS Charter.

15   Article 4(1) made Canada reluctant to ratify the ACHR. See the recent commentary of the National Association of Women and the Law: http://www.nawl.ca/ratifying_am.htm. Other potentially problematic provisions of the ACHR for Canada include the prohibition on prior censorship (AmDR art. 13 (4)) and the broad provision on the right of reply (AmDR art. 14). See Report of the Senate Standing Committee, above note 12 at 14–15, citing comments made by former Minister of Foreign Affairs Lloyd Axworthy in 1999.

16   ETS no. 5.

17   Article 27(1) permits derogation "in time of war, public danger, or other emergency that threatens the independence or security of a State Party."

18   Under art. 27(2), non-derogable rights are art. 3 (right to juridical personality), art. 4 (right to life), art. 5 (right to humane treatment), art. 6 (freedom from slavery), art. 9 (freedom from *ex post facto* laws), art.12 (freedom of conscience and religion), art.17 (rights of the family), art.18 (right to a name), art. 19 (rights of the child), art. 20 (right to nationality), and art. 23 (right to participate in government).

19   For an interpetation of the scope of art. 27(2), see *Advisory Opinion OC-8/87* (1987) I/A Court HR Series A no. 8.

There are two protocols to the ACHR. The Additional Protocol to the ACHR in the Area of Economic, Social and Cultural Rights 1988 (ACHR-OP1)[20] deals with economic, social and cultural rights.[21] Like the ICESCR, the ACHR-OP1 provides for progressive implementation of its obligations:

> The States Parties . . . undertake to adopt the necessary measures, both domestically and through international co-operation, especially economic and technical, to the extent allowed by their available resources, and taking into account their degree of development, for the purpose of achieving progressively and pursuant to their internal legislations, the full observance of the rights recognized in this Protocol.[22]

And like the ICESCR, the ACHR-OP1 permits restrictions and limitations on the rights it proclaims:

> The State Parties may establish restrictions and limitations on the enjoyment and exercise of the rights established herein by means of laws promulgated for the purpose of preserving the general welfare in a democratic society only to the extent that they are not incompatible with the purpose and reason underlying those rights.[23]

The rights proclaimed under the ACHR-OP1 include the right to work (article 6), the right to fair conditions of work (article 7), trade union rights (article 8), the right to social security (article 9), the right to health (article 10), the right to a healthy environment (article 11), the right to food (article 12), the right to education (article 13), the right to benefits of culture (article 14), the right to the formation and protection of families (article 15), the rights of children (article 16), the protection of the elderly (article 17), and the protection of the handicapped (article 18).

The second protocol is the Protocol to the ACHR to Abolish the Death Penalty 1990 (ACHR-OP2).[24] The ACHR-OP2 prohibits the death penalty without exception unless a state party has declared, at the time of ratification or accession, that it reserves the right to apply the death penalty in wartime for extremely serious crimes of a military nature and in accordance with international law.

---

20 OAS TS no. 69. Canada is not a state party.
21 Few recall today that the Ninth International Conference of American States, which created the OAS, adopted the non-binding American Charter of Social Guarantees 1948. It contained thirty-eight articles on the social rights of workers and their families.
22 ACHR-OP1, above note 19, art. 1.
23 Ibid., art. 5.
24 OAS TS no. 73. Canada is not a state party.

4) Other OAS Human Rights Instruments

The OAS and its antecedent, the Pan American Union, have generated treaties on a wide range of human rights issues. Four deserve particular mention. The first is the Inter-American Convention to Prevent and Punish Torture 1985.[25] The definition of torture in the treaty is distinctive:

> For the purposes of this Convention, torture shall be understood to be any act intentionally performed whereby physical or mental pain or suffering is inflicted on a person for purposes of criminal investigation, as a means of intimidation, as personal punishment, as a preventive measure, as a penalty, or for any other purpose. Torture shall also be understood to be the use of methods upon a person intended to obliterate the personality of the victim or to diminish his physical or mental capacities, even if they do not cause physical pain or mental anguish. The concept of torture shall not include physical or mental pain or suffering that is inherent in or solely the consequence of lawful measures, provided that they do not include the performance of the acts or use of the methods referred to in this article.[26]

Like the CAT, the Inter-American Convention creates state obligations to investigate and punish acts of torture (articles 8 and 12) and to compensate torture victims (article 9).

A second treaty of note is the Inter-American Convention on the Prevention, Punishment and Eradication of Violence against Women 1994.[27] This is the only multilateral treaty of its kind. The Convention defines violence against women as "any act or conduct, based on gender, which causes death or physical, sexual or psychological harm or suffering to women, whether in the public or the private sphere."[28] States parties undertake "to pursue, by all appropriate means and without delay, policies to prevent, punish and eradicate such violence" (article 7) and to adopt various specific progressive measures (article 8).

A third major OAS human rights treaty is the Inter-American Convention on the Forced Disappearance of Persons 1994.[29] It too is the only multilateral treaty of its kind. The treaty is discussed in Chapter Seven.

---

25   OAS TS no. 67. Canada is not a state party.
26   Article 2.
27   (1994) 33 ILM 1534. Canada is not a state party, despite having urged its adoption in the early 1990s shortly after becoming a member of the OAS.
28   Article 1.
29   (1994) 33 ILM 1429. Canada is not a state party.

Another key OAS human rights treaty is the Inter-American Convention on the Elimination of All Forms of Discrimination Against Persons with Disabilities 1999.[30] Article 1 of the Convention defines disability as follows:

The term 'disability' means a physical, mental, or sensory impairment, whether permanent or temporary, that limits the capacity to perform one or more essential activities of daily life, and which can be caused or aggravated by the economic and social environment.

Article 2(b) provides:

A distinction or preference adopted by a state party to promote the social integration or personal development of persons with disabilities does not constitute discrimination provided that the distinction or preference does not in itself limit the right of persons with disabilities to equality and that individuals with disabilities are not forced to accept such distinction or preference.

States parties to the Convention are obliged to take a wide array of legal and policy measures to eliminate discrimination against and stereotypes about persons with disabilities (articles 3–5). They must also report to a specialized supervisory committee, discussed in Chapter Fifteen.

There are also OAS treaties on the following subjects: the nationality of women,[31] political rights of women,[32] civil rights of women,[33] diplomatic asylum,[34] territorial asylum,[35] and terrorism.[36]

Several OAS non-treaty sources of human rights are also worthy of note. They include the Cartagena Declaration on Refugees 1984,[37] the

30   GA res. 1608 (1999). Canada is not a state party.
31   OAS Convention on the Nationality of Women 1933 [1991] CanTS no. 28.
32   Inter-American Convention on the Granting of Political Rights to Women 1948 [1991] CanTS no. 29.
33   OAS Convention on the Granting of Civil Rights to Women 1948 [1991] CanTS no. 30.
34   OAS Convention on Diplomatic Asylum 1954, International Conferences of American States, 2d Supplement, 1942–1954 at 334. Canada is not a state party.
35   OAS Convention on Territorial Asylum 1954, International Conferences of American States, 2d Supplement, 1942–1954 at 345. Canada is not a state party.
36   Inter-American Convention Against Terrorism 2002. Canada was the first OAS member state to ratify the treaty. It has not yet been published in the CanTS.
37   Adopted at a colloquium held in Cartagena, Colombia from 19–22 November 1984. The Declaration recommended extending the UN's definition of refugee (discussed in Chapter Seven) to include persons who flee their country "because their lives, safety or freedom have been threatened by generalized violence, foreign aggression, internal conflicts, massive violation of human rights or other circum-

Declaration of Principles on Freedom of Expression 2000,[38] and the Inter-American Democratic Charter 2001.[39] The Inter-American Commission on Human Rights recently approved a draft American Declaration on the Rights of Indigenous Peoples.[40] The draft is currently under consideration by the OAS Committee on Juridical and Political Affairs.

B. EUROPEAN INSTRUMENTS

Three intergovernmental systems deal with human rights in Europe: the Council of Europe, the EU, and the Organization for Security and Co-operation in Europe (OSCE). Though Canada is not geographically European, it has observer status at the Council of Europe and has been a full member of the OSCE since its inception. This section will review the main instruments adopted by these intergovernmental organizations. Of the three organizations, the Council of Europe is by far the most influential in the area of human rights. However, the OSCE has arguably had greater influence on Canada due to the depth and duration of Canada's participation.

1) The Council of Europe

a) The Statute of the Council of Europe

The Council is constituted by the Statute of the Council of Europe 1949.[41] The statute makes few express references to human rights. Article 1(1)(a) proclaims that the aim of the Council of Europe is to "achieve a greater unity between its members for the purpose of safeguarding and realising the ideals and principles which are their common heritage and facilitating their economic and social progress." Article 1(2)(a) then provides that this aim is to be pursued in part by agreements and common action "in the maintenance and further realisation of human rights and fundamental freedoms." Article 3 provides

---

stances which have seriously disturbed public order." Many Latin American states have incorporated this broader definition into their domestic legislation. UNHCR, *Protecting Refugees: A Field Guide for NGOs* (Geneva: Atar SA, 1999) at 17.

38   Approved by the Inter-American Commission on Human Rights during its 108th regular session, 19 October 2000.

39   Adopted 11 September 2001 by the OAS General Assembly.

40   Approved by the Commission on 26 February 1997 at its 133rd session, 95th regular session.

41   ETS no. 1.

that every member of the Council of Europe is required to "accept the principles of the rule of law and of the enjoyment by all persons within its jurisdiction of human rights and fundamental freedoms, and collaborate sincerely and effectively in the realisation of the aim of the Council as specified in [article 1]."

b) The European Convention for the Protection of Human Rights and Fundamental Freedoms

The Council of Europe's Convention for the Protection of Human Rights and Fundamental Freedoms 1950 (ECHR),[42] now revised,[43] was the first multilateral treaty to deal comprehensively with human rights of a civil and political nature.[44] The treaty covers:

- the right to life (article 2);
- the prohibition of torture (article 3);
- the prohibition of slavery and forced labour (article 4);
- the right to liberty and security (article 5);
- the right to a fair trial (article 6);
- the principle of no punishment without law (article 7);
- the right to respect for private and family life (article 8);
- freedom of thought, conscience and religion (article 9);
- freedom of expression (article 10);
- freedom of assembly and association (article 11);
- the right to marry (article 12);
- the right to an effective remedy (article 13); and
- the prohibition of discrimination (article 14).

The ECHR is supplemented by protocols adding, among other things: rights to property and to free elections (Protocol 1); mobility rights and freedom from imprisonment for debt (Protocol 4); rights to appeal in criminal cases and to compensation for wrongful conviction (Protocol 7); and the right of non-discrimination on any ground (Protocol 12). All Council of Europe member states are parties to the ECHR but not necessarily to the additional protocols.

Although the ECHR bears closest resemblance to the ICCPR, neither the ECHR nor its additional protocols includes the right of self-

---

42 Above note 16.
43 The text of the ECHR has been amended by Protocols no. 3 (ETS no. 45), 5 (ETS no. 55), 8 (ETS no. 118), and 11 (ETS no. 155), which entered into force on 21 September 1970, 20 December 1971, 1 January 1990, and 1 November 1998 respectively.
44 On the ECHR generally, see D. Harris et al., *Law of the European Convention on Human Rights*, 2d ed. (London: Butterworths, 2001).

determination, a minority rights clause, the right to recognition as a person before the law, a prohibition on war propaganda or hate speech, the right to a nationality, the right against self-incrimination, or any special rights for children.[45] The derogation clause in ECHR article 15 provides a relatively high threshold for legitimate derogation[46] and pre-scribes a short list of non-derogable rights.[47]

c) The European Social Charter
The primary Council of Europe treaty dealing with economic, social, and cultural rights is the European Social Charter (revised) 1996 (EurSC).[48] Its closest UN equivalent is the ICESCR. Like the ICESCR, the EurSC sets out overriding policy objectives aimed at creating the conditions in which the declared rights and principles can be achieved. It establishes few enforceable or justiciable rights.[49] The treaty's ratifi-cation process is particularly interesting. States parties accept at least six of nine selected articles and an additional sixteen or more of their choice.[50] Only a few states have accepted all of the EurSC's rights.

d) Other Council of Europe Human Rights Treaties
Like the OAS, the Council of Europe has generated a wide variety of human rights instruments. Perhaps the best known European human rights treaty besides the ECHR is the European Convention for the Pre-vention of Torture and Inhuman or Degrading Treatment or Punish-

---

45   Most rights included in the ECHR, above note 16, are proclaimed in substantial-ly similar terms in the ICCPR. But the ECHR definitions of the right to life (art. 6), the right to a fair trial (art. 14), the right to marry (art. 23), and political rights (art. 25) contain significant differences from their ICCPR equivalents. See the discussion in Chapter Ten.

46   ECHR, *ibid.*, art. 15(1) permits derogation in time of "war or other public emer-gency threatening the life of the nation."

47   *Ibid.*, art. 15(2) declares as non-derogable the right to life ("except in respect of deaths resulting from lawful acts of war"), the prohibition on torture, the prohi-bition on slavery, and the protection from retroactive criminal laws (unless they were "criminal according to the general principles of law recognized by civilized nations").

48   ETS no. 163. The EurSC was preceded by the European Social Charter 1961 (ETS no. 35), the Additional Protocol to the Charter 1988 (ETS no. 128), the Protocol Amending the European Social Charter 1991 (ETS no. 142), and the Additional Protocol Providing for a System of Collective Complaints 1995 (ETS no. 158). The purpose of the EurSC was to bring all revisions up to date and introduce new rights such as the right to housing (art. 31) and the right to pro-tection against sexual harassment in the workplace (art. 26).

49   See the discussion in Chapter Fifteen.

50   See EurSC, above note 48, Part III, art. A(1)(b) and (c).

ment 1987.[51] It does not create any substantive norms but merely incorporates by reference the prohibition on torture in ECHR article 3. The treaty establishes and sets out the procedures for the European Committee for the Prevention of Torture and Inhuman or Degrading Treatment or Punishment (discussed in Chapter Fifteen).

A second important Council of Europe treaty is the European Charter for Regional or Minority Languages 1992.[52] The purpose of the Charter is to promote and protect minority languages in Europe. States undertake obligations to promote the use of regional or minority languages in public life, including in the areas of education (article 8), the administration of justice (article 9), public services (article 10), media (article 11), cultural activities (article 12), and economic and social life (article 13). Like other Council of Europe treaties, the Charter allows states to choose to adhere to only some of its provisions.

The Framework Convention for the Protection of National Minorities 1995[53] is the first multilateral human rights treaty focused on minority rights since the League of Nations era. It includes a variety of rights ranging from basic civil and political rights to unique norms such as freedom from forced assimilation (article 5(2)) and the right to use one's surname and first names in the minority language (article 11(1)).

A fourth Council of Europe treaty of note is the unique Convention for the Protection of Human Rights and Dignity of the Human Being with Regard to the Application of Biology and Medicine 1997,[54] including its additional protocols on human cloning[55] and the transplantation of organs and tissues of human origin.[56] Notable provisions of the Convention include articles 2 ("the interests and welfare of the human being shall prevail over the sole interest of society or science"), 5 (the

---

51 ETS no. 126. There have been two protocols to the convention: Protocol 1 (1993) ETS no. 151; and Protocol 2 (1993) ETS no. 152. Protocol 1 opens the treaty for signature by non-member states of the Council of Europe.

52 ETS no. 148.

53 ETS no. 157. The Convention is open to non-member states at the invitation of the Council of Europe's Committee of Ministers. On minority rights in Europe generally, see P. Cumper & S. Wheatley, eds., *Minority Rights in the "New" Europe* (The Hague: M. Nijhoff, 1999).

54 ETS no. 164.

55 Additional Protocol to the Convention for the Protection of Human Rights and Dignity of the Human Being with regard to the Application of Biology and Medicine, on the Prohibition of Cloning Human Beings 1998, ETS no. 168.

56 Additional Protocol to the Convention on Human Rights and Biomedicine Concerning Transplantation of Organs and Tissues of Human Origin 2002, ETS no. 186. The Protocol is not yet in force.

right to prior informed consent except in emergency), 11 (a prohibition on discrimination on basis of genetic make-up), 13 (limited genetic engineering), and 14 (limited use of medically assisted procreation techniques). To date, there is no equivalent UN, OAS, or AU instrument other than the non-binding Universal Declaration on the Human Genome and Human Rights 1997.[57] The cloning protocol prohibits "any intervention seeking to create a human being genetically identical to another human being, whether living or dead" (article 1) and rules out any possible exception to the prohibition (article 2). The protocol on transplantation of human organs and tissues obliges states parties to ensure equitable access to transplantation services (article 3) and prohibits the removal of organs or tissue from a living person other than for the therapeutic benefit of the recipient and only where there is no suitable organ or tissue available from a deceased person and no comparably effective alternative therapeutic method (article 9).

The Council of Europe has also produced treaties on: the rights of refugees,[58] the protection of individuals with regard to the automatic processing of personal data,[59] the exercise of children's rights,[60] cybercrime,[61] and terrorism.[62] Some of these treaties are also open for accession to non-member states of the Council of Europe.[63] Canada is party to very few Council of Europe treaties.[64]

---

57 Adopted unanimously and by acclamation by the General Conference of UNESCO at its 29th session on 11 November 1997.

58 See, for example, European Agreement on Transfer of Responsibility for Refugees 1980, ETS no. 107; and Protocol to the European Convention on Consular Functions concerning the Protection of Refugees 1967, ETS no. 61A. The latter is not yet in force.

59 Additional Protocol to the Convention for the Protection of Individuals with regard to Automatic Processing of Personal Data, Regarding Supervisory Authorities and Transborder Data Flows 2001, ETS no. 181. The Protocol is not yet in force.

60 European Convention on the Exercise of Children's Rights 1996, ETS no. 160.

61 See, for example, Convention on Cybercrime 2001, ETS no. 185; and Additional Protocol to the Convention on Cybercrime, Concerning the Criminalisation of Acts of a Racist and Xenophobic Nature Committed through Computer Systems 2003, ETS no. 189. Neither treaty is yet in force.

62 See, for example, European Convention on the Suppression of Terrorism 1977, ETS no. 90.

63 See, for example, European Agreement on the Abolition of Visas for Refugees 1959, ETS no. 31, which is open for signature by non-Council members that are party to the UN Convention relating to the Status of Refugees 1951.

64 But, see, for example, the Convention on the Transfer of Sentenced Persons 1983 [1985] CanTS no. 9, which aims to assist in the rehabilitation of prisoners by permitting them to serve sentences in their own country so that they can be in contact with family and friends.

2) European Union Instruments

The EU has produced few treaties containing human rights guarantees. However, all EU member states have ratified the ECHR and accepted the jurisdiction of the European Court of Human Rights. In addition, the European Court of Justice has found that respect for fundamental rights is an integral part of the EU's general principles.[65]

The Treaty of Amsterdam 1997 inserted a new article 6 into the revised Treaty on European Union, reaffirming that the EU

> is founded on the principles of liberty, democracy, respect for human rights and fundamental freedoms, and the rule of law, principles which are common to the Member States.

Article 7 provides that member states violating human rights in a "serious and persistent" manner may have their EU membership suspended.

The EU has also produced a Charter of Fundamental Rights 2000.[66] The Charter was intended to be a treaty, but disagreements over its content prevented that, and it remains non-binding. Both the European Parliament and the EU Commission have urged that it be formalized as a binding instrument.

The Charter is far-reaching. It establishes rights well beyond those included in the ECHR, including: the right to conscientious objection to military service (article 10(2)); a prohibition on trafficking in humans (article 5(3)); respect for academic freedom (article 13); freedom to conduct a business (article 16); and rights for children, the elderly, and the disabled (articles 24–26). The Charter also covers some important political rights, including the right to good administration (article 41), the right of access to documents (article 42), and the right of petition (articles 43–44).

The Charter forms part of a draft EU constitution now under negotiation by member states. If the draft constitution is adopted, the Charter will become law.

---

65   For an assessment of the relevant cases, see J. Weiler, "Protection of Fundamental Human Rights within the Legal Order of the Coummunities" in R. Bernhardt & J. Jolowicz, eds., *International Enforcement of Human Rights* (New York: Springer-Verlag, 1987) at 113. More generally see N. Neuwahl & A. Rosas, eds., The *European Union and Human Rights* (The Hague: Kluwer Academic Publishers, 1995).

66   The Charter was proclaimed at the EU Council meeting in Nice in 2000.

3) Instruments of the Organization for Security and Cooperation in Europe

Although not a treaty, the Final Act of the Conference on Security and Cooperation in Europe 1975 (better known as the Helsinki Final Act)[67] was a very significant human rights instrument during the Cold War. Under its terms, the West accepted Soviet authority in the USSR and its satellites, and the USSR committed itself to basic international human rights standards including, most importantly, the UDHR. The Helsinki Final Act was signed by thirty-three European countries as well as by the US and Canada.[68]

At least two of the Act's so-called "Guiding Principles" addressed human rights. Principle VII provided that participating states would act in conformity with the purposes and principles of the UN Charter and the UDHR, and that they would also fulfil their obligations

> as set forth in the international declarations and agreements in this field, including *inter alia* the International Covenants on Human Rights, by which they may be bound.

Principle VIII addressed equal rights and self-determination of peoples. Principle X was also important. It stipulated that the legislation enacted by participating states would have to "conform with their obligations under international law."

Although never binding, the Helsinki Final Act had a significant influence on government human rights policy and legislation in OSCE member states, and was frequently invoked by human rights NGOs.[69] Today the OSCE continues to play an important role on issues of democracy and human rights.[70]

C. AFRICAN UNION INSTRUMENTS

The African Union (AU) was formerly known as the Organization of African Unity (OAU). It is the youngest of all multilateral human rights

---

67 (1975) 14 ILM 1292.

68 Canada signed on 1 August 1975. On 21 November 1990, Canada also signed the OSCE Charter of Paris for a New Europe 1990, by which it affirmed its commitment to the consolidation of democracy, human rights, and the rule of law in all OSCE member states.

69 See generally T. Buergenthal, "The CSCE Rights System" (1993) 25 Geo. Wash. J. Int'l & Econ. L. 333.

70 See the discussion in Chapter Sixteen.

systems. Although the AU's legal framework for human rights protection is expanding, it remains weak compared to its European and Inter-American equivalents. Canada is not a member of the AU.

1) The Constitutive Act of the African Union

The Constitutive Act of the African Union 2000[71] replaces the OAU Charter 1963,[72] and with it the OAU. Article 4(m) of the Constitutive Act lists "respect for democratic principles, human rights, the rule of law, and good governance" as core principles of the AU. Article 4(h) of the Act authorizes the AU "to intervene in a Member State pursuant to a decision of the Assembly in respect of grave circumstances, namely: war crimes, genocide and crimes against humanity." Interventions require a decision by the AU's Assembly of Heads of State and Government.

2) The African Charter on Human and Peoples' Rights and its Protocols

The African Charter on Human and Peoples' Rights 1981 (AfrCHPR)[73] is the main human rights treaty of the AU system.[74] It came into force in 1986 and has been ratified or acceded to by all AU member states. Like the Constitutive Act of the African Union, the AfrCHPR emphasizes throughout the importance of respecting tradition and cultural practices.[75]

The AfrCHPR has many distinguishing features. First, unlike the ACHR and the ECHR, it encompasses civil, political, economic, social and cultural rights in a single instrument. Second, the AfrCHPR contains no derogation clause.

---

71 OAU doc. CAB/LEG/23.15.
72 479 UNTS 39. The OAU Charter, like the UN Charter, made passing reference to human rights without prescribing human rights. Article 2(1)(e) established as an objective of the OAU the promotion of international co-operation "having due regard to the Charter of the United Nations and the Universal Declaration of Human Rights."
73 OAU doc. CAB/LEG/67/3 rev. 5.
74 On the AfrCHPR generally, see M. Evans & R. Murray, eds., *The African Charter on Human and Peoples' Rights: The System in Practice, 1986–2000* (Cambridge: Cambridge University Press, 2002).
75 See, for example, arts. 17(3) ("the promotion and protection of morals and traditional values recognized by the community shall be the duty of the State") and 18(2) ("The State shall have the duty to assist the family which is the custodian of morals and traditional values recognized by the community").

Third, the AfrCHPR includes many implicit and explicit duties. An example of an implicit duty is article 27(2), which provides that AfrCHPR rights are to be exercised "with due regard to the rights of others, collective security, morality and common interest." Examples of explicit duties include article 29(1), which requires individuals to respect their parents at all times and to maintain them in case of need, and article 29(4), which requires individuals "to preserve and strengthen social and national solidarity, particularly when the latter is threatened." These duties, like those of the AmDR, are non-justiciable.[76]

Fourth, unlike any other major human rights treaty, the AfrCHPR establishes both individual and "peoples'" rights. These latter rights go well beyond self-determination. For instance, the AfrCHPR explicitly recognizes a right to development (article 22) and a right to national peace and security (article 23). Some of the enumerated peoples' rights are decidedly political in tone. For example, article 20(3) provides: "All peoples shall have the right to the assistance of the States parties to the present Charter in their liberation struggle against foreign domination, be it political, economic or cultural." Article 21(5) provides: "States parties to the present Charter shall undertake to eliminate all forms of foreign economic exploitation particularly that practiced by international monopolies so as to enable their peoples to fully benefit from the advantages derived from their national resources."

A fifth characteristic of the AfrCHPR is the unusually specific and broad range of obligations it creates for states parties. For example, states parties must "promote and ensure through teaching, education and publication" the respect of the AfrCHPR's rights (article 25). They must also "allow the establishment of appropriate national institutions entrusted with the promotion and protection" of the AfrCHPR's rights (article 26).

A sixth and particularly notorious characteristic of the AfrCHPR is the extreme limitations it attaches to many of the very rights it proclaims. Limitations in the treaty generally apply to political expression rights and not those involving the administration of justice or bodily integrity. For example, article 8 on freedom of conscience and religion provides that "no one may, subject to law and order, be submitted to measures restricting the exercise of these freedoms." Similarly, article 10(1) provides an individual with a right to free association "provided that he abides by the law." The obvious problem with limitations such

---

76 See generally M. Mutua, "The Banjul Charter and the African Cultural Fingerprint: An Evaluation of the Language of Duties" (1995) 35 Virginia Journal of International Law 339.

as these is that the law itself may be unfair, thus negating the possibility of beneficial reliance on the right.

Since the coming into force of the AfrCHPR, two additional protocols have been adopted. The Protocol to the AfrCHPR on the Establishment of an African Court on Human and Peoples' Rights 1998 is discussed in Chapter Fifteen. It does not amend or supplement any of the rights enumerated in the AfrCHPR. The other protocol is the Protocol to the AfrCHPR on the Rights of Women in Africa 2003 (AfrCHPR Women's Protocol).[77] It contains provisions on, *inter alia*, the elimination of discrimination against women (article 2), the elimination of harmful practices such as female genital mutilation and scarification (article 5), rights in relation to marriage (articles 6–7), the right to education and training (article 12), health and reproductive rights (article 14), and widows' and inheritance rights (articles 20–21). The African Commission on Human and Peoples' Rights will supervise implementation of the AfrCHPR Women's Protocol upon its coming into force, pending the establishment of the African Court on Human and Peoples' Rights.

3) Other African Union Human Rights Instruments

In addition to the AfrCHPR and its protocols, the OAU has adopted a small number of specialized treaties, including treaties on specific aspects of refugee problems,[78] the elimination of mercenaries,[79] and the rights and welfare of children.[80]

---

77 AU doc. CAB/LEG/23.18. The protocol is not yet in force. Fifteen ratifications are required for it to come into force.

78 The OAU Convention Governing the Specific Aspects of Refugee Problems in Africa 1969, 1001 UNTS 45. The treaty repeats the definition found in the UN Convention relating to the Status of Refugees 1951, but also covers persons forced to leave their country "owing to external aggression, occupation, foreign domination or events seriously disturbing public order in either part or the whole of his country of origin or nationality."

79 The OAU Convention for the Elimination of Mercenaries in Africa 1972, OAU doc. CM/433/Rev.L, Annex 1.

80 The African Charter on the Rights and Welfare of the Child 1990, OAU doc. CAB/LEG/24.9/49.

CHAPTER 7

RELATED FIELDS: INTERNATIONAL LABOUR, REFUGEE, HUMANITARIAN AND CRIMINAL LAW

Human rights do not exist in a legal vacuum. As explained in Chapter One, international human rights law developed in part from the older disciplines of international labour and humanitarian law. Human rights did not overtake these fields. They continue to exist as separate but related areas of law. Similarly, the fields of international refugee protection and international criminal law overlap significantly with, but exist independently of, human rights.

The purpose of this chapter is to introduce international labour, refugee, humanitarian, and criminal law. The treatment of these areas is necessarily summary. We describe only the main instruments and issues.

A. INTERNATIONAL LABOUR LAW

Two basic human rights guarantees — freedom of association and freedom from forced labour — serve as the cornerstones of international labour law. Yet the main source of international labour law is not human rights treaties but the many conventions of the International Labour Organization (ILO). Though the ILO conventions we consider below are human-rights-related, most ILO conventions concern matters beyond human rights. The North American Agreement on Labour

Cooperation 1993 (NAALC),[1] another source of international labour law, is of special relevance to Canada. We examine it below, too.

1) Conventions of the International Labour Organization

The ILO was established in 1919 and its constitution adopted in 1946.[2] The Philadelphia Declaration 1944 concerning the aims and purposes of the ILO, which is annexed to the constitution, refers to various human rights including freedom of expression and association. To date the ILO has sponsored over 180 labour rights conventions, many of which are broadly ratified.[3] Canada is party to thirty ILO conventions, twenty-eight of which are still in force.

The ILO has declared eight of its conventions "fundamental." They are:

- the Forced Labour Convention (No. 29) 1930,[4]
- the Freedom of Association and Protection of the Right to Organize Convention (No. 87) 1948,[5]
- the Right to Organize and Collective Bargaining Convention (No. 98) 1949,[6]
- the Equal Remuneration Convention (No. 100) 1951,[7]
- the Abolition of Forced Labour Convention (No. 105) 1957,[8]
- the Discrimination (Employment and Occupation) Convention (No. 111) 1958,[9]
- the Minimum Age Convention (No. 138) 1973,[10] and
- the Worst Forms of Child Labour Convention (No. 182) 1999.[11]

The significance of this "fundamental" designation is explained in the ILO's Declaration of Fundamental Principles and Rights at Work 1998:

---

1 [1994] CanTS no. 4.
2 Constitution of the International Labour Organization 1946 [1946] CanTS no. 48.
3 The ILO also formulates international labour standards in the form of non-binding recommendations. Like the conventions, the ILO's recommendations are adopted at annual meetings of the International Labour Conference. Since 1919, the ILO has adopted more than 185 recommendations.
4 39 UNTS 55. Canada is not a state party.
5 [1973] CanTS no. 14.
6 96 UNTS 257. Canada is not a state party.
7 [1973] CanTS no. 37.
8 [1960] CanTS no. 21.
9 362 UNTS 31. Canada is a state party, but the treaty is not published in CanTS. See http://www.treaty-accord.gc.ca/Treaties_CLF/Details.asp?Treaty_ID=104044.
10 1015 UNTS 297. Canada is not a state party.
11 [2001] CanTS no. 2. Child labour is currently one of the ILO's major preoccupations.

[A]ll Members, even if they have not ratified the Conventions in question, have an obligation arising from the very fact of membership in the [ILO], to respect, to promote and to realize, in good faith and in accordance with the Constitution, the principles concerning the fundamental rights which are the subject of those Conventions.

The ILO has established two important conventions concerning indigenous peoples: the Convention Concerning the Protection and Integration of Indigenous and Other Tribal and Semi-Tribal Populations in Independent Countries (No. 107) 1957 and the Convention Concerning Indigenous and Tribal Peoples in Independent Countries (No. 169) 1989.[12] These are the only binding multilateral treaties regarding the rights of indigenous peoples. Convention 169 is generally considered an improvement on Convention 107, and was in fact aimed at overcoming criticisms of the assimilationist and paternalistic approach of the latter.[13] Still, aboriginal groups in Canada and other states have successfully opposed broad ratification of these conventions. They are generally considered inimical to the group rights claims of indigenous peoples.[14]

2) The North American Agreement on Labour Cooperation

In 1993, the United States, Mexico, and Canada adopted the North American Agreement on Labour Cooperation (NAALC) as a side accord to the North American Free Trade Agreement 1992 (NAFTA).[15]

---

12   See also: the Recruiting of Indigenous Workers Convention (No. 50) 1936; the Contracts of Employment (Indigenous Workers) Convention (No. 64) 1939; the Penal Sanctions (Indigenous Workers) Convention (No. 65) 1939; the Contracts of Employment (Indigenous Workers) Convention (No. 86) 1947; and the Abolition of Penal Sanctions (Indigenous Workers) Convention (No. 104) 1955. All of these treaties have been "shelved or withdrawn," according to the ILO website.

13   Convention 107 was closed to further ratifications when Convention 169 came into force in September 1991. It will cease to be in force with respect to any state that becomes party to Convention 169.

14   There are only thirteen states parties to Convention 169. On indigenous opposition to Conventions 107 and 169 generally, see S. Venne, *Our Elders Understand Our Rights: Evolving International Law Regarding Indigenous Peoples* (Penticton, BC: Theytus Books Ltd., 1998) at 71, 92; and C. Magallanes, "International Human Rights and the Impact of Domestic Law on Indigenous Peoples' Rights in Australia, Canada and New Zealand," in P. Havemann, ed., *Indigenous Peoples' Rights in Australia, Canada and New Zealand* (Auckland: Oxford University Press, 1999) at 235–76.

15   [1994] CanTS no. 2. Neither the NAFTA itself, nor any agreement of the World Trade Organization, expressly mentions labour rights.

The NAALC arose primarily out of the concerns of Canadian and US unions about weak Mexican labour protections.

The NAALC does not create international labour norms or require states parties to change their laws. Instead, it requires parties to maintain "high labour standards" and to strive to improve them (article 2), and to ensure access to "fair, equitable, and transparent" mechanisms for the effective enforcement of those standards (article 5). Parties must act in accordance with eleven key labour principles set out in Annex 1 to the NAALC. The principles are divided into three tiers. The first tier deals with freedom of association, collective bargaining, and the right to strike. The second tier concerns forced labour, pay equity, employment discrimination, compensation in case of injury or illness, and protection of migrant labour. The third tier addresses child labour, minimum wages, and occupational safety. Some of the eleven principles, such as workers' compensation and protections for migrant workers, extend beyond the areas declared "fundamental" by the ILO.

Canada has now entered into similar labour accords with Chile and Costa Rica as side agreements to its free trade pacts with those countries.[16] It has not, however, entered into such an accord with Israel, its only other free trade partner.

B. INTERNATIONAL REFUGEE PROTECTION LAW

International refugee law is at once a sub-field of international human rights law and an independent field.[17] Many leading human rights treaties already address refugee-related rights including protection from expulsion,[18] the right to leave any country,[19] the right to asy-

---

16 Canada-Chile Agreement on Labour Cooperation 1997 [1997] CanTS no. 52; and Canada-Costa Rica Agreement on Labour Cooperation 2001 (not yet listed in the CanTS). The proposed Free Trade Agreement of the Americas — a hemispheric free trade agreement — will likely include a separate labour accord as well.

17 See generally: E. Feller *et al.*, eds., *Refugee Protection in International Law* (Cambridge: Cambridge University Press, 2003); A. Helton, *The Price of Indifference: Refugees and Humanitarian Action in the New Century* (Oxford: Oxford University Press, 2002); G. Goodwin-Gill, *The Refugee in International Law*, 2d ed. (New York: Oxford University Press, 1996); J. Hathaway, *The Law of Refugee Status* (Toronto: Butterworths, 1991).

18 See, for example, International Covenant on Civil and Political Rights 1966 (ICCPR), [1976] CanTS no. 47, art. 13; American Convention on Human Rights 1969 (ACHR), OAS TS no. 36, art. 22(5)–(6); European Convention on Human Rights 1950 (ECHR), ETS no. 5, Protocol 4 (1963) art. 3 and Protocol 7 (1984) art. 1.

19 See, for example, Universal Declaration of Human Rights 1948 (UDHR), GA res. 217 (III), art.13(2); ICCPR, *ibid.*, art. 12(2).

lum,[20] and the right to nationality.[21] There are also two UN statelessness treaties, namely the UN Convention relating to the Status of Stateless Persons 1954[22] and the UN Convention on the Reduction of Statelessness 1961.[23] Canada is a party to the later treaty but not the earlier one. Canada has also recently entered a bilateral treaty with the US for cooperation in the examination of refugee status claims from nationals of third countries.[24]

Significant though these treaties are, the field of international refugee law is dominated by the UN Convention Relating to the Status of Refugees 1951 (Refugee Convention),[25] as amended by the Protocol Relating to the Status of Refugees 1967.[26] Article 1 of the Refugee Convention defines a refugee as someone who

---

20 See, for example, UDHR, *ibid.*, art. 14, ACHR, above note 18, art. 22(7). See also the limits placed on the right of asylum in the African Charter on Human and Peoples' Rights 1981 (AfrCHPR), OAU doc. CAB/LEG/67/3 rev. 5, art. 23(2), obligating states parties to ensure that:

> (a) any individual enjoying the right of asylum under 12 of the present Charter shall not engage in subversive activities against his country of origin or any other State party to the present Charter;
> (b) their territories shall not be used as bases for subversive or terrorist activities against the people of any other State party to the present Charter.

See also ECHR, above note 18, art. 16, which permits states parties to impose restrictions "on the political activity of aliens."

21 See, for example, UDHR, above note 19, art. 15; ICCPR, above note 18, art. 24(3); ACHR, above note 18, art. 20.

22 360 UNTS 117. The treaty provides various rights for stateless persons (for example, access to courts, property rights, religious freedom) while imposing certain obligations on them (for example, compliance with laws and regulations of the host country).

23 [1978] CanTS no. 32. The treaty requires states parties to grant citizenship to stateless persons in certain instances.

24 Agreement between the Government of Canada and the Government of the United States of America for Cooperation in the Examination of Refugee Status Claims from Nationals of Third Countries 2002. The agreement is not yet listed in the CanTS.

25 [1969] CanTS no. 6. At the time of its accession, Canada placed the following reservation:

> Canada interprets the phrase 'lawfully staying' as referring only to refugees admitted for permanent residence: refugees admitted for temporary residence will be accorded the same treatment with respect to the matters dealt with in Articles 23 [public relief] and 24 [labour legislation and security] as is accorded visitors generally.

Recall that the Refugee Convention is now complemented by various regional equivalents. See Chapter Six.

26 [1969] CanTS no. 29. The Refugee Convention covers only persons who became refugees prior to 1 January 1951. The 1967 protocol allows persons who had become refugees after that date to be treated as refugees too.

owing to well-founded fear of being persecuted for reasons of race, religion, nationality, membership of a particular social group or political opinion, is outside the country of his nationality and is unable, or owing to such fear, is unwilling to avail himself of the protection of that country; or who, not having a nationality and being outside the country of his former habitual residence as a result of such events, is unable or, owing to such fear, is unwilling to return to it.

This definition expressly includes persons having a nationality and those not having one (i.e., stateless persons), provided that the other criteria are met. Explicitly excluded from eligibility for refugee status and protection are persons suspected of having committed a crime against peace, a war crime, a crime against humanity, a serious non-political crime outside the country of refuge prior to her admission to that country as a refugee, or an act contrary to the purposes and principles of the UN (article 1(6)(F)). The refugee definition also implicitly excludes anyone with a fear of persecution based on gender or sexual orientation.[27]

The main protection afforded to eligible refugees under the Refugee Convention is the right of *non-refoulement* (article 33), meaning the right not to be returned to a country where one's life or person would be endangered.[28] Other entitlements include freedom of religion (article 4), the right of association (article 15), access to courts (article 16), rights to work (articles 17–19), a right to housing (article 21), a right to education (article 22), freedom of movement (26), and the right not be expelled from the country of refuge in the absence of any threat to national security or public order (article 32). Article 7(1) provides: "Except where this Convention contains more favourable provisions, a Contracting State shall accord to refugees the same treatment as is accorded to aliens generally."

---

27 Canada has recognized gender and sexual orientation as particular "social groups" falling within the Convention definition. See D. Galloway, *Immigration Law* (Toronto: Irwin Law, 1997) at 267–69. The Office of the UN High Commissioner for Refugees has adopted a similar policy.

28 Non-refoulement rights are also included in ACHR, above note 18, art. 22(8); the Convention Against Torture and Other Cruel, Inhuman or Degrading Treatment or Punishment 1984 (CAT), [1987] CanTS no. 36, art. 3; and the Protocol Additional to the Geneva Conventions of 12 August 1949, and Relating to the Protection of Victims of International Armed Conflicts 1977 (GC Protocol I), [1991] CanTS no. 2, art. 73. Note also the decision of the Human Rights Committee in *Kindler v. Canada*, discussed in Chapters Four and Ten, in which it was held that extradition by an ICCPR state party can violate the treaty where there is a "real risk" that the extradited person's rights under the Covenant will be violated in the receiving state. See *Kindler v. Canada* (1993), Comm. no. 470/1991 at para. 13.2.

Because the Refugee Convention's definition of refugee includes only persons *outside* their country of nationality or habitual residence (that is, persons who have crossed an international border), it excludes "internally displaced persons" (IDPs). IDPs may be described as

> persons or groups of persons who have been forced or obliged to flee or to leave their homes or places of habitual residence, in particular as a result of or in order to avoid the effects of armed conflict, situations of generalized violence, violations of human rights or natural or human-made disasters, and who have not crossed an internationally recognized State border.[29]

There is an increasing recognition that IDPs require their own legal protections under international law to address the particular threats they face.[30]

C. INTERNATIONAL HUMANITARIAN LAW

International humanitarian law has been described as the human rights component of the law of war. The ambition of international humanitarian law is to lessen the brutality of war by placing restraints on its legitimate conduct. The two branches of humanitarian law are sometimes described as the law of The Hague (which governs the conduct of hostilities between belligerents)[31] and the law of Geneva (which safeguards non-combatants and those otherwise exempt from treatment as combatants).[32] The Law of Geneva is the focus of this section, as it is most directly linked to human rights.

---

29 F. Deng, "Guiding Principles on Internal Displacement," UN doc. E.CN.4/1998/53/Add. 2.

30 There are an estimated 17 million IDPs in the world today, as compared to an estimated 13 million refugees.

31 See Chapter One. See also: the Convention on the Prohibition of the Development, Production, Stockpiling and Use of Chemical Weapons and on their Destruction 1992 [1997] CanTS no. 44, and the Convention on the Prohibition of the Use, Stockpiling, Production and Transfer of Anti-Personnel Mines and their Destruction 1997 [1999] CanTS no. 4.

32 International humanitarian law also focuses on the protection of property. See, for example, the Geneva Convention relative to the Protection of Civilian Persons in Time of War 1949, below note 39, art. 147; GC Protocol I, above note 28, arts. 53 and 85(4)(d); the Protocol Additional to the Geneva Conventions of 12 August 1949, and Relating to the Protection of Victims of Non-International Armed Conflicts 1977 (GC Protocol II), [1991] CanTS no. 2, art. 16. See also the UNESCO Convention for the Protection of Cultural Property in the Event of Armed Conflict 1954 [1999] CanTS no. 52, and its two protocols.

1) Relation to International Human Rights Law

The preamble to the UDHR declares that human rights are the "foundation of freedom, justice and peace" and "essential to promote the development of friendly relations between nations." It also declares, "if man is not to be compelled to have recourse, as a last resort, to rebellion against tyranny and oppression . . . human rights should be protected by the rule of law. . . ." Leading human rights instruments also include prohibitions on war and hate speech.[33] The message is that the most assured means to avoid war — whether inter-state (international) or intra-state (internal) — is the effective protection of human rights.[34]

Recent years have seen a partial convergence of international human rights and humanitarian law, particularly in the development of modern international criminal law.[35] This can be traced primarily to the end of the Cold War, the proliferation of violent internal armed conflicts in many parts of the world, and the recognized need to afford better protection to the victims of such conflicts.[36] Convergence has perpetuated longstanding confusion about the respective scope of application of international human rights and humanitarian law. Many people continue to think that human rights law only applies in times of peace and that only humanitarian law applies in times of war. In fact, international human rights law applies in peace and war, serving to complement and reinforce the protections afforded by international humanitarian law.

---

33 See, for example, UDHR, above note 19, art. 7, ICCPR, above note 18, art. 20, ACHR, above note 18, art. 13(5).

34 See also the Charter of the United Nations 1945 (UN Charter), [1945] CanTS no. 7, preamble, which provides in part:

> We the Peoples of the United Nations determined to save succeeding generations from the scourge of war, which twice in our lifetime has brought untold sorrow to mankind, and to reaffirm faith in fundamental human rights, in the dignity and worth of the human person, in the equal rights of men and women and of nations large and small. . . .

35 On the relationship between international human rights and humanitarian law generally, see R. Provost, *International Human Rights and Humanitarian Law* (Cambridge: Cambridge University Press, 2002). See also M. Freeman, "International Law and Internal Armed Conflicts: Clarifying the Interplay Between Human Rights and Humanitarian Protections" (2000) Journal of Humanitarian Assistance (http://www.jha.ac/articles/a059.htm).

36 Perhaps the most significant attempt to tackle this problem is the UN's effort to elaborate "fundamental standards of humanity." See Report of the Secretary-General, "Minimum Humanitarian Standards," UN doc. E/CN.4/1998/87. See also D. Petrasek, "Moving Forward on the Development of Minimum Humanitarian Standards" (1998) 92 AJIL 561.

2) Types of Conflict

Before examining which human rights and humanitarian norms are applicable in armed conflict, it is necessary to distinguish among conflict situations. International law recognizes four types of conflict, each of which is governed by a different set of legal norms.

Situations of Internal Tensions and Disturbances. The term "internal tensions and disturbances" refers to situations that fall short of armed conflict but involve the use of force and other repressive measures by government to maintain or restore public order or public safety. A non-exhaustive list of examples is found in article 1(2) of the GC Protocol II,[37] and includes "riots, isolated and sporadic acts of violence and other acts of a similar nature."[38] Only international human rights law applies in such situations, subject to permissible limitations or derogations.

International Armed Conflict. This term describes armed conflict between two or more states. Such conflicts are governed by the central provisions of international humanitarian law, particularly the Geneva Conventions[39] and the GC Protocol I.[40] In addition, most human rights guarantees remain applicable, subject, as always, to permissible derogations and limitations.

Wars of National Liberation. Article 1(4) of the GC Protocol I requires wars of national liberation to be treated in the same manner as international armed conflicts. Specifically, article 1(4) extends coverage to armed conflicts in which

---

37   Above note 32. Canada placed a statement of understanding upon ratification:

> The Government of Canada understands that the undefined terms used in Additional Protocol II which are defined in Additional Protocol I shall, so far as relevant, be construed in the same sense as those definitions. The understandings expressed by the Government of Canada with respect to Additional Protocol I shall, as far as relevant, be applicable to the comparable terms and provisions contained in Additional Protocol II.

38   Article 1(2) expressly states that GC Protocol II, above note 32, does not apply to situations of tensions and disturbances.

39   Geneva Convention for the Amelioration of the Condition of the Wounded and Sick in Armed Forces in the Field 1949 [1965] CanTS no. 20 (GC1); Geneva Convention for the Amelioration of the Condition of Wounded, Sick, and Shipwrecked Members of Armed Forces at Sea 1949 [1965] CanTS no. 20 (GC2); Geneva Convention relative to the Treatment of Prisoners of War 1949 [1965] CanTS no. 20 (GC3); and Geneva Convention relative to the Protection of Civilian Persons in Time of War 1949 [1965] CanTS no. 20 (GC4).

40   Above note 28. Canada made two reservations, ten statements of understanding, and one declaration to GC Protocol I. For details, consult the CanTS.

peoples are fighting against colonial domination and alien occupation and against racist regimes in the exercise of their right to self-determination, as enshrined in the Charter of the United Nations and the Declaration on Principles of International Law concerning Friendly Relations and Cooperation among States in accordance with the Charter of the United Nations.

Thus, the laws of human rights and humanitarian law that apply to international armed conflict apply equally to wars of national liberation.[41]

Internal Armed Conflict. This term refers to all armed conflicts that may not be characterized as either international armed conflicts or wars of national liberation.[42] Human rights law applies in such conflicts, subject to permissible limitations and derogations. In addition, the provisions of article 3 common to each of the Geneva Conventions (Common Article 3),[43] and the provisions of the GC Protocol II, apply in such conflicts.

3) The Law of Geneva

a) The Geneva Conventions and the GC Protocol I

The Geneva Conventions enjoy almost universal adherence and likely represent customary international law. Article 2 common to each of the Geneva Conventions makes it clear that, with the exceptions of Common Article 3 and the Martens Clause,[44] the Conventions are addressed exclusively to armed conflicts between states. Common Article 3, which builds upon the Martens Clause, provides that parties to "armed conflict(s) not of an international character" must apply certain minimum standards to "persons taking no active part in the hostilities." Such persons include "members of armed forces who have laid down

---

41 But different legal norms would apply in a state that is not party to the GC Protocol I, since the Geneva Conventions do not cover wars of national liberation.

42 GC Protocol II, above note 32, art. 1(1).

43 Common Article 3 expressly applies "in the case of armed conflict not of an international character occurring in the territory of one of the High Contracting Parties."

44 The Martens Clause provides that the parties to any armed conflict must act "in accordance with the principles of the law of nations derived from the usages established among civilized peoples, from the laws of humanity and the dictates of public conscience." The clause first appeared in the preamble to the Hague Convention (II) with Respect to the Laws and Customs of War on Land 1899. It was later included in GC1 art. 63, GC2 art. 62, GC3 art. 142, GC4 art. 158, GC Protocol I, above note 28, art. 1, and the preamble to the GC Protocol II, above note 32.

their arms and those placed *hors de combat* by sickness, wounds, detention, or any other cause."[45]

Common Article 3 establishes an affirmative obligation to collect and care for the wounded and sick, and expressly prohibits certain acts against "persons taking no active part in the hostilities, including members of armed forces who have laid down their arms and those placed *hors de combat* by sickness, wounds, detention, or any other cause." The prohibited acts are violence to life and person, in particular murder of all kinds, mutilation, cruel treatment and torture; taking of hostages; outrages upon personal dignity, in particular humiliating and degrading treatment; and the passing of sentences and the carrying out of executions without previous judgment pronounced by a regularly constituted court affording due process.

The rest of the Geneva Conventions apply to international armed conflicts, and in particular to those groups identified in the title of each Convention; thus, to the wounded and sick in the field (GC1), to the wounded and sick at sea (GC2), to prisoners of war (GC3), and to civilians under the control of another state in the context of an armed conflict (GC4). These groups are generally referred to in each treaty by the term "protected person," in whose favour states parties to the particular treaty assume various obligations.[46] For example, under the GC3, the "Detaining Power" must provide "humane treatment" to prisoners of war (article 13), and must abstain from adverse discrimination against them (article 16) and "physical and mental torture" of them (article 17). Similarly, under the GC4 — arguably the most important of the Geneva Conventions from a human rights perspective — the "Occupying Power" may not apply measures of brutality (article 32), carry out collective punishment and reprisals against civilians (article 33), take hostages (article 34), or effect "individual or mass forcible transfers" (article 49).[47]

---

45   Common Article 3 further provides that such persons must in all circumstances be treated humanely "without any adverse distinction founded on race, colour, religion or faith, sex, birth or wealth, or any other similar criteria."

46   Although each Convention focuses on a particular protected group, there are many articles common to each of the Geneva Conventions. See generally H. Coursier, *Course of Five Lessons on the Geneva Conventions* (Geneva: International Committee of the Red Cross, 1963) at 24–37.

47   See also art. 11 of the Draft UN Declaration on the Rights of Indigenous Peoples 1993, UN doc. E/CN.4/Sub.2/1993/29/Annex I, which provides:

> Indigenous peoples have the right to special protection and security in periods of armed conflict. States shall observe international standards, in particular the Fourth Geneva Convention of 1949, for the protection of civilian populations in circumstances of emergency and armed conflict, and shall not: (a)

The GC Protocol I applies not only to international conflicts but also to liberation wars carried out in pursuit of the right of self-determination.[48] It expands the protections available under the Geneva Conventions and provides that the Protocol supplements "other applicable rules of international law relating to the protection of fundamental human rights during international armed conflict" (article 72). For example, GC Protocol I article 75 creates robust due process protections, similar to those applicable under human rights treaties, for persons "arrested, detained or interned for actions related to the armed conflict."

The Geneva Conventions and the GC Protocol I make a fundamental distinction between "grave breaches" — which trigger individual criminal responsibility — and other breaches. The category of grave breaches is of particular interest because it most closely approximates the category of human rights violations. Some grave breaches are common to all four of the Geneva Conventions,[49] some are found only in selected Geneva Conventions,[50] some are found only in the GC4,[51] and the lion's share are found only in the GC Protocol I.[52] To constitute a grave breach, the underlying act must have been committed against protected persons or property.

Recruit indigenous individuals against their will into the armed forces and, in particular, for use against other indigenous peoples; (b) Recruit indigenous children into the armed forces under any circumstances; (c) Force indigenous individuals to abandon their lands, territories or means of subsistence, or relocate them in special centres for military purposes; (d) Force indigenous individuals to work for military purposes under any discriminatory conditions.

48   Article 1(4). The adoption of GC Protocol I, above note 28, art. 1(4) proved extremely controversial. The article was ultimately adopted by a vote and not by consensus, and was consciously targeted at the situations then existing in South Africa and Israel. It specifically sought to confer prisoner-of-war status on "national liberation movement" combatants involved in those conflicts.

49   These are: wilful killing, torture or inhuman treatment, and wilfully causing great suffering or serious injury to body or health. See, for example, GC4, above note 39, art. 130.

50   These are: extensive destruction and appropriation of property not justified by military necessity and carried out unlawfully and wantonly (in GC1, GC2, and GC4); compelling a prisoner of war or a protected civilian to serve in the armed forces of the hostile power (in GC3 and GC4); and willfully depriving a prisoner of war or a protected person of the rights or fair and regular trial prescribed in the Geneva Conventions (in GC3 and GC4).

51   These are: unlawful deportation or transfer of a protected person; unlawful confinement of a protected person; and the taking of hostages.

52   See arts. 11 and 85, which add a long list of new crimes (for example, medical experimentation) and declare certain violations of the Hague Conventions and other international humanitarian law treaties to be grave breaches.

b) The GC Protocol II

The main purpose of the GC Protocol II is to expand upon the protections of Common Article 3 in respect of non-international armed conflicts (other than liberation struggles). While the GC Protocol II improves upon the self-described "minimum" protections afforded by Common Article 3, its coverage is not nearly as broad as the Geneva Conventions or the GC Protocol I.

From a human rights perspective, the most important components of the GC Protocol II are Parts II, III, and IV. Part II contains provisions concerning humane treatment of persons who do not take part in or who have ceased to take part in hostilities. Specifically, article 4(2) supplements the prohibitions contained in Common Article 3 by adding prohibitions against, *inter alia*, collective punishment, terrorism, slavery, pillage, and threats to carry out these acts. Part II also provides special protections for children (article 4(3)) and persons whose liberty has been restricted (article 5), and sets out a fairly rigorous set of standards regarding the prosecution and punishment of conflict-related criminal offences (article 6).

Part III provides for the humane treatment of the wounded, sick, and shipwrecked (article 7) and protects the person and property of medical and religious personnel (articles 9–12).

The most relevant provisions of Part IV are those prohibiting attacks or violent threats against civilians (article 13(2)), prohibiting starvation of civilians (article 14), protecting works containing dangerous forces ("dams, dykes and nuclear electrical generating stations") (article 15), and prohibiting forced displacement of civilians (article 17).

Despite the seriousness of the offences listed in the GC Protocol II, none are defined as "grave breaches" and hence do not establish a basis for individual criminal responsibility. The situation has changed, however, since the establishment of the International Criminal Tribunal for the former Yugoslavia (ICTY), the International Criminal Tribunal for Rwanda (ICTR), and the International Criminal Court.[53]

The biggest challenge in seeking to rely on the GC Protocol II is its very restrictive conditions of application. GC Protocol II article 1(1) only covers internal armed conflicts which take place

> in the territory of a High Contracting Party between its armed forces and dissident armed forces or other organized armed groups which, under responsible command, exercise such control over a part of its

---

53 See the section on "International Criminal Law" below.

territory as to enable them to carry out sustained and concerted military operations and to implement [this Protocol].[54]

Although article 1(1) states that it does not modify the conditions of application of Common Article 3, the fact is that Common Article 3 establishes a lower threshold than that found in the GC Protocol II. Unlike article 1(1), Common Article 3 does not provide a detailed definition of internal armed conflicts, but simply refers to them as "armed conflict[s] not of an international character occurring in the territory of one of the High Contracting Parties."[55]

The GC Protocol II is also notoriously difficult to apply because states engaged in internal armed conflicts rarely accept that it applies to their situation. They prefer to classify armed belligerents as terrorists or criminals so as not to confer on them any beneficial legal status. Thus the GC Protocol II, established to supplement the rudimentary protections of Common Article 3, can often prove an unreliable source of protection for victims of internal armed conflict.[56]

D. INTERNATIONAL CRIMINAL LAW

1) Relation to International Human Rights and Humanitarian Law

As explained in Chapter One, the modern origins of international criminal law may be traced to the trials of Nuremberg and Tokyo following the Second World War. Today the field of international criminal law is one of the most dynamic and rapidly evolving areas of international law.

---

54   The ICTY Appeals Chamber has further refined this definition, *inter alia*, in its landmark decision, *Prosecutor v. Tadic* (1995), Case no. IT-94-1-AR72, Decision on Interlocutory Appeal, ICTY Appeals Chamber. Among other things, the Appeals Chamber provided useful clarifications regarding the appropriate geographic and temporal frames of reference for internal armed conflicts.

55   For an analysis of the conditions of application of Common Article 3, see paras. 215–20 of the International Court of Justice's decision in the *Case Concerning Military and Paramilitary Activities in and Against Nicarauga (Nicaragua v. USA)*, [1986] ICJ Rep 14.

56   For a summary of the longstanding debates among international lawyers and scholars regarding the reputedly high threshold of application of the GC Protocol II (and the general unwillingness of states to acknowledge its application to their domestic circumstances) see A. Carillo, "*Hors de Logique*: Contemporary Issues in International Humanitarian Law as Applied to Internal Armed Conflict" (1999) 15 American University International Law Review 1 at 67–90.

Broadly speaking, the term "international criminal law" refers to international law that assigns criminal responsibility to individuals for certain serious offences or that obliges states to criminalize certain conduct. The notion of group or state criminal responsibility is mostly rejected by contemporary international law.[57]

International criminal law closely overlaps with parts of both international human rights and humanitarian law. For example, the Convention on the Prevention and Punishment of the Crime of Genocide 1948 (Genocide Convention)[58] is a human rights treaty but makes genocide an international crime for individuals acting in a public or private capacity. Similarly, the CAT makes torture a crime for individuals acting in a public capacity. Humanitarian law is no different. As noted earlier, the Geneva Conventions and the GC Protocol I distinguish "grave breaches" (which create international criminal responsibility) from other breaches (which do not).

The statutes of international criminal tribunals are another important source of international criminal law. The fact that a particular form of conduct is not punishable under the statute of an international criminal tribunal does not mean, however, that it is not a crime under international law. Most international crimes have not been included in the mandate of an international criminal tribunal. Instead, treaties and custom have been the primary sources of international criminal law.

2) Genocide, Crimes Against Humanity, and War Crimes

Although there are numerous international crimes, since Nuremberg and Tokyo three crimes have come to dominate the field: genocide, crimes against humanity, and certain types of war crimes. These have been codified, with only minor variation, in the statute of every modern international or mixed criminal tribunal. Each is examined below. Particular attention is given to the definitions of these crimes found in the Rome Statute of the International Criminal Court 1998 (Rome Statute)[59] since it will become — if it is not already — the standard for defining them. The Rome Statute, together with the Elements of Crimes (ICC Elements)[60] and Rules of Procedure and Evidence (ICC Rules),[61] drew

---

57   See S. Ratner & J. Abrams, *Accountability for Human Rights Atrocities in International Law*, 2d ed. (Oxford: Oxford University Press, 2001) [Ratner, *Accountability*] at 16–17.

58   [1949] CanTS no. 27.

59   [2002] CanTS no. 13.

60   UN doc. PCNICC/2000/1/Add.2 (2000).

61   UN doc. PCNICC/2000/1/Add.1 (2000).

directly from the statutes and jurisprudence of the ICTY and the ICTR. Both the ICC Elements and the ICC Rules are intended to assist the International Criminal Court. They are not, however, binding on the Court and remain subordinate to the Rome Statute.

a) Genocide

The Genocide Convention was the first human rights treaty adopted by the UN.[62] It declares genocide to be a crime under international law. Article 2 of the Genocide Convention defines the crime as

> any of the following acts committed with intent to destroy, in whole or in part, a national, ethnic, racial or religious group, as such:
> (a) Killing members of the group;
> (b) Causing serious bodily or mental harm to members of the group;
> (c) Deliberately inflicting on the group conditions of life calculated to bring about its physical destruction in whole or in part;
> (d) Imposing measures intended to prevent births within the group; or
> (e) Forcibly transferring children of the group to another group.[63]

Thus, genocide consists of two elements: intent to destroy a protected group in whole or in part, and the commission of a prohibited act. If either element is absent, the conduct does not amount to genocide.[64]

---

62 The Genocide Convention, above note 58, was adopted on 9 December 1948, one day earlier than the UDHR. The term "genocide" was invented by Raphael Lemkin, a Jewish refugee from Poland. See R. Lemkin, *Axis Rule in Occupied Europe* (Washington, D.C.: Carnegie Endowment for International Peace, 1944). On the crime of genocide generally, see W. Schabas, *Genocide in International Law: The Crime of Crimes* (Cambridge: Cambridge University Press, 2000).

63 This definition of genocide has almost certainly attained customary status. Among other things, it has been adopted as the definition of genocide in the Statute of the International Criminal Tribunal for the former Yugoslavia 1993 (ICTY Statute), UN doc. S/Res./827 (1993), as amended (art. 4); the Statute of the International Criminal Tribunal for Rwanda 1994 (ICTR Statute), UN doc. S/Res./955 (1994), as amended (art. 2); and the Rome Statute, above note 59 (art. 6). See generally Ratner, *Accountability*, above note 57 at 41–42.

64 Contrast the narrow definition of the Genocide Convention with the broad definition articulated in art. 7 of the Draft UN Declaration on the Rights of Indigenous Peoples 1993, above note 47:

> Indigenous peoples have the collective and individual right not to be subjected to ethnocide and cultural genocide, including prevention of and redress for: (a) Any action which has the aim or effect of depriving them of their integrity as distinct peoples, or of their cultural values or ethnic identities; (b) Any action which has the aim or effect of dispossessing them of their lands, territories or resources; (c) Any form of population transfer which has the aim or effect of vio-

Thus, the convention's definition of genocide does not cover killing with the intention of destroying a political group.[65] Nor does it cover the killing of a significant percentage of the members of a particular ethnic group in the absence of an intention to destroy that group because of its ethnicity ("as such").[66] It is, however, unclear what percentage of a target group must be destroyed in order to qualify as destruction "in part."[67]

Other articles in the Genocide Convention set out the various forms of participation that might constitute acts of genocide (article 3), the principle of individual responsibility (article 4), the obligation of states parties to criminalize the act of genocide (article 5), the core rules on jurisdiction and extradition (articles 6 and 7),[68] and referral to the International Court of Justice in cases of disputes (article 9).[69]

For several decades after its adoption, the Genocide Convention was neglected.[70] Even as genocides occurred, the UN and other international organizations remained focused on the Cold War and other con-

---

lating or undermining any of their rights; (d) Any form of assimilation or integration by other cultures or ways of life imposed on them by legislative, administrative or other measures; (e) Any form of propaganda directed against them.

65 But in *Prosecutor v. Jean-Paul Akayesu* (1998), Case no. ICTR-96-4-T, Judgment, ICTR Trial Chamber, at para. 516 [*Akayesu*], the ICTR suggested that the list of protected groups in the Genocide Convention is not exhaustive, and that its drafters intended to protect "any stable and permanent group."

66 Modern international criminal tribunals recognize that intention can be determined by inference, having regard to contextual facts such as the pattern of atrocities, the extent of planning, and the total number of victims. See, for example, *Akayesu*, above note 65 at paras. 485, 533–48.

67 But see *Prosecutor v. Krstic* (2001), Case no. IT-98-33, Judgment, ICTY Trial Chamber, at para. 634; *Prosecutor v. Jelisic* (1999), Case no. IT-95-10, Judgment, ICTY Trial Chamber, at para. 82; *Prosecutor v. Kayishema and Ruzindana* (1999), Case no. ICTR-95-I, Judgment and Sentence, ICTR Trial Chamber, at paras. 96–97. These cases examine the meaning of "in part."

68 Note that the Genocide Convention, like the International Convention on the Suppression and Punishment of the Crime of Apartheid 1973 (Apartheid Convention) 1015 UNTS 243 (art. 5), contemplated but did not establish an international criminal tribunal. Art. 6 of the Genocide Convention, above note 58, provides:

Persons charged with genocide . . . shall be tried by a competent tribunal of the State in the territory of which the act was committed, or by such international penal tribunal as may have jurisdiction with respect to those Contracting Parties which shall have accepted its jurisdiction.

69 The first such referral was made in *Case Concerning Application of the Convention on the Prevention and Punishment of the Crime of Genocide (Bosnia and Herzegovina v. Yugoslavia)* (Preliminary Objections), [1996] ICJ Rep 4.

70 The one prominent exception was the 1961 trial of Adolf Eichmann in Israel. See generally H. Arendt, *Eichmann in Jerusalem: A Report on the Banality of Evil* (New York: Penguin Books, 1963).

temporary crimes such as apartheid. However, with the end of the Cold War and the establishment of the ICTY, the ICTR, and the International Criminal Court — all of which exercise jurisdiction over the crime of genocide — the Genocide Convention has been reinvigorated and made internationally enforceable. Its reinvigoration is also attributable in part to the genocide trials that have been held in recent years in many European countries, as well as in Canada and other parts of the world.[71]

b) Crimes Against Humanity

The term "crime against humanity" was probably first used by the Allied Powers during the First World War to decry the Armenian genocide in 1915–18. As a legal term, it first appeared in the IMT Charter (article 6(c)).[72] Today the category of crimes against humanity is recognized in the Convention on the Non-Applicability of Statutory Limitations to War Crimes and Crimes Against Humanity 1968 (article 1(b)),[73] the ICTY Statute (article 5), the ICTR Statute (article 3),[74] the Rome Statute (article 7), regional instruments,[75] and domestic criminal laws.[76]

Historically the category of crimes against humanity required a nexus to armed conflict; there was no concept of crimes against humanity committed in peacetime. IMT Charter article 6(c), for example, defined crimes against humanity as follows:

> [M]urder, extermination, enslavement, deportation, and other inhumane acts committed against any civilian population, before or during the war, or persecutions on political, racial or religious grounds in execution of or in connection with any crime within the jurisdiction of the Tribunal [namely, war crimes and crimes against peace], whether or not in violation of the domestic law of the country where perpetrated.

---

71   Although most domestic genocide trials have concerned Second World War crimes, there is an increasing number of cases involving acts of genocide committed in Bosnia and Rwanda. See generally L. Reydams, *Universal Jurisdiction: International and Municipal Legal Perspectives (Oxford Monographs in International Law Series)* (New York: Oxford University Press, 2003) at cc. 4–17.

72   Charter of the International Military Tribunal 1945 (IMT Charter), 82 UNTS 280.

73   754 UNTS 73.

74   ICTY Statute, above note 63; ICTR Statute, above note 63. The ICTY and ICTR have, of course, refined the definition of crimes against humanity through their jurisprudence. Much of that jurisprudence is now reflected in the ICC Elements.

75   See, for example, the Council of Europe's Convention on the Non-Applicability of Statutory Limitations to War Crimes and Crimes Against Humanity 1974, ETS no. 82.

76   See the discussion in Chapter Eleven of the *Crimes Against Humanity and War Crimes Act*, SC 2000, c. 24.

But today, the nexus to armed conflict has mostly disappeared. As currently defined in the ICTR Statute and the Rome Statute, the definition of crimes against humanity has no nexus to armed conflict.[77] This is unlikely to change in the post-Rome Statute era.

Like genocide, a crime against humanity consists of more than the isolated commission of a proscribed act such as torture or killing. There must also exist a particular context. Specifically, under the definitions of crimes against humanity employed in the ICTY Statute, the ICTR Statute, and the Rome Statute, proscribed acts constitute crimes against humanity only if "committed as part of a widespread or systematic attack directed against any civilian population, with knowledge of the attack."[78] The individual perpetrator need only have a general level of knowledge about the attack.[79]

As for the proscribed acts themselves, article 7(1) of the Rome Statute lists the following:

- murder;
- extermination;[80]

---

77   See also art. 1(b) of the UN Convention on the Non-Applicability of Statutory Limitations to War Crimes and Crimes Against Humanity 1968, above note 73. The ICTY Statute, which preceded the ICTR Statute and the Rome Statute, included the nexus.

78   Rome Statute, above note 59, art. 7(2) provides:

> "Attack directed against any civilian population" means a course of conduct involving the multiple commission of [enumerated acts] against any civilian population, pursuant to or in furtherance of a State or organizational policy to commit such attack.

> Among other things, this definition — and in particular the phrase "State or organizational policy" — makes clear that crimes against humanity do not require an element of state action, as they did under the IMT Charter. Non-state actors such as rebel armies may also perpetrate crimes against humanity. This has been confirmed in *Prosecutor v. Tadic* (1997), Case no. IT-94-1, Judgment, ICTY Trial Chamber, at paras. 654–55, and *Prosecutor v. Kupreskic et al.* (2000), Case no. IT-95-16, Judgment, ICTY Trial Chamber, at paras. 551–52.

79   See the introduction to the crimes against humanity section in the ICC Elements. It provides in part that the knowledge requirement

> should not be interpreted as requiring proof that the perpetrator had knowledge of all characteristics of the attack or the precise details of the plan or policy of the State or organization. In the case of an emerging widespread or systematic attack against a civilian population, the intent clause of the last element indicates that this mental element is satisfied if the perpetrator intended to further such an attack.

80   Rome Statute, above note 59, art. 7(2)(b) provides that extermination "includes the intentional infliction of conditions of life, *inter alia* the deprivation of access

- enslavement;[81]
- deportation or forcible transfer of persons;[82]
- imprisonment "or other severe deprivation of physical liberty in violation of fundamental rules of international law";
- torture;[83]
- rape,
- sexual slavery, enforced prostitution, forced pregnancy,[84] enforced sterilization, or other comparably grave forms of sexual violence;
- persecution;[85]
- forced disappearance of persons;[86]
- apartheid; and
- "other inhumane acts of a similar character intentionally causing great suffering, or serious injury to body or to mental or physical health."

These acts are elaborated upon in the ICC Elements.

c) War Crimes

As its name suggests, war crimes may only be committed in times of war. In this respect, war crimes are narrower in scope than crimes

---

to food and medicine, calculated to bring about the destruction of part of a population."

81 *Ibid.*, art. 7(2)(c) provides that enslavement means "the exercise of any or all of the powers attaching to the right of ownership over a person and includes the exercise of such power in the course of trafficking in persons, in particular women and children." As noted below, slavery also constitutes an international crime in its own right, independent of the category of crimes against humanity.

82 *Ibid.*, art. 7(2)(d) provides that "deportation or forcible transfer of population" means the "forced displacement of the persons concerned by expulsion or other coercive acts from the area in which they are lawfully present, without grounds permitted under international law."

83 *Ibid.*, art. 7(2)(e) essentially adopts the CAT definition of torture. But it eliminates the state action requirement; the torture need not be carried out by or at the instigation of a public official or by a person acting in a public capacity. As noted below, torture also constitutes an international crime in its own right.

84 *Ibid.*, art. 7(2)(f) provides that forced pregnancy means "the unlawful confinement of a woman forcibly made pregnant, with the intent of affecting the ethnic composition of any population or carrying out other grave violations of international law."

85 *Ibid.*, art. 7(2)(g) provides that persecution means "the intentional and severe deprivation of fundamental rights contrary to international law by reason of the identity of the group or collectivity."

86 *Ibid.*, art. 2(i) essentially adopts the definition of forced disappearance used in the Inter-American Convention on the Forced Disappearance of Persons 1994. As noted below, forced disappearance may also constitute an international crime in its own right.

against humanity and genocide, which may be committed both in peacetime and wartime. War crimes are described in a wide range of sources, including international humanitarian law treaties (discussed above), the IMT Charter,[87] the Convention on the Non-Applicability of Statutory Limitations to War Crimes and Crimes Against Humanity 1968,[88] the ICTY Statute,[89] the ICTR Statute,[90] the Rome Statute,[91] regional instruments,[92] and domestic criminal laws.[93] To constitute a war crime, the act in question must have been committed "as part of a plan or policy or as part of a large-scale commission of such crimes" (Rome Statute article 8(1)).

As explained earlier, different international legal norms apply to international armed conflicts and wars of national liberation on the one hand, and internal armed conflicts on the other. Concerning international conflicts, the Rome Statute lists a total of twenty-six different violations, including eight "grave breaches of the Geneva Conventions of 12 August, 1949" (article 8(a)) and eighteen "other serious violations

---

87   IMT Charter, above note 72, art. 6(b) defines war crimes as

> violations of the laws or customs of war [including] murder, ill-treatment or deportation to slave labour or for any other purpose of civilian population of or in occupied territory, murder or ill-treatment of prisoners of war or persons on the seas, killing of hostages, plunder of public or private property, wanton destruction of cities, towns or villages, or devastation not justified by military necessity.

88   Article 1(a) of the treaty, above note 73, covers:

> War crimes as they are defined in the Charter of the International Military Tribunal, Nurnberg, of 8 August 1945 and confirmed by resolutions 3 (1) of 13 February 1946 and 95 (I) of 11 December 1946 of the General Assembly of the United Nations, particularly the 'grave breaches' enumerated in the Geneva Conventions of 12 August 1949 for the protection of war victims.

Note that this definition excludes the concept of war crimes committed in the course of an internal armed conflict.

89   The ICTY Statute, above note 63, sets out two provisions on war crimes: "grave breaches of the Geneva Conventions of 1949" (art. 2) and "violations of the laws or customs of war" (art. 3). Article 2 provides an exhaustive list of eligible crimes, but art. 3 does not.

90   Given that the events in Rwanda related to a an internal conflict, the ICTR Statute only applies to violations of Common Article 3 or the GC Protocol II. It does not include the category of grave breaches, which are limited to contexts of international conflict.

91   See the discussion immediately below.

92   See, for example, Convention on the Non-Applicability of Statutory Limitations to War Crimes and Crimes Against Humanity 1974, above note 75.

93   See, for example, the discussion in Chapter Eleven regarding the *Crimes Against Humanity and War Crimes Act*, SC 2000, c. 24.

of the laws and customs applicable in international armed conflict, within the established framework of international law" (article 8(b)). The latter include a variety of war crimes listed under the Hague Conventions and the GC Protocol I. They also include some more recent war crimes including attacks on UN peacekeepers (article 8(2)(b)(iii)) and the forcible recruitment of child soldiers (article 8(2)(b)(xxvi)).

The Rome Statute lists sixteen war crimes pertaining to internal armed conflicts. These include four "serious violations of Article 3 common to the four Geneva Conventions of 12 August 1949" (article 8(c))[94] and twelve "other serious violations of the laws and customs applicable in armed conflicts not of an international character" (article 8(e)).[95] While this list is short in comparison to that applicable in international conflicts, it nevertheless represents a significant advance and constitutes the only treaty-based criminalization of such conduct.[96]

3) Other International Crimes

There are additional international crimes that exist independently of genocide, crimes against humanity, and war crimes. Many of these are drawn from international human rights law. None is included as a stand-alone crime within the jurisdiction of any international criminal tribunal.

Slavery is one of the oldest international crimes and its prohibition is without question part of customary law. The key treaties on slavery are the Slavery Convention 1926,[97] as modified by the Protocol Amending the Slavery Convention 1953[98] (collectively Slavery Convention), and the Supplementary Convention on the Abolition of Slavery, the Slave Trade, and Institutions and Practices Similar to Slavery 1956 (Supple-

---

94   There are four war crimes listed under Rome Statute, above note 59, art. 8(c): violence to life and person, outrages upon personal dignity, taking of hostages, and the passing of sentences and carrying out of executions without previous judgment by a properly constituted tribunal. These crimes must have been committed "against persons taking no active part in the hostilities, including members of armed forces who have laid down their arms and those placed hors de combat by sickness, wounds, detention or any other cause."

95   Article 8(f), *ibid.*, stipulates that the war crimes enumerated under art. 8(e) must have been committed in "armed conflicts that take place in the territory of a State when there is protracted armed conflict between governmental authorities and organized armed groups or between such groups."

96   It may be recalled that neither Common Article 3 nor the GC Protocol II establishes individual criminal responsibility; they merely prohibit certain forms of conduct.

97   [1928] CanTS no. 5.

98   [1953] CanTS no. 26.

mentary Convention).[99] The Slavery Convention requires states parties to impose "severe penalties" for persons who enslave others or engage in the slave trade (article 6). The Supplementary Convention requires states parties to abolish institutions and practices similar to slavery (articles 1–2),[100] criminalize and punish persons engaging in the trading of slaves (article 3),[101] and criminalize and punish persons who enslave or induce enslavement (article 6).[102] Related to slavery are acts of forced labour. The principal treaties are the ILO's Forced Labour Convention (No. 29) 1930[103] and the Abolition of Forced Labour Convention (No. 105)

---

99 [1963] CanTS no. 7. The preamble to the Supplementary Convention states its purpose in relation to the Slavery Convention:

> Having decided, therefore, that the Convention of 1926, which remains operative, should now be augmented by the conclusion of a supplementary convention designed to intensify national as well as international efforts towards the abolition of slavery, the slave trade and institutions and practices similar to slavery. . . .

100 Article 1 of the Supplementary Convention, *ibid.*, defines such institutions and practices to include debt bondage, serfdom, and

> (c) Any institution or practice whereby:
> (i) A woman, without the right to refuse, is promised or given in marriage on payment of a consideration in money or in kind to her parents, guardian, family or any other person or group; or
> (ii) The husband of a woman, his family, or his clan, has the right to transfer her to another person for value received or otherwise; or
> (iii)A woman on the death of her husband is liable to be inherited by another person;
>
> (d) Any institution or practice whereby a child or young person under the age of 18 years, is delivered by either or both of his natural parents or by his guardian to another person, whether for reward or not, with a view to the exploitation of the child or young person or of his labour.

101 Article 7(c) of the Supplementary Convention, *ibid.*, provides that the slave trade

> means and includes all acts involved in the capture, acquisition or disposal of a person with intent to reduce him to slavery; all acts involved in the acquisition of a slave with a view to selling or exchanging him; all acts of disposal by sale or exchange of a person acquired with a view to being sold or exchanged; and, in general, every act of trade or transport in slaves by whatever means of conveyance.

102 Article 7(a) of the Supplementary Convention, *ibid.*, defines slavery as "the status or condition of a person over whom any or all of the powers attaching to the right of ownership are exercised." A slave is a person in that status or condition.

103 Above note 4. Forced labour is defined in art. 2 of the 1930 Convention as "all work or service which is exacted from any person under the menace of any penalty and for which the said person has not offered himself voluntarily." It excludes military service, prison labour, and forced labour carried out as part of

1957.[104] Although neither convention criminalizes acts of forced labour, certain instances of forced labour may constitute international crimes.[105]

Apartheid was established as an international crime by article 3 of the International Convention on the Suppression and Punishment of the Crime of Apartheid 1973.[106] Although the definition of apartheid is broad enough to cover many forms of official racist conduct,[107] states

---

a "normal civic obligation" or "in cases of emergency ... and in general any circumstance that would endanger the existence or the well-being of the whole or part of the population" (art. 2). Similar exclusions are found in ICCPR, above note 18, art. 8(3)(b)–(c) and ACHR, above note 18, art. 6(2)–(3).

104 Above note 8. The 1957 Convention only addresses forced labour that is carried out

(a) as a means of political coercion or education or as a punishment for holding or expressing political views or views ideologically opposed to the established political, social or economic system;

(b) As a method of mobilising and using labour for purposes of economic development;

(c) As a means of labour discipline;

(d) As a punishment for having participated in strikes; [or]

(e) As a means of racial, social, national or religious discrimination.

See also, for example, ICCPR, *ibid.*, art. 8(3)(a) and ACHR, *ibid.*, art. 6(2).

105 See the Convention for the Suppression of the Traffic in Persons and of the Exploitation of the Prostitution of Others 1950, 96 UNTS 271. It establishes individual criminal responsibility for anyone who entices persons into prostitution or who exploits prostitutes (arts. 1–2). See also the Optional Protocol to the Convention on the Rights of the Child on the Sale of Children, Child Prostitution, and Child Pornography 2000 (CRC-OP-SC), GA res. 54/263, especially arts. 3 (states parties must ensure that the sale of children, child prostitution and child pornography are covered under their criminal laws) and 4 (states parties must establish jurisdiction over the offences whenever they are commited in their territory, and may establish jurisdiction on the basis of the nationality principle or the passive personality principle). See also the Convention on the Elimination of All Forms of Discrimination Against Women 1979 (CEDAW), [1982] CanTS no. 31, art. 6, which requires states parties to suppress trafficking in women; and the Inter-American Convention on International Traffic in Minors 1994, OAS TS no. 79, arts. 7–11, which set out the penal aspects of the treaty.

106 Above note 68. Canada is not a party to the treaty. Note that art. 1 of the treaty refers to apartheid as a crime against humanity. So do art. 1(b) of the UN Convention on the Non-Applicability of Statutory Limitations to War Crimes and Crimes Against Humanity 1968, above note 72, and arts. 7(1)(j) and 7(2)(h) of the Rome Statute, above note 59.

107 Article 2 provides that the crime of apartheid

shall include similar policies and practices of racial segregation and discrimination as practised in southern Africa [provided that they are] committed for the purpose of establishing and maintaining domination by one racial group of persons over any other racial group of persons and systematically oppressing them.

and non-state actors have generally treated it as applying only to the former regime in South Africa.[108]

Torture is criminalized both in the CAT and the Inter-American Convention to Prevent and Punish Torture 1985.[109] See the discussions of each treaty in Chapters Five and Six, respectively.

While some consider *forced disappearance* to be an international crime, it is probably only a crime under Inter-American law at present. The crime is defined most comprehensively in the unique Inter-American Convention on the Forced Disappearance of Persons 1994.[110] Article 2 provides

> forced disappearance is considered to be the act of depriving a person or persons of his or their freedom, in whatever way, perpetrated by agents of the state or by persons or groups of persons acting with the authorization, support, or acquiescence of the state, followed by an absence of information or a refusal to acknowledge that deprivation of freedom or to give information on the whereabouts of that person, thereby impeding his or her recourse to the applicable legal remedies and procedural guarantees.

This definition was adopted in the Rome Statute which, as already noted, includes forced disappearance as one of the acts that may give rise to a crime against humanity (article 7(1)(i) and 7(2)(i)).

As to the crime of *aggression* (also known as "**crimes against peace**"), the Rome Statute authorizes the International Criminal Court to exercise jurisdiction over the crime, but only after its definition is formally negotiated and adopted by the Court's Assembly of States Parties. This has not yet happened. As things stand, the IMT Charter definition of crimes against peace is the only internationally recognized instance of its invocation.[111]

---

108 Ratner, *Accountability,* above note 57 at 122–23.

109 Inter-American Convention to Prevent and Punish Torture 1985, OAS TS no. 67.

110 (1994) 33 ILM 1429. The Convention was influenced by the prior UN General Assembly Declaration on the Protection of All Persons from Enforced Disappearances 1992.

111 The IMT Charter, above note 72, somewhat controversially treated the category of crimes against peace (essentially a category of *jus ad bellum*) as a crime for which there could be individual, as opposed to state, responsibility under international law. It was considered the worst crime and the foundation or prerequisite for all other international crimes committed during the Second World War.

Finally, there are many other offences against international law that are partially connected to human rights law. Examples include transnational organized crime,[112] terrorism,[113] crimes committed against internationally protected persons,[114] and piracy.[115]

---

112 See, for example, Convention against Transnational Organized Crime 2000, GA res. 55/25, annex I; Protocol Against the Smuggling of Migrants by Land, Sea and Air, Supplementing the UN Convention against Transnational Organized Crime 2000, GA res. 55/25, annex III; and Protocol to Prevent, Suppress and Punish Trafficking in Persons, Especially Women and Children, Supplementing the United Nations Convention Against Transnational Organized Crime 2000, GA res. 55/25, annex II. Canada ratified all of these conventions in 2002, but they have not yet been added to the CanTS.

113 See, for example, International Convention for the Suppression of Terrorist Bombings 1997 [2002] CanTS no. 8; International Convention for the Suppression of the Financing of Terrorism 1999 [2002] CanTS no. 9.

114 See, for example, Convention on the Prevention and Punishment of Crimes Against Internationally Protected Persons, Including Diplomatic Agents 1973 [1977] CanTS no. 43.

115 See, for example, Convention on the High Seas 1958, 450 UNTS 11. Canada is not a state party.

PART TWO

THE CANADIAN RECEPTION OF INTERNATIONAL HUMAN RIGHTS LAW

CHAPTER 8

GENERAL PRINCIPLES OF CANADIAN RECEPTION LAW

The very essence of an international human rights obligation is that the state to which it applies undertakes to give effect to it in its domestic law. At this point in our legal history, human beings continue to be governed chiefly — indeed, almost exclusively — by the internal laws of states. Therefore, international laws for the benefit of human beings must be received into domestic law if they are to be more than empty promises.

How exactly this reception of international human rights law occurs is, from an international law perspective, a matter of some indifference. The important thing is that states meet their international obligations. What steps they take to do so are generally up to them. Thus some states give direct effect to international human rights law in their domestic laws, while others require implementation of such obligations, usually by legislation, before their nationals can rely on them. Neither of these reception schemes is, as a matter of international law, inferior or superior to the other. What matters is the scheme's effectiveness in securing the human rights guarantees to which the state is bound.

The Canadian reception system is notable for the lack of explicit provisions on the status of international human rights law (or, for that matter, international law in general) in the written constitution. In this Canada may seem to compare unfavourably to such states as the Czech Republic, Colombia, Japan, South Africa, Spain, and many others whose constitutions make explicit reference to international human rights obligations. This unfavourable impression is exacerbated, perhaps, when one recalls that it is an unwritten rule of Canadian law that treaties that purport to affect the rights of citizens require legislative implementation before the courts will give them domestic effect. In spite of these seeming obstacles, Canada's reception system is arguably among the most effective in the world at securing the human rights of its citizens. How this can be so will become clear in the course of this and the following chapters.

In the absence of constitutional or statutory provisions governing the reception of international law in Canada, the question becomes one of common law. Therefore we must occasionally turn to English law to understand the Canadian position. The same is true in many other Commonwealth countries, notably Australia, New Zealand, and certain African and Caribbean states. But even without explicit constitutional provisions governing the reception of international law, Canada's constitution has shaped Canadian reception law from a distance. The law of federalism has significant consequences for the implementation of treaties generally, and human rights treaties in particular. And the entrenchment of certain human rights guarantees in the *Charter* is the principal (but certainly not the only) means by which Canada discharges its international human rights obligations.

A. THE FOUR PILLARS OF CANADIAN RECEPTION LAW

The Canadian reception system, like its counterparts in the UK and other Commonwealth jurisdictions, consists of four pillars: the judicial notice of international law by domestic courts, the interpretive presumption that domestic law conforms with the state's international obligations, the incorporation of customary international law by the common law, and the necessity of implementing treaties by primary or secondary legislation.

1) Judicial Notice of International Law

In the law of evidence, judicial notice is the power of courts to accept the truth of certain propositions without proof. Usually this power is considered in relation to the proof of facts,[1] but there is also a doctrine

---

1   See D. Paciocco & L. Stuesser, *The Law of Evidence*, 3d ed. (Toronto: Irwin Law, 2002) at 386.

of judicial notice of law.[2] This doctrine not only permits but requires courts to take judicial notice of forms of law to which they must give effect, including statutes, secondary legislation, the common law, and international law. By contrast, Canadian courts do not take judicial notice of foreign law, i.e., the domestic law of foreign states. Foreign law must be proved.[3] The common law's different treatment of foreign and international law was succinctly explained by Lauterpacht: international law need not be proved in common law courts simply because "it is not foreign law."[4] This distinction between foreign law and international law is not peculiar to Canada and other common law countries. "There is not a legal system in the world where international law is treated as 'foreign law.' It is everywhere part of the law of the land; as much as contracts, labour law or administrative law."[5]

While it is clear as a matter of practice that Canadian courts consider themselves free, if not obliged, to consider relevant international treaties, customs, and principles in the course of their decision-making, there is nevertheless a paucity of direct authority for doing so. The leading Canadian case is The Ship "North" v. The King, in which the Supreme Court of Canada expressly approved a lower court's application of the international law of hot pursuit, saying "The right of hot pursuit . . . being part of the law of nations was properly judicially taken notice of and acted upon by the learned judge."[6] Though recent cases rarely make the point so clearly,[7] commentators agree that Canadian courts must

2   Judicial notice of law is originally a common law doctrine but has been declared in certain statutes, for example Canada Evidence Act RSC 1985 c. C-5 s. 18. These declaratory provisions do not mention international law; however, judicial notice of international law remains a common law rule.

3   See J. Castel & J. Walker, Canadian Conflict of Laws, 5th ed., looseleaf (Markham, Ontario: Butterworths, 2002) at s. 7.1.

4   H. Lauterpacht, "Is International Law Part of the Law of England?" [1939] Transactions of the Grotius Society 51 at 59.

5   R. Higgins, "The Relationship Between International and Regional Human Rights Norms and Domestic Law" in Developing Human Rights Jurisprudence, vol. 5 (London: Commonwealth Secretariat, 1993) at 16 [Higgins, "Domestic Law"]. Of course, international laws that do not bind the state (for example, treaties to which the state is not a party) are not "the law of the land." Non-binding international laws are not the same as foreign law, but they are analogous to it.

6   (1906) 37 SCR 385 at 394.

7   But see: Post Office v. Estuary Radio Ltd., [1968] 2 QB 740 (CA) at 756–57 [Post Office]; Jose Pereira E. Hijos, S.A. v. Canada (Attorney General), [1997] 2 FC 84 (TD) [Jose Pereira E. Hijos, S.A.]; Re Secession of Quebec, [1998] 2 SCR 217 at para. 109 [Re Secession of Quebec]; Quebec (Minister of Justice) v. Canada (Minister of Justice) (2003), 228 DLR (4th) 63 (Que CA) at paras. 106–16 [Quebec (Minister of Justice)].

take judicial notice of international law.[8] More importantly, judicial practice reveals that Canadian courts regularly do so.

Questions of international human rights law in Canada sometimes arise before administrative decision-makers or tribunals instead of courts. Whether such bodies must also take judicial notice of international law is an unsettled question. The answer probably depends on the decision-maker's enabling legislation. As is so often the case in administrative law, the ultimate question is what the legislature intended. If the legislature empowered the decision-maker to decide questions of law, this power can and usually should be read as including questions of international law.[9] Even if the decision-maker's powers are more limited, however, he or she may be required to consider international law. In *Baker v. Canada (Minister of Citizenship and Immigration)*, the Supreme Court of Canada reversed an immigration officer's decision on a reasonableness standard of review on the ground that his decision was "inconsistent with the values underlying the grant of the discretion."[10] Among these values were the rights of children at international law. The extent to which administrative decision-makers may or must give effect to international law is an evolving area of Canadian law. Future developments are difficult to foresee. What is clear, however, is that legislatures rarely if ever intend to empower their delegates to violate international law. In principle, then, administrative decisions

---

8   The lengthiest treatment is G. van Ert, *Using International Law in Canadian Courts* (The Hague: Kluwer Law International, 2002) at 30–40 [van Ert, *Using International Law*]. See also: R. St. J. Macdonald, "The Relationship between Domestic Law and International Law in Canada" in R. St. J. Macdonald *et al.*, eds., *Canadian Perspectives on International Law and Organization* (Toronto: University of Toronto Press, 1974): 88 at 111–14; A. Bayefsky, *International Human Rights Law: Use in Canadian Charter of Rights and Freedoms Litigation* (Toronto: Butterworths, 1992) at 138–39; G.P. Heckman, "International Human Rights Law Norms and Discretionary Powers: Recent Developments" (2003) 16 Canadian Journal of Administrative Law and Practice 31 at 33n7. In English law, see *Halsbury's Laws of England*, 4th ed. vol. 17 (London: Butterworths, 1976) at para. 100 and M. Shaw, *International Law*, 3d ed. (Cambridge: Cambridge University Press, 1991) at 111.

9   See for instance *National Corn Growers Association v. Canada (Import Tribunal)*, [1990] 2 SCR 1324 [*National Corn Growers*] in which the court approved the tribunal's resort to international trade law to interpret a federal statute. Recent commentators have observed, ". . . if Parliament is presumed to intend conformity with Canada's international obligations, it makes little sense to assume that it granted administrative decision-makers discretion to ignore these obligations": J. Brunnée & S. Toope, "A Hesitant Embrace: The Application of International Law by Canadian Courts" [2002] Canadian Yearbook of International Law 3 at 38n155 [Brunnée & Toope, "A Hesitant Embrace"].

10   [1999] 2 SCR 817 at para. 65 [*Baker*].

that do so should be reversible on a correctness standard, a reasonableness standard (as in *Baker*), and even a patently unreasonable standard.[11] To avoid error, administrative decision-makers — especially
those considering human rights questions — should inform themselves of applicable international norms.

2) The Presumption of Conformity with International Law

It is an ancient and firmly established rule of legal construction that
common law courts will endeavour to interpret domestic law so as to
conform with the requirements of international law and the comity of
nations.[12] The classic statement of this rule is from Maxwell's *On the
Interpretation of Statutes*: "[E]very statute is to be so interpreted and
applied, as far as its language admits, as not to be inconsistent with the
comity of nations, or with the established rules of international law."[13]
In the words of a Canadian commentator,

> It is not lightly to be assumed that the legislature intends to put the
> state in default internationally or to enact a statute in contravention
> of international law. Therefore, if at all possible, and unless the con-
> trary clearly appears, a statute must be interpreted so as to conform
> with international law.[14]

This interpretive rule has been frequently affirmed and applied in Canadian courts. In the *Arrow River* case, Riddell J.A. observed that "the Sovereign will not be considered as enacting anything that will conflict
with his plain duty, unless the language employed in the statute is perfectly clear and explicit, admitting of no other interpretation."[15] In
Daniels v. White and the Queen, Pigeon J. applied "the rule of construction that Parliament is not presumed to legislate in breach of a treaty or

---

11 A contrary view was taken by Wilson J. (concurring) in *National Corn Growers*,
above note 9 at 1349. See the discussion in van Ert, *Using International Law*,
above note 8 at 115–16, 134–35.

12 For a discussion of the history and application of the presumption in Anglo-Canadian law, see van Ert, *ibid.* at 99–136. See also R. Sullivan, *Sullivan and Driedger on
the Construction of Statutes*, 4th ed. (Markham: Butterworths, 2002) at 421–39 [*Sullivan and Driedger*, 4th ed.].

13 Sir Peter Benson Maxwell, *On the Interpretation of Statutes*, 1st ed. (London:
Sweet & Maxwell, 1875) at 122.

14 D.C. Vanek, "Is International Law Part of the Law of Canada?" (1960) 8 UTLJ
251 at 259.

15 *Arrow River & Tributaries Slide & Boom Co. Ltd. v. Pigeon Timber Co. Ltd.* (1930–1),
66 OLR 577 (Supreme Court of Ontario Appellate Division) at 579 [*Arrow River*].

in any manner inconsistent with the comity of nations and the established rules of international law."[16] In *R. v. Zingre*, Dickson J. (as he then was) interpreted a provision of the *Canada Evidence Act* in the light of a century-old treaty "because the contrary view would result in the purpose of the 1880 Treaty being completed frustrated." He went on to describe it as "the duty of the Court, in interpreting the 1880 Treaty and section 43 of the *Canada Evidence Act* to give them a fair and liberal interpretation with a view to fulfilling Canada's international obligations."[17] In *Ordon Estate v. Grail*, Iacobucci and Major JJ. observed,

> Although international law is not binding upon Parliament or the provincial legislatures, a court must presume that legislation is intended to comply with Canada's obligations under international instruments and as a member of the international community. In choosing among possible interpretations of a statute, the court should avoid interpretations that would put Canada in breach of such obligations.[18]

In *Baker v. Canada (Minister of Citizenship and Immigration)*, L'Heureux-Dubé J. for the majority of the Supreme Court of Canada observed that while treaties require domestic implementation before taking direct effect in Canadian law, "the values reflected in international human rights law may help inform the contextual approach to statutory interpretation and judicial review."[19] L'Heureux-Dubé J. went on to approve the following description of the presumption:

> [T]he legislature is presumed to respect the values and principles enshrined in international law, both customary and conventional.

---

16 [1968] SCR 517 at 541 [*Daniels*]. Pigeon J. went on to say, "It is a rule that is not often applied, because if a statute is unambiguous, its provisions must be followed even if they are contrary to international law. . . ." This part of Pigeon J.'s dictum was emphasized by LeBel J. for the Court in *Schreiber v. Canada (Attorney General)*, 2002 SCC 62 at para. 50 [*Schreiber*]. With respect, the dictum is mistaken and should not be given such weight. Contrary to Pigeon J.'s conclusion, the presumption is very frequently applied by Canadian courts and other courts in the common law tradition. Although as a matter of domestic law Canadian legislatures are sovereign to violate international law, they very rarely intend to do so and are almost always presumed by our courts not to do so.

17 [1981] 2 SCR 392 at 407, 409–10 [*Zingre*].

18 [1998] 3 SCR 437 at para. 137 [*Grail*]. On the meaning of the first phrase in this quotation, see the discussion later in this chapter.

19 *Baker*, above note 10 at para. 70. See also *R. v. Sharpe*, [2001] 1 SCR 45 at para. 175 per L'Heureux-Dubé, Bastarache, and Gonthier JJ. and *114957 Canada Ltée (Spraytech, Société d'arrosage) v. Hudson (Town)*, [2001] 2 SCR 241 at para. 30 [*Spraytech v. Hudson*] per L'Heureux-Dubé, Gonthier, Bastarache, and Arbour JJ., in which *Baker* is depicted in terms of the presumption of conformity.

These constitute a part of the legal context in which legislation is enacted and read. In so far as possible, therefore, interpretations that reflect these values and principles are preferred.[20]

In *Canadian Foundation for Children, Youth and the Law v. Canada (Attorney General)*, McLachlin C.J. for the majority found that *Criminal Code* section 43 (which provides a defence to parents and schoolteachers who use reasonable force against children by way of correction) was not unconstitutionally vague for the purpose of *Charter* section 7, in part because its content could be adduced by interpreting it in conformity with the CRC and the ICCPR.[21] The chief justice affirmed the presumption, looked to the relevant treaty provisions, and concluded: "From these international obligations, it follows that what is 'reasonable under the circumstances' will seek to avoid harm to the child and will never include cruel, inhuman or degrading treatment."[22] These cases are only a few among the many Canadian and Commonwealth authorities in support of the presumption as a tool of legal interpretation.

The presumption applies to most if not all forms of Canadian law. It is most often applied to primary legislation, that is, statutes enacted by the federal and provincial legislatures. The presumption also applies to delegated legislation[23] and prerogative acts.[24] Whether the presumption applies to the common law is somewhat contentious. It has been said that courts will not readily reshape the common law in the image of the state's treaty obligations.[25] For courts to do so may risk obviating the need for implementing legislation, contrary to the implementation requirement (discussed below). Nevertheless, recent cases have declared that courts will strive to develop the common law consistently with the state's treaty obligations.[26] As for the state's customary obli-

---

20 R. Sullivan, *Driedger on the Construction of Statutes*, 3d ed. (Toronto: Butterworths, 1994) at 330 (L'Heureux-Dubé J.'s emphasis removed).

21 2004 SCC 4 [*Canadian Foundation*].

22 *Ibid.* at paras. 31–32.

23 See for instance *Schavernoch v. Foreign Claims Commission*, [1982] 1 SCR 1092 and *R. v. Secretary of State for the Home Department, ex p. Brind*, [1991] 1 AC 696.

24 *Post Office*, above note 7 at 757.

25 *Malone v. Metropolitan Police Commissioner*, [1979] Ch 344 (Eng.) at 379.

26 In *Attorney-General v. Guardian Newspapers (No. 2)*, [1990] 1 AC 109 at 283–84 [*Guardian*], Lord Goff stated, "I conceive it to be my duty, when I am free to do so, to interpret the law in accordance with the obligations of the Crown under this treaty." The "law" in question here was common law. See also *R. v. Lyons and others*, [2002] 3 WLR 1562 at para. 27 per Lord Hoffmann, and *Jose Pereira E. Hijos S.A.*, above note 7 at para. 20. Commentators have approved this approach: see M. Hunt, *Using Human Rights Law in English Courts* (Oxford: Hart Publishing, 1998) at 150 [Hunt, *Using Human Rights Law*] and Brunnée & Toope, "A Hesitant Embrace," above note 9 at 26.

gations, courts have long incorporated these directly into the common law (as described below). The doctrine of incorporation is, in a sense, simply an application of the presumption of conformity to the common law.

There have been suggestions in the past that the presumption is subject to certain rather artificial restrictions. Much English and some Canadian case law has held that courts may not consult a treaty in the course of statutory interpretation unless the statute is somehow ambiguous on its face. This rule is inconsistent with earlier formulations of the presumption (such as Maxwell's, quoted above) and was rightly rejected by the Supreme Court of Canada in *National Corn Growers v. Canada (Import Tribunal)*.[27] The reasons of Gonthier J. on this point merit quotation:

> . . . it is reasonable to make reference to an international agreement at the very outset of the inquiry to determine if there is any ambiguity, even latent, in the domestic legislation. The Court of Appeal's suggestion that recourse to an international treaty is only available where the provision of the domestic legislation is ambiguous on its face is to be rejected. . . . In *Schavernoch v. Foreign Claims Commission*, [1982] 1 S.C.R. 1092, this Court had occasion to comment upon the circumstances in which it is proper for the courts to consult an underlying international agreement. Though the language used by Estey J. is perhaps not explicit, I do not understand his remarks to mean that consultation of the treaty is proper only where it appears that the text to be interpreted is ambiguous on its face. At page 1098 of his decision, he writes:
>
> > If one could assert an ambiguity, either patent *or latent*, in the Regulations it might be that a court could find support for making reference to matters external to the Regulations in order to interpret its terms. . . . [Emphasis added]
>
> The suggestion that recourse can be had to an underlying international agreement where a latent ambiguity can be asserted implies that there is no need to find a patent ambiguity before consultation of the agreement is possible. As a latent ambiguity must arise out of matters external to the text to be interpreted, such an international agreement may be used, as I have just suggested, at the preliminary stage of determining if an ambiguity exists.[28]

---

27   *National Corn Growers*, above note 9.
28   *Ibid.* at 1371–73.

In short, Canadian courts need not find an ambiguity on the face of the statute before having recourse to a relevant treaty obligation. They may look at the treaty directly. If their comparison of the treaty and the statute reveals a latent ambiguity in the latter, the court will construe the legislation in conformity with international law unless it can be shown that the legislature intended otherwise.[29]

Two recent decisions of the Supreme Court of Canada may seem to conflict with *National Corn Growers* on this point. In *CanadianOxy Chemicals Ltd. v. Canada (Attorney General)*, Major J. said, "It is only when genuine ambiguity arises between two or more plausible readings, each equally in accordance with the intentions of the statute, that the courts need to resort to external interpretive aids."[30] This dictum was affirmed and enlarged upon in *Bell ExpressVu Limited Partnership v. Rex*,[31] in which Iacobucci J. quoted Major J.[32] and added that, similarly, "[o]ther principles of interpretation, such as the strict construction of penal statutes and the '*Charter* values' presumption, only receive application where there is ambiguity as to the meaning of a provision."[33] If Canadian treaty obligations are properly described as "external interpretive aids," Major J.'s dictum may conflict with *National Corn Growers*. Likewise, if the presumption of conformity is among the principles of interpretation Iacobucci J. excludes from consideration without a finding of ambiguity, this too may conflict with *National Corn Growers*.

In our view, these cases may be reconciled. The literal conflict between *CanadianOxy* and *National Corn Growers* is admittedly stark. We suggest, however, that a Canadian treaty obligation (whether implemented or not) is not an "external interpretive aid" but rather forms part of the legal context in which the legislation was enacted.[34] As Iacobucci

---

29 Prominent English commentators have sought to liberate English law from the patent ambiguity requirement in much the same way as Gonthier J. accomplished in *National Corn Growers*. See generally Hunt, *Using Human Rights Law*, above note 26, and Higgins, "Domestic Law," above note 5 at 20.

30 [1999] 1 SCR 743 at para. 14 [*CanadianOxy*].

31 2002 SCC 42 [*Bell ExpressVu*].

32 *Ibid.* at para. 29.

33 *Ibid.* at paras. 28.

34 Sullivan observes that international law constitutes "a part of the legal context in which legislation is enacted and read": *Sullivan and Driedger*, 4th ed., above note 12 at 422. In *Rahaman v. Canada (Minister of Citizenship and Immigration)*, [2002] 3 FC 537 at para. 35, Evans J.A. observed, "Nowadays, there is no doubt that, even when not incorporated by an Act of Parliament into Canadian law, international norms are part of the context within which domestic statutes are to be interpreted. . . ." Further support for this proposition may be found in *Re Secession of Quebec*, above note 7 at para. 27, in which the Court rejected the

J. emphasized in *Bell ExpressVu*, the modern approach to statutory interpretation insists that an Act be read in its entire context.[35] In any case there were no international instruments before the court in *CanadianOxy* and it is doubtful that Major J. had them in mind. Iacobucci J.'s dictum in *Bell ExpressVu* is perhaps easier to reconcile with *National Corn Growers*, for both cases insist upon a finding of ambiguity before applying a principle of interpretation. What the latter case established is that this ambiguity may either be patent (clear on the face of the statute), or latent (discoverable upon consultation of the relevant treaty). Iacobucci J.'s reasons in *Bell ExpressVu* did not reject Gonthier J.'s patent/latent distinction. Indeed, Iacobucci J. did not consider *National Corn Growers* at all, and the case before him had no international law element.

There have occasionally been suggestions that the presumption only applies to implementing legislation, i.e., legislation to give domestic legal effect to a treaty. Such a rule ignores one of the main purposes of the presumption, namely to prevent courts from violating Canadian treaty obligations by misconstruing statutes that were not intended to break international law. This risk is just as real (if not more real) for ordinary legislation as it is for implementing legislation. Therefore the presumption should apply to all legislation. And it does.[36]

The presumption of conformity applies in respect of any rule of international law binding on Canada. Ordinarily such rules derive from treaties to which Canada is a party. But binding international laws may also derive from customary international law, and the presumption applies equally in such instances.[37]

---

submission that international law elements of the reference were non-justiciable, saying, "The questions posed by the Governor in Council, as we interpret them, are strictly limited to aspects of the legal framework in which that democratic decision [i.e. whether to secede from Canada] is to be taken." Similarly a Canadian treaty obligation, the subject-matter of which overlaps with a statute, may be seen as part of the statute's legal framework.

35   *Bell ExpressVu*, above note 31 at paras. 26–27.

36   Examples are plentiful. In *Spraytech v. Hudson*, above note 19 at paras. 31–32, the majority construed Quebec's *Cities and Towns Act* RSQ c. C-19 in the light of the precautionary principle, without suggesting that the legislation intended to implement that principle. In *Canadian Foundation*, above note 21, the majority applied the presumption to *Criminal Code* RSC 1985 c. C-46 s. 43 — a provision that predated both treaties with which it was presumed to comply.

37   For example, *Re Powers of Ottawa (City) and Rockcliff Park (Village) to Levy Rates on Foreign Legations and High Commissioners' Residences*, [1943] SCR 208 [*Re Foreign Legations*] (statute presumed consistent with customary international law of sovereign immunity); *Spraytech v. Hudson*, *ibid.* (statute presumed consistent with customary "precautionary principle").

There are two other cases where the presumption should apply. Where a treaty has been ratified by Canada but has not yet come into force,[38] it is not yet, strictly speaking, binding on Canada. Yet the presumption should apply. VCLT article 18(b) requires Canada and other states parties to refrain from acts which would defeat the object and purpose of a treaty pending its entry into force. A Canadian judgment that is inconsistent with a treaty ratified by Canada but not yet in force may place Canada in default of that treaty when it comes into force. Such a judgment may also place Canada in violation of VCLT article 18(b), depending on the nature and seriousness of the inconsistency. Courts may avoid these results by applying the presumption of conformity. Similarly, in the case of treaties requiring both signature and ratification, a treaty signed but not yet ratified by Canada is not yet binding on it. Here, too, VCLT article 18(a) requires states to refrain from acts that would defeat the object and purpose of a treaty until they have made clear their intention not to become parties. While not every domestic judgment inconsistent with a treaty Canada has signed will necessarily defeat that treaty's object and purpose, there may be instances where a judgment delays or complicates Canada's ratification of the treaty — for instance, by requiring additional legislative action by Parliament or the provinces to undo the effect of the court's decision. The risk of this is especially great in respect of human rights treaties, whose object and purpose is, generally speaking, to bring the domestic laws of states parties to an agreed-upon international standard. It may therefore be appropriate, in proper cases, to apply the presumption of conformity in respect of signed but as-yet-unratified treaties.[39]

As we have noted, the orthodox understanding of the presumption of conformity is that it applies only in respect of binding international norms.[40] It is arguable, however, that the presumption may or should also apply to certain non-binding international instruments. In *United*

---

38   See the discussion of signature, ratification, and entry into force in Chapter Three.

39   Parliament itself has recognized that the presumption of conformity is properly applicable, at least in respect of human rights treaties, from the moment Canada signs. The *Immigration and Refugee Protection Act* SC 2001 c. 27 s. 3(3)(f) provides that it is to be construed and applied in a manner that complies with "international human rights instruments to which Canada is signatory" — not a party.

40   There is something of an exception, however, for international comity. Common law courts have often affirmed that they will demonstrate, where possible, deference and respect for other states even the absence of a legal obligation to do so, for example *Zingre*, above note 17 at 401. This includes applying a presumption that legislation is intended to preserve the comity of nations: *Daniels*, above note 16 at 541.

States of America v. Burns,[41] the Supreme Court of Canada took note of anti-death-penalty resolutions of the UN Commission on Human Rights, and Canada's support for them, in finding that extraditing fugitives to the US without assurances that the death penalty would not be imposed on them was unconstitutional in all but exceptional cases.[42] While the court did not explicitly apply the presumption of conformity, its approach is similar. Yet there are good reasons not to apply the presumption of conformity to non-binding international instruments. Canadian foreign relations may be prejudiced by such an approach. If Canadian diplomats and politicians need worry about the domestic legal effects of actions which, as a matter of international law, are non-binding, they may hesitate to take positions they might otherwise adopt. Furthermore, it would be difficult to determine which non-binding international acts and statements should attract the presumption and which should not. While the distinction between binding and non-binding international instruments is quite clear, there is no obvious or accepted hierarchy among non-binding instruments.

The presumption of conformity is rebuttable. Nothing in Canadian constitutional law prevents Parliament or the provincial Legislatures from enacting legislation that violates international law.[43] If a litigant can show that a given provision was indeed intended to breach a Canadian treaty obligation, contravene Canada's obligations under customary international law, or defy international comity, the presumption is rebutted and the court will construe the legislation according to its terms. It will then be for the Canadian government to live with the international legal consequences. The difficulty for litigants seeking to rebut the presumption is clear: Canadian legislatures very rarely embark upon such an unlawful or confrontational course.[44]

While the presumption of conformity with international law is a powerful interpretive tool, its bounds must be kept in mind. The presumption does not apply unless a real or potential conflict between domestic and international law can be shown. Thus in *Quebec (Commission des droits de la personne et des droits de la jeunesse) v. Maksteel*

---

41   [2001] 1 SCR 283 [*Burns*].
42   *Ibid.* at para. 84.
43   See the discussion of legislatures under the heading "Reception and the Separation of Powers," below.
44   Brunnée & Toope have described the presumption as placing an "onus . . . on Canadian courts" to interpret Canadian law consistently with international law: Brunnée & Toope, "A Hesitant Embrace," above note 9 at 51. In our view, the onus is not on the court but on the party attempting to rebut the presumption.

Québec Inc., Deschamps J. for the majority rejected the appellant's reliance on the ICESCR and other international materials "because there is no actual or potential conflict between the interpretation of section 18.2 that has been adopted and the instruments cited by the appellant."[45] Similarly in *Bouzari v. Iran*, the plaintiff's attempt to rely on the presumption failed because, in the words of Swinton J., "the legislation . . . is consistent with both customary international law respecting state immunity and Canada's treaty obligations. Therefore . . . there is no need to read in a further exception in order to comply with international law."[46] A related point is that the fact that a given enactment omits to implement or reflect some international norm does not necessarily mean that Canada is in default, for Canada may have discharged its obligation in other legislation or by other means.

3) The Incorporation of Customary International Law

It is a well-established, though rarely invoked, doctrine that norms of customary international law are directly enforceable as rules of the common law.[47] The doctrine is known as incorporation.[48] Incorporation applies only to customary norms. As explained below, in Canada and other Commonwealth countries treaty-based norms generally require implementation by statute.

Incorporation was established as a rule of the common law in the eighteenth century.[49] In his famous *Commentaries on the Laws of England*, William Blackstone declared that "the law of nations . . . is here adopted in it's [sic] full extent . . . and is held to be a part of the law of

---

45   2003 SCC 68 at para. 44; see also para. 73 (per Bastarache J.).

46   [2002] OJ No. 1624 (SCJ) at para. 42 [*Bouzari*]; otherwise unreported (Court File No. 00-CV-201372). As we write, an appeal of this decision is under reserve at the Court of Appeal for Ontario.

47   See generally van Ert, *Using International Law*, above note 8 at 137–70.

48   Another term that is sometimes used is "adoption."

49   The ancient English authorities include: *Buvot v. Barbuit* (1737), Cas. T. Talb. 281, 25 ER 777; *Triquet v. Bath* (1764), 3 Burr. 1478, 97 ER 936; *Heathfield v. Chilton* (1767), 4 Burr. 2015, 98 ER 50. See also *Duke of Brunswick v. The King of Hanover* (1844), 6 Beav. 1, 49 ER 724, *Emperor of Austria v. Day and Kossuth* (1861), 2 Giff. 628, 66 ER 263. Early American incorporation authorities include: *Nathan v. Commonwealth of Virginia*, 1 US (1 Dall.) 77 (1781); *Respublica v. De Longchamps*, 1 US (1 Dall.) 111 (Pa. 1784); *Ross v. Rittenhouse*, 2 US (2 Dall.) 160 (Pa. 1792); *Hensfield's Case*, 11 F. Cas. 1099 (C.C.D.Pa. 1793); *United States v. Ravara*, 2 US (2 Dall.) 297 (Pa. 1793); *Talbot v. Janson*, 3 US (3 Dall.) 133 (1795); *United States v. Smith*, 18 US (5 Wheat.) 153 (1820).

the land."[50] In England, the reach of the doctrine was the subject of some dispute in the late nineteenth and early twentieth centuries,[51] but ultimately won robust affirmation by Lord Denning in the Court of Appeal[52] and later by the House of Lords.[53] While later English authorities are, of course, only persuasive, some earlier ones are binding.[54]

In any case, the incorporation doctrine was powerfully affirmed in Canadian law by the Supreme Court of Canada in *Saint John v. Fraser-Brace Overseas*.[55] Like the earlier incorporation case *Re Foreign Legations*,[56] which the court relied on, *Fraser-Brace* concerned the power of a municipality to tax property owned by a foreign state. Applying the customary international law of sovereign immunity as Canadian law, the Court affirmed the lower court's finding that such property was immune from taxation. Rand J.'s powerful affirmation of the incorporation doctrine has gone unjustly neglected. He declared:

> It is obvious that the life of every state is, under the swift transformations of these days, becoming deeply implicated with that of the others in a *de facto* society of nations. If in 1767 Lord Mansfield, as in *Heathfield v. Chilton* . . . could say, "The law of nations will be carried as far in England, as any where," in this country, in the 20th century, in the presence of the United Nations and the multiplicity of impacts with which technical developments have entwined the entire globe, we cannot say anything less. . . . [To] say that precedent is now required for every proposed application to matter which differs only in accidentals, that new concrete instances must be left to legislation or convention, would be a virtual repudiation of the concept of inherent adaptability which has maintained the life of the common law, and a retrograde step in evolving the rules of international intercourse. However slowly and meticulously they are to be fashioned they must be permitted to meet the necessities of increasing interna-

---

50   Sir William Blackstone, *Commentaries on the Laws of England*, vol. 4 (Chicago: University of Chicago Press, 1979) at 67.

51   See van Ert, *Using International Law*, above note 8 at 138–42.

52   *Trendtex Trading v. Bank of Nigeria*, [1977] 1 QB 529 (CA) [*Trendtex Trading*].

53   *I° Congreso del Partido*, [1983] 1 AC 244 (HL).

54   This is the effect of another type of reception, namely the reception of English law into Canada. See P. Hogg, *Constitutional Law of Canada*, looseleaf ed. (Scarborough: Carswell, 1997) at c. 2. Thus an English case that predates the applicable reception date is law in Canada unless overruled by a competent Canadian court since its reception.

55   [1958] SCR 263 [*Fraser-Brace*].

56   *Re Foreign Legations*, above note 37. See the discussion of this much maligned judgment in van Ert, *Using International Law*, above note 8 at 142–45.

tional involvements. It is the essence of the principle of precedent that new applications are to be determined according to their total elements including assumptions and attitudes, and in the international sphere the whole field of the behaviour of states, whether exhibited in actual conduct, conventions, arbitrations or adjudications, is pertinent to the determination of each issue.[57]

In this passage, Rand J. not only affirms a leading English incorporation authority, but goes on to explain and approve the philosophical justification of the doctrine. The common law must be permitted to develop according to "the behaviour of states." It would be "a retrograde step" for courts to insist upon precedent, legislation, or a treaty before giving effect to customary international law.[58]

Another leading Canadian case applying the incorporation doctrine is *Re Regina and Palacios*,[59] a judgment of the Court of Appeal for Ontario. The main question in the appeal was whether the respondent, a former Nicaraguan diplomat charged with drug offences, was entitled to diplomatic immunity. Since the Vienna Convention on Diplomatic Relations 1961, such questions have usually been answered by treaty. But Blair J.A. found the treaty ambiguous on this point, and resorted instead to the customary international law which the 1961 treaty sought to codify.[60] Blair J.A. began by observing that the Supreme Court of Canada's judgment in *Re Foreign Legations* established that "the immunities and privileges of diplomats recognized by customary international law were . . . incorporated by the domestic law of Canada."[61] Blair J.A. went on to consider the customary rule that diplomatic immunity extends after termination of a diplomat's duties to give him a reasonable time to leave the host state. He found that this reasonableness rule was recognized as forming part of the common law in two nineteenth-century English cases.[62] To resolve the ambiguity in the treaty, Blair J.A. applied the customary/common law rule.

---

57   *Fraser-Brace*, above note 55 at 268–69.
58   Similarly in *Trendtex Trading*, above note 52 at 554, Lord Denning declared, "If this court today is satisfied that the rule of international law on a subject has changed from what it was 50 or 60 years ago, it can give effect to that change — and apply the change in our English law — without waiting for the House of Lords to do it."
59   (1984) 45 OR (2d) 269 (Ont CA) [*Palacios*].
60   *Ibid.* at 278.
61   *Ibid.* at 274. See also *Palacios* at 276: "Treaties, unlike customary international law, only become part of municipal law if they are expressly implemented by statute."
62   *Ibid.* at 275; the English authorities are *Magdalena Steam Navigation Co. v. Martin* (1859), 2 El. & El. 94, 121 ER 36 and *Musurus Bey v. Gadban et al.* [1894] 2 QB 352.

The incorporation doctrine has been affirmed, if only in *obiter*, in other recent cases.[63] The most recent consideration of incorporation by the Supreme Court of Canada also affirms the doctrine, though again only in *obiter*. In *Re Canada Labour Code*,[64] La Forest J. for the majority considered the state of the sovereign immunity doctrine in Canada prior to Parliament's enactment of the *State Immunity Act*.[65] His view was that the common law of Canada conformed with the restrictive doctrine of state immunity as it had developed in customary international law in the late twentieth century, and that the effect of the *State Immunity Act* was to codify and clarify the theory rather than to alter its substance.[66] In support of this proposition, La Forest J. cited the leading House of Lords authority on incorporation, *I° Congreso del Partido*.[67] As Lord Wilberforce explained in that case, the incorporation doctrine replaced the old common law rule of blanket immunity with the new restrictive doctrine that had taken root in modern customary international law.

As we saw in Chapter Three, most rules of customary international law may be modified or set aside by treaty, but *jus cogens* norms may not. While the VCLT is not explicit on this point, it is clear that *jus cogens* is, in effect, an entrenched form of custom.[68] Thus, *jus cogens* norms should be incorporated by the common law in the same way as ordinary customary international laws. Yet the Supreme Court of Canada has sent mixed signals about the domestic legal status of *jus cogens*.

In *Suresh v. Canada (Minister of Citizenship and Immigration)*,[69] the court discussed *jus cogens* in the course of its consideration of torture and refoulement to torture in international law. While discussing the "principles of fundamental justice" element of *Charter* section 7, the court considered whether the prohibition of torture constitutes a peremptory norm of international law.[70] The proper way to frame such

---

63   See, for example, *Jose Pereira E. Hijos, S.A.*, above note 7; *Suresh v. Canada (Minister of Citizenship and Immigration)*, [2000] 2 FC 592 at para. 32 (FCA) rev'd, [2002] 1 SCR 3 [*Suresh*], *Mack v. Canada (Attorney General)* (2001), 55 OR (3d) 113 at para. 32 (CA Ont.), *Bouzari*, above note 46 at para. 39.

64   [1992] 2 SCR 50 [*Re Canada Labour Code*].

65   RSC 1985 c. S-18.

66   *Re Canada Labour Code*, above note 64 at 73–74.

67   Above note 53.

68   See the discussion of custom in Chapter Three.

69   *Suresh* (SCC), above note 63.

70   The relevance of this question is far from clear, given that art. 3 of the Convention Against Torture and Other Cruel, Inhuman or Degrading Treatment or Punishment 1984 (CAT), [1987] CanTS no. 36 explicitly forbids Canada from extraditing people to states where there are substantial grounds for believing that they would be in danger of being subjected to torture.

a discussion, in our view, is to begin with the question, "Could two states validly conclude a treaty permitting each to torture the others' nationals?" Instead, the court embarked on a summary and inconclusive consideration of treaties, General Assembly declarations, domestic laws, judicial decisions, and academic works, from which it concluded that the prohibition on torture is an "emerging, if not established peremptory norm" that "cannot be easily derogated from."[71] With respect, this conclusion is mistaken in two ways. First, whether the prohibition on torture is *jus cogens* or not,[72] it is a rule elaborately set out in a treaty to which Canada is a party, namely the CAT. Second, there is no such thing in international law as "hard-to-derogate-from" norms. A norm is either customary, in which case it may be derogated from by treaty or subsequent custom, or peremptory, in which case it may not be derogated from. In our respectful view, to the extent that it addresses *jus cogens*, *Suresh* must be treated as a mistake.

The question of *jus cogens* was considered again, more briefly, in *Schreiber v. Canada (Attorney General)*.[73] Schreiber was arrested by the RCMP following a German extradition request. He attempted to sue Germany in an Ontario court for alleged personal injuries of a non-bodily nature. His action was dismissed in reliance on the federal *State Immunity Act*.[74] On appeal, Schreiber argued that the Act made an exception to the rule of state immunity for cases of non-bodily injury. Amnesty International intervened to argue that the right to the protection of mental integrity and to compensation for its violation was a peremptory norm of international law which prevails over the doctrine of sovereign immunity.[75] In rejecting this argument, LeBel J. found that such a peremptory norm had not been established.[76] No doubt that is true, but it misses the larger point: even if such a peremptory norm did exist, it would not prevent Parliament from legislating inconsistently with it. Rules of *jus cogens* control what kind of treaties the Canadian executive can enter into, not what kind of laws Canadian legislatures can enact. *Jus cogens* cannot be invoked to invalidate or "disapply" statutes for the simple reason that the common law (of which rules of

---

71 *Suresh*, (SCC) above note 63 at para. 65.
72 Other courts have found that it is: *R. v. Bow Street Metropolitan Stipendiary Magistrate and others, ex parte Pinochet Ugarte (No. 3)*, [1999] 2 WLR 827 at para. 28; *Prosecutor v. Furundzija* (1998), Case no. IT-95-17/1-T (ICTY) at para. 153.
73 Above note 16.
74 Above note 65.
75 *Schreiber*, above note 16 at para. 48.
76 *Ibid.* at para. 49; see also para. 17.

jus cogens are a part) is ousted by statute. However, courts interpreting Canadian legislation should vigorously apply the presumption of conformity in respect of rules of *jus cogens*, for Canadian legislatures rarely if ever intend to violate peremptory norms of international law. In short, a litigant wishing to rely on a rule of *jus cogens* against a Canadian statute may not argue that the statute is invalid, but only that it ought to be interpreted consistently with international law. This argument should almost always succeed, for it is inconceivable that Parliament or a provincial Legislature would intend to violate a rule of customary international law that has gained peremptory status.[77] The problem with *Schreiber's* treatment of *jus cogens* is that the court seemingly entertained the possibility that, had the purported peremptory norm been proven, it could be relied on by the court to invalidate or "disapply" the *State Immunity Act*.[78]

4) The Implementation of Treaties

"Treaties, unlike customary international law, only become part of municipal law if they are expressly implemented by statute."[79] But why does Canadian law draw this distinction? If custom is incorporated directly into the common law, why should treaty law be any different?

The short answer is that treaty-making is a prerogative of the Crown, and under our system of constitutional monarchy the Crown may only legislate in Parliament.[80] If treaties did not require implementation by legislation, but simply took direct effect in Canadian law, the federal government could bypass the democratic process and make laws binding upon Canadians simply by making treaties with foreign states. In the famous words of Sir Robert Phillimore in the leading English case on this point, "This is a use of the treaty-making prerogative of the Crown which I believe to be without precedent, and in principle contrary to the laws of the constitution."[81]

The general rule, therefore, is that treaties are not part of Canadian law unless they have been implemented by statute.[82] Arguably, howev-

---

77 This assumes, of course, that the rule upon which the litigant relies really is a norm of *jus cogens*; whether this is so is a matter the court must determine for itself.

78 See also *Suresh* (FCA), above note 63, in which the court seems to have entertained the same argument.

79 *Palacios*, above note 59 at 276 per Blair J.A.

80 For a longer answer, see van Ert, *Using International Law*, above note 8 at 172–75.

81 *The Parlement Belge*, [1878–9] 4 PD 129 at 154.

82 *Baker*, above note 10 at para. 69.

er, there are exceptions to this rule. The use of the supposedly unimplemented Convention on the Rights of the Child 1989 as one way of challenging the minister's administrative decision-making in *Baker v. Canada* was seen by a minority of the Supreme Court of Canada as possibly granting "the executive the power to bind citizens without the necessity of involving the legislative branch."[83] Even if that is not so (and the majority of the Court held it was not), it seems clear that the presumption of conformity with international law gives some degree of indirect legal effect to unimplemented treaties, particularly when used to control administrative decision-makers.[84] Another possible exception to the implementation rule may be the legitimate expectations doctrine. In *Minister for Immigration and Ethnic Affairs v. Teoh*,[85] the High Court of Australia found that the government's ratification of the CRC created a legitimate expectation to certain procedural rights — even though Australia had not implemented the treaty. The Australian federal government responded, with breathtaking candour, by issuing a statement declaring that people should not expect the government of Australia to act in accordance with its treaty obligations unless they have been enacted into domestic law.[86] *Teoh* has not been followed in Canada (it was pointedly ignored in *Baker*) but has won some support in England.[87]

Legislative competence to implement treaties is subject to the ordinary division of powers.[88] Thus a treaty whose subject-matter falls within federal jurisdiction must be implemented by Parliament, a treaty within provincial jurisdiction must be implemented by the provincial Legislatures, and a treaty falling within both jurisdictions must be implemented by all of Canada's legislatures.[89]

---

83   *Ibid.* at para. 80 per Iacobucci and Cory JJ. We say "supposedly unimplemented" because the court treated it that way, though in fact the CRC has prompted abundant federal and provincial legislative activity. See, for example, *Canadian Foundation*, above note 21 at para. 9, where McLachlin C.J.C. briefly surveys enactments implementing the Convention on the Rights of the Child 1989 (CRC), [1992] CanTS no. 3, art. 3(1)'s "best interests of the child" principle.

84   See the discussion in van Ert, *Using International Law*, above note 8 at 207–26.

85   (1994–95) 183 CLR 273 (HCA) [*Teoh*].

86   See M. Allars, "One Small Step for Legal Doctrine, One Giant Leap Towards Integrity in Government: *Teoh's* Case and the Internationalization of Administrative Law" (1995) 17 Sydney Law Review 204 at 217.

87   *R. v. Secretary of State for the Home Dept., ex parte Ahmed*, [1999] Imm AR 22 (Eng. CA); see also *Thomas v. Baptiste*, [1999] 3 WLR 249 (PC).

88   *Attorney General for Canada v. Attorney General for Ontario (Labour Conventions)*, [1937] AC 326 (PC) [*Labour Conventions*].

89   See the discussion "Reception and the Division of Powers," below.

It remains to consider what implementation consists in. The only rule is that the implementing instrument must be a law,[90] whether primary (for example a federal or provincial statute) or secondary (for example statutory regulations). There are no other formal requirements. The legislature is left the greatest possible leeway to take whatever action it deems necessary or desirable to give domestic effect to a treaty.[91] In *Pfizer Inc. v. Canada*, Lemieux J. cited nine different "implementation techniques" chosen by Parliament to implement the WTO Agreement,[92] including amendments and repeals of statutory provisions, the addition of new substantive provisions, the authorization of regulatory powers to implement parts of the treaty, and the imposition of limits on pre-existing ministerial powers consistent with the requirements of the treaty.[93]

Not all implementing legislation is obviously so. Parliament or the provincial Legislatures may enact, amend, or repeal legislation for the purpose of implementing a Canadian treaty obligation without referring to the treaty in the text of the enactment. Indeed, in respect of

---

90   As Lord Atkin noted in *Labour Conventions*, above note 88 at 347–48, while the government may seek Parliamentary approval of a treaty it wishes to ratify, such an expression of approval does not operate as law. See also *Mastini v. Bell Telephone of Canada* (1971), 18 DLR (3d) 215 (Ex Ct) at 217. For Canadian practice on seeking Parliamentary approval of treaties before ratification, see van Ert, *Using International Law*, above note 8 at 68–71.

91   Sullivan has recently drawn a distinction between two types of implementation, dubbed "incorporation by reference" and "harmonization": *Sullivan and Driedger*, 4th ed., above note 12, at 430–39. The former involves, in effect, quotation from or citation of the underlying treaty so as to give it domestic effect "without being changed in any way": Sullivan at 430. The latter "attempts to harmonize the international law rules . . . with the terminology, concepts, institutions and interpretation rules of domestic law": Sullivan at 431. This distinction is not found in previous editions of *Driedger on the Interpretation of Statutes* nor in other leading Canadian and English works on statutory interpretation. Nor has it been recognized in the case law. In our view, the distinction is largely unhelpful. The two types of implementation are in fact only two of an almost infinite variety of ways in which legislatures may implement treaty obligations. Actual implementing legislation is often difficult to fit into either category. Even if an enactment can be described as "harmonizing" or "incorporating by reference," the description does little work. The presumption of conformity applies to all implementing (and non-implementing) legislation, however characterized.

92   Agreement Establishing the World Trade Organization 1994 (1994) 33 ILM 114, implemented by the *World Trade Organization Implementation Act* SC 1994, c. 47.

93   [1999] 4 FC 441 (FCTD) at para. 30.

human rights treaties this is usually the case.[94] Courts and litigants must also bear in mind that legislation that was not originally intended to implement a treaty may later be relied upon by the federal government as its means of doing so. As a Department of Justice lawyer has helpfully explained,

> Canada's method of implementing its treaty obligations means that they are often scattered throughout several statutes, at both federal and provincial levels, and that there is frequently no signal as to when a law implements a treaty obligation. The problem is particularly acute when existing law is relied upon for ratification purposes.[95]

Before ratifying treaties that touch on domestic laws (as human rights treaties invariably do), the federal government consults internally, as well as with the provinces, territories, aboriginal groups, and others to determine what legislative changes, if any, would be needed to meet the treaty's requirements. If the conclusion is that existing legislation suffices, no new enactments will be brought.[96] Whatever existing legislation is relied upon in reaching that conclusion becomes, in effect,

---

94 In *Core document forming part of the reports of States Parties: Canada* (1998) UN doc. HRI/CORE/1/Add.91 at para. 138, which forms part of Canada's reports to UN treaty bodies, Canada explains Canadian human rights implementation practice as follows:

> Some human rights matters fall under federal jurisdiction, others under provincial and territorial jurisdiction. Therefore, human rights treaties are implemented by legislative and administrative measures adopted by all jurisdictions in Canada. It is not the practice in any jurisdiction in Canada for one single piece of legislation to be enacted incorporating a particular international human rights convention into domestic law (except, in some cases, regarding treaties dealing with specific human right issues, such as the 1949 Geneva Conventions for the protection of war victims). Rather, many laws and policies, adopted by federal, provincial and territorial governments, assist in the implementation of Canada's international human rights obligations.

95 E. Eid, "Interaction Between International and Domestic Human Rights Law: A Canadian Perspective," paper presented to the Sino-Canadian International Conference on the Ratification and Implementation of Human Rights Covenants: Beijing, China, October 2001, at 8–9. The author is senior counsel in the human rights law section of the federal Department of Justice. The paper is available from: http://www.icclr.law.ubc.ca/Publications/Reports/E-Eid.PDF.

96 *Ibid.* at 4. Eid notes that where there is uncertainty as to whether a domestic measure conforms with a proposed treaty obligation, a legal opinion may be sought. Where a gap between the existing domestic law and the proposed treaty obligation is found, the federal government may choose either to seek amendment of the domestic legislation or enter a reservation to the treaty: Eid at 4–5.

implementing legislation: it is legislation that gives effect to Canada's treaty obligations, even though its original purpose was not to do so. The fact that implementing legislation can be so hard to identify is one compelling reason why courts should apply the presumption of conformity when construing Canadian laws.

B. RECEPTION AND THE SEPARATION OF POWERS

The Supreme Court of Canada has observed that the separation of powers under the Canadian constitution is not strict, but is nevertheless there.[97] The federal and provincial cabinets, which sit at the pinnacle of their respective executive branches, are drawn from and responsible to Parliament or the provincial Legislatures, i.e., the legislative branch. The judiciary, while strictly independent from government, may nevertheless share certain judicial functions with administrative tribunals and other executive decision-makers. Despite this overlap, it is still meaningful to speak, in broad terms, of the separation of powers in Canada. What follows is a consideration of the role and responsibilities of the executive, legislative, and judicial organs of the Canadian state in the reception of international human rights law.

While the Canadian state is a subject of international law, and therefore bound by its requirements, the various organs that make up the state are not. Rather, international law treats the state as a unity, consistent with its recognition as a single legal person in international law.[98] Yet the fact that international law does not address itself to the executive, legislative, and judicial organs of states directly does not mean these organs should feel free to disregard it. While these organs cannot themselves be liable for violations of international law, their internationally unlawful acts can attract vicarious liability to the state as a whole.

That an act of the executive, legislative, or judicial organs of the state is lawful as a matter of domestic law will not excuse the state as a whole from international liability. A state may not plead its internal law to excuse non-performance of its international obligations. This rule has been recognized in the jurisprudence of the Permanent Court of

---

97   *Cooper v. Canada (Canadian Human Rights Commission)*, [1996] 3 SCR 854 at paras. 10–11 per Lamer C.J.

98   J. Crawford, *The International Law Commission's Articles on State Responsibility: Introduction, Text and Commentaries* (Cambridge: Cambridge University Press, 2002) at para. 6 to commentary to art. 2 (p. 83).

International Justice[99] and the International Court of Justice,[100] in the awards of arbitral tribunals,[101] and in judgments of the Supreme Court of Canada.[102] It has also been codified, in respect of treaty obligations, in the Vienna Convention on the Law of Treaties 1969 (VCLT).[103] The rule is now being further codified in the ongoing work of the International Law Commission. The Commission's Draft Articles on State Responsibility[104] include the following articles of note:

Article 1

Responsibility of a State for its internationally wrongful acts

Every internationally wrongful act of a State entails the international responsibility of that State.

Article 3

Characterization of an act of a State as internationally wrongful

The characterization of an act of a State as internationally wrongful is governed by international law. Such characterization is not affected by the characterization of the same act as lawful by internal law.

Article 4

Conduct of organs of a State

1. The conduct of any State organ shall be considered an act of that State under international law, whether the organ exercises legislative,

---

99 For example *S.S. "Wimbledon" Case* (1923), PCIJ Series A, no. 1 at 29–30; *Greco-Bulgarian "Communities" Case* (1930), PCIJ Series B, no. 17 at 32; *Treatment of Polish Nationals Case* (1932), PCIJ series A/B, no. 44 p. 4 at 24.

100 For example *Reparations for Injuries Suffered in the Service of the United Nations* [1949] ICJ Rep 174 at 180; *Anglo-Norwegian Fisheries case (United Kingdom v. Norway)* [1951] ICJ Rep 116 at 132; *Nottebohm case (Preliminary Objection)* [1953] ICJ Rep 111 at 123; *Applicability of the Obligation to Arbitrate under Section 21 of the United Nations Headquarters Agreement Case* [1988] ICJ Rep 12 at para. 57.

101 For example "Alabama" Arbitration (1872) in J. Moore, *International Arbitrations*, vol. 4 (Washington: Government Printing Office, 1898) at 4144, 4156–57; *Norwegian Shipowners' Claims (Norway v. United States of America)* (1922) I RIAA 309 at 331; *Tinoco case (United Kingdom v. Costa Rica)* (1923) I RIAA 371 at 386; *Shufeldt Claim* (1930) II RIAA 1081 at 1098; *Wollemborg Claim* (1956) XIV RIAA 283 at 289; *Flegenheimer Claim* (1958) XIV RIAA 327 at 360.

102 *Zingre*, above note 17 at 410 per Dickson J., *R. v. Malmo-Levine*, 2003 SCC 74 at para. 271 [*Malmo-Levine*].

103 [1980] CanTS no. 37. See art. 27: "A party may not invoke the provisions of its internal law as justification for its failure to perform a treaty."

104 Crawford, above note 98.

executive, judicial or any other functions, whatever position it holds in the organization of the State, and whatever its character as an organ of the central government or of a territorial unit of the State.

2.   An organ includes any person or entity which has that status in accordance with the internal law of the State.

Article 32

Irrelevance of internal law

The responsible State may not rely on the provisions of its internal law as justification for failure to comply with its obligations under this Part.

In short, while the executive, legislative, and judicial branches of the Canadian state are not themselves bound by international law, their acts may constitute breaches of international law for which Canada as a whole will be internationally responsible. This point must be borne in mind when considering the roles of Canadian executives, legislatures, and courts in the reception system.

1) The Executive

The executive is the broadest of the constitution's three branches. It encompasses the Crown, the cabinet, the civil service, related government agencies, and certain administrative tribunals. These executive organs exist in both federal and provincial incarnations. An appropriate synonym for the executive is simply "government."[105]

We have noted that executive acts inconsistent with Canada's international obligations may put Canada in violation of international law. Whether such internationally unlawful acts are also violations of Canadian law is a matter of some uncertainty. In most cases, the executive's powers derive from primary or delegated legislation. Since legislation is presumed not to violate international law, a legislation-based executive act that violates international law may be controllable by judicial review.[106] Not every executive act is derived from statute, however. The executive possesses certain common law powers, notably royal prerog-

---

105 It is strictly incorrect to use "government" synonymously with Parliament or a provincial Legislature, for example "The federal government passed a law . . ."; legislative power under the *Constitution Act 1867*, 30 & 31 Vict. c. 3, is granted to Parliament and the provincial Legislatures, not to the federal and provincial executives.

106 *Baker*, above note 10, offers some authority for this proposition, though the question remains unsettled.

atives. The extent to which these acts may be subject to judicial review, either for inconsistency with international law or on other grounds, is uncertain. In principle, prerogatives are susceptible to such review. As Laskin J.A. declared in *Black v. Chrétien*, "the expanding scope of judicial review and of Crown liability make it no longer tenable to hold that the exercise of a prerogative power is insulated from judicial review merely because it is a prerogative and not a statutory power."[107] What remains unclear is whether certain exercises of the prerogative (such as treaty-making and foreign affairs) are non-justiciable,[108] and whether inconsistency with international law is a ground for challenging prerogative acts at all. One matter that is seemingly established now is that executive acts, whatever their nature, are reviewable on *Charter* grounds.[109]

The most important function of the executive in Canadian reception law is the negotiation and assumption of treaty obligations. At common law, the power to assume treaty obligations forms part of the royal prerogative over foreign affairs. In Canada, this rule has not been altered by the constitution or by statute, so treaty-making remains a purely executive act.[110] Most provinces acknowledge that the power to make treaties rests exclusively with the federal executive, even though there is no explicit provision of the constitution to this effect. Yet Quebec has sometimes taken the view that the treaty power is divided between the federal and provincial Crowns according to the division of legislative powers in sections 91–92 of the *Constitution Act 1867*.[111] In practice, however, the federal government is wholly responsible for negotiating and concluding treaties, including human rights treaties.[112]

---

107 (2001) 54 OR (3d) 215 (Ont CA) at para. 47.

108 See the discussion in Chapter Thirteen. See also van Ert, *Using International Law*, above note 8 at 93–97.

109 *Operation Dismantle v. The Queen*, [1985] 1 SCR 441, *Schmidt v. The Queen*, [1987] 1 SCR 500. See also *Chua v. Minister of National Revenue*, [2001] 1 FC 608 (FCTD), supplemental reasons [2001] 1 FC 641 (FCTD).

110 See generally M. Copithorne, "National Treaty Law and Practice: Canada" in M. Leigh *et al.*, eds., *National Treaty Law and Practice: Canada, Egypt, Israel, Mexico, Russia, South Africa* (Washington, DC: American Society of International Law, 2003): 1–32 [Copithorne, "National Treaty Law"].

111 The matter has yet to be judicially considered. See G. van Ert, "The Legal Character of Provincial Agreements with Foreign Governments" (2001) 42 Les Cahiers de Droit 1093.

112 This has not stopped the Quebec government from purporting to bind itself, by decree, to certain international human rights instruments. See, for example, REIQ (1984–9) no. 1978(8) at 836 (CERD), *Arrêté en conseil no. 1438-76* (21 April 1976) (ICCPR) and *Décret no. 1676-91*, G.O.Q. 1992. II. 51 (CRC). This

This is not to say that the provincial executives have no role in the conclusion of Canadian human rights treaties. They have a very important role — on the domestic plane. Questions of human rights frequently fall within the legislative jurisdiction of the provinces. As a practical matter, then, the federal government must often consult with the provincial governments before assuming new international human rights obligations. For if these obligations need implementation by provincial legislation, the federal government must rely on its provincial counterparts to introduce and support such legislation in their respective Legislatures. The complexity of this process is the main reason why *Labour Conventions* is unpopular with some commentators. The provinces themselves are presumably quite happy with this scheme, for it gives them a say (however indirectly) in the treaty-making process. It is notable that the federal government itself has never seriously challenged *Labour Conventions*, and that a seemingly effective infrastructure for dealing with intergovernmental human rights matters has been in place since the mid-1970s.[113]

2) The Legislatures

The legislative branch of the Canadian constitution consists of Parliament and the provincial Legislatures.[114]

In *Ordon Estate v. Grail*, Iacobucci and Major JJ. observed, "Although international law is not binding upon Parliament or the provincial legislatures, a court must presume that legislation is intended to comply with Canada's obligations under international instruments and as a member of the international community."[115] As we noted earlier, it is true to say that international law does not bind Parliament or the provincial legislatures, but this must not be taken as a

---

practice has been judicially noticed by the Quebec Court of Appeal and may seemingly be relied on by Quebec litigants: *Quebec (Minister of Justice)*, above note 7 at para. 87.

113 For an explanation of the origins and work of the Federal-Provincial-Territorial Continuing Committee on Human Rights, see K. Bell, "From Laggard to Leader: Canadian Lessons on a Role for U.S. States in Making and Implementing Human Rights Treaties" (2002) 5 Yale Human Rights & Development Law Journal 255 [Bell, "From Laggard to Leader"].

114 The three territorial assemblies do not fit easily into this category, for their jurisdiction is not grounded directly in the constitution but is delegated by Parliament. They may therefore lack the residual sovereignty to violate international law described below.

115 *Grail*, above note 18 at para. 137.

denial of the bindingness of international law on the Canadian state itself. A violation of international law by Act of Parliament is a breach of Canada's obligations and may attract international responsibility to Canada as a whole.

In spite of this, the common law rule continues to be that legislatures are capable of violating international law. In the English tradition, Parliament is said to be sovereign, meaning that it may legislate on any matter and the validity of its legislation may not be challenged in a court of law or elsewhere. Thus Cockburn C.J. observed that there is "no judicial body in the country by which the validity of an act of parliament could be questioned. An act of the legislature is superior in authority to any court of law."[116] Thoroughgoing parliamentary sovereignty has never existed in Canada because our written constitution generally forbids Parliament from legislating in provincial jurisdiction and vice versa. And in 1982 parliamentary sovereignty was further curtailed by the *Canadian Charter of Rights and Freedoms*. Thus parliamentary sovereignty does not exist in its purest form in Canada. Yet Canadian legislatures retain a residual sovereignty to do anything that is not forbidden by the written constitution.[117] Since nothing in the written constitution expressly forbids legislatures from enacting laws which violate international law, Parliament and the Legislatures may do so. The power of our legislatures to violate international law has been frequently affirmed.[118]

In theory, then, Canadian legislatures may enact laws that break international law and Canadian courts are powerless to stop them. But what is the actual significance of this theoretical power? Parliament and the provincial Legislatures rarely if ever set out to violate international law — and especially not international human rights law — in

---

116 *Ex p. Canon Selwyn* (1872) 36 JP 54 at 55 (Eng QB).

117 *Arrow River & Tributaries Slide & Boom Co. Ltd. v. Pigeon Timber Co. Ltd.*, [1932] SCR 495 at 510, *British Columbia Electric Railway Co. Ltd. v. The King*, [1946] AC 527 (PC) at 542, *Daniels*, above note 16 at 539. Recent jurisprudence of the Supreme Court of Canada suggests that legislative sovereignty may be further abridged in Canada by unwritten constitutional principles, though this area of the law is still very much in development. See *Re Remuneration of Judges of the Provincial Court of Prince Edward Island*, [1997] 3 SCR 3, *Re Secession of Quebec*, above note 7 and *Mackin v. New Brunswick (Minister of Finance)*, [2002] 1 SCR 405.

118 See, for instance, *Re Foreign Legations*, above note 37 at 231 per Duff C.J. and *Capital Cities Communications v. CRTC*, [1978] 2 SCR 141 at 173 per Laskin C.J. In both these cases the affirmations of parliamentary sovereignty were *obiter dicta*. This does not detract from their authority, but simply underscores how rare it is for Parliament to intentionally violate international law.

the course of their enactments. Knowing this, Canadian courts presume that legislation was not intended to violate international law. The merits of this presumption are at least threefold. First, it almost always accords with the legislature's actual intent; on the rare occasion that a real conflict between international law and a domestic statute arises, it is usually attributable to legislative inattention rather than legislative intent. Second, the presumption avoids judicial pronouncements which may jeopardize Canada's relations with foreign states and treaty partners. Third, the presumption places the onus of proving legislative intent to violate international law on the person arguing for the internationally unlawful interpretation.

Though Canadian legislatures are sovereign as a matter of Canadian law to violate international law, their primary role in the reception system is to implement it. As we have seen, treaties need legislation to take direct effect in Canadian law. But the great majority of treaties ratified by the federal government each year go unimplemented, for the simple reason that they do not purport to affect Canada's internal laws and therefore do not need implementation. It is only when the subject-matter of a treaty seeks to regulate or affect the domestic laws of the states parties that implementation is needed.

Human rights treaties are, of course, the leading example of treaties that purport to affect domestic law, and yet they rarely receive express legislative implementation. There are several explanations for this. One reason is that Canada's domestic laws are frequently respectful of human rights "as is" and therefore do not need amendment to satisfy the requirements of new human rights obligations. A second reason is that some international human rights provisions impose obligations of conduct rather than obligations of result, and therefore do not lend themselves to express implementation.[119] But the most important reason seems to be the practice of the federal and provincial governments to survey and bring required amendments to their legislation before the federal government ratifies a human rights treaty.[120] In a sense, international human rights treaties are implemented in advance. Were it otherwise, Canada would be at risk of making promises internationally that it could not keep domestically. As we have noted, this practice makes it difficult to know what is implementing legislation and what is not.[121]

---

119 See the discussion of the ICESCR in Chapter Four.
120 See Copithorne, "National Treaty Law," above note 110 at 5, and Brunnée & Toope, "A Hesitant Embrace," above note 9 at 22–24.
121 See C. Heyns & F. Viljoen, *The Impact of the United Nations Human Rights Treaties on the Domestic Level* (The Hague: Kluwer Law International, 2002) at

Finally, recall that legislative jurisdiction to implement treaties is divided according to the ordinary division of powers (as explained below). This is particularly important in respect of human rights treaties, whose ratification is the responsibility of the federal government but whose implementation often falls, at least in part, to the provincial Legislatures.

3) The Judiciary

The judiciary consists principally of courts, whether federal or provincial, established under sections 92(14), 96, and 101 of the *Constitution Act 1867*. The judiciary may also consist, for our purposes, of administrative tribunals and other delegated decision-makers exercising quasi-judicial powers.

Like the other organs of the Canadian state, the judiciary may, by its decisions, bring Canada into violation of international law. Awareness of this risk is no doubt one of the reasons why Canadian courts apply the presumption of conformity and incorporate customary international law into the common law. Yet the judiciary's primary commitments are to the constitution and to legislative intent. If it may be clearly demonstrated that the legislature intended to violate international law by its enactment, and if that enactment is constitutional, Canadian courts will give effect to it. Thus there is a potential conflict between Canada's international obligations and the judiciary's responsibility, in domestic law, to uphold the constitution and give effect to legislative intent. But this conflict is more theoretical than real since, as already noted, Canadian legislatures rarely violate international law and even more rarely intend to do so.

The judiciary discharges Canada's obligations under international law in two main ways. First, the courts give effect to customary international law by incorporating it into Canadian common law. Second (and more commonly), Canadian courts construe domestic legislation (whether implementing or non-implementing, primary or secondary) consistently with Canada's treaty commitments. To know what those treaty commitments are and what they mean, our courts take judicial notice of their existence[122] and interpret them according to the international rules of

---

118 [Heyns & Viljoen, *Impact of UN Human Rights Treaties*] and I. Weiser, "Effect in Domestic Law of International Human Rights Treaties Ratified Without Implementing Legislation" in *The Impact of International Law on the Practice of Law in Canada* (The Hague: Kluwer Law International, 1999) at 132.

122 See the discussion of judicial notice, above.

treaty interpretation set out in VCLT articles 31–32.[123] Canadian courts should keep in mind that their failure to develop the common law in the light of custom, or to interpret legislation in conformity with Canadian treaty obligations, may place Canada in breach of international law and bring international responsibility upon the Canadian state.[124]

Some human rights treaties specifically refer to the role of judicial organs in giving effect to the rights protected by them. CAT article 2(1) provides, "Each State Party shall take effective legislative, administrative, judicial or other measures to prevent acts of torture in any territory under its jurisdiction." Similarly, CRC article 3(1) declares, "In all actions concerning children, whether undertaken by public or private social welfare institutions, courts of law, administrative authorities or legislative bodies, the best interests of the child shall be a primary consideration."[125]

The Quebec Court of Appeal has admirably appreciated the significance of this latter provision for Canadian courts. In *Quebec (Minister of Justice) v. Canada (Minister of Justice)*, the court observed:

> From the outset, it is important . . . to immediately point out that article 3 of the *Convention on the Rights of the Child*, which sets forth the guiding principle and philosophy, is also aimed at the decisions of courts, not only those of legislative bodies. The judges eventually responsible for applying the [*Youth Criminal Justice Act*] and, to do so, for interpreting it, will be at the front line of its application.[126]

This image of Canadian courts situated on the first line of application of Canada's international human rights obligations is not only correct as a matter of international law but commendable as a matter of policy. In an influential series of judicial colloquia on international human rights law, leading Commonwealth and American judges have enunciated a similar position. The first meeting, held in Bangalore, India in

---

123 *Pushpanathan v. Canada (Minister of Citizenship and Immigration)*, [1998] 1 SCR 982 at paras. 51–53.

124 See Lord McNair, *The Law of Treaties* (Oxford: Clarendon Press, 1961) at 345–55 and Higgins, "Domestic Law," above note 5 at 16. A British government report from 1884 (quoted in McNair at 335) observed, "a State is always responsible for a breach of its treaties, and it is immaterial in what particular way the breach has arisen."

125 See also the Convention on the Elimination of All Forms of Discrimination Against Women 1979 (CEDAW), [1982] CanTS no. 31, art. 15(2): "States Parties shall accord to women, in civil matters, a legal capacity identical to that of men and the same opportunities to exercise that capacity. In particular, they shall . . . treat [women] equally in all stages of procedure in courts and tribunals."

126 Above note 7 at para. 132.

1988, concluded with the issuance of the Bangalore Principles. The following principles are of particular relevance to the judiciary:

7. It is within the proper nature of the judicial process and well-established judicial functions for national courts to have regard to international obligations which a country undertakes — whether or not they have been incorporated into domestic law — for the purpose of removing ambiguity or uncertainty from national constitutions, legislation or common law.

8. However, where national law is clear and inconsistent with the international obligations of the State concerned, in common law countries the national court is obliged to give effect to national law. In such cases the court should draw such inconsistency to the attention of the appropriate authorities since the supremacy of national law in no way mitigates a breach of an international legal obligation which is undertaken by a country.

9. It is essential to redress a situation where, by reason of traditional legal training which has tended to ignore the international dimension, judges and practising lawyers are often unaware of the remarkable and comprehensive developments of statements of international human rights norms. . . .

10. These views are expressed in recognition of the fact that judges and lawyers have a special contribution to make in the administration of justice in fostering universal respect for fundamental human rights and freedoms.[127]

The Bangalore Principles have been developed, strengthened and expanded upon in subsequent colloquia. In 1989 the colloquium issued the Harare Declaration of Human Rights, point three of which declares,

Subject always to any clearly applicable domestic law to the contrary, it is within the proper nature of the judicial process for national courts to have regard to international human rights norms — whether or not incorporated into domestic law and whether or not a country is party to a particular convention where it is declaratory of customary international law — for the purpose of resolving ambiguity or uncertainty in national constitutions and legislation or filling gaps in the common law.[128]

---

127 "Bangalore Principles" in *Developing Human Rights Jurisprudence: The Domestic Application of International Human Rights Norms* (London: Commonwealth Secretariat, 1988).

128 "Harare Declaration of Human Rights" in *Developing Human Rights Jurisprudence*, vol. 2 (London: Commonwealth Secretariat, 1989) at 11.

For the tenth anniversary of the Bangalore Principles, the colloquium returned to Bangalore and produced an even more powerful declaration of the role of the judiciary in the implementation and advancement of international human rights law.[129] Point two of the 1998 declaration described the "moral principle of each individual's personal and equal autonomy and human dignity" as being "in the keeping of the judiciary." The presumption of conformity with international law was cast in particularly strong terms at point three:

> It is the vital duty of an independent, impartial and well-qualified judiciary, assisted by an independent, well-trained legal profession, to interpret and apply national constitutions and ordinary legislation in harmony with international human rights codes and customary international law, and to develop the common law in the light of the values and principles enshrined in international human rights law.

This depiction of the presumption of conformity as a duty of the judiciary, rather than merely a tool of statutory interpretation, finds support in Canadian and English case law. In *Zingre*, Dickson J. (as he then was) described it as "the duty of the Court, in interpreting the 1880 Treaty and section 43 of the *Canada Evidence Act* to give them a fair and liberal interpretation with a view to fulfilling Canada's international obligations."[130] In *Corocraft v. Pan American Airways*, Lord Denning M.R. called it "the duty of these courts to construe our legislation so as to be in conformity with international law and not in conflict with it."[131] Likewise in *Attorney-General v. Guardian Newspapers (No. 2)*, Lord Goff stated, "I conceive it to be my duty, when I am free to do so, to interpret the law in accordance with the obligations of the Crown under this treaty."[132]

C. RECEPTION AND THE DIVISION OF POWERS

In Canada, legislative competence to implement treaties is subject to the ordinary division of powers as set out in sections 91 and 92 of the

---

129 "The Challenge of Bangalore: Making Human Rights a Practical Reality" in *Developing Human Rights Jurisprudence*, vol. 8 (London: INTERIGHTS & Commonwealth Secretariat, 2001) at 267–70.
130 *Zingre*, above note 17 at 409–10.
131 [1968] 3 WLR 1273 (CA) at 1281.
132 *Guardian*, above note 26 at 283–84.

Constitution Act 1867. This was decided in the famous *Labour Conventions* case.[133] Parliament enacted legislation[134] purporting to implement certain ILO conventions in accordance with the Labour Part of the Treaty of Versailles 1919.[135] The legislation was part of the Bennett government's scheme to lift Canada out of the Great Depression. Some provinces challenged the legislation, saying it was properly within provincial jurisdiction. That was clearly so, but the Dominion (as the Federal Government was then known) contended that Parliament had plenary power to implement treaties ratified by Canada. Lord Atkin for the Privy Council disagreed. The only explicit provision in the *British North America Act 1867* dealing with treaty implementation was section 132, which gave Parliament jurisdiction to implement treaties

> necessary or proper for performing the Obligations of Canada or any Province thereof, as part of the British Empire, towards Foreign Countries, arising under Treaties between the Empire and such Foreign Countries . . .

Lord Atkin found that the conventions in question were not "empire treaties" but obligations which Canada had acquired for itself in exercise of its newly-won independence in international affairs.[136] Therefore section 132 had no application. Lord Atkin also rejected the argument, for the purpose of this case at least, that these conventions could be implemented under Parliament's "Peace, Order, and Good Government" power. Lord Atkin observed:

> For the purposes of ss. 91 and 92, i.e., the distribution of legislative powers between the Dominion and the Provinces, there is no such thing as treaty legislation as such. The distribution is based on classes of subjects: and as a treaty deals with a particular class of subjects so will the legislative power of performing it be ascertained. . . . It would be remarkable that while the Dominion could not initiate legislation however desirable which affected civil rights in the Provinces, yet its Government not responsible to the Provinces nor controlled by provincial Parliaments need only agree with a foreign country to enact such legislation: and its Parliament would be forthwith clothed with

---

133 Above note 88.

134 *Weekly Rest in Industrial Undertakings Act* SC 1935 c. 14; *Minimum Wages Act* SC 1935 c. 44; *Limitation of Hours of Work Act* SC 1935 c. 63.

135 [1919] CanTS no. 4.

136 *Statute of Westminster* 1931 RSC 1985 App. II No. 27. See also the Balfour Declaration 1926.

authority to affect provincial rights to the full extent of such agreement . . . . In other words the Dominion cannot merely by making
promises to foreign countries clothe itself with legislative authority
inconsistent with the constitution which gave it birth.[137]

It is important to emphasize that Lord Atkin did not deny Parliament could ever implement a treaty under its "Peace, Order, and Good
Government" (POGG) power. He denied only that these treaties could
be implemented this way. Indeed, he explained the earlier Privy Council decision in *Re Regulation and Control of Radio Communication*[138] as
an application of Parliament's POGG power to implement a treaty in a
case where the subject-matter of the treaty (broadcasting) fell within
neither section 91 or section 92. Similarly, in *Attorney General for
Ontario v. Canada Temperance Foundation*,[139] Lord Simon observed that
implementing legislation that "must from its inherent nature be the
concern of the Dominion as a whole" will fall within Parliament's
POGG jurisdiction. This judgment is wholly consistent with *Labour
Conventions*, for the point of the latter case is that treaty implementation occurs according to the established division of powers — which
includes Parliament's power to legislate for the peace, order, and good
government of Canada. Use of the POGG power to implement a treaty
was approved by the Supreme Court of Canada in *R. v. Crown Zeller-
bach Canada Ltd.*[140]

The significance of *Labour Conventions* for the implementation of
human rights treaties can hardly be overstated. Many if not most
human rights treaties touch on matters falling within provincial legislative jurisdiction.[141] Though it is always open to the federal government
to argue that a given human rights treaty falls within Parliament's
POGG power, it has never done so. The chief practical result of *Labour
Conventions* has been that the federal government must frequently
delay ratification of major human rights treaties to ensure that provincial legislation is in compliance.[142] Another way of making provision
for Canada's federal nature is to negotiate the addition of a "federal

---

137 *Labour Conventions*, above note 88 at 351–52.
138 [1932] AC 304 (PC).
139 [1946] AC 193 (PC) at 205.
140 [1988] 1 SCR 401. See also *Malmo-Levine*, above note 102 at para. 72.
141 Notably *Constitution Act 1867*, above note 105, ss. 92(13) ("Property and Civil
     Rights in the Province") and 92(16) ("Generally all Matters of a merely Local or
     Private Nature in the Province").
142 See I. Bernier, *International Legal Aspects of Federalism* (London: Longman,
     1973) at 152–58 and Heyns & Viljoen, *Impact of UN Human Rights Treaties*,
     above note 121 at 118.

clause" to the treaty in question. A federal clause is a treaty provision permitting federal states like Canada to participate only partially in the treaty, depending on the extent to which the state's sub-federal units have implemented it.[143] Similar results may be had by entering a federalism reservation upon ratifying or acceding to a treaty. However, federal clauses and reservations often meet with resistance, especially in respect of human rights treaties. There are no federal state clauses in any of the major UN human rights treaties, nor has Canada entered federalism reservations to any of these.[144]

For all this, it is far from clear that *Labour Conventions* has seriously impeded Canada's adherence to international human rights treaties. To the contrary, it has been argued that the decision has made Canada a leader in implementing human rights treaties by requiring "fluid consultation" between the federal and provincial levels of government.[145] Similarly, it has been suggested that Canada's division of powers contributes to "stronger awareness of, and commitment to, the aspirations of international human rights."[146]

D. RECEPTION OF OTHER INTERNATIONAL LAW SOURCES

To this point, our discussion of Canadian reception law has focused on the two predominant sources of international law, namely treaties and custom. As we saw in Chapter Three, these are not the only sources of international law. They are, however, the only sources which are subject to elaborate common law reception rules. We turn now to consider the role of other sources of international law in the Canadian reception system. Also considered here is so-called "soft law."

---

143 See, for example, the American Convention on Human Rights 1969 (ACHR), OAS TS no. 36, art. 28.

144 But Canada did enter a federal state reservation to the *Convention on the Nationality of Married Women* 1957 [1960] CanTS no. 2: "Inasmuch as under the Canadian constitutional system legislative jurisdiction in respect of political rights is divided between the provinces and the Federal Government, the Government of Canada is obliged, in acceding to this *Convention*, to make a reservation in respect of rights within the legislative jurisdiction of the provinces."

145 Bell, "From Laggard to Leader," above note 113 at 268.

146 J. Cameron, "Federalism, Treaties and International Human Rights under the Canadian Constitution" (2002) 48 Wayne Law Review 1 at 50.

1) General Principles of Law

As we saw in Chapter Three, courts and tribunals may use general principles of law to fill gaps in treaty and customary law by elaborating, by analogy to widely-accepted domestic law rules, a suitable international law rule. An example was suggested by La Forest J. in *R. v. Finta*: the principle that ignorance of the law is no excuse.[147]

Given the provenance of general principles in the domestic laws of "civilized nations," and their lacuna-filling role in judicial decision-making, it is not surprising that Anglo-Canadian reception law provides no guidance on how (or if) they apply domestically. Assuming that Canada is a "civilized nation," such general principles should exist in Canadian law already, without implementation or incorporation from international law. We know of no Canadian or Commonwealth case in which a disparity was identified between domestic law and a general principle of law recognized by civilized nations. Were such a case to arise, our tentative view would be that general principles ought to be incorporated by the common law or used in statutory interpretation to inform the presumption of conformity. But such a disparity between Canadian law and general principles of law is unlikely to be found.[148]

Though general principles rarely if ever arise in Canadian case law, they are adverted to by the *Charter*. Section 11(g) provides that any person charged with an offence has the right "not to be found guilty on account of any act or omission unless, at the time of the act or omission, it constituted an offence under Canadian or international law or was criminal according to the general principles of law recognized by the community of nations." Read literally, the phrasing of section 11(g) is redundant, for "international law" includes "the general principles of law recognized by the community of nations." It seems that the intent behind section 11(g)'s wording was to implement ICCPR article 15(2), which limits the protection from retroactive criminal laws granted by article 15(1) so as not to extend to "the trial and punishment of any person for any act or omission which, at the time when it was committed, was criminal according to the general principles of law recognized by the community of nations."[149]

---

147 [1994] 1 SCR 701 at 763 [*Finta*].

148 See Brunnée & Toope, "A Hesitant Embrace," above note 9 at 12.

149 For more on *Charter* s. 11(g), see Chapter Ten under "Rights in Criminal Proceedings."

2) Judicial Decisions

As explained in Chapter Three, judicial decisions are a subsidiary means for the determination of rules of law. The use of judicial decisions is, of course, entirely familiar to Canadian judges and lawyers working in the common law tradition. Reliance on judicial decisions as a subsidiary source of international law has therefore excited no controversy here. Nor has any rule developed, comparable to the implementation requirement or the incorporation doctrine, to describe the reception of international judicial decisions into Canadian law. Instead, the courts have had regard to such decisions as appropriate without treating them as binding. That approach is quite correct. Since judicial decisions have no formal precedential value in international law, there is no reason why they should have any in Canadian law. Instead, courts called upon to consider international judicial decisions should do so carefully and respectfully, but with the confidence to reach a different conclusion where international law or the case at bar demands it.

Canadian courts must also bear in mind the impact of their own decisions on the development of international law. When a domestic court considers international legal questions it does so not only as an organ of its domestic legal system but also as a part of the international judiciary.[150] The phrase "judicial decisions" refers not only to decisions of international courts and arbitrators, but also to domestic courts considering questions of international law. Thus, as La Forest J. observed in *R v. Finta*, a Canadian judge's interpretation of international law "bears some force internationally."[151] In particular, decisions on questions of international law by domestic courts help shape custom.

3) Scholarly Writings

As noted in Chapter Three, another subsidiary source of international law described in the Statute of the International Court of Justice 1945 (ICJ Statute) is "the teachings of the most highly qualified publicists of the various nations,"[152] that is, scholarly writings. The Canadian (and

---

150 I. Brownlie, *Principles of Public International Law*, 5th ed. (1998) at 584, 708.

151 *Finta*, above note 147 at 774. "In applying international law, domestic courts are not merely engaged in the internalization of international norms into the domestic legal system. They are also involved in the continuous process of the development of international law, particularly customary law": Brunnée & Toope, "A Hesitant Embrace," above note 9 at 56–57.

152 [1945] CanTS no. 7 art. 38(1)(d). See the discussion in Chapter Three.

indeed, the international) approach to scholarly writings was admirably explained by La Forest J. in *R. v. Finta*:

> It is instructive at this point to say something about the utility of the views of learned writers . . . in determining the applicable international law. They are extremely useful, of course, in bringing before the Court the various relevant sources of law, and as Lord Alverstone observed in *West Rand Central Gold Mining Co. v. The King*, [1905] 2 K.B. 391, at p. 402, they also render "valuable service in helping to create the opinion by which the range of the consensus of civilized nations is enlarged." But, as he went on to add (at p. 402), "in many instances their pronouncements must be regarded rather as the embodiments of their views as to what ought to be . . . the conduct of nations *inter se*, than the enunciation of a rule or practice as universally approved or assented to [by nation states] as to be fairly termed . . . 'law.'" In a word, international conventions and the practices adopted and approved as law by authoritative decision makers in the world community, along with the general principles of law recognized by civilized countries are what constitute the principal sources of international law. The pronouncements of learned writers on international law are extremely useful in setting forth what these practices and principles are, but the personal views of learned writers in the field, though useful in developing consensus, are of a subsidiary character in determining what constitutes international law.[153]

In short, Canadian reception of scholarly writings follows the international approach. They are not treated as themselves a source of law (either international or Canadian) but may be used in proper cases to help elucidate what the law is.

4) Soft Law

The concept of soft law was introduced in Chapter Four. While all soft law is soft (non-binding), some is softer than others. For example, the UN High Commissioner for Refugees Handbook on Procedures and Criteria for Determining Refugee Status is widely recognized as an authoritative and important resource for immigration authorities and the courts that review their determinations. As La Forest J. explained in *Canada (Attorney General) v. Ward*, "While not formally binding on signatory states, the Handbook has been endorsed by the states which are members of the Executive Committee of the UNHCR, including

---

153 *Finta*, above note 147 at 761–62.

Canada, and has been relied upon by the courts of signatory states."[154]
The Handbook must be counted among the firmer instances of soft law.

Not every variety of soft law enjoys such stature, however. Courts
and litigants must not think that the existence of the descriptor "soft
law" justifies or lends credibility to unprincipled reliance on any internationally-derived document or statement. Brunnée and Toope argue
that soft law is potentially relevant and persuasive for the purposes of
statutory interpretation and judicial review, but should not attract the
presumption of conformity.[155] We agree with this approach. Among the
non-binding international materials that have been considered by
Canadian courts are resolutions of the UN General Assembly, the general comments and "views" (decisions) of UN treaty bodies established
under various UN human rights treaties, and the declarations of important international organizations or conferences.

It is sometimes easier to say what soft law is not than what it is.
Treaties and customs binding on Canada at international law are certainly not soft law.[156] Likewise, a treaty to which Canada is bound but which
it has not expressly implemented in domestic law is not soft law; it may
be called non-binding as a matter of Canadian law[157] but it is clearly is
binding at international law. A treaty to which Canada is not bound (for
example, the ECHR) is not soft law. Though such a treaty is non-binding on Canada it is nevertheless binding on the states parties to it.
Travaux préparatoires (works preparatory to the conclusion of treaties)
may perhaps be called soft law until the treaty to which they are preparatory is adopted and opened for signature, but not afterwards.[158]

---

154 [1993] 2 SCR 689 at 713–14.

155 Brunnée & Toope, "A Hesitant Embrace," above note 9 at 20, 52–54.

156 This mistake is made by L. LeBel and G. Chao, "The Rise of International Law
in Canadian Constitutional Litigation: Fugue or Fusion? Recent Developments
and Challenges in Internalizing International Law" (2002) 16 Supreme Court
Law Review (2d) 23. The authors state (at 29) that many international conventions "include aspirational declarations, programmes of action, guidelines, and
protocols, also known as 'soft law.'" Later (at 44) they equate custom with soft
law. Both these passages are, with respect, mistaken. No provision in a treaty ratified by Canada is properly described as soft law. Canada's act of ratification
expresses to the world its intent to be bound by the treaty. Likewise, customary
international law is binding on all states and cannot in any sense be equated
with soft law. These errors appear to be informed by a more grievous error (at
62), namely the authors' belief that "international law is generally non-binding."

157 Even this is an oversimplification, given the presumption of conformity.

158 These were described as soft law by the Court of Appeal for Quebec in *Quebec
(Minister of Justice)*, above note 7 at paras. 121–22.

CHAPTER 9

RECEPTION THROUGH THE *CHARTER* AND OTHER HUMAN RIGHTS LAWS

As a country with a constitution "similar in principle to that of the United Kingdom,"[1] Canada originally had no constitutional or statutory instruments guaranteeing human rights. Under the English constitutional model of the nineteenth century, Parliament was sovereign to enact any law and no court could question the validity of Parliament's enactments. The prevailing conception of human rights in this legal tradition was, by contemporary standards, somewhat narrow. Yet its historical influence can hardly be overstated. It consisted of civil liberties such as freedom of speech and religion, habeas corpus, the right to a fair hearing or trial, freedom from trespass to the person or property, and the right to a remedy from an independent judiciary for violation of these and other rights. Civil liberties occasionally received recognition in legislation, but for the most part they were common law doctrines elaborated and protected by the courts. The only guarantees of the continuance of these rights lay in the forbearance of the legislature and the vigilance of the judiciary.

In the minds of some, that was the way it should be — even the way it had to be. As the leader of the opposition, Lester Pearson, observed while speaking against the federal government's proposed Bill of Rights,

> [F]reedoms are not guaranteed by words, even words in a constitution, let alone by words in an ordinary, normal act of parliament. . . .

---

1   *Constitution Act 1867*, 30 & 31 Vict. c. 3, preamble.

Incorruptible and respected courts enforcing laws made by free men in parliament assembled and dealing with specific matters, with specific sanctions to enforce their observance; these are the best guarantees of our rights and liberties. This is the tried and tested British way, and this is a better course to follow than the mere pious affirmation of general principles, to which some political societies are addicted.[2]

But this view rapidly lost ground in Canada as the twentieth century wore on. The change in attitude was driven in no small part by the rise of international human rights law, as the prime minister of the day, Mr Diefenbaker, made clear in his speech in support of the draft Bill:

We have today, in effect, although never adopted by Canada, a universal declaration of human rights which was passed by the United Nations. It contains 30 articles. Its preamble sets forth clearly and unmistakably, as does the preamble of the United Nations Charter, the greatness of human rights and the determinant that the preservation of human rights is on the peace of the world. . . . This measure that I introduce is the first step on the part of Canada to carry out the acceptance either of the international declaration of human rights or of the principles that actuated those who produced that noble document.[3]

The feeling that human rights required explicit legislative protection continued to attract support, resulting in the enactment of anti-discrimination laws and statutory bills of rights throughout the country and culminating in the constitutional entrenchment of human rights protection in the *Canadian Charter of Rights and Freedoms*.

A. THE *CANADIAN CHARTER OF RIGHTS AND FREEDOMS*

1) International Law Origins

Though one would hardly know it by reading the leading cases, the *Charter*'s roots in international human rights law run deep. Impetus for the enactment of constitutionally-protected rights came in large part

---

2   Mr Pearson, *House of Commons Debates* (4 July 1960) at 5661. As prime minister, Mr Pearson changed his view and supported Pierre Trudeau's proposal of an entrenched human rights charter.

3   Mr Diefenbaker, *House of Commons Debates* (1 July 1960) at 5644–45. By "never adopted," Mr Diefenbaker may have meant that the UDHR had never been explicitly implemented by statute.

from the post-war development of human rights law in such instruments as the UN Charter, the UDHR, the CERD, the ICCPR, and the ICESCR.[4] Early drafts of the *Charter* made reference to the UDHR and the ICCPR.[5] Many of the *Charter's* provisions correspond closely in meaning and wording to articles of the UDHR, the ICCPR, the ECHR, and other leading human rights treaties.[6] It is also notable that while the idea of enshrining rights in the written constitution is inevitably inspired in part by American constitutional history, the substance of the *Charter's* provisions far more closely resembles these international instruments than the US *Bill of Rights*.

While the *Charter's* international parentage is clear, the legal significance of this fact is less so. The *Charter* is not explicitly implementing legislation but, as we saw in Chapter Eight, legislation can implement international obligations without making express reference to the underlying treaty. In our view, there is simply no denying that the *Charter* is the principal means by which Canada's obligations under international human rights law are given domestic legal effect. The government of Canada has itself often said so in international forums.[7] Canadian courts have occasionally drawn the same conclusion. In *R. v. Big M Drug Mart*, Belzil J.A. observed, "That these fundamental freedoms were entrenched in the *Charter* in conformity with Canada's

---

4   See for instance the 1968 position paper by the then minister of justice, Mr Trudeau, reproduced in A. Bayefsky, *Canada's Constitution Act 1982 & Amendments: A Documentary History*, 2 vols. (Toronto: McGraw-Hill Ryerson, 1989), vol. 1 at 53. See also A. Bayefsky, *International Human Rights Law: Use in Canadian Charter of Rights and Freedoms Litigation* (Toronto: Butterworths, 1992) at 33–38.

5   Bayefsky, *International Human Rights Law*, above note 4 at 36–37.

6   See Chapter Ten and the table of concordance at Appendix 1.

7   In *Core document forming part of the reports of States Parties: Canada* (1998) UN doc. HRI/CORE/1/Add.91 at para. 137, which forms part of Canada's reports to UN treaty bodies, Canada explains the implementing role of the *Charter* as follows:

> International conventions that Canada has ratified do not automatically become part of the law of Canada. Rather, treaties that affect the rights and obligations of individuals are implemented by domestic law. To some extent, human rights treaties are implemented by constitutional law, including the *Canadian Charter of Rights and Freedoms*, which applies to all governments in Canada. To a considerable extent, they are implemented by legislative and administrative measures.

> Similarly, in its submissions to the UN Human Rights Committee, Canada has observed that the *Charter* does not directly incorporate the ICCPR but is nevertheless the primary mechanism used by Canada to ensure domestic implementation of its ICCPR obligations: *Fourth Periodic Report of Canada to the UN Human Rights Committee*, 15 October 1997, UN Doc. CCPR/C/103/Add.5 at para. 22.

commitment in the ICCPR cannot be doubted."[8] Similarly, in *Mack v. Canada (Attorney General)*, Cumming J. declared, "Undoubtedly, the *Charter* gives effect to many of Canada's obligations under international law."[9] Thus far, however, the Supreme Court of Canada's pronouncements on this point have been somewhat opaque.[10]

2) The *Charter*'s Uncertain Reception Rules

As we attempted to show in Chapter Eight, the rules by which international law is received into Canadian law are largely settled. Customary international law is incorporated into the common law, treaties need implementation to take direct effect in domestic law, courts take judicial notice of all forms of international law, and legislation is presumed not to violate Canada's international obligations. One area of continued uncertainty, however, is the reception of international human rights law through the *Charter*. Apart from some specific comments on the relevance of international law in interpreting *Charter* sections 1 and 7 (considered below), the Supreme Court of Canada has so far failed to elaborate a satisfactory and consistently-applied approach for the use of international human rights law in *Charter* interpretation.

This failure is not for lack of trying. The first chief justice of the *Charter* era, Dickson C.J., displayed an enthusiasm for and commitment to international human rights law both in his decisions and his extra-judicial addresses and writings. The problem with Dickson C.J.'s approach to *Charter* reception rules is that he was too successful: rather than elaborating a single theory for the application of international human rights law to the *Charter*, Dickson C.J. came up with two rather different theories.

It is easiest to tell the story backwards. In *Slaight Communications v. Davidson*,[11] Dickson C.J. for the majority of the court affirmed the following passage from his dissenting reasons in *Re Public Service Employee Relations Act*:

---

8   [1984] 1 WWR 625 (Alta CA) at 655.

9   (2001) 55 OR (3d) 113 (SCJ) at para. 35. Appeal dismissed: (2002) 60 OR (3d) 737 (CA). Leave to appeal to Supreme Court of Canada refused without reasons 24 April 2003.

10   An exception is this observation by L'Heureux-Dubé J. in *R. v. Ewanchuk*, [1999] 1 SCR 330 at para. 73: "Our *Charter* is the primary vehicle through which international human rights achieve a domestic effect." But she made this comment in concurring reasons to which only Gonthier J. subscribed.

11   [1989] 1 SCR 1038 at 1056 [*Slaight*].

> The content of Canada's international human rights obligations is, in my view, an important indicia of the meaning of the "full benefit of the *Charter's* protection." I believe that the *Charter* should generally be presumed to provide protection at least as great as that afforded by similar provisions in international human rights documents which Canada has ratified.[12]

The reader will recognize this rule from Chapter Eight. It is the presumption of conformity, according to which legislation is presumed by the court interpreting it not to have intended to violate the state's obligations under international law. Curiously, Dickson C.J. did not identify it as such, but that is clearly what it is. Thus the *Charter's* provisions will "generally" be presumed to conform with, if not surpass, the requirements of "similar provisions" in human rights "documents which Canada has ratified" (i.e., treaties to which Canada is a party). This stipulation indicates that human rights treaties to which Canada is not a party, such as the ECHR, are not objects of the presumption. Rather, the presumption applies only to Canada's binding international human rights obligations.

Like all interpretive presumptions, the *Slaight* presumption is rebuttable. The word "generally" serves to emphasize this. One means of rebutting it is to show that the international instrument upon which a party relies is too dissimilar in content to the relevant *Charter* provision. This is the meaning of Dickson C.J.'s phrase "similar provisions in international human rights documents." In our view, this similarity rule is simply one means of expressing the more general reason for rebutting an interpretive presumption, namely that other factors (legislative history, inconsistency with other provisions, inconsistency with the other official language versions of the text, etc.) indicate clear legislative intent not to conform with the requirements of the treaty. This similarity requirement must not be applied formalistically. The fact that an international instrument expresses a given human right in different words than the *Charter* should not, without more, rebut the presumption. The ultimate question a court must ask itself is, "Is this international human right among those protected by the *Charter?*"

The *Slaight* presumption is an admirable rule for the reception of international human rights law in Canada's constitution. As we have suggested, the presumption is supported by the history of the *Charter* itself, for the *Charter* was inspired by the development of international rights law and the need to bring Canada's laws into conformity with

---

12   [1987] 1 SCR 313 at 349 [*Re PSERA*].

its treaty obligations. The presumption is also strongly grounded in Canadian and Commonwealth interpretive practice.[13] Moreover, it accords with the vital distinction between binding and non-binding international sources. The presumption could benefit from some minor adjustments around the edges. For instance, it should apply not only to treaties to which Canada is a party but also to customary rules of international human rights law, for these are equally binding on Canada. Furthermore, it should apply to treaties ratified by Canada but not yet in force, and, in proper cases, to treaties signed but not yet ratified by Canada.[14] Both these suggestions may be characterized as friendly amendments to Dickson C.J.'s doctrine, for they are simply logical extensions of his reasoning.

In spite of its great merits, the *Slaight* approach to *Charter* interpretation has not attracted much support from the Supreme Court of Canada in subsequent cases. At least one reason for this is that the passage approved by the court in *Slaight* is an excerpt from a much longer discussion in *Re Public Service Employee Relations Act* which has come to predominate later treatments of international human rights law in *Charter* cases.[15] Regrettably, that discussion elaborated a rather more tentative and complicated approach to international human rights law. Dickson C.J. seems to have acknowledged the weaknesses of *Re PSERA* by quoting from it so selectively in *Slaight*. Here is the relevant passage of *Re PSERA* in its entirety:

> International law provides a fertile source of insight into the nature and scope of the freedom of association of workers. Since the close of the Second World War, the protection of the fundamental rights and freedoms of groups and individuals has become a matter of international concern. A body of treaties (or conventions) and customary norms now constitutes an international law of human rights under which the nations of the world have undertaken to adhere to the standards and principles necessary for ensuring freedom, dignity and social justice for their citizens. The *Charter* conforms to the spirit of this contemporary international human rights movement, and it incorporates many of the policies and prescriptions of the various international documents pertaining to human rights. The various sources of international human rights law — declarations, covenants,

---

13 G. van Ert, *Using International Law in Canadian Courts* (The Hague: Kluwer Law International, 2002) at 102–19.

14 For an explanation, see the discussion of the presumption of conformity in Chapter Eight.

15 *Re PSERA*, above note 12.

conventions, judicial and quasi-judicial decisions of international tribunals, customary norms — must, in my opinion, be relevant and persuasive sources for interpretation of the *Charter's* provisions.

In particular, the similarity between the policies and provisions of the *Charter* and those of international human rights documents attaches considerable relevance to interpretations of those documents by adjudicative bodies, in much the same way that decisions of the United States courts under the *Bill of Rights*, or decisions of the courts of other jurisdictions are relevant and may be persuasive. The relevance of these documents in *Charter* interpretation extends beyond the standards developed by adjudicative bodies under the documents to the documents themselves. As the Canadian judiciary approaches the often general and open textured language of the *Charter*, "the more detailed textual provisions of the treaties may aid in supplying content to such imprecise concepts as the right to life, freedom of association, and even the right to counsel." J. Claydon, "International Human Rights Law and the Interpretation of the Canadian Charter of Rights and Freedoms" (1982), 4 *Supreme Court L.R.* 287, at p. 293.

Furthermore, Canada is a party to a number of international human rights Conventions which contain provisions similar or identical to those in the *Charter*. Canada has thus obliged itself internationally to ensure within its borders the protection of certain fundamental rights and freedoms which are also contained in the *Charter*. The general principles of constitutional interpretation require that these international obligations be a relevant and persuasive factor in *Charter* interpretation. As this Court stated in *R. v. Big M Drug Mart Ltd.*, [1985] 1 S.C.R. 295, at p. 344, interpretation of the *Charter* must be "aimed at fulfilling the purpose of the guarantee and securing for individuals the full benefit of the *Charter's* protection." The content of Canada's international human rights obligations is, in my view, an important indicia of the meaning of "the full benefit of the *Charter's* protection." I believe that the *Charter* should generally be presumed to provide protection at least as great as that afforded by similar provisions in international human rights documents which Canada has ratified.

In short, though I do not believe the judiciary is bound by the norms of international law in interpreting the *Charter*, these norms provide a relevant and persuasive source for interpretation of the provisions of the *Charter*, especially when they arise out of Canada's international obligations under human rights conventions.[16]

---

16   *Ibid.* at 348–50.

There are two very different approaches to *Charter* reception law here. Part of the passage enunciates the presumption of conformity as affirmed in *Slaight*. The rest, however, advocates a "relevant and persuasive" approach to international human rights law.

The relevant and persuasive approach is essentially comparative. Rather than requiring courts and litigants to presume from the outset the identity of the *Charter*'s guarantees with similar provisions in Canada's human rights treaties, this approach merely permits courts and litigants to draw on international human rights law where they consider it helpful or interesting to do so — and otherwise ignore it. Dickson C.J.'s reference to the US *Bill of Rights* jurisprudence is telling. Obviously the case law of a foreign state is not binding on Canada. It should only be used in a comparative way. Similarly, the relevant and persuasive approach looks to international human rights law in a merely comparative manner. We saw in Chapter Eight that it is an error to equate international law with foreign law. Dickson C.J. appears to commit that error here. Another notable feature of this approach is that it seems not to require that the "various sources of international human rights law" considered during *Charter* interpretation be binding on Canada. This follows from the essentially comparative character of this interpretive strategy; why insist that the international law at issue be binding on Canada when one's use of it is purely comparative? By permitting courts to look to any human rights instrument, whether binding or not, the relevant and persuasive approach encourages courts to put Canada's binding obligations on a par with non-binding (and therefore ignorable) instruments.

Subsequent case law from the Supreme Court of Canada has rarely invoked the relevant and persuasive approach explicitly.[17] Yet the court's use of international sources suggests that it has taken this comparative approach to heart.[18] The court has frequently had regard to non-binding international instruments in the course of *Charter* interpretation, often without adverting to their non-binding character or defending their relevance.[19] The practice has earned the court criticism

---

17   But see *R. v. Zundel*, [1992] 2 SCR 731 at 811, *R. v. Sharpe*, [2001] 1 SCR 45 at paras. 175–79, *United States of America v. Burns*, [2001] 1 SCR 283 at para. 80 [*Burns*], and *R. v. Advance Cutting & Coring Ltd.*, [2001] 3 SCR 209 at para. 14 [*Advance Cutting*].

18   See generally J. Brunnée & S. Toope, "A Hesitant Embrace: The Application of International Law by Canadian Courts" [2002] Canadian Yearbook of International Law 3.

19   For example, *Advance Cutting*, above note 17 at para. 13 (AfrCHPR); *B.(R.) v. Children's Aid Society of Metropolitan Toronto*, [1995] 1 SCR 315 at para. 35 (AfrCHPR); *Mitchell v. Canada (Minister of National Revenue)*, [2001] 1 SCR 911

from international lawyers and legal academics.[20] The criticism is not that the court should ignore non-binding instruments, but rather that it should show more enthusiasm for Canada's actual obligations and explain its recourse to non-binding materials when it feels the need to consult them.

There may be a way of reconciling the relevant and persuasive approach with the *Slaight* presumption. William Schabas interprets *Re PSERA* as "a rather sophisticated doctrine distinguishing between two categories of international sources," namely binding and non-binding instruments and materials:

> In a general sense, international human rights instruments were part of the *Charter's* context of adoption . . . and "provide a relevant and persuasive source for interpretation of the provisions of the *Charter*." In the case of international human rights norms to which Canada is a party, Chief Justice Dickson said he believed "the *Charter* should generally be presumed to provide protection at least as great as that afforded by similar provisions in international human rights documents."[21]

This interpretation of Dickson C.J.'s meaning is not entirely supported by his reasons in *Re PSERA*, for he clearly placed customary international law (which is binding) in the "relevant and persuasive" category. But perhaps that was simply an oversight. Schabas' reading may be what Dickson C.J. intended.

Whether it is wholly consistent with Dickson C.J.'s *dicta* or not, this interpretation of *Re PSERA* is far preferable to the rather unstructured approach to international law that characterizes current *Charter* analysis. This approach would treat binding international human rights laws (whether treaty-based or customary) as presumptively protected by the *Charter*, and non-binding instruments (be they treaties to

---

at paras. 81–83 (various non-binding international instruments concerning indigenous rights).

20 See, for example, W. Schabas, "International Human Rights Law and the Canadian Courts" in T. Cromwell *et al.*, eds., *Human Rights in the 21st Century: Propsects, Institutions and Processes* (Montreal: Les Éditions Thémis, 1996) at 21, S. Toope, "Keynote Address: Canada and International Law" in *The Impact of International Law on the Practice of Law in Canada: Proceedings of the 27th Annual Conference of the Canadian Council on International Law* (The Hague: Kluwer Law International, 1999) at 33.

21 W. Schabas, "Twenty-Five Years of Public International Law at the Supreme Court of Canada" (2000) 79 CBR 174 at 186. See also W. Schabas, *International Human Rights Law and the Canadian Charter*, 2d ed. (Scarborough: Carswell, 1996) at 231–32.

which Canada is not a party; resolutions of the General Assembly, the Commission on Human Rights and other UN organs; the general comments, concluding observations, and views of UN treaty bodies;[22] communiqués of international meetings, etc.) as not presumptively within the *Charter's* guarantees but still potentially relevant and persuasive sources for *Charter* interpretation. The present authors strongly endorse this approach.

There is yet another approach to international legal norms espoused by the Supreme Court of Canada in some cases. The court sometimes explains its resort to international law as providing "context" for judicial decision-making. Similarly, the court has described itself as looking to "international values" to inform statutory interpretation. As L'Heureux-Dubé J. observed in a non-*Charter* case, *Baker v. Canada (Minister of Citizenship and Immigration)*, "the values reflected in international human rights law may help inform the contextual approach to statutory interpretation and judicial review."[23] Similarly, the Court in *Suresh v. Canada (Minister of Citizenship and Immigration)* spoke of "Canada's international obligations and values as expressed in '[t]he various sources of international human rights law'"[24] and observed that the statute in question had to be considered in its "international context."[25] What effect if any this emphasis on values and context may have on *Charter* interpretation is still unclear. Framing the discussion in these terms could be helpful in some cases but harmful in others. It could be helpful in cases where the presumption of conformity is, for whatever reason, inapplicable, and yet resort to international law still seems warranted. Yet the invocation of international context or values must not distract judges from the bindingness of certain international instruments and the consequential need to interpret

---

22 While the views of treaty bodies authorized to consider individual communications are not strictly binding, they are nevertheless entitled to considerable weight given the expertise of these bodies and the adjudicative fashion in which complaints are heard. See J. Harrington, "How Canadian Lawyers Can Contribute to the Effectiveness of the UN Human Rights Committee" (forthcoming paper in the 2002 proceedings of the Annual Conference of the Canadian Council of International Law).

23 [1999] 2 SCR 817 at para. 70; see also *114957 Canada Ltée (Spraytech, Société d'arrosage) v. Hudson (Town)*, [2001] 2 SCR 241 at para. 30. Similarly, in *Rahaman v. Canada (Minister of Citizenship and Immigration)*, [2002] 3 FC 537 (FCA) at para. 35, Evans J.A. observed, "Nowadays, there is no doubt that, even when not incorporated by an Act of Parliament into Canadian law, international norms are part of the context within which domestic statutes are to be interpreted. . . ."

24 [2002] 1 SCR 3 at para. 46 [*Suresh*].

25 *Ibid.* at para. 59.

domestic law in conformity with their requirements wherever possible. When Canada is subject to a relevant international legal obligation, it will not suffice to discharge that duty that our courts merely consider it under the rubric of "context" or "values."

While the general interpretive approach to international law and the *Charter* remains somewhat uncertain, the Supreme Court of Canada has made some notable pronouncements on the relevance of international law in interpreting *Charter* sections 7 and 1.

a) International Law and Section 7

Section 7 provides, "Everyone has the right to life, liberty and security of the person and the right not to be deprived thereof except in accordance with the principles of fundamental justice." The first part of this provision finds parallels in international human rights law.[26] But it is the latter phrase, "principles of fundamental justice," which the Supreme Court of Canada has sought to interpret in the light of international law.

In *Re s. 94(2) of the Motor Vehicle Act*, Lamer J. (as he then was) elaborated his residuary theory of the relationship between *Charter* section 7 and sections 8–14, whereby the latter sections are seen as illustrative of deprivations of rights contrary to fundamental justice and section 7 is a residuary provision to catch similarly unlawful deprivations. "Thus," explained Lamer J.,

> ss. 8 to 14 provide an invaluable key to the meaning of "principles of fundamental justice." Many have been developed over time as presumptions of the common law, others have found expression in the international conventions on human rights. All have been recognized as essential elements of a system for the administration of justice which is founded upon a belief in "the dignity and worth of the human person" . . . and on "the rule of law". . .[27]

This observation that the meaning of "principles of fundamental justice" may be elucidated in part by reference to Canada's obligations under international human rights law has been affirmed by the court in later cases.[28]

---

26   See the discussion of the right to life, liberty and security of the person in Chapter Ten.

27   *Re s. 94(2) of the Motor Vehicle Act*, [1985] 2 SCR 486 at 503 [*Re Motor Vehicle Act*]. See also 512.

28   See *R. v. Kindler*, [1991] 2 SCR 779 at 791 (per Lamer C.J., Sopinka J. dissenting) and *Burns*, above note 17 at para. 79 (unanimously).

The importance of international law in construing section 7 was reaffirmed by the Supreme Court of Canada in *Suresh* in the following terms:

> The inquiry into the principles of fundamental justice is informed not only by Canadian experience and jurisprudence, but also by international law, including *jus cogens*. This takes into account Canada's international obligations and values as expressed in "[t]he various sources of international human rights law — declarations, covenants, conventions, judicial and quasi-judicial decisions of international tribunals, [and] customary norms": *Burns*, at paras. 79–81; *Reference re Public Service Employee Relations Act (Alta.)*, [1987] 1 S.C.R. 313, at p. 348, per Dickson C.J. (dissenting); see also *Re B.C. Motor Vehicle Act, supra*, at p. 512; *Slaight Communications Inc. v. Davidson*, [1989] 1 S.C.R. 1038, at pp. 1056–57; *R. v. Keegstra*, [1990] 3 S.C.R. 697, at p. 750; and *Baker, supra*.[29]

Here, Lamer J.'s dictum in *Re Motor Vehicle Act* is considerably (and, in our view, correctly) expanded. The court here speaks of international law in general. This clearly includes customary international law (of which *jus cogens* is a part). It also includes human rights treaties, and may even include non-human-rights treaties.[30] One uncertainty here is whether the court would permit the phrase "principles of fundamental justice" to be interpreted in the light of any treaty or only treaties to which Canada is a party.

Suresh also includes the following statement about the role of international law in determining the content of "principles of fundamental justice":

> International treaty norms are not, strictly speaking, binding in Canada unless they have been incorporated into Canadian law by enact-

---

29   *Suresh*, above note 24 at para. 46.

30   In her dissenting reasons in *R v. Malmo-Levine*, 2003 SCC 74 at para. 270 [*Malmo-Levine*], Arbour J. assumed that non-human rights treaties may inform the inquiry into the principles of fundamental justice, but found that in the case before her Canada's international narcotics obligations were not helpful in construing s. 7:

> > In many instances, Canada's treaty obligations will be apposite to a s. 7 analysis. Indeed, in some cases an examination of international law will provide indispensable insight into the scope and content to be given to the "principles of fundamental justice". . . . This is not the case here, however. Given the nature of the harm principle, Canada's treaty obligations are not particularly helpful in demonstrating the existence or application of the principle as a principle of fundamental justice.

> The majority did not speak to this point.

ment. However, in seeking the meaning of the Canadian Constitution, the courts may be informed by international law. Our concern is not with Canada's international obligations qua obligations; rather, our concern is with the principles of fundamental justice. We look to international law as evidence of these principles and not as controlling in itself.[31]

This is a perfectly reasonable approach to elucidating the principles of fundamental justice for the purposes of *Charter* section 7. Were this approach to be adopted in respect of the *Charter* as a whole, however, it might sound a death knell for Dickson C.J.'s *Slaight* presumption. The fact that Canada has undertaken certain international obligations, and that it has done so according to its good faith belief that Canadian law satisfies those obligations, is the driving force behind the *Slaight* presumption and the presumption of conformity in general. If one sets knowledge of Canada's legal obligations wholly aside in construing the *Charter*, one is left with no reason to resort to international law save curiosity. Such an approach would undermine one of the *Charter*'s great purposes, namely to secure for Canadians in their domestic law the rights and freedoms that are their due under international law.

The Supreme Court of Canada's most recent section 7 jurisprudence has further elaborated on the meaning of "principles of fundamental justice" and, in so doing, has again resorted to international law. In *Canadian Foundation for Children, Youth and the Law v. Canada (Attorney General),*[32] the appellants argued that the best interests of the child rule, found in CRC article 3(1) and elsewhere in international and Canadian law, constituted a principle of fundamental justice for the purpose of section 7, and that *Criminal Code* section 43 deprived children of their security of the person contrary to this principle by creating a defence to assault for parents and schoolteachers who use force by way of correction. McLachlin C.J. for the majority of the court explained that a principle of fundamental justice must meet three criteria: (1) it must be a legal principle; (2) there must sufficient consensus that the alleged principle is vital or fundamental to our societal notion of justice; and (3) it must be capable of being identified with precision and applied to situations in a manner that yields predictable results.[33] McLachlin C.J. then applied this test to the best interests of the child rule. She found that the rule is indeed a legal principle, not-

---

31   *Suresh*, above note 24 at para. 60.
32   2004 SCC 4 [*Canadian Foundation*].
33   *Ibid.* at para. 8; see also *Malmo-Levine*, above note 30 at para. 113.

ing its enunciation in CRC article 3(1) and CEDAW articles 5(b) and 16(1)(d), as well as in federal and provincial statutes. She went on, however, to find that the rule was not "vital or fundamental to our societal notion of justice," noting that CRC article 3(1) calls it "a primary consideration" not "the primary consideration" and that it may be subordinated to other concerns in appropriate contexts.[34]

The rule that the content of section 7's "principles of fundamental justice" is to be determined in part by Canada's obligations under international law is to be applauded. The rule helps give section 7 some discernable meaning founded on custom (which is a universal source of international legal norms) and treaty (which is a consensually-adopted form of international obligation). What is more, the rule simply makes sense, for it is hard to imagine how the deprivation of a person's life, liberty, or security of the person contrary to international human rights law could ever be described as consistent with the principles of fundamental justice.

b) International Law and Section 1

Section 1 provides, "The *Canadian Charter of Rights and Freedoms* guarantees the rights and freedoms set out in it subject only to such reasonable limits prescribed by law as can be demonstrably justified in a free and democratic society." This provision, which both guarantees and limits *Charter* rights, was famously interpreted by Dickson C.J. in *R. v. Oakes*[35] to mean that a party seeking to justify a legislative limitation of a *Charter* right prescribed by law must show:

1) that the legislation pursues a sufficiently important objective to justify the limitation;
2) that the legislation is rationally connected to the objective;
3) that the legislation impairs the right no more than necessary to meet the objective; and
4) that the legislation is proportionate, that is, its deleterious effects are outweighed by its salutary objective.[36]

Decided cases, from *Oakes* itself onwards, have shown how international law may inform the first and fourth elements of the section 1 inquiry.

---

34 *Canadian Foundation, ibid.* at paras. 9–10. See also para. 11, in which McLachlin C.J. found that the rule does not meet the third criterion, either.
35 [1986] 1 SCR 103.
36 We have rephrased the fourth step in the *Oakes* analysis in the light of *Dagenais v. CBC*, [1994] 3 SCR 835.

In *Oakes*, Dickson C.J. invoked Canadian treaty obligations in support of his view that the legislative objective at issue was pressing and substantial. *Oakes* concerned the constitutionality of a so-called reverse onus provision in federal narcotics legislation. The Crown described Parliament's objective as to curb drug trafficking by facilitating the conviction of traffickers. In finding this to be a sufficiently important objective to justify limitation of *Charter* section 11(d)'s presumption of innocence, Dickson C.J. took judicial notice of and relied on two narcotics treaties to which Canada is a party.[37]

In *Slaight Communications v. Davidson*, Dickson C.J. again looked to international law in the course of section 1 analysis. The case concerned a man unjustly dismissed from his job. An adjudicator appointed pursuant to the *Canada Labour Code* ordered the man's former employer to give him a letter of recommendation and not to communicate with the man's potential future employers except by sending a copy of the letter. The Supreme Court of Canada held that these orders infringed *Charter* section 2(b)'s freedom of expression guarantee but were justified under section 1. At the section 1 stage, Dickson C.J. observed:

> Given the dual function of section 1 identified in *Oakes* [of both guaranteeing and limiting rights], Canada's international human rights obligations should inform not only the interpretation of the content of the rights guaranteed by the *Charter* but also the interpretation of what can constitute pressing and substantial section 1 objectives which may justify restrictions upon those rights. Furthermore, for the purposes of this stage of the proportionality inquiry, the fact that a value has the status of an international human right, either in customary international law or under a treaty to which Canada is a State Party, should generally be indicative of a high degree of importance attached to that objective.[38]

Here, unlike in *Oakes*, the international law at issue was rights-related. Dickson C.J. noted Canada's ratification of the ICESCR and its "com-

---

37 The Protocol for Limiting and Regulating the Cultivation of the Poppy Plant, the Production of, International and Wholesale Trade in, and Use of Opium 1953 456 UNTS 3 and the Single Convention on Narcotic Drugs 1961 [1964] CanTS no. 30.

38 *Slaight*, above note 11 at 1056–57. These comments were made at the "deleterious effects" stage of the s. 1 inquiry, though they clearly address the "pressing and substantial" stage as well. Indeed, it has been suggested that this latter stage is, in effect, a restatement of the "pressing and substantial" requirement and therefore redundant: P. Hogg, *Constitutional Law of Canada*, looseleaf ed. (Scarborough: Carswell, 1997) at section 35.12.

mitment therein to protect, *inter alia*, the right to work in its various dimensions found in Article 6 of that treaty."[39]

Dickson C.J. again turned to international human rights law in the companion hate speech cases of *R. v. Keegstra*[40] and *Canada (Human Rights Commission) v. Taylor*.[41] In *Keegstra*, the chief justice observed,

> Generally speaking, the international human rights obligations taken on by Canada reflect the values and principles of a free and democratic society, and thus those values and principles that underlie the *Charter* itself. . . . Moreover, international human rights law and Canada's commitments in that area are of particular significance in assessing the importance of Parliament's objective under section 1.[42]

Dickson C.J. went on to say that "[n]o aspect of international human rights has been given attention greater than that focused upon discrimination" and to quote at some length from anti-discrimination provisions of the CERD, the ICCPR, and the ECHR. On the legal effect of the first two treaties for Canada (which is a party to both), Dickson C.J. said "CERD and ICCPR demonstrate that the prohibition of hate-promoting expression is considered to be not only compatible with a signatory nation's guarantee of human rights, but is as well an obligatory aspect of this guarantee."[43] In conclusion, Dickson C.J. declared,

> . . . Canada, along with other members of the international community, has indicated a commitment to prohibiting hate propaganda, and in my opinion this Court must have regard to that commitment in investigating the nature of the government objective behind section 319(2) of the *Criminal Code*. That the international community has collectively acted to condemn hate propaganda, and to oblige State Parties to CERD and ICCPR to prohibit such expression, thus emphasizes the importance of the objective behind section 319(2) and the principles of equality and the inherent dignity of all persons that infuse both international human rights and the *Charter*.[44]

The chief justice made similar comments in *Taylor*, as well as noting that Taylor's communication to the UN Human Rights Committee under the ICCPR-OP1 had been rejected on the ground that Taylor and

---

39   *Slaight, ibid.* at 1056.

40   [1990] 3 SCR 697 [*Keegstra*]. See also *R. v. Andrews*, [1990] 3 SCR 870.

41   [1990] 3 SCR 892 [*Taylor*].

42   *Keegstra*, above note 40 at 750.

43   *Ibid.* at 754.

44   *Ibid.* at 754–55.

his political party advocated racial or religious hatred. "This conclusion," said Dickson C.J., "is indicative of the approach taken in the realm of international human rights, and thus emphasizes the substantial weight which must be given the aim of preventing the harms caused by hate propaganda."[45]

Even this brief survey reveals the profound mark Dickson C.J. left on section 1 jurisprudence.[46] But his reliance on international law (including but not limited to international human rights law) in elucidating section 1 is, at first blush, somewhat incongruous. One thinks of modern international law as guaranteeing human rights; why, then, should it be of such relevance at the stage of *Charter* analysis which determines their limits? The answer, of course, is that delineating the boundaries of a right is an essential part of defining the right as a whole. The truth of this is acknowledged in section 1 which, as Dickson C.J. so often emphasized, both guarantees and justifies limits to the *Charter*'s rights. Dickson C.J.'s method was to look to international human rights law both to elucidate the right and to determine its limits. This approach is in keeping with his belief, articulated in *Re PSERA* and, with greater force, in *Slaight*, that the *Charter* should conform to similar provisions of Canada's international obligations.

B. OTHER CANADIAN HUMAN RIGHTS PROVISIONS

Inevitably, discussion of human rights protection in Canada focuses on the *Charter*. But many other legislative enactments protect the human rights of Canadians. These other enactments share in the task of discharging the legislative dimension of Canada's international human rights obligations. These laws come in three varieties: bills of rights, anti-discrimination provisions, and laws which combine the two in a single act, charter, or code. Confusingly, many Canadian anti-discrimination laws describe themselves as "Human Rights Acts," with the result that Canadian anti-discrimination law is known as "human rights law" when in fact human rights goes well beyond anti-discrimination. In this section and throughout this work, we use "human rights" to

---

45   *Taylor*, above note 41 at 920.
46   Dickson C.J. is not the only Supreme Court judge to invoke international law during the s. 1 inquiry. See, for example, *Ross v. New Brunswick School District No. 15*, [1996] 1 SCR 825 at paras. 97–98 per La Forest J.

mean human rights in their entirety and "anti-discrimination" to mean what in Canadian discourse is known as "human rights law."

Non-*Charter* enactments for the protection of human rights are, technically speaking, ordinary Acts of Parliament and the provincial Legislatures. That is to say that, unlike the *Charter*, bills of rights and anti-discrimination codes are not entrenched in the written constitution. And yet the Supreme Court of Canada has recognized the "quasi-constitutional" status of such legislation for the purposes of statutory interpretation.[47] The legal significance of this special status was explained, in the context of anti-discrimination law, by McIntyre J. in *Winnipeg School Division No. 1 v. Craton*:

> Human rights [anti-discrimination] legislation is of a special nature and declares public policy regarding matters of general concern. It is not constitutional in nature in the sense that it may not be altered, amended, or repealed by the Legislature. It is, however, of such a nature that it may not be altered, amended, or repealed, nor may exceptions be created to its provisions, save by clear legislative pronouncement.[48]

Similarly, in *Insurance Corporation of British Columbia v. Heerspink*, Lamer J. (as he then was) described a provincial human rights code as "a fundamental law."[49] He wrote:

> When the subject matter of a law is said to be the comprehensive statement of the "human rights" of the people living in that jurisdiction, then there is no doubt . . . that the people of that jurisdiction have through their legislature clearly indicated that they consider that law, and the values it endeavours to buttress and protect, are, save their constitutional laws, more important than all others. Therefore, short of that legislature speaking to the contrary in express and unequivocal language . . . , it is intended that the [Human Rights] Code supersede all other laws when conflict arises.[50]

These passages reveal a certain similarity between the interpretive approach to quasi-constitutional legislation and the presumption of

---

47   For bills of rights, see for example *Singh v. Minister of Employment and Immigration*, [1985] 1 SCR 177 [*Singh*]. For anti-discrimination codes, see *Canada (Attorney General) v. Mossop*, [1993] 1 SCR 554 at 612.

48   [1985] 2 SCR 150 at 156. See also *Ontario Human Rights Commission v. Simpson Sears Ltd.*, [1985] 2 SCR 536 at 546–47.

49   [1982] 2 SCR 145 at 158 [*Heerspink*].

50   *Ibid.* at 157–58.

conformity: both approaches are premised on the presumption that the legislation intends to preserve and conform to some underlying norm, whether it be a particular human right or a relevant international obligation. This comparison must not be taken too far. The presumption of conformity may not be applied to invalidate or "disapply" an enactment that unavoidably conflicts with an international norm. By contrast, Canadian courts give quasi-constitutional legislation priority over ordinary legislation, even when that legislation is enacted after the quasi-constitutional legislation.

A curious feature of Canadian jurisprudence under quasi-constitutional human rights and anti-discrimination legislation is how rarely international law has been invoked or relied upon to interpret it. There can be no doubt that the presumption of conformity applies to such enactments. If it applies to a limitation provision of the *Canada Shipping Act*,[51] it must surely also apply to human rights and anti-discrimination laws. And yet, with some exceptions, Canadian courts and tribunals have tended not to look to international law when construing such provisions. Lack of familiarity with international human rights law may be one reason. Another may be that most quasi-constitutional laws in Canada are anti-discrimination codes. Only the *Canadian Bill of Rights*, the *Quebec Charter of Human Rights and Freedoms*, the *Alberta Bill of Rights*, the *Saskatchewan Human Rights Code*, and the *Yukon Human Rights Act* go beyond anti-discrimination measures to address other human rights. While there is no shortage of international treaties, jurisprudence and scholarship on the topic of discrimination, the federal and provincial human rights codes address the question so thoroughly that reference to international sources may so far have seemed unnecessary. One finds a similar phenomenon in the Supreme Court of Canada's equality jurisprudence under *Charter* section 15: the court has frequently considered international anti-discrimination provisions, but in the course of section 1 analysis or in some context other than section 15 itself.[52] Such complacency may be unwarranted. In its concluding observations on Canada's fourth report to the Human Rights Committee, the Committee expressed concern with the inadequacy of Canadian remedies for violations of ICCPR articles 2, 3, and 26, and recommended that Canadian legislation be amended so as to guarantee access to a competent tribunal and to an effective remedy in all cases of discrimination.[53]

---

51   *Ordon Estate v. Grail*, [1998] 3 SCR 437 at paras. 137–38.
52   See van Ert, *Using International Law*, above note 13 at 249–50.
53   Human Rights Committee, *Concluding Observations of the Human Rights Committee, Canada: 07/04/99* (1999) UN doc. CCPR A/54/40 at para. 9.

1) *Canadian Bill of Rights*

The sorry history of the *Canadian Bill of Rights*[54] does not merit lengthy treatment. As we have seen, the *Bill* was envisaged by the government of the day as a partial response to the need for Canada to meet the evolving human rights requirements of international law. Yet it suffered from significant weaknesses. As an Act of Parliament, it applied only in areas of federal jurisdiction. As an ordinary rather than a constitutional enactment, the *Bill's* power to set aside the doctrine of implied repeal and render inoperative legislation that conflicted with it was a matter of continued uncertainty. (The quasi-constitutional approach to human rights legislation, described above, won support in *R. v. Drybones*[55] and in certain dissents by Laskin J.,[56] but did not firmly take hold until the early 1980s, by which time the *Bill's* provisions had been largely superseded by the *Charter*.)

Another weakness of the *Bill* (or rather its interpretation by the Supreme Court of Canada) was that it protected only rights existing in Canada at the time of its enactment. Unlike the rest of the constitution, which Lord Sankey famously described as "a living tree capable of growth and expansion within its natural limits,"[57] the *Bill* was said not to be concerned with "'human rights and fundamental freedoms' in any abstract sense but rather with such rights and freedoms as existed in Canada immediately before the statute was enacted."[58] Tarnopolsky was of the view that this interpretation of the *Bill* "merely camouflages the fact that the judges of the Supreme Court are giving their own interpretations to the words used" instead of giving effect to Parliament's intent.[59] This approach also excluded from judicial consideration all reference to such significant developments in international human rights law as the ICCPR, the ICESCR, and the CERD, all of which were concluded and acceded to by Canada after the *Bill's* enactment.

Just when the *Bill* seemed dead and buried, a judgment of the Supreme Court of Canada appeared to reinvigorate it. In *Singh v. Min-*

---

54 SC 1960 c. 44.

55 [1970] SCR 282.

56 See: *R v. Hogan*, [1975] 2 SCR 574 at 597–98 (Laskin J. dissenting); *R v. Burnshine*, [1975] 1 SCR 693 at 714 (Laskin J. dissenting); *Miller and Cockriell v. The Queen*, [1977] 2 SCR 680 at 686 (Laskin C.J. concurring in the result but dissenting on this point).

57 *Edwards v. Attorney-General for Canada*, [1930] AC 124 at 136 (PC).

58 *Robertson and Rosetanni v. The Queen*, [1963] SCR 651 at 654 per Ritchie J.; see also *Authorson v. Canada (Attorney General)*, 2003 SCC 39 at para. 10 [*Authorson*].

59 W. Tarnopolsky, *The Canadian Bill of Rights*, 2d ed. (Toronto: McClelland and Stewart, 1975) at 159.

ister of Employment and Immigration,[60] the majority of the court allowed several immigration appeals in reliance on *Charter* section 7 while the minority allowed them on the basis of section 2(3) of the *Bill of Rights*. Beetz J. (for the minority) noted that *Charter* section 26 preserves "any other rights or freedoms that exist in Canada" and pleaded that the Bill and other rights-protecting instruments not be allowed to "fall into neglect."[61] Wilson J. (for the majority) relied on the *Charter* yet paused to observe that "the recent adoption of the *Charter* by Parliament and nine of the ten provinces as part of the Canadian constitutional framework has sent a clear message to the courts that the restrictive attitude which at times characterized their approach to the *Canadian Bill of Rights* ought to be re-examined."[62] These comments suggest that there may be room for fresh approaches to the *Bill* informed by international law. Thus far, however, the *Bill* has played a disappointingly small role in the reception and implementation of Canadian human rights obligations.

The latest chapter in the history of the *Bill of Rights* is the decision of the Supreme Court of Canada in *Authorson v. Canada (Attorney General)*.[63] Disabled war veterans sued the federal government for non-payment of interest on accounts held in trust for them. In its defence, the government relied on legislation enacted by Parliament disentitling the veterans to the amounts owed. The veterans challenged the legislation as inconsistent with the *Bill of Rights*.[64] The Supreme Court of Canada affirmed that where federal legislation conflicts with the *Bill*, the *Bill* applies and the legislation is inoperative unless it is expressly declared to operate notwithstanding the *Bill*. Yet the court found no inconsistency between the *Bill* and the impugned legislation.

2) Canadian Human Rights Act

The *Canadian Human Rights Act* (*CHRA*) is federal anti-discrimination legislation.[65] It applies to federal and federally-regulated institutions (for example, the federal government, Crown corporations, banks, the armed forces) and to subjects of federal regulation (for example, federal works per *Constitution Act 1867* section 91(10)(a)). Unlike the *Char-*

---

60   *Singh*, above note 47.
61   *Ibid.* at 224.
62   *Ibid.* at 209.
63   *Authorson*, above note 58.
64   *Ibid.* at para. 32.
65   RSC 1985 c. H-6.

ter's equality guarantees, which apply only to the federal and provincial legislatures and governments,[66] the anti-discrimination provisions of the *CHRA* extend throughout the federally-regulated public and private sectors. Responsibility for enforcing the Act falls to the Canadian Human Rights Commission and the Canadian Human Rights Tribunal.[67]

The *CHRA* is a significant legislative means by which Canada implements its anti-discrimination obligations at international law. Canada's core document (which forms part of Canadian reports to UN treaty bodies) explains that "Many of the international human rights instruments that Canada has ratified are directed against discrimination. . . . An important means of implementing this feature of international obligations is through human rights legislation (or human rights codes)."[68]

In spite of the *CHRA*'s implementing function, few decisions of the Canadian Human Rights Tribunal have relied on or referred to international human rights law, jurisprudence, or scholarship.[69] There are, however, some exceptions.

In *Stanley v. Canada (Royal Canadian Mounted Police)*,[70] female RCMP employees alleged that a policy requiring prisoners in lock-up to be guarded by persons of the same sex constituted sex discrimination. The arbitrator agreed that a *prima facie* case of discrimination contrary to the *CHRA* had been established, but found that the impugned policy was reasonably necessary to protect inmate privacy when undressed or using the toilet. The RCMP could therefore avail itself of the "bona fide occupational requirement" defence. In determining the privacy interest of inmates, the arbitrator relied in part on ICCPR article 17(1), which protects against "arbitrary or unlawful interference with [one's] privacy" and the ICCPR's preamble, which recognizes the inherent dignity of the person.[71] The arbitrator also relied on ICCPR article 10(a), which requires states parties to treat all persons deprived of their liberty "with humanity and with respect for the inherent digni-

---

66 *Charter* s. 32(1). For this purpose, federal includes territorial. See *Charter* s. 32(1)(a).

67 See the discussion of anti-discrimination mechanisms in Chapter Thirteen.

68 Canada, *Core document forming part of the reports of States Parties: Canada* (1998), above note 7 at para. 130.

69 This is in spite of the Canadian Human Rights Commission's recognition that "[i]nternational human rights standards are becoming an increasingly important source of interpretation for Canadian human rights law": Canadian Human Rights Commission, *Annual Report 2001* (Ottawa: Minister of Public Works and Government Services, 2002) at 7.

70 (1987) 8 CHRR paras. 29978-30247 [*Stanley*].

71 *Ibid.* at paras. 30166–67.

ty of the human person."[72] Finally, the arbitrator considered the non-binding UN Standard Minimum Rules for the Treatment of Prisoners,[73] but could not conclude with certainty that the relevant provision (article 53) sought to protect prisoners' privacy rights.[74]

International human rights law was also relied on by the tribunal in *Nealy v. Johnston*.[75] The facts of this dispute resemble those of *Taylor*: a racist organization employed telephones to spread hate messages contrary to *CHRA* section 13(1). The tribunal concluded that section 13(1) infringed freedom of expression contrary to *Charter* section 2(b) but was saved by section 1. In its section 1 analysis the tribunal invoked CERD article 4(a), which requires states parties to "declare an offence punishable by law all dissemination of ideas based on racial superiority or hatred. . . ," and the decision of the Human Rights Committee in *Taylor and the Western Guard Party v. Canada* that Taylor's complaint was inadmissible given Canada's obligation under ICCPR article 20(2) to prohibit the advocacy of racial or religious hatred.[76] The tribunal concluded,

> As the decision of the Human Rights Committee of the United Nations shows, section 13(1) of the *Canadian Human Rights Act* is an important element in the Canadian response to the challenge of international human rights obligations and outweighs any concern to protect the dissemination of hate messages. It would be a perverse result if the objects of such a provision which reflect both the consensus of the international community and an ideal of responsible democracy in which the dignity of both individuals and groups is to be respected were to be impugnable as antithetical to the values of "a free and democratic society."[77]

3) Provincial and Territorial Human Rights Laws

a) *Quebec Charter of Human Rights and Freedoms*
In many ways the most ambitious human rights enactment in Canadian law is Quebec's *Charter of Human Rights and Freedoms*.[78] Like the

---

72 *Ibid.* at para. 30179.
73 Adopted by the First United Nations Congress on the Prevention of Crime and the Treatment of Offenders (Geneva, 1955) and approved by ECOSOC res. 663 C (XXIV) (1957) and ECOSOC res. 2076 (LXII) (1977).
74 *Stanley*, above note 70 at paras. 30181–85.
75 (1989) 10 CHRR D/6450 paras. 45598–45701 [*Nealy*].
76 *Taylor and the Western Guard Party v. Canada* (1983), Comm. no. 104/1981, Rep HRC 231.
77 *Nealy*, above note 75 at para. 45690.
78 RSQ c. C-12 [*Quebec Charter*].

Canadian *Charter*, the *Quebec Charter* protects such basic civil rights and freedoms as life, liberty, religion, expression, association, and due process. Like the *Canadian Human Rights Act* and similar provincial enactments, the *Quebec Charter* prohibits discrimination in public life and the workplace and creates a human rights tribunal to enforce these prohibitions. Yet the *Quebec Charter* goes further. It recognizes certain economic and social rights,[79] and includes some novel and unusually-expressed human rights guarantees.[80] All of its protections save those in respect of economic and social rights supersede later enactments unless the contrary is expressly provided for.[81]

Quebec courts and tribunals have embraced the use of international human rights in their interpretations of the *Quebec Charter*. In *Quebec (Commission des droits de la personne et des droits de la jeunesse) v. Montréal (Ville)*, the Court of Appeal for Quebec described the adoption of human rights laws, both federally and provincially, as having occurred "in an international context of affirmation of human rights and freedoms."[82] The court went on to approve the relevant and persuasive approach to international human rights law in respect of the *Quebec Charter*, saying, "In the case of the *Quebec Charter*, the importance attached to different international human rights texts during the work preparatory to its adoption and the similarity of the language used in Quebec and international standards illustrate the usefulness of recourse to the latter."[83] Similarly, Quebec's human rights tribunal has described international human rights law as the interpretive backdrop of its decisions,[84] a description adopted by the Court of Appeal.[85] The presump-

---

79 *Ibid.* at chapter IV.

80 For example, *ibid.*, s. 2 (every human being whose life is in peril has a right to assistance) and s. 44 (every person has a right to information to the extent provided by law).

81 *Ibid.* s. 52.

82 (1998) 36 CCEL (2d) 196 at para. 65 (Que CA) [*Montréal (Ville)*]. The French reads "dans un contexte international d'affirmation des droits et libertés de la personne." See also *2747-3174 Québec Inc. v. Quebec (Régie des permis d'alcool)*, [1996] 3 SCR 919 at paras. 238–40 per L'Heureux-Dubé J. (concurring).

83 *Montréal (Ville)*, *ibid.* at para. 65. The French reads, "Dans le cas de la Charte québécoise, l'importance accordée à différents textes du droit international des personnes lors des travaux préparatoires à son adoption et la similarité du langage utilisé dans les normes québécoises et internationales illustrent l'utilité du recours à ces dernières."

84 *Commission des droits de la personne et droits de la jeunesse du Québec v. Maison des jeunes*, [1998] RJQ 2549 at para. 41.

85 *Gosselin v. Quebec (Attorney General)*, [1999] RJQ 1033 at para. 32.

tion of conformity has been cited as one reason why courts may have recourse to international law in interpreting the *Quebec Charter*.[86]

The justiciability of the *Quebec Charter*'s social and economic rights guarantees was considered by the Supreme Court of Canada in *Gosselin v. Quebec (Attorney General)*.[87] Gosselin, a welfare recipient, alleged that Quebec social assistance legislation violated, *inter alia*, section 45 of the *Quebec Charter*. McLachlin C.J. for the majority held that Chapter IV (the economic and social rights chapter) was not a basis for judicial review of legislation.[88] The legislative language was insufficiently precise to indicate the legislature's intent to permit judicial review founded on these provisions. McLachlin C.J. compared the *Quebec Charter*'s qualified wording to the language used in the ICESCR and UDHR and concluded from this comparison that section 45 was "highly equivocal."[89] And yet McLachlin C.J. emphasized that Chapter IV creates rights and that violations of these rights may not go wholly unremedied. Though Chapter IV rights are not grounds for invalidating legislation, they can still be the basis of declaratory relief.[90]

b) Human Rights Provisions in the Common Law Jurisdictions

The first Canadian jurisdiction to enact a comprehensive statutory scheme for the protection of human rights was Saskatchewan in 1947.[91] The Saskatchewan Act combined protection for fundamental freedoms such as speech, assembly, religion, and association with anti-discrimination provisions. The current *Saskatchewan Human Rights Code* pre-

---

86 *Dufour v. Centre hospitalier St-Joseph de la Malbaie*, [1992] RJQ 825 (TDPQ) at 835.

87 [2002] 4 SCR 429 [*Gosselin* SCC].

88 *Ibid.* at para. 92.

89 *Ibid.* at para. 93. This is a striking passage. Normally when a Canadian or Commonwealth judge takes note of a treaty obligation and finds a related legislative provision to be ambiguous, she replies by presuming the legislature intended the enactment to conform with the treaty. Here, McLachlin C.J. invokes Canada's human rights obligations to inform an interpretation of s. 45 which significantly undermines the legal weight of that section. One might understandably view McLachlin C.J.'s approach here as a failure to apply the presumption. There are, however, more charitable readings. Though McLachlin C.J. did not explicitly say so, the structure of her discussion is consistent with a finding that the legislature's weak language effectively rebutted the presumption of conformity. Alternatively, it may be that the nature of ICESCR obligations (which are mostly obligations of conduct rather than obligations of result; see Chapter Four) informed the chief justice's conclusions.

90 *Gosselin* SCC, *ibid.* at paras. 95–96. See the discussion in Chapter Thirteen.

91 *Saskatchewan Bill of Rights Act* SS 1947 c. 35.

serves these protections.[92] The Court of Appeal for Saskatchewan has described the *Code* in terms of international human rights protection and enforcement, and has held that "Saskatchewan legislation, for the most part, gives effect to the rights protected in the [ICCPR]."[93]

Ontario enacted its human rights code in 1962.[94] The *Code* incorporated among its provisions certain anti-discrimination protections found in earlier enactments.[95] The preamble to the *Code* begins, "Whereas recognition of the inherent dignity and the equal and inalienable rights of all members of the human family is the foundation of freedom, justice and peace in the world and is in accord with the Universal Declaration of Human Rights as proclaimed by the United Nations . . . ." The first clause of this passage repeats nearly word-for-word the opening words of the UDHR.[96]

Like Saskatchewan and Quebec, Alberta possesses both a human rights code and a bill of rights. The two enactments were adopted in 1972.[97] The *Alberta Bill of Rights* closely resembles the *Canadian Bill of Rights* in its protections of liberty, security of the person, enjoyment of property, equality, religion, speech, assembly, association, and the press. The two bills also share the same rule of construction, namely that every law shall be construed and applied as not to abrogate, abridge, or infringe the protected rights and freedoms.[98] However, the *Alberta Bill* does not particularize this rule of construction, as the *Canadian Bill* does, to protect such legal rights as habeas corpus, fair hearings, and the presumption of innocence.[99]

Manitoba's *Human Rights Code* declares in its preamble that "Manitobans recognize the individual worth and dignity of every member of the human family, and this principle underlies the Universal Declaration of

---

92 *Saskatchewan Human Rights Code* SS 1979 c. S-24.1.

93 *Canadian Odeon Theatres Ltd. v. Human Rights Commission (Saskatchewan) and Huck*, [1985] 3 WWR 717 at 736 (Sask CA). See also *Saskatchewan (Human Rights Commission) v. Prince Albert Elks Club Inc.*, [2003] 3 WWR 1 (Sask CA) at para. 30.

94 SO 1961-2 c. 93. Now the *Human Rights Code* RSO 1990 c. H.19.

95 See the *Racial Discrimination Act* 1944 SO 1944 c. 51, the *Fair Employment Practices Act* 1951 SO 1951 c. 24, the *Female Employees Fair Remuneration Act* 1951 SO 1951 c. 26, and the *Fair Accommodations Practices Act* 1954 SO 1954 c. 28.

96 The only difference is that the UDHR repeats the preposition "of": "Whereas recognition of the inherent dignity and of the equal and inalienable rights of all members of the human family. . . ."

97 *Alberta Bill of Rights* SA 1972 c. 1 (now RSA 2000 c. A-14); *Individual's Rights Protection Act* RSA 1980 c. I-2 (now the *Alberta Human Rights, Citizenship and Multiculturalism Act* SA 1996 c. H-11.7).

98 *Alberta Bill of Rights, ibid.*, s. 2; *Canadian Bill of Rights,* above note 54, s. 2.

99 *Canadian Bill of Rights, ibid.*, s. 2(a)–(g).

Human Rights, the *Canadian Charter of Rights and Freedoms*, and other solemn undertakings, international and domestic, that Canadians honour."[100] This language not only invokes the UDHR explicitly but also recognizes Canada's commitment to other international human rights laws. The *Code* goes on to prohibit discrimination in Manitoba in broad terms.

Prince Edward Island's *Human Rights Act* begins similarly. Its preamble affirms, in the words of the UDHR's preamble, that recognition of the dignity, equality, and rights of all is the foundation of freedom, justice, and peace in the world "and is in accord with the Universal Declaration of Human Rights." The preamble goes on to note that the original 1968 Prince Edward Island *Human Rights Act* "was passed by the legislature of this province in response to" the UDHR.[101]

Similarly, the Yukon *Human Rights Act*[102] makes several references to the UDHR and Canada's "international undertakings." The preamble recognizes "[t]hat Canada is a party to the United Nations' *Universal Declaration of Human Rights* and other international undertakings having as their object the improvement of human rights in Canada and other nations of the world."[103] The preamble also recognizes the "responsibility" of the Yukon government "to encourage an understanding and recognition of human rights that is consistent with Canada's international undertakings," and declares it to be "just and consistent with Canada's international undertakings to recognize and make special provisions for the unique needs and cultural heritage of the aboriginal peoples of the Yukon." The Act goes on, at section 1(c), to include the promotion of principles underlying the *Charter*, the UDHR, and "other solemn undertakings, international and national, which Canada honours" as an object of the Act. The substantive provisions of the Act include a bill of rights (Part 1) and anti-discrimination provisions (Part 2).

The other Canadian provinces and territories have all enacted anti-discrimination provisions, though without reference to international human rights law.[104] None has enacted broader "bills of rights."

---

100 *Human Rights Code* CCSM c. H175 preamble.
101 *Human Rights Act* RSPEI 1988 c. H-12. See *Condon v. Prince Edward Island* (2002), 214 Nfld & PEIR 244.
102 SY 1987 c. 3.
103 Strictly speaking this is incorrect: Canada is not a "party" to the UDHR because that instrument is a resolution of the UN General Assembly, not a treaty.
104 *Human Rights Code* RSBC 1996 c. 210 (British Columbia); *Human Rights Code* RSNB 1973 c. H-11 (New Brunswick); *Human Rights Code* RSN 1990 c. H-14 (Newfoundland); *Northwest Territories Fair Practices Act* RSNWT 1988 c. F-2 (Northwest Territories); *Human Rights Act* RSNS 1989 c. 214 (Nova Scotia). See also *Nunavut Act* SC 1993 c. 28 s. 29(1).

C. IMPLIED RIGHTS AND PUBLIC POLICY

Two other strains of human rights protection may be found in Canadian law, though their authority and continued significance is unclear.

The first is the so-called implied bill of rights. Pre-*Charter* judgments of the Supreme Court of Canada sometimes suggested that certain fundamental freedoms could not be abridged either by Parliament or the provincial Legislatures.[105] There is also some post-*Charter* authority for this approach.[106] This theory has always been very difficult to reconcile with the concept of parliamentary sovereignty which, before the enactment of the *Charter*, remained a central feature of Canadian constitutional arrangements. In our view, the implied bill of rights theory is intellectually unsatisfying. Rights protection is simply not possible to read into the 1867 constitution, given its derivation from British constitutional tradition. Furthermore, the content of the implied bill of rights was very narrow and pales in comparison to the *Charter* and other Canadian human rights instruments.

The second strain of human rights protection is more plausible. In *Re Drummond Wren* (1945),[107] Mackay J. was faced with a covenant in a deed of land forbidding the land's sale to "Jews or persons of objectionable nationality." The judge held the covenant to be void as inconsistent with Canadian public policy. In determining that policy, Mackay J. looked not only to provincial anti-discrimination legislation but also to sources of international human rights law, then in their infancy. He quoted from the preamble of the UN Charter, and noted that, under articles 1 and 55, "Canada is pledged to promote 'universal respect for, and observance of, human rights and fundamental freedoms for all without distinction as to race, sex, language or religion.'"[108] He also took notice of the Atlantic Charter 1941,[109] noting that Canada had subscribed to it and that it recognized "the principles of freedom from fear and freedom of worship."[110] Mackay J. also relied on resolutions

---

105 *Re Alberta Statutes*, [1938] SCR 100 at 133–34 per Duff C.J.; *Saumur v. City of Quebec*, [1953] 2 SCR 299; *Switzman v. Elbling*, [1957] SCR 285 at 307 (per Rand J.) and 328 (per Abbott J.). But see *Attorney General of Canada and Dupond v. Montreal*, [1978] 2 SCR 770 at 796 per Beetz J.

106 For example *OPSEU v. Ontario (Attorney General)*, [1987] 2 SCR 2.

107 [1945] OR 778 [*Re Drummond Wren*].

108 *Ibid.* at 781.

109 [1942] CanTS no. 1. The Charter was a joint declaration on the purposes of the war issued by Britain and the US during a meeting in Newfoundland.

110 *Re Drummond Wren*, above note 107 at 781.

against racism adopted by international conferences and statements made by the Allied leaders promising accountability for the perpetrators of the Holocaust. He observed that "common law courts have, by their actions over the years, obviated the need for rigid constitutional guarantees in our policy by their wise use of the doctrine of public policy as an active agent in the promotion of the public weal" and concluded that he would not be "breaking new ground" but "applying well-recognized principles" by avoiding the impugned covenant.[111]

Though the correctness of *Re Drummond Wren* was once questioned,[112] it surely cannot be today. Human rights, either as implemented in domestic laws or expressed in international instruments to which Canada is a party or which enunciate customary international law, must appropriately be viewed as an expression of public policy, as that phrase is used in Canadian jurisprudence. While *Re Drummond Wren* is a contracts case, the principle that human rights form part of Canadian public policy surely extends beyond contract to any area of the law where public policy may arise.

---

111 *Ibid.* at 783.
112 *Re Noble and Wolf* [1948] OR 579. But see *Bhadauria v. Seneca College* (1979), 27 OR (2d) 142 at 147–49 per Wilson J.A. and *Seneca College v. Bhadauria,* [1981] 2 SCR 181 at 192 per Laskin C.J.

RECEPTION OF SPECIFIC INTERNATIONAL HUMAN RIGHTS

We observed in Chapter Eight that courts and counsel are often too quick to find that international human rights norms are not implemented in Canadian law. We argued that the absence of explicit implementing legislation must not be equated with non-implementation. In short, the concept of implementation is more subtle than is sometimes thought. The purpose of this chapter is to put this subtler conception of implementation into practice. We do so by isolating twenty human rights or groups of related human rights and describing them as they exist in both international and Canadian law. By so doing we are able to identify which domestic laws serve an implementing function by giving effect to Canada's international human rights obligations. We end this chapter with a discussion of international and Canadian provisions governing derogations from human rights norms.

It is not always easy to say whether the constitutional, quasi-constitutional, statutory, or common laws of Canada meet international requirements. Like all legal questions, this one often leaves room for reasonable disagreement. Accordingly, we do not attempt to pass judgment on Canada's domestic human rights record in respect of all the rights discussed below. But we do not hesitate to identify points of past and present difficulty where we see fit.

Each right or group of rights is addressed separately. First the right is described as it appears in instruments binding on Canada at international law, namely the UDHR, the ICCPR, the ICESCR, the CERD, the CEDAW, the CAT, the CRC, certain ILO treaties, the AmDR, and other binding instruments.[1] Next, the right is discussed as it appears in the main non-binding instruments, notably the ACHR and its protocols, the ECHR and its protocols, the EurSC,[2] the AfrCHPR and the AfrCHPR Women's Protocol, and other relevant instruments.[3] Finally, the right is examined as it appears in Canadian law. There is, admittedly, a certain artificiality to this approach, for many of the rights considered here do not easily stand alone but depend upon and overlap with others.

Canada's practice in international law is such that the distinction we draw between binding and non-binding instruments accords closely (but not exactly) to the distinction between UN instruments and instruments elaborated by regional human rights systems. Generally speaking, Canada participates very heavily in the UN treaty system and very little in the Inter-American and Council of Europe systems. This overlap between "binding" and "UN" on the one hand, and "non-binding" and "regional" on the other, is subject to one important exception: the AmDR. As explained in Chapter Six, the AmDR originated as a non-binding declaration but has since been held by the Inter-American Court of Human Rights to be an enunciation of human rights obligations binding on Canada and other parties to the Charter of the Organization of American States 1948.[4] The Canadian government acknowledges the binding character of the AmDR and recognizes the competence of the Inter-American Commission on Human Rights to entertain petitions from Canadians alleging violations of the AmDR.[5] We therefore include it within our discussions of binding instruments.

The AmDR is not the only formally non-binding instrument we treat as binding for the purposes of this chapter. As explained in Chapter Four, the UDHR is technically non-binding (being a resolution of the UN General Assembly), yet most of its provisions are widely considered to represent customary international law. Throughout this chapter we treat the UDHR as a binding instrument. We take the same approach to the ILO's so-called fundamental conventions,[6] whether Canada is a

---

1   On the bindingness of the UDHR and the AmDR, see the discussion immediately below.

2   We have omitted the Charter of Fundamental Rights of the European Union, which for the moment is not legally binding on EU member states.

3   We have omitted the MWC from our discussion. For more on the MWC, see Chapter Five.

4   [1990] CanTS no. 23.

5   See "Canada and the Inter-American Human Rights System," statement by Ambassador Peter M. Boehm, permanent representative of Canada to the OAS, 2 December 1999, OAS doc. OEA/Ser.G, CP/CAJP-1596/99.

6   See the discussion of the ILO in Chapter Seven.

party to them or not. We adopt this approach because the ILO does, but we acknowledge that it remains controversial in some quarters.

Three of the instruments considered below — the UDHR, the AmDR, and the *Charter* — include general limitations provisions applicable to all the rights and freedoms they proclaim. UDHR article 29(2) provides:

> In the exercise of his rights and freedoms, everyone shall be subject only to such limitations as are determined by law solely for the purpose of securing due recognition and respect for the rights and freedoms of others and of meeting the just requirements of morality, public order and the general welfare in a democratic society.

AmDR article 28 provides:

> The rights of man are limited by the rights of others, by the security of all, and by the just demands of the general welfare and the advancement of democracy.

Finally, *Charter* section 1 provides:

> The *Canadian Charter of Rights and Freedoms* guarantees the rights and freedoms set out in it subject only to such reasonable limits prescribed by law as can be demonstrably justified in a free and democratic society.

The reader should bear these limitation provisions in mind in the discussions that follow.

With some exceptions, we are forced by space constraints to limit our discussion of the international human rights described below to a survey of the relevant treaty provisions. We wish to emphasize, however, that an appreciation of the complete international legal position requires consideration of international custom, the jurisprudence of international courts and treaty bodies,[7] and international legal scholarship. Similarly, our discussion of the applicable Canadian law is necessarily somewhat brief. We make no attempt to address *Charter*

---

7   This material is readily accessible online and has been examined in countless academic texts and commentaries. See, for example, M. Castan, S. Joseph, & J. Schultz, *The International Covenant on Civil and Political Rights: Cases, Materials, and Commentary* (Oxford: Oxford University Press, 2000) and N. Jayawickrama, *The Judicial Application of Human Rights Law: National Regional and International Jurisprudence* (Cambridge: Cambridge University Press, 2002). For a summary of the workings and the Canadian jurisprudence of the Human Rights Committee, see J. Harrington, "How Canadian Lawyers Can Contribute to the Effectiveness of the UN Human Rights Committee" (forthcoming paper in the 2002 proceedings of the Annual Conference of the Canadian Council of International Law).

jurisprudence in general, or to provide a complete account of such vast disciplines as Canadian labour or family law.

A. FREEDOM OF THOUGHT, CONSCIENCE AND RELIGION

This fundamental freedom encompasses thought on all matters, personal conviction, and the belief in and practice of religion, broadly construed.

1) In Binding Instruments

UDHR article 18 provides, "Everyone has the right to freedom of thought, conscience and religion; this right includes freedom to change his religion or belief, and freedom, either alone or in community with others and in public or private, to manifest his religion or belief in teaching, practice, worship and observance."

Freedom of thought, conscience and religion is protected in ICCPR article 18(1) in language similar to UDHR article 18.[8] Other ICCPR provisions protect against impairment of the freedom to adopt a religion or belief[9] and recognize the liberty of parents and guardians to ensure the religious and moral education of their children in conformity with their own convictions.[10] ICCPR article 18(3) provides, "Freedom to manifest one's religion or beliefs may be subject only to such limitations as are prescribed by law and are necessary to protect public safety, order, health, or morals or the fundamental rights and freedoms of others."

CERD article 5(d)(vii) requires states parties to guarantee the right of everyone, "without distinction as to race, colour, or national or ethnic origin," to equal enjoyment of freedom of thought, conscience and religion.

CRC article 14(1) requires states parties to "respect the right of the child to freedom of thought, conscience and religion." CRC article 14(2) requires states parties to "respect the rights and duties of the parents and, when applicable, legal guardians, to provide direction to the child in the exercise of his or her right in a manner consistent with the evolving capacities of the child." Finally, article 14(3) permits only such limitations on the right to manifest one's religion or beliefs "as are prescribed by law and are necessary to protect public safety, order, health or morals, or the fundamental rights and freedoms of others."

---

8   See ICCPR General Comment 22 (1993) at paras. 1–11.

9   International Covenant on Civil and Political Rights 1966 (ICCPR), [1976] CanTS no. 47, art. 18(2).

10   *Ibid.*, art. 18(4).

AmDR article 3 declares the right of every person "freely to profess a religious faith, and to manifest and practice it both in public and in private." There is no express guarantee of freedom of conscience in the AmDR.

2) In Non-Binding Instruments

ACHR article 12 declares the right of everyone to freedom of conscience and religion subject only to limits prescribed by law that are necessary to protect public safety, order, health, or morals, or the rights and freedoms of others. ACHR article 13 guarantees freedom of thought and expression.

ECHR article 9(1) guarantees freedom of thought, conscience and religion in terms very similar to UDHR article 18, while article 9(2) provides that "[f]reedom to manifest one's religion or beliefs shall be subject only to such limitations as are prescribed by law and are necessary in a democratic society in the interests of public safety, for the protection of public order, health or morals, or for the protection of the rights and freedoms of others."

AfrCHPR article 8 provides simply, "Freedom of conscience, the profession and free practice of religion shall be guaranteed. No one may, subject to law and order, be submitted to measures restricting the exercise of these freedoms." Freedom of thought is not expressly mentioned.

3) In Canadian Law

Unlike the UN instruments, the *Charter* does not treat freedom of thought, conscience and religion together. *Charter* section 2 guarantees "freedom of conscience and religion" at paragraph (a) and "freedom of thought, belief, opinion and expression, including freedom of the press and other media of communication" at paragraph (b). That difference in presentation aside, it is clear that these provisions of the *Charter* are Canada's principal means of fulfilling its international undertakings to protect freedom of thought, conscience and religion. Other Canadian laws that serve to implement Canada's obligations under this heading include section 1(c) and (d) of the *Canadian Bill of Rights* (which omits mention of freedom of conscience) and certain provincial and territorial bills of rights.[11]

---

11   *Yukon Human Rights Act* SY 1987 c. 3 ss. 3, 4; *Alberta Bill of Rights* RSA 2000 c. A-14 s. 1(c) and (d); *Saskatchewan Human Rights Code* SS 1979 c. S-24.1 ss. 4, 5; *Quebec Charter of Human Rights and Freedoms*, RSQ c. C-12, s. 3 [*Quebec Charter*].

Schabas has observed that Canadian courts have found resort to international human rights provisions useful in *Charter* section 2 analysis in part because that section is so succinct; the more detailed international instruments may help elucidate the *Charter*'s meaning.[12] An example of this occurs in the reasons of Tarnopolsky J.A. for the Court of Appeal for Ontario in R. v. *Edwards Books and Art Ltd*:

> It will be noted that the right [in ICCPR article 18] is defined as including not only the right to have or adopt a religion or belief of one's choice, but also to be able to "manifest" the religion or belief "in worship, observance, practice and teaching." The pertinent part of the definition of the word "manifest" in *Webster's New World Dictionary* provides: "to make clear or evident; show plainly; reveal; evince." The *Oxford Dictionary* definition is as follows: "To make evident to the eye or to the mind; to show plainly; to display (a quality, condition, feeling, etc.); to reveal the presence of, evince." It is manifest, to use the term in another connotation, that all religions require their adherents to observe the tenets of that religion by various practices which would appear to others to have a purely secular significance. . . . Such observations, when practised as part of a religious observance, have to be considered within the scope of one's religious freedom. This is so even though what is a religious practice for people of one religion is secular for those of another and vice versa.[13]

This interpretation of *Charter* section 2(a) to include the ability to manifest one's religion or belief, as provided by ICCPR article 18, was affirmed by the majority of the Supreme Court of Canada on appeal. As Dickson C.J. put it, Tarnopolsky J.A.'s definition of freedom of religion to include the freedom to manifest and practice one's religion "anticipated conclusions which were reached by this court in the *Big M Drug Mart* case" (which had not been decided at the time Tarnopolsky J.A. wrote).[14]

To justify his resort to ICCPR article 18 in construing *Charter* section 2(a), Tarnopolsky J.A. invoked the presumption of conformity:

> Both a textual comparison and a review of the evidence before the Special Joint Committee of the Senate and House of Commons on the Constitution, 1981–82, confirm that the International Covenant on

---

12 W. Schabas, *International Human Rights Law and the Canadian Charter*, 2d ed. (Scarborough: Carswell, 1996) at 132.

13 (1984) 48 OR (2d) 395 at 421 (CA) [*Edwards Books* CA], also reported under the name R. v. *Videoflicks Ltd. et al*.

14 R. v. *Edwards Books and Art Ltd.*, [1986] 2 SCR 713 at 735 [*Edwards*]; R. v. *Big M Drug Mart Ltd.*, [1985] 1 SCR 295.

Civil and Political Rights was an important source of the terms chosen [for *Charter* section 2]. Since Canada ratified that covenant in
1976, with the unanimous consent of the federal and provincial governments, the covenant constitutes an obligation upon Canada under
international law, by article 2 thereof, to implement its provisions
within this country. Although our constitutional tradition is not that
a ratified treaty is self-executing within our territory, but must be
implemented by the domestic constitutional process . . . nevertheless,
unless the domestic law is clearly to the contrary, it should be interpreted in conformity with our international obligations. Therefore,
article 18 of the covenant is pertinent to our consideration of the definition of freedom of conscience and religion under the *Charter*.[15]

The present authors respectfully agree with this approach.

The Supreme Court of Canada has held that freedom of religion
under the *Charter* encompasses the right of parents to educate their children according to their own religious beliefs,[16] and that this right includes
the right of parents to make medical treatment decisions for their children on religious grounds.[17] These decisions appear to be consistent with
Canada's obligation under ICCPR article 18(4) to respect the liberty of
parents to ensure the religious and moral education of their children in
conformity with their own convictions.[18] One may wonder, however,
whether CRC article 14(2) imposes a more child-centred approach to this
right. That article requires states parties to respect the rights and duties
of parents or guardians to "provide direction" to children in the exercise
of their own freedom of thought, conscience and religion "in a manner
consistent with the evolving capacities of the child." The apparent divergence between the two treaties on this point has been a source of controversy internationally,[19] but has not yet been considered in Canadian law.

B. FREEDOM OF OPINION AND EXPRESSION

International and Canadian law alike protect this freedom while
acknowledging permissible limits on some types of expression.

---

15 *Edwards Books* CA, above note 13 at 420.
16 *R. v. Jones*, [1986] 2 SCR 284 [*Jones*].
17 *B.(R.) v. Children's Aid Society of Metropolitan Toronto*, [1995] 1 SCR 315 at para.
    105 [*Children's Aid*].
18 See also International Covenant on Economic, Social and Cultural Rights 1966
    (ICESCR), [1996] CanTS no. 46, art. 13(3).
19 See G. van Bueren, *The International Law on the Rights of the Child* (Dordrecht:
    Martinus Nijhoff, 1995) at 152, 155–59 [van Bueren, *International Law*].

1) In Binding Instruments

UDHR article 19 guarantees the right of everyone to freedom of opinion and expression, including freedom to hold opinions without interference and to seek, receive, and impart information and ideas through any media and regardless of frontiers.

These freedoms are affirmed and elaborated upon in ICCPR article 19(1) and (2).[20] The ICCPR also imposes certain restrictions on freedom of expression (but not freedom of opinion) in recognition of the "special duties and responsibilities" that freedom of expression carries with it. These restrictions "shall only be such as are provided by law and are necessary" for respect of the rights or reputations of others, or for protection of national security or of public order, or of public health or morals.[21] There are further restrictions on freedom of expression in ICCPR article 20: states parties are required to prohibit by law any propaganda for war[22] and any advocacy of national, racial, or religious hatred constituting incitement to discrimination, hostility, or violence.[23]

Children enjoy freedom of expression under CRC article 13(1) in terms identical to those used in ICCPR article 19(2). Curiously, however, children's freedom of opinion is not enshrined in the CRC. The omission is probably of no legal consequence for Canada given that children come within the term "everyone" in ICCPR article 19(1). Canada and other states parties to the CRC must also assure "to the child who is capable of forming his or her own views the right to express those views freely in all matters affecting the child, the views of the child being given due weight in accordance with the age and maturity of the child."[24] This provision serves to recognize that, where children are concerned, mere protection from state interference is not always enough to guarantee freedom of expression. Children may also need positive action to facilitate their self-expression in criminal trials, custody hearings, and other proceedings involving them.[25]

The CERD also guarantees freedom of opinion and expression, but subject to important limits on hate speech. Article 5(d)(viii) requires

---

20   See generally ICCPR General Comment 10 (1983) and ICCPR General Comment 11 (1983).
21   ICCPR, above note 9, art. 19(3)(a) and (b).
22   *Ibid.*, art. 20(1).
23   *Ibid.*, art. 20(2); see also Universal Declaration of Human Rights 1948 (UDHR), GA res. 217 (III) (1948), art. 7.
24   Convention on the Rights of the Child 1989 (CRC), [1992] CanTS no. 3, art. 12(1); see also art. 12(2).
25   van Bueren, *International Law*, above note 19 at 131-2.

states parties to guarantee the right of everyone, "without distinction as to race, colour, or national or ethnic origin" to equal enjoyment of freedom of opinion and expression. Yet CERD article 4(a) expresses states parties' condemnation of racist propaganda and requires states parties to make "all dissemination of ideas based on racial superiority or hatred" and "incitement to racial discrimination" an "offence punishable by law." The definition of racial discrimination in CERD article 1(1) is broad. It includes "any distinction, exclusion, restriction or preference based on race, colour, descent, or national or ethnic origin."

AmDR article 4 recognizes the right to "freedom of investigation, of opinion, and of expression and dissemination of ideas, by any medium whatsoever." It includes no express prohibition of war propaganda or hate speech.

2) In Non-Binding Instruments

ACHR article 13(1) guarantees "freedom of thought and expression" in terms very similar to ICCPR article 19(2). Also like the ICCPR, the ACHR requires that propaganda for war and advocacy of hatred "be considered as offences punishable by law."[26] The ACHR also prohibits indirect restrictions on expression "such as the abuse of government or private controls over newsprint, radio broadcasting frequencies, or equipment used in the dissemination of information."[27] Prior censorship of public entertainments is expressly permitted under ACHR article 13(4) "for the sole purpose of regulating access to them for the moral protection of childhood and adolescence." Article 14(1) provides that persons injured by "inaccurate or offensive statements or ideas disseminated to the public" by legally-regulated media have a right "to reply or to make correction using the same communications outlet," subject to conditions established by law.

ECHR article 10(1) recognizes the right of everyone to freedom of expression in terms similar to UDHR article 19. A qualification is added: states parties may nevertheless require the licensing of broadcasting, television, or cinema enterprises. The right to free expression is limited by article 10(2), which enunciates the standard grounds of limitation in the ECHR (national security, public safety, prevention of disorder or crime, protection of health or morals, and protection of the health of others), but adds to this list limits based on "the protection

---

26   American Convention on Human Rights 1969 (ACHR), 1969 OAS TS no. 36, art. 13(5).

27   *Ibid.*, art. 13(3).

of the reputation or rights of others, for preventing the disclosure of information received in confidence, or for maintaining the authority and impartiality of the judiciary." The ECHR contains no express prohibition of war propaganda or hate speech, yet the European Court of Human Rights has found that states may more easily justify interference with expression when it involves hate or appeals to violence.[28]

AfrCHPR article 9 recognizes the right of every individual to receive information and the right to express and disseminate his opinions "within the law." There is no express prohibition of war propaganda or hate speech.

3) In Canadian Law

Charter section 2(b) guarantees everyone "freedom of thought, belief, opinion and expression, including freedom of the press and other media of communication." We have already observed that section 2(b) differs from most international instruments by including "thought" as part of its freedom of expression guarantee rather than its guarantee of freedom of religion and conscience. This appears to be a distinction without a difference. Clearly, *Charter* section 2(b) is the primary means by which Canada discharges its obligations to safeguard freedom of opinion and expression. Similar guarantees are found in section 1(d) of the *Canadian Bill of Rights* and in certain provincial and territorial enactments.[29]

The *Charter* makes no reference to war propaganda or hate speech. In respect of war propaganda (which Canada is required by ICCPR article 20(1) to prohibit by law), there is no law of Canada which explicitly prohibits it.[30] Canada appears to be in breach of the ICCPR to this extent.[31] In its first state report to the Human Rights Committee, Cana-

---

28   C. Ovey & R. White, *Jacobs and White, The European Convention on Human Rights*, 3d ed. (Oxford: Oxford University Press, 2002) at 280–82.

29   *Yukon Human Rights Act*, above note 11, s. 4; *Alberta Bill of Rights*, above note 11, s. 1(d); *Saskatchewan Human Rights Code*, above note 11, s. 5; *Quebec Charter*, above note 11, s. 3.

30   Note that the Supreme Court of Canada's jurisprudence on *Charter* s. 2(b) has tended to avoid internal limitations on free expression. Thus a law implementing art. 20 would probably infringe s. 2(b) and need to pass s. 1 scrutiny to be valid.

31   *Criminal Code*, RSC 1995 c. C-46, s. 319 (which prohibits hate propaganda) is not, in our view, broad enough to prohibit war propaganda. That section speaks of inciting or promoting hatred against "any identifiable group" where "identifiable group" means "any section of the public distinguished by colour, race, religion or ethnic origin." It is difficult to see how a foreign state, against which war is advocated, might be described as a section of the public. Furthermore, it is a well-established rule of statutory interpretation that criminal provisions are to be read narrowly.

da admitted that there is no law prohibiting propaganda for war and that an individual or organization may, therefore, legally disseminate such propaganda. Canada noted, however, that the government itself cannot do so without violating ICCPR article 20. But Canada seems already to have violated article 20 simply by failing to implement that commitment in Canadian law.[32] In their consideration of Canada's first state report, some members of the Human Rights Committee noted this and sought clarification of Canada's position.[33] The matter has not been taken up in subsequent Canadian state reports.

Turning to hate speech, sections 318–320.1 of the *Criminal Code* prohibit the promotion of genocide, the incitement and promotion of hatred, and the distribution of hate propaganda. The constitutionality of section 319 (the hate speech prohibition) was upheld by the Supreme Court of Canada in *R. v. Keegstra*.[34] Keegstra was an anti-Semite who used his position as a high school teacher to spread his racist views. He was charged under section 319(2), which prohibits the wilful promotion of hatred of identifiable groups other than in private conversation. Both the majority and the dissent agreed that section 319(2) infringed *Charter* section 2(b). Yet the majority upheld the law under section 1, while the dissent would have invalidated it. The reasons of both are illuminating.

Dickson C.J. (with Wilson, L'Heureux-Dubé, and Gonthier JJ.) upheld the legislation. He considered first whether section 2(b) was infringed by the hate speech provisions. He noted that international agreements to which Canada is a party (namely the ICCPR and the CERD), along with the equality and multiculturalism provisions of the *Charter*, supported the view that section 2(b) itself should be internally limited "so as not to extend to communications which seriously undermine the equality, security and dignity of others."[35] Yet he preferred to grant section 2(b) a "large and liberal interpretation," saying that *Charter* section 1 is "especially well suited to the task of balanc-

---

32 "For article 20 to become fully effective there ought to be a law making it clear that propaganda and advocacy as described therein are contrary to public policy and providing for an appropriate sanction in case of violation. The Committee, therefore, believes that States parties which have not yet done so should take the measures necessary to fulfil the obligations contained in article 20 . . .": ICCPR General Comment 11 (1983) at para. 2.

33 Human Rights Committee, *Concluding Observations: Canada* (1980) UN doc. A/35/40 at para. 171.

34 [1990] 3 SCR 697 [*Keegstra*].

35 *Ibid.* at 733.

ing" competing values for the purpose of rights limitation.[36] Turning next to section 1, Dickson C.J. began by rejecting the American approach to freedom of speech, as advocated by the dissent. Here again he invoked Canada's international obligations, saying that

> the international commitment to eradicate hate propaganda and, most importantly, the special role given equality and multiculturalism in the Canadian Constitution necessitate a departure from the view, reasonably present in America at present, that the suppression of hate propaganda is incompatible with the guarantee of free expression.[37]

Having made these brief but significant references to international law, Dickson C.J. went on to address the international position at length. Having already established "a great deal of support . . . for the conclusion that the harm caused by hate propaganda represents a pressing and substantial concern in a free and democratic society," he added that reference to international human rights principles also offers guidance with respect to assessing the legislative objective at this stage of the constitutional analysis.[38] "Generally speaking," said Dickson C.J.,

> the international human rights obligations taken on by Canada reflect the values and principles of a free and democratic society, and thus those values and principles that underlie the *Charter* itself (*Reference re Public Service Employee Relations Act (Alta.)*, [1987] 1 S.C.R. 313, per Dickson C.J., at p. 348). Moreover, international human rights law and Canada's commitments in that area are of particular significance in assessing the importance of Parliament's objective under section 1. As stated in *Slaight Communications Inc. v. Davidson, supra,* at pp. 1056–57:
>
> > . . . Canada's international human rights obligations should inform not only the interpretation of the content of the rights guaranteed by the *Charter* but also the interpretation of what can constitute pressing and substantial section 1 objectives which may justify restrictions upon those rights.
>
> In the context of justifying an infringement of section 2(b), the majority in *Slaight* made a point of noting that a value enjoying status as an international human right is generally to be ascribed a high degree of importance under section 1 of the *Charter* (pp. 1056–57).[39]

---

36 *Ibid.* at 734.
37 *Ibid.* at 744.
38 *Ibid.* at 749.
39 *Ibid.* at 750.

Having thus established the relevance of international law to the section 1 inquiry, Dickson C.J. surveyed Canada's obligations to combat racism and hatred under the CERD and the ICCPR, concluding that "the protection provided freedom of expression by [these treaties] does not extend to cover communications advocating racial or religious hatred."[40] After briefly canvassing ECHR article 10 and the case law arising from it, Dickson C.J. returned to Canada's binding obligations. He observed that the CERD and the ICCPR "demonstrate that the prohibition of hate-promoting expression is considered to be not only compatible with a signatory nation's guarantee of human rights, but is as well an obligatory aspect of this guarantee."[41] In our view, Dickson C.J.'s recognition of Canada's legal obligation to prohibit hate speech is what most differentiates — and recommends — his approach over that of the dissent.[42] Dickson C.J. concluded that "finding the correct balance between prohibiting hate propaganda and ensuring freedom of expression has been a source of debate internationally" but

> . . . Canada, along with other members of the international community, has indicated a commitment to prohibiting hate propaganda, and in my opinion this Court must have regard to that commitment in investigating the nature of the government objective behind section 319(2) of the *Criminal Code*. That the international community has collectively acted to condemn hate propaganda, and to oblige State Parties to CERD and ICCPR to prohibit such expression, thus emphasizes the importance of the objective behind section 319(2) and the principles of equality and the inherent dignity of all persons that infuse both international human rights and the *Charter*.[43]

---

40   *Ibid.* at 752. See ICCPR General Comment 11 (1983) at para. 2.

41   *Keegstra, ibid.* at 754.

42   Dickson C.J.'s approach is also, in our view, a notable repudiation of the "relevant and persuasive" approach to international law and the *Charter* (see Chapter Nine). Dickson C.J. did not simply consider international norms or values. Rather, he carefully distinguished binding (CERD and ICCPR) from non-binding (ECHR) instruments, reiterated the obligatory nature of the former on Canada as a matter of international law, and informed his interpretation of *Charter* s. 1 accordingly. Though Dickson C.J. did not give direct legal effect to these treaties, he did give them a degree of legal weight. By upholding the impugned legislation (as he went on to do), Dickson C.J. effectively applied the presumption of conformity to the *Charter*, for he avoided an interpretation of the *Charter* which, by invalidating Canada's hate propaganda laws, would have placed Canada in default of its international obligations.

43   *Keegstra,* above note 34 at 754–55.

In dissent, McLachlin J. (Sopinka J. concurring, La Forest J. concurring in part) took a rather different approach to Canada's international obligations. Her analysis posited two 'approaches' to freedom of expression, the American and the international: "On the international approach, the objective of suppressing hatred appears to be sufficient to override freedom of expression. In the United States, it is necessary to go much further and show clear and present danger before free speech can be overridden."[44] Whatever the truth in this analysis, it ought to be beside the point. American law is not binding on Canada, while the international law at issue in *Keegstra* (namely the CERD and the ICCPR) is. And yet, in a striking repudiation of the presumption of conformity, McLachlin J. concluded that the *Charter* "follows the American approach."[45] It must be noted that this conclusion came in McLachlin J.'s section 2(b) analysis; it need not have led to a finding that the hate propaganda provisions were unconstitutional, for there remained the possibility of saving them at section 1. Indeed, McLachlin J.'s result was no different than Dickson C.J.'s at this point: both agreed that the impugned provisions infringed section 2(b). Nevertheless, McLachlin J.'s reasoning is notably less solicitous of Canada's international human rights obligations than that of the chief justice.[46] This "take it or leave it" approach to international law returns in McLachlin J.'s section 1 analysis:

> Canada's international obligations, and the accords negotiated between international governments may well be helpful in placing *Charter* interpretation in a larger context. Principles agreed upon by free and democratic societies may inform the reading given to certain of its guarantees. It would be wrong, however, to consider these obligations as determinative of or limiting the scope of those guarantees. The provisions of the *Charter*, though drawing on a political and social philosophy shared with other democratic societies, are uniquely Canadian. As a result, considerations may point, as they do in this case, to a conclusion regarding a rights violation which is not necessarily in accord with those international covenants.[47]

---

44 *Ibid.* at 822.
45 *Ibid.*
46 Even McLachlin J.'s language serves to deny or play down the legal nature of the CERD and ICCPR. She speaks of the "international approach," the "international experience," the "international tradition," and the "international viewpoint" rather than speaking simply of "international law," "international obligations," and "international requirements."
47 *Keegstra* above note 34 at 838.

This passage takes the "relevant and persuasive approach," criticized in Chapter Nine, to its extreme but logical conclusion: the relegation of international legal norms to merely comparative documents of no legal significance for *Charter* interpretation. McLachlin J. went on to find that the impugned legislation was not saved by section 1 and was therefore invalid. She claimed, however, not to be of the view "that any measures taken to implement Canada's international obligations to combat racial discrimination and hate propaganda must necessarily be unconstitutional" for those obligations "are general in nature" and need not be fulfilled by means of *Criminal Code* section 319(2).[48] Yet it is unclear from her reasons what McLachlin J. thought could be done to implement Canada's obligation to prohibit by law (ICCPR article 20(2)) and criminalize (CERD article 4) hate propaganda without violating the *Charter*.

The question of hate propaganda in international law arose again in *R. v. Zundel*,[49] in which a Holocaust denier was accused of spreading false news contrary to *Criminal Code* section 181. This provision originated from a thirteenth-century English law intended to protect the "great men of the realm" from slander. The majority of the Supreme Court of Canada held that section 181 infringed *Charter* section 2(b) and was not saved by section 1. In coming to this conclusion the majority noted that section 181 was not required to implement Canada's international human rights obligations.[50] The dissenting judges would have saved section 181 at the section 1 stage. They relied in part on the ICCPR and CERD, which "serve to emphasize the important objective of section 181 in preventing the harm caused by calculated falsehoods which are likely to injure the public interest in racial and social tolerance."[51]

The Human Rights Committee has found Canada in violation of its ICCPR obligations in cases arising from Quebec's language laws. In *Ballantyne, Davidson and McIntyre v. Canada*,[52] the Committee found

---

48 *Ibid.* at 838–39.
49 [1992] 2 SCR 731 [*Zundel*].
50 *Ibid.* at 764. The majority's exact words were, "It is noteworthy that no suggestion has been made before this Court that Canada's obligations under the international human rights conventions to which it is a signatory require the enactment of any provision(s) other than that section which was under review in *Keegstra*: s. 319. The retention of s. 181 is not therefore necessary to fulfil any international obligation undertaken by Parliament." The reader will note the errors in this passage. It is the Crown, not Parliament, that undertakes international obligations. And for "signatory" the majority clearly means "party."
51 *Ibid.* at 811.
52 (1993) Comm. nos. 359/1989 and 385/1989/Rev.1 [*Ballantyne*].

that Quebec's commercial sign laws, which at the time prohibited advertising in English, unnecessarily restricted the complainants' right to freedom of expression under ICCPR article 19(2). The Committee noted that a state may choose one or more official languages but may not exclude, outside the spheres of public life, the freedom to express oneself in a language of one's choice.[53] The Committee reached the same conclusion one year later in another complaint, *Singer v. Canada*.[54] Quebec's current legislation provides that commercial advertising must be in French, but may also be in another language provided that French is markedly predominant.[55] It is notable that in *Ballantyne*, the Human Rights Committee observed that the goal of protecting Canada's vulnerable francophone minority could have been achieved without restricting freedom of expression by requiring that advertising be in both French and English.

The Canadian law of defamation may act as a limit on free expression. See the discussion of the right to privacy, below.

C. FREEDOM OF PEACEFUL ASSEMBLY

Though widely acknowledged as a basic civil liberty, the right to assemble has generated relatively little international and Canadian legal attention.

1) In Binding Instruments

UDHR article 20(1) recognizes the right of everyone to "peaceful assembly." ICCPR article 21 does the same, adding that no restrictions may be placed on the exercise of this right "other than those imposed in conformity with the law and which are necessary in a democratic society in the interests of national security or public safety, public order (*ordre public*), the protection of public health or morals or the protection of the rights and freedoms of others." The right to peaceful assembly is also recognized in CERD article 5(d)(ix) and CRC article 15(1). AmDR article 21 provides, "Everyone has the right to assemble peaceably with others in a formal public meeting or an informal gathering, in connection with matters of common interest of any nature."

---

53   *Ibid.* at para. 11.4.
54   (1994) Comm. no. 455/1991 [*Singer*].
55   *Charter of the French Language* RSQ c. C-11 s. 58.

2) In Non-Binding Instruments

ACHR article 15 recognizes the "right of peaceful assembly, without arms." The right is limited in words that repeat the limitation in ICCPR article 21 almost exactly. The right is also recognized in EHCR article 11(1), subject to the standard ECHR rights limitation in article 11(2) and a further proviso that article 11 "shall not prevent the imposition of lawful restrictions on the exercise of these rights by members of the armed forces, of the police or of the administration of the State." AfrCHPR article 11 grants every individual "the right to assemble freely with others" subject to "necessary restrictions provided for by law in particular those enacted in the interest of national security, the safety, health, ethics and rights and freedoms of others."

3) In Canadian Law

Charter section 2(c) guarantees everyone the fundamental freedom of "peaceful assembly." Similarly, section 1(e) of the *Bill of Rights* protects "freedom of assembly." The freedom is also protected in certain provincial instruments.[56]

Hogg observes that the qualification "peaceful" in *Charter* section 2(c) is not found in the *Bill of Rights'* counterpart to this provision, and that this addition brings the *Charter* closer to the first amendment of the US *Constitution*.[57] In our view, the better comparison is with the UDHR and ICCPR provisions, which employ the very same wording.[58] The word "peaceful" acts as an internal limit on the right; section 2(c) is the only "fundamental freedom" subject to an explicit internal limitation. This is all the more notable given that the freedoms guaranteed by section 2 are negative rather than positive in nature, that is, they require state restraint not state action.

The right of peaceful assembly has generated surprisingly little Canadian case law. The Supreme Court of Canada has yet to consider *Charter* section 2(c), nor have courts of appeal considered it in any depth.[59]

---

56 *Yukon Human Rights Act*, above note 11, s. 5; *Alberta Bill of Rights* , above note 11, s. 1(e); *Saskatchewan Human Rights Code,* above note 11, s. 6; *Quebec Charter*, above note 11, s. 3.

57 P. Hogg, *Constitutional Law of Canada*, looseleaf ed. (Scarborough: Carswell, 1997) at s. 41.2 [Hogg, *Constitutional Law*].

58 See Chapter Nine.

59 See K. Norman, "Freedom of Peaceful Assembly and Freedom of Association" in G. Beaudoin & E. Mendes, *The Canadian Charter of Rights and Freedoms*, 3d ed (Montreal: Wilson & Lafleur, 1996) at 299–307.

Perhaps the leading case on freedom of assembly in Canada is *Attorney General of Canada and Dupond v. Montreal*,[60] a pre-*Charter* decision in which the Court declined to strike down a city bylaw restricting public assembly saying,

> The right to hold public meetings on a highway or in a park is unknown to English law. Far from being the object of a right, the holding of a public meeting on a street or in a park may constitute a trespass against the urban authority in whom the ownership of the street is vested even though no one is obstructed and no injury is done; it may also amount to a nuisance.[61]

No reference to Canada's international obligations was made. One must seriously doubt whether *Dupond* remains good law after the enactment of the *Charter*.

D. FREEDOM OF ASSOCIATION

The human right freely to associate with others is a broad one. Yet it has particular resonance in the context of rights of workers to unionize, to bargain collectively, and to strike. This is particularly so in Canadian law, where many of the most contentious cases on the ambit of freedom of association have arisen from the labour law context. For more on international labour law, see Chapters Seven and Eleven.

1) In Binding Instruments

UDHR article 20(1) provides that everyone has the right to "freedom of peaceful assembly and association." Article 20(2) adds that no one may be compelled to belong to an association.

ICCPR article 22(1) provides, "Everyone shall have the right to freedom of association with others, including the right to form and join trade unions for the protection of his interests."[62] Article 22(2) limits this right on the grounds of national security or public safety, public order, the protection of public health or morals, or the protection of the rights and freedoms of others, and adds that article 22 "shall not pre-

---

60   [1978] 2 SCR 770 [*Dupond*].
61   *Ibid.* at 797.
62   The specific right to form and join trade unions is also protected in UDHR, above note 23, art. 23(4); ICESCR, above note 18, art. 8(1)(a); and the International Convention on the Elimination of All Forms of Racial Discrimination 1966 (CERD) [1970] CanTS no. 28, art. 5(e)(ii).

vent the imposition of lawful restrictions on members of the armed forces and of the police in their exercise of this right." Article 22(3) provides that nothing in article 22 shall authorize states parties to the ILO Freedom of Association and Protection of the Right to Organize Convention (No. 87) 1948[63] (of which Canada is one) to take "legislative measures which would prejudice, or to apply the law in such a manner as to prejudice, the guarantees provided for in that Convention." CRC article 15 recognizes the right of the child to freedom of association.

Freedom of association is both recognized and curtailed by the CERD. Article 5(d)(ix) affirms the right of everyone, without distinction, to equality before the law in the enjoyment of freedom of association. Yet article 4(b) requires states parties to "declare illegal and prohibit organizations . . . which promote and incite racial discrimination" and to "recognize participation in such organizations . . . as an offence punishable by law." Thus freedom of association in the CERD does not extend to association with racist organizations, which must be banned by Canada and other states parties.

Two of the ILO's eight "fundamental conventions"[64] concern freedom of association: the Freedom of Association and Protection of the Right to Organize Convention (No. 87) 1948[65] (to which Canada is a party) and the Right to Organize and Collective Bargaining Convention (No. 98) 1949[66] (to which Canada is not a party).

Convention No. 87 protects the freedoms of association and organization of workers and employers. Article 2 provides that workers and employers, "without distinction whatsoever," have the right to establish and join organizations of their own choosing without previous authorization. Article 8 provides that in exercising their rights workers, employers, and their respective organizations shall respect the law of the land, but that the law of the land "shall not be such as to impair, nor shall it be so applied as to impair, the guarantees provided for in this Convention." Article 9(1) provides that national laws and regulations may determine the "extent to which the guarantees provided for in this Convention shall apply to the armed forces and the police."

---

63 [1973] CanTS no. 14.
64 "Fundamental conventions" are treated by the ILO as binding even on non-parties. See the discussion of the ILO in Chapter Seven. See also Y. Poisson & A. Torobin, "The Right to Organize and Collective Bargaining: Canada and International Labour Organization Convention 98" (1999) 2 Workplace Gazette 86 at 88, and B. Burkett, J. Craig, & S. Gallagher, "Canada and the ILO: Freedom of Association since 1982" (2003) 10 Canadian Labour and Employment Law Journal 231 at 239.
65 Above note 63.
66 96 UNTS 257.

Convention No. 98 protects the right to organize and to bargain collectively. Article 1 guarantees workers "adequate protection against acts of anti-union discrimination," particularly in respect of acts which make employment subject to quitting or not joining a union and to the dismissal or prejudicing of workers for their union activities. Article 2 protects against interference by employers' organizations in workers' organizations, or vice versa. Article 4 commits states parties to taking appropriate measures to encourage and promote the development of collective bargaining. Like Convention No. 87, this convention allows states parties to determine by domestic laws or regulations the application of these principles to the armed forces and the police.[67]

Like the ICCPR, AmDR article 22's guarantee of free association explicitly includes unions: "Everyone has the right to associate with others to promote, exercise and protect his legitimate interests of a political, economic, religious, social, cultural, professional, labour union or other nature."

As we noted in Chapter Seven, labour rights, including freedom of association, are addressed in the NAALC (the labour side-accord to NAFTA).[68] NAALC article 1(b) declares one of the treaty's objectives to be to "promote, to the maximum extent possible, the labour principles set out in Annex 1." This annex includes among its principles freedom of association and protection of the right to organize, the right to bargain collectively, and the right to strike. Yet the treaty's protection of these rights is notably qualified. The chapeau to Annex 1 explains that the states parties are committed to promote the listed labour principles "subject to each Party's domestic law." Similarly, article 2 of the treaty affirms "full respect for each Party's constitution" and recognizes "the right of each Party to establish its own domestic labour standards." Arguably, these provisions oust any attempt to expand the scope of freedom of association in domestic law by reference to the treaty.

2) In Non-Binding Instruments

ACHR article 16(1) recognizes "the right to associate freely" for various purposes including "labour"; the word "union" is not specified.[69]

---

67   See also art. 6: "This Convention does not deal with the position of public servants engaged in the administration of the state, nor shall it be construed as prejudicing their rights or status in any way."

68   See also similar labour side-accords with Chile and Costa Rica, discussed in Chapter Seven.

69   But see Additional Protocol to the American Convention on Human Rights in the Area of Economic, Social and Cultural Rights 1988 (ACHR-OP1), OAS TS no. 69, art. 8 (on trade union rights).

ECHR article 11(1) explicitly includes "the right [of everyone] to form and to join trade unions for the protection of his interests" in its freedom of association guarantee. AfrCHPR article 10 recognizes the right of every individual to free association "provided he abides by the law" but makes no reference to labour rights.

3) In Canadian Law

The most important provision implementing Canada's international obligation to guarantee freedom of association is *Charter* section 2(d), which provides that everyone has the "fundamental freedom" of "freedom of association." In *Professional Institute of the Public Service of Canada v. Northwest Territories (Commissioner)*, Sopinka J. described "four separate propositions" arising from the Supreme Court of Canada's jurisprudence on section 2(d):

> . . . first, that s. 2(d) protects the freedom to establish, belong to and maintain an association; second, that s. 2(d) does not protect an activity solely on the ground that the activity is a foundational or essential purpose of an association; third, that s. 2(d) protects the exercise in association of the constitutional rights and freedoms of individuals; and fourth, that s. 2(d) protects the exercise in association of the lawful rights of individuals.[70]

More recently, the majority of the court has noted that there will be occasions where a given activity does not fall within Sopinka J.'s third and fourth rules, yet prohibition of that activity may nevertheless infringe section 2(d).[71]

The meaning and extent of section 2(d) has been determined largely in the context of labour disputes. As we have seen, international labour law has much to say on the content of freedom of association. Thus, section 2(d) has been, and continues to be, a testing-ground for the reception of international law by the *Charter*. Earlier jurisprudence of the Supreme Court of Canada did not hesitate to depart from international norms in construing section 2(d). Later cases, however, may suggest a new willingness to conform to the international law of freedom of association.

In *Re Public Service Employee Relations Act (Alberta)*,[72] the majority of the Supreme Court of Canada held that freedom of association as

---

70 [1990] 2 SCR 367 at 401–2.
71 *Dunmore v. Ontario (Attorney General)*, [2001] 3 SCR 1016 at para. 16 [*Dunmore*].
72 [1987] 1 SCR 313 [*Re PSERA*].

guaranteed by *Charter* section 2(d) does not include a positive right to strike and to bargain collectively. Le Dain J. specifically denied that these rights are fundamental, describing them instead as "the creation of legislation, involving a balance of competing interests in a field which has been recognized by the courts as requiring a specialized expertise."[73] In dissent, Dickson C.J. relied heavily on international labour law, particularly Convention No. 87 and decisions of the ILO Committee on Freedom of Association (which hears complaints of alleged breaches of freedom of association).[74] He held that Canada "has undertaken as a binding international obligation to protect to some extent the associational freedoms of workers within Canada" and that this obligation "goes beyond merely protecting the formation of labour unions and provides protection of their essential activities — that is of collective bargaining and the freedom to strike."[75]

There can be little doubt that the majority's interpretation of freedom of association in *Re PSERA* is at odds with that of the ILO. Decisions of the Committee on Freedom of Association have described the rights to strike and to bargain collectively as fundamental human rights. As we have seen, "breaches" of Convention No. 98 by ILO member states are treated as justiciable by the ILO even in respect of states not parties to that treaty. The inconsistency of Canada's section 2(d) jurisprudence with Canada's international obligations has been commented upon by the Committee on Freedom of Association.[76] While

---

73 *Ibid.* at 391.
74 For more on the complaint process, see the discussion of international labour law mechanisms in Chapter Sixteen and Burkett *et al.*, above note 64.
75 *Re PSERA*, above note 72, at 359.
76 For example, in a case brought against Canada before the ILO Committee on Freedom of Association, the Committee observed:

> Finally, the Committee notes that the Supreme Court of Canada held in 1987 that the *Constitution Act* does not guarantee the right to strike, and that the freedom of association guaranteed by the *Canadian Charter of Rights*, which is enshrined in the *Constitution*, does not embody the right to strike. The Committee certainly respects the judgement of the highest court of Canada, but points out that this is a different forum and that the Committee's mandate is to evaluate, with a view to making a recommendation to the Governing Body, whether certain situations of fact and/or legislation are in conformity with the principles of freedom of association, as established in international Conventions.

The Committee concluded that, in spite of the Supreme Court's jurisprudence, Canada acted contrary to the principles of freedom of association by ordering striking postal workers back to work: *Complaint Against the Government of Canada Presented by the Canadian Labour Congress (CLC) and the Postal, Telegraph and Telephone International (PTTI)*, Freedom of Association cases vol. LXXII 1989 Series B no 3, report no. 268 case no. 1451 at paras. 103–4.

Canada generally has no obligation at international law to constitution-alize human rights, a final determination by the highest court in the land that there is no domestic legal remedy for a legislative failure to protect workers' rights to bargain collectively and to strike will violate international law to the extent that those rights are among Canada's international obligations.

Another controversy surrounding the meaning and reach of section 2(d) has been whether it includes the freedom not to associate. The *Charter* does not expressly guarantee such a right, but is it implicit in section 2(d)? We have seen that UDHR article 20(2) provides that no one may be compelled to belong to an association, but that this provision is not repeated in the ICCPR or other UN treaties. In *Lavigne v. OPSEU*, La Forest J. relied on UDHR article 20 in support of his conclusion that freedom of association included freedom from forced association, saying these freedoms "are not distinct rights, but two sides of a bilateral freedom which has as its unifying purpose the advancement of individual aspirations."[77] The inclusion of a right not to associate in *Charter* section 2(d) was affirmed in *R. v. Advance Cutting & Coring Ltd.*[78] Bastarache J. (dissenting on other grounds) invoked UDHR article 20, ICESCR article 8(1)(a) (on the right of everyone to "join the trade union of his choice"), and even AfrCHPR article 10 to support his conclusion. He also noted that the absence of the right not to be compelled to associate from the "international covenants" (presumably the ICCPR and the ICESCR) does not "minimize the negative right," for "the specificity of the international covenants did not replace the broad principles enunciated in the Universal Declaration."[79] Though the judges split on many other points, eight of the nine agreed that section 2(d) includes a right not to associate.

The Supreme Court of Canada reaffirmed its earlier case law on the scope of section 2(d) in the trade union context in *Delisle v. Canada (Deputy Attorney General)*.[80] Delisle was an RCMP officer and president of an RCMP employee association in Quebec. He challenged federal legislation excluding RCMP officers from the public service labour relations regime. His challenge failed. Bastarache J. for the majority affirmed that section 2(d) protects the rights of workers to form an independent employee association and to exercise in association the lawful rights of its members. But he declined to find that section 2(d)

---

77   [1990] 2 SCR 211 at 319.
78   [2001] 3 SCR 209 [*Advance Cutting*].
79   *Ibid.* at para. 14; see also the reasons of LeBel J. at paras. 192–94.
80   [1999] 2 SCR 989 [*Delisle*].

requires the inclusion of workers or associations in any particular statutory trade union regime. In short, the exclusion of RCMP officers from trade union representation and all it entails (collective bargaining, grievance procedures, prohibitions of unfair labour practices, etc.) did not infringe section 2(d). In dissent, Cory and Iacobucci JJ. emphasized that this appeal was not about the right to strike or to bargain collectively, yet they found that the exclusion of RCMP officers from the statutory regime was "anti-associational" and therefore contrary to section 2(d). Cory and Iacobucci JJ. noted (without seemingly drawing much from it) that the "fundamental freedom of the individual simply to participate in a union is widely recognized . . . in international covenants to which Canada is a party."[81]

Delisle is an unsatisfying case from the perspective of international labour and human rights law. The majority gave no consideration to Canada's obligations at all. The dissent referred to international norms in passing but gave them no clear weight. In particular, neither side gave any serious consideration to the fact that ILO Conventions Nos. 87 and 98 permit states to limit freedom of association in respect of the armed forces and the police. Had the court held that the exclusion of RCMP members from the statutory regime infringed section 2(d) but was saved under section 1 given the pressing and substantial importance of assuring reliable police services, this decision would seemingly have been consistent with Canada's international obligations.

From an international law perspective, surely the most intriguing section 2(d) case is *Dunmore v. Ontario (Attorney General)*.[82] Ontario enacted legislation to bring agricultural workers within the province's labour relations regime. In particular, the legislation extended trade union and collective bargaining rights to formerly-excluded workers. One year and one provincial election later, however, the Ontario legislature repealed that legislation and thereby returned agricultural workers to their excluded status. Workers challenged this repeal and won. For the majority of the Supreme Court of Canada, Bastarache J. held the repealing legislation to be an infringement of section 2(d) not justified by section 1.

At the outset of his reasons, Bastarache J. explained that his analysis of freedom of association under the *Charter* "aims to protect the full range of associational activity contemplated by the *Charter* and to honour Canada's obligations under international human rights law" —

---

81   *Ibid.* at para. 69; see also paras. 71 and 141.
82   *Dunmore*, above note 71.

thus setting a rather different tone than *Delisle*.[83] Bastarache J. began by establishing that the protection offered by section 2(d) is not limited to activities performable by individuals alone but includes activities that are collective in nature. He described this collective dimension of section 2(d) as "consistent with developments in international human rights law, as indicated by the jurisprudence of the Committee of Experts on the Application of Conventions and Recommendations and the ILO Committee on Freedom of Association."[84] Bastarache J. went on to conclude that the exclusion of agricultural workers from the Ontario labour relations scheme infringed section 2(d), calling this conclusion "not only implied by Canadian *Charter* jurisprudence but . . . also consistent with international human rights law."[85] He invoked Convention No. 87 articles 2 and 10, noting that Canada was a party to the convention and that its "broadly worded provisions confirm . . . that discriminatory treatment implicates not only an excluded group's dignity interest, but also its basic freedom of association."[86] Bastarache J. next invoked the Right of Association (Agriculture) Convention (No. 11) 1921,[87] an ILO convention to which Canada is not a party. But that did not discourage Bastarache J. from referring to it: "Although provincial jurisdiction has prevented Canada from ratifying Convention No. 11, together these conventions provide a normative foundation for prohibiting any form of discrimination in the protection of trade union freedoms."[88] This "foundation" was "fortified," in Bastarache J.'s view, by yet another ILO Convention to which Canada is not a party, namely the Rural Workers' Organization Convention (No. 141) 1975.

It is important to note the limits of Bastarache J.'s formulation of section 2(d). While he described the "freedom to organize" as lying "at

---

83 *Ibid.* at para. 13. The seeming inconsistencies between *Delisle* and *Dunmore* are discussed in Hogg, above note 57 at section 41.3(b).

84 *Dunmore*, *ibid.* at para. 16.

85 *Ibid.* at para. 27.

86 *Ibid.*

87 38 UNTS 153.

88 *Dunmore*, above note 71 at para. 27. This passage is somewhat troubling. In principle, a court should not look behind the reason why Canada has declined to ratify a given treaty and decide what legal effect should be given to that refusal. This is particularly so where the reason is said to be (as here) a constitutional one, namely divided legislative competence in the area of labour relations. Furthermore, the use of an unratified treaty to "provide a normative foundation" for domestic legal decision-making seems inconsistent with the repeated refusals of Canadian courts to give legal effect to Canada's actual treaty obligations unless they are implemented by legislation.

the core of the *Charter's* protection of freedom of association,"[89] he nevertheless acknowledged, and did not explicitly doubt, the court's jurisprudence denying constitutional status to the rights to strike and to bargain collectively.[90] *Dunmore* certainly does not overturn *Re PSERA* and related cases. Yet the case reveals both an openness to and a fluency in international labour law reminiscent of Dickson C.J.'s dissent in *Re PSERA*. In the words of recent commentators, *Dunmore* suggests two possible paths: "Down one path lies an expansion of the *Dunmore* ruling toward the broad guarantees embodied in the Freedom of Association Conventions. Along the second path lies a confirmation of the principles set out in [*Re PSERA*]. . . . At this early stage, it is not possible to predict with certainty which path Canadian courts will follow."[91]

This discussion has unavoidably focused on the *Charter*. It must be recalled, however, that the enactments that most immediately implement (or fail to implement) Canada's obligation to protect freedom of association in the labour law context are the federal and provincial labour laws. This is alluded to in the preamble to Part I of the *Canada Labour Code*, which refers to Canada's ratification of Convention No. 87 and its assumption of "international reporting responsibilities in this regard."[92] While federal and provincial labour legislation recognizes freedom of association and protects it in significant ways, certain categories of workers (notably agricultural and domestic workers) remain excluded from the coverage of labour relations legislation in some provinces,[93] and the right to strike is not explicitly recognized in legislation.[94]

E. DEMOCRATIC RIGHTS

This heading includes election rights, civil service participation rights, and rights in political life.

---

89   *Ibid.* at para. 37.
90   *Ibid.* at para. 17.
91   B. Burkett, J. Craig, & S. Gallagher, "Canada and the ILO: Freedom of Association since 1982" (2003) 10 Canadian Labour and Employment Law Journal 231 at 268.
92   *Canada Labour Code* RSC 1985 c. L-2 Part I preamble.
93   For example *Labour Relations Code* RSA 2000 c. L-1 s. 4(2), *Industrial Relations Act* RSNB c. I-4 s. 1(1). Ontario's legislative response to *Dunmore*, the *Agricultural Employees Protection Act* 2002 SO 2002 c. 16, guarantees freedom of association for individual agricultural workers but does not extend to the certification of unions, collective bargaining, or the right to strike.
94   See G. Adams, *Canadian Labour Law*, 2d ed, looseleaf (Aurora, Ontario: Canada Law Book Inc., 1993) at section 11.80–100.

1) In Binding Instruments

The UN instruments guarantee citizens several rights in respect of elec-tions.[95] Citizens have the right to vote in genuine periodic elections[96] and the right to stand for such elections.[97] Such elections shall be conducted by secret ballot[98] and held according to universal and equal suffrage.[99] The UN instruments also declare everyone's right to equal access to the pub-lic service of his country,[100] and a more general right to participate in gov-ernment, directly or through freely chosen representatives.[101] CEDAW article 7(c) adds to these rights a right of women to participate, on equal terms with men, in non-governmental organizations and associations.[102]

AmDR article 20 recognizes the right of every person of legal capacity to participate in the government of his country, directly or through representatives, and to take part in "honest, periodic and free" popular elections conducted by secret ballot. There is no explicit right of equal access to the public service.

2) In Non-Binding Instruments

The ACHR guarantees the rights to "take part in the conduct of public affairs,"[103] to "vote and to be elected in genuine periodic elections,"[104] and to "have access, under general conditions of equality, to the public service of his country."[105] Democratic rights are notably absent from the

---

95 See ICCPR General Comment 25 (1996).
96 UDHR, above note 23, art 21(3); ICCPR, above note 9, art. 25(b); CERD, above note 62, art. 5(c); Convention on the Elimination of All Forms of Discrimina-tion Against Women 1979 (CEDAW), [1982] CanTS no. 31, art. 7(a).
97 ICCPR, ibid., art. 25(b); CERD, ibid., art. 5(c); CEDAW, ibid., art. 7(a).
98 UDHR, above note 23, art. 21(3); ICCPR, ibid., art. 25(b).
99 UDHR, ibid., art. 21(3); ICCPR, ibid., art. 25(b); CERD, above note 62, art. 5(c); CEDAW, above note 96, art. 7.
100 UDHR, ibid., art. 21(2); ICCPR, ibid., art. 25(c); CERD, ibid., art. 5(c); CEDAW, ibid., art. 7(b).
101 UDHR, ibid., art. 21(1); ICCPR, ibid., art. 25(a); CERD, ibid., art. 5(c).
102 See also the Convention on the Political Rights of Women 1952 [1957] CanTS no. 3, which provides that women shall be entitled to vote in all elections on equal terms with men without any discrimination (art. 1); that women shall be eligible for election to all publicly elected bodies, established by national law, on equal terms with men, without any discrimination (art. 2); and that women shall be entitled to hold public office and to exercise all public functions, established by national law, on equal terms with men, without any discrimination (art. 3).
103 ACHR, above note 26, art. 23(1)(a).
104 ACHR, ibid., art. 23(1)(b).
105 Ibid., art. 23(1)(c).

ECHR, but article 3 of ECHR Protocol No. 1 (1952) provides that states parties will hold free elections at reasonable intervals by secret ballot, under conditions which will ensure the free expression of the opinion of the people in the choice of the legislature. The AfrCHPR guarantees citizens the right to participate freely in the government of their country[106] and the right to equal access to the public service,[107] but does not explicitly recognize the rights to vote and to stand for election.

3) In Canadian Law

The right to vote is guaranteed to Canadian citizens by *Charter* section 3. The *Charter* right extends only to federal and provincial elections[108] although the right to vote in other elections, referenda, or plebiscites may, of course, be conferred by ordinary legislation. The international requirement of periodic elections is fulfilled by *Charter* section 4, which requires fresh elections for the House of Commons and the provincial legislatures at least every five years, with a possible exception for times of real or apprehended war, invasion, or insurrection. The international requirement that elections be "genuine" is not found explicitly in the *Charter*, though section 5's requirement that Parliament and each legislature sit at least once every twelve months may go some ways towards satisfying this obligation. More importantly, the Supreme Court of Canada has repeatedly affirmed that the purpose of *Charter* section 3 is the effective representation of citizens.[109]

As we noted at the outset of this chapter, *Charter* rights are subject to reasonable limits as described by section 1. Thus the *Canada Elections Act* disqualifies non-citizens, citizens under eighteen years of age on polling day, and certain electoral officers.[110] The Act also purports to disqualify "every person who is imprisoned in a correctional institution serving a sentence of two years or more,"[111] but the Supreme Court of Canada held that provision to be an unjustified limitation on voting

---

106 African Charter on Human and Peoples' Rights 1981 (AfrCHPR), OAU doc. CAB/LEG/67/3 rev. 5, art. 13(1).
107 *Ibid.*, art. 13(2).
108 *Haig v. Canada*, [1993] 2 SCR 995 [*Haig*].
109 *Re Provincial Electoral Boundaries (Saskatchewan)*, [1991] 2 SCR 158 at 183; *Haig, ibid.* at 1031; *Harvey v. New Brunswick (Attorney General)*, [1996] 2 SCR 876 at para. 24; *Thomson Newspaper Co. v. Canada (Attorney General)*, [1998] 1 SCR 877 at para. 82; *Figueroa v. Canada (Attorney General)*, 2003 SCC 37 at para. 21 [*Figueroa*].
110 SC 2000 c. 9 ss. 3–4.
111 *Ibid.*, s. 4(c).

rights in *Sauvé v. Canada (Chief Electoral Officer)*.[112] The dissent in *Sauvé* noted the UN Human Rights Committee's General Comment on ICCPR article 25, in which the Committee observed that restrictions of prisoners' right to vote must be "proportionate to the offence and the sentence" — thereby implying that such limits are permissible.[113] The dissent also looked to ECHR jurisprudence for support of its view that the impugned restriction on the right to vote was justifiable.[114] It appears that the majority in *Sauvé* interpreted *Charter* section 3 in a way that in fact exceeds Canada's international obligation to protect voting rights.

The right to stand for election is also protected by *Charter* section 3, which guarantees every citizen the right to be qualified for membership in the House of Commons or a provincial legislature. In *Harvey v. New Brunswick (Attorney General)*,[115] the Supreme Court of Canada upheld a New Brunswick law that expelled from the legislature and disqualified for five years any person convicted of engaging in a corrupt or illegal practice. The majority held that the law infringed section 3 but was justified under section 1. The right to stand for municipal or other elections is not explicitly protected by the *Charter* but may no doubt be read into it, and may also find protection in ordinary or quasi-constitutional legislation.[116]

The drawing of electoral boundaries has been considered by the UN Human Rights Committee and the Supreme Court of Canada. The Committee has observed that such boundaries "should not distort the distribution of voters or discriminate against any group and should not exclude or restrict unreasonably the right of citizens to choose their representatives freely."[117] Faced with a challenge to Saskatchewan's provincial electoral boundaries, the Supreme Court of Canada held that *Charter* section 3 does not require perfect parity of voting power between electors; deviations from absolute parity that are consistent with the principle of effective representation do not infringe section 3.[118] The Court did not consider the Committee's observations in its

---

112 2002 SCC 68 [*Sauvé*]. The provision in question was actually RSC 1985 c. E-2 as amended, but the current legislation repeats the prior enactment word for word on this point.

113 ICCPR General Comment 25 at para. 14. Quoted in *Sauvé, ibid.* at para. 133.

114 See *Sauvé, ibid.* at paras. 127–29.

115 Above note 109.

116 See, for example, *Quebec Charter*, above note 11, s. 22, which guarantees every legally capable and qualified person "the right to be a candidate and to vote at an election."

117 ICCPR General Comment 25 (1996) at para. 21.

118 *Re Provincial Electoral Boundaries (Saskatchewan)*, above note 109, at 184–85.

reasons, but its reasoning strikes the present authors as consistent with the Committee's interpretation of the ICCPR.

The right of citizens to have equal access to their country's public service is not explicitly declared in the *Charter* or any other Canadian human rights instruments. Yet the right implicates anti-discrimination provisions in the *Charter* and the federal and provincial human rights codes. In *Lavoie v. Canada*, the majority of the Supreme Court of Canada relied on UDHR article 21(2) and ICCPR article 25(c) to support its conclusion that legislation granting Canadian citizens preferential treatment in the federal civil service breached section 15(1) but was saved by section 1.[119] The majority noted that these international instruments required only that citizens enjoy equal access to the public service. The majority invoked these instruments at the "sufficiently important objective" stage of the *Oakes* test, and noted that a rule is not non-discriminatory simply because it reflects an international consensus as to the appropriate limit on equality rights. Such a consideration is "highly relevant" in section 1 analysis, but is not part of the section 15(1) equality analysis.[120]

The right to participate directly or indirectly in government is another right not explicitly enunciated in the *Charter* or in any Canadian statute. Yet it is clearly established in Canadian law and political culture. A passage from the Supreme Court of Canada's judgment in *Figueroa v. Canada (Attorney General)* is instructive. The court described "the central focus of section 3" as "the right of each citizen to participate in the electoral process" and continued,

> This signifies that the right of each citizen to participate in the political life of the country is one that is of fundamental importance in a free and democratic society and suggests that s. 3 should be interpreted in a manner that ensures that this right of participation embraces a content commensurate with the importance of individual participation in the selection of elected representatives in a free and democratic state.[121]

Note also that the federal *Employment Equity Act* applies to most of the federal public service.[122] The Act requires employers to identify and

---

119 *Lavoie v. Canada*, [2002] 1 SCR 769 at para. 56 [*Lavoie*]; see also para. 46.

120 *Ibid.* at para. 48.

121 *Figueroa*, above note 109, at para. 26. Also of note is *Re Secession of Quebec*, [1998] 2 SCR 217 at paras. 135–36, where the court particularly noted the participation of the Quebec population in Canadian political and governmental life in the course of its discussion of the international law right to self-determination.

122 SC 1995 c. 44. On application to the public service, see s. 4(1). On employers' equity obligations, see s. 5.

eliminate employment barriers against women, aboriginal peoples, persons with disabilities, and members of visible minorities, and to institute positive policies and make reasonable accommodations to ensure such persons appropriate representation in the workforce.

F. MOBILITY RIGHTS

The rights considered under this heading concern mobility into, out of, and within states.[123]

1) In Binding Instruments

The UN instruments[124] recognize four rights under the rubric of mobility: (1) freedom of movement within the territory of a state;[125] (2) free choice of residence within the territory of a state;[126] (3) freedom to leave any country, including one's own;[127] and (4) the right to enter one's own country.[128] The first three rights may only be restricted by states to protect national security, public order, public health or morals, and the rights and freedoms of others.[129] As for the right to enter one's own country, states may not deprive anyone of this right arbitrarily.[130] Mobility rights also receive brief consideration in CERD article 5(d)(i)–(ii) and CEDAW article 15(4). The latter provision requires states parties to accord mobility rights equally to men and women.

AmDR article 8 declares the right of every person to "fix his residence within the territory of the state of which he is a national, to move about freely within such territory, and not to leave it except by his own will."

2) In Non-Binding Instruments

ACHR article 22 treats the themes of mobility, asylum, and expulsion together. The mobility rights provisions generally resemble those of the

---

123 On asylum and expulsion, see the discussion at of international refugee protection in Chapter Eleven.
124 See ICCPR General Comment 27.
125 UDHR, above note 23, art. 13; ICCPR, above note 9, art. 12(1).
126 UDHR, *ibid.*, art. 13; ICCPR, *ibid.*, art. 12(1).
127 UDHR, *ibid.*, art. 13; ICCPR, *ibid.*, art. 12(2).
128 UDHR, *ibid.*, art. 13; ICCPR, *ibid.*, art. 12(4).
129 ICCPR, *ibid.*, art. 12(3).
130 *Ibid.*, art. 12(4).

ICCPR, with the exception of article 22(4) which permits states to restrict mobility "in designated zones for reasons of public interest." Mobility rights are protected in articles 2 and 3(2) of ECHR Protocol No. 4 (1968). Protection from expulsion is provided by ECHR Protocol No. 4 articles 3–4 (in respect of nationals) and ECHR Protocol No. 7 article 1 (in respect of aliens). Like the ACHR, AfrCHPR article 12 treats mobility, asylum, and expulsion together.

3) In Canadian Law

The mobility rights of Canadian citizens and, to a lesser extent, permanent residents of Canada are protected by *Charter* section 6. There are notable divergences between section 6 and international law. Yet the Supreme Court of Canada has observed that section 6 "closely mirrors the provisions of several human rights instruments to which Canada is a party"[131] and has described section 6 as "grounded in a concern with fundamental human rights."[132]

Section 6(1) guarantees the right of every citizen of Canada to enter, remain in, and leave Canada. The fact that this right applies only to citizens makes it only a partial implementation of the ICCPR's requirements in respect of freedom to leave, for ICCPR article 12(2) requires that everyone, citizens and non-citizens alike, be free to leave any country. Likewise, section 6(1) may not completely satisfy ICCPR article 12(4)'s requirement that no one be arbitrarily deprived of the right to enter his country.[133] If the *Charter* is wanting in this regard, the deficiency is seemingly corrected by section 19 of the *Immigration and Refugee Protection Act*,[134] which provides that Canadian citizens and persons registered as Indians under the *Indian Act* have the right to enter and remain in Canada in accordance with the Act, and permanent residents are permitted to enter Canada upon proving their status.[135] The extradition of Canadian citizens to face trial in foreign countries

---

131 *Canadian Egg Marketing Board v. Richardson*, [1998] 3 SCR 157 at para. 58 [*Richardson*].

132 *Ibid.* at para. 59.

133 See Human Rights Committee, General Comment 27 (1999) at para. 20, which suggests that the right to enter "his own country" is broader than the concept of "country of his nationality."

134 SC 2001 c. 27.

135 In two cases, Canada's deportation of permanent residents on the ground of criminal convictions has been found not to violate ICCPR, above note 9, art. 12(4): *Stewart v. Canada* (1996), Comm. no 538/1993 and *Canepa v. Canada* (1997), Comm. no 558/1993.

has been held to infringe section 6(1), but to be a justifiable limit on the right (partly on the ground that Canada's international obligations under extradition treaties should be respected).[136]

Charter section 6(2) guarantees the rights of Canadian citizens and permanent residents to move to and take up residence, and to pursue a livelihood, in any province. The broader application of this subsection may reflect ICCPR article 12(1), which guarantees liberty of movement and choice of residence to everyone lawfully within the state's territory. Yet the international formulation appears to be broader than section 6(2).

Charter section 6(4) appears to permit provincial laws which discriminate against non-residents for the purpose of ameliorating social or economic disadvantage in areas of underemployment. The consistency of this section with Canada's international obligations is questionable.

Section 6 may not be the only *Charter* provision implicating mobility rights. In *Godbout v. Longueuil (City)*, La Forest J. (L'Heureux-Dubé and McLachlin JJ. concurring) invoked the right to liberty of movement and freedom to choose one's residence, as expressed in ICCPR article 12, in support of his conclusion that the liberty element of *Charter* section 7 includes protection for an "irreducible sphere of personal autonomy."[137] This interpretation did not attract majority acceptance, however. The rest of the court preferred to resolve the case without reference to section 7.

G. RIGHT TO LIFE, LIBERTY AND SECURITY OF THE PERSON

Life has been called the supreme right.[138] Liberty and security of the person cannot be far behind. Under the heading of life, liberty and security of the person fall a number of human rights concerns, including capital punishment, slavery, extradition, forcible confinement, and more. In this section we describe the general right as it exists in international law, then consider its treatment in Canadian law (particularly in the context of extradition cases). More specific deprivations of liberty and security (such as arrest and criminal proceedings) are addressed later in this chapter.

---

136 *Re Federal Republic of Germany and Rauca* (1983), 41 OR (2d) 225; *United States v. Cotroni*, [1989] 1 SCR 1469; *United States v. Burns*, [2001] 1 SCR 283 [*Burns*].
137 [1997] 3 SCR 844 at para. 69 [*Godbout*].
138 ICCPR General Comment 6 (1982) at para. 1.

1) In Binding Instruments

UDHR article 3 declares, in terms eminently familiar to Canadian lawyers, "Everyone has the right to life, liberty and security of the person." AmDR article 1 says effectively the same thing.[139] UDHR article 4 reinforces the right to liberty by prohibiting slavery, servitude, and the slave trade.

The ICCPR treats the right to life separately from the right to liberty and security of the person. Article 6(1) provides that every human being has "the inherent right to life." It continues, "This right shall be protected by law. No one shall be arbitrarily deprived of his life." The rest of article 6 defines and limits the power of states parties to impose the death penalty. The death penalty may be imposed only for the most serious crimes. It may not be imposed retroactively. It may not be imposed contrary to the ICCPR or the Genocide Convention. It may only be carried out pursuant to a final judgment by a competent court.[140] It must be coupled with a right to seek pardon or commutation of the sentence.[141] It shall not be imposed on minors or pregnant women.[142] Finally, nothing in article 6 shall be invoked to delay or prevent the abolition of capital punishment by states parties.[143] As explained in Chapter Four, these provisions do not prohibit the death penalty. They instead regulate it and may implicitly urge its abolition. ICCPR-OP2 prohibits the death penalty within the jurisdiction of states parties to it and requires those states to abolish it. Canada is not a party to this treaty.[144]

The right to liberty and security of the person is expressed chiefly in ICCPR article 9(1) but also in article 8.[145] The latter article is a broad prohibition of slavery, the slave trade, servitude, and certain forms of forced or compulsory labour.[146] Article 9(1) declares everyone's right to

---

139 "Every human being has the right to life, liberty and the security of his person."
140 ICCPR, above note 9, art. 6(2).
141 *Ibid.*, art. 6(4).
142 *Ibid.*, art. 6(5).
143 *Ibid.*, art. 6(6).
144 For more on the Second Optional Protocol to the International Covenant on Civil and Political Rights, Aiming at the Abolition of the Death Penalty 1989 (ICCPR-OP2), 999 UNTS 302 and the death penalty in general, see Chapter Four.
145 See ICCPR General Comment 8 (1982) 95.
146 Forms of labour excluded from the definition of forced or compulsory labour include: hard labour imposed as punishment for crime; work or service that is not hard labour but is imposed by lawful court order on a detained or conditionally released person; military service; service required in cases of emergency; and work or service which forms part of normal civil obligations: ICCPR, above note 9, art. 8(3)(a)–(c).

liberty and security of the person and adds that no one shall be deprived of liberty "except on such grounds and in accordance with such procedures as are established by law." Article 9 goes on to treat specific rights concerning deprivations of liberty, which we treat under separate headings, below.

CRC article 6 recognizes the child's inherent right to life and requires states parties to ensure to the maximum extent possible the survival and development of the child.

2) In Non-Binding Instruments

Like the ICCPR, the ACHR treats the right to life and the right to liberty and security of the person separately. Article 4(1) provides that every person "has the right to have his life respected" and adds that this right shall be protected by law and "in general, from the moment of conception." As explained in Chapter Six, this provision is often cited as a reason why Canada has not become a party to the ACHR.[147] Article 4(1) also provides that no one shall be arbitrarily deprived of life. Articles 4(2) and 4(3) regulate use of the death penalty. These provisions require, *inter alia*, that the application of the death penalty shall not be extended to crimes to which it does not presently apply, and that it shall not be re-established in states that have prohibited it. Article 4(5) prohibits capital punishment of minors and pregnant women, and also prohibits the punishment in respect of those over seventy. ACHR article 6(1) prohibits slavery, involuntary servitude, the slave trade, and "traffic in women." Article 6 goes on to prohibit forced or compulsory labour in terms similar to ICCPR article 8(3). Finally, article 7(1) recognizes the right of every person to "personal liberty and security" while article 7(2) provides that deprivation of physical liberty must occur according to pre-existing constitutional or ordinary law. A protocol to abolish the death penalty was concluded in 1990.[148]

ECHR article 2 provides that everyone's right to life shall be protected by law and that no one shall be deprived of his life intentionally save upon conviction for a capital offence. This article has been

---

147 See also W. Schabas, "Substantive and Procedural Issues in the Ratification by Canada of the American Convention on Human Rights" (1991) 12 Human Rights Law Journal 405 and W. Schabas, "Canadian Ratification of the American Convention on Human Rights" (1998) 16 Netherlands Quarterly of Human Rights 315.

148 Protocol to the American Convention on Human Rights to Abolish the Death Penalty 1990 (ACHR-OP2), OAS TS no. 73.

supplemented by ECHR Protocol No. 6 (1983) which abolishes the death penalty except in respect of acts committed in time of war or of imminent threat of war,[149] and more recently by ECHR Protocol No. 13 (2002) which abolishes the death penalty entirely.[150] ECHR article 4 prohibits slavery and forced or compulsory labour in terms similar to ICCPR article 8. ECHR article 5 guarantees the right of everyone to liberty and security of the person, and provides that no one shall be deprived of his liberty save "in accordance with a procedure prescribed by law" and in specified cases. These cases include lawful detention after conviction by a competent court, lawful arrest or detention for non-compliance with a court order or other legal obligation, lawful arrest or detention upon reasonable suspicion of having committed an offence, lawful detention for medical reasons, and lawful arrest or detention to prevent unauthorized entry or stay in the country.

AfrCHPR article 4 describes human beings as "inviolable" and declares that every human being shall be entitled to respect for his life and the integrity of his person. Furthermore, no one may be arbitrarily deprived to this right. Article 6 grants everyone "the right to liberty and to security of his person" and adds that no one may be deprived of his freedom "except for reasons and conditions previously laid down by law." Similarly, article 5 requires states to prohibit, *inter alia*, slavery and the slave trade. Article 4 of the AfrCHPR Women's Protocol declares that every woman is entitled to respect for her life and the integrity and security of her person and includes specific provisions concerning violence against women.

3) In Canadian Law

Charter section 7 declares, "Everyone has the right to life, liberty and security of the person and the right not to be deprived thereof except in accordance with the principles of fundamental justice." Section 7 is, in principle, subject to the general limit on *Charter* rights expressed in section 1. Yet the "principles of fundamental justice" qualification acts as an internal limit on the right, and the Supreme Court of Canada has said in *obiter* that a breach of section 7 will only be justified under section 1 in exceptional cases.[151]

---

149 ECHR Protocol No. 6 ETS 114 arts. 1–2.
150 ECHR Protocol No. 13 ETS 187 art. 1.
151 *Re BC Motor Vehicle Act*, [1985] 2 SCR 486 at 518; *Burns*, above note 136 at para. 133.

Section 7 is usually treated as enunciating a single right — the right not to be deprived of life, liberty and security of the person except in accordance with the principles of fundamental justice.[152] Nevertheless, the individual elements of the right warrant consideration in the light of international human rights law.

The right to life is not, on the face of section 7, absolutely guaranteed by the *Charter*. Section 7 appears only to guarantee that no one shall be deprived of life except according to fundamental justice. The matter has never been directly considered in Canada because the death penalty has not been imposed here since 1962. It was abolished as a sentence under the *Criminal Code* in 1976 and for all other offences (for example treason) in 1998.[153] Furthermore, the Supreme Court of Canada has treated cases involving the extradition of fugitives to retentionist states (i.e., those that still retain the death penalty) under the liberty and security of the person elements of section 7, on the ground that it is the foreign state and not Canada that might impose the death penalty in these cases and the *Charter* does not apply to foreign states.[154] (By contrast, the Human Rights Committee has dealt with extradition cases under ICCPR article 6, the right to life.) In short, there is surprisingly little jurisprudence on the right to life element of section 7.

The Supreme Court of Canada has emphasized that the concepts of liberty and security of the person must be kept "analytically distinct to the extent possible."[155] Yet in *Charter* jurisprudence as in the international instruments, there is a degree of overlap. The liberty interest in section 7 was once thought to be restricted to freedom from physical restraint. It seems now to be established, however, that liberty is also engaged "where state compulsions or prohibitions affect important and fundamental life choices."[156] Similarly, the security interest in section 7 includes but is not restricted to physical integrity.[157] It includes "overlong subjection to the

---

152 For an unorthodox interpretation of s. 7, see *Gosselin v. Quebec (Attorney General)*, 2002 SCC 84 at paras. 307–87 per Arbour J. [*Gosselin*].

153 *Act to amend the National Defence Act and to make consequential amendments to other Acts* SC 1998 c. 35.

154 *Kindler v. Canada (Minister of Justice)*, [1991] 2 SCR 779 at 831 per La Forest J. [*Kindler*].

155 *Blencoe v. British Columbia (Human Rights Commission)*, [2000] 2 SCR 307 at para. 48 [*Blencoe*].

156 *Ibid.* at para. 49. See also *Godbout*, above note 137 at para. 66.

157 *R. v. Morgentaler (No. 2)*, [1988] 1 SCR 30; *Rodriguez v. British Columbia*, [1993] 3 SCR 519. In a different context, La Forest J. (dissenting) observed, "The security of nationals is the essence of sovereignty and the most basic obligation a state owes its citizens": *Chan v. Canada (Minister of Employment and Immigration)*, [1995] 3 SCR 593 at 630.

vexations and vicissitudes of a pending criminal accusation"[158] and serious state-imposed psychological stress in non-criminal contexts.[159]

The Supreme Court of Canada's section 7 jurisprudence on the extradition of fugitives to the United States, where they may face the death penalty, has frequently — and unevenly — engaged with international human rights law. In 1991, the court gave judgment in the companion cases of *Kindler v. Canada (Minister of Justice)*[160] and *Re Ng Extradition*.[161] Kindler and Ng were wanted in the US for murder and kidnapping. Kindler had in fact been tried and convicted, but escaped before sentencing. Ng had not yet stood trial. Both were apprehended in Canada and ordered extradited by the minister of justice following lengthy extradition proceedings. In neither case did the minister exercise his statutory power to seek assurances from the US, pursuant to article 6 of the Canada-US Extradition Treaty 1971,[162] that the death penalty would not be imposed or carried out. The Supreme Court of Canada held that to surrender the fugitives to the US without assurances seriously affected their liberty and security interests but was consistent with the principles of fundamental justice. La Forest J. noted an international "trend for abolition" of capital punishment but no actual prohibition of it in international law. He also found that to extradite without assurances did not shock the conscience of the Canadian people.[163] In dissent, Sopinka J. found an infringement of section 7, holding that circumstances in which extradition may breach section 7 were not limited to those that "shock the conscience." Also in dissent, Cory J. relied heavily on the concept of human dignity, as expressed in international law and Canadian international practice, in support of his finding that the extraditions infringed the prohibition of cruel and unusual punishment in *Charter* section 12.[164]

Following these appeals, Kindler and Ng took their cases to the Human Rights Committee. So did a third fugitive in Canada, Cox. The Committee considered the cases under ICCPR articles 6 and 7 (the

---

158 *Mills v. The Queen*, [1986] 1 SCR 863 at 919–20 per Lamer J.

159 *New Brunswick (Minister of Health and Community Services) v. G.(J.)*, [1999] 3 SCR 46 [*New Brunswick*].

160 *Kindler*, above note 154.

161 [1991] 2 SCR 858 [*Ng*].

162 [1976] CanTS no. 3.

163 *Kindler*, above note 154 at 833–34, 839. La Forest J. wrote for himself and L'Heureux-Dubé and Gonthier JJ. McLachlin J. (as she then was) concurred in the result. Lamer C.J., Sopinka and Cory JJ. dissented.

164 See the discussion of torture and cruel, inhuman or degrading treatment or punishment, below.

right to life and the prohibition of cruel, inhuman or degrading treatment or punishment) and found that the extraditions of Kindler and Cox were consistent with Canada's obligations under the ICCPR, but that the extradition of Ng was not. In *Kindler*,[165] the Committee confirmed that extradition by a state party can violate the ICCPR where there is a "real risk" that the extradited person's rights under the Covenant will be violated in the receiving state.[166] The Committee also urged abolitionist states like Canada to consider their own abolitionist stance when deciding whether to seek assurances under extradition treaties.[167] These points made, the Committee determined that ICCPR article 6 did not require Canada to seek assurances against the death penalty before extraditing Kindler. Nor did ICCPR article 7 require Canada to seek such assurances in this case. This provision (said the Committee) must be read in the light of ICCPR article 6(2), which does not prohibit the death penalty nor deem it necessarily to be cruel, inhuman or degrading treatment or punishment.[168] The Committee came to similar conclusions in *Cox*.[169] In *Ng*,[170] the Committee again found no violation of article 6 but found that gas asphyxiation (the method of execution employed in the jurisdiction in which Ng faced the death penalty) was cruel and inhuman treatment. Canada therefore violated its ICCPR obligations by failing to seek assurances in Ng's case.

When, in 2001, the Supreme Court of Canada had occasion to revisit its jurisprudence on extradition to retentionist states, one might have expected the court to consider these important Human Rights Committee views. Yet the judgment of the court in *United States of America v. Burns* made no reference to them.[171] Instead, the court invoked a hodgepodge of other international materials, mostly nonbinding, in support of its conclusion that section 7 in fact does require the minister of justice to seek assurances against the death penalty in all but exceptional cases. While we applaud the result of *Burns* (which, for all the court's protestations to the contrary, effectively overrules *Kindler* and *Ng*), the reasoning in the case, and the court's use of international law and materials, is unsatisfying. The court declared that abolition of the death penalty had "emerged as a major Canadian initiative

165 *Kindler v. Canada* (1993), Comm. no. 470/1991 UN doc. CCPR/48/D/470/1991 [*Kindler* HRC].

166 *Ibid.* at para. 13.2.

167 *Ibid.* at para. 14.5.

168 *Ibid.* at para. 15.1.

169 *Cox v. Canada* (1994), Comm. no. 539/1993.

170 *Ng v. Canada* (1993), Comm. no. 469/1991.

171 *Burns*, above note 136.

at the international level"[172] yet glossed over the fact that Canada has not ratified the one UN treaty dedicated to abolishing the death penalty, namely the ICCPR-OP2.[173] Instead, the court relied on the existence of other abolitionist treaties — to which Canada is equally not a party[174] — and various other non-binding declarations, some of which are of doubtful relevance.[175] Ultimately the court conceded that there was no "international law norm against the death penalty, or against extradition to face the death penalty," yet found nevertheless that the "evidence" (that is, the international materials considered by the court) shows "significant movement towards acceptance internationally of a principle of fundamental justice that Canada has already adopted internally, namely the abolition of capital punishment."[176] If Canada had already adopted abolition "internally" as a principle of fundamental justice, one wonders what the relevance was of the various international materials marshalled by the court.

A new chapter was recently added to this story by the decision of the Human Rights Committee in *Judge v. Canada*.[177] Judge was an American who escaped from prison and fled to Canada after being sentenced to death for two counts of first-degree murder. He was convicted of two robberies in Vancouver and was sentenced to ten years' imprisonment. Unlike Kindler, Ng, and Cox, who were all extradited to the US, Judge was deported there. The difference is crucial, for while Canada may make extradition proceedings subject to assurances from the receiving country that the fugitive will not face the death penalty, no such procedure exists, formally at least, for deportation orders. The Human Rights Committee concluded that for states that have abolished the death penalty, there is an obligation not to expose a person to the real risk of its application, and that this obligation applies to extradition and deportation cases alike.[178] Thus Canada was found to have vio-

---

172 *Ibid.* at heading to para. 79.
173 *Ibid.* at para. 87.
174 Protocol to the American Convention on Human Rights to Abolish the Death Penalty, above note 148; European Convention on Human Rights 1950 (ECHR), Protocol No. 6 (1983) ETS 114.
175 *Burns*, above note 136 at paras. 84–88.
176 *Ibid.* at para. 89. Note that the court elevates the abolition of capital punishment to the status of a "principle of fundamental justice." Yet earlier in the judgment (at para. 8) the court declines to find that extraditions without assurances will always violate s. 7 — even though they will obviously always infringe on a person's liberty and security of the person, and will never be in accordance with the principle of fundamental justice that capital punishment should be abolished!
177 (2003) Comm. No. 829/1998 [*Judge*].
178 *Ibid.* at para. 10.4.

lated Judge's right to life under ICCPR article 6(1). The Committee also found Canada in violation of article 6(1) for deporting Judge before he had the opportunity to appeal the rejection of his application for a stay of deportation.[179]

We have seen that the "principles of fundamental justice" component of section 7 finds no direct parallel in the international instruments. Though analogies may be drawn to ICCPR prohibitions of arbitrary deprivation of life and arbitrary arrest or detention,[180] section 7's internal limit on the right to life, liberty, and security of the person remains a Canadian innovation. It appears that the framers of the *Charter* understood this phrase to be roughly synonymous with the concept of natural justice as established in Anglo-Canadian administrative law. The idea, it seems, was that courts should review deprivations of life, liberty, and security for procedural insufficiencies but not for substantive errors.[181] This is seemingly consistent with ICCPR article 9(1) which, as we have seen, permits deprivations of the right to liberty and security of the person "on such grounds and in accordance with such procedures as are established by law." However, the Supreme Court of Canada soon established that the "principles of fundamental justice" were both procedural and substantive.[182]

From the perspective of international human rights law, substantive review under section 7 has produced mixed results. We noted in Chapter Nine that section 7, as interpreted in *Re Motor Vehicle Act* and later cases, is one means by which international law may find vindication through the *Charter*. This approach to section 7 not only enriches the *Charter* with obligations and values drawn from international law, but also provides some ascertainable content to the frequently elusive concept of "principles of fundamental justice." Yet the "balancing exercise" that has come to characterize substantive review under section 7 has not always produced satisfactory human rights results. *Suresh* is the

---

179 This finding suggests that s. 48(2) of the *Immigration and Refugee Protection Act*, above note 134, which provides that removal orders "must be enforced as soon as is reasonably practicable," may be inconsistent with the ICCPR. A court could avoid this undesirable conclusion, of course, by reading s. 48(2) in the light of the ICCPR as required by the presumption of conformity and s. 3(3)(f). On the presumption, see Chapter Eight.

180 See ICCPR, above note 9, arts. 6(1) and 9(1).

181 Hogg, above note 54, at s. 44.10(a).

182 *Re s. 94(2) of the Motor Vehicle Act*, [1985] 2 SCR 486 [*Re Motor Vehicle Act*]. On how to determine whether a given rule or proposition amounts to a principle of fundamental justice for the purpose of *Charter* s. 7, see *R. v. Malmo-Levine*, 2003 SCC 74 at paras. 110–29.

prime example. There, the Supreme Court of Canada held that "in exceptional circumstances, deportation to face torture might be justified, either as a consequence of the balancing process mandated by section 7 of the *Charter* or under section 1."[183] This conclusion is not only inconsistent with Canada's treaty obligations,[184] but it contradicts *obiter dicta* in earlier cases.[185] Quite apart from these considerations, it is a disturbing interpretation of the *Charter*.[186] It is very much to be hoped that courts will in future exercise the remarkable discretion that our "principles of fundamental justice" jurisprudence gives them in ways that are informed by and consistent with Canada's international human rights obligations.

This discussion has inevitably focused on the *Charter*. Yet section 7 is far from being the only means by which Canada satisfies its international obligations to protect the human right to life, liberty and security of the person. Federally and in some provincial jurisdictions, bills of rights include life, liberty and security among their protections.[187] But the laws that most directly protect the lives, liberty, and security of Canadians are the various criminal law prohibitions against homicide, confinement, and assault. Depending on how broadly one defines liberty and security, countless other non-criminal statutes might also be cited as implementing this right. Common law tort actions may also play a role in vindicating individuals' rights to life, liberty and security.[188] While these statutory and common-law rules may not explicitly implement Canada's treaty commitments, the fundamental role they play in discharging those commitments underscores yet again how

---

183 *Suresh v. Canada (Minister of Citizenship and Immigration)*, [2002] 1 SCR 3 at para. 78 [*Suresh*]; see also para. 58.

184 See the discussion of the CAT in Chapter Five and the discussion of the right to protection from torture and cruel, inhuman, or degrading treatment or punishment, below.

185 *R. v. Schmidt*, [1987] 1 SCR 500 at 522 per La Forest J. [*Schmidt*]; *Kindler*, above note 154 at 851 per McLachlin J.

186 The decision of the Human Rights Committee in *Judge*, above note 177, described above, casts further doubt on the soundness of *Suresh*, above note 183.

187 *Canadian Bill of Rights* SC 1960 c. 44 s. 1(a); *Quebec Charter*, above note 11, s. 1; *Alberta Bill of Rights*, above note 11, s. 1(a).

188 See the discussion of common law remedies in Chapter Thirteen. See also M. Ratner & B. Stephens, *International Human Rights Litigation in U.S. Courts* (Irvington-on-Hudson, NY: Transnational Publishers, 1996) at 38 for a chart comparing international human rights violations to corresponding tort actions. See also C. Scott, *Torture as Tort: Comparative Perspectives on the Development of Transnational Human Rights Litigation* (Oxford: Hart Publishing, 2001).

mistaken it is to conclude that a human rights treaty is "unimplemented" simply because it is not explicitly implemented.

H. RIGHT TO PROPERTY AND PROPERTY-RELATED RIGHTS

International and Canadian law both offer some degree of protection for property rights, subject to limitations in the public interest.

1) In Binding Instruments

The UN instruments guarantee three types of property or property-related right: the right to own property and not to be arbitrarily deprived of it;[189] the right to "protection of the moral and material interests resulting from any scientific, literary or artistic production," (intellectual property rights);[190] and the right not to be discriminated against on the ground of property[191] or in the exercise of it.[192]

AmDR article 23 recognizes the right of every person "to own such property as meets the essential needs of decent living and helps to maintain the dignity of the individual and of the home." This is a rather different property guarantee than UDHR article 17, for it does not protect ownership itself so much as guarantee a minimum standard of living. Like UDHR article 27(2), AmDR article 13 declares that every person has the right to "the protection of his moral and material interests as regards his inventions or any literary, scientific or artistic works of which he is the author."

2) In Non-Binding Instruments

ACHR article 21(1) recognizes the right to the use and enjoyment of one's property but adds that the law may subordinate such use and enjoyment to the interest of society. Article 21(2) forbids deprivation of

---

189 UDHR, above note 23, art. 17. See also ICCPR, above note 9, art. 17, which forbids arbitrary or unlawful interference with one's privacy, family, home, or correspondence, and CEDAW, above note 96, art. 15(2), which requires states parties to accord women legal capacity identical to that of men.

190 UDHR, ibid., art. 27(2); ICESCR, above note 18, art. 15(c).

191 ICCPR, above note 9, art. 26; ICESCR, ibid., art. 2(2); CRC, above note 24, art. 2(1).

192 CERD, above note 62, art. 5(d)(v), 5(d)(vi); CEDAW, above note 96, art. 15(2), 16(1)(h).

property "except in payment of just compensation, for reasons of public utility or social interest, and in the cases and according to the forms established by law." Article 21(3) requires states parties to prohibit by law usury "and other forms of exploitation of man by man." No definition of usury or elaboration of "other forms of exploitation" is given.

The European and African instruments also guarantee property rights subject to the public interest. Article 1 of the ECHR First Protocol (1952)[193] declares that natural and legal persons are entitled to the peaceful enjoyment of their possessions and may not be deprived of their possessions "except in the public interest and subject to the conditions provided for by law and by the general principles of international law." These provisions are declared not to impair the state's right to enforce laws controlling the use of property in the general interest or to secure payment of taxes and other contributions or penalties. Similarly, AfrCHPR article 14 declares that the right of property shall be guaranteed and may only be encroached upon "in the interest of public need or in the general interest of the community and in accordance with the provisions of appropriate laws."

3) In Canadian Law

Explicit protection of property rights is notably absent from the *Charter*. The Supreme Court of Canada has hesitated to bring such protection into the *Charter* through other sections.[194]

The contrast to section 1(a) of the *Canadian Bill of Rights* is striking.[195] That provision recognizes and declares the right of the individual to enjoyment of property, and the right not to be deprived thereof except by due process of law. The strength of section 1(a) is perhaps in question following the decision of the Supreme Court of Canada in *Authorson v. Canada (Attorney General)*.[196] A representative plaintiff in a class action by disabled veterans tried to rely on the *Bill of Rights* to challenge legislation that limited the Crown's liability for gross mismanagement of the veterans' pensions and other benefits. The courts below found the legislation inconsistent with the veterans' right,

---

193 European Convention on Human Rights 1950 (ECHR), Protocol No. 1 (1952), ETS no. 9.

194 See for example *Re ss. 193 and 195.1 of the Criminal Code*, [1990] 1 SCR 1123 at 1170–1.

195 See also *Alberta Bill of Rights*, above note 11, s. 1(a) and *Human Rights Act* RSY 1986 (Supp.) c. 11 s. 51.

196 2003 SCC 39.

declared in *Bill of Rights* section 1(a), not to be deprived of the enjoyment of property except by due process of law. The Supreme Court of Canada overruled the lower courts, finding that the due process protections in section 1(a) do not protect against expropriation of property by the passage of unambiguous legislation.

Perhaps the best places to look for property rights protections in Canadian law are ordinary statutes and the common law. An entire part of the *Criminal Code* is devoted to offences against rights of property.[197] Intellectual property rights are protected by federal legislation.[198] Federal and provincial expropriation legislation compensates and provides procedural protections to property-owners facing government expropriation.[199] The common law has long recognized and protected the rights of natural persons to own, inherit, and dispose of property in various forms. Canadian courts, like their English counterparts, generally construe expropriation statutes according to the presumption that the expropriating authority must observe due process[200] and pay compensation.[201] Until recently, tax statutes were interpreted strictly in the taxpayer's favour.[202] Property rights protections are also found in Quebec civil law.

In contrast to the UN instruments, Canadian law has not recognized property as a prohibited ground of discrimination either under *Charter* section 15(1) or in federal and provincial anti-discrimination laws. However, discrimination in the exercise of property rights (for example, refusing to sell to a person on account of her nationality) is prohibited in federal and provincial human rights codes.

---

197 *Criminal Code*, above note 31, Part IX. Not all the offences under Part IX are orthodox property offences. For example, s. 365 makes pretending fraudulently to practice "witchcraft, sorcery, enchantment or conjuration" a summary offence!

198 For example *Copyright Act* RSC 1985 c. C-42, *Industrial Design Act* RSC 1985 c. I-9, *Patent Act* RSC 1985 c. P-4, *Trade-marks Act* RSC 1985 c. T-13.

199 For example *Expropriation Act* RSC 1985 c. E-21, *Expropriation Act* RSBC 1996 c. 125, *Expropriations Act* RSO 1990 c. E.26, *Expropriation Act* RSQ c. E-24, etc.

200 *Harrison v. Carswell*, [1976] 2 SCR 200 at 219.

201 *Manitoba Fisheries Ltd. v. The Queen*, [1979] 1 SCR 101 at 109; *Wells v. Newfoundland*, [1999] 3 SCR 199 at para. 47. See also *Attorney-General v. De Keyser's Royal Hotel*, [1920] AC 508 (Eng HL) at 542.

202 For example *Partington v. Attorney-General* (1869), LR 4 HL 100 (HL) per Lord Cairns; now see *Corporation Notre-Dame de Bon-Secours v. Quebec*, [1994] 3 SCR 3.

I. RIGHTS TO PRIVACY AND REPUTATION

The themes of privacy and respect for one's reputation are intimately linked, and are usually treated together in international human rights instruments.

1) In Binding Instruments

UDHR article 12 declares, "No one shall be subjected to arbitrary interference with his privacy, family, home or correspondence, nor to attacks upon his honour and reputation. Everyone has the right to the protection of the law against such interference or attacks."

ICCPR article 17 repeats this provision almost word for word.[203] Privacy is also protected by ICCPR article 14(1), which provides an exception to the rule of public hearings in criminal cases where "the interest of the private lives of the parties so requires." The privacy rights of children are reaffirmed by CRC article 16 in the same terms as used in the ICCPR. Furthermore, CRC article 40(2)(b)(vii) guarantees the rights of children accused of crimes to have their privacy fully respected at all stages of the proceedings.

AmDR article 5 declares the rights of every person to "the protection of the law against abusive attacks upon his honour, his reputation, and his private and family life." Similarly, articles 9 and 10 guarantee the inviolability of a person's home and correspondence, respectively.

2) In Non-Binding Instruments

ACHR article 11, entitled "Right to privacy," recognizes in article 11(1) everyone's right "to have his honour respected and his dignity recognized" and provides in article 11(2) and (3) protection against arbitrary or abusive interference with private life, family, home, or correspondence. Article 14(1) entitles persons injured by inaccurate or offensive statements or ideas disseminated publicly by legally-regulated media a "right to reply or to make a correction using the same communications outlet." Article 14(3) requires, for the "effective protection of honour and reputa-

---

203 The only difference is the addition of the word *unlawful*: "(1) No one shall be subjected to arbitrary interference with his privacy, family, home or correspondence, nor to unlawful attacks upon his honour and reputation. (2) Everyone has the right to the protection of the law against such interference or attacks." For more on ICCPR, above note 9, art. 17, see ICCPR General Comment 16 (1988).

tion," that publishers and other media outlets have "a person responsible who is not protected by immunities or special privileges."

ECHR article 8(1) provides, "Everyone has the right to respect for his private and family life, his home and his correspondence." Article 8(2) limits interference with this right by public authorities except in accordance with law and as "necessary in a democratic society in the interests of national security, public safety or the economic well-being of the country, for the protection of health or morals, or for the protection of the rights and freedoms of others." There is no explicit privacy guarantee in the AfrCHPR.

3) In Canadian Law

Guarantees of privacy and reputation are found throughout the Canadian legal order, from the *Charter* to ordinary statutes to common law doctrines of some antiquity. And yet there is no explicit constitutional or statutory protection of the basic human right to be free from invasions of privacy and attacks upon one's reputation. Here is yet another example of an international human right that is implicitly but not explicitly implemented in Canadian law.

There is no explicit guarantee of privacy in the *Charter*. The closest thing is section 8, "Everyone has the right to be secure against unreasonable search or seizure." In the leading case, *Hunter v. Southam*,[204] the Supreme Court of Canada held that the interest that section 8 seeks to protect is not limited to the protection of property or the prevention of trespass. Rather, section 8 protects a person's reasonable expectation of privacy. The court looked to American rather than international law in reaching this conclusion. Yet the Supreme Court has cited the international provisions.[205] Later jurisprudence has established the "constitutional significance"[206] of privacy in cases involving property searches,[207] body searches,[208] and searches or seizures of private information.[209]

---

204 [1984] 2 SCR 145.
205 For example *Edmonton Journal v. Alberta (Attorney General)*, [1989] 2 SCR 1326 [*Edmonton Jounal*] at 1377 per La Forest J. (dissenting in part), citing the ICCPR, UDHR, and ECHR.
206 *Ibid.* at 1376.
207 For example *R. v. Genest*, [1989] 1 SCR 59.
208 For example *R. v. Beare*, [1988] 2 SCR 387 [*Beare*]; *R. v. Dyment*, [1988] 2 SCR 417 [*Dyment*].
209 For example *Dyment, ibid.*; *Thomson Newspapers Ltd. v. Canada (Director of Investigation and Research)*, [1990] 1 SCR 425 (lesser expectation of privacy in respect of business documents); *R. v. O'Connor*, [1995] 4 SCR 411 [*O'Connor*].

Section 8 may not be the only *Charter* provision implicating the right to privacy. Though the position has not yet attracted majority support, several minority judgments of the Supreme Court of Canada have suggested that the liberty and security of the person elements of section 7 encompass a right to privacy.[210] Privacy may also be a pressing and substantial legislative reason for limiting other *Charter* rights, notably freedom of expression.[211]

Privacy is also protected in Canada by a variety of quasi- and non-constitutional provisions. Section 5 of the *Quebec Charter* provides, "Every person has a right to respect for his private life." In *Godbout v. Longueuil (City)*,[212] the Supreme Court of Canada relied on section 5 to invalidate a municipal resolution that imposed a residency requirement on city employees, finding that an employee's choice of residence is an aspect of his or her right to privacy. Specific guarantees of privacy, including limits on privacy rights, may be found in several federal and provincial privacy statutes,[213] and in the *Criminal Code*.[214] Furthermore, the elaboration of privacy rights in international and constitutional law may be spreading to the common law.[215] In *Douglas v. Hello! Ltd.*,[216] Sedley LJ found that the common law's traditional rejection of a stand-alone right to privacy had been overtaken by such developments as the recognition of privacy rights in the ECHR and the implementation of those rights in the UK *Human Rights Act 1998*. There is also Canadian authority to suggest an emerging tort of invasion of privacy.[217] Some jurisdic-

---

210 *Beare*, above note 208 at 412 per La Forest J.; *Children's Aid*, above note 17 at 369 per La Forest J.; *O'Connor, ibid.* at para. 118 per L'Heureux-Dubé J.; *M. (A.) v. Ryan*, [1997] 1 SCR 157 at para. 80 per L'Heureux-Dubé J.

211 For example *Edmonton Journal*, above note 205 at 1345; see also at 1374 per La Forest J. (dissenting in part), citing the internal limits to free expression enunciated in the ICCPR and the ECHR.

212 *Godbout*, above note 137.

213 For example *Privacy Act* RSC 1985 c. P-21, *Personal Information Protection and Electronic Documents Act* SC 2000 c. 5, *Freedom of Information and Protection of Privacy Act* RSBC 1996 c. 165, *Freedom of Information and Protection of Privacy Act* RSO 1990 c. F.31, *An Act Respecting Access to Documents Held by Public Bodies and the Protection of Personal Information* RSQ 1982 c. A-2.1 (Quebec).

214 *Criminal Code*, above note 31, Part VI (invasion of privacy).

215 In Quebec, see the *Civil Code* SQ 1991 c. 64 arts. 35–41 (respect of reputation and privacy).

216 [2001] QB 967 (Eng CA).

217 *Ontario (Attorney General) v. Dieleman* (1994), 20 OR (3d) 229 (Gen. Div.). See the discussion in B. McIsaac, R. Shields, & K. Klein, *The Law of Privacy in Canada* (Scarborough: Carswell, 2000) at heading 2.4.1.

tions have decided not to wait for the common law to develop. They have created statutory torts to remedy interferences with privacy.[218]

Like the right to privacy, the right to legal protection from attacks on one's honour and reputation finds no explicit mention in the *Charter*. Yet in *Hill v. Church of Scientology of Toronto*, the Supreme Court of Canada observed that "the good reputation of the individual represents and reflects the innate dignity of the individual, a concept which underlies all the *Charter* rights. It follows that the protection of the good reputation of the individual is of fundamental importance to our democratic society."[219] The court went on to affirm, consistently with the international position, that "reputation is intimately related to the right to privacy."[220] *Hill* is also notable for its conclusion that the common law of defamation, which is the principal legal means by which reputation is protected in Canada's common law jurisdictions,[221] complies with *Charter* values and needs no judicial alteration or legislative amendment. The protection of reputation in most Canadian jurisdictions therefore remains largely a matter of common law. Though it is an unorthodox use of the term, there is a sense in which the common law of defamation "implements" Canada's international obligations in respect of the right to reputation.

J. RIGHTS IN RESPECT OF ARREST, DETENTION AND IMPRISONMENT

We group under this heading international and Canadian provisions that grant procedural and substantive rights in the event of arrest, detention or imprisonment. Protection from torture and cruel, inhuman or degrading treatment or punishment is addressed separately later in the chapter.

1) In Binding Instruments

UDHR article 9 provides in part that no one shall be subject to arbitrary arrest or detention. The ICCPR reaffirms this[222] and expands upon it by adding the right to be informed upon arrest of the reasons for the arrest

---

218 *Privacy Act* RSBC 1996 c. 373 s. 1(1); *Privacy Act* RSS 1978 c. P-24 s. 2; *Privacy Act* CCSM c. P125 s. 2(1); *Privacy Act* RSNL 1990 c. P-22 s. 3(1).
219 [1995] 2 SCR 1130 at para. 120 [*Hill*].
220 *Ibid.* at para. 121.
221 For Quebec, see note 215, above.
222 ICCPR, above note 9, art. 9(1). On art. 9 generally, see ICCPR General Comment 8 (1982) and ICCPR General Comment 9 (1982).

and to be promptly informed of any charges.[223] Furthermore, ICCPR article 9 requires states parties to provide a means of challenging without delay the lawfulness of one's detention,[224] declares that persons awaiting trial shall not generally be detained in custody but may be released subject to guarantees such as bail,[225] and provides that victims of unlawful arrest or detention shall have an enforceable right to compensation.[226] Article 10(1) adds that all persons deprived of liberty shall be treated with humanity and with respect for the inherent dignity of the human person. Finally, article 11 forbids imprisonment "merely on the ground of inability fulfil a contractual obligation."

CRC article 37(b) provides that no child shall be deprived of liberty unlawfully or arbitrarily, and that the arrest, detention or imprisonment of a child shall be in conformity with the law and shall be used only as a measure of last resort. Further, the arrest, detention or imprisonment of a child shall be for the shortest appropriate period. Other provisions of the CRC recognize a child's right to be promptly informed of the charges against her,[227] to challenge the legality of her detention,[228] and to be treated humanely while deprived of her liberty.[229]

AmDR article 25 protects against arbitrary arrest. It provides, among other things, that no person may be deprived of liberty except in the cases and according to the procedures established by pre-existing law, that those deprived of liberty have the right to challenge the legality of their detainment without delay, and that detained persons have the right to humane treatment while in custody. Article 25 also forbids deprivations of liberty for "nonfulfillment of obligations of a purely civil character."

2) In Non-Binding Instruments

ACHR article 7(3) provides that no one shall be subject to arbitrary arrest or imprisonment. Article 7(4) adds that anyone detained shall be informed of the reasons for his detention and shall be promptly notified of the charges against him. Article 7(6) declares that detained persons shall be entitled to "recourse to a competent court, in order that the court may decide without delay on the lawfulness of his arrest or detention and order his release if the arrest or detention is unlawful."

---

223 ICCPR, ibid., art. 9(2).
224 Ibid., art. 9(4).
225 Ibid., art. 9(3).
226 Ibid., art. 9(5).
227 CRC, above note 24, art. 40(2)(b)(ii).
228 Ibid., art. 37(d).
229 Ibid., art. 37(c).

Article 8(2)(b) guarantees accused persons "prior notification in detail" of the charges against them.

ECHR article 5(1) declares everyone's right to liberty and security of the person and provides that no one shall be deprived of liberty save in specified cases and "in accordance with a procedure prescribed by law." The specified cases (art. 5(1)(a)–(f)) include lawful detention after conviction, lawful arrest, or detention for non-compliance with a lawful court order or to secure fulfilment of a legal obligation, and lawful arrest or detention of a person reasonably suspected of having committed an offence. Article 5(2) requires that an arrested person be informed promptly of the reasons for his arrest and of any charge against him. Article 5(3) guarantees suspects either trial within a reasonable time or release pending trial, and provides that release pending trial may be conditioned by guarantees to appear. Article 5(4) entitles arrested or detained persons to challenge the lawfulness of their detention and be released if the detention is not lawful. Article 5(5) provides an enforceable right to compensation to victims of arrest or detention in contravention of article 5. Finally, article 6(3)(a) guarantees everyone charged with a criminal offence the right to be informed promptly and in detail of the nature and cause of the accusation against him.

The weakest guarantor of the civil rights described under this heading is the AfrCHPR. Article 6 affirms the right to liberty and security of the person, and provides that no one "may be deprived of his freedom except for reasons and conditions previously laid down by law. In particular, no one may be arbitrarily arrested or detained." The AfrCHPR contains no explicit provisions on the right to be informed of the reason for one's arrest or detention, the right to be informed of criminal charges, or the right to challenge the legality of one's detention.

3) In Canadian Law

There is great overlap between the international and Canadian laws of arrest, detention and imprisonment. This is unsurprising, for the rights described under this heading have enjoyed some form of protection in Anglo-American law for centuries, and have gained international currency in part through the influence of that tradition.

Charter section 9 provides, "Everyone has the right not to be arbitrarily detained or imprisoned." Similarly, section 2(a) of the *Canadian Bill of Rights* requires that no law of Canada be construed and applied so as to authorize or effect the arbitrary detention, imprisonment, or exile of any person. Unlike the UDHR and ICCPR, these provisions refer to detention but not to arrest. Yet the Supreme Court of Canada has held that detention connotes some form of compulsory restraint and may include arrest.[230] Detention will be arbitrary when there are no criteria, express or implied, governing it.[231] Note that *Charter* section 9 is subject to the limitation in section 1; some forms of arbitrary detention may be justified.[232]

Charter section 10 sets out the legal rights of arrested or detained persons. Similar provisions occur in section 2(c) of the *Bill of Rights*. Arrested or detained persons have the right to be "informed promptly" of the reasons behind their arrest or detention.[233] (If they are charged with an offence, they have the right to be informed without unreasonable delay of the specific offence.)[234] Arrested or detained persons have the right to retain and instruct counsel without delay[235] and to be informed of that right.[236] This provision may exceed international requirements, which generally provide that the right to counsel arises at the trial stage.[237] Finally, arrested or detained persons have the right to have the validity of their detention determined by way of habeas corpus and to be released if their detention is not lawful.[238] One might expect this provision to satisfy the requirements of ICCPR section 9(4) since a draft of that provision actually used the words "in the nature of *habeas corpus*."[239]

Charter section 11(e) affirms the right of persons charged with an offence not to be denied reasonable bail without just cause.[240] A simi-

---

230 *Chromiak v. The Queen*, [1980] 1 SCR 471 at 478; see also *R. v. Therens*, [1985] 1 SCR 613 at 631.

231 *R. v. Hufsky*, [1988] 1 SCR 621 at 633 [*Hufsky*].

232 For example *Hufsky*, where police "spot-checks" of drivers for drunkenness and traffic violations was found to be arbitrary detention per s. 9 but justified under s. 1.

233 *Charter* s. 10(a); *Bill of Rights*, above note 187, s. 2(c)(i).

234 *Charter* s. 11(a).

235 *Charter* s. 10(b); *Bill of Rights*, above note 187, s. 2(c)(ii).

236 *Charter*, ibid.

237 But see more expansive readings of the right to counsel in *Murray v. United Kingdom* (1996), 22 EHRR 29 [*Murray*]; *Imbrioscia v. Switzerland* (1993), 17 EHRR 441; *De Voituret v. Uruguay* (1984), Comm. no. 109/1981; *Kelly v. Jamaica* (1996), Comm no. 537/1993.

238 *Charter* s. 10(c); *Bill of Rights*, above note 187, s. 2(c)(iii).

239 N. Jayawickrama, *The Judicial Application of Human Rights Law: National Regional and International Jurisprudence* (Cambridge: Cambridge University Press, 2002) at 416 n.168. But see *Chahal v. United Kingdom* (1996), 23 EHRR 413, in which the European Court of Human Rights found that, in the circumstances of that case, habeas corpus was in fact not enough to meet the requirements of European Convention on Human Rights 1950 (ECHR), ETS no. 5, art. 5(4). The case was complicated by the government's refusal to divulge certain materials on the ground of national security.

240 Note that today the term "judicial interim release" is used in preference to "bail" in the *Criminal Code*; s. 11(e) is understood to refer to such release schemes: *R. v. Pearson*, [1992] 3 SCR 665 at 690 [*Pearson*].

lar provision is found in *Bill of Rights* section 2(f). These provisions correspond to ICCPR article 9(3), which provides in part that persons awaiting trial shall not generally be detained in custody but may be subject to guarantees to appear for trial. The requirement that bail be "reasonable" was first declared in Anglo-Canadian law by section 10 of the *Bill of Rights* 1689, which forbade "excessive" bail.[241] The reasonableness requirement in section 11(e) refers both to the reasonableness of the quantum and of any other terms imposed.[242] There will be "just cause" for denying bail where denial is "necessary to promote the proper functioning of the bail system and is not undertaken for any purpose extraneous to the bail system."[243]

The requirement that persons deprived of their liberty be treated with humanity and respect for their human dignity, expressed internationally in ICCPR article 10(1) and AmDR article 25, finds no explicit parallel in Canadian law. There is some authority, however, for invoking the prohibitions of cruel and unusual punishment in *Charter* section 12 and *Bill of Rights* section 2(b) to challenge prison conditions.[244] And the requirements of humanity and human dignity are touched upon by certain provisions of the *Corrections and Conditional Release Act*.[245] Section 3(a) speaks of "the safe and humane custody and supervision of offenders." Section 70 requires the Correctional Service of Canada to take all reasonable steps to ensure that penitentiaries, the penitentiary environment, and the living and working conditions of inmates are "free of practices that undermine a person's sense of personal dignity."

Another ICCPR requirement not expressly guaranteed by the *Charter* is the "enforceable right" of victims of "unlawful arrest or detention" to compensation (art. 9(5)).[246] The jurisprudence of the Human Rights Committee has established that "unlawful" means contrary to ICCPR article 9, whether the detention is lawful under domestic law or not.[247] "Unlawful" presumably also means contrary to domestic law even in the absence of a violation of the ICCPR. At common law, an action for damages is available for the tort of false imprisonment (wrongful deten-

---

241 1 William & Mary sess. 1 c. 6.
242 *Pearson*, above note 240 at 689.
243 *Ibid.* at 693.
244 *McCann v. The Queen*, [1976] 1 FC 570 (TD); *R. v. McC.(T.)* (1991), 4 OR (3d) 203 (Prov Div).
245 SC 1992 c. 20.
246 See the discussion of compensation payments for human rights violations in Chapter Thirteen.
247 *A. v. Australia* (1997), Comm. no. 560/1993 at para. 9.

tion).[248] The "imprisonment" will not be "false" if the perpetrator acted with legal justification, such as under the *Criminal Code*.[249] The existence of this common law action may not be enough to satisfy article 9(5)'s requirements, judging by the Human Rights Committee's decision in *Portorreal v. Dominican Republic*, where the Committee was of the view that compensation was owed for an arrest that failed to meet the requirement, in ICCPR article 9(2), that the arrested person be informed of the reasons for his arrest.[250] This approach would seemingly require any infringement of *Charter* sections 9 and 10 to be remedied in part by compensatory damages. Though the remedial power of courts under *Charter* section 24(1) is broad enough to permit damage awards, Canadian courts rarely make them.[251]

Curiously, many Canadian jurisdictions continue to have legislation in place permitting the imprisonment of debtors — not because this practice is still condoned but simply because the legislation has never been repealed. Nevertheless, these statutes go unused today and the imprisonment of debtors has become "a legal backwater of little interest to lawyers or legislators."[252] The mere existence of these hoary statutes probably does not bring Canada into international default. There can hardly be any doubt that any attempt to imprison a debtor today would result in a successful constitutional challenge to the legislation.[253]

K. RIGHTS IN CRIMINAL PROCEEDINGS

We have grouped under this heading a number of familiar rights in criminal proceedings. They are:

- the right to counsel;

---

248 See A. Linden, *Canadian Tort Law*, 7th ed. (Markham, Ontario: Butterworths, 2002) at 49–52.

249 See *Criminal Code*, above note 31, ss. 494–95 on the lawfulness of arrests without warrant.

250 See *Portorreal v. Dominican Republic* (1987), Comm. no. 188/84.

251 On the reasons for this, see K. Roach, *Constitutional Remedies in Canada*, looseleaf ed. (Aurora, Ontario: Canada Law Book Inc., 1994–) at c. 11.

252 C. Dunlop, *Creditor-Debtor Law in Canada*, 2d ed (Scarborough: Carswell, 1995) at 111–12. In *R. v. Whitfield* [1970] SCR 46 at 52–53, Hall J. (dissenting) suggested in *obiter* that the English *Debtors Act* (1869) 32-3 Vict. c. 62 s. 4 abolished imprisonment for debt in Canada. But this must be mistaken, for that Act does not purport to extend to Canada.

253 "Debtors' prison for impoverished people is a Dickensian concept that in civilized countries has largely been abolished": *R. v. Wu*, 2003 SCC 73 at para. 2 per Binnie J.

- the right to trial within a reasonable time;
- the right to a fair and public hearing by an impartial and independent tribunal;
- the right to examine witnesses;
- the right to an interpreter;
- the presumption of innocence;
- the privilege against self-incrimination;
- the right to benefit from lesser punishments;
- protection from retroactive laws; and
- protection from double jeopardy.

1) In Binding Instruments

UDHR article 10 declares that everyone is entitled in full equality to a fair and public hearing by an independent and impartial tribunal in the determination of criminal charges. Article 11(1) affirms everyone's right "to be presumed innocent until proved guilty according to law in a public trial at which he has had all the guarantees necessary for his defence." Article 11(2) forbids convictions on account of acts or omissions which did not constitute penal offences under national or international law at the time they were committed. That same article also provides that a penalty heavier than the one applicable at the time the offence was committed shall not be imposed.

The ICCPR affirms, expands upon, and adds to these criminal proceedings rights.[254] The presumption of innocence is affirmed.[255] So, too, is the protection against the imposition of heavier penalties than those applicable when the offence was committed.[256] Retroactive criminal laws are forbidden,[257] but this prohibition shall not prejudice the trial and punishment of persons whose acts or omissions, at the time they were committed, were criminal according to "the general principles of law recognized by the community of nations."[258] The right to a fair and public hearing by an impartial and independent tribunal is affirmed and elaborated upon.[259] Certain "minimum guarantees" for criminal defendants are declared, including rights to counsel and the prepara-

---

254 See generally ICCPR General Comment 13 (1984).
255 ICCPR, above note 9, art. 14(2).
256 *Ibid.*, art. 15(1).
257 *Ibid.*, art. 15(1).
258 *Ibid.*, art. 15(2).
259 *Ibid.*, art. 14(1).

tion of a defence,[260] the right to be tried without undue delay,[261] the right to be present at one's criminal trial,[262] the right to examine opposing witnesses,[263] the right to an interpreter if necessary[264] and the right not to be compelled to testify against oneself or to confess guilt.[265] ICCPR article 14(7) forbids double jeopardy: no one shall be liable to be tried or punished again for an offence for which he has already been finally convicted or acquitted. Article 15(1) provides that if, following the offence, provision is made by law for the imposition of a lighter penalty, the offender shall benefit thereby.

CRC article 40(1) declares that states parties recognize:

> the right of every child alleged as, accused of, or recognized as having infringed the penal law to be treated in a manner consistent with the promotion of the child's sense of dignity and worth, which reinforces the child's respect for the human rights and fundamental freedoms of others and which takes into account the child's age and the desirability of promoting the child's reintegration and the child's assuming a constructive role in society.

To this end, article 40(2) reaffirms many of the human rights protected in the UDHR and ICCPR as they apply to children. These include the presumption of innocence,[266] the right of the child to be informed of the charges against her,[267] the right to a fair hearing before an independent and impartial authority,[268] the right to have the matter determined without delay,[269] the privilege against self-incrimination[270] and the right to examine witnesses.[271] The CRC also confirms the child's right to counsel and the right to challenge the legality of her detention.[272]

---

260 *Ibid.*, art. 14(3)(b) and (d).

261 *Ibid.*, art. 14(3)(c). Canada was found by the Human Rights Committee to be in violation of this art. (and art. 14(5), "Everyone convicted of a crime shall have the right to his conviction and sentence being reviewed by a higher tribunal according to law") in a case where a person's appeal from conviction was delayed over two and half years due to administrative error: *Pinkney v. Canada* (1981), Comm. no. 27/1977 (R.7/27) at 101 [*Pinkney*].

262 ICCPR, *ibid.*, art. 14(3)(d).

263 *Ibid.*, art. 14(3)(e).

264 *Ibid.*, art. 14(3)(f); see also art. 14(3)(a).

265 *Ibid.*, art. 14(3)(g).

266 CRC, above note 24, art. 40(2)(b)(i).

267 *Ibid.*, art. 40(2)(b)(ii).

268 *Ibid.*, art. 40(2)(b)(iii).

269 *Ibid.*, art. 40(2)(b)(iii).

270 *Ibid.*, art. 40(2)(b)(iv).

271 *Ibid.*, art. 40(2)(b)(iv).

272 *Ibid.*, art. 37(d).

The presumption of innocence, the right to an "impartial and public hearing," and the right "to be tried by courts previously established in accordance with pre-existing laws" are recognized by AmDR article 26.[273] The right to be tried "without undue delay" is recognized in article 25, as is the right not to be subjected to retroactive criminal laws.[274]

2) In Non-Binding Instruments

Almost all of the rights considered under this heading find expression in both the ACHR and the ECHR, while only some are addressed in the AfrCHPR. The right to counsel is protected in all three instruments.[275] The right to trial within a reasonable time is protected in the ACHR and the ECHR,[276] but not in the AfrCHPR. The right to a fair and public hearing is secured by the ACHR and the ECHR, as is the right to an independent and impartial tribunal.[277] The AfrCHPR is seemingly less demanding: article 7(1) recognizes the right to have one's cause heard but omits mention of fairness, publicity, or judicial independence. Judicial independence is affirmed, however, in AfrCHPR article 26. The right to an interpreter, if needed, is recognized in ACHR article 8(3)(a) and ECHR article 6(3)(e). The presumption of innocence is guaranteed in all three instruments.[278] The privilege against self-incrimination finds protection in ACHR article 8(3)(g) and AfrCHPR article 7(1)(d) but is not explicitly stated in the ECHR.[279] ACHR article 9 protects against retroactive criminal laws while also guaranteeing convicted persons the benefit of any lesser punishment provided by law subsequent to the commission of the offence. ECHR article 7 forbids convictions under retroactive laws but does not include the "*in mitius*" principle, that a criminal provision which is less severe than the previously applicable provision is to be applied retrospectively.[280] The AfrCHPR provides no

273 See also American Declaration on the Rights and Duties of Man 1948 (AmDR), OAS res. XXX (1948), art. 18, providing a right to resort to the courts to ensure respect for one's legal rights.
274 "No person may be deprived of his liberty except in the cases and according to the procedures established by pre-existing law."
275 ACHR, above note 26, art. 8(2)(d), 8(2)(e); ECHR, above note 239, art. 6(3)(c); AfrCHPR, above note 106, art. 7(1)(c).
276 ACHR, ibid., arts. 7(5), 8(1); ECHR, ibid., art. 5(3).
277 ACHR, ibid., art. 8(1), 8(5); ECHR, ibid., art. 6(1).
278 ACHR, ibid., art. 8(2); ECHR art. 6(2); AfrCHPR, above note 106, art. 7(1)(b).
279 Nevertheless, the European Court of Human Rights has held that the privilege forms part of art. 6's notion of fair procedure: *Murray*, above note 237, at para. 45; *Saunders v. United Kingdom* (1996), 23 EHRR 313 at para. 68.
280 See *G v. France* (1996), 21 EHRR 288. Such a provision has been included in art. 49(1) of the Draft Charter of Fundamental Rights of the European Union 2000.

explicit protection against retroactive criminal laws and no provision guaranteeing the benefit of lighter criminal sanctions. Finally, protection against double jeopardy is provided by ACHR article 8(4) and article 4(1) of ECHR Protocol No. 7 (1984).

3) In Canadian Law

Human rights are never wholly uncontroversial. Yet as human rights go, the rights considered here are among the least disputed. Though these rights gained constitutional force in Canada only relatively recently, most have long histories in ordinary statutes and the common law. This is not a textbook on criminal law, and we make no attempt to engage the voluminous jurisprudence these fundamental rights have generated under the *Charter* or other laws. Rather, our aim is to highlight the high degree of overlap (and modicum of divergence) between the international and Canadian protection of these rights.

The *Charter* explicitly guarantees almost all of the international criminal law rights considered under this heading. We have already considered the right to retain and instruct counsel without delay and to be informed of that right.[281] Most of the other rights in question here fall under section 11: the right to be tried within a reasonable time;[282] the right to a fair and public hearing by an independent and impartial tribunal;[283] the privilege against self-incrimination;[284] the presumption of innocence;[285] the right to benefit from lesser punishments;[286] the right to protection from retroactive laws;[287] and the right to protection from double jeopardy.[288] The right to an interpreter, which in Canada extends not only to accused persons but also to "a party or witness in any proceedings," is guaranteed by *Charter* section 14.

Two provisions in *Charter* section 11 are of particular note from a reception-law perspective. First, section 11(f)'s guarantee of the benefit of trial by jury for certain serious offences finds no international par-

---

281 *Charter* s. 10(b); see the discussion of rights in respect of arrest, detention and imprisonment, above.
282 *Charter* s. 11(b). In a pre-*Charter* communication to the Human Rights Committee, Canada was found in breach of its ICCPR obligations to try people without undue delay: *Pinkney*, above note 261.
283 *Charter* s. 11(d).
284 *Charter* ss. 11(c) and 13.
285 *Charter* s. 11(d).
286 *Charter* s. 11(i).
287 *Charter* s. 11(g).
288 *Charter* s. 11(h).

allel. The jury, for the most part, is an institution peculiar to common law jurisdictions. Second, the protection from retroactive criminal laws afforded by section 11(g) refers to offences under "international law" or acts "criminal according to the general principles of law recognized by the community of nations" (repeating ICCPR article 15(2)). The wording of section 11(g) is, on its face, redundant: an act recognized as criminal "according to the general principles of law recognized by the community of nations" must also be an offence under "international law."[289] Furthermore, it is unclear what the phrase "according to the general principles of law recognized by the community of nations" is aimed at. It appears to refer to the source of international law known as general principles.[290] Yet specific criminal offences are not contemplated by such principles; it is more likely, then, that the phrase is intended to refer to customary international law. These uncertainties aside, it is fairly clear that section 11(g) permits an exception to the rule that Parliament may not enact retroactive criminal offences, namely that Parliament may do in respect of offences under international law. Thus, if an act is or becomes a criminal offence under international law, but is not so under Canadian law, Parliament may legislate to make it retroactively so.

The right to examine witnesses, as declared in ICCPR article 14(3)(e), is not explicitly provided for in the *Charter*. However, the Supreme Court of Canada has confirmed that the right of accused persons to cross-examine adverse witnesses and generally to make full answer and defence to the charges against them is assured by the *Charter*.[291] "The right of the innocent not to be convicted is dependent on the right to present full answer and defence. This, in turn, depends on being able to call the evidence necessary to establish a defence and to challenge the evidence called by the prosecution."[292] The power to compel witnesses to attend court and give evidence is provided by the subpoena provisions of the *Criminal Code*.[293]

---

289 An earlier draft of s. 11(g) lacked this redundancy: "Any person charged with an offence has the right . . . not to be found guilty on account of any act or omission that at the time of the act or omission did not constitute an offence under Canadian or international law."

290 See Chapter Three.

291 This right has been located in *Charter* s. 11(d) (*R. v. Corbett*, [1988] 1 SCR 670) and s. 7 (*R. v. Stinchcombe*, [1991] 3 SCR 326, *R. v. Potvin*, [1989] 1 SCR 525 at 544).

292 *R. v. Seaboyer*, [1991] 2 SCR 577 at 608.

293 *Criminal Code*, above note 31, ss. 698–708.

L. RIGHTS IN CIVIL PROCEEDINGS

The right to a fair and public hearing by an independent and impartial tribunal, considered above in the criminal context, also applies to civil proceedings. Other rights of note in the civil context, but discussed elsewhere in this work, are equality before the law,[294] the right to a remedy,[295] and, when children are involved, the best interests of the child.[296]

1) In Binding Instruments

UDHR article 10 declares, "Everyone is entitled in full equality to a fair and public hearing by an independent and impartial tribunal, in the determination of his rights and obligations."[297]

ICCPR article 14(1) provides that "[i]n the determination of . . . his rights and obligations in a suit at law, everyone shall be entitled to a fair and public hearing by a competent, independent and impartial tribunal established by law." Article 14(1) goes on to permit exclusion of the press and public from all or part of a trial for reasons of morals, public order, or national security in a democratic society, or where the interest of the private lives of the parties so requires, or "to the extent strictly necessary in the opinion of the court in special circumstances where publicity would prejudice the interests of justice." Article 14(1) concludes by requiring the publication of civil (and criminal) judgments except in certain family-law contexts.

CRC article 12(2) requires states parties to provide children with "the opportunity to be heard in any judicial and administrative proceedings" affecting them, either directly or through a representative. Similarly, states parties must assure "to the child who is capable of forming his or her own views the right to express those views freely in all matters affecting the child, the views of the child being given due weight in accordance with the age and maturity of the child."[298]

---

294 See the discussion of equality rights, below.
295 See the discussion in Chapters Twelve and Thirteen.
296 See the discussion of family and children's rights, below.
297 For an elaboration of the requirements of independence and impartiality, see the "Bangalore Principles of Judicial Conduct 2002," being annex 1 of Commission on Human Rights, *Report of the Special Rapporteur on the Independence of Judges and Lawyers* (2003) UN doc. E/CN.4/2003/65. By resolution 2003/43, the UN Commission on Human Rights noted the Principles and brought them "to the attention of Member States, the relevant United Nations organs and inter-governmental and non-governmental organizations for their consideration."
298 CRC, above note 24, art. 12(1).

AmDR article 18 provides in part that every person may have access to the courts to ensure respect for his legal rights. The article is headed, "Right to a fair trial."

2) In Non-Binding Instruments

ACHR article 8(1) guarantees everyone a hearing by a "competent, independent and impartial tribunal, previously established by law . . . for the determination of his rights and obligations of a civil, labour, fiscal or any other nature." The ECHR's guarantee of a "fair and public hearing within a reasonable time by an independent and impartial tribunal established by law" applies to both civil and criminal proceedings.[299] The AfrCHPR recognizes every individual's right "to have his cause heard," including the right to "an appeal to competent national organs against acts of violating his fundamental rights as recognized and guaranteed by conventions, laws, regulations and customs in force."[300]

3) In Canadian Law

There are important constitutional and statutory provisions affirming and giving effect to fairness rights in Canadian civil proceedings. The Supreme Court of Canada has held that *Charter* section 7 will afford protection outside of the criminal context to civil proceedings in which a person's right to life, liberty, or security of the person is engaged.[301] Similarly, section 2(e) of the *Canadian Bill of Rights* makes no distinction between civil and criminal proceedings in declaring that no law of Canada shall be construed so as to "deprive a person of the right to a fair hearing in accordance with the principles of fundamental justice for the determination of his rights and obligations." Stronger still is

---

299 ECHR, above note 239, art. 6(1).
300 AfrCHPR, above note 106, art. 7(1).
301 Section 7 "is not limited solely to purely criminal or penal matters. There are other ways in which the government, in the course of the administration of justice, can deprive a person of their s. 7 rights to liberty and security of the person": *New Brunswick*, above note 159 at para. 65 (child protection proceedings). In *Singh v. Minister of Employment and Immigration*, [1985] 1 SCR 177, Wilson J. held that the *Immigration Act* violated refugee claimants' rights under *Charter* s. 7 by failing to accord them sufficient procedural guarantees (notably the opportunity to state one's case and to know the case one has to meet). See also *Children's Aid*, above note 16 at 341 per Lamer C.J.

section 23 of the *Quebec Charter*, which provides in part, "Every person has a right to a full and equal, public and fair hearing by an independent and impartial tribunal, for the determination of his rights and obligations." Countless other statutes could be cited as instances of these principles put into practice. Ultimately, however, all these provisions are informed by, and even declaratory of, basic principles of procedural fairness, public courts, and judicial independence adopted and developed in Canadian jurisprudence. The topic is best addressed from the perspective of the principles themselves.

The notion of fairness in Canadian law has its origins in the concept of natural justice, as expressed by the Latin maxims *nemo judex in re sua* (no one shall be a judge in his own cause) and *audi alteram partem* (hear the other side). With notable exceptions,[302] these principles were historically treated as standards for judicial, rather than administrative, decision-making procedures. The rise of administrative law in the twentieth century widened the reach of natural justice beyond courts and court-like bodies to encompass the panoply of administrative decision-makers now active in modern states. At the same time, English and Canadian courts broadened the scope of natural justice to embrace a potentially wider range of concerns under the heading of "procedural fairness."[303] Today, Canadian law generally guarantees procedurally fair hearings not only in court-based civil proceedings but also in a wide variety of administrative matters. Fairness has its limits, however. The degree of procedural fairness applicable to a particular administrative tribunal will depend upon the nature and function of that body. Not all administrative bodies are under a duty to act fairly. And with the exception of constitutional and quasi-constitutional matters, allegations of unfairness will only be admitted on procedural, not substantive, grounds.[304]

The international law requirement of public hearings is vindicated in Canada by a long tradition of open courts in both civil and criminal proceedings. In *Edmonton Journal v. Alberta (Attorney General)*,[305] Cory J. observed that courts must be "open to public scrutiny and to public criticism of their operation,"[306] citing Blackstone among others. He

---

302 For example *Dr Bentley's Case* (1723), 93 ER 698 (KB); *Cooper v. Board of Works for Wandsworth District* (1863), 143 ER 414 (CP).

303 For example *Ridge v. Baldwin*, [1964] AC 40 (HL); *Nicholson v. Haldimand Norfolk (Regional) Police Commissioners*, [1979] 1 SCR 311; *Knight v. Indian Head School Division No. 19*, [1990] 1 SCR 653 [*Knight*].

304 See generally D. Mullan, *Administrative Law* (Toronto: Irwin Law, 2001) at c. 8.

305 *Edmonton Journal*, above note 205.

306 *Ibid.* at 1337.

went on to affirm Dickson J.'s dictum that in Canadian court proceedings "covertness is the exception and openness the rule."[307]

The requirement that tribunals in civil proceedings be independent and impartial also has a long history in Canada. We have already touched on the principle of impartiality in our discussion of natural justice: decision-makers must not have a personal interest in the outcome of legal disputes they preside over, and must give a fair hearing to both sides of the dispute. The principle of independence is that decision-makers should be free from control by, or inappropriate influences from, the state or others. The establishment of judicial independence in Anglo-Canadian law is often said to begin with the *Act of Settlement 1700*,[308] which provided that judges shall hold office during good behaviour and shall not be subject to removal from office except by Parliament. This provision is reproduced in section 99(1) of the *Constitution Act 1867*. But constitutional protection of judicial independence in Canada goes beyond the written constitution. The Supreme Court of Canada has declared judicial independence to be an unwritten principle of the Canadian constitution[309] derived from the constitution's similarity in principle to that of the United Kingdom.[310] Though intimately associated with the judicial function, independence is not an exclusively judicial value; it must also be observed in certain forms of administrative decision-making.[311] One ground upon which to challenge the fairness of certain administrative decisions is to question the decision-maker's independence.[312]

M. PROTECTION FROM TORTURE AND CRUEL, INHUMAN OR DEGRADING TREATMENT OR PUNISHMENT

Under this heading we consider the prohibition of torture and other grave forms of mistreatment.

---

307 *Attorney General of Nova Scotia v. MacIntyre*, [1982] 1 SCR 175 at 185.

308 12 & 13 Will. 3 c. 2.

309 *Re Remuneration of Judges of the Provincial Court of Prince Edward Island*, [1997] 3 SCR 3; *Mackin v. New Brunswick (Minister of Finance)*, [2002] 1 SCR 405.

310 *Constitution Act 1867* (UK) 30 & 31 Vict. c. 3, preamble.

311 The degree of independence required of a particular government decision-maker or tribunal is determined by its enabling statute. See *Ocean Port Hotel Ltd. v. British Columbia (General Manager, Liquor Control and Licensing Branch)*, [2001] 2 SCR 781.

312 For example *Bell Canada v. Canadian Telephone Employees Association*, 2003 SCC 36, where the challenge failed.

1) In Binding Instruments

UDHR article 5 provides that no one shall be subjected to torture or to cruel, inhuman or degrading treatment or punishment. ICCPR article 7 repeats these words and adds specific protection against unconsensual medical or scientific experimentation.[313] CRC article 37(a) provides that no child shall be subjected to torture or other cruel, inhuman or degrading treatment or punishment.

The pre-eminent statement of the international community's condemnation of torture and other forms of serious ill-treatment is the CAT.[314] Among its provisions are a definition of torture, a requirement that states parties take effective measures to prevent acts of torture in their jurisdictions, a prohibition on expelling, returning, or extraditing persons to states where there are substantial grounds for believing they would be in danger of being subjected to torture, and a requirement that statements gained by means of torture be inadmissible as evidence (save in proceedings against the alleged torturer). For more on the CAT, see the discussion in Chapter Five.

AmDR article 26 provides in part that persons accused of an offence have the right not to receive "cruel, infamous or unusual punishment."

2) In Non-Binding Instruments

ACHR article 5(2) provides that no one shall be subjected to torture or to cruel, inhuman or degrading punishment or treatment. ECHR article 3 provides that no one shall be subjected to torture or to inhuman or degrading treatment or punishment. Both the Inter-American and the European treaty systems have been supplemented by specific treaties prohibiting torture.[315] AfrCHPR article 5 guarantees every individual the right to respect of his or her inherent dignity, and adds that all forms of "exploitation and degradation of man," particularly "torture, cruel, inhuman or degrading punishment and treatment," shall be prohibited. Specific protection against cruel, inhuman or degrading punishment and treatment of women is provided by article 4(1) of the AfrCHPR Women's Protocol.

---

313 See ICCPR General Comment 7 (1982).

314 Convention Against Torture and Other Cruel, Inhuman or Degrading Treatment or Punishment 1984 (CAT), [1987] CanTS no. 36.

315 Inter-American Convention to Prevent and Punish Torture 1985 OAS TS no. 67; European Convention for the Prevention of Torture and Inhuman or Degrading Treatment or Punishment 1987 ETS no. 126. See also the two protocols to the European Convention: ETS nos. 151, 152. See the discussion of these treaties in Chapter Six.

3) In Canadian Law

The principal measures relied on by Canada to implement its international obligations in respect of torture and cruel, inhuman or degrading punishment or treatment are the *Charter* and the *Criminal Code*.[316]

Charter section 12 provides, "Everyone has the right not to be subjected to any cruel and unusual treatment or punishment." In theory, this right is limited by section 1. Yet it seems unlikely that section 1 has any application to section 12.[317] Recall that Canada is obliged under CAT article 2(2) not to permit any justification of torture whatsoever. For the Crown to advance a section 1 justification in a torture case would, in our view, be contrary to Canada's CAT obligations. For a court to accept such an argument would also place Canada in violation of international law.

The wording of section 12 has troubled Canadian courts even before adoption of the *Charter*, for a similar provision is found in section 2(b) of the *Canadian Bill of Rights*.[318] The wording came to Canadian law through the English *Bill of Rights 1689*, which declared "That excessive Bail ought not to be required, nor excessive Fines imposed; nor cruel and unusual Punishments inflicted."[319] This archaic but familiar formulation was regrettably preserved by the framers of the *Charter*. One difficulty with the phrase is that, if taken literally, it gives the bizarre result that habitual acts of cruelty are constitutionally permissible. This conjunctive reading was once endorsed by the Supreme Court of Canada,[320] but has since been set aside in favour of an interpretation that treats "cruel and unusual" as a "compendious expression of a norm."[321]

---

316 See generally Canada, *Fourth Report on the Convention against Torture and Other Cruel, Inhuman or Degrading Treatment or Punishment* (2002) UN doc. CAT/C/55/Add. 8.

317 Hogg considers that s. 12 may be an absolute right that cannot ever be justifiably limited: Hogg, *Constitutional Law*, above note 57 at s. 35.14(f). This was also the view of McIntyre and Le Dain JJ. in *R. v. Smith*, [1987] 1 SCR 1045 at 1085 and 1111 [*Smith*], respectively. The majority, however, considered and rejected a s. 1 justification.

318 ". . . no law of Canada shall be construed or applied so as to . . . impose or authorize the imposition of cruel and unusual treatment or punishment."

319 1 Will. & Mary, sess. 2, c. 2, s. 10 (UK); see *Smith*, above note 317 at 1061 per Lamer J. See also the *Eighth Amendment to the American Constitution*.

320 *Miller and Cockriell v. The Queen*, [1977] 2 SCR 680 [*Miller*] at 706 per Ritchie J., who noted that capital punishment had been part of English law "from time immemorial" and part of Canadian law since Confederation, and therefore could not be called "unusual."

321 *Smith*, above note 317 at 1067 (per Lamer J.) and 1088 (per McIntyre J., dissenting), adopting the reasons of Laskin C.J. in *Miller*.

Another problem with the wording of section 12 is that, on its face at least, it is narrower than the corresponding international instruments (notably the ICCPR and the CAT). The international instruments expressly prohibit torture and also prohibit cruel, inhuman or degrading treatment or punishment. While the prohibition of torture is easily read into section 12,[322] and the word "cruel" already appears there, the words "inhuman or degrading" are more difficult to read in. This has led Tarnopolsky to suggest that caning (for example) might well be considered inhuman or degrading as a matter of international law but not necessarily cruel and unusual under section 12.[323] In spite of these differences of expression between section 12 and the international instruments, Canada's position before the Committee Against Torture and other treaty bodies is that section 12 and other *Charter* provisions fully implement Canada's obligation to prohibit torture and cruel, inhuman or degrading treatment or punishment. In our view, Canada is correct to take this view before international bodies and should adopt the same position before Canadian courts.[324]

The great reliance which Canada places on section 12 in its reports to treaty bodies is in some tension with the limits on section 12 advanced by the Crown and accepted by the courts in leading section 12 cases. In *United States of America v. Burns*,[325] the Supreme Court of Canada confirmed earlier decisions declaring that section 12 cannot be invoked to prevent extradition to countries that may subject the fugitive to cruel and unusual treatment or punishment. The court considered and rejected the decision of the European Court of Human Rights

---

322 See, for example, *Suresh*, above note 183 at para. 51.
323 W. Tarnopolsky, "A Comparison Between the Canadian Charter of Rights and Freedoms and the International Covenant on Civil and Political Rights" (1982) 8 Queens LJ 211 at 219. In *Canadian Foundation for Children, Youth and the Law v. Canada (Attorney General)*, 2004 SCC 4 [*Canadian Foundation*], the Supreme Court of Canada found that using instruments in the course of child corporal punishment is an assault for which *Criminal Code*, above note 31, s. 43 provides no defence. While the Court did not find s. 43 in violation of *Charter* s. 12 or any other *Charter* provision, it made clear that s. 43 must be presumed to conform to Canada's international obligations. See the discussion of family and children's rights, below.
324 While the Supreme Court of Canada has never explicitly declared that *Charter* s. 12 is to be interpreted in conformity with Canada's treaty obligations, one may find some support for that approach in *Smith*, above note 317 at 1061, where Lamer J. (as he then was) quotes ICCPR art. 7 and cites UDHR art. 5 and ECHR art. 3 at the outset of his account of the history of s. 12.
325 *Burns*, above note 136 at paras. 50–57.

in *Soering v. The United Kingdom*,[326] which held that the guarantee against subjection to torture or to inhuman or degrading treatment or punishment in ECHR article 3 is violated when a state extradites someone to a state where there are substantial grounds for believing that that person faces a real risk of being subjected to torture or to inhuman or degrading treatment or punishment. Rather than follow *Soering* — the rationale of which tracks CAT article 3(1) — the court found that section 12 had no application in such cases because the potential acts of a foreign government are too causally remote from the Canadian extradition process. Although the court admitted that Canada's decision to extradite "would be a necessary link in the chain of causation," it declared that "the proper place for the 'state responsibility' debate is under section 7."[327] We have already noted that section 12 appears to be an absolute right. It is not limited internally and seems unlikely to be limited by section 1. By contrast, section 7 is limited internally and may even be limited by section 1. The effect of *Burns*, therefore, is to weaken the *Charter's* protection of persons requested for extradition by states with questionable human rights records.[328]

A troubling example of the weak protection that *Charter* section 7 offers, in the extradition context, to persons at risk of torture is the decision of the Supreme Court of Canada in *Suresh v. Canada (Minister of Citizenship and Immigration)*.[329] Suresh was a Convention refugee alleged by Canada to belong to a terrorist organization. He was ordered

---

326 (1989) 11 EHRR 439.

327 The court reaffirmed this approach in respect of torture in *Suresh*, above note 183 at para. 53.

328 Quite a different approach to s. 12 was described by Cory J. (Lamer C.J. concurring) in dissent in *Kindler*, above note 154. The learned judge surveyed European jurisprudence in favour of subjecting extradition decisions to review under ECHR, above note 239, art. 3 (at 820–24) and held that s. 12 likewise imposes an obligation on Canada not to extradite a person to face cruel and unusual treatment of punishment (in this case, the death penalty). Cory J. observed (at 827),

> Canada has committed itself in the international community to the recognition and support of human dignity and to the abolition of the death penalty. These commitments were not lightly made. They reflect Canadian values and principles. Canada cannot, on the one hand, give an international commitment to support the abolition of the death penalty and at the same time extradite a fugitive without seeking the very assurances contemplated by the Treaty. To do so would mean that Canada either was not honouring its international commitments or was applying one standard to the United States and another to other nations. Neither alternative is acceptable. Both would contravene Canadian values and commitments.

329 *Suresh*, above note 183.

deported. He relied on section 7 — presumably because *Burns* rendered section 12 unavailable to him — and argued that the deportation order was unconstitutional because there were substantial grounds for believing he was in danger of being subjected to torture upon his return to Sri Lanka. He invoked CAT articles 2(2) and 3(1). He no doubt also relied on *R. v. Schmidt*, in which La Forest J. invoked torture as an extreme example of the kind of treatment which, if engaged in by a foreign state, would render extradition to that state an infringement of section 7. La Forest went further, declaring:

> Situations falling fall short of [torture] may well arise where the nature of the criminal procedures or penalties in a foreign country sufficiently shocks the conscience as to make a decision to surrender a fugitive for trial there one that breaches the principles of fundamental justice enshrined in section 7.[330]

Admittedly this dictum was *obiter*, but one might have expected it to carry great weight. Yet in *Suresh*, the Supreme Court of Canada came to quite a different result. The unattributed judgment of the Court declared, in stark conflict with earlier jurisprudence and Canada's international human rights obligations,[331] that "in exceptional circumstances, deportation to face torture might be justified" under the *Charter* "either as a consequence of the balancing process mandated by section 7 . . . or under section 1."[332] Thus the court in *Suresh* has seemingly established that deportation to face torture is not necessarily a violation of the *Charter*. *Suresh* is described in Canada's fourth report to the Committee Against Torture. At the time of writing, that report has not yet been examined. When it is, we feel certain that the *Suresh* decision will come in for serious criticism. It is richly deserved. *Suresh* pays lip service to Canada's obligations under the CAT and other instruments while failing to give them domestic effect.

Canada's principal CAT obligations are implemented by section 269.1 of the *Criminal Code*. Section 269.1(1) makes it an indictable offence for officials, or persons acting at their instigation or with their consent or acquiescence, to inflict torture. "Official" means a peace offi-

---

330 *Schmidt*, above note 185 at 522. See also *Kindler*, above note 154 at 832 (per La Forest J.) and 851 (per McLachlin J.).

331 See, for example, *Khan v. Canada* (1994), Comm. no. 15/1994 (Committee Against Torture).

332 *Suresh*, above note 183 at para. 78. See also the companion case *Ahani v. Canada (Minister of Citizenship and Immigration)*, [2002] 1 SCR 72, in which this reasoning was applied in finding the relevant provisions of the *Immigration Act* constitutional and upholding the minister's decision to deport Ahani.

cer, a public officer, a member of the Canadian Forces, or persons in foreign states exercising the powers of such officials, whether the person exercises powers in or outside Canada.[333] The definition of torture closely follows that found in CAT article 1(1).[334] There is no defence of superior authority or exceptional circumstances.[335] Statements obtained by torture are inadmissible in evidence in proceedings within federal jurisdiction, except as evidence that the statement was obtained by torture.[336] Other *Criminal Code* provisions concerning offences against the person may be invoked in respect of certain forms of cruel, inhuman or degrading treatment or punishment falling short of torture.[337]

Other legislative and administrative measures also serve to give effect to Canada's obligations in respect of torture and cruel, inhuman or degrading treatment or punishment. The *Crimes Against Humanity and War Crimes Act* includes torture in the definition of crimes against humanity.[338] The *Immigration and Refugee Protection Act* confers refugee protection to persons at risk of torture or other forms of cruel and unusual treatment or punishment.[339] The Yukon *Torture Prohibition Act* makes torture a tort and provides that Yukon public officials, and those who act with their consent or acquiescence, will be liable in damages to any person upon whom they inflict torture.[340] These statutory provisions are complemented by regulatory and administrative provisions governing the use of force by police and correctional agencies.[341]

N. EQUALITY RIGHTS

International and Canadian equality provisions come in several forms. There are guarantees of equality before the law and equal protection of the law. There are prohibitions on discrimination, both generally and

---

333 *Criminal Code*, above note 31, s. 269.1(2).

334 *Ibid.*, s. 269.1(2).

335 *Ibid.*, s. 269.1(3).

336 *Ibid.*, s. 269.1(4).

337 Canada, *Fourth Report on the Convention Against Torture and Inhuman or Degrading Treatment or Punishment* (2002), above note 316 at para. 14.

338 SC 2000 c. 24 ss. 4, 6.

339 Above note 134, ss. 95(1)(b), 97(1)(a)–(b).

340 RSY 2002 c. 222 s. 1. This appears to be the only Canadian law giving explicit effect to the requirement in CAT, above note 314, art. 14 that torture victims have "an enforceable right to fair and adequate compensation."

341 Canada, *Fourth Report on the Convention Against Torture and Inhuman or Degrading Treatment or Punishment* (2002), above note 316 at paras. 14–19.

on specified grounds. There are specific guarantees of gender equality. And there are provisions permitting affirmative action ("special measures") to achieve equality for vulnerable groups.

1) In Binding Instruments

The UDHR both guarantees equality and prohibits discrimination. Article 7 declares, "All are equal before the law and are entitled without any discrimination to equal protection of the law. All are entitled to equal protection against any discrimination in violation of this Declaration and against any incitement to such discrimination." Article 2 provides that everyone is entitled to the UDHR's rights and freedoms "without distinction of any kind, such as race, colour, sex, language, religion, political or other opinion, national or social origin, property, birth or other status."

Similarly, ICCPR article 26 declares the principles of equality before the law and equal protection of the law, then goes on to require the law to "prohibit any discrimination and guarantee to all persons equal and effective protection against discrimination on any ground such as race, colour, sex, language, religion, political or other opinion, national or social origin, property, birth or other status."[342] In addition to these provisions, ICCPR article 3 requires states to ensure the equal right of men and women to the enjoyment of all ICCPR rights.[343] A similar provision appears in ICESCR article 3.

CRC article 2(1) requires states parties to respect and ensure children's rights without discrimination of any kind, irrespective of the child's or his or her parent's or legal guardian's status. Article 2(2) requires states parties to ensure that the child is protected against discrimination or punishment on the basis of the status, activities, expressed opinions, or beliefs of the child's parents, legal guardians, or family members.

Equality and non-discrimination have been the subject of two leading UN treaties, namely the CERD and the CEDAW. The major equality and non-discrimination provisions of these treaties are summarized below. For more, see Chapter Five.

By CERD article 2(1), states parties condemn racial discrimination and undertake to pursue a policy of eliminating racial discrimination and promoting understanding among the races. To this end, states par-

---

342 See also ICCPR, above note 9, art. 2(1).
343 See: ICCPR General Comment 4 (1981); ICCPR General Comment 18 (1989); ICCPR General Comment 28 (2000).

ties undertake not to engage in acts or practices of racial discrimination[344] or to sponsor, defend, or support racial discrimination.[345] States parties also assume positive obligations to take effective measures to review governmental policies and to amend, rescind, or nullify discriminatory laws and regulations,[346] to prohibit racial discrimination by any persons, group, or organization,[347] and to encourage "integrationist multiracial organizations and movements and other means of eliminating barriers between races."[348] CERD article 2(2) commits states parties, "when the circumstances so warrant," to take special and concrete measures to ensure the adequate development and protection of certain racial groups or individuals belonging to them.

CEDAW article 2 declares that states parties condemn discrimination against women in all its forms and agree "to pursue by all appropriate means and without delay a policy of eliminating discrimination against women." To this end, states parties undertake a series of anti-discrimination obligations.[349] Article 4(1) excludes certain forms of affirmative action from the definition of discrimination but requires that they be discontinued when their objectives are met. Article 15 requires states parties to accord women equality with men before the law[350] and legal capacity identical to that of men (particularly in contract and property matters).

AmDR article 1 declares that all persons are equal before the law and have the rights and duties established in the AmDR without distinction as to race, sex, language, creed, or any other factor.

2) In Non-Binding Instruments

The ACHR includes both a non-discrimination guarantee, in article 1, and a general equality guarantee in article 24. The latter article declares, "All persons are equal before the law. Consequently, they are entitled, without discrimination, to equal protection of the law."[351]

---

344 CERD, above note 62, art. 2(1)(a).

345 *Ibid.*, art. 2(1)(b).

346 *Ibid.*, art. 2(1)(c).

347 *Ibid.*, art. 2(1)(d).

348 *Ibid.*, art. 2(1)(e).

349 CEDAW, above note 96, art. 2(a)–(g).

350 *Ibid.*, art. 15(1).

351 See also the Inter-American Convention on the Elimination of All Forms of Discrimination Against Persons with Disabilities 1999 OAS doc. AG/RES. 1608, 7 June 1999.

ECHR article 14 provides that the enjoyment of the rights and free-doms set forth in the treaty "shall be secured without discrimination on any ground such as sex, race, colour, language, religion, political or other opinion, national or social origin, association with a national minority, property, birth or other status." Unlike other international human rights instruments, however, the ECHR does not couple this non-discrimination provision with a general equality guarantee. Article 1(1) of the ECHR Protocol No. 12 (2000), which as we write is not yet in force, would correct this deficiency by providing that the enjoyment of "any right set forth by law" shall be secured without discrimination on any ground. The preamble to this protocol reaffirms that "the prin-ciple of non-discrimination does not prevent States Parties from taking measures in order to promote full and effective equality, provided that there is an objective and reasonable justification for those measures."

AfrCHPR article 2 provides that everyone is entitled to the rights and freedoms recognized and guaranteed in the treaty "without distinc-tion of any kind such as race, ethnic group, colour, sex, language, reli-gion, political or any other opinion, national and social origin, fortune, birth or other status." Article 3(1) provides that every individual shall be equal before the law, while article 3(2) provides that every individual shall be entitled to equal protection of the law. Article 18(3) provides that the state "shall ensure the elimination of every discrimination against women and also ensure the protection of the rights of the woman and the child as stipulated in international declarations and conventions." In keeping with the AfrCHPR's mission of protecting both individuals' and peoples' rights, article 19 declares, "All peoples shall be equal; they shall enjoy the same respect and shall have the same rights. Nothing shall justify the domination of a people by another." Specific provisions concerning women's equality are found in the AfrCHPR Women's Protocol, notably in articles 2(1) (anti-discrimination) and 8 (access to justice and equal protection before the law).

3) In Canadian Law

As we noted in Chapter Nine, while Canadian laws and judgments tend to meet or exceed international equality requirements, those requirements themselves rarely attract the attention of Canadian courts and tribunals.

The starting-point, as is so often the case, is the *Charter*. Section 15(1) provides,

> Every individual is equal before and under the law and has the right
> to the equal protection and equal benefit of the law without discrim-

ination and, in particular, without discrimination based on race, national or ethnic origin, colour, religion, sex, age or mental or physical disability.

This compendious provision covers the main themes of contemporary international equality law: equality before the law, equal protection of the law, protection from discrimination, and equality of the sexes.[352]

The structural similarities between *Charter* section 15(1) and ICCPR article 26 are remarkable. Both provisions begin with a general equality guarantee, then add specified heads of prohibited discrimination. There are, however, notable differences between the two provisions.

First, section 15(1) supplements the international guarantees of equality before the law and equal protection of the law with further guarantees of equality under the law and equal benefit of the law. It is unclear what, if anything, these extra guarantees actually add to those found in international human rights law.

More important differences lie in the discrimination guarantees of the two provisions. The prohibited grounds of discrimination expressly provided for in *Charter* section 15(1) include many, but not all, of those found in the ICCPR and other UN instruments. Likewise, section 15(1) provides protection against discrimination on the basis of grounds not explicitly required by the ICCPR or Canada's other treaty obligations. The prohibited grounds of race, colour, sex, religion, and national origin are common to both *Charter* section 15(1) and ICCPR article 26. The prohibited grounds of age and mental or physical disability are found expressly in *Charter* section 15(1) but not in ICCPR article 26, though article 26 may be broad enough to include such grounds, for it includes grounds "such as" those listed and also provides an open-ended ground of "other status." Similarly, though *Charter* section 15(1) does not expressly include such ICCPR grounds as language, political, or other opinion, social origin, property, or birth, it may still offer such protection by analogy. The jurisprudence of section 15(1)[353] confirms that it protects against discrimination on the basis of

---

352 Further protection for equality of the sexes is found in *Charter* s. 28: "Notwithstanding anything in this *Charter*, the rights and freedoms referred to in it are guaranteed equally to male and female persons." See also *Constitution Act 1982*, being Schedule B to the *Canada Act* 1982 (UK), c. 11, s. 35(4): "Notwithstanding any other provision of this *Act*, the aboriginal and treaty rights referred to in subsection (1) are guaranteed equally to male and female persons."

353 For example *Andrews v. Law Society of British Columbia*, [1989] 1 SCR 143 [*Andrews*].

grounds analogous to those expressly provided for.[354] The Supreme Court of Canada and other Canadian courts have shown themselves quite willing to extend the reach of section 15(1) through the recognition of such analogous grounds as marital status,[355] citizenship,[356] and sexual orientation.[357]

The leading case on section 15(1) is *Law v. Canada (Minister of Employment and Immigration)*.[358] Speaking for the unanimous court, Iacobucci J. explained that the general approach to section 15(1) involves three issues: (1) whether the impugned provision imposes differential treatment between the claimant and others, in purpose or effect; (2) whether one or more of the listed or analogous grounds of discrimination are the basis for the differential treatment; and (3) whether the impugned provision has a purpose or effect that is discriminatory within the meaning of the equality guarantee. Elaborating on this latter point, Iacobucci J. emphasized the necessity of showing a conflict between the purpose or effect of the impugned law and the purpose of section 15(1).[359] He described that purpose as

> to prevent the violation of essential human dignity and freedom through the imposition of disadvantage, stereotyping, or political or social prejudice, and to promote a society in which all persons enjoy equal recognition at law as human beings or as members of Canadian society, equally capable and equally deserving of concern, respect and consideration.[360]

Iacobucci J. went on to identify four "contextual factors" which may indicate that the impugned provision demeans the claimant's dignity: pre-existing disadvantage, stereotyping, prejudice or vulnerability; correspondence or lack thereof between the basis of the claim and the actual need, capacity or circumstances of the claimant and others; the

---

354 Where a ground of discrimination is expressly prohibited by ICCPR, above note 9, art. 26 or another Canadian human rights treaty, and is not among the so-called enumerated grounds of s. 15(1), it should be possible to bolster one's argument for recognition of the ground as analogous by reference to the treaty. This would be an application of Dickson C.J.'s *Slaight* presumption, discussed in Chapter Nine (*Slaight Communications v. Davidson*, [1989] 1 SCR 1038 [*Slaight*]). We are not aware of any case that has addressed this point.

355 *Miron v. Trudel*, [1995] 2 SCR 418 [*Miron*].

356 *Andrews*, above note 353; *Lavoie*, above note 119.

357 *Egan v. Canada*, [1995] 2 SCR 513.

358 [1999] 1 SCR 497 [*Law*].

359 *Ibid.* at para. 41.

360 *Ibid.* at para. 51.

ameliorative purposes or effects of the impugned provision; and the nature of the interest affected.[361]

The *Charter's* equality guarantee preserves scope for affirmative action. Section 15(2) provides that section 15(1) "does not preclude any law, program or activity that has as its object the amelioration of conditions of disadvantaged individuals or groups including those that are disadvantaged because of race, national or ethnic origin, colour, religion, sex, age or mental or physical disability." This exclusion from judicial review of measures aimed at encouraging equality appears to be broadly consistent with the international position. It is notable, however, that similar international provisions require affirmative measures such as these to be temporary and wound up once they have achieved their objectives.[362]

The *Charter* applies only to the federal and provincial legislatures and executives,[363] and therefore does not suffice to meet Canada's international obligations to eliminate discrimination in private transactions. Complementing section 15(1) are the federal and provincial anti-discrimination laws and enforcement mechanisms described in Chapters Nine and Thirteen. Among the requirements of these laws are pay equity,[364] non-harassment,[365] and the requirement that employers justify employment-related distinctions as *bona fide* occupational requirements.[366] Other statutory provisions also protect and promote equality and non-discrimination in Canada.[367] Anti-discrimination may also be a rule of the common law.[368]

---

361 For more on the *Law* test and s. 15(1) generally, see R. Sharpe, K. Swinton, & K. Roach, *The Charter of Rights and Freedoms*, 2d ed (Toronto: Irwin Law, 2002).

362 For example CERD, above note 62, art. 2(2); CEDAW, above note 96, art. 4(1).

363 *Charter* s. 32.

364 For example *Canadian Human Rights Act*, RSC 1985, c. H-6, s. 11(1); *Pay Equity Act* RSQ E-12.001; *Employment Standards Act 2000*, SO 2000 c. 41 s. 42; *Human Rights Code* RSBC 1996 c. 210 s. 12.

365 For example *Canadian Human Rights Act*, *ibid.*, s. 14.

366 For example *ibid.*, ss. 15(1), 15(2).

367 *Canadian Bill of Rights*, above note 187, s. 1 recognizes and declares the human rights and fundamental freedoms stated therein "without discrimination by reason of race, national origin, colour, religion or sex"; *Employment Equity Act* SC 1995 c. 44 requires employers to identify and eliminate employment barriers against women, aboriginal peoples, persons with disabilities, and members of visible minorities, and to institute positive policies and make reasonable accommodations to ensure such persons appropriate representation in the workforce.

368 See the discussion of *Re Drummond Wren*, [1945] OR 778 in Chapter Nine. See also *RWDSU v. Dolphin Delivery Ltd*, [1986] 2 SCR 573 on the *Charter's* relation to the common law. On the existence of a common law tort of discrimination, see the discussion of anti-discrimination mechanisms in Chapter Thirteen.

O. RIGHTS OF PEOPLES AND MINORITIES

We assemble under this heading three different but related topics: the human right to self-determination, the rights of aboriginal peoples under international and Canadian law, and the cultural and linguistic rights of minorities.

1) In Binding Instruments

The major UN instruments do not address the rights of peoples and minorities in great depth. The UDHR makes no explicit reference to such rights at all; its concern is with persons not peoples. For the most part, the ICCPR and ICESCR follow the same approach. The great exception, of course, is common article 1 on the right of all peoples to self-determination, which we considered in Chapter Four. Also of note is ICCPR article 27, which provides that persons belonging to ethnic, religious, or linguistic minorities "shall not be denied the right, in community with the other members of their group, to enjoy their own culture, to profess and practise their own religion, or to use their own language."[369] A similar provision in respect of children is found in CRC article 30.

One notable aspect of CRC article 30 is that it distinguishes "persons of indigenous origin" from other minorities. This is a rare instance of a UN treaty making mention of the particular circumstances of indigenous peoples (as they are known in international law).

The rights of peoples and minorities are not addressed by the AmDR.

2) In Non-Binding Instruments

The only significant UN-based instrument in this area is the non-binding and unadopted UN Draft Declaration on the Rights of Indigenous Peoples 1993.[370] The draft is a product of the UN Working Group on Indigenous Populations, a group in which the Canadian government

---

369 See the discussion in Chapter Four. See ICCPR General Comment 12 (1984) and ICCPR General Comment 23 (1994). Self-determination and the rights of indigenous peoples have been considered by the Committee on the Elimination of Racial Discrimination, even though the CERD does not explicitly address these matters. See CERD General Recommendation XXI (1996) and CERD General Recommendation XXIII (1997).
370 UN doc. E/CN.4/Sub.2/1993/29/Annex I.

and Canadian aboriginal peoples have been heavily involved.[371] While the UN Commission on Human Rights has set the end of 2004 as a target for the General Assembly to adopt the draft, major disagreements continue to hamper that effort. Particularly controversial, from the perspective of states, is the draft's description of indigenous groups as peoples with a right of self-determination.

The rights of peoples and minorities are neglected by both the ACHR and the ECHR. By contrast, the AfrCHPR affirms the rights of all peoples to existence and self-determination,[372] declares that colonized or oppressed peoples have the right to free themselves,[373] and provides that all peoples shall have the right to the assistance of states parties in their liberation struggle against foreign domination, be it political, economic, or cultural.[374]

While the main Inter-American and European human rights instruments do not address the rights of peoples and minorities, other instruments within these systems do. A draft American Declaration on the Rights of Indigenous Peoples was approved by the Inter-American Commission on Human Rights in 1997[375] and will likely be adopted by the OAS General Assembly.[376] The Council of Europe system includes treaties for the protection of regional or minority languages and national minorities.[377]

As noted in Chapter Seven, the ILO has attempted, with limited success, to elaborate treaty norms in respect of indigenous peoples. Its first attempt, the Indigenous and Tribal Populations Convention (No. 107) 1957, was criticized for implicitly endorsing an assimilationist model of

---

371 See C. Magallanes, "International Human Rights and the Impact on Domestic Law on Indigenous Peoples' Rights in Australia, Canada and New Zealand" in P. Havemann, ed., *Indigenous Peoples' Rights in Australia, Canada and New Zealand* (Auckland: Oxford University Press, 1999) at 235–76. See also P. Thornberry, *Indigenous Peoples and Human Rights* (Manchester: Manchester University Press, 2002). See also the discussion in Chapter Fourteen.

372 AfrCHPR, above note 106, art. 20(1).

373 *Ibid.*, art. 20(2).

374 *Ibid.*, art. 20(3).

375 Proposed American Declaration on the Rights of Indigenous Peoples (approved by the Inter-American Commission on Human Rights on 26 February 1997, at its 1333rd session, 95th Regular Session), OEA/Ser/L/V/.II.95 Doc.6 (1997).

376 See OAS General Assembly res. 1851 (XXXII-0/02), adopted at the fourth plenary session (4 June 2002), affirming the General Assembly's intent to adopt the proposed declaration.

377 European Charter for Regional or Minority Languages 1992 ETS no. 148; Framework Convention for the Protection of National Minorities 1995 ETS no. 157. See the discussion of these treaties in Chapter Six.

indigenous rights. The ILO later revised Convention No. 107 along anti-assimilation lines with the Indigenous and Tribal Peoples in Independent Countries Convention (No. 169) 1989. Yet many indigenous representatives were dissatisfied by the process leading to the convention, and called on states not to ratify it. Canada is not a party to Convention No. 169.

3) In Canadian Law

Canadian law has engaged the questions of peoples' and minorities' rights — often unsatisfactorily — for centuries. From the *Royal Proclamation 1763* to the *Constitution Act 1982* and beyond, the rights of aboriginal peoples and religious and linguistic minorities have been a constant preoccupation of Canadian lawmakers. A survey of this vast and complex body of law is well beyond the scope of this work. We address only the leading Canadian provisions and judgments as they relate to international law.

The right to self-determination of peoples was considered in some detail by the Supreme Court of Canada in its unanimous, unattributed judgment in *Re Secession of Quebec*.[378] The federal government referred three questions to the court, one of which asked whether there is a right to self-determination under international law giving Quebec the right to secede unilaterally from Canada. The court described the right of peoples to self-determination as "so widely recognized in international conventions that the principle has acquired a status beyond 'convention' and is considered a general principle of international law"[379] and went on to note its affirmation in several UN treaties and other instruments. The court noted the difficulties inherent in identifying a particular group as a "people" for the purpose of self-determination, and declined to decide whether the Quebec population, in whole or in part, constituted a people.[380] Instead, the court held that international law generally requires the right to self-determination to be fulfilled within existing states and consistently with their territorial integrity. In the court's words:

> There is no necessary incompatibility between the maintenance of the territorial integrity of existing states, including Canada, and the right of a "people" to achieve a full measure of self-determination. A state whose government represents the whole of the people or peo-

---

378 *Re Secession*, above note 121.
379 *Ibid.* at para. 114. Presumably by "general principle" the court meant "rule of custom."
380 *Ibid.* at paras. 123–25.

ples resident within its territory, on a basis of equality and without discrimination, and respects the principles of self-determination in its own internal arrangements, is entitled to the protection under international law of its territorial integrity.[381]

The court went on to find that the circumstances in Quebec were not such as to create a right to external self-determination (i.e., secession) at international law, for the Quebec population was neither a colonial nor an oppressed people.[382] The court's findings in *Re Secession* have not deterred the Quebec legislature from affirming the "right of the Québec people to self-determination" and declaring the Quebec people to be "the holder of rights that are universally recognized under the principle of equal rights and self-determination of peoples."[383] Parliament also responded to *Re Secession*, enacting the so-called *Clarity Act* by which the House of Commons is empowered to scrutinize provincial secession proposals, either before or after the holding of a provincial secession referendum, to determine whether they are sufficiently clear to allow the federal government to enter secession negotiations.[384] If either the referendum question or result is deemed unclear by the Commons, the government may not negotiate with the would-be secessionist province.

The leading provisions of Canadian law for the protection of minorities (be they ethnic, religious, or linguistic, but excluding, for the moment, aboriginal peoples) are found in the *Charter* and the *Constitution Act 1867*. We must distinguish from the outset between Canada's so-called founding nations (its historic anglophone and francophone populations) and other groups. The anglophone and francophone groups enjoy a somewhat privileged position in Canadian constitutional law.[385] At Confederation, the politically predominant ethnic groups in the country were of British extraction (English-speaking and mostly Protestant Christian) and of French origin (French-speaking and almost entirely Catholic). Accommodating the rights of these linguistic and religious groups — each of whom found itself in the majority in some parts of the country but in the minority elsewhere

---

381 *Ibid.* at para. 130.
382 *Ibid.* at paras. 131–38.
383 *Act Respecting the Exercise of the Fundamental Rights and Prerogatives of the Quebec People and the Quebec State* RSQ, c. E-20.2, s. 1.
384 *An Act to Give Effect to the Requirement for Clarity as Set Out in the Opinion of the Supreme Court of Canada in the Quebec Secession Reference* SC 2000 c. 26.
385 This has been acknowledged, in respect of constitutionally-protected religious education rights (which strongly overlap with language divisions), in *Re Bill 30*, [1987] 1 SCR 1148 at 1164 (per Wilson J.) and 1206 (per Estey J.) [*Re Bill 30*].

— was a major preoccupation of the Fathers of Confederation. This translated into certain linguistic[386] and religious[387] guarantees in the *British North America Act 1867*. Additional linguistic guarantees were entrenched by the *Charter*.[388]

The privileging of certain religious groups by the *Constitution Act 1867* has been condemned by the Human Rights Committee as a violation of the ICCPR. In *Waldman v. Canada*,[389] the Committee heard a communication from an Ontarian who complained that provincial law discriminated against him by providing public funding to Roman Catholic but not to Jewish schools. The Committee noted that Ontario's legislation was required by section 93 of the *Constitution Act 1867*, and noted the Supreme Court of Canada's decisions in *Re Bill 30*[390] and *Adler v. Ontario*[391] that the *Charter* cannot be used to invalidate other provisions of the constitution.[392] Yet the Committee affirmed that if a state party to the ICCPR makes public funding available to religious schools it must do so without discrimination. Having found no reasonable and objective criteria to justify the differential treatment between the Roman Catholic faith and Waldman's religion, the Committee found a violation of Waldman's right to equal and effective protection against discrimination (ICCPR article 26). The case is an illustration of the rule that a state may not plead its internal law — even its constitutional law — to excuse non-performance of its international obligations. It is also an illustration

---

386 *Constitution Act 1867*, above note 310, s. 133 (on bilingualism in Parliament, the Quebec legislature, and the courts of Canada and Quebec).

387 *Ibid.*, s. 93. Now repealed in respect of Quebec by *Constitution Act 1867* s. 93A.

388 See *Charter* ss. 16 (establishing English and French as the official languages of Canada and New Brunswick), 16.1 (on the equality and rights of English and French linguistic communities in New Brunswick), 17–18 (on the use of English and French in the debates, proceedings, statutes, records, and journals of Parliament and the New Brunswick legislature), 19 (on the use of English and French in Canadian and New Brunswick courts), 20 (on the right to use English and French in communications with Canadian and New Brunswick government institutions), 21 (saving other constitutional provisions on the English and French languages), 22 (saving any legal or customary right or privilege acquired or enjoyed either before or after the coming into force of the *Charter* with respect to languages other than English and French), and 23 (on minority language educational rights).

389 (1999) Comm. no. 694/1996 [*Waldman*].

390 *Re Bill 30*, above note 385.

391 [1996] 3 SCR 609 [*Adler*].

392 See also *Charter* s. 29: "Nothing in this *Charter* abrogates or derogates from any rights or privileges guaranteed by or under the Constitution of Canada in respect of denominational, separate or dissentient schools."

of the non-enforceable nature of Human Rights Committee views,[393] for while Waldman prevailed before the Committee the impugned constitutional provisions remain unchanged.

Another constitutional provision of relevance to Canadian minority groups is *Charter* section 27, which provides that the *Charter* "shall be interpreted in a manner consistent with the preservation and enhancement of the multicultural heritage of Canadians." The relationship between section 27 and Canada's international obligations was noted by three judges of the Supreme Court of Canada in *R. v. Zundel*.[394] Speaking in dissent, Cory and Iacobucci JJ. (Gonthier J. concurring) described ICCPR article 27 as the model for *Charter* section 27 and noted that both provisions stress "the importance of tolerance and respect for the dignity of human beings."[395] While the Supreme Court of Canada has occasionally relied on section 27,[396] it may be correct to say that it is an interpretive rather than a substantive provision and therefore cannot be infringed.[397]

Though section 27 is the only explicit *Charter* provision on the protection of minorities (excluding linguistic minorities protected by sections 16–23), it is not the only constitutional means of protecting minority rights in Canada. Other *Charter* provisions (particularly sections 2 and 15), while addressed particularly to individuals, may also serve to advance the rights of minority groups. Furthermore, the Supreme Court of Canada has identified the protection of minorities as an unwritten principle of the Canadian constitution,[398] though it remains to be seen how this principle may play out in particular cases.

Ordinary statutes also play a role in protecting peoples and minorities in Canada. Anti-discrimination laws, though directed at the protection of individuals, also benefit minority groups as a whole. The hate speech prohibitions in the *Criminal Code* serve, in an indirect way, to protect minority rights to enjoy one's own culture, profess and practice one's own religion, and use one's own language.[399] The federal *Multiculturalism Act* declares it to be the policy of the Government of Canada to

---

393 See the discussion of treaty bodies in Chapter Fourteen.
394 *Zundel*, above note 49.
395 *Ibid.*, at 815–16.
396 See, for example, *Keegstra*, above note 34 at 757; *Adler*, above note 391; *Edwards*, above note 14.
397 See *Roach v. Canada (Minister of State for Multiculturalism and Citizenship)*, [1994] 2 FC 406 (FCA).
398 *Re Secession*, above note 121 at paras. 79–82.
399 *Criminal Code*, above note 31, ss. 318–320.1. See the discussion of freedom of expression, above, Section B.

"recognize and promote the understanding that multiculturalism reflects the cultural and racial diversity of Canadian society and acknowledges the freedom of all members of Canadian society to preserve, enhance and share their cultural heritage."[400] The Act declares several other multiculturalism-related policies, including the promotion of full and equitable participation by individuals and communities of all origins in Canadian society,[401] the encouragement of respect and inclusiveness in Canadian institutions,[402] and the preservation and enhancement of languages other than English and French, while strengthening the status and use of the official languages of Canada.[403] The Act's preamble refers to Canada's equality and anti-discrimination commitments under the CERD and its obligations under ICCPR article 27. Multiculturalism provisions also exist in several provinces.[404]

Turning now to the rights of aboriginal peoples, we have noted that there is relatively little international law on the subject. Domestically, the rights of Canada's aboriginal peoples have often been described as *sui generis*,[405] and indeed the consititutional and statutory sources of Canadian aboriginal law are, for the most part, peculiar to Canada. The leading provisions — notably section 35 of the *Constitution Act 1982*, earlier constitutional laws of relevance to aboriginal peoples,[406] and the *Indian Act*[407] — have no direct international counterparts.[408] And yet international law is often in the background of aboriginal laws and claims in Canada. From the beginning of European settlement in Canada, agreements between aboriginal peoples and the Crown have been

---

400 *Canadian Multiculturalism Act* RSC 1985 c. 24 (4th Supp.) s. 3(1)(a).
401 *Ibid.*, s. 3(1)(c).
402 *Ibid.*, s. 3(1)(f).
403 *Ibid.*, s. 3(1)(i).
404 *Multiculturalism Act* RSBC 1996 c. 321, *Human Rights, Citizenship and Multiculturalism Act* RSA 2000 c. H-14, *Multiculturalism Act* SS 1997 c. M-23.01, *Manitoba Multiculturalism Act* CCSM c. M223, *Multiculturalism Act* RSNS 1989 c. 294. See also *Quebec Charter*, above note 11, s. 43: "Persons belonging to ethnic minorities have a right to maintain and develop their own cultural interests with the other members of their group."
405 Of its own kind; unique. See, for example, *Delgamuukw v. British Columbia*, [1997] 3 SCR 1010 at paras. 112–15 on the *sui generis* nature of aboriginal title and *Guerin v. The Queen*, [1984] 2 SCR 335 at 382 on the *sui generis* nature of aboriginal rights.
406 See *Constitution Act 1930*, 20–21 George V, c. 26 (UK) and *Manitoba Act 1870*, 33 Victoria, c. 26 (CA).
407 RSC 1985 c. I-5.
408 This is not to deny, of course, the role that these laws may play in discharging Canada's obligations under ICCPR art. 27.

dubbed treaties. Indeed they have often borne the hallmarks of treaties, though they do not today constitute treaties in the international sense of the word.[409] The description of aboriginal communities as "peoples" and "nations" derives in part from historic and contemporary notions of the sovereign character or international claims of indigenous populations. The right of aboriginal peoples to self-government, which is ostensibly recognized by the federal government[410] but has not yet been held to form part of section 35(1) of the *Constitution Act 1982*, has strong parallels with the international right of self-determination. Aboriginal rights have been the subject of treaties between Canada and the US.[411] Furthermore, aboriginal Canadians have been active in the international arena, particularly in UN and ILO initiatives to establish international indigenous legal norms.

The UN Human Rights Committee has twice found Canada in violation of ICCPR article 27 in cases involving aboriginal peoples. In *Lovelace v. Canada*,[412] a woman born and registered as a Maliseet Indian lost her status under the *Indian Act* by marrying a non-Indian. Lovelace challenged her loss of status on several grounds, some of which the Committee could not consider because Canada was not a party to the ICCPR when she lost her status. However, the Committee found a continuing, and therefore justiciable, violation of Lovelace's minority rights under ICCPR article 27. Parliament finally enacted legislation to amend the offending provision of the *Indian Act* in 1985.[413] The second finding of a violation of article 27 came in *Lubicon Lake Band v. Canada*.[414] The chief and members of the Lubicon Lake Band, a Cree Indian band in northern Alberta, alleged violations of their right

---

409 Vienna Convention on the Law of Treaties 1968 (VCLT), [1980] CanTS no. 37, art. 2(1)(a) defines "treaty" as an international agreement concluded between states.

410 See Canada, *Aboriginal Self-Government* (Ottawa: Indian Affairs and Northern Development, 1995).

411 For example *Jay Treaty* 1794 1 British and Foreign State Papers 784, *Migratory Birds Convention* 1916 [1917] UKTS no. 7.

412 (1981) Comm. no. R.6/24.

413 *Act to Amend the Indian Act* SC 1985 c. 27. 19. This amendment has not been enough to satisfy the Human Rights Committee. In its most recent *Concluding Observations on Canada*, the Committee expressed its concern about ongoing discrimination against aboriginal women and noted that while amendments had been brought following *Lovelace* to restore Indian status to many women, "this amendment affects only the woman and her children, not subsequent generations, which may still be denied membership in the community." The Committee recommended that Canada address these issues: Human Rights Committee, *Concluding Observations: Canada* (1999) UN doc. CCPR/C/79/Add.105 at para. 19.

414 (1990) Comm. no. 167/1984.

to self-determination under ICCPR article 1. The band was in a protracted dispute with the federal and provincial governments over oil and gas exploration projects in areas the band claimed as its traditional territory. While the Committee held that alleged violations of article 1 were not within the purview of the Optional Protocol process (which is directed at individuals' rather than peoples' rights), it nevertheless found that historical inequities and recent developments threatened the way of life and culture of the band and constituted a violation of article 27. The Lubicon Lake dispute is ongoing.[415]

The principle of self-government is cherished by aboriginal peoples and accepted by the federal government, yet remains contentious at the level of implementation. The main vehicle for aboriginal self-governance in Canada remains the *Indian Act*, which recognizes bands and defines the powers of band councils. Many aboriginals and others question whether bands operating under the Act — which is a statutory regime of delegated powers imposed by Parliament and which lacks or is inconsistent with many features of traditional aboriginal self-government — may truly be characterized as self-governing. The *Indian Act* is not the only aboriginal governance regime in Canada. Other regimes, founded on modern land claims and self-government agreements, are in place in respect of Inuit peoples[416] and several First Nations communities.[417] Negotiations for self-government, often but not always in the context of land claims agreements, are ongoing.

The recently-concluded land claims and self-government agreement between the Governments of Canada and the Northwest Territories and the Tlicho (or Dogrib) people[418] is of particular interest. Chapter 7.13 of the agreement, entitled "International Legal Obligations," includes a series of provisions concerning the rights and duties of the Tlicho people in respect of Canadian obligations under international law. The Tlicho are granted the right to be heard by the federal government before Canada consents to be bound by a treaty that may

---

415 See Amnesty International, "'Time is wasting': Respect for the land rights of the Lubicon Cree long overdue,"AMR 20/001/2003 (April 2003).

416 See *Nunavut Land Claims Agreement* 1993, *Nunavut Land Claims Agreement Act* SC 1993 c. 29, and *Nunavut Act* SC 1993 c. 28.

417 For example *James Bay and Northern Quebec Agreement* 1975, *Sechelt Indian Band Self-Government Act* SC 1986 c. 27, *Inuvialuit Final Agreement* 1994, *Western Arctic (Inuvialuit) Claims Settlement*, SC 1984 c. 24, *First Nations Land Management Act* SC 1999 c. 24, *Nisga'a Final Agreement* 1999, *Nisga'a Final Agreement Act* SC 2000 c. 7.

418 *Land Claims and Self-Government Agreement Among the Tlicho and the Government of the Northwest Territories and the Government of Canada*, 25 August 2003 [*Tlicho Agreement*].

affect Tlicho rights,[419] and the right to be consulted by Canada in the development of positions taken by Canada before international tribunals in cases involving Tlicho law or actions.[420] The Tlicho also incur obligations under the agreement. They are required to bring their laws or other exercises of power into conformity with Canada's international obligations.[421] This requirement is subject to mediation and arbitration proceedings in the event that Canada and the Tlicho disagree over whether there is in fact a breach.[422] Furthermore, if an international tribunal finds Canada to be in breach of an international legal obligation, and that breach is attributable to the Tlicho, the Tlicho government shall, at the request of the government of Canada, remedy the breach to enable Canada to perform the obligation.[423] Other agreements exist between the federal government and aboriginal groups touching matters of international law,[424] but none is as extensive as the Tlicho Agreement.

P. RIGHTS TO LEGAL PERSONALITY AND NATIONALITY

These rights resemble each other in at least one important respect. The right to legal personality is the necessary precursor to every other right an individual may hold under her domestic legal system. Likewise, in an era when individuals remain largely objects, rather than subjects, of international law, nationality is the essential prerequisite for the vindication of most internationally-derived rights.

---

419 *Ibid.*, cl. 7.13.2.
420 *Ibid.*, cl. 7.13.5.
421 *Ibid.*, cl. 7.13.3.
422 *Ibid.*, cl. 7.13.4.
423 *Ibid.*, cl. 7.13.6.
424 For example *Nisga'a Final Agreement* 1999 ch. 9 s. 96 (Canada to consult Nisga'a in respect of the formulation of positions relating to international agreements that may significantly affect migratory birds or their habitat within the Nass Area), *Nunavut Land Claims Agreement* 1993 art. 5.9.2 (Canada to include Inuit representation in discussions leading to the formulation of government positions in relation to an international agreement relating to Inuit wildlife harvesting rights in the Nunavut Settlement Area), *James Bay and Northern Quebec Agreement* 1975 s. 24.4.27(i) (Co-ordinating Committee including Native and government members may submit recommendations to responsible provincial or federal minister on positions to be adopted in international and intergovernmental negotiations relating to wildlife management involving the Territory).

1) In Binding Instruments

On the right to legal personality, UDHR article 6 provides, "Everyone has the right to recognition everywhere as a person before the law." ICCPR article 16 repeats, in substance, UDHR article 6. CEDAW article 15(2) requires states parties to accord to women, in civil matters, a legal capacity identical to that of men and the same opportunities to exercise that capacity, particularly in respect of contracts, property, and judicial procedure. AmDR article 17 provides, "Every person has the right to be recognized everywhere as a person having rights and obligations, and to enjoy the basic civil rights."

The right to nationality has received more extensive international attention. UDHR article 15 provides that everyone has the right to a nationality and that no one shall be arbitrarily deprived of his nationality nor denied the right to change his nationality. ICCPR article 24(3) gives effect to the right to a nationality by providing that every child has the right to acquire a nationality. This should not be thought of as exclusively a child's right, however. CERD article 5(d) requires states parties to guarantee "the right to nationality" to everyone equally, without distinction as to race, colour, or national or ethnic origin. CEDAW article 9(1) requires states parties to grant women equal rights with men to acquire, change, or retain their nationality and requires that neither marriage to an alien nor change of nationality by the husband during marriage shall automatically affect the nationality of the wife.[425] CEDAW article 9(2) provides that states parties shall grant women equal rights with men with respect to the nationality of their children. CRC article 7 provides that children shall have the right to acquire a nationality. Finally, AmDR article 19 declares that every person has "the right to the nationality to which he is entitled by law and to change it, if he so wishes, for the nationality of any other country that is willing to grant it to him."

Persons without a nationality are known as stateless. As noted in Chapter Seven, Canada is a party to the Convention on the Reduction of Statelessness 1961[426] and is required under it to grant Canadian nationality to stateless persons in certain cases.

---

425 Marriage and nationality are the subject of a separate Convention on the Nationality of Married Women 1957 [1960] CanTS no. 2.
426 [1978] CanTS no. 32.

2) In Non-Binding Instruments

ACHR article 3, entitled "Right to juridical personality," provides that every person has "the right to recognition as a person before the law." AfrCHPR article 5 provides in part that every individual shall have the right to "the recognition of his legal status." Legal personality is not addressed in the ECHR or its protocols.

ACHR article 20(1) recognizes the right of every person to a nationality. Article 20(2) provides that every person has the right to the nationality of the state in which he was born "if he does not have the right to any other nationality." This is an anti-statelessness provision. Finally, ACHR article 20(3) provides that no one shall be arbitrarily deprived of his nationality or of the right to change it. The right to nationality is not addressed in the ECHR or its protocols,[427] or in the AfrCHPR.

The Convention Relating to the Status of Stateless Persons 1954[428] defines stateless persons and accords them various civil, political, economic, and social rights. Canada is not a party to this treaty.

3) In Canadian Law

Outside of Quebec, it is difficult to find a positive statement in Canadian law affirming the right to recognition as a person before the law. Within Quebec, article 1 of the *Civil Code* provides, "Every human being possesses juridical personality and has the full enjoyment of civil rights"[429] and section 1 of the *Quebec Charter* declares that every human being possesses juridical personality. These provisions have no parallels federally or in the common law provinces. The legal personality of natural persons seems simply to be presumed in the common law tradition. Thus the common law of contract provides clear rules on the contractual incapacity of certain persons (for example minors and the mentally disordered) but offers little direct authority on the contractual capacity of persons in general. Another class of persons upon whom the common law historically imposed legal incapacities (contractual and otherwise) was women. Such incapacities were famously decried by Lord Sankey in *Edwards v. Attorney-General for Canada* as "relic[s] of days more barbarous than ours."[430] Yet even *Edwards* does not enunciate a general rule that human beings are presumed to have legal personality.

---

427 But see the European Convention on Nationality 1997 ETS no. 166.
428 360 UNTS 117.
429 *Civil Code*, above note 215, art. 1. See also s. 1 of the *Quebec Charter*, above note 11.
430 [1930] AC 124 (PC) at 128 [*Edwards*].

The grant of Canadian nationality is governed by the *Citizenship Act*,[431] which serves in part to implement Canada's obligations under the Convention on the Reduction of Statelessness 1961. For instance, section 4(1) extends Canadian citizenship (which, for our purposes, is the same as nationality) to foundlings as required by article 2 of the 1961 Convention. Similarly, section 9(1)(a) permits a Canadian citizen to renounce her citizenship only if she is or will become a citizen of a country other than Canada, as required by article 7(1)(a). Under the federal government's Bill C-18 (which, at time of writing, is still before Parliament), the role of the *Citizenship Act* in implementing Canada's obligations under the 1961 Convention would be even more clear. As well as repeating the existing anti-statelessness provisions, clause 11 of the bill requires the minister to grant Canadian citizenship to stateless persons in prescribed circumstances. The Department of Citizenship and Immigration describes clause 11 as ensuring Canada's obligations under the 1961 Convention.[432]

Q. STANDARD OF LIVING RIGHTS

Under this heading we address the rights to an adequate standard of living, social security, social insurance, and health.

1) In Binding Instruments

Most of the UDHR's guarantees fall within the category of civil and political rights. Yet, as we saw in Chapter Four, the UDHR also acknowledges and provides protections for some economic and social rights. UDHR article 22 declares that everyone, "as a member of society, has the right to social security." That article goes on to declare that everyone is "entitled to realization, through national effort and international co-operation, and in accordance with the organization and resources of each State, of the economic, social and cultural rights indispensable for his dignity and the free development of his personality." The content of economic and social rights is described in part by article 25(1), which provides that everyone has the right to "a standard of living adequate for the health and well-being of himself and of his

---

431　RSC 1985 c. C-29.

432　Citizenship and Immigration Canada, *Citizenship of Canada Act: Bill C-18 Clause by Clause Analysis* (November 2002) at 22.

family, including food, clothing, housing and medical care and necessary social services" as well as the right to "security in the event of unemployment, sickness, disability, widowhood, old age or other lack of livelihood in circumstances beyond his control."

The rights to social security, an adequate standard of living, and health are recognized in ICESCR articles 9, 11, and 12.[433] Article 9 declares that states parties recognize the right of everyone to social security, including social insurance. In article 11(1) states parties recognize everyone's right to "an adequate standard of living for himself and his family, including adequate food, clothing and housing, and to continuous improvement of living conditions." The article also pledges states parties to "take appropriate steps to ensure the realization of this right, recognizing to this effect the essential importance of international co-operation based on free consent." Article 11(2) specifically addresses the problem of hunger. States parties, recognizing the "fundamental right of everyone to be free from hunger," shall take measures needed to improve food production, conservation and distribution and to ensure an equitable distribution of world food supplies in relation to need. Article 12(1) declares that state parties "recognize the right of everyone to the enjoyment of the highest attainable standard of physical and mental health." The rest of the article specifies steps to be taken to achieve the full realization of this right, including those necessary for children's health; the improvement of environmental and industrial hygiene; the prevention, treatment, and control of disease; and "the creation of conditions which would assure to all medical service and medical attention in the event of sickness."[434]

The rights to social security, an adequate standard of living, and health arise in other UN instruments. CERD article 5(e)(iv) requires states parties to guarantee the right to public health, medical care, social security, and social services to everyone equally, without distinction as to race, colour, or national or ethnic origin. CEDAW article 11(1)(e) requires states parties to ensure, on a basis of equality of men and women, the right to social security and paid leave. CRC article 26(1) recognizes for every child the right to benefit from social security, including social insurance. CRC article 24(1) recognizes "the right of the child to the enjoyment of the highest attainable standard of health" and declares that states parties "shall strive to ensure that no

433 See ICESCR General Comment 3 (1990); ICESCR General Comment 4 (1991); ICESCR General Comment 9 (1998); ICESCR General Comment 12 (1999); ICESCR General Comment 14 (2000).
434 ICESCR, above note 18, art. 12(2)(a)–(d).

child is deprived of his or her right of access to such health care services." Article 24(2) requires states parties to "pursue full implementation of this right" and, in particular, to take appropriate measures in respect of specific child-related health matters.

AmDR article 16 declares that every person has the right to "social security which will protect him from the consequences of unemployment, old age, and any disabilities arising from causes beyond his control that make it physically or mentally impossible for him to earn a living." Article 11 provides that every person has the right to "the preservation of his health through sanitary and social measures relating to food, clothing, housing and medical care, to the extent permitted by public and community resources."

2) In Non-Binding Instruments

Standard of living rights are not addressed in the ACHR, but are found in ACHR-OP1.[435] Article 9(1) provides that everyone shall have the right to "social security protecting him from the consequences of old age and of disability which prevents him, physically or mentally, from securing the means for a dignified and decent existence." Article 9(2) stipulates certain minimum requirements of social security coverage for employed persons. While there is no express right to an adequate standard of living in the Protocol, there are specific guarantees in respect of health,[436] the environment,[437] and food[438] which cover much the same ground. The health provisions include an affirmation of the right to health,[439] the recognition of health as "a public good,"[440] and specific commitments in respect of primary health care, health care services, disease prevention and treatment, education, and the needs of "the highest risks groups" and the poor.[441]

There are no provisions on standard of living rights in the ECHR or its protocols. But they are extensively addressed in the EurSC,[442] which includes articles on the protection of health, social security,

---

435 Above note 69.
436 *Ibid.*, art. 10.
437 *Ibid.*, art. 11.
438 *Ibid.*, art. 12.
439 *Ibid.*, art. 10(1).
440 *Ibid.*, art. 10(2).
441 *Ibid.*, art. 10(2)(a)–(f).
442 For more on the EurSC's operation and its revisions, see the discussion in Chapter Six.

social and medical assistance, and the right to benefit from social welfare services.[443]

The AfrCHPR makes no reference to the rights to social security, an adequate standard of living or health. However, the AfrCHPR Women's Protocol includes provisions on health and reproductive rights,[444] food security,[445] adequate housing,[446] and the environment.[447]

3) In Canadian Law

A literal reading of the *Charter* and Canada's other constitutional laws suggests that standard of living rights are implemented outside constitutional law, if at all. Yet litigants have, on occasion, suggested more subtle interpretations. We begin by considering the *Charter* jurisprudence in this area, then turn to ordinary statutes.

The susceptibility of standard of living rights (and economic and social rights generally) to judicial review on *Charter* grounds remains an open question. The matter was first considered in *Irwin Toy Ltd. v. Quebec (Attorney General)*.[448] There, the majority of the court observed that "economic rights as generally encompassed by the term 'property' are not within the perimeters of the section 7 guarantee" but added:

> This is not to declare, however, that no right with an economic component can fall within "security of the person." Lower courts have found that the rubric of "economic rights" embraces a broad spectrum of interests, ranging from such rights, included in various international covenants, as rights to social security, equal pay for equal work, adequate food, clothing and shelter, to traditional property — contract rights. To exclude all of these at this early moment in the history of *Charter* interpretation seems to us to be precipitous.[449]

Similar observations were made in *Gosselin v. Quebec (Attorney General)*,[450] where the justiciability of standard of living rights was directly before the court. Gosselin was a welfare recipient who sued the Quebec

---

443 European Social Charter (revised) 1996 (EurSC), ETS no. 163, arts. 11–14.

444 Protocol to the African Charter on Human and Peoples' Rights on the Rights of Women in Africa 2003 (AfrCHPR Women's Protocol), AU doc. CAB/LEG/23.18, art. 14.

445 *Ibid.*, art. 15.

446 *Ibid.*, art. 16.

447 *Ibid.*, art. 18.

448 [1989] 1 SCR 927 [*Irwin Toy*].

449 *Ibid.* at 1003–4.

450 *Gosselin*, above note 152.

government in class proceedings. She contended that Quebec social assistance legislation infringed *Charter* sections 7 and 15(1) and section 45 of the *Quebec Charter* because it paid roughly two-thirds less income support to claimants under the age of thirty unless they participated in education or work experience programmes. The majority of the Supreme Court of Canada found no violation of either the *Charter* or the *Quebec Charter*. Speaking for the majority, McLachlin C.J. considered whether section 7 could apply to protect economic and social rights. She noted that *Irwin Toy* left the question open and observed,

> Even if section 7 could be read to encompass economic rights, a further hurdle emerges. Section 7 speaks of the right not to be deprived of life, liberty and security of the person, except in accordance with the principles of fundamental justice. Nothing in the jurisprudence thus far suggests that section 7 places a positive obligation on the state to ensure that each person enjoys life, liberty or security of the person. Rather, section 7 has been interpreted as restricting the state's ability to deprive people of these. Such a deprivation does not exist in the case at bar.[451]

Even still, McLachlin C.J. refused to close off the possibility that section 7 may "one day" be interpreted to include positive obligations.[452] In dissent, Bastarache J. denied that section 7 could ever extend to economic rights,[453] LeBel J. left the point open,[454] and L'Heureux-Dubé and Arbour JJ. found that section 7 did indeed include economic rights.[455]

While the majority in *Gosselin* was anxious not to prejudice future *Charter* development in the light of economic and social rights, it did not hesitate to foreclose most such developments in respect of the *Quebec Charter*. Section 45, which falls within the *Quebec Charter*'s economic and social rights chapter, declares, "Every person in need has a right, for himself and his family, to measures of financial assistance and to social measures provided for by law, susceptible of ensuring such person an acceptable standard of living." The majority held that section 45, and several other sections within the economic and social rights chapter, "are limited in such a way as to put the specific legislative measures or framework adopted by the legislature beyond the reach of judicial review. These provisions require the state to take steps to make the Chapter IV

---

451 *Ibid.* at paras. 80–81.
452 *Ibid.* at para. 82. On positive and negative rights, see Chapter Two.
453 *Ibid.* at paras. 202–23.
454 *Ibid.* at para. 414.
455 *Ibid.* at paras. 141–43 (L'Heureux-Dubé J.) and 311–13 (Arbour J.).

rights effective, but they do not allow for the judicial assessment of the adequacy of those steps."[456] The majority did allow, however, that breaches of Chapter IV rights may be the basis of declaratory relief.[457]

Whether standard of living rights are guaranteed constitutionally or quasi-constitutionally, and whether those rights are satisfactorily implemented in Canadian law, are separate (if overlapping) questions. The concept of implementation is more difficult to gauge in the context of economic, social and cultural rights than elsewhere, given that they are often non-justiciable. Yet in its state reports under the ICESCR,[458] Canada argues that Canadian law does indeed satisfy Canada's obligations in respect of standard of living rights. Among the federal measures relied on by Canada are Employment Insurance, the Canada Health and Social Transfer, the Canada Pension Plan, the National Housing Act, Old Age Security, the National Child Benefit, the Labour Force Development Strategy, income supplements for seniors, economic assistance to refugees, various projects targeted at aboriginal peoples, the Court Challenges Programme, and of course Canada's universal health care system. Among the provincial measures relied on in Canada's state reports are various welfare enactments, specific benefits in respect of families, shelter, the handicapped and pensioners, landlord and tenant legislation, school meals and community kitchen programmes, homelessness initiatives, and much more.

It is difficult — perhaps impossible — to say whether these and other statutory and administrative measures fully implement Canada's obligations in respect of standard of living rights. But whether they do so in full or not, they clearly play their part.[459] This is all the more reason for Canadian courts and litigants to consider the ICESCR and other relevant international obligations when construing social legislation.

---

456 *Ibid.* at para. 92.

457 See the discussion of common law remedies in Chapter Thirteen.

458 The most recent is Canada, *Third Report on the International Covenant on Economic, Social and Cultural Rights* (1998) UN Doc. E/1994/104/Add.17.

459 The role of welfare legislation in implementing Canadian treaty obligations was acknowledged, if not in these terms, by the Court of Appeal for British Columbia in *M.B. v. British Columbia*, [2002] 5 WWR 327 (damages phase; judgment on liability), [2001] 5 WWR 6, reversed 2003 SCC 53). The question before the court was the deductibility of welfare benefits from a tort award against the Crown. The Crown contended that unless the deduction were allowed, the tort victim/welfare recipient would be doubly compensated. Mackenzie J.A. rejected this view. He noted (at paras. 107–8) that social assistance benefits are not gratuitous but are paid by statutory obligation and reflect "a broader sense of social obligation" expressed in UDHR, above note 23, art. 25(1) and ICESCR, above note 18, arts. 9 and 11. Mackenzie J.A. observed, "Consistent with the *Declara-*

R. FAMILY AND CHILDREN'S RIGHTS

This heading includes the right to marry, protections for families, mothers and children, and provisions enunciating the best interests of the child principle.

1) In Binding Instruments

UDHR article 16(3) declares the family to be "the natural and fundamental group unit of society" and provides that it is "entitled to protection by society and the State." The right of men and women of full age to marry and to found a family is protected by article 16(1), which also provides that these rights are "without any limitation due to race, nationality or religion" and that men and women are "entitled to equal rights as to marriage, during marriage and at its dissolution." Article 16(2) requires that marriage be entered into only with the "free and full consent of the intending spouses." UDHR article 25(2) recognizes, without elaboration, that motherhood and childhood "are entitled to special care and assistance," and adds that all children, "whether born in or out of wedlock, shall enjoy the same social protection."

ICCPR article 23(1) repeats UDHR article 16(3)'s description of the family and its entitlements.[460] Articles 23(2) and (3) reaffirm the UDHR's provisions on the right to marry and to found a family and the requirement of consensual marriages. Article 23(4) goes further. Rather than merely declaring the entitlement of spouses to equal marriage rights, it provides that states parties shall "take appropriate steps to ensure equality of rights and responsibilities of spouses as to marriage, during marriage and at its dissolution." Article 23(4) goes on to provide that, in the event of marriage dissolution, "provision shall be made for the necessary protection of any children." ICCPR article 24(1) provides that every child shall have without discrimination "such measures of protection as are required by his status as a minor, on the part of his family, society and the State."[461] ICCPR article 24(2) requires children to be registered at birth and named.

---

tion and the *Covenant*, the *BC Benefits Act* can be taken as a recognition by the Legislature of a general obligation to relieve poverty and the right of those in need to receive adequate support for their health and well being." Similarly, Prowse J.A. noted (at para. 78) that the claimant's legal entitlement to welfare benefits is reinforced by the UDHR and the ICESCR.

460 See ICCPR General Comment 19 (1990).

461 See ICCPR General Comment 17 (1989).

The family, mothers, and children are addressed in ICESCR article 10. Article 10(1) reaffirms that the family is "the natural and fundamental group unit of society" and repeats the requirement of mutual consent in marriage. It adds that the "widest possible protection and assistance should be accorded to the family . . . particularly for its establishment and while it is responsible for the care and education of dependent children." Article 10(2) exhorts states parties to accord special protection to mothers during a reasonable period before and after childbirth, and recognizes that during that time working mothers should be accorded paid leave or leave with adequate social security benefits. Article 10(3) urges states parties to take "[s]pecial measures of protection and assistance" on behalf of all children and youth, particularly in the field of child labour standards.

CERD article 5(d)(iv) requires states parties to guarantee the right to marriage and choice of spouse to everyone equally, without distinction as to race, colour, or national or ethnic origin.

Marriage is treated extensively in the CEDAW.[462] Article 16(1) requires states parties to take "all appropriate measures" to eliminate discrimination against women "in all matters relating to marriage and family relations." In particular, states parties must ensure, on the basis of male-female equality, the same right to enter into marriage;[463] the same right freely to choose a spouse and to marry only with free and full consent;[464] the same rights and responsibilities during marriage and at its dissolution;[465] the same rights and responsibilities as parents, irrespective of marital status;[466] the same rights "to decide freely and responsibly on the number and spacing of their children and to have access to the information, education and means to enable them to exercise these rights";[467] the same rights and responsibilities with regard to guardianship, wardship, trusteeship, and adoption of children;[468] the same personal rights as husband and wife, including the right to choose a family name, a profession, and an occupation;[469] and the same rights for both spouses in respect of the ownership, acquisition, management,

---

462 See also Convention on Consent to Marriage, Minimum Age for Marriage and Registration of Marriages 1962 521 UNTS 231.
463 CEDAW, above note 96, art. 16(1)(a).
464 *Ibid.*, art. 16(1)(b).
465 *Ibid.*, art. 16(1)(c).
466 *Ibid.*, art. 16(1)(d).
467 *Ibid.*, art. 16(1)(e).
468 *Ibid.*, art. 16(1)(f).
469 *Ibid.*, art. 16(1)(g).

administration, enjoyment, and disposition of property.[470] CEDAW article 16(2) provides that child marriages shall have no legal effect and that a minimum marriage age shall be established and marriage registration shall be made compulsory. Finally, CEDAW article 11(2) requires states parties to "take appropriate measures" to prevent discrimination against women on the grounds of marriage. In particular, article 11(2)(a) provides that states parties shall take appropriate measures to prohibit "discrimination in dismissals on the basis of marital status."

The CEDAW also contains important provisions on maternity. Article 11(2) requires states parties to "take appropriate measures" to prevent discrimination against women on the grounds of maternity. In particular, states parties shall take appropriate measures to prohibit dismissal on the grounds of pregnancy or maternity leave;[471] to introduce maternity leave with pay or with comparable social benefits without loss of former employment, seniority, or social allowances;[472] to encourage "supporting social services to enable parents to combine family obligations with work responsibilities," in particular through child-care facilities;[473] and to provide special protection to women during pregnancy in types of work proved to be harmful to them.[474] While the CEDAW contains no specific provisions on children's rights, it does affirm the best interests of the child principle in articles 5(b) and 16(1)(d).

While these and other UN instruments contain significant protections for children, today the pre-eminent statement of the rights of children at international law is the CRC.[475] The CRC is the lengthiest of the six main UN human rights treaties. We do not attempt to address it in detail.[476] One of the treaty's guiding principles is enunciated in article 3(1):

> In all actions concerning children, whether undertaken by public or private social welfare institutions, courts of law, administrative authorities or legislative bodies, the best interests of the child shall be a primary consideration.

Another principle that resounds throughout the CRC is respect for the rights of parents and guardians. Article 5 provides that states parties

---

470 *Ibid.*, art. 16(1)(h).
471 *Ibid.*, art. 11(2)(a).
472 *Ibid.*, art. 11(2)(b).
473 *Ibid.*, art. 11(2)(c).
474 *Ibid.*, art. 11(2)(d).
475 For more on the CRC and its optional protocols, see Chapter Five. See also the various General Comments of the Committee on the Rights of the Child.
476 See van Bueren, *International Law*, above note 19.

shall "respect the responsibilities, rights and duties" of parents and other guardians "to provide, in a manner consistent with the evolving capacities of the child, appropriate direction and guidance in the exercise by the child of the rights recognized in the present Convention." Several provisions of the CRC recognize and elaborate upon the right of the child not to be separated from his parents except where such separation is in his or her best interest.[477] The civil rights of children are restated and, in some cases, extended by the CRC.[478] Article 12(1) requires states parties to "assure to the child who is capable of forming his or her own views the right to express those views freely in all matters affecting the child, the views of the child being given due weight in accordance with the age and maturity of the child." This hearing requirement attaches to "any judicial and administrative proceedings affecting the child."[479] The obligation of states parties to protect the child from all forms of abuse and neglect is stated in several provisions.[480] There are articles governing adoption,[481] maintenance payments,[482] education,[483] school discipline,[484] and other matters of particular interest to children.[485] The special needs of refugee children,[486] children with disabilities,[487] and minority or indigenous children[488] are the subject of separate articles. Capital pun-

---

477 See generally CRC, above note 24, arts. 9, 10, 20.
478 For example, ibid., arts. 6, 7, 14, 15, 16, 37, 40(2).
479 Ibid., art. 12(2).
480 For example, ibid., arts. 11, 19, 34, 35, 36.
481 Ibid., art. 21. Canada has entered the following reservation to art. 21: "With a view to ensuring full respect for the purposes and intent of article 20 (3) and article 30 of the Convention, the Government of Canada reserves the right not to apply the provisions of article 21 to the extent that they may be inconsistent with customary forms of care among aboriginal peoples in Canada." Canada recently informed the Committee on the Rights of the Child that it does not intend to withdraw this reservation. See Committee on the Rights of the Child, Concluding Observations: Canada (2003) UN doc. CRC/C/15/Add.215 at para. 6.
482 CRC, ibid., art. 27(4).
483 Ibid., arts. 28–29.
484 Ibid., art. 28(2).
485 For instance, ibid., art. 17(c) declares that states parties shall encourage the production and dissemination of children's books.
486 Ibid., art. 22.
487 Ibid., art. 23.
488 Ibid., art. 30. Canada has entered the following statement of understanding to art. 30:
    It is the understanding of the Government of Canada that, in matters relating to aboriginal peoples of Canada, the fulfilment of its responsibilities under article 4 of the Convention must take into account the provisions of article 30. In particular, in assessing what measures are appropriate to implement the rights recognized in the Convention for aboriginal children, due regard

ishment of children is prohibited, and conditions imposed on the deprivation of a child's liberty.[489] Finally, CRC article 40 addresses at length the rights of children accused or convicted of crimes.[490]

AmDR article 6 declares, "Every person has the right to establish a family, the basic element of society, and to receive protection therefor." Article 7 reads, "All women, during pregnancy and the nursing period, and all children have the right to special protection, care and aid."

2) In Non-Binding Instruments

ACHR article 17 concerns the rights of the family. Article 17(1) affirms that the family is the natural and fundamental group unit of society and is entitled to protection by society and the state.[491] The right of men and women to marry is affirmed in article 17(2), and the free and full consent of the intending spouses is required by article 17(3). States parties are required by article 17(4) to "take appropriate steps" to ensure equality of rights and "adequate balancing of responsibilities" between spouses "as to marriage, during marriage, and in the event of its dissolution." In such event, "provision shall be made for the necessary protection of any children solely on the basis of their own best interests." Two further protections for children are given by the ACHR. Article 17(5) provides that the law shall recognize equal rights for children born in and out of wedlock. Article 19 provides that every minor child has "the right to the measures of protection required by his condition as a minor on the part of his family, society, and the state." Family and children's rights are further elaborated upon in ACHR-OP1 articles 15 and 16. Among the rights recognized are the right of everyone to form a family in accordance with domestic law,[492] special care and assistance

---

must be paid to not denying their right, in community with other members of their group, to enjoy their own culture, to profess and practice their own religion and to use their own language.

489 CRC, *ibid.*, art. 37. Canada has entered the following reservation to art. 37(c): "The Government of Canada accepts the general principles of article 37(c) of the Convention, but reserves the right not to detain children separately from adults where this is not appropriate or feasible." Canada recently informed the Committee on the Rights of the Child of its efforts towards the removal of this reservation. The Committee regretted "the rather slow process": Committee on the Rights of the Child, *Concluding Observations: Canada* (2003), above note 481, at para. 6.

490 For a consideration of the CRC's protocols, see Chapter Five.

491 See also ACHR-OP1, above note 69, art. 15(1).

492 *Ibid.*, art. 15(2).

to mothers,[493] and the right of every child "to the protection that his status as a minor requires from his family, society and the State."[494]

ECHR article 12 provides that men and women of marriageable age have the right to marry and to found a family "according to the national laws governing the exercise of this right." Nothing in the ECHR or its protocols addresses the rights of mothers or children. There are, however, provisions on these themes in EurSC articles 7, 8, and 17. There is also a separate European instrument on children's rights.[495]

AfrCHPR article 18(1) extends protection to the family as "the natural unit and basis of society." Article 18(3) requires states to "ensure the elimination of every discrimination against women and also ensure the protection of the rights of the woman and the child as stipulated in international declarations and conventions." Further protections for children are provided in a separate OAU convention.[496] The AfrCHPR includes no marriage guarantee and no explicit protection to mothers or children beyond article 18(3). Article 6 of the AfrCHPR Women's Protocol requires marriage to be consensual and requires states parties to encourage monogamy while protecting the rights of women in marriage and family, including in polygamous marriages. Rights upon separation, divorce, and annulment are provided by article 7.

3) In Canadian Law

The law of marriage in Canada is undergoing fundamental change. The traditional definition of marriage derives from common law. In *Hyde v. Hyde and Woodmansee*, Lord Penzance defined marriage as "the voluntary union for life of one man and one woman, to the exclusion of all others."[497] The only statutory provisions on marriage rights in Canada, for the moment, are the *Criminal Code* and the *Marriage (Prohibited Degrees) Act*.[498] The former criminalizes bigamy[499] while the latter prohibits marriages between lineally related persons (whether by consanguinity or adoption) and between brothers and sisters.[500] The received

---

493 *Ibid.*, art. 15(3)(a).
494 *Ibid.*, art. 16.
495 European Convention on the Exercise of Children's Rights 1996 ETS no. 160.
496 African Charter on the Rights and Welfare of the Child 1990 OAU Doc. CAB/LEG/24.9/49 (1990).
497 (1866) LR 1 P & D 130 at 133.
498 We are excluding provincial legislation on the solemnization of marriage (*Constitution Act 1867*, above note 310, s. 92(12)).
499 *Criminal Code*, above note 31, s. 290.
500 SC 1990 c. 46 s. 2(2).

definition of marriage is changing, however. The heterosexual definition of marriage has been held unconstitutional in three Canadian
provinces on the ground of its discriminatory exclusion of same-sex
couples.[501] Rather than appeal these decisions, the federal government
announced its intent to introduce legislation in Parliament to replace
the common law definition of marriage with one which permits marriage between same-sex couples.[502] The Attorney General of Canada
has referred its draft marriage bill to the Supreme Court of Canada to
test its constitutionality. At the time of writing, that reference has yet
to be heard.

The right to divorce is established by the federal *Divorce Act*.[503]
Though the terms of that Act appear somewhat demanding, in practice
divorces are quite freely available in Canada. It is also possible to seek
annulment of one's marriage, that is, to argue that it was never valid in
the first place. But it is easier simply to seek a divorce. The Supreme
Court of Canada has held that marital status is an analogous ground for
the purposes of the *Charter*'s equality guarantee.[504] While the context
of this decision was discrimination against unmarried partners, it no
doubt also applies to prevent discrimination against divorced persons.

Many federal and provincial statutes discharge, to varying degrees,
Canada's obligations to accord special protection to mothers before and
after childbirth. Employment standards legislation in the provinces
creates rights to pregnancy leave prior to the expected birth date[505] and
to parental leave following the birth or adoption of a child.[506] Furthermore, up to fifty weeks of parental benefits payments are available
under the federal *Employment Insurance Act*.[507] Discrimination on the
grounds of pregnancy or child-birth constitutes sex discrimination

---

501 *Lingue Catholique pour les droits de l'homme v. Hendricks*, [2004] QJ No. 2593
    (QL) (CA); *EGALE Canada Inc. v. Canada (Attorney General)*, [2003] 7 WWR 22
    (BCCA); *Halpern v. Canada (Attorney General)* (2003), 172 OAC 276 (CA).
502 Parliament's jurisdiction over the definition of marriage derives from s. 91(26)
    of the *Constitution Act 1867*, above note 310.
503 SC 1986 c. 4.
504 *Miron*, above note 355.
505 For example, *Employment Standards Code* RSA 2000 c. E-9 ss. 45–49; Ontario
    Employment Standards Act, above note 364, ss. 46–47; *Labour Standards Code*
    RSNS 1989 c. 246 ss. 59 and 59A.
506 For example *Employment Standards Act* RSBC 1996 c. 113 s. 51; Ontario *Employ-
    ment Standards Act*, ibid., s. 48; *Act Respecting Labour Standards* RSQ c. N-1.1 s.
    81.10. Only female employees are entitled to parental leave in Alberta.
507 SC 1996, c. 23, s. 23.

under the *Canadian Human Rights Act*[508] and provincial human rights codes.[509]

The implementation of children's rights in Canadian law has been a subject of much legislative and judicial activity in the years following Canada's ratification of the CRC. Today, the best interests of the child principle is enacted in the child welfare legislation of every province and territory.[510] Federally, the principle is applied in the *Divorce Act*,[511] the *Youth Criminal Justice Act*,[512] and the *Immigration and Refugee Protection Act*.[513] The inclusion of the best interests principle in the latter Act is presumably in response to both Canada's CRC obligations and the decision of the Supreme Court of Canada in *Baker v. Canada (Minister of Citizenship and Immigration)*, in which the Supreme Court of Canada relied on CRC article 3(1) to find that certain discretionary immigration decisions must "consider children's best interests as an important factor, give them substantial weight, and be alert, alive and sensitive to them."[514] In its recent *Concluding Observations on Canada*,[515] the Committee on the Rights of the Child made several recommendations concerning implementation of the treaty. In particular, the Committee recommended that the best interests of the child principle be "integrated in all revisions of legislation concerning children, legal procedures in courts, as well as in judicial and administrative decisions and in projects, programs and services which have an impact on children," and that Canada continue its efforts to establish a system of juvenile justice that fully integrates the provisions and principles of the CRC and other relevant international standards.

---

508 *Canadian Human Rights Act*, above note 364, s. 3(2).

509 For example *Saskatchewan Human Rights Code*, above note 11, s. 2(1)(o).

510 See J. Wilson, *Wilson on Children and the Law* (Toronto: Butterworths, 1994) at 3.94–95.

511 Above note 503, ss. 16(8), 16(10), 17(5), 17(9).

512 SC 2002 c. 1 ss. 25(8), 27(1), 30(3), 30(4) [*YCJA*]. See also *Quebec (Minister of Justice) v. Canada (Minister of Justice)* (2003), 228 DLR (4th) 63 (Que CA) at para. 135 [*Quebec (Minister of Justice)*], in which the Court of Appeal for Quebec observed that the specific reference, in the Act's preamble, to the CRC and to the rights and freedoms of young people "necessarily forces decision-makers . . . to consider the best interests of the young person at the administrative or judicial stage in every decision they must make in the young person's regard." The court went on (at para. 136) to hold that all references to interests other than the child's well-being must be read, interpreted, and applied in the light of CRC art. 3.

513 *Immigration and Refugee Protection Act*, above note 134, ss. 25, 28, 60, 68, and 69.

514 [1999] 2 SCR 817 at para. 75.

515 Committee on the Rights of the Child, Concluding Observations: Canada (2003), above note 481.

The Committee also recommended that Parliament repeal *Criminal Code* section 43, which creates a defence of reasonable corrective force for parents and teachers accused of assaulting children. Since this recommendation was made, in *Canadian Foundation for Children, Youth and the Law v. Canada (Attorney General)* the Supreme Court of Canada upheld the constitutionality of section 43 but interpreted it to provide a defence only to "minor corrective force of a transitory and trifling nature." It does not apply to children under two or teenagers, nor to discipline using objects or involving blows to the head. It does not permit corporal punishment of any form by teachers, though it does permit them "reasonably [to] apply force to remove a child from a classroom or secure compliance with instructions." It does not protect degrading, inhuman, or harmful conduct. And it does not protect conduct "stemming from the caregiver's frustration, loss of temper or abusive personality" but must instead be corrective in nature.[516]

In arriving at these conclusions about the scope of section 43, the court engaged extensively with Canada's obligations under the CRC and other treaties. McLachlin C.J. for the majority noted that neither the CRC nor the ICCPR explicitly requires Canada to ban all forms of corporal punishment.[517] Yet she observed that section 43 should be interpreted to conform with these treaties, and quoted CRC article 37(a) and ICCPR article 7 (both of which prohibit torture or other cruel, inhuman or degrading treatment or punishment) and CRC article 19(1) (on protecting children from abuse and neglect). McLachlin C.J. then observed, "From these international obligations, it follows that what is 'reasonable under the circumstances' will seek to avoid harm to the child and will never include cruel, inhuman or degrading treatment."[518]

McLachlin C.J. also looked to the work of the Human Rights Committee, noting that it "has expressed the view that corporal punishment of children in schools engages [ICCPR] article 7's prohibition of degrading treatment or punishment" but that it "has not expressed a similar opinion regarding parental use of mild corporal punishment."[519] She went on to observe that the "[c]ontemporary social consensus" is that the use of corporal punishment by teachers is not acceptable, and that this consensus "is consistent with Canada's international obligations, given the findings of the Human Rights Committee." While McLachlin C.J. engaged with the Human Rights Committee's observa-

---

516 *Canadian Foundation*, above note 323 at para. 40.
517 *Ibid.* at para. 33.
518 *Ibid.* at para. 32.
519 *Ibid.* at para. 33.

tions in some detail, she did not look to those of the Committee on the Rights of the Child. This point was made by Arbour J. in dissent. She explained the origin and role of the Committee and quoted its criticism of a UK provision similar to *Criminal Code* section 43. She also quoted the Committee's Concluding Observations on Canada from both 1995 and 2003, noting that "the Committee has not recommended clarifying these laws so much as abolishing them entirely."[520] Clearly Arbour J. gave more weight to the Committee's views than did the majority. What is less clear is whether the Committee's views represent a simple interpretation of the CRC's requirements or rather exceed those requirements. By disregarding the Committee and affirming that the CRC does not explicitly require Canada to ban child corporal punishment, the majority leaves the impression that it considered the Committee's approach to have gone further than the CRC requires.

Several provisions of the federal *Youth Criminal Justice Act*[521] have been held by the Quebec Court of Appeal to be consistent with Canada's obligations under the ICCPR and the CRC. In *Quebec (Minister of Justice) v. Canada (Minister of Justice)*,[522] the government of Quebec referred six questions to the Court of Appeal challenging the Act. Along with questions on Parliament's jurisdiction to enact the law and the law's compliance with *Charter* sections 7 and 15(1), Quebec asked whether its general objectives[523] and its specific provisions concerning youth justice court,[524] the imposition of adult sentences for certain offences,[525] the publication of a young person's identity,[526] and the possible imprisonment of young people with adults[527] were compatible with the CRC and the ICCPR. After considering the justiciability of these questions,[528] the Court of Appeal answered each challenge in turn and ultimately concluded that there was no incompatibility between any provisions of the Act and Canada's treaty obligations.[529]

---

520 *Ibid.* at paras. 186–88.
521 YCJA, above note 512.
522 *Quebec (Minister of Justice)*, above note 512.
523 YCJA, above note 512, ss. 3, 38, 39, and 83.
524 *Ibid.*, ss. 13 and 67.
525 *Ibid.*, ss. 61, 62, 64, 70, and 72.
526 *Ibid.*, ss. 75 and 110(2)(b).
527 *Ibid.*, ss. 76 and 92.
528 See the discussion of justiciability in Chapter Thirteen.
529 However, the court went on to find certain provisions of the Act in violation of *Charter* s. 7 and not saved by s. 1. Rather than appeal this decision, the federal government plans to introduce amending legislation.

S. RIGHT TO EDUCATION

Both the right to education and its proper aims are addressed in international human rights law.

1) In Binding Instruments

UDHR article 26(1) declares that everyone has the right to education. Education shall be free, "at least in the elementary and fundamental stages." Such elementary education shall be compulsory, while "[t]echnical and professional education shall be made generally available and higher education shall be equally accessible to all on the basis of merit." Article 26(2) declares that the objects of education shall be "the full development of the human personality" and "the strengthening of respect for human rights and fundamental freedoms." Education shall promote "understanding, tolerance and friendship among all nations, racial or religious groups, and shall further the activities of the United Nations for the maintenance of peace."[530] Article 26(3) provides that parents have "a prior right to choose the kind of education that shall be given to their children."[531]

The ICESCR reaffirms and elaborates on UDHR article 26.[532] The right to education is recognized, and its dual objectives of fully developing the human personality (including "the sense of its dignity") and strengthening respect for human rights and fundamental freedoms are agreed upon by the states parties. States parties further agree on the role of education in enabling all persons to participate effectively in a free society and to promote friendship, tolerance, and international peace.[533] States parties "recognize" that primary education shall be compulsory and free, secondary education shall be generally available and accessible, and higher education shall be equally accessible on the

---

530 See also the UDHR, above note 23, preamble, which declares as an objective of the UDHR that "every individual and every organ of society, keeping this Declaration constantly in mind, shall strive by teaching and education to promote respect for these rights and freedoms. . . ."

531 See also ICCPR, above note 9, art. 18(4): "The States Parties to the present Covenant undertake to have respect for the liberty of parents and, when applicable, legal guardians to ensure the religious and moral education of their children in conformity with their own convictions."

532 See ICESCR General Comment 11 (1999) and ICESCR General Comment 13 (1999).

533 ICESCR, above note 18, art. 13(1).

basis of capacity.[534] States parties also recognize that free secondary and higher education shall be progressively introduced,[535] that "fundamental education" for those who have not completed primary education "shall be encouraged or intensified as far as possible," and that "the development of a system of schools at all levels shall be actively pursued, an adequate fellowship system shall be established, and the material conditions of teaching staff shall be continuously improved."[536] States parties undertake to respect the liberty of parents and guardians to opt for private schools for their children, and to ensure the religious and moral education of their children in conformity with their own convictions.[537]

CERD article 5(e)(v) requires states parties to guarantee the right to education and training to everyone equally, without distinction as to race, colour, or national or ethnic origin.

CEDAW article 10 declares that states parties shall take "all appropriate measures to eliminate discrimination against women in order to ensure to them equal rights with men in the field of education." In particular, states parties shall ensure, on a basis of equality of men and women: the same conditions for career and vocational guidance, for access to studies, and for the achievement of diplomas;[538] access to the same curricula, examinations, teaching staff with qualifications of the same standard, and school premises and equipment of the same quality;[539] the elimination of stereotyped conceptions of the roles of men and women at all levels and in all forms of education;[540] the same opportunities to benefit from scholarships and grants;[541] the same opportunities for continuing education;[542] the reduction of female student drop-out rates and the organization of programmes for girls and women who have left school prematurely;[543] the same opportunities to participate in physical education;[544] and access to "specific educational information to help to ensure the health and well-being of families, including information and advice on family planning."

---

534 Ibid., art. 13(2)(a)–(c).
535 Ibid., art. 13(2)(b)–(c).
536 Ibid., art. 13(2)(d)–(e).
537 Ibid., art. 13(3).
538 CEDAW, above note 96, art. 10(a).
539 Ibid., art. 10(b).
540 Ibid., art. 10(c).
541 Ibid., art. 10(d).
542 Ibid., art. 10(e).
543 Ibid., art. 10(f).
544 Ibid., art. 10(g).

The education rights of children are addressed in CRC articles 28 and 29.[545] The right of the child to education is recognized.[546] States parties shall "progressively and on the basis of equal opportunity": make primary education compulsory and free;[547] encourage different forms of secondary education, make these accessible to every child, and "take appropriate measures such as the introduction of free education and offering financial assistance";[548] make higher education accessible to all on the basis of capacity;[549] make educational and vocational information and guidance available and accessible to all children;[550] and encourage regular attendance.[551] States parties shall also "take all appropriate measures to ensure that school discipline is administered in a manner consistent with the child's human dignity and in conformity with the present Convention,"[552] and "promote and encourage international co-operation in matters relating to education," with particular account to be taken of the needs of developing countries.[553] The objects of the child's education are addressed in CRC article 29. These include those enunciated in the UDHR and ICESCR, and further values such as respect for one's parents and for the environment.

AmDR article 12 declares the right of every person to an education "based on the principles of liberty, morality and human solidarity" which will "prepare him to attain a decent life, to raise his standard of living, and to be a useful member of society." This right includes the right to equality of opportunity and the right to "at least" free primary education.

2) In Non-Binding Instruments

The ACHR contains no express provisions on education rights. However, ACHR-OP1 article 13 closely follows ICESCR article 13's provisions on education — with the notable difference that the ICESCR's mandatory language ("shall") is replaced throughout with hortatory terms ("should," "ought").

---

545 See CRC General Comment 1 (2001).
546 CRC, above note 24, art. 28(1).
547 *Ibid.*, art. 28(1)(a).
548 *Ibid.*, art. 28(1)(b).
549 *Ibid.*, art. 28(1)(c).
550 *Ibid.*, art. 28(1)(d).
551 *Ibid.*, art. 28(1)(e).
552 *Ibid.*, art. 28(2).
553 *Ibid.*, art. 28(3).

ECHR Protocol No. 1 (1952)[554] article 2 provides that no one shall be denied the right to education, and that the state shall respect the rights of parents to ensure such education and teaching in conformity with their own religious and philosophical convictions. The EurSC includes provisions on vocational training in article 10, but does not address education more generally.

AfrCHPR article 17(1) declares that every individual shall have the right to education. It does not elaborate. However, AfrCHPR Women's Protocol article 12 includes specific provisions on the elimination of discrimination in education and the promotion of female literacy and education.

3) In Canadian Law

There is no express constitutional right to education in Canada, though certain constitutional provisions address education matters. Section 93 of the *Constitution Act 1867* protects the right to denominational schools in certain provinces. This scheme was found by the Human Rights Committee in *Waldman v. Canada* to be a violation of the equality rights of religious minorities.[555] Further education rights are found in *Charter* section 23, which guarantees certain education rights to minority language groups. Like the section that attracted criticism in *Waldman*, the rights created by section 23 do not extend to all language minorities but only to those specified, namely English- and French-speakers. That does not necessarily mean that section 23 is inconsistent with international law, however, for international law recognizes the right of states to use official languages.[556]

The most significant constitutional provision concerning education is section 93 of the *Constitution Act 1867*, which makes education a matter of provincial jurisdiction.[557] The right of children to attend school is guaranteed by the various provincial statutes. Indeed, school attendance is generally compulsory unless the child receives acceptable instruction at home or is otherwise legally excused from attendance.[558]

---

554 Above note 193.
555 *Waldman*, above note 389. For more on *Waldman*, see the discussion of the rights of peoples and minorities, above.
556 See, for example, *Ballantyne*, above note 52 at para. 11.4.
557 Except for the schooling of aboriginal children. See the *Indian Act*, above note 407, ss. 114–22. The federal government also helps fund post-secondary education.
558 See A. Brown & M. Zuker, *Education Law*, 3d ed. (Toronto: Thomson Carswell, 2002) at 204–5.

The constitutionality of compulsory school attendance laws was confirmed by the Supreme Court of Canada in *R. v. Jones*, where it was emphasized that the impugned law compelled attendance at a state-certified, but not necessarily state-run, school.[559] Similar allowance for private or home schooling is made in other provincial Schools Acts.

The objectives of education, as enunciated in the ICESCR and the AmDR, are generally not to be found in provincial education laws. In particular, the goals of strengthening respect for human rights and promoting peace and human solidarity are not explicitly implemented by legislation. However, school curricula on such themes as multiculturalism and racial tolerance may serve to give effect to these obligations.

Criminal Code section 43 provides in part that schoolteachers are justified in using force by way of correction toward a pupil if the force does not exceed what is reasonable under the circumstances. This has been interpreted by the Supreme Court of Canada to permit teachers "reasonably [to] apply force to remove a child from a classroom or secure compliance with instructions" but not to permit corporal punishment.[560] The court observed that this interpretation of section 43 is consistent with the views of the UN Human Rights Committee on corporal punishment of children in schools and ICCPR article 7's prohibition of degrading treatment or punishment.[561]

T. RIGHTS TO CULTURE, THE ARTS AND SCIENCE

International instruments describe participation in the cultural life of the community and enjoyment of the arts and sciences as human rights.

1) In Binding Instruments

UDHR article 27(1) declares that everyone has the right "freely to participate in the cultural life of the community, to enjoy the arts and to share in scientific advancement and its benefits."[562] ICESCR article 15 reaffirms UDHR article 27 and declares states parties' respect for aca-

---

559 *Jones*, above note 16.
560 *Canadian Foundation*, above note 323, at para. 40.
561 *Ibid.* at paras. 33, 38.
562 See also UDHR, above note 23, art. 27(2) (intellectual property), discussed under the heading of property and property-related rights, above, Section H.

demic and creative freedom[563] and their recognition of the benefits of international contacts and co-operation in scientific and cultural fields.[564] CERD article 5(e)(vi) requires states parties to guarantee the right to equal participation in cultural activities without distinction as to race, colour, or national or ethnic origin. AmDR article 13 provides that every person has the right "to take part in the cultural life of the community, to enjoy the arts, and to participate in the benefits that result from intellectual progress, especially scientific discoveries." Every person also has the right to the protection of his moral and material interests in respect of his inventions or works.

2) In Non-Binding Instruments

The ACHR contains no express provisions on culture and science rights save article 26, quoted earlier,[565] but ACHR-OP1 article 14 closely restates ICESCR article 15. Neither the ECHR nor the EurSC contain any provisions on culture or science, but a separate European Cultural Convention 1954 requires states parties to take appropriate measures to safeguard and to encourage the development of culture.[566] AfrCHPR article 17(2) declares that every individual may freely take part in the cultural life of his community.

3) In Canadian Law

The rights to participate in cultural life, to enjoy the arts, and to share in scientific progress do not readily lend themselves to legislative protection.[567] Though expressed positively, Canada's main obligation under these provisions may be not to hinder people's participation in and enjoyment of these pursuits. The federal *Multiculturalism Act*, discussed earlier, is of note.[568] So, too, is the federal *Status of the Artist Act*.[569] It declares the federal government's recognition of the importance of artists, their role in Canadian society and cultural industries, and the importance of compensating them for their work.[570] The Act also

---

563 ICESCR, above note 18, art. 15(3).
564 *Ibid.*, art. 15(4).
565 See the discussion of the right to education, above.
566 ETS no. 18, art. 1.
567 Intellectual property rights are an exception. See the discussion of property and property-related rights, above.
568 See the discussion of the rights of peoples and minorities, above.
569 SC 1992 c. 33 [*Artist Act*].
570 *Ibid.*, s. 2.

affirms artists' freedoms of association and expression.[571] The Act goes on to establish the framework for a collective bargaining regime for professional artists working as independent contractors in the federal jurisdiction. Other policies and programmes relied on by Canada in its reports to the Economic, Social and Cultural Rights Committee include support of the Canadian Broadcasting Corporation, science and research agencies such as the National Research Council, the Natural Sciences and Engineering Research Council and the Social Sciences and Humanities Research Council, federal scholarship programmes, and the federal/provincial SchoolNet initiative.

Scientific, artistic, and cultural matters fall heavily within provincial jurisdiction. Provincial initiatives in these domains include multiculturalism laws and policies,[572] provincial arts councils, public universities, libraries and museums, and a great variety of artistic, cultural, and heritage events. Many of these initiatives and activities emphasize Canadian aboriginal cultures and heritage.

U. DEROGATIONS

As explained in Chapter Two, some human rights treaties permit derogations from their guarantees in times of national and public emergency.[573] Derogation is not a human right; rather, it is a right of states. It is, however, a narrow right that must be exercised proportionately and without discrimination.

1) In Binding Instruments

Canada and other states parties have a right of derogation from certain civil and political rights under ICCPR article 4(1):

> In time of public emergency which threatens the life of the nation and the existence of which is officially proclaimed, the States Parties to the present Covenant may take measures derogating from their obligations under the present Covenant to the extent strictly required by the exigencies of the situation, provided that such measures are not

---

571 *Ibid.*, ss. 3 and 8.
572 See the discussion of the rights of peoples and minorities, above, Section O.
573 See the discussion of the limited not absolute nature of human rights in Chapter Two. See also ICCPR General Comment 5 (1981) at 110 and ICCPR General Comment 29 (2001).

inconsistent with their other obligations under international law and do not involve discrimination solely on the ground of race, colour, sex, language, religion or social origin.

Article 4(2) goes on to stipulate that no derogation may be made from ICCPR articles 6 (right to life), 7 (prohibition of torture and cruel, inhuman, or degrading treatment or punishment), 8(1) (freedom from slavery), 8(2) (freedom from servitude), 11 (no imprisonment for debt), 15 (protection from retroactive criminal laws), 16 (right to legal recognition), and 18 (freedom of thought, conscience and religion). Note also the internal limitations of the right to derogation in article 4(1) itself: it may not be exercised in a discriminatory manner nor contrary to the state's other international obligations (such as those imposed by international humanitarian law). Finally, article 4(3) requires states parties who avail themselves of the right of derogation to inform other states parties "of the provisions from which it has derogated and of the reasons by which it was actuated."

No other instrument binding on Canada contains a derogation provision.

2) In Non-Binding Instruments

ACHR article 27 provides for the "suspension" of certain of the treaty's guarantees in time of "war, public danger, or other emergency that threatens the independence or security of a State Party." The provision is somewhat broader than its ICCPR counterpart, but the list of rights excluded from derogation by ACHR article 27(2) is longer than that found in ICCPR article 4(2). There may be no suspension of articles 3 (right to juridical personality), 4 (right to life), 5 (right to humane treatment), 6 (freedom from slavery), 9 (freedom from *ex post facto* laws), 12 (freedom of conscience and religion), 17 (rights of the family), 18 (right to a name), 19 (rights of the child), 20 (right to nationality), and 23 (right to participate in government), "or of the judicial guarantees essential for the protection of such rights."

ECHR article 15(1) permits derogations "to the extent strictly required by the exigencies of the situation, provided that such measures are not inconsistent with its other obligations under international law." Article 15(2) excludes derogations from articles 2 (right to life), 3 (prohibition of torture), 4(1) (prohibition of slavery) and 7 (protection from retroactive criminal laws). EurSC article 30 permits derogations from any of its provisions in time of war or other public emergency threatening the life of the nation.

3) In Canadian Law

Canada has implemented its ICCPR right of derogation by means of the federal *Emergencies Act*.[574] The Act's preamble is instructive:

> WHEREAS the safety and security of the individual, the protection of the values of the body politic and the preservation of the sovereignty, security and territorial integrity of the state are fundamental obligations of government;
>
> AND WHEREAS the fulfilment of those obligations in Canada may be seriously threatened by a national emergency and, in order to ensure safety and security during such an emergency, the Governor in Council should be authorized, subject to the supervision of Parliament, to take special temporary measures that may not be appropriate in normal times;
>
> AND WHEREAS the Governor in Council, in taking such special temporary measures, would be subject to the *Canadian Charter of Rights and Freedoms* and the *Canadian Bill of Rights* and must have regard to the *International Covenant on Civil and Political Rights*, particularly with respect to those fundamental rights that are not to be limited or abridged even in a national emergency;

This subjection of governmental powers exercisable under the Act to the *Charter*, the *Bill of Rights* and the ICCPR is implicit throughout the Act. The Act does not invoke the notwithstanding clauses of *Charter* section 33 or *Bill of Rights* section 2 (described below). Nor does it expressly derogate from any rights not subject to derogation under ICCPR article 4(1). Indeed, the powers granted to the Governor in Council in the event of the various forms of national emergency defined by the Act (public welfare emergency, public order emergency, international emergency, and war emergency) appear quite insufficient to authorize derogation from such internationally non-derogable rights as life, freedom from torture, and freedom of thought. Furthermore, section 4(b) explicitly provides that nothing in the Act shall be construed or applied so as to confer on the Governor in Council the power to make orders or regulations providing for the detention, imprisonment, or internment of Canadian citizens or permanent residents on

---

574 RSC 1985 c. 22 (4th Supp.). While the Act is federal, it clearly contemplates incursions into provincial jurisdiction in times of emergency, as permitted under the emergency branch of the peace, order and good government power (*Constitution Act 1867*, above note 310, s. 91). See *Re Anti-Inflation Act (Canada)*, [1976] 2 SCR 373.

the basis of race, national or ethnic origin, colour, religion, sex, age, or mental or physical disability.

The *Emergencies Act* is not the only Canadian law permitting derogation from human rights. Section 33 of the *Charter* empowers Parliament or the provincial legislatures to legislate "notwithstanding" sections 2 and 7–15 if they do so by express enactment. Similar notwithstanding clauses are found in section 2 of the *Canadian Bill of Rights*, section 52 of the *Quebec Charter*, section 2 of the *Alberta Bill of Rights*,[575] and section 44 of the *Saskatchewan Human Rights Code*.[576] *Charter* section 33 is the most elaborate provision. While section 33(1) grants Parliament and the Legislatures the power to derogate from some of the *Charter's* most fundamental guarantees, section 33(3) terminates the effect of such a derogation five years after it comes into force (unless the legislature specifies an earlier date.) However, section 33(4) and (5) permit the derogation to be re-enacted, subject to the same five-year limit.

Nothing in section 33 or any of the provincial notwithstanding clauses explicitly limits their use to times of public emergency threatening the life of the nation, as required by ICCPR article 4(1). Non-emergency uses of these provisions are likely to violate international law.

Charter section 33 has rarely been invoked, with two major exceptions. In 1982 Quebec enacted a law retroactively applying *Charter* section 33 to every law then in force in Quebec.[577] This extraordinary enactment was in protest of the adoption of the 1982 constitutional amendments without Quebec's assent. New Quebec legislation also routinely invoked section 33 until a change of government in 1985. These Quebec laws must surely have put Canada in violation of ICCPR article 4. While the new government abandoned the practice of resorting to section 33 as a matter of course, the National Assembly did invoke it in respect of a law prohibiting the use of English in commercial signs.[578] This use of section 33 (as well as section 52 of the *Quebec Charter*) was challenged before the Human Rights Committee in *Ballantyne, Davidson and McIntyre v. Canada*.[579] The complainants were English-speaking Quebec residents who argued that the province's commercial sign laws unnecessarily restricted their right to freedom of expression under ICCPR article 19(2). They also submitted that the

---

575 *Alberta Bill of Rights*, above note 11.
576 *Saskatchewan Human Rights Code*, above note 11.
577 *Act Respecting the Constitution Act, 1982* SQ 1982 c. 21.
578 *Act to Amend the Charter of the French Language* SQ 1988 c. 54.
579 *Ballantyne*, above note 52.

invocation of the federal and provincial notwithstanding clauses deprived them of a domestic remedy for the infringement of their rights.

In reply, Canada[580] made some intriguing arguments about the nature of *Charter* section 33. Canada argued that the existence of section 33 is not *per se* contrary to Canada's obligations under ICCPR article 4. Rather, it submitted, "Canada's obligation is to ensure that Section 33 is never invoked in circumstances which are contrary to international law. The Supreme Court of Canada has itself stated that 'Canada's international human rights obligations should [govern] . . . the interpretation of the content of the rights guaranteed by the Charter'." Thus, argued Canada, section 33 could never be invoked to permit acts clearly prohibited by international law. Accordingly, Canada submitted that section 33 is compatible with the ICCPR.[581] Canada repeated these submissions in the later case of *Singer v. Canada.*[582] While the Human Rights Committee noted these submissions, it drew no conclusions in respect of them.

This was not the first time Canada had taken this position on section 33 before the Human Rights Committee. In a supplementary report to the Committee in 1984, a Canadian representative explained,

> In the view of the Federal Government, any resort to section 33 would have to be compatible with Canada's international obligations, which would be invoked if there were any real derogation from the rights and freedoms set out in the Canadian *Charter*. Canada was obliged to report to the Human Rights Committee and was a party to the Optional Protocol so that anyone seeking to assert a right would be able to have recourse to the Committee if deprived of a remedy under section 33.[583]

---

580 It appears that both the federal and Quebec governments made submissions to the Committee. The arguments to be discussed here are attributed to the "State party," i.e., Canada.

581 *Ballantyne*, above note 52 at para. 8.4. The passage quoted by Canada is from *Slaight*, above note 354 at 1056–57: "Given the dual function of s. 1 identified in *Oakes*, Canada's international human rights obligations should inform not only the interpretation of the content of the rights guaranteed by the *Charter* but also the interpretation of what can constitute pressing and substantial s. 1 objectives which may justify restrictions upon those rights." Note that Canada used the word "govern" before the Committee, while the Supreme Court of Canada used "inform."

582 *Singer*, above note 54 at para. 5.4.

583 UN doc. CCPR/C/SR.559 at para. 28, quoted in Schabas, above note 12 at 73.

This *Ballantyne* approach to section 33 has never been confirmed by Canadian courts. It has much to recommend it. As Canada rightly argued, an internationally-informed limit on section 33 would reconcile it with Canada's ICCPR obligations by allowing Canadian courts to supervise and review invocations of section 33 by our legislatures for consistency with international human rights law. Furthermore, the *Ballantyne* doctrine is easily reconciled with established reception law principles. The doctrine is simply an application of the *Slaight* presumption that the *Charter* conforms to international human rights law.[584] In our view, the *Ballantyne* doctrine should govern all invocations of notwithstanding clauses by Canadian legislatures. The rationale for the rule in respect of section 33 is identical in the case of provincial derogation provisions: all are presumed not to violate Canada's international obligations under ICCPR article 4 and other binding rules of international law.

---

584 On the *Slaight* presumption, see the discussion of the *Charter* in Chapter Nine.

RECEPTION OF INTERNATIONAL LABOUR, REFUGEE, HUMANITARIAN AND CRIMINAL LAWS

The many rights and groups of rights described in Chapter Ten are the pre-eminent rights enjoyed by human beings at international law. They are not, however, the only international laws relating to human rights. As we saw in Chapter Seven, the fields of international labour, refugee protection, humanitarian and criminal law are closely related to human rights. In this chapter we briefly consider Canada's laws concerning these related fields.

A. INTERNATIONAL LABOUR LAW

As explained in Chapter One, international labour law is at once a precursor to and a subset of general international human rights law. The international labour regime, elaborated principally by the ILO, is a vast area of law in which Canada has participated in fairly limited ways. Canada is a party to only 30 of the over 180 ILO conventions. Of the ILO's eight "fundamental conventions," Canada is a party to only five.[1]

---

1   Canada is not a party to ILO Conventions Nos. 29 (forced labour), 98 (collective bargaining), and 138 (minimum age). On fundamental conventions, see the discussion of international labour law in Chapter Seven.

And yet the Canadian labour movement has made frequent use of ILO complaints mechanisms.[2]

ILO conventions are not the only source of international labour law. The major UN human rights treaties and other instruments binding on Canada provide important protections for labour and labour-related rights. These include the rights to work,[3] to favourable working conditions,[4] to pay equity,[5] to rest and leisure,[6] and to freedom of association[7] including trade unionism.[8] Canada has also undertaken international labour law obligations, though rather weak ones, under the NAALC and similar agreements with its other free trade partners.[9]

It is not a simple matter — nor one within the scope of this book — to determine the extent to which international labour law is or is not implemented in Canadian law. We made a partial attempt to do so, in respect of freedom of association, in Chapter Ten. We also consider labour law promotion and protection mechanisms in Chapter Thirteen. To complete the task, one would have to look well beyond the *Charter* into federal and especially provincial legislation on such matters as working conditions, health and safety regulations, working hours, statutory holidays, minimum wages, non-discrimination, and more. An important starting-point for such an inquiry would be materials related to Canada produced by the ILO, such as the observations of the Committee of Experts on the Application of Conventions and Recom-

---

2   See B. Burkett, J. Craig, & S. Gallagher, "Canada and the ILO: Freedom of Association since 1982" (2003) 10 Canadian Labour and Employment Law Journal 231 [Burkett & Gallagher, "Canada and the ILO"].

3   Universal Declaration of Human Rights 1948 (UDHR), GA res. 217 (III) (1948), art. 23(1); International Covenant on Economic, Social and Cultural Rights 1966 (ICESCR), [1976] CanTS no. 46, art. 7; International Convention on the Elimination of All Forms of Racial Discrimination 1966 (CERD), [1970] CanTS no. 28, art. 5(e)(i); Convention on the Elimination of All Forms of Discrimination Against Women 1979 (CEDAW), [1982] CanTS no. 31, art. 11(1)(a); American Declaration on the Rights and Duties of Man 1948 (AmDR), OAS res. XXX (1948), art. 14.

4   UDHR, *ibid.*; ICESCR, *ibid.*; CERD, *ibid.*; CEDAW, *ibid.*, art. 11(1)(f).

5   UDHR, *ibid.*, art. 23(2); ICESCR, *ibid.*, art. 7(a)(i); CERD, *ibid.*; CEDAW, *ibid.*, art. 11(1) (d).

6   UDHR, *ibid.*, art. 24; ICESCR, *ibid.*, art. 7 (d); Convention on the Rights of the Child 1989 (CRC), [1992] CanTS no. 3, art. 31; AmDR, above note 3, art. 15.

7   UDHR, *ibid.*, art. 20; International Covenant on Civil and Political Rights 1966 (ICCPR), [1976] CanTS no. 47, art. 22(1); CERD, above note 3, art 5(d)(ix); CRC, *ibid.*, art. 15(1); AmDR, *ibid.*, art. 22. See the discussion of freedom of association in Chapter 10.

8   UDHR, *ibid.*, art. 23(4); ICCPR, *ibid.*, art. 22 (1); ICESCR, above note 3, art. 8(1)(a); CERD, *ibid.*, art. 5 (e)(ii); AmDR, *ibid.*, art. 22.

9   See the discussion in Chapter Seven.

mendations, the reports of the Conference Committee on the Application of Conventions and Recommendations, and the jurisprudence of the Committee on Freedom of Association.[10] Those who have considered the question tend to agree that Canada's implementation of international labour law standards is impressive but incomplete.[11]

B. INTERNATIONAL REFUGEE PROTECTION

UDHR article 14(1) declares everyone's right to seek and to enjoy in other countries asylum from persecution. There are few other provisions on asylum in the main UN human rights treaties[12] for the simple reason that asylum is the subject of a separate (and older) UN treaty regime: the Convention relating to the Status of Refugees 1951[13] and its 1967 Protocol.[14] It will be recalled from Chapter Seven that Canada is a party to both instruments.[15]

The principal means by which Canada purports to implement its obligations under these treaties is the *Immigration and Refugee Protection Act*.[16] Section 3(2)(b) of the Act declares that one of its objectives with respect to refugees is "to fulfil Canada's international legal obligations with respect to refugees and affirm Canada's commitment to international efforts to provide assistance to those in need of resettlement." Section 3(3) provides that the Act is to be construed and applied in a manner that "furthers the domestic and international

---

10   The observations, reports, and decisions of these bodies can be found on the ILO website (http://www.ilo.org).

11   See Burkett & Gallagher, "Canada and the ILO," above note 2; J. Dorsey, "International Labour Conventions and the I.L.O.: Application in British Columbia" (1985) 43 The Advocate 619; R. McCallum, "Domestic Constitutions, International Law, and the International Labour Organization: An Australian and Canadian Case Study" (1994-5) 20 Queen's LJ 301; Y. Poisson & A. Torobin, "The Right to Organize and Collective Bargaining: Canada and International Labour Organization Convention 98" (1999) 2 Workplace Gazette 86.

12   But see the protection from expulsion provision in ICCPR, above note 7, art. 13.

13   [1969] CanTS no. 6.

14   [1969] CanTS no. 29.

15   For more on international refugee protection in Canada, see: L. Waldman, *Immigration Law and Practice*, looseleaf ed. (Markham: Butterworths, 1992–); M. von Sternberg, *The Grounds of Refugee Protection in the Context of International Human Rights and Humanitarian Law: Canadian and United States Case Law Compared* (The Hague: Martinus Nijhoff, 2002); D. Galloway, *Immigration Law* (Toronto: Irwin Law, 1997).

16   SC 2001 c. 27.

interests of Canada" and "complies with international human rights instruments to which Canada is signatory."[17] Refugee protection is dealt with by Part 2 of the Act which, at section 96, defines "Convention refugee" in terms that implement the definition of refugee at international law.[18] Other provisions of Part 2 give effect to not only the relevant provisions of the Refugee Convention and the Protocol but also the CAT.[19] The Supreme Court of Canada has acknowledged that the *Immigration Act* (the predecessor legislation to the *Immigration and Refugee Protection Act*) served as implementing legislation for the Refugee Convention.[20] The courts must surely come to the same conclusion in respect of the current legislation. This is not to say that the new Act perfectly or completely implements Canada's refugee protection obligations, but only that it is the principal legislative means by which Canada purports to do so. For more on the Act, see the discussion of refugee protection mechanisms in Chapter Thirteen.

C. INTERNATIONAL HUMANITARIAN LAW

As explained in Chapter Seven, humanitarian law is divided between the law of The Hague (which governs the conduct of hostilities between belligerents) and the law of Geneva (which protects non-combatants and similar persons). Breaches of Hague law and Geneva law are offences under Canadian law. Certain violations of the laws and customs of war constitute war crimes and are indictable offences for the purposes of sections 4(1) and 6(1) of the *Crimes Against Humanity and War Crimes Act*.[21] Grave breaches of the Geneva Conventions (including the GC Protocol I) are indictable offences under section 3(1) of the *Geneva Conventions Act*.[22] Other breaches of international humanitarian law constitute offences under the *Crimes Against Humanity and War Crimes Act*.[23] Other

---

17   *Ibid.*, s. 3(3)(a) and (f).
18   See L. Waldman, *The Definition of Convention Refugee* (Markham: Butterworths, 2001).
19   See the discussion of refugee protection mechanisms in Chapter Thirteen.
20   *Pushpanathan v. Canada (Minister of Citizenship and Immigration)*, [1998] 1 SCR 982 at para. 4.
21   SC 2000 c. 24 [*CAHWCA*].
22   RSC c. G-3. The GC Protocols I and II were implemented in Canadian law by the *Act to Amend the Geneva Conventions Act, the National Defence Act, and the Trade-Marks Act* RS 1990 c. 14.
23   See the offences of crimes against humanity and genocide in *CAHWCA*, above note 21, ss. 4(1) and 6.

laws by which Canada implements its international humanitarian law obligations include the *Anti-Personnel Mines Convention Implementation Act*[24] and the *Chemical Weapons Convention Implementation Act*.[25]

These statutes are not the only means by which Canada gives domestic effect to its international humanitarian law obligations. A more immediate means of assuring Canadian compliance with the laws of war is to train Canadian Forces personnel in those rules. This is the responsibility of the Office of the Judge Advocate General. The Office's *Law of Armed Conflict at the Operational and Tactical Level* is a remarkable guide to the law of armed conflict. The manual's introduction provides this laudable explanation of the bindingness of international humanitarian law on Canadian Forces members:

> The obligations binding on Canada in accordance with Customary International Law and Treaties to which Canada is a party are binding not only upon the Government and the CF [Canadian Forces] but also upon every individual. Members of the CF are obliged to comply and ensure compliance with all International Treaties and Customary International Law binding on Canada. This manual assists CF members in meeting those obligations.[26]

The Office of the Judge Advocate General includes a directorate of international law which provides legal advice to the Department of National Defence, the Canadian Forces, and the federal government on matters involving international law and international military operations.

D. INTERNATIONAL CRIMINAL LAW

There is inevitable overlap between international criminal law and international humanitarian law. As explained in Chapter Seven, the main branches of modern international criminal law are genocide, war crimes, and crimes against humanity. Other important international criminal prohibitions include torture, slavery, and terrorism.

Canada was at the forefront of the international effort to establish the International Criminal Court, and was also the first country to implement the Rome Statute of the International Criminal Court

---

24 SC 1997 c. 33.
25 SC 1995 c. 25.
26 Office of the Judge Advocate General (Canada), *The Law of Armed Conflict at the Operational and Tactical Level* (B-GG-005-027/AF-021, 5 September 2001) at i.

1998[27] into domestic law. The *Crimes Against Humanity and War Crimes Act*[28] is a comprehensive scheme to give domestic effect to the treaty's substantive and procedural provisions. In a Department of Justice press release issued upon introduction of the bill in Parliament, the proposed legislation was described as "comprehensive implementation legislation" that "would implement in Canada the Rome Statute of the International Criminal Court."[29] The Act does indeed appear to meet Canada's obligations under that treaty. It creates the offences of genocide, crimes against humanity, and war crimes[30] based on customary and conventional international law,[31] including the Rome Statute. It asserts Canadian jurisdiction over these offences on the bases of the nationality, territorial, passive personality, and universal principles.[32] It implements the Rome Statute offences of breach of responsibility by military commanders and other superiors.[33] It makes available to accused persons all defences established in Canadian and international law, the latter defences in accordance with the Rome Statute.[34] The Act also creates offences to protect the integrity of the processes of the International Criminal Court[35] and to ensure that proceeds from offences under the Act can be restrained, seized, or forfeited.[36] Finally, the Act implements Canada's obligation, under Rome Statute article 89, to arrest and surrender persons sought by the International Criminal Court for trial.[37]

Even before Parliament implemented the Rome Statute, Canadian courts were active in the areas of war crimes and crimes against humanity. Following recommendations made by the Commission of Inquiry on War Criminals (the Deschênes Commission), Parliament enacted amendments to the *Criminal Code* and other federal statutes to facilitate the detection, prosecution and deportation of perpetrators of genocide,

---

27 [2002] CanTS no. 13.
28 *CAHWCA*, above note 21.
29 Department of Justice, "Canada Introduces New Act to Implement International Criminal Court," press release of 10 December 1999.
30 *CAHWCA*, above note 21, ss. 4(1), 6(1).
31 *Ibid.*, ss. 4(3), 6(3).
32 Territorial jurisdiction is established under *CAHWCA, ibid.*, ss. 4–5. Other forms of jurisdiction are established under *CAHWCA* s. 8. On these principles, see Chapter Eighteen.
33 *Ibid.*, ss. 5(1) and (2), 7(1) and (2).
34 *Ibid.*, ss. 11, 14.
35 *Ibid.*, ss. 16–26.
36 *Ibid.*, s. 31.
37 *Ibid.*, ss. 47–53 (amending the *Extradition Act* to allow for surrender to the International Criminal Court).

war crimes and crimes against humanity. The Crown's attempts to prosecute such crimes under the *Criminal Code* were a failure, due in large part to the interpretation of the relevant *Criminal Code* provisions given by the Supreme Court of Canada in the much-criticized decision of *R. v. Finta*.[38] After *Finta*, the federal government shifted its focus from criminal prosecution of war criminals to revocation of citizenship and deportation. In this area, the government has enjoyed greater success. The jurisprudence of the Federal Court of Canada, arising from appeals under the Refugee Convention's "exclusion clause" (art. 1F(a)),[39] has been applauded for its good grasp of the relevant international law and its prescience in reaching decisions later confirmed, in other contexts, by the ICTY and ICTR.[40]

The international crime of terrorism was brought to the top of the world agenda with the massive terrorist attacks on the US of 11 September 2001. Acting under Chapter VII of the UN Charter, the UN Security Council adopted Resolution 1373, which requires all states to take a variety of measures to prevent and suppress terrorism. Canada and other states responded to Resolution 1373 by enacting new laws to fight terrorism. The *Anti-Terrorism Act*[41] amended the *Criminal Code* and several other statutes to introduce new measures for the investigation and prosecution of terrorist and terrorism-related acts.

The *Criminal Code* now defines "terrorist activity" to mean either an offence under the several anti-terrorism treaties to which Canada is a party, or an act or omission, in or outside Canada,

---

38   [1994] 1 SCR 701 [*Finta*]. In *Finta*, the acquittal of the accused was upheld by a majority of the Supreme Court of Canada. The majority of the court held, *inter alia*, that the trial judge did not err in instructing the jury that the Crown must prove not only the *mens rea* of the underlying offences but also that he knew his acts constituted war crimes and/or crimes against humanity. See K. Raman, "The Future of the Nuremburg Promise" (1994) 28 CR (4th) 392; I. Cotler, "War Crimes Law and the *Finta* Case" (1995) 6 Supreme Court LR (2d) 577. The *Criminal Code* provisions on which *Finta* was based were repealed by *CAHWCA*, *ibid.*, s. 42.

39   Article 1F(a) explicitly excludes from eligibility for refugee status and protection persons suspected of having committed a crime against peace, a war crime, a crime against humanity, a serious non-political crime outside the country of refuge prior to her admission to that country as a refugee, or acts contrary to the purposes and principles of the UN. See Chapter Seven.

40   J. Rikhof, "War Crimes Law, As Applied in Canada" in R. Wiggers & A. Griffiths, eds., *Canada and International Humanitarian Law: Peacekeeping and War Crimes in the Modern Era* (Halifax: Centre for Foreign Policy Studies, Dalhousie University, 2002) at 121–66.

41   SC 2001 c. 41.

(i) that is committed

    (A) in whole or in part for a political, religious or ideological purpose, objective or cause, and

    (B) in whole or in part with the intention of intimidating the public, or a segment of the public, with regard to its security, including its economic security, or compelling a person, a government or a domestic or an international organization to do or to refrain from doing any act, whether the public or the person, government or organization is inside or outside Canada, and

(ii) that intentionally

    (A) causes death or serious bodily harm to a person by the use of violence,

    (B) endangers a person's life,

    (C) causes a serious risk to the health or safety of the public or any segment of the public,

    (D) causes substantial property damage, whether to public or private property, if causing such damage is likely to result in the conduct or harm referred to in any of clauses (A) to (C), or

    (E) causes serious interference with or serious disruption of an essential service, facility or system, whether public or private, other than as a result of advocacy, protest, dissent or stoppage of work that is not intended to result in the conduct or harm referred to in any of clauses (A) to (C). . . .[42]

Included within this definition of terrorist activity are conspiracies, attempts, threats, counselling, and being an accessory after the fact. Terrorist groups are also defined.[43] Other provisions in the terrorism amendments to the *Criminal Code* rely on these definitions to create new offences such as financing terrorist activities,[44] participating in the activities of terrorist groups,[45] facilitating terrorist activity,[46] and harbouring or concealing terrorists.[47]

Another new addition to the *Criminal Code* is the investigative hearing procedure.[48] A peace officer investigating a terrorism offence

---

42   *Criminal Code*, RSC 1985 c. C-46, s. 83.01(1).

43   A terrorist group is defined as either "an entity that has as one of its purposes or activities facilitating or carrying out any terrorist activity" or an entity on a list established by the Governor in Council under s. 83.05.

44   *Criminal Code*, above note 42, ss. 83.02–83.04.

45   *Ibid.*, ss. 83.18.

46   *Ibid.*, s. 83.19.

47   *Ibid.*, ss. 83.23.

48   *Ibid.*, ss. 83.28.

may apply to a judge for an "order for the gathering of information" from the person named in the order. If the judge is satisfied that the Attorney General of Canada has consented and that there are reasonable grounds to believe that a terrorism offence has been or will be committed, and that information concerning the offence is likely to be obtained, she may make an order requiring a person to attend and be examined by the Crown before a judge. In short, the procedure gives the Crown a means of compelling information from named persons at the investigative (pre-trial) stage of criminal proceedings.

Yet another novel feature of the *Anti-Terrorism Act* is the introduction of "preventive arrest" powers that permit police to arrest and impose conditions of release on suspected terrorists, even without a warrant in certain cases.[49]

These and other aspects of the Act have excited controversy and concern among lawyers, legal academics, human rights activists, and members of Canada's Muslim and Arab communities.[50] Some worry that the definition of terrorist activity is broad enough to capture legitimate forms of dissent. Another concern is that the investigative hearing procedure establishes an inquisitorial scheme that offends against the right to a fair hearing before an independent and impartial tribunal. Critics are also concerned about the misuse of preventive detention and the fact that suspects lack the right to be informed of the case against them. These concerns and others may soon be addressed by the Supreme Court of Canada, which recently heard a constitutional challenge to parts of the Act.[51] As we write, the court's decision is under reserve.

War crimes, crimes against humanity, and terrorism are not the only international crimes addressed in Canadian law. Torture is contrary to *Criminal Code* section 269.1.[52] Slavery and the slave trade are not explicitly prohibited in any federal statute, but are clearly barred by *Charter* section 7.

---

49 *Ibid.*, s. 83.3.
50 See R. Daniels, P. Macklem & K. Roach, eds., *The Security of Freedom: Essays on Canada's Anti-terrorism Bill* (Toronto: University of Toronto Press, 2001).
51 *Re Application Under s. 83.28 of the Criminal Code*, 2004 SCC 42, aff'g 2003 BCSC 1172, heard 10–11 December 2003.
52 See the discussion of protection from torture and cruel, inhuman or degrading treatment or punishment in Chapter Ten.

PART THREE

THE PROMOTION AND PROTECTION OF HUMAN RIGHTS

CHAPTER 12

STATE RESPONSIBILITY FOR BREACHES OF INTERNATIONAL HUMAN RIGHTS LAW

A. NATURE AND SCOPE OF STATE RESPONSIBILITY

It is a basic principle of international law, if not of law itself, that wrongful acts entail the responsibility of the wrongdoer.[1] The international law of state responsibility is customary in origin but has been the subject of an important codification project by the International Law Commission since 1949. Recently the Commission adopted the final text of its Draft Articles on Responsibility of States for Internationally Wrongful Acts 2001 (Draft Articles).[2] Draft Articles article 2 provides that internationally wrongful state conduct consists of an action or omission attributable to the state under international law and constituting a breach of an international obligation of the state. State breaches of international human rights obligations are, of course, among those breaches that will entail the state's responsibility.

---

1   "[I]t is a principle of international law, and even a general conception of law, that any breach of an engagement involves an obligation to make reparation": *Chorzów Factory (Germany v. Poland) (Merits)* (1928), PCIJ Series A no. 17 at 29. The court also observed (at 47), "[R]eparation must, as far as possible, wipe out all the consequences of the illegal act and re-establish the situation which would, in all probability, have existed if that act had not been committed."
2   UN doc. A/CN.4/L.602/Rev. 1 (2001). The Draft Articles are not binding and must be used with care. However, many of their provisions are widely accepted as declaratory of existing customary international law.

The nature of a state's responsibility for violations of human rights obligations was considered by the Inter-American Court of Human Rights in the landmark case of *Velásquez Rodríguez v. Honduras*.[3] The case concerned a Honduran student who was allegedly detained without warrant and tortured by police. He subsequently disappeared. The Court unanimously declared Honduras in violation of several articles of the ACHR and ordered the state to pay fair compensation to Velásquez's next-of-kin. In arriving at this result, the court considered ACHR article 1(1), by which states parties "undertake to respect the rights and freedoms recognized" in the convention and "to ensure to all persons subject to their jurisdiction the free and full exercise of those rights and freedoms" without discrimination. The court made the following observations:

> The obligation to ensure the free and full exercise of human rights is not fulfilled by the existence of a legal system designed to make it possible to comply with this obligation — it also requires the government to conduct itself so as to effectively ensure the free and full exercise of human rights . . . .[4]
>
> According to Article 1(1), any exercise of public power that violates the rights recognized by the Convention is illegal. Whenever a State organ, official or public entity violates one of those rights, this constitutes a failure of the duty to respect the rights and freedoms set forth in the Convention . . . .[5]
>
> An illegal act which violates human rights and which is initially not directly imputable to a State (for example, because it is the act of a private person or because the person responsible has not been identified) can lead to international responsibility of the State, not because of the act itself, but because of the lack of due diligence to prevent the violation or to respond to it as required by the Convention . . . .[6]
>
> The State has a legal duty to take reasonable steps to prevent human rights violations and to use the means at its disposal to carry out a serious investigation of violations committed within its jurisdiction, to identify those responsible, to impose the appropriate punishment and to ensure the victim adequate compensation.
>
> This duty to prevent includes all those means of a legal, political, administrative and cultural nature that promote the protection of human rights and ensure that any violations are considered and treat-

---

3   (1988) I/A Court HR Series C no. 4 [*Velásquez Rodríguez*].
4   *Ibid.* at para. 167.
5   *Ibid.* at para. 169.
6   *Ibid.* at para. 171.

ed as illegal acts, which, as such, may lead to the punishment of those responsible and the obligation to indemnify the victims for damages.[7]

The essence of *Velásquez Rodríguez* has been affirmed in a widely-endorsed report adopted by the UN Commission on Human Rights,[8] according to which a state's obligation to respect, ensure respect for, and enforce international human rights and humanitarian law includes, *inter alia*, a state's duty to:

a) take appropriate legal and administrative measures to prevent violations;
b) investigate violations and, where appropriate, take action against the violator in accordance with domestic and international law;
c) provide victims with equal and effective access to justice irrespective of who may be the ultimate bearer of responsibility for the violation;
d) afford appropriate remedies to victims; and
e) provide for or facilitate reparation to victims.

We consider this report an accurate account of the law of state responsibility for human rights violations.

B. ATTRIBUTION OF CONDUCT TO THE STATE

A state is an artificial entity composed, in most cases, of many thousands of individual actors. To establish whether state responsibility attaches to a given act, one must first determine whose acts may be attributed to the state as a matter of international law. This is known as attribution or imputability.[9]

A state's responsibility may be triggered by persons acting on its behalf. In principle, the conduct of any state organ, be it of legislative, executive, judicial, or other nature, is attributable to the state under international law.[10] Likewise, the conduct of persons who are not state organs but who exercise governmental authority is attributable to the

---

7 *Ibid.* at paras. 174–5.
8 *Basic Principles and Guidelines on the Right to a Remedy and Reparation for Victims of Violations of International Human Rights and Humanitarian Law*, annexed to M. C. Bassiouni, "The Right to Restitution, Compensation and Rehabilitation For Victims of Gross Violations of Human Rights and Fundamental Freedoms: Final Report," UN doc. E/CN.4/2000/62 (2000).
9 See generally J. Currie, *Public International Law* (Toronto: Irwin Law, 2001) at 393–405.
10 Draft Articles, above note 2, art. 4.

state.[11] In short, states will generally be considered responsible under international human rights law for the acts or omissions of their officials, broadly defined. Whether or not an official's unlawful conduct was authorized by the state is irrelevant; responsibility is strict.[12] It suffices to show that the official carried out the act or omission in an official capacity. It is no defence for a state to assert that the official's conduct was prohibited by domestic law.[13]

The conduct of private persons not acting on behalf of the state generally will not attract state responsibility. There are, however, at least three exceptions. First, private acts may be attributed to the state where the state directs or controls the impugned conduct.[14] Second, private acts may be attributed to the state where a person or group exercises elements of governmental authority in the absence or default of the official authorities.[15] A third exception is where the state acknowledges and adopts the impugned conduct.[16] Otherwise, conduct by private actors will generally not be attributable to the state and will therefore not attract state responsibility under international law.[17] It remains to be seen whether the general rule against state attribution for private conduct will hold over time. It is not without its detractors.[18]

C. DEFENCES

States may invoke certain defences, described in the Draft Articles as "circumstances precluding wrongfulness," to excuse or justify what would

---

11   *Ibid.*, art. 5.
12   *Ibid.*, art. 7.
13   *Ibid.*, art. 32.
14   *Ibid.*, art. 8 and accompanying commentary.
15   *Ibid.*, art. 9 and accompanying commentary.
16   *Ibid.*, art. 11 and accompanying commentary.
17   But see *Mouvement Burkinabe des Droits de l'Homme v. Burkina Faso* (2001), Comm. 204/97 at para. 42, in which the African Commission on Human and Peoples' Rights found state responsibility even where neither the state nor its agents committed the violation. The state was found liable on the basis of the African Charter on Human and Peoples' Rights 1981 (AfrCHPR), OAU doc. CAB/LEG/67/3 rev. 5, art. 1, which requires states parties to "give effect to" the rights contained therein.
18   See generally A. Clapham, *Human Rights in the Private Sphere* (Oxford: Clarendon Press, 1993). The women's human rights movement has also given this issue more prominence and urgency. The "public/private" distinction works against women disproportionately, since most discrimination and mistreatment against women occurs in the private sphere, whether within or outside of the home. See generally J. Peters & A. Wolper, eds., *Women's Rights, Human Rights: International Feminist Perspectives* (New York: Routledge, 1995) at c. 13–17.

otherwise constitute breaches of international human rights law. Available defences include consent,[19] *force majeure*,[20] necessity,[21] "supervening impossibility of performance,"[22] distress,[23] and "fundamental change of circumstances."[24] None of these defences relieves a state from meeting its obligations once the circumstances in question have ceased to exist.[25] And none may be invoked in defence of breaches of *jus cogens*.[26]

D. REMEDIES FOR BREACHES OF INTERNATIONAL HUMAN RIGHTS LAW

State responsibility under international human rights law is delictual or civil in nature, not criminal. A state that breaches its human rights obligations cannot be the subject of international criminal proceedings, but may face civil proceedings such as those conducted by the International Court of Justice and the European and Inter-American human

---

19 Vienna Convention on the Law of Treaties 1968 (VCLT), [1980] CanTS no. 37, arts. 54–59; Draft Articles, above note 2, art. 20.

20 Draft Articles, *ibid.*, art. 23 refers to "the occurrence of an irresistible force or of an unforeseen event, beyond the control of the State, making it materially impossible in the circumstances to perform the obligation." The International Law Commission's commentary to art. 23 notes that *force majeure* may be due to "human intervention" including loss of control over a portion of territory due to insurrection. However, the loss of control has to be akin to impossibility and not constitute merely increased difficulty of performance.

21 Draft Articles, *ibid.*, art. 25 provides that this defence may not be invoked unless the measure purported to be necessary is the only way for the state to safeguard an essential interest against a "grave and imminent peril" and does not seriously impair an essential interest of the state or of other states. The article further provides that necessity may not be invoked as a defence if the state has contributed to the situation of necessity.

22 VCLT, above note 19, art. 61. The impossibility must be physical ("disappearance or destruction of an object indispensable for the execution of the treaty").

23 Draft Articles, above note 2, art. 24. This defence is limited to situations of imminent peril faced by individuals (not states) and which do not allow time for deliberation.

24 VCLT, above note 19, art. 62 provides that a fundamental change of circumstances must have been unforeseen by the parties at the time the treaty was ratified, and may not be invoked as a ground for terminating or withdrawing from a treaty "unless the existence of those circumstances constituted an essential basis of the consent of the parties to be bound by the treaty . . . and the effect of the change is radically to transform the extent of obligations still to be performed under the treaty." The article further provides that the fundamental change must not have resulted from a breach by the party invoking it.

25 Draft Articles, above note 2, art. 27(2).

26 *Ibid.*, art. 26.

rights courts. A state in breach of international human rights law may also be civilly liable before its own courts and tribunals according to its domestic law. In short, state breaches of international human rights law entail a civil remedy.

International human rights law treats the question of remedy as an independent human right, and states undertake to implement that right in their domestic laws just as they undertake to implement such basic rights as freedom of expression, liberty, privacy, and equality. The right to a remedy is expressly guaranteed in several UN and regional instruments.[27] UDHR article 8 provides, "Everyone has the right to an effective remedy by the competent national tribunals for acts violating the fundamental rights granted him by the constitution or by law." While the UDHR speaks of violations of fundamental rights in general, ICCPR article 2(3)(a) requires states parties to ensure effective remedies for violations of the rights and freedoms recognized in the ICCPR itself. Article 2(3) goes on to require states parties to ensure that claimants' rights shall be determined "by competent judicial, administrative or legislative authorities, or by any other competent authority provided for by the legal system of the State,"[28] and to ensure that remedies, when granted, shall be enforced.[29] The ICCPR also includes remedial provisions in respect of particular human rights violations.[30] Right to remedy provisions are also found in other UN[31] and regional[32]

---

27 As we saw in Chapter Ten, most human rights instruments also recognize the procedural right of access to a fair hearing.

28 International Covenant on Civil and Political Rights 1966 (ICCPR), [1976] CanTS no. 47, art. 2(3)(b)

29 *Ibid.*, art. 2(3)(c)

30 Article 9(5) recognizes "an enforceable right to compensation" for anyone unlawfully arrested or detained. Article 14(6) requires victims of miscarriages of justice to be "compensated according to law."

31 See, for example, International Convention on the Elimination of All Forms of Racial Discrimination 1966 (CERD), [1970] CanTS no. 28, art. 6, which includes a guarantee to obtain "just and adequate reparation or satisfaction for any damage suffered" as a result of racial discrimination. A similar provision is found in Convention on the Elimination of All Forms of Discrimination Against Women 1979 (CEDAW), [1982] CanTS no. 31, art. 2(c). Convention Against Torture and Other Cruel, Inhuman or Degrading Treatment or Punishment 1984 (CAT), [1987] CanTS no. 36, art. 14 has perhaps the broadest provision. It affords torture victims redress and "an enforceable right to fair and adequate compensation, including the means for as full rehabilitation as possible." The article also guarantees compensation for a torture victim's dependants in the event of the victim's death.

32 See, for example, American Convention on Human Rights 1969 (ACHR), OAS TS no. 36, arts. 10, 25, and 63(1); European Convention on Human Rights 1950 (ECHR), ETS no. 5, arts. 13 and 41. The remedial rights expressed in these instru-

instruments. Many international humanitarian law[33] and labour law[34] instruments also include a right to remedy.

The international law recognition of the right to a fair hearing and the right to a remedy means that the obligation to provide redress for state violations of other human rights falls, in the first instance, to the wrongdoing state itself, by means of mechanisms provided for in its domestic law. It is only when the state has failed to afford a victim the required relief that the matter may come before supranational bodies. This is known as the exhaustion of domestic (or local) remedies. It is a requirement of all international bodies charged with monitoring or adjudicating upon state compliance with international human rights law.[35]

While the right to a remedy for breaches of international human rights law is clearly established, the remedial jurisdiction of international adjudicative and treaty bodies varies widely.[36] Furthermore, uncertainty and inconsistency mark the actual remedial practices of these bodies.[37] The domestic law of remedies is far more settled, though the availability of such remedies in respect of violations of international human rights law is not always clear. If the state in question requires legislative implementation of international law, a human rights claimant may need either to show that explicit implementation has occurred or rely on similar domestic provisions as effectively implementing the international right. Canada is an example of a state in which international human rights obligations are rarely implemented expressly, requiring claimants seeking to vindicate their treaty-based human rights to anchor their claims in general Canadian law (supported, in proper cases, by the presumption of conformity with international law).[38]

---

ments have received detailed treatment (and expansion) in the jurisprudence of the Inter-American Commission and Court of Human Rights and the European Court of Human Rights. See D. Shelton, *Remedies in International Human Rights Law* (Oxford: Oxford University Press, 1999) at 23–36 [Shelton, *Remedies*].

33 See, for example, the Protocol Additional to the Geneva Conventions of 12 August 1949, and Relating to the Protection of Victims of International Armed Conflicts 1977 (GC Protocol I), [1991] CanTS no. 2, art. 75.

34 See, for example, arts. 15(2), 16(4), and 16(5) of the ILO's Indigenous and Tribal Peoples in Independent Countries Convention (No. 169) 1989.

35 N. Udombana, "So Far, So Fair: The Local Remedies Rule in the Jurisprudence of the African Commission on Human and Peoples' Rights" (2003) 97 AJIL 1 at 6–12.

36 See Chapters Fourteen and Fifteen.

37 See generally Shelton, *Remedies*, above note 32.

38 On the presumption of conformity, see Chapter Eight.

CHAPTER 13

CANADIAN HUMAN RIGHTS MECHANISMS

It is a well-established rule of international law that international tribunals will not entertain claims against a state unless the claimant has exhausted all remedies available under the state's domestic law.[1] And as we saw in Chapter Twelve, the right to a domestic remedy for violations of international human rights law is itself a human right to which states parties to UN and other human rights treaties must give effect. With these two principles in mind, we turn now to consider Canadian mechanisms for the promotion and protection of human rights.

Means of remedying violations of human rights are at the forefront of this discussion. Yet the concept of remedy discussed here is broader than the traditional notion of judicial remedies in Canadian law. This breadth reflects the international approach, which contemplates not only judicial but also legislative, administrative, and political action to ensure the protection and promotion of human rights norms.[2]

---

1 The rule is customary: *Interhandel Case (Switzerland v. United States)*, [1959] ICJ Rep 27.

2 In Canada, *Core Document Forming Part of the Reports of States Parties: Canada* (1998) UN doc. HRI/CORE/1/Add.91 at para. 90, Canada notes that responsibility for the protection of human rights in Canada is shared between the legislative, executive, and judicial branches of government.

A. THE RIGHT TO A REMEDY IN CANADIAN LAW

In Canadian law, the maxim "No right without a remedy" is well-established in common law and is also given effect by statutes and the *Charter*. The principle was famously enunciated by Holt C.J. in the old English case of *Ashby v. White*:

> If the plaintiff has a right, he must of necessity have a means to vindicate and maintain it, and a remedy if he is injured in the exercise or enjoyment of it; and indeed it is a vain thing to imagine a right without a remedy; for want of right and want of remedy are reciprocal.[3]

These words, and the principle they capture, have frequently been affirmed in Canadian cases.[4] In respect of *Charter* violations, section 24(1) provides, "Anyone whose rights or freedoms, as guaranteed by this *Charter*, have been infringed or denied may apply to a court of competent jurisdiction to obtain such remedy as the court considers appropriate and just in the circumstances."[5] The breadth of this section has frequently been affirmed by the Supreme Court of Canada. In *R. v. Mills*, McIntyre J. observed that it is "difficult to imagine language which could give the court a wider and less fettered discretion."[6] The Supreme Court of Canada has recently emphasized that courts must use section 24(1) to craft remedies that are both responsive and effective.[7]

B. JUDICIAL MECHANISMS

We examine under this heading judicial remedies for human rights violations available under the *Charter*, quasi-constitutional and ordinary

---

3   (1703) 92 ER 126 at 136 (Eng QB).
4   For example *Orchard v. Tunney*, [1957] SCR 436 at 447; *R. v. Mills*, [1986] 1 SCR 863 at 971–72 [*Mills*]; *Rahey v. The Queen*, [1987] 1 SCR 588 at 630; *Doucet-Boudreau v. Nova Scotia (Minister of Education)*, 2003 SCC 62 at para. 25 [*Doucet-Boudreau*].
5   Included with this broad remedial power is a more specific provision, without parallel in international law, requiring courts to exclude evidence obtained contrary to the *Charter* if its admission would bring the administration of justice into disrepute: *Charter* s. 24(2).
6   *Mills*, above note 4, at 965. See also *Doucet-Boudreau*, above note 4, at para. 24.
7   "[A] purposive approach to remedies requires at least two things. First, the purpose of the right being protected must be promoted: courts must craft *responsive* remedies. Second, the purpose of the remedies provision must be promoted: courts must craft *effective* remedies": *Doucet-Boudreau*, *ibid.* at para. 25 (Iacobucci and Arbour JJ.'s emphasis).

statutes, and the common law. Excluded from this discussion are anti-discrimination mechanisms, which we address separately below. Before addressing these judicial remedies, we consider the justiciability of claims founded on international human rights law.

1) Justiciability of International Law Claims

While both international and Canadian law affirm the right to an effective remedy for rights violations, this does not mean that violations of international human rights law are directly justiciable in Canadian courts. A justiciable question may be defined as one that a court of law is prepared to answer.[8] Courts have found certain questions to be non-justiciable for a variety of reasons including mootness, lack of standing, and the inappropriateness of the court as a forum for resolving certain disputes. The conventional wisdom is that questions arising from international law are not justiciable in Canadian courts unless the international norm at issue has been implemented into Canadian law.

This approach oversimplifies to the point of error. The implementation requirement only applies to treaties. Matters of customary international law are automatically incorporated into the common law and are therefore justiciable like other common law rules.[9] As for treaty law, Canadian court practice is more welcoming of international law arguments than is sometimes suggested. In responding to the contention that so-called "pure" questions of international law are not justiciable, the Supreme Court of Canada in Re Secession of Quebec[10] noted that it has looked to international law in a number of previous cases "to determine the rights or obligations of some actor within the Canadian legal system." Furthermore, a narrow approach to justiciability fails to take account of the strong interpretive presumption that domestic law conforms with Canadian treaty obligations.[11] Longstanding Anglo-Canadian judicial practice makes clear that unimplemented treaty obligations are justiciable to the extent required to apply the presumption of conformity. Thus, while a litigant may not be able to place direct reliance on a right guaranteed by a Canadian treaty obligation, he is permitted to raise that right and rely on it for the purposes of interpreting a

---

8 "The notion of justiciability is concerned with the appropriateness of courts deciding a particular issue, or instead deferring to other decision-making institutions like Parliament": *Re Canada Assistance Plan (British Columbia)*, [1991] 2 SCR 525 at 545.

9 See the discussions of implementation and incorporation in Chapter Eight.

10 [1998] 2 SCR 217 at para. 22 [*Re Secession*].

11 See the discussion of the presumption of conformity in Chapter Eight.

domestic provision. Finally, there is a distinction to be drawn between actions that rely on an international norm to advance a domestic legal claim and actions that rely on international law to challenge the government's conduct of foreign affairs. The first type of action is justiciable along the lines set out above. The justiciability of the second type of action is a somewhat complicated question and is beyond the scope of this chapter, but there are grounds for asserting its justiciability as well, at least in *Charter* cases.[12]

There is therefore no blanket rule that claims founded on international human rights law are non-justiciable before Canadian courts. There are, however, certain limits on the extent to which litigants may rely on international human rights law in Canadian proceedings. If the alleged infringement derives from treaty (as will usually be the case), proof of treaty infringement alone will seemingly not suffice to found a judicial remedy.[13] The claimant must show that the right in question has been implemented into domestic law, thus turning an infringement of international law into a domestically unlawful act. Alternatively, the claimant may argue that domestic law (whether that law is implementing legislation or not) must be interpreted in such a way as to avoid violating the claimant's rights under international human rights law. In the rare case of alleged violations of customary international human rights norms, the claimant may invoke the doctrine of incorporation to rely directly on the customary norm as a rule of common law. In short, whether the claimant relies on treaty or custom, she must demonstrate some degree of overlap between the international norm and domestic law, for it is ultimately domestic law that founds the claim for remedy.

This is, in our view, an accurate account of the current Canadian legal position. Yet development in the law of justiciability, as in law generally, is to be expected. Justiciability is not a fixed concept but a "con-

---

12   The traditional rule is that foreign affairs are non-justiciable. See *Rustomjee v. The Queen* (1876), 2 QBD 69 at 74 and *R. v. Vincent* (1993), 80 CCC (3d) 256 at 269 (Ont CA). In constitutional matters, this rule has been supplanted by the *Charter*: *Operation Dismantle v. The Queen*, [1985] 1 SCR 441. Outside the *Charter* context, however, the courts continue to decline to review governmental conduct of foreign affairs, for example *Council of Civil Service Unions v. Minister for the Civil Service*, [1985] 1 AC 374 (HL) at 418, *Black v. Chrétien* (2001), 54 OR (3d) 215 (CA) at para. 52, *Blanco v. Canada*, 2003 FCT 263. But see the dissent of Wright J. in *Aleksic et al. v. Attorney General of Canada* (2002), 215 DLR (4th) 720 (Ont Div Ct) at paras. 11 and 14. See also M. Buhler, "The Emperor's New Clothes: Defabricating the Myth of 'Act of State' in Anglo-Canadian Law" in C. Scott, ed. *Torture as Tort: Comparative Perspectives on the Development of Transnational Human Rights Litigation* (Oxford: Hart Publishing, 2001) at 343.

13   But see the discussion of declaratory relief below.

tingent and fluid notion dependent on various assumptions concerning the role of the judiciary in a given place at a given time as well as on its changing character and evolving capacity."[14] An example of such development may be *Quebec (Minister of Justice) v. Canada (Minister of Justice)*, in which the Quebec Court of Appeal agreed to consider the Quebec Government's request for a declaration of incompatibility between federal legislation and Canadian treaty obligations.[15] In the end, the court found no incompatibility, but the fact that the court was prepared to make such a declaration suggests that Canadian judicial thinking about the justiciability of international law may be developing in important (and laudable) ways.[16]

For the most part, the doctrine of justiciability is a self-imposed limit on the power of judges to decide cases. But non-justiciability may also arise by statute. An example of this is the *State Immunity Act*,[17] section 3(1) of which grants immunity to foreign states and officials from the jurisdiction of Canadian courts except as provided by the Act. The Act's exceptions include waiver,[18] proceedings that relate to the foreign state's commercial activity,[19] death or personal injury occurring in Canada,[20] and damage to or loss or property occurring in Canada.[21] Even with these exceptions, the Act is a significant obstacle to human rights claimants seeking remedies against foreign states and officials in Canadian courts.[22] Yet it is also the means by which Canada implements its obligations under the international law of sovereign immunity.[23] This consideration, combined with the fact that the limit on

---

14   P. Macklem & C. Scott, "Constitutional Ropes of Sand or Justiciable Guarantees? Social Rights in a New South African Constitution" (1992) 141 U. Pa. L.R. 1 at 27.
15   (2003) 228 DLR (4th) 63 (Que CA) [*Re Youth Criminal Justice Act*].
16   For more on declaratory relief, see the discussion of common law and equitable remedies below.
17   RSC 1985 c. S-18.
18   *Ibid.*, s. 4.
19   *Ibid.*, s. 5.
20   *Ibid.*, s. 6(a).
21   *Ibid.*, s. 6(b).
22   See, for example, *Bouzari v. Iran*, [2002] OJ No. 1624 (SCJ), in which the plaintiffs' action against Iran claiming damages for torture was found to be barred by Act s. 3(1). An appeal from this decision is pending. See also *Schreiber v. Canada (Attorney General)*, [2002] 3 SCR 269, though the merits of Mr Schreiber's claim are less obvious.
23   The law of sovereign immunity originates from international custom, and was therefore directly incorporated into Canadian common law until Parliament enacted the *State Immunity Act*. See *Re Canada Labour Code*, [1992] 2 SCR 50 at 102–5 per La Forest J. Were a lacuna discovered in the Act, the customary international

justiciability here is not self-imposed but is a law of Parliament, may make it difficult for Canadian courts to see how they could loosen the shackles of justiciability in matters of sovereign immunity. But the law of sovereign immunity, like the customary international law from which it derives, is not fixed. It may develop to take greater account of human rights standards. Indeed, there are signs that it is doing so.[24]

2) *Charter* Remedies

If the victim of a violation of international human rights law can show that the internationally unlawful act also amounts to a *Charter* violation, she may have access to a variety of remedies.[25] Canadian governments are not immune from such remedies, for the *Charter* explicitly applies to them: section 32(1).

The ultimate remedy for a *Charter* violation, or any violation of the constitution, is invalidity. Section 52(1) of the *Constitution Act 1982* provides that the constitution, as defined in that section, "is the supreme law of Canada" and that "any law that is inconsistent with the provisions of the Constitution is, to the extent of the inconsistency, of no force or effect." Upon finding such an inconsistency, the court may make a declaration of immediate invalidity, or may delay invalidity in proper cases.[26] Section 52(1) also permits the court to "read down" legislation that would otherwise be unconstitutional, or to "read in" terms needed to preserve the legislation's constitutionality. As the wording of section 52(1) itself suggests, courts need not declare an entire Act invalid if only part of it is unconstitutional; the offending provision may be severed from the rest.

These variations on the theme of invalidity may provide effective remedies for some human rights violations. But in many cases such legislative remedies do not suffice. The *Charter* recognizes this by provid-

---

law of sovereign immunity as incorporated by common law would presumably fill it. For an example of this, see *Re Regina and Palacios* (1984), 45 OR (2d) 269 (CA).

24　For example, Rome Statute of the International Criminal Court 1998 (Rome Statute), [2002] CanTS no. 13, art. 27 treats official capacity as an irrelevant consideration in determining an individual's international criminal responsibility. And in *R. v. Bow Street Metropolitan Stipendiary Magistrate and others, ex parte Pinochet Ugarte (No. 3)*, [1999] 2 WLR 827 (HL), the majority of the House of Lords held that sovereign immunity only protects state officials in the exercise of official functions and that torture, being expressly prohibited by international law, is not such a function.

25　See K. Roach, *Constitutional Remedies in Canada*, looseleaf ed. (Aurora, Ontario: Canada Law Book Inc., 1994–).

26　For example *Re Manitoba Language Rights*, [1985] 1 SCR 721.

ing a distinct remedial provision in respect of *Charter* rights. Section 24(1) provides that anyone whose *Charter* rights or freedoms have been "infringed or denied" may "obtain such remedy as the court considers appropriate and just in the circumstances." The connection between this provision and Canada's obligations under international human rights law was noted in *R. v. Mills* by Lamer J. (as he then was), who observed that section 24(1) "establishes the right to a remedy as the foundation stone for the effective enforcement of *Charter* rights" consistently with UDHR article 8 and ICCPR article 2(3).[27] The breadth of remedies available under section 24(1) is clear from its wording and affirmed by decided cases. Yet, outside of the criminal law context, the courts have tended to prefer declarations over injunctive relief or similarly intrusive remedies. The courts have likewise avoided awards of damages and costs, though section 24(1) itself does not exclude them.[28] In criminal matters, section 24(1) permits stays of proceedings, the quashing of judicial decisions including warrants and committals, and other forms of relief.

Section 24(1) is not the *Charter*'s only remedial provision. Section 24(2) provides that evidence obtained in a manner that infringes or denies *Charter* rights or freedoms "shall be excluded if it is established that, having regard to all the circumstances, the admission of it in the proceedings would bring the administration of justice into disrepute." This is a departure from the common law position, which admitted illegally-obtained evidence if it was relevant.[29] Another *Charter* remedial provision is section 10(c), which constitutionalizes the common law right of *habeas corpus*.

3) Quasi-Constitutional Remedies: Bills of Rights

Statutory bills of rights exist at the federal level and in some provinces. As quasi-constitutional legislation, bills of rights may render conflicting statutes "inoperative" to the extent of their inconsistency with the protected rights.[30] For more on statutory bills of rights, see Chapter Nine.

---

27   *Mills*, above note 4 at 881 per Lamer J. (dissenting but not on this point).

28   See *Mackin v. New Brunswick (Minister of Finance)*, [2002] 1 SCR 405 at paras. 78–81.

29   See D. Paciocco & L. Stuesser, *The Law of Evidence*, 2d ed. (Toronto: Irwin Law, 1999) at c. 9.

30   For example *R. v. Drybones*, [1970] SCR 282, *Singh v. Minister of Employment and Immigration*, [1985] 1 SCR 177, *Authorson v. Canada (Attorney General)*, 2003 SCC 39 (all cases under the *Canadian Bill of Rights*).

The remedial provisions of the *Quebec Charter of Human Rights and Freedoms* (*Quebec Charter*) are of especial interest. Section 52 of the *Quebec Charter* provides that no Act may derogate from the rights and freedoms guaranteed in sections 1 to 38 unless it does so expressly. We have noted that the *Quebec Charter* differs from every other human rights instrument in Canada in that it extends some protection to economic and social rights.[31] These provisions, found in sections 39 to 48, are excluded from the ambit of section 52 and therefore may not give rise to declarations of invalidity. Yet the Supreme Court of Canada has affirmed that declaratory relief is available for breaches of these rights. In *Gosselin v. Quebec (Attorney General)*, McLachlin C.J. for the majority made the following observations:

> While it is true that courts lack the power to strike down laws that are inconsistent with the social and economic rights provided in Chapter IV of the *Quebec Charter*, it does not follow from this that courts are excused from considering claims based upon these rights. Individuals claiming their rights have been violated under the *Charter* are entitled to have those claims adjudicated, in appropriate cases. The *Quebec Charter* is a legal document, purporting to create social and economic rights. These may be symbolic, in that they cannot ground the invalidation of other laws or an action in damages. But there is a remedy for breaches of the social and economic rights set out in Chapter IV of the *Quebec Charter*: where these rights are violated, a court of competent jurisdiction can declare that this is so.[32]

This decision opens up a curious imbalance in Canadian human rights law: certain economic and social rights are justiciable and may be the subject of declaratory relief in Quebec but in no other Canadian jurisdiction.

Section 49 of the *Quebec Charter* is also of note. It entitles victims of unlawful interferences with *Quebec Charter* rights "to obtain the cessation of such interference and compensation for the moral and material prejudice resulting therefrom," including the possibility of punitive damages.

4) Criminal Law Remedies

Not every human rights infringement is a criminal act. And yet the criminal law plays an essential role in respect of the most serious human rights violations. In Canada, the *Criminal Code* gives effect to Canada's obligations to punish and prevent grave human rights viola-

---

31 See the discussion of the *Quebec Charter* in Chapter Nine.
32 *Gosselin v. Quebec (Attorney General)*, [2002] 4 SCR 429 at para. 96.

tions through the recognition of offences protecting life[33] and liberty[34] and criminalizing torture[35] and other assaults.[36]

Certain sentencing provisions of the *Criminal Code* are also notable from a remedial perspective. A court, upon sentencing or discharging an offender, may order him to make restitution to persons who suffer bodily harm or property damage as a result of the commission of the offence or the arrest or attempted arrest of the offender.[37] Offenders are also required to pay a "victim surcharge" which is intended to increase revenues for provincial and territorial victim services.[38] Sentencing courts shall also consider statements by victims describing the harm done to them or loss suffered by them due to the offence.[39] If the victim so requests, the court will permit him to read the statement or present it in any other manner the court considers appropriate.[40] If the victim is dead, ill or otherwise incapable of making a statement, the statement may be made by the victim's spouse, common-law partner, relative, guardian, or care-giver.[41]

5) Judicial Review

We do not ordinarily think of judicial review of administrative action as a statutory remedy. Its origins lie in the prerogative writs of *mandamus*, *certiorari*, prohibition, and *quo warranto*. But these writs have been abolished in most Canadian jurisdictions and replaced with a statutory procedure usually called an application for judicial review.[42] While the remedy is now statutory, the substantive law of judicial review remains largely common law in nature.[43]

---

33 *Criminal Code* RSC 1985 c. C-46, ss. 229–40 (offences of murder, manslaughter, and infanticide).
34 *Ibid.*, ss. 279–86 (offences of kidnapping, forcible confinement, hostage-taking, and abduction).
35 *Ibid.*, s. 269.1.
36 *Ibid.*, ss. 265–69.
37 *Ibid.*, ss. 738–741.2.
38 *Ibid.*, s. 737.
39 *Ibid.*, s. 722(1). See also s. 672.5(14).
40 *Ibid.*, s. 722(2.1).
41 *Ibid.*, s. 722(4)(b).
42 For example *Federal Court Act* RSC 1985 c. F-7 s. 18.1(1), *Judicial Review Procedure Act* RSO 1990 c. J.1 s. 2(1), *Judicial Review Procedure Act* RSBC 1996 c. 241 s. 2(1). See S. Blake, *Administrative Law in Canada*, 3d ed. (Markham: Butterworths, 2001) at 159–65.
43 See generally D. Mullan, *Administrative Law* (Toronto: Irwin Law, 2001).

Decisions and acts of administrative decision-makers that violate international law should, in principle, be controllable by judicial review. This follows from the presumption of conformity with international law.[44] Since the statute or regulation under which the decision-maker acts is presumed to conform to Canadian obligations under treaty and custom, violations of those obligations by the decision-maker are contrary to the legislature's intent and exceed the decision-maker's powers. To apply the presumption of conformity to control administrative decision-making on international law grounds is consistent with the pragmatic and functional approach to judicial review, for the central inquiry of the pragmatic and functional approach is legislative intent.[45]

There is no direct Canadian authority for the proposition that violations of international law by administrative decision-makers may be controlled by judicial review. Yet the judgment of the Supreme Court of Canada in *Baker v. Canada (Minister of Citizenship and Immigration)* supports this approach. There, the majority of the court looked to Canada's obligations under the CRC (among other factors) in determining that the administrative decision under review was unreasonable. The decision-maker's failure to have regard to the CRC and other international norms concerning children was one way in which his decision was found to be "inconsistent with the values underlying the grant of discretion."[46]

It is helpful to recall the potential consequences of violations of international law by administrative officials, boards, and tribunals. Such acts bring the risk of Canadian legal liability before international courts and arbitral bodies. They may also bring diplomatic and political difficulties for the Canadian government. And they will necessitate executive or legislative intervention to cure the administrative default. To apply the presumption of conformity in such circumstances is not simply a matter of good interpretive practice but also an accurate account of legislative intent in almost every instance.

While judicial review is itself a remedy, further remedies flow from it. A court that grants the claimant's application for judicial review may quash the administrative decision in issue, prohibit the decision-maker

---

44   See the discussion of the presumption of conformity in Chapter Eight, and J. Brunnée & S. Toope, "A Hesitant Embrace: The Application of International Law by Canadian Courts" [2002] Canadian Yearbook of International Law 3 at 38 n. 155.

45   See *Pushpanathan v. Canada (Minister of Citizenship and Immigration)*, [1998] 1 SCR 982 at para. 26, and *Dr. Q v. College of Physicians and Surgeons of British Columbia*, 2003 SCC 19 at para. 21.

46   [1999] 2 SCR 817 at paras. 65, 69–71 [*Baker*].

from taking certain acts, or order it to take acts it would not otherwise take. It may also make a declaration.

6) Other Statutory Remedies

Statutory remedies for infringements of internationally-recognized human rights are found in numerous other federal and provincial statutes. A few examples include federal and provincial Elections Acts (creating electoral offences to protect voting rights),[47] the federal *Corrections and Conditional Release Act* (requiring humane treatment of inmates and establishing an inmate grievance procedure),[48] and federal and provincial Expropriation Acts (regulating governmental deprivations of property).

7) Common Law and Equitable Remedies

The availability of common law and equitable remedies for human rights violations depends upon identifying a cause of action under which the human rights claim may be subsumed. The mere breach of a statutory human rights provision will not necessarily be actionable at common law.[49] There are, however, several established torts that a human rights claimant may rely on. The intentional torts of trespass to the person (battery, assault, and forcible confinement) may correspond to such human rights violations as deprivations of life, liberty and security of the person; arbitrary arrest and detention; and torture. The torts of defamation and malicious prosecution may afford remedies to unlawful attacks on a person's honour and reputation. The statutory tort of violation of privacy may be invoked to remedy interferences with privacy in British Columbia, Saskatchewan, Manitoba, and Newfoundland and Labrador.[50] The tort of misfeasance in public office, recently considered by the Supreme Court of Canada in *Odhavji Estate*

---

47   For example, *Canada Elections Act* SC 2000 c. 9 part 19.

48   SC 1992 c. 20 ss. 3(a), 69, 90, 91.

49   *Seneca College of Applied Arts and Technology v. Bhadauria*, [1981] 2 SCR 181 [*Bhadauria*] (discussed below); see also *The Queen v. Saskatchewan Wheat Pool*, [1983] 1 SCR 205, in which it was held that breach of statutory duty is not a tort in Canadian common law.

50   *Privacy Act* RSBC 1996 c. 373 s. 1(1) (BC); *Privacy Act* RSS 1978 c. P-24 s. 2 (Sask.); *Privacy Act* CCSM c. P125 s. 2(1) (Man.); *Privacy Act* RSNL 1990 c. P-22 s. 3(1) (NL).

v. Woodhouse,[51] may offer human rights claimants relief in a wide variety of cases based on deliberate, unlawful conduct by public officials.

Identifying a cause of action is only the first step. Claimants seeking common law or equitable remedies for human rights violations must next determine the liability of the opposing party to such actions. Historically, the Crown enjoyed immunity from tort claims and other matters, but today the federal and provincial governments are in principle liable in tort.[52] This includes direct liability and vicarious liability in respect of Crown servants or agents. While Crown liability is the norm today, statutory exceptions and conditions continue to exist in a variety of areas. Claimants against governments must also beware of limitations statutes. These can be especially short in respect of municipal governments. Apart from these considerations, human rights claimants must bear in mind the availability of defences, of which both the Crown and private parties may avail themselves.

The remedies most likely to be of interest to human rights claimants are damages, specific relief, and declaratory relief.

The most common form of damage award in successful tort actions (and common law actions generally) is compensatory damages, meaning an award of money that will as nearly as possible put the victim in the position she would have been in but for the wrongdoer's wrong. Compensatory damages may be pecuniary or non-pecuniary. Pecuniary damages are those that can be measured in money. They include economic losses such as lost wages and lost employment opportunities and losses due to personal injury or death. Non-pecuniary damages compensate for harms that are not readily measurable in money, such as pain and suffering or mental anguish. Also included within this heading are aggravated damages, which may be awarded to compensate victims of particularly malicious or high-handed misconduct. Victims of human rights abuses may also seek punitive (or "exemplary") damages. Punitive damages are non-compensatory in nature; rather than compensating for the victim's loss, they seek to punish the wrongdoer for his conduct. Punitive damages may be claimed over and above compensatory claims.[53]

---

51 2003 SCC 69. See also *Roncarelli v. Duplessis*, [1959] SCR 121.

52 See generally P. Hogg & P. Monahan, *Liability of the Crown*, 3d ed (Scarborough: Carswell, 2000) [Hogg & Monahan, *Liability*].

53 On damages generally, see J. Cassels, *Remedies: The Law of Damages* (Toronto: Irwin Law, 2000).

Specific relief includes injunctions and orders for specific performance of legal obligations.[54] These remedies are available in principle against private parties. As for the Crown, the common law rule is that coercive forms of relief (injunction, specific performance, and remedies in the nature of *mandamus*, prohibition, and *certiorari*) are not available against it. This rule is now declared in statutes in every Canadian jurisdiction. In lieu of such remedies, human rights claimants and others may seek declaratory relief. Note, however, that Crown immunity does not extend to the Crown's servants and officials. Ministers, public servants, and corporate Crown agents may in principle be the object of injunctive and related forms of relief.[55]

As its name indicates, declaratory relief consists of a declaration by the court of the legal relations between the parties. Declarations are available against the Crown, and are frequently relied on in constitutional challenges. But even in non-constitutional matters, declaratory relief may be a powerful remedy for human rights claimants. While there is technically nothing coercive about a declaration, governments rarely ignore declaratory judgments against them. We noted earlier that human rights claimants seeking to rely on common law or equitable remedies must identify a cause of action under which the human rights claim may be subsumed. That is not the case for declarations. While a plaintiff must show standing, and must also show that the question is real and not theoretical, he need not demonstrate facts entitling him to seek damages or other coercive relief.[56]

This raises the intriguing prospect of declaratory relief in respect of simple violations of international law. By "simple violations of international law," we mean those that do not coincide with violations of domestic law, and are therefore not directly actionable, but are nevertheless relevant to Canadian law. The justiciability of such questions has been affirmed by the Supreme Court of Canada and the Court of Appeal for Quebec in reference cases. In *Re Secession of Quebec*,[57] the Supreme Court was asked whether international law gave Quebec a

---

54 These are equitable, not common law remedies. While the distinction between equitable and common law remedies remains important for some purposes, it is not relevant for ours.

55 On Crown liability to specific relief, see Hogg & Monahan, *Liability*, above note 52 at 31–34.

56 *Dyson v. Attorney-General (No. 1)*, [1911] 1 KB 410 (Eng CA) at 417, *Dyson v. Attorney-General (No. 2)*, [1912] 1 Ch 158 (CA) at 166–68, *Russian Commercial and Industrial Bank v. British Bank for Foreign Trade*, [1921] 2 AC 438 (HL) at 448, *Solosky v. The Queen*, [1980] 1 SCR 821 at 830.

57 *Re Secession*, above note 10 at para. 22.

right unilaterally to secede from Canada, and whether there was an international law right to self-determination that gave Quebec such a right. When challenged on its jurisdiction to answer such questions, the court affirmed that it had jurisdiction over international law questions "to determine the rights or obligations of some actor within the Canadian legal system," and noted that the question "does not ask an abstract question of 'pure' international law but seeks to determine the legal rights and obligations of . . . institutions that clearly exist as part of the Canadian legal order."[58] In *Quebec (Minister of Justice) v. Canada (Minister of Justice)*,[59] the Government of Quebec referred several questions to the Quebec Court of Appeal concerning the federal *Youth Criminal Justice Act*.[60] Most of the questions were challenges of the legislation's constitutionality, but two inquired about the compatibility of the law with Canadian obligations under the ICCPR and the CRC. The court concluded, following *Re Secession*, that these questions were properly before it. In particular, the Court of Appeal noted that while its answers to the questions would have no international legal force, they would indirectly affect the *Charter* questions before them.[61]

While references and declaratory judgments are not technically the same, they are very similar. Both are advisory rather than coercive in nature. Both may be brought in the absence of facts amounting to a cause of action. In short, these reference cases may provide authority for claimants seeking a declaration that their human rights, as established in international law, have been violated.[62]

Perhaps a more direct authority (because it concerns declarations not advisory opinions) is the judgment of the Federal Court of Appeal in *Montana Band of Indians v. Canada*.[63] The plaintiff Indian bands sought declarations of their rights under both constitutional and international law. In respect of the latter, they sought a declaration that ICCPR articles 1 and 27 were binding on Canada and applicable to them.[64] The trial

---

58   *Ibid.* at paras. 22–23.
59   *Re Youth Criminal Justice Act*, above note 15.
60   SC 2002 c. 1 [*YCJA*].
61   *Re Youth Criminal Justice Act*, above note 15 at paras. 111–16.
62   But see *Re Indian Residential Schools*, [2000] 9 WWR 437 (Alta QB) at paras. 68–73, where Nation J. struck out pleadings seeking a declaration that the residential school system constituted a breach of the Genocide Convention on the ground that "a non-legal or political code of conduct" (i.e., the Convention) could not be the basis for declaratory relief. With respect, Nation J. was mistaken to characterize a treaty as non-legal.
63   [1991] 2 FC 30 (CA) [*Montana Band*].
64   *Ibid.* at 37.

judge struck out the plaintiffs' amended statement of claim for failing to identify the plaintiffs' grievance against the Crown. The Court of Appeal unanimously overturned this decision, holding that for the purpose of declaratory relief there was no need to point to a specific breach. What is interesting about this judgment is what it does not say: nowhere in the judgment is any objection raised to the propriety of seeking declaratory relief in respect of a Canadian treaty obligation.

Persuasive support for declaratory relief in such cases is found in the Bangalore Principles 1988, the eighth principle of which urges courts to draw inconsistencies between international and domestic law "to the attention of the appropriate authorities since the supremacy of national law in no way mitigates a breach of an international legal obligation which is undertaken by a country."[65]

C. ANTI-DISCRIMINATION MECHANISMS

We saw in Chapter Nine that federal, provincial, and territorial laws prohibit public and private forms of discrimination in their respective jurisdictions. These prohibitions are enforced by a variety of statutory human rights commissions, boards, and tribunals.

The procedures and structures of these bodies vary from jurisdiction to jurisdiction, though they share many common features.[66] Individuals may initiate a complaint to the human rights commission.[67] In some jurisdictions, the commission may also initiate complaints of its own motion.[68] Upon receipt of a complaint, the commission will

---

65   "Bangalore Principles" in *Developing Human Rights Jurisprudence: The Domestic Application of International Human Rights Norms* (London: Commonwealth Secretariat, 1988) at x. See the discussion of the judiciary in Chapter Eight.

66   See generally R. Zinn & P. Brethour, *The Law of Human Rights in Canada: Practice and Procedure*, looseleaf (Aurora, Ontario: Canada Law Book Inc., 1996) at c. 17 [Zinn & Brethour, *The Law of Human Rights*].

67   For example, *Canadian Human Rights Act* RSC 1985 c. H-6 s. 40(1); *Human Rights Code* RSBC 1996 c. 210 s. 21(1); *Human Rights, Citizenship and Multiculturalism Act* RSA 2000 c. H-14 s. 20(2); *Human Rights Code* RSO 1990 c. H.19 s. 32; *Quebec Charter of Human Rights and Freedoms*, RSQ c. C-12, s. 74 [*Quebec Charter*]; *Human Rights Act* RSNS 1989 c. 214 s. 29. In the Northwest Territories and Nunavut, complaints are addressed to an officer appointed pursuant to the *Fair Practices Act* RSNWT 1988 c. F-2 s. 7. (On the application of Northwest Territories law in Nunavut, see the *Nunavut Act*, SC 1993 c. 28, s. 29(1).)

68   For example, *Canadian Human Rights Act*, ibid., s. 40(3); *Human Rights Code* (RSO), ibid., s. 32; *Human Rights Act* (RSNS), ibid., s. 29.

appoint an investigator[69] and may (or sometimes must) attempt to reach a settlement.[70] Often the investigator or the commission is empowered to dismiss certain complaints, for instance: those that are not within the commission's jurisdiction;[71] those that are without merit;[72] those made in bad faith;[73] and those in which the victim does not consent to continuing the complaint.[74] Complaints that are not dismissed are referred to a tribunal[75] or panel[76] or board of inquiry[77] for hearing, decision, and (where appropriate) remedy. Some of these decision-making bodies are empowered by provincial inquiries legislation,[78] while others exercise powers under the human rights codes they enforce.[79]

The remedies available from these bodies include monetary and non-monetary forms of relief.[80] Monetary remedies typically include compensation for lost wages, lost employment opportunities, expenses incurred, and hurt feelings or mental anguish, and may include punitive damages in cases of wilful or reckless violations of anti-discrimination provisions. Complainants have a general duty to mitigate their damages. Non-monetary remedies include cease and desist orders in respect of the discriminatory conduct, compliance orders to prevent

---

69 For example, *Canadian Human Rights Act*, *ibid.*, s. 43(1); *Human Rights Code* (RSBC), above note 67, s. 29(1); *Human Rights Code* (RSO), *ibid.*, s. 33.

70 For example, *Canadian Human Rights Act*, *ibid.*, s. 47; *Human Rights, Citizenship and Multiculturalism Act*, above note 67, s. 20(1); *Human Rights Code* (RSO), *ibid.*, s. 33; *Human Rights Act* RSPEI 1988 c. H-12 s. 22.

71 For example, *Canadian Human Rights Act*, *ibid.*, s. 41(b); *Human Rights Code* (RSBC), above note 67, s. 27(1)(a); *Human Rights Code* (RSO), *ibid.*, s. 34(1).

72 For example, *Human Rights Code* (RSBC), *ibid.*, s.27(1)(c); *Human Rights, Citizenship and Multiculturalism Act*, above note 67, s. 20(1); *Human Rights Act* RSNB 1973 c. H-11 s. 18(2).

73 For example, *Canadian Human Rights Act*, above note 67, s. 41(d); *Human Rights Code* (RSBC), *ibid.*, s. 27(1)(e); *Human Rights Code* (RSO), above note 67, s. 34(1).

74 For example, *Human Rights Code* (RSBC), *ibid.*, s. 21(5); *Human Rights Code* RSN 1990 c. H-14 s. 20(3).

75 The procedure in British Columbia, Saskatchewan, Ontario, Quebec, and federally.

76 The procedure in Alberta, Manitoba, Prince Edward Island, and the Yukon.

77 The procedure in New Brunswick, Nova Scotia, and Newfoundland and Labrador. In the Northwest Territories and Nunavut, an officer with the powers of a board established under the *Public Inquiries Act* RSNWT 1988 c. P-14 hears the complaint: *Fair Practices Act*, above note 67, s. 7(5).

78 For example *Human Rights Act* (RSNS), above note 67, s. 34(1); *Human Rights Act* (RSPEI), above note 70, s. 26; *Human Rights Code* (RSN), above note 74, s. 27(1).

79 For example *Canadian Human Rights Act*, above note 67, ss. 48.1–48.9; *Human Rights, Citizenship and Multiculturalism Act*, above note 67, s. 32; *Quebec Charter*, above note 67, Parts II (Commission) and VI (Tribunal).

80 See Zinn & Brethour, *The Law of Human Rights*, above note 66 at c. 16.

future breaches (including mandatory affirmative action programmes and sensitivity training for staff), orders for the reinstatement of employees fired for discriminatory reasons, and mandatory apologies to victims. Human rights commissions tend to have a broad discretion in the development of appropriate non-monetary remedies.

The existence of statutory anti-discrimination regimes appears to pre-empt the development of the common law in the field covered by the statute. In *Seneca College of Applied Arts and Technology v. Bhadauria*,[81] the Supreme Court of Canada struck out a statement of claim, based on the alleged tort of discrimination, on the ground that the existence of such a tort was excluded by the Ontario *Human Rights Code*.[82] The Code was described as a comprehensive provision for remedying discriminatory practices which ousted any common law development in the area. In reaching this conclusion, the court overruled the Court of Appeal for Ontario, which had found a common law tort of discrimination.[83] Laskin C.J.'s reasoning in *Bhadauria* suggests that where human rights codes are less than comprehensive, or do not invest exclusive jurisdiction in the statutory bodies they create, they will not inhibit common law development in areas untouched by legislation.[84] Note also that the *Bhadauria* rule (that discriminatory practices are not actionable at common law where statutory schemes have intervened), may be displaced by statute. The British Columbia *Civil Rights Protection Act* renders actionable in tort without proof of damage any conduct or communication by a person that has as its purpose interference with the civil rights of a person or class of persons by promoting hatred or contempt or notions of superiority or inferiority on the basis of colour, race, religion, ethnic origin, or place of origin.[85]

D. INVESTIGATIVE MECHANISMS

The front line in investigative fact-finding in Canada is, of course, the country's federal, provincial, and municipal police forces. But as we noted earlier, not all human rights violations are criminal. The investigation of human rights complaints sometimes falls to other bodies. Under this heading we consider three such bodies: commissions of

---

81 *Bhadauria*, above note 49.
82 RSO 1970 c. 318.
83 (1979) 27 OR (2d) 142.
84 See *Lajoie v. Kelly*, [1997] 3 WWR 181 (Man QB).
85 RSBC 1996 c. 49.

inquiry, coroners' inquests and similar proceedings, and ombudsman offices. All these mechanisms have, to differing degrees, the investigatory functions, decision-making powers, and structural independence associated with judicial bodies, yet lack judicial remedial powers and procedures. Though not remedial in the strictest sense of the word, the work of these investigative mechanisms is an important part of the promotion and protection of human rights in Canada.

1) Commissions of Inquiry

Commissions of inquiry are established by governments as responses to particular controversies[86] or ongoing public concerns.[87] They are usually established by order in council under powers provided by statute.[88] They generally possess subpoena powers and the authority to conduct public and *in camera* hearings. Though established at the impetus of government, commissions of inquiry are intended to be independent of it.[89] For this reason they are often presided over by acting or former judges. The essence of these commissions is their mandate to inquire into and report upon events or issues of public importance, with a view to stimulating effective governmental and public policy responses to their findings and recommendations.[90]

Commissions of inquiry have often been established in response to proven or alleged human rights abuses. Recent examples include: the wrongful conviction inquiries in the cases of Donald Marshall Jr.[91] and Thomas Sophonow;[92] the disturbances at the Kingston Prison for

---

86   For example Commission of Inquiry on the Blood System in Canada (reported 1997).

87   For example Royal Commission Inquiry into Civil Rights (reported 1968), Royal Commission on Bilingualism and Biculturalism (reported 1967–70), Royal Commission on Aboriginal Peoples (reported 1996), Commission on the Future of Health Care in Canada (reported 2002).

88   For example *Inquiries Act* RSC 1985 c. I-11, *Public Inquiries Act* RSO 1990 c. P.41, *Inquiry Act* RSBC 1996 c. 224. But see *Masters v. Ontario* (1994), 18 OR (3d) 551 (Div Ct), where an inquiry was described as being conducted under the "prerogative" of the premier of Ontario.

89   See T. Witelson, "Declaration of Independence: Examining the Independence of Federal Public Inquiries" in A. Manson & D. Mullan, eds., *Commissions of Inquiry: Praise or Reappraise?* (Toronto: Irwin Law, 2003) at 301–60.

90   Manson & Mullan, *ibid.*, at 4.

91   Nova Scotia, *Royal Commission on the Donald Marshall, Jr., Prosecution: Commissioners Report: Findings and Recommendations* (Halifax: The Commission, 1989).

92   *The Inquiry Regarding Thomas Sophonow: The Investigation, Prosecution, and Consideration of Entitlement to Compensation* (Winnipeg: Statutory Publications, 2001).

Women;[93] the torture and killing of a local teenager by Canadian Forces in Somalia;[94] and the police killing of aboriginal protester Dudley George.[95] Human rights have also been the subject of commissions of broader scope, such as the Commission of Inquiry on War Criminals[96] and the Royal Commission on Aboriginal Peoples.[97] Like the ombudsman proceedings and coroners' inquests that they in some ways resemble, commissions of inquiry offer human rights claimants an opportunity to investigate alleged violations and put their concerns on record. Commissions of inquiry may also result in substantive recommendations for redress, though governments in Canada are somewhat notorious for disregarding their reports (particularly in the case of large-scale thematic commissions like the Royal Commission on Aboriginal Peoples).

2) Coroners and Medical Examiners

In cases of human rights abuses causing death, investigations and inquests by coroners or medical examiners may help provide answers.[98] Coroners and medical examiners do not determine criminal or civil responsibility for the deaths they investigate. Instead, their role is to ascertain the facts of death, including the identity of the deceased and how, when, where, and by what means the deceased died. Coroners and med-

---

93   Canada, *Commission of Inquiry into Certain Events at the Prison for Women in Kingston* (Ottawa: Public Works and Government Services Canada, 1996).

94   See Canada, *Dishonoured Legacy: The Lessons of the Somalia Affair: Report of the Commission of Inquiry into the Deployment of Canadian Forces to Somalia* (Ottawa: The Commission, 1997).

95   See Ministry of the Attorney General (Ontario), "Ontario Government Announces Public Inquiry Into the Death of Dudley George," News Release 12 November 2003. Among those calling for an inquiry into the George affair was the UN Human Rights Committee. See Human Rights Committee, *Concluding Observations: Canada* (2003) UN doc. CCPR/C/79/Add.105 (1999) at para. 11.

96   See Canada, *Commission of Inquiry on War Criminals Report* (Ottawa: Supply and Services Canada, 1986), better known as the Deschênes Commission.

97   See Canada, *Report of the Royal Commission on Aboriginal Peoples* (Ottawa: The Commission, 1996).

98   The role of coroners and medical examiners is similar but their organization and qualifications differ. The coroner system is rooted in the common law and was historically non-medical, with autopsies performed by pathologists. The modern medical examiner system integrates pathologists and other medical experts into the investigative process. Most Canadian provinces and territories continue to operate a coroner system. Medical examiner systems are in place in Alberta, Manitoba, Nova Scotia, and Newfoundland. Coroners in Ontario are licensed physicians, but this is not a requirement in all coroner jurisdictions.

ical examiners do not investigate all deaths; only those that are unnatural, unexpected, unexplained, or warrant investigation for other reasons.

Coroners and medical examiners in Canada have statutory powers to conduct investigations and inquests into deaths. Their investigative powers generally include viewing or taking possession of bodies, entering and inspecting places where bodies are or were, inspecting places the deceased was prior to death, disinterring or exhuming remains, inspecting and extracting information from records or writings relating to the deceased, and seizing things material to the investigation.[99] A coroner's inquest is a court proceeding to determine the facts of death. Guided by the presiding coroner, a jury (summoned in the same way as criminal juries) hears evidence from witnesses and determines the facts. The jury does not assign fault, but may make recommendations to prevent similar deaths in the future. These recommendations are published in the verdict. Coroners' inquests are mandatory when a person dies in custody,[100] but are otherwise at the discretion of the investigating coroner. Similar proceedings take place in medical examiner jurisdictions, though they are often conducted by a judge sitting without a jury.[101]

3) Ombudsman and Similar Bodies

The word "ombudsman" is Swedish for representative.[102] An ombudsman is an independent, objective investigator of people's complaints against government agencies and other organizations. The International Ombudsman Institute describes the role of the ombudsman as

> to protect the people against violation of rights, abuse of powers, error, negligence, unfair decisions and maladministration in order to

---

99 For example *Coroners Act* RSBC 1996 c. 72 s. 15; *Coroners Act* RSO 1990 c. C.37 s. 16; *Fatality Inquiries Act* RSA 2000 c. F-9 ss. 21, 28; *Coroners Act* SS 1999 c. C-38.01 ss. 11–15.

100 For example *Coroners Act* (RSBC), *ibid.*, s. 10; *Coroners Act* (RSO), *ibid.*, s. 10(4); *Coroners Act* (SS), *ibid.*, s. 20.

101 For example *Fatality Inquiries Act* RSA 2000 c. F-9 ss. 35(2) (jury optional), *Fatality Investigations Act* SNS 2001 c. 31 s. 27(3) (judge alone), *Fatality Inquiries Act* CCSM c. F52 s. 26(1) (judge alone).

102 In Swedish, the suffix –man in ombudsman is not masculine. While backformations such as ombudsperson and ombuds exist in English, the term ombudsman remains prevalent in Canada both in English and French, for example Forum of Canadian Ombudsman, International Ombudsman Institute (University of Alberta), Ombudsman Ontario, L'ombudsman des Services français de Radio-Canada. The Quebec government ombudsman is called protecteur du citoyen in French and ombudsman in English.

improve public administration and make the government's actions more open and the government and its servants more accountable to members of the public.[103]

Historically, the office of ombudsman was created by statute for the purpose of addressing complaints against government. Today, ombudsman offices are found not only in government but also in public or publicly-regulated institutions such as universities, Crown corporations, and banks, and even in the private sector. The ombudsman role is often served by bodies going under a different name, such as commissioner or investigator.

In many countries, the protection of human rights is central to the ombudsman's task. In Canada, the human rights responsibilities of ombudsman offices and similar bodies are less explicit but still important. In particular, federal and provincial complaints commissioners in respect of privacy rights and police conduct offer human rights victims an important forum to be heard and to gain redress for their grievances.

There is no federal ombudsman for Canada. There are, however, several federal agencies and commissions that fill this role. They include the Commissioner of Official Languages,[104] the Information Commissioner,[105] the Privacy Commissioner,[106] the Communications Security Establishment Commissioner,[107] the Correctional Investigator,[108] the Canadian Forces Ombudsman,[109] the Commission for Public Complaints Against the RCMP,[110] and the Military Police Complaints Commission.[111]

Most Canadian provinces and territories have created ombudsman offices by statute.[112] These tend to have broad jurisdiction over govern-

---

103 International Ombudsman Institute web site (http://www.law.ualberta.ca/centres/ioi).
104 See *Official Languages Act* RSC 1985 c. 31 (4th Supp.) Part IX.
105 See *Access to Information Act* RSC 1985 c. A-1 ss. 54–66.
106 See *Privacy Act* RSC 1985 c. P-21 ss. 53–67.
107 See *National Defence Act* RSC 1985 c. N-5 Part V.1.
108 See *Corrections and Conditional Release Act*, above note 48, Part III.
109 The position of Ombudsman is an Order in Council appointment under s. 5 of the *National Defence Act*, above note 107. The Office of the Ombudsman and its mandate are set out in Ministerial Directives Respecting the Ombudsman for the Department of National Defence and the Canadian Forces (5 September 2001).
110 *Royal Canadian Mounted Police Act* RSC 1985 c. R-10 Part VI.
111 See *National Defence Act*, above note 107, Part IV Division 1.
112 *Ombudsman Act* RSBC 1996 c. 340, *Ombudsman Act* RSA 2000 c. O-8, *Ombudsman Amendment Act* SA 2003 c. 30, *Ombudsman and Children's Advocate Act* RSS 1978 c. O-4, *Ombudsman Act* CCSM c. O45, *Ombudsman Act* RSO 1990 c. O.6, *Public Protector Act* RSQ c. P-32, *Ombudsman Act* SNB c. O-5, *Ombudsman Act*

ment-related complaints within the province or territory. In some provinces, separate bodies exist to address issues of specific public interest, such as health services[113] and police complaints.[114]

Ombudsman complaints processes vary from office to office, but all strive for accessibility. Complaints may usually be initiated by correspondence or by filling out a simple form. Many ombudsman offices now have presences on the Internet.

E. POLITICAL MECHANISMS

As important as legal and administrative avenues are for promoting and protecting human rights in Canada, they have not supplanted direct political action, either by politicians and the civil servants who work under them or by the advocates who target them. Some of the political measures discussed in this section are more or less permanent, such as parliamentary committees and government departments. Others, such as reparations payments, are *ad hoc* responses to particular human rights issues. Finally, we briefly note the importance of Canada's cultural inclination towards human rights protection.

1) Parliamentary and Ministerial Action

Particularly since the advent of the *Charter*, Canadian politicians have embraced the concept of human rights with notable enthusiasm. Substantiated allegations of human rights abuses are likely to attract political attention, both federally and provincially. For this reason, lobbying government ministers and members of Parliament or the provincial legislatures can sometimes be an effective means of promoting and protecting human rights in Canada. The following discussion focuses on the federal level, where important parliamentary and ministerial mechanisms exist for addressing human rights concerns. But human rights

---

RSNS 1989 c. 327, *Citizens' Representative Act* SNL 2001 c. C-14.1, *Ombudsman Act* RSY 2002 c. 163.

113 For example Quebec's Health and Social Services Ombudsman (see *Act respecting the Health and Social Services Ombudsman* RSQ P-31.1).

114 Commissions and other civilian bodies charged with hearing, investigating, and reviewing complaints against the police are found throughout the country, for example Office of the Police Complaint Commissioner (BC), Police Complaints Investigator (Saskatchewan), Special Investigations Unit (Ontario), Commissaire à la déontologie policière (Quebec), Nova Scotia Police Commission.

advocacy at the provincial level is also important, for, as we have seen in previous chapters, many human rights issues fall within provincial jurisdiction.

Debate on human rights issues, both in Canada and abroad, occurs in Parliament almost without stop. Parliamentary committees are the main forums for these discussions. In the Senate, the work of the Human Rights Committee and the Legal and Constitutional Affairs Committee is most immediately relevant. Three other Senate committees — Aboriginal Peoples, Foreign Affairs, and National Security and Defence — also have mandates that frequently touch upon human rights matters. In the Commons, the two most important committees from a human rights perspective are Justice and Human Rights, and Foreign Affairs and International Trade. The latter committee has a Subcommittee on Human Rights and International Development. Other Commons committees in which human rights are frequently addressed are: Aboriginal Affairs, Northern Development and Natural Resources; Citizenship and Immigration; Human Resources Development and the Status of Persons with Disabilities; and National Defence and Veterans Affairs.[115] Apart from these standing committees, legislative committees are sometimes struck to consider particular bills. The main role of committees in the parliamentary process is to scrutinize proposed legislation. However, parliamentary committees often undertake their own research on matters of interest to them and publish their findings and views in public reports. An example is the recent Senate Human Rights Committee report recommending Canadian adherence to the ACHR.[116]

Committees are not the only place for human rights discussion in Parliament, of course. The legislative floor itself is available to Senators and MPs, though the parliamentary agenda is so tightly controlled by the government that opportunities to speak at any length are rare. When such opportunities do arise, the quality of debate can be disappointing. Senate debates are often more informed than those in the Commons, but misgivings about the Senate's legitimacy as an unelected body cast a shadow over everything it does. In spite of all this, lob-

---

115 As we write, Paul Martin has succeeded Jean Chrétien as prime minister and announced reforms to Parliament and government departments which may affect the organization of committees. Up-to-date committee information for both the Senate and the Commons may be found on Parliament's web site, http://www.parl.gc.ca.

116 Standing Senate Committee on Human Rights, "Enhancing Canada's Role in the OAS: Canadian Adherence to the American Convention on Human Rights" (May 2003).

bying Senators and MPs can be effective in promoting and protecting human rights. William Sampson, a Canadian who was tortured and sentenced to death in Saudi Arabia, credited his eventual release in part to the efforts of two MPs, the Hon. Dan McTeague (Pickering-Ajax-Uxbridge) and Stéphane Bergeron (Verchères-Les-Patriotes).[117]

Government ministries and agencies are a sometimes overlooked forum for the promotion and protection of human rights in Canada. Within the Department of Justice, a Human Rights Law Section of twenty lawyers advises the federal government on human rights. The work of this section includes examining bills and regulations for consistency with the *Charter*,[118] advising government lawyers in rights-related litigation, representing Canada in individual complaints before UN treaty bodies, and educating lawyers on human rights law.[119] Another federal department, Canadian Heritage, runs the Human Rights Program.[120] The Program is the federal government's main human rights promotional initiative. It carries out educational and promotional activities to the public and within government, and funds independent human rights projects. The Program is also responsible for co-ordinating provincial and territorial involvement in Canada's reports to UN treaty bodies. Human rights promotion is also an important aspect of the work of the Canadian International Development Agency (CIDA), an agency under the Department of Foreign Affairs and International Trade. Among CIDA's objectives are to strengthen "the capacity of organizations that protect and promote human rights in order to enhance each society's ability to address rights concerns and strengthen the security of the individual."[121]

In cases of especial urgency or notoriety, individual ministers may personally intervene to protect human rights victims or protest abuses. The recent case of Zahra Kazemi is an illustration. Kazemi was a Canadian journalist arrested in Iran while taking photographs outside a Tehran prison during student-led protests. Kazemi was severely beaten during police interrogation. She later died from her injuries. Canada's

---

117 Evidence of William Sampson before the Standing Committee on Foreign Affairs and International Trade, 6 November 2003.

118 As required by s. 4.1(1) of the *Department of Justice Act* RSC 1985 c. J-2.

119 N. Baer, "The Rights Stuff" (2002) 2 Justice Canada no. 2 (available online at http://canada.justice.gc.ca/en/dept/pub/jc).

120 See http://www.pch.gc.ca/progs/pdp-hrp.

121 Canadian International Development Agency, "Government of Canada Policy for CIDA on Human Rights, Democratization and Good Governance" (December 1996) at 4.

foreign affairs minister denounced Kazemi's death as "a flagrant violation of her rights under international human rights law and a breach of obligations that Iran owes to the international community" and urged Iran to return Kazemi's body to her family in Montreal.[122] Upset with Iran's handling of the Kazemi affair, Canada recalled its ambassador[123] and later called upon the UN Commission on Human Rights to investigate the matter.[124] It is hard to say how successful these Canadian interventions were. They have so far failed to convince Iran to repatriate Kazemi's remains. But the Kazemi affair seems to have provoked an important power struggle between fundamentalist and reformist elements in Iran.[125] It can at least be said that the minister's interventions on behalf of the Kazemi family drew international attention to what might otherwise have become yet another forgotten human rights violation.

Unfortunately, stories of ministerial and governmental inaction in the face of human rights abuses may also be cited. In 2001, Canadian William Sampson appeared on Saudi Arabian television and confessed responsibility for two car bombings. Sampson later informed Canadian diplomats that he had been forced to confess under torture and that he was being mistreated in prison, yet government officials insisted publicly that he had not been mistreated.[126] Sampson and a British co-accused were sentenced in a secret trial to death by public beheading, while other accused Britons were sentenced to lengthy jail terms. All were granted clemency by the Saudi king and released in August 2003. While British diplomatic efforts on behalf of the prisoners were praised,[127] Canadian efforts were panned by Sampson and his family.[128] The terrifying story of Maher Arar may be another instance of Canadian inaction, although as we write the details of the Arar affair remain unclear.[129]

---

122 Department of Foreign Affairs and International Trade, "Graham Seeks Justice for Death of Zahra Kazemi," News Release No. 104, 21 July 2003.
123 "Canada recalls ambassador from Iran," CBC News (http://www.cbc.ca), 25 July 2003.
124 "Canada wants UN help in Kazemi case," CBC News (http://www.cbc.ca), 28 August 2003.
125 "Murder trial sparks Iran row," BBC News (http://news.bbc.co.uk), 8 October 2003.
126 M. Jimenez, "Ottawa knew of Sampson's torture," Globe and Mail, 13 August 2003.
127 British efforts reportedly included personal intervention by Prince Charles: "Prince Charles instrumental in freeing Sampson: U.K. papers," CBC News (http://www.cbc.ca), 11 August 2003.
128 For example "Ottawa no help, says father of man in Saudi jail," CBC News (http://www.cbc.ca), 10 January 2003; "Canadian government failed me: Sampson," CBC News (http://www.cbc.ca), 7 November 2003.
129 Arar is a Syrian-born Canadian who was arrested at JFK airport in New York and deported to the Middle East, where he was held in a Syrian jail for nearly a year

2) Compensation Payments for Human Rights Violations

ICCPR article 14(6) requires Canada to compensate persons wrongfully convicted of criminal offences unless it is proved that the miscarriage of justice is wholly or partly attributable to the convict himself. Given this legal obligation, the subject of compensation payments for wrongfully convicted persons should seemingly not appear under the heading "political mechanisms." Yet Canada has no legislative framework in place to implement the right to compensation for wrongful conviction. Instead, the compensation of wrongfully convicted persons in Canada proceeds on an *ex gratia* basis — payments are made out of magnanimity not legal obligation. In spite of the existence of federal-provincial guidelines on compensating wrongfully convicted and imprisoned persons, the compensation process in Canada remains essentially a political one.[130] Compensation payments have been made in respect of such well-known wrongful conviction cases as Donald Marshall, Guy Paul Morin, David Milgaard, and Thomas Sophonow, but the method of compensation is characterized by inconsistency and uncertainty.[131]

Ex gratia compensation payments have been employed in Canada as redress for other human rights abuses. In 1988, the federal government, belatedly and after long negotiations with an NGO representing Japanese-Canadians, offered "symbolic redress payments" of $21,000

---

and claims to have been tortured. The latest media reports suggest that American officials acted on information they had received from the RCMP — information the RCMP had not shared with the Canadian government. The result was the bizarre spectacle of Canada making an official protest against American action in which the RCMP itself appears to have played a contributing role. See J. Sallot, "Chrétien was kept in the dark about Arar," *Globe and Mail*, 9 January 2003. As this book went to press, Arar's demands for a public inquiry were acceded to by the federal government.

130 See 1988 Federal-Provincial Guidelines on Compensation for Wrongfully Convicted and Imprisoned Persons, discussed in H. Kaiser, "Wrongful Conviction and Imprisonment: Towards an end to the Compensatory Obstacle Course" (1989) 9 Windsor Yearbook of Access to Justice 96. Though the guidelines were formulated having regard to the International Covenant on Civil and Political Rights 1966 (ICCPR), [1976] CanS no. 47, art. 14(6), and in some ways go further than that article requires, their non-binding nature must put into question whether Canada has met its ICCPR obligations. See Human Rights Committee, *Concluding Observations: Canada* (1980) UN doc. CCPR A/35/4 at para. 178.

131 A graphic illustration of this is the Sophonow case. After being awarded compensation to be jointly paid by the federal and Manitoba governments, Manitoba delayed payment while suing the city of Winnipeg for its share of the payment, and Sophonow was forced to sue Manitoba to collect his full compensation: "Still owed millions, Sophonow sues province," CBC News (http://www.cbc.ca), 17 June 2002.

to eligible Canadians of Japanese ancestry who were forcibly relocated, interned, or deported, or suffered property loss, or were "otherwise deprived of the full enjoyment of fundamental rights and freedoms" during the Second World War. Accompanying these payments was a sum of $12 million to be administered by the National Association of Japanese Canadians for "activities to promote the educational, social and cultural well-being of the community or that promote human rights" and a further sum of $12 million to support the creation of the Canadian Race Relations Foundation.[132]

A rather different compensation scheme has been announced for victims of physical and sexual abuse in Indian residential schools. As an alternative to litigation, claimants may now apply to a federal department, Indian Residential Schools Resolution Canada, for compensation. Claimants complete a form describing the abuses they suffered and submit it to an adjudicator whose task is to quantify the money value of the claim. After this decision has been rendered, claimants may reject the compensation and pursue litigation or accept it and sign a release precluding future claims against the government in respect of the abuses in question. Claimants who accept compensation are not precluded from pursuing further litigation for loss of language and culture (assuming such claims are actionable).[133]

Other ethnocultural communities within Canada continue to seek compensation and other forms of redress for historic human rights violations. In 1994, the federal government rejected claims for redress made by the Chinese Canadian National Council, the German Canadian Congress, the Canadian Jewish Congress, the National Association of Canadians of Origins in India, the National Congress of Chinese Canadians, the National Congress of Italian Canadians, the Ukrainian Canadian Congress, and the Canadian Ukrainian Civil Liberties Association. Speaking in the House of Commons on the matter, the secretary of state for multiculturalism acknowledged that "some Canadian ethnocultural communities found their loyalty questioned, their freedom restrained and their lives disrupted" in the "crisis atmosphere of war" and that some past Canadian immigration practices were "at odds with our shared commitment to human justice." But she nevertheless

---

132 Department of Canadian Heritage, *Final Report on the Implementation of the Japanese Canadian Redress Agreement, 1988* (Ottawa: Department of Canadian Heritage, November 1997) at 5.

133 Indian Residential Schools Resolution Canada, "New Dispute Resolution Process Launched for Abuse Claims at Indian Residential Schools," News Release 6 November 2003. See http://www.irsr-rqpi.gc.ca.

refused the requested compensation, which she described as totalling hundreds of millions of dollars.[134]

ICCPR article 9(5) requires states parties to make an enforceable right to compensation available to victims of unlawful arrest or detention. As we saw in Chapter Ten, such compensation is available by means of tort actions for false imprisonment and is also available, theoretically at least, under *Charter* section 24(1).[135]

3) Symbolic Reparation

Symbolic reparation encompasses non-material forms of reparation that aim to commemorate and restore dignity to the victims of human rights abuses. Such measures may include public apologies, the erection of monuments and other memorials, the establishment of national days of remembrance, the expunging of criminal records, the renaming of public places, and other gestures of atonement and reconciliation.[136]

Since the late 1980s Canadian governments have made several high-profile official apologies, expressions of regret, and acknowledgements of past wrongs.[137] In 1988 the prime minister of the day, Brian Mulroney, officially apologized from the floor of the House of Commons to Canadians of Japanese ancestry who were deported, interned, and mistreated by the Canadian government during the Second World War.[138] In 1998, the federal government released a "statement of recon-

---

134 Ms Finestone, *House of Commons Debates* (14 December 1994) at 9065–66. A group representing Canadians of Chinese ancestry continued their search for compensation through the courts. Their claims in respect of the so-called Chinese head tax were rejected: *Mack v. Canada (Attorney General)* (2002), 60 OR (3d) 737 (CA), leave to appeal refused 24 April 2003.

135 See the discussion of rights in respect of arrest, detention and imprisonment in Chapter Ten.

136 A report adopted by the Commission on Human Rights describes a similar concept, "satisfaction and guarantees of non-repetition," as involving (in part): cessation of continuing violations; verification of the facts and disclosure of the truth; an official declaration or a judicial decision restoring the dignity, reputation, and rights of the victim; apology and acceptance of responsibility; and commemorations and tributes to the victims. See *Basic Principles and Guidelines on the Right to a Remedy and Reparation for Victims of Violations of International Human Rights and Humanitarian Law*, annexed to M. Bassiouni, "The Right to Restitution, Compensation and Rehabilitation For Victims of Gross Violations of Human Rights and Fundamental Freedoms: Final Report" UN doc. E/CN.4/2000/62 (2000).

137 See S. Alter, "Apologising for Serious Wrongdoing: Social, Psychological and Legal Considerations: Final Report for the Law Commission of Canada" (Ottawa: Law Commission, 1999).

138 Mr Mulroney, *House of Commons Debates* (22 September 1988) at 19500.

ciliation" with Canadian aboriginal peoples which, while not explicitly apologizing to them,[139] acknowledged that "our history with respect
to the treatment of Aboriginal people is not something in which we can
take pride" and formally expressed the government's "profound regret
for past actions of the federal government which have contributed to
these difficult pages in the history of our relationship together."[140] In
1999, the premier of Quebec, Lucien Bouchard, apologized in the
National Assembly to the so-called Duplessis orphans and offered them
financial compensation.[141] Most recently, the Queen, on the advice of
the Canadian government, issued a Royal Proclamation acknowledging
"the trials and suffering" of the Acadian people as a result of their mass
deportation by the British government in the 1750s.[142] While the
proclamation is not an apology,[143] it appears to have been warmly
received by Acadian Canadians.

Other forms of symbolic reparation have sometimes been offered
together with the gestures described above. The Bouchard government's apology to the Duplessis orphans included an offer to issue
them birth certificates bearing their real names. The *Royal Proclamation
on Deportation* declares 28 July 2005, and every 28 July thereafter, as a
day of commemoration of the Great Upheaval (as the Acadian deportation is known).

Another notable form of symbolic reparation is the repatriation of
human remains from Canadian museums to aboriginal communities.
Many Canadian museums hold skeletal remains of pre-contact peoples

---

139 The statement did, however, apologize to those aboriginal peoples who were victims of sexual and physical abuse in residential schools.

140 "Statement of Reconciliation" in *Gathering Strength — Canada's Aboriginal Action
Plan* (Ottawa: Department of Indian Affairs and Northern Development, 7 January 1998).

141 Mr Bouchard, *Journal des débats de l'Assemblée nationale* (4 March 1999) at
14h10. The Duplessis orphans were five to six thousand Quebec orphans during
the premiership of Maurice Duplessis who, in a scheme to qualify for extra federal aid money, were declared mentally ill by the Quebec government and con-
fined for years to church-run psychiatric institutions. Many were physically and
sexually abused. The orphans accepted a settlement in 2001: "Duplessis orphans
accept Quebec's final offer" CBC News (http://www.cbc.ca) 1 July 2001.

142 Canada, *Royal Proclamation on Deportation*, 9 December 2003.

143 The proclamation makes no apology and expresses no regret. It also expressly
excludes any legal or financial liability: "Whereas this Our present Proclamation
does not, under any circumstances, constitute a recognition of legal or financial
responsibility by the Crown in right of Canada and of the provinces and is not,
under any circumstances, a recognition of, and does not have any effect upon,
any right or obligation of any person or group of persons . . . ."

in their collections, and are prepared to repatriate them, along with associated mortuary objects, to individuals or communities who can demonstrate rights to them.[144] While acts of repatriation do not necessarily involve any acknowledgement of wrongdoing on the part of the museum, the government, or anyone else, the restoration of ancestral remains to the communities from which they derive has an undeniably restorative element for aboriginal communities attempting to retrace their heritage and culture.[145]

4) Canada's Human Rights Culture

A fundamental, if intangible, element in the protection of human rights in Canada is its political culture. Though such claims can only be supported anecdotally, it seems that a great many Canadians take for granted the notions of tolerance, equality, pluralism, and human dignity that underpin human rights law. Expressions of prejudice (particularly towards gay and lesbian people, women and certain racial groups) remain tolerated, and even condoned, in some quarters. Yet extremist politics do not thrive here. To the contrary, accusations of extremism and intolerance have been very damaging to certain right-wing political parties over the last ten years. Though it is difficult to assess in concrete terms the impact of Canada's human-rights-friendly culture, its role in protecting human rights here must not be disregarded.

F. LABOUR LAW MECHANISMS

Federally and in the provinces, labour relations boards regulate collective bargaining and exercise remedial powers to correct unfair labour practices. To the extent that labour rights and human rights overlap, labour relations boards may serve as a forum for remedying human rights violations.

Labour relations boards are administrative tribunals created by statute and composed of members experienced in labour relations. In

---

144 See, for example, Canadian Museum of Civilization, "Human Remains Policy," 1992 (updated 2000).

145 See Assembly of First Nations & Canadian Museums Association, "Turning the Page: Forging New Partnerships Between Museums and First Peoples — Task Force Report" (Ottawa: Assembly of First Nations and Canadian Museums Association, 1992).

most jurisdictions, labour relations boards operate in tripartite panels consisting of an employer representative, an employee representative, and a neutral chair. The system is intended to offer a speedy, inexpensive, and effective forum for labour dispute resolution. To this end, labour relations hearings strive to be more informal and flexible than judicial proceedings.[146]

Conduct which interferes with freedom of association, the right to organize, or freedom of collective bargaining, or which violates other statutory labour protections, constitutes an unfair labour practice and may be remedied by application to the relevant labour relations board.[147] Available remedies include orders for reinstatement, compensation, and cessation of unfair practices. In most jurisdictions, board orders are enforceable as orders of the court.[148]

G. REFUGEE PROTECTION MECHANISMS

Human rights play a significant role in the determination of refugee protection claims under the *Immigration and Refugee Protection Act* (IRPA).[149] The *IRPA*'s objectives with respect to refugees include fulfilling Canada's international legal obligations[150] and establishing procedures that uphold Canada's respect for the human rights and fundamental freedoms of all human beings.[151] The *IRPA* is to be construed and applied in a manner that complies with international human rights instruments to which Canada is a signatory.[152]

Eligible refugee protection claims are heard orally by members of the Refugee Protection Division of the Immigration and Refugee Board.[153]

---

146 G. Adams, *Canadian Labour Law*, 2d ed, looseleaf (Aurora, Ontario: Canada Law Book Inc., 1993) at c. 5 [Adams, *Canadian Labour Law*].

147 Most jurisdictions distinguish between private and public sector employees and operate separate but similar statutory regimes for the latter.

148 Adams, *Canadian Labour Law*, above note 146 at c. 10.

149 SC 2001 c. 27 [*IRPA*].

150 *Ibid.*, s. 3(2)(b).

151 *Ibid.*, s. 3(2)(e).

152 *Ibid.*, s. 3(3)(f).

153 Ineligible claims include those from: persons recognized as Convention refugees by another country to which they can be returned; persons already determined to be protected persons; persons determined inadmissible on grounds of security, human rights violations, serious criminality, or organized criminality; and persons who have had a previous refugee protection claim rejected or found ineligible for referral. See *IRPA*, above note 149, s. 101(1).

Claims are accepted if the claimant is a Convention refugee or a person in need of protection.[154] A Convention refugee is a refugee as defined in article 1 of the Convention Relating to the Status of Refugees 1951 as amended by the Protocol Relating to the Status of Refugees 1967.[155] A person in need of protection is a person whose removal would subject her personally to a danger of torture within the meaning of CAT article 1, or a risk to her life or to cruel and unusual treatment or punishment.[156] Persons in need of protection may also be persons prescribed by regulation.[157] In short, past or potential violations of the claimant's human rights are central to the Refugee Protection Division's determination.

Under the IRPA, unsuccessful refugee claimants are supposed to enjoy a right of appeal to the Refugee Appeal Division.[158] As we write, however, the IRPA's appeal provisions have yet to come into force. Until they do, the only recourse for claimants who feel their claims have been improperly refused is judicial review with leave of the Federal Court.[159] Leave is not readily given, however, and reviewing courts tend to show deference to decisions of the Immigration and Refugee Board. Appeals from Federal Court decisions may be made in cases where a "serious question of general importance is involved."[160] Further appeals to the Supreme Court of Canada are by leave. All these levels of appeal and review provide further opportunities to raise human rights concerns — in the rare cases that go this far through the courts.

Unsuccessful refugee claimants are ordered removed from Canada. Claimants under removal orders may apply to the Minister of Immigration for protection to prevent their removal, a process known as pre-removal risk assessment (PRRA). Applicants must base their PRRA applications on new evidence arising after the rejection of their refugee protection claims, or new evidence that was not reasonably available or that they could not reasonably have been expected in the circumstances to have presented at the hearing.[161] PRRA applicants may make

---

154 Ibid., s. 107(1).
155 Ibid., s. 96 implements the Convention definition of refugee in Canadian law. See also Chapter Seven.
156 Ibid., s. 97(1). See that section for applicable conditions.
157 Ibid., s. 97(2).
158 Ibid., s. 110(1).
159 Ibid., s. 72.
160 Ibid., s. 74(d).
161 Ibid., s. 113(a). An example of evidence that the applicant could not reasonably have been expected to present at the hearing is evidence of spousal abuse by a woman whose initial refugee protection claim was linked to her spouse's claim.

written submissions to explain the risk they face if removed from Canada. The PRRA process presents another opportunity to raise human rights concerns, subject to the limitations described above.

Unsuccessful refugee claimants and others who do not meet the *IRPA*'s requirements may request an exemption on the grounds of "humanitarian and compassionate" or "public policy" considerations. *IRPA* section 25(1) provides,

> The Minister shall, upon request of a foreign national who is inadmissible or who does not meet the requirements of this Act, and may, on the Minister's own initiative, examine the circumstances concerning the foreign national and may grant the foreign national permanent resident status or an exemption from any applicable criteria or obligation of this Act if the Minister is of the opinion that it is justified by humanitarian and compassionate considerations relating to them, taking into account the best interests of a child directly affected, or by public policy considerations.

The inclusion of the best interests of the child as a consideration was seemingly prompted by the requirements of CRC article 3(1) and the decision of the Supreme Court of Canada in *Baker v. Canada (Minister of Citizenship and Immigration).*[162] Here, too, human rights concerns are at the forefront of the *IRPA* process.

Human rights are also a factor in determining the admissibility of certain persons to Canada irrespective of the *IRPA*'s other provisions. *IRPA* section 35(1) provides that permanent residents and foreign nationals are inadmissible "on grounds of violating human or international rights" if they have committed, outside Canada, offences referred to in the *Crimes Against Humanity and War Crimes Act.* Also inadmissible are senior officials in the service of governments that, in the minister's opinion, engage or have engaged in "terrorism, systematic or gross human rights violations, or genocide, a war crime or a crime against humanity." Refugee claims by persons deemed inadmissible on grounds of violating human or international rights are ineligible for referral to the Refugee Protection Division.[163] Likewise, such persons may not seek protection under the PRRA scheme.[164] There is no appeal from the determination that a person is inadmissible on grounds of vio-

---

162 *Baker*, above note 46.
163 *IRPA*, above note 149, s. 101(1)(f)
164 *Ibid.*, s. 112(3)(a).

lating human or international rights,[165] though judicial review is available in the usual way.

H. MILITARY JUSTICE MECHANISMS

We saw in Chapter Eleven that violations of international humanitarian law are criminal offences in Canada. Such offences may be tried in the ordinary courts or, in the case of persons subject to Canadian military law, in the military justice system.

The *National Defence Act* creates a system of military justice applicable to members of the armed forces and other persons subject to military law under the Act.[166] Persons subject to military law remain subject to all the duties and liabilities of ordinary citizens.[167] The substantive and procedural rules of military law are known as the *Code of Service Discipline*. Among the service offences punishable under the *Code of Service Discipline* are all offences punishable under the *Criminal Code* or any other Act of Parliament, whether committed in Canada or abroad.[168] Thus violations of international humanitarian law, as implemented in Canada by the *Geneva Conventions Act*,[169] the *Crimes Against Humanity and War Crimes Act*[170] and other laws, are punishable under military law.

The administration of military justice in the Canadian Forces is under the superintendence of the Judge Advocate General.[171] There are two forms of service tribunal: summary trial (for relatively minor offences) and trial by court martial (for more serious offences). Trials by general courts martial are presided by military judges appointed by the Governor in Council[172] and are conducted before a panel of five members.[173] The military judge determines all questions of law or mixed law and fact,[174] while the members of the panel determine the

---

165 *Ibid.*, s. 64(1).

166 *National Defence Act*, above note 107.

167 *R. v. MacKay*, [1980] 2 SCR 370 at 390; see also *National Defence Act*, ibid., s. 71.

168 *National Defence Act*, ibid., s. 130(1).

169 RSC 1985 c. G-3.

170 SC 2000 c. 24 ss. 4, 6.

171 *National Defence Act*, above note 107, s. 9.2(1).

172 *Ibid.*, s. 165.21(1).

173 *Ibid.*, s. 167.

174 *Ibid.*, s. 191.

court martial's finding by a vote of the majority of its members.[175] Other forms of courts martial also exist.[176] Persons tried and found guilty by courts martial have a right to appeal to the Court Martial Appeal Court.[177] Appeals from that court to the Supreme Court of Canada are by leave.[178]

---

175 *Ibid.*, s. 192(1) and (2).
176 See *National Defence Act*, *ibid.*, ss. 169–78.
177 *Ibid.*, ss. 230, 234–37.
178 *Ibid.*, s. 245.

CHAPTER 14

UN HUMAN RIGHTS MECHANISMS

The UN system for the promotion and protection of human rights is the largest and most universal of all multilateral systems. It includes judicial, quasi-judicial, and non-judicial mechanisms. Although the UN has existed for less than sixty years, and its human rights bodies for less than that, it is hard to imagine the world in its absence. Despite many imperfections, it is essential. And overall, if slowly, it is improving itself and the world around it.

A. TREATY BODIES

1) Overview

Most of the major UN human rights treaties or their related protocols include undertakings by states parties to accept the oversight of specialized international committees known as treaty bodies.[1] The pur-

---

1   The only exception is the Committee on Economic, Social and Cultural Rights, which was not established by treaty but by ECOSOC under Resolution 1985/17 (1985). While the ICESCR did not contemplate the establishment of a supervisory committee, it did require states parties to submit periodic reports to the UN Secretary-General (art. 16).

pose of these bodies is to ensure the compliance of states parties with their treaty obligations.[2] There are currently seven treaty bodies:

- the Human Rights Committee (which monitors compliance with the ICCPR),[3]
- the Committee on Economic, Social and Cultural Rights (which monitors compliance with the ICESCR),[4]
- the Committee against Torture (which monitors compliance with the CAT),[5]
- the Committee on the Elimination of Racial Discrimination (which monitors compliance with the CERD),[6]
- the Committee on the Rights of the Child (which monitors compliance with the CRC and its optional protocols),[7]
- the Committee on the Elimination of Discrimination against Women (which monitors compliance with the CEDAW),[8] and

---

2   On treaty bodies generally, see A. Bayefsky, *The UN Human Rights Treaty System: Universality at the Crossroads* (New York: Transnational Publishers, 2001) [Bayefsky, *Universality*]; and M. O'Flaherty & P. Bhagwati, *Human Rights and the UN: Practice Before the Treaty Bodies* (The Hague: Martinus Nijhoff, 2002).

3   Active since 1977, the Human Rights Committee is the most influential of all UN treaty bodies. It is not to be confused with the Commission on Human Rights, discussed later in this chapter. On the work of the Committee generally, see K. Yound, *The Law and Process of the UN Human Rights Committee* (Ardsley, NY: Transnational Publishers, 2002); S. Joseph et al., *The International Covenant on Civil and Political Rights: Cases, Materials, and Commentary* (New York: Oxford University Press, 2000); and D. McGoldrick, *The Human Rights Committee: Its Role in the Development of the International Covenant on Civil and Political Rights* (Oxford: Clarendon Press, 1994).

4   On the work of the Committee on Economic, Social and Cultural Rights generally, see S. Leckie, "The Committee on Economic, Social and Cultural Rights: Catalyst for Change in a System Needing Reform" in *The Future of UN Human Rights Treaty Monitoring*, P. Alston & J. Crawford, eds. (Cambridge: Cambridge University Press, 2000) [Alston, *Future of UN*] at c. 6.

5   On the Committee against Torture generally, see P. Burns, "The Committee against Torture," in *The UN Human Rights Treaty System in the 21st Century*, A. Bayefsky, ed. (The Hague: Kluwer Law International, 2000) [Bayefsky, *21st Century*].

6   The Committee was the first UN treaty body in operation. It held its first meeting in 1970. On the Committee on the Elimination of Racial Discrimination generally, see M. Banton, "Decision-taking on the Committee on the Elimination of Racial Discrimination" in Alston, *Future of UN*, above note 4 at c. 3.

7   On the Committee on the Rights of the Child generally, see G. Lansdown, "The Reporting Process under the Convention on the Rights of the Child," in Alston, *Future of UN, ibid.* at c. 5.

8   On the Committee on the Elimination of Discrimination against Women generally, see M. Bustelo, "The Committee on the Elimination of Discrimination against Women at the Crossroads" in Alston, *Future of UN, ibid.* at c. 4.

- the Committee on the Protection of the Rights of All Migrant Workers and Members of Their Families (which monitors compliance with the MWC).[9]

No treaty bodies were established under the Genocide Convention or the International Convention on the Suppression and Punishment of the Crime of Apartheid 1973.[10]

Each UN treaty body is composed of expert members elected by the states parties. Members serve in a personal or independent capacity. Canadians have served on the Human Rights Committee and the Committee Against Torture.[11]

Four kinds of procedures fall within the jurisdiction of various of the treaty bodies:

1) review of periodic reports submitted by states parties;
2) investigation of systematic violations;
3) review of petitions filed by one state against another; and
4) review of petitions made by individuals against states parties.

For a graphic representation of the mandates and procedures of UN treaty bodies, see Table 14.1 below.[12]

Canadian acceptance of, and participation in, these treaty body procedures is significant but not complete. Canada is required to provide periodic reports to all of the treaty bodies with the exception of the committee established under the MWC, to which Canada is not a party. Canada is subject to investigation for systemic violations of human rights under the CAT and the Optional Protocol to the CEDAW 1999

---

9   The Committee held its first session in March 2004.

10 But note that art. 9 of the Apartheid Convention, GA res. 3068 (XXVIII), did establish a so-called "Group of Three." The group — disbanded in 1995 — consisted of three members of the Commission on Human Rights. Its mandate was to consider reports submitted by states parties in accordance with art. 7 of the Convention. The Group was authorized to meet either before or after each annual session of the Commission on Human Rights to consider the reports submitted in accordance with art. 7.

11 Three Canadians have served as members of the Human Rights Committee: Walter Tarnopolsky (1976–83), Gisèle Côté-Harper (1983–84) and Maxwell Yalden (1997–present). Peter Burns has been a member of the Committee Against Torture since 1987 and its chair since 1998.

12 See page 399. The quasi-judicial procedures established by the ILO and UNESCO are not included on the chart. They are not technically "treaty bodies" in the sense of being established under and responsible for monitoring a particular treaty. ILO procedures are discussed in Chapter Sixteen, and the UNESCO procedures are discussed later in this chapter.

(CEDAW-OP),[13] but not under the Optional Protocol to the CAT 2002 (CAT-OP),[14] to which it is not a party. Canada is subject to the inter-state complaint and review mechanism under the ICCPR, the CAT, and the CERD, and to the individual complaint and review mechanism under the ICCPR-OP1, the CAT, and the CEDAW-OP. To date Canada has chosen not to participate in the CERD individual complaint mechanism.[15]

2) State Reporting Procedures

All the major human rights treaties establish a mandatory reporting system under which states parties submit periodic reports regarding the measures they have taken to meet the treaty's requirements. Treaty bodies typically require reports at two- to five-year intervals. They may also request states parties to submit information on an urgent basis regarding situations of particular concern. States are expected to make their reports widely available to the public.[16]

Each treaty body has adopted "general comments" (sometimes called "general recommendations") which serve as interpretive aids for states parties in drafting their reports. General comments are often quite detailed, leaving little doubt as to the conclusions a treaty body will ultimately reach on many issues. States parties have no formal means to participate in the development or drafting of general comments, though they are free to criticize them.[17]

The typical reporting procedure is as follows. First, the state party submits a report. The report may be accompanied by a "core document" applicable to reports before all treaty bodies.[18] The treaty body then examines the report, along with information obtained from UN and other sources. Great reliance is placed on information received from NGOs and other civil society organizations, which increasingly prepare their own

---

13   GA res. A/RES/54/4 (2000). Canada acceded to the Protocol in 2002. The treaty is not listed in the CanTS as of this writing.

14   (2003) 42 ILM 26.

15   In the Committee on the Elimination of Racial Discrimination's most recent Concluding Observations regarding Canada's periodic reports under the CERD, the Committee asked Canada to consider making the necessary declaration under CERD art. 14 to permit individual complaints. Committee on the Elimination of Racial Discrimination, *Concluding Observations: Canada* (2002).

16   See, for example, MWC art. 73(4).

17   For example, various states objected to ICCPR General Comment no. 24 (1994) on reservations to the treaty. See Human Rights Committee Report, UN doc. A/51/40 (1996).

18   See, for example, *Core Document Forming Part of the Reports of States Parties: Canada*, UN doc. HRI/CORE/1/Add.91 (1998).

parallel reports known as "shadow reports."[19] Next the treaty body prepares a "list of issues" which it sends to the state. The issues can be quite
specific and demanding at times.[20] The state then has an opportunity to
submit a written reply. Later a formal public session, generally lasting one
day, is held at UN offices in Geneva or New York at which the state's
report and any subsequent clarifications it has made are questioned and
discussed.[21] Finally, the treaty body meets in private and adopts "concluding observations" for submission to the state and inclusion in its
annual report to the General Assembly.[22] A few treaty bodies have
reviewed state parties' performances even in the absence of a report.[23]

Many states produce very thorough reports. But some states treat
the process of drafting reports as an exercise in disingenuous self-

---

19 See, for example, Report Submitted by the Aboriginal Legal Services of Toronto
to the UN Committee on the Elimination of Racial Discrimination, 16 July 2002,
available at: http://aboriginallegal.ca/docs/shadow_report.htm. More generally
see S. Grant, "The NGO Role: Implementing, Expanding Protection and Monitoring the Monitors" in Bayefsky, *21st Century*, above note 5.

20 For example, the list of issues recently submitted to Canada by the Committee
on Economic, Social and Cultural Rights included the following:

> Does the Government agree that repealing protective legislation without
> replacing it would be inconsistent with article 2 of the Covenant? Provide
> details as to how Governments have dealt with this issue under the *Charter*,
> and explain what the Government's position was in *Ferrel v. Attorney-General
> of Ontario* and *Dunmore v. Ontario*. . . .
>
> For provinces applying a "work for welfare" scheme, such as Quebec and
> Ontario, please provide information concerning the application of labour
> standards, including minimum wage and any discriminatory criteria that are
> applied, such as age. . . .

UN doc. E/C.12/Q/CAN/1 (1998) at paras. 5 and 25 respectively.

21 Canada's Department of Foreign Affairs and International Trade presents the
reports. This means that some criticisms and questions concerning provincial
implementation of certain human rights go unanswered, except on the occasions
when provincial representatives join the delegation. See, for example, Committee on Economic, Social and Cultural Rights, *Concluding Observations: Canada*
(1999) at para. 377:

> [I]n the light of the federal structure of Canada and the extensive provincial
> jurisdiction, the absence of any expert particularly representing the largest
> provinces, other than Quebec, significantly limited the potential depth of the
> dialogue on key issues.

22 Treaty bodies may also be required to co-operate in the reporting process with
the ILO or other UN bodies. See, for example, MWC art. 74(2) and (5).

23 See the Comparative Summary of the Working Methods of the Treaty Bodies
(January 2001): http://66.36.242.93/methods/working_methods_summary.php.

assessment done without consulting the most closely concerned NGOs.[24] Some states have included only constitutional and statutory quotations in their reports. There have been serious delays by states in fulfilling their treaty reporting obligations, sometimes in good faith and other times not.[25] States with bad human rights records are often responsible for the most severe delays, and there are many states that have never submitted a report to any treaty body.[26] Yet if states did start to fulfill their reporting obligations in a timely manner, it is far from clear that the treaty bodies could cope with the extra caseload.[27]

All of the treaty bodies' concluding observations contain a section on "positive aspects" of a state party's performance prior to a concluding section on "principal areas of concern and recommendations." Most concluding observations on Canada have praised its general commitment to human rights. But treaty bodies have also criticized Canada on many issues. The most frequent criticisms relate to Canada's treatment of Aboriginal peoples. For example, the Committee on Economic, Social and Cultural Rights recently expressed concern at the "gross disparity" between Aboriginals and the majority of Canadians with respect to the enjoyment of ICESCR rights:

> There has been little or no progress in the alleviation of social and economic deprivation among aboriginal people. In particular, the Committee is deeply concerned at the shortage of adequate housing, the endemic mass unemployment and the high rate of suicide, especially among youth, in the aboriginal communities. Another concern

24   Canada's state reports are prepared by the federal government, usually in collaboration with the provincial and territorial governments and relevant NGOs.

25   Canada was three years late in filing its third periodic report under the CAT. Committee against Torture, *Concluding Observations: Canada* (2001) at para. 55. It was six years late in filing its thirteenth periodic report under the CERD. Committee on the Elimination of Racial Discrimination, *Concluding Observations: Canada* (2002) at para. 316.

26   For example, as of 2002, 54 states parties had reports more than five years overdue to the Human Rights Committee, and 33 states parties had never filed a single report. Human Rights Committee, Annual Report, UN doc. A/57/40 (2002) at paras. 68–69.

27   The budgets of treaty bodies are very small. They are approximately 500 times smaller than the budgets of the International Criminal Tribunal for the Former Yugoslavia (ICTY) or the International Criminal Tribunal for Rwanda (ICTR). The work is part-time (no more than a few weeks each year) and unpaid. Most treaty bodies have only a few staff to support them in their work. See E. Evatt, "Ensuring Effective Supervisory Procedures: The Need for Resources" in Alston, *Future of UN*, above note 4 at c. 21. See also M. Schmidt, "Servicing and Financing Human Rights Supervision" in Alston, *Future of UN*, above note 4 at c. 22.

is the failure to provide safe and adequate drinking water to aboriginal communities on reserves. The delegation of the State party conceded that almost a quarter of aboriginal household dwellings required major repairs and lacked basic amenities.[28]

Rates of female and child poverty have been another subject of concern. The Committee on the Elimination of Discrimination against Women recently stated:

> While appreciating the federal Government's various anti-poverty measures, the Committee is concerned about the high percentage of women living in poverty, in particular elderly women living alone, female lone parents, aboriginal women, older women, women of colour, immigrant women and women with disabilities, for whom poverty persists or even deepens, aggravated by the budgetary adjustments made since 1995 and the resulting cuts in social services. The Committee is also concerned that those strategies are mostly directed towards children and not towards these groups of women.[29]

---

28 Committee on Economic, Social and Cultural Rights, *Concluding Observations: Canada* (1999) at para. 392. See also Human Rights Committee, *Concluding Observations: Canada* (1999) at para 230:

> The Committee notes that, as the State party acknowledged, the situation of the aboriginal peoples remains 'the most pressing human rights issue facing Canadians.' In this connection, the Committee is particularly concerned that the State party has not yet implemented the recommendations of the Royal Commission on Aboriginal Peoples (RCAP). With reference to the conclusion by RCAP that without a greater share of lands and resources institutions of aboriginal self-government will fail, the Committee emphasizes that the right to self-determination requires, *inter alia*, that all peoples must be able to dispose freely of their natural wealth and resources and that they may not be deprived of their own means of subsistence (art. 1, para. 2). The Committee recommends that decisive and urgent action be taken towards the full implementation of the RCAP recommendations on land and resource allocation. The Committee also recommends that the practice of extinguishing inherent aboriginal rights be abandoned as incompatible with article 1 of the Covenant.

29 Committee on the Elimination of Discrimination against Women, *Concluding Observations: Canada* (2003) at para. 357. See also Human Rights Committee, *Concluding Observations: Canada* (1999) at para. 242:

> The Committee is concerned that many women have been disproportionately affected by poverty. In particular, poverty among single mothers, who suffer a very high rate of poverty, leaves their children without the protection to which they are entitled under the Covenant. While the delegation expressed a strong commitment to address this inequality in Canadian society, the Committee is concerned that many of the programme cuts in recent years have exacerbated such inequalities and harmed women and other disadvan-

Another subject of concern has been Canada's treatment of refugee claimants and their families. The Committee against Torture recently urged Canada to enhance the effectiveness of the remedies to protect the rights granted by CAT article 3(1):

> Noting the assurances that the proposed new Immigration and Refugee Act provides for a pre-removal risk assessment 'available to all persons under a removal order,' the Committee encourages the State party to ensure that the proposed new legislation permits in-depth examination by an independent entity of claims, including those from persons already assessed as security risks. The Committee urges the State party to ensure that obstacles to the full implementation of article 3 are removed, so that an opportunity is given to the individual concerned to respond before a security risk decision is made, and that assessments of humanitarian and compassionate grounds are made without demanding a fee from a person who seeks protection.[30]

Many treaty bodies have also expressed concern about the ability of the federal government to ensure comprehensive domestic implementation of its treaty obligations.[31] But these are only examples. A full survey of

---

taged groups. The Committee recommends a thorough assessment of the impact of recent changes in social programmes on women and that action be undertaken to redress any discriminatory effects of these changes.

See also Committee on the Rights of the Child, *Concluding Observations: Canada* (1996) at para. 561:

The Committee is concerned by the emerging problem of child poverty, especially among vulnerable groups. It is also worried by the increasing number of children who are brought up by single parent families, or in other problematic environments. While appreciating the programs already set up, the Committee emphasizes the need for special programmes and services to provide the necessary care, especially in terms of education, housing and nutrition, for such children.

30 Committee against Torture, *Concluding Observations: Canada* (2001) at paras. 58–59. See also Committee on Economic, Social and Cultural Rights, *Concluding Observations: Canada* (1999) at para. 412:

The Committee views with concern the plight of thousands of 'Convention refugees' in Canada, who cannot be given permanent resident status for a number of reasons, including the lack of identity documents, and who cannot be reunited with their families for a period of five years.

31 See, for example, Committee on the Rights of the Child, *Concluding Observations: Canada* (1996) at para. 558:

The Committee, while taking note of the statement, reflected in the report of the State party, that the federal nature of Canada is a complicating factor in the implementation of the Convention, and that the exact division of respon-

treaty body concluding observations on Canada is beyond the scope of this book.

3) Investigation of Systematic Violations

The CAT, the CEDAW-OP, and the CAT-OP provide unique in-country investigative powers to their respective treaty bodies.[32] Article 20 of the CAT gives the Committee Against Torture the power to initiate confidential investigations of a state party when there is reliable information that torture is being "systematically practiced" by that state party. The Committee will first invite the state to reply to the allegations. Thereafter, it may undertake a further confidential inquiry that can include an on-site, consensual visit to the state, and the transmission of findings to that state. The whole process is confidential unless the state consents to publication of a summary account of the investigation in the Committee's annual report. CAT article 28 permits states parties to opt out of the article 20 procedure by making a formal declaration to that effect.[33] In practice, the Committee only has enough funds to con-

---

sibilities between federal, provincial and territorial governments over matters affecting children may involve an element of uncertainty, stresses that Canada is bound to observe fully the obligations assumed by ratifying the Convention. The Committee is concerned that sufficient attention has not been paid to the establishment of a permanent monitoring mechanism that will enable an effective system of implementation of the Convention in all parts of the country. Disparities between provincial or territorial legislation and practices that affect the implementation of the Convention are a matter of concern to the Committee.

See also Committee on Economic, Social and Cultural Rights, *Concluding Observations: Canada* (1999) at para. 387:

The Committee heard ample evidence from the State party suggesting that Canada's complex federal system presents obstacles to the implementation of the Covenant in areas of provincial jurisdiction. The Committee regrets that, unless a right under the Covenant is implicitly or explicitly protected by the Canadian *Charter* through federal-provincial agreements, or incorporated directly in provincial law, there is no legal redress available to either an aggrieved individual or the Federal Government where provinces have failed to implement the Covenant.

32   The Human Rights Committee has occasionally requested states parties to receive an investigative mission in circumstances where it failed to reply to requests for information. The Committee only has sufficient funds to conduct at most one visit per year. See *Report of the Human Rights Committee*, UN doc. A/56/40 (2001) at para. 202.

33   Canada did not make such a declaration upon ratification.

duct one in-country visit per year.[34] By contrast, the European Committee for the Prevention of Torture is able to conduct approximately twenty visits per year. It has a budget almost twenty-five times that of the UN Committee Against Torture.[35]

CEDAW-OP article 8 creates a similar procedure to CAT article 20. The procedure allows the Committee on the Elimination of Discrimination against Women to initiate confidential investigations in cases of "grave or systematic violations" of the CEDAW. As with the CAT procedure, the Committee first invites the state party to submit observations on the allegations before considering whether to conduct a further inquiry that could include an in-country visit. Following any such inquiry and/or visit, the Committee forwards its findings to the state party, which has six months to respond. All information remains confidential unless the state party consents to its publication.[36] States parties may opt out of the article 8 procedure by making an appropriate declaration under CEDAW-OP article 10 at the time of ratification or accession.[37]

The CAT-OP was inspired by the detention centre inspection mechanisms of the International Committee of the Red Cross and the European Committee for the Prevention of Torture. The treaty opened for signature on 1 January 2003 and requires twenty ratifications to come into force. The core purpose of the CAT-OP is to prevent torture and other cruel, inhuman or degrading treatment or punishment. Article 2(1) establishes the Sub-Committee on Prevention, an independent sub-committee of the Committee against Torture composed of ten elected independent experts, while article 3 requires states parties to maintain at the domestic level one or more "national preventive mechanisms." The Sub-Committee on Prevention will have the authority to conduct in-country inspections of detention facilities and provide assistance and recommendations to national preventive mechanisms and states parties. Articles 12 and 14 of the CAT-OP require states parties to fully co-operate with the Sub-Committee on Prevention before, during, and after any

---

34   "Note by the Secretary-General on Effective Implementation of Human Rights Instruments," UN doc. A/57/56 (2002) at para. 21. The Committee Against Torture's budget in 2002 was a mere US$172,500.

35   The European Committee for the Prevention of Torture's budget for 2002 was approximately US$4 million. Council of Europe, "Programme of Activities for 2002" at 30–33.

36   CEDAW-OP, above note 13, art. 9.

37   Canada did not make such a declaration at the time of its ratification.

in-country visit.[38] Article 13 requires the Sub-Committee to establish a programme of regular visits, which are to be conducted by at least two Sub-Committee members and any experts they may invite from a pre-established roster. Recommendations and observations of the Sub-Committee must be communicated confidentially to the state party, but states parties may also consent to publication.[39] If a state party refuses to fully co-operate with the Sub-Committee on Prevention or fails to act on its recommendations, the Committee against Torture (acting on the advice of the Sub-Committee) may bring the matter to public attention after the state party has had an opportunity to explain its actions.[40]

The national preventive mechanisms under the CAT-OP are to be accorded powers to make unannounced visits to detention centres and examine persons held there, to make recommendations to the state party, and to submit proposals and observations on relevant legislation.[41] Article 20 requires states parties to provide national preventive mechanisms full access and co-operation in fulfilling their mandate, including the right to meet and share information directly with the Sub-Committee on Prevention. Article 22 requires states parties to publish and disseminate the annual reports issued by national preventive mechanisms. States parties may, however, make a declaration upon joining the treaty that would allow their treaty obligations to be postponed for up to a maximum of five years (article 24). The mandatory nature of the visits by national mechanisms could raise constitutional concerns for federal states like Canada, since the CAT-OP extends to all parts of a federal state without any limitation or exception and reservations to the protocol are barred.[42]

4) Individual Petition Procedures

The Human Rights Committee, the Committee Against Torture, the Committee on the Elimination of Racial Discrimination, the Committee on the Elimination of Discrimination against Women, and the Committee on the Protection of the Rights of All Migrant Workers and Members of Their Families all operate individual petition procedures.

---

38 But art. 14(2) permits a state party to temporarily prevent visitation of a particular place of detention on urgent and compelling grounds of national defence, public safety, natural disaster or serious disorder.
39 CAT-OP, above note 14, art. 16(1)–(2).
40 Ibid., art. 16(4).
41 Ibid., art. 19.
42 Ibid., arts. 29–30.

Victims, family members, and NGOs are permitted to present petitions (known as "communications"). The petition procedures are only available to individuals subject to the jurisdiction of a state that is party to the ICCPR-OP1 (in the case of the Human Rights Committee) or the CEDAW-OP (in the case of the Committee on the Elimination of Discrimination against Women), or that has accepted the relevant body's jurisdiction under CAT article 22 (in the case of the Committee Against Torture), CERD article 14 (in the case of the Committee on the Elimination of Racial Discrimination), or MWC article 77 (in the case of the Committee on the Protection of the Rights of All Migrant Workers and Members of Their Families). There are no individual petition procedures available under the ICESCR or the CRC.[43] The CERD individual petition procedure is by far the least used (excluding the MWC procedure, which is not yet up and running). A very small percentage of CERD states parties have made declarations allowing for individual petitions, and there have been less than twenty-five individual cases since the petition system began operating in 1982.[44] The Human Rights Committee has received by far the most individual petitions.[45]

There are generally two stages to a treaty body's treatment of an individual petition: admissibility and consideration on the merits. Most petitions are rejected at the admissibility stage. The burden of proof of admissibility rests, naturally, on the applicant. For a petition to be admissible, a number of criteria must be satisfied. First, there is typically a bar on anonymous submissions. Second, the petition must be in writing and must involve facts that occurred after the date when the petition procedure came into force against the concerned state. Third, the petition must not have been previously examined by the treaty body in question. Fourth, consideration of any matter that is being examined under another international procedure of investigation

---

43   The Commission on Human Rights recently appointed an independent expert on the question of a draft optional protocol to the ICESCR. See his most recent report, UN doc. E/CN.4/2003/53 at para. 76. There he affirms an earlier Commission on Human Rights resolution calling for the establishment of an open-ended working group of the Commission tasked with elaborating an optional protocol to the ICESCR that would permit individual complaints (albeit only for "gross, unmistakable violations").

44   See Report of the Committee on the Elimination of Racial Discrimination, UN doc. A/56/18 (2001) at 111. The Committee has, however, developed new procedures for itself, including an early warning and urgent action procedure.

45   Almost half of all registered communications, however, have related to just two countries: Jamaica and Uruguay. J. Donnelly, *Universal Human Rights in Theory and Practice*, 2d ed. (Ithaca: Cornell University Press, 2003) at 135.

or settlement is generally barred.[46] Fifth, the petition must not be manifestly ill-founded nor constitute an abuse of the rules of procedure for submission.[47] Finally, and most importantly, all available and sufficient domestic remedies must have been exhausted. The purpose of this rule is to allow states an adequate opportunity to resolve the matter internally, since treaty body procedures are not intended to replace domestic mechanisms. The burden of proof of exhaustion of domestic remedies falls upon the applicant, who must make a *prima facie* case as to domestic exhaustion or alternatively as to why exhaustion is not possible in the particular state. Thereafter the burden passes to the state to establish that an effective domestic remedy was, and remains, available. The exhaustion requirement is generally interpreted in a liberal and flexible manner, and may be waived explicitly or implicitly (as by failure to reply in a timely manner) by the responding state.

Upon receipt of an admissible complaint, the treaty body will review it in private. Letters and documentation submitted by the complainant will remain confidential. In some cases, interim measures may be granted to avoid "irreparable damage" to the complainant.[48] Treaty bodies do not conduct oral hearings between the individual applicant and the respondent state, but instead forward the complaint to the state, permitting it three to six months to respond. The treaty body then makes a final determination on the matter in closed session, whether or not the state chose to contest the complaint. The "views" (that is, the conclusions) of the body are then forwarded to the state party and the complainant, and eventually to the UN General Assembly. The views of a treaty body are not binding but merely hortatory; treaty bodies have no power to order specific remedies for violations but only to make general findings and recommendations.[49] Actions recommended by the Human Rights Committee have included conducting a full public investigation, bringing the perpetrators to justice, paying compensa-

---

46   This is to prevent a case from becoming the subject of various procedures at the same time. Usually the applicant can prevent dismissal on this ground if she withdraws the case from the other procedure.

47   This means, for example, that the complaint must make out a *prima facie* case relating to rights guaranteed by the particular treaty, and she must not make false declarations or use slanderous language.

48   See J. Harrington, "International Human Rights Law in Canada's Courts: The Ahani Case" (2003) 29 CCIL Bulletin 7. Harrington reviews how Canadian courts recently refused to recognize or abide by an interim injunction made by the Human Rights Committee calling on Canada to halt deportation of an Iranian man.

49   For example, a treaty body can call on a state to pay compensation as a remedy for a particular violation, but it can neither bind a state nor specify the quantum.

tion, providing restitution, providing medical treatment, ensuring non-repetition of the violation, changing legislation, and ensuring various case-specific forms of remedy such as release from jail or commutation of a death sentence.[50] Some treaty bodies have established a Special Rapporteur for the Follow-up of Views, to monitor the implementation of their recommendations, but they only have the power to shame.[51] Unless domestic law provides otherwise, the views of treaty bodies are not enforceable as judgments before domestic courts.

Several dozen complaints have been made against Canada before the Human Rights Committee for violations of the ICCPR. About half of these were deemed inadmissible. Of the admissible cases, there have been several findings against Canada, most of which have involved multiple breaches of the ICCPR.[52] Canada's record of compliance with the Committee's recommendations has been mixed.[53] Just over a dozen

---

50   D. Shelton, *Remedies in International Human Rights Law* (Oxford: Oxford University Press, 1999) at 142–44 [Shelton, *Remedies*].

51   See, for example, Human Rights Committee, Rules of Procedure, UN doc. A/56/40, vol. I (2001) Rule 95. The Human Rights Committee also notes cases of non-compliance in its annual report.

52   See *Lovelace v. Canada* (1981), Comm. no. R.6/24 [finding: violation of arts. 2, 3, 12, 23, 26, and 27]; *Lubicon Lake Band v. Canada* (1990), Comm. no. 167/1984 [finding: violation by Canada of arts. 1 and 27]; *Pinkney v. Canada* (1981), Comm. no. 27/1977 (R.7/27) [finding: violation of arts. 10(1), 10(2), 14(3)(c), 14(5), and 17(1)]; *Ballantyne, Davidson and MacIntyre v. Canada* (1993), Comm. nos. 359/1989 and 385/1989/Rev.1 [finding: violation of arts. 19, 26, 27]; *Singer v. Canada* (1994), Comm. no. 455/1991 [finding: violation of art. 19(2)]; *Gauthier v. Canada* (1999), Comm. no. 633/1995 [finding: violation of art. 19(2)–(3)]; *Waldman v. Canada* (1999), Comm. no. 694/1996 [finding: violation of art. 26]; *Ng v. Canada* (1993), Comm. no. 469/1991 [finding: violation of arts. 6 and 10]; and *Judge v. Canada* (2003), Comm. no. 829/1998 [finding: violation of art. 6(1)]. The admissible cases in which the Human Rights Committee found against the applicant are: *Kindler v. Canada* (1993), Comm. no. 470/1991 [finding: no violation of arts. 6 or 7]; *Cox v. Canada* (1994), Comm. no. 539/1993 [finding: no violation of arts. 6, 7, 14, or 26]; *Canepa v. Canada* (1997), Comm. no. 558/1993 [finding: no violation of arts. 7, 12(4), 17, 23]; *Stewart v. Canada* (1996), Comm. no. 538/1993 [finding: no violation of arts. 12(4), 17, 23]; *Van Duzen v. Canada* (1982), Comm. no. 50/1979 [finding: no violation of art. 15(1)]; *MacIsaac v. Canada* (1982), Comm. no. 55/1979 [finding: no violation of art. 15(1)]; *Bhinder v. Canada* (1989), Comm. no. 208/1986 [finding: no violation of arts. 18, 26]; *Ross v. Canada* (2000), Comm. no. 736/1997 [finding: no violation of arts. 18, 19]; and *Marshall et al. v. Canada* (1991), Comm. no. 205/1986 [finding: no violation of art. 25(a)]. Many of these cases are examined in Chapter Ten.

53   See generally J. Harrington, "Punting Terrorists, Assassins and Other Undesirables: Canada, the Human Rights Committee and Requests for Interim Measures of Protection" (2003) 48 McGill Law Journal 2.

complaints against Canada have been filed with the Committee Against Torture for alleged violations of the CAT. Most were found inadmissible. Of the admissible cases, only one finding has been made in favour of the applicant.[54]

A surprisingly high number of states have never been the subject of individual complaint under any of the relevant treaty body procedures. What's more, where complaints are made, in many cases treaty bodies receive insufficient cooperation from the state party. On the whole, however, individual petition procedures have been reasonably effective mechanisms and their potential for enhanced enforcement remains great. The Human Rights Committee, in particular, has developed a useful jurisprudence that has deepened understanding of many human rights.

5) Inter-State Petition Procedures

ICCPR article 41, CAT article 21, CERD article 11, and MWC article 76 all provide for inter-state complaint mechanisms. Only the CERD inter-state mechanism is mandatory; the others are optional. There is no inter-state complaint mechanism under the ICESCR, the CEDAW, or the CRC.

Inter-state complaint procedures typically operate as follows: a state party makes an allegation against another state party (assuming both have recognized the competence of the particular treaty body to handle inter-state petitions);[55] the responding state is given a few months to reply; if the states fail to resolve the question in an amicable manner, the case is referred to the relevant treaty body, which can appoint, with the states' consent, a conciliation mechanism to make non-binding findings. To date, no state has filed an inter-state complaint with a treaty body, and thus the relevance of these procedures is questionable. Possible reasons for the non-use of these procedures include fear that a complaint against another state will adversely affect diplomatic relations, concern that it will incite retaliation by the other state, and doubt that the procedures are effective.

---

54 See *Khan v. Canada* (1994), Comm. no. 15/1994, in which the Committee Against Torture found that Canada had violated CAT art. 3. The Committee held that there were substantial grounds for believing that the applicant, Mr. Khan, would be in danger of being subjected to torture if Canada were to expel or forcibly return him to Pakistan. Canada expelled him.

55 It is irrelevant whether there has been any direct or indirect injury to the complaining state or any of its nationals. The basis for the complaint is simply that the state party in violation has broken its promise to the other not to violate the treaty in question.

6) Evolution of the Treaty Body System

As we have seen, the UN treaty body system is organized on a treaty-by-treaty basis. In 2002 the members of all of the treaty bodies convened the first-ever "inter-committee" meeting, principally to discuss the harmonization of working methods. Since 1984 there has also been an annual meeting of the chairpersons of the treaty bodies. But these meetings are insufficient to overcome the treaty body system's high degree of complexity and duplication. Some commentators have suggested that there need to be two consolidated treaty bodies, one for examining state reports under all treaties to which a state is party, and one for examining individual and inter-state complaints and conducting in-country investigations.[56] So far, however, the idea has been rejected. Instead, treaty body members have proposed only minor changes, such as to permit states to submit an expanded core document to complement their periodic reports under each treaty.[57]

B. THE ECONOMIC AND SOCIAL COUNCIL

The UN Charter established the Economic and Social Council (ECOSOC) as an intergovernmental body under the authority of the General Assembly. It is composed of the representatives of fifty-four member states each elected for a three-year term. ECOSOC conducts studies and makes recommendations on a broad array of issues to do with human rights and "economic, social, cultural, educational, health and related matters." It is also responsible for co-ordinating and, to some extent, programming the activities of the UN. In its early years, ECOSOC took a number of key decisions concerning human rights. Most importantly, it established the Commission on Human Rights and the Commission on the Status of Women, discussed below.

---

56   Bayefsky recommended that the Commission on Human Rights establish an open-ended working group to elaborate a draft omnibus optional protocol to the seven (at the time, six) major UN human rights treaties. She suggested that the purpose of the protocol would be to establish the two consolidated treaty bodies. Bayefsky, *Universality*, above note 2 at 2. See also the Report of the Secretary-General entitled "Strengthening of the United Nations: An Agenda for Further Change," UN doc. A/57/387 (2002). The report proposes that treaty bodies better co-ordinate their activities, standardize their reporting requirements, and permit each state to produce a single report summarizing its adherence to all treaties to which it is a party (para. 51).

57   See "Report of the Chairpersons of the Human Rights Treaty Bodies on their Fifteenth Meeting," UN doc. A/58/350 (2003) at para. 7.

Table 14.1: UN Treaty Bodies

	ICCPR	ICESCR	CAT	CERD	CRC	CEDAW	MWC
States parties and remaining signatories	149 and 8 (ICCPR-OP1: 104 and 5) (ICCPR-OP2: 50 and 7)	146 and 7	132 and 12 (CAT-OP: 2 and 20)	166 and 8	191 and 2 (CRC-OP-SC: 57 and 61) (CRC-OP-SC: 64 and 60)	172 and 2 (CEDAW-OP: 53 and 32)	23 and 10
Canadian participation	ICCPR: state party since 1976. (ICCPR-OP1: state party since 1976.) (Not state party to ICCPR-OP2.)	State party since 1976	State party since 1987. (Not state party to CAT-OP.)	State party since 1970	State party since 1991. (State party to CRC-OP-SC since 2000 — in force for Canada since 2002). (Not state party to CRC-OP-SC.)	State party since 1982. (State party to CEDAW-OP since 2002 — in force for Canada since 2003.)	Not a state party
Number of committee members	18	18	10	18	18	23	10 (but will go to 14 once there are 41 states parties)
Who elects committee members	States parties	ECOSOC	States parties	States parties	States parties	States parties	States parties
Duration of appointment	4 years, renewable	4 years, renewable	2 years, renewable	4 years, renewable	4 years, renewable	4 years, renewable	4 years, renewable
State reporting obligations	Art. 40	Art. 16	Art. 19	Art. 9	Art. 44	Art. 18	Art. 73

	ICCPR	ICESCR	CAT	CERD	CRC	CEDAW	MWC
Periodicity of reporting obligation[58]	Upon request (but generally once every 4 years)	Every 5 years	Every 4 years	Every 2 years	Every 5 years	Every 4 years	Every 5 years
Inter-state complaint mechanism	Art. 41: optional declaration	N/A	Art. 21: optional declaration	Art. 11: not optional	N/A	N/A	Art. 76: optional declaration
Individual complaint mechanisms	Applies to all states parties to ICCPR-OP1	N/A	Art. 22: optional declaration. 52 states have made declaration	Art. 14: optional declaration. 40 states have made declaration	N/A	Applies to all CEDAW-OP states parties	Art. 77: optional declaration: states have made declaration
Authority to examine systematic violations	N/A	N/A	Art. 20 with opt out under art. 28. Also applies to all CAT-OP states parties.	N/A	N/A	Art. 8 of CEDAW-OP with opt out under art. 10	N/A
Referral to International Court of Justice for interpretation disputes	N/A	N/A	Art. 30: possible to opt out	Art. 22: possible to opt out	N/A	Art. 29: possible to opt out	N/A

58   Usually states have to submit their first report within one or two years of becoming a state party.

More recently, ECOSOC established the Commission on Crime Prevention and Criminal Justice. It consists of forty state members elected by ECOSOC on the basis of equitable geographical distribution. Its main function is to formulate international policies and make recommendations in the field of crime prevention and criminal justice, particularly in the areas of terrorism, corruption, human trafficking, crime prevention in urban areas, and reforms to the administration of criminal justice. The Commission's annual session in Vienna offers states a forum for debating these issues and developing action plans and standards. The Commission also prepares periodic UN congresses on the prevention of crime and the treatment of offenders, and formulates draft resolutions for action by ECOSOC on issues within its competence.

ECOSOC also recently established the Permanent Forum on Indigenous Issues.[59] The Forum consists of sixteen independent experts, including eight indigenous representatives.[60] Its mandate is to provide advice and recommendations to ECOSOC on issues affecting indigenous peoples, and assist in the co-ordination of relevant activities and initiatives pertaining to the human rights of indigenous peoples. The key initiatives it tracks are the Sub-Commission on the Promotion and Protection of Human Rights' Working Group on Indigenous Populations,[61] the Commission on Human Rights' Working Group on the Draft Declaration on the Rights of Indigenous Peoples 1993,[62] and the Special Rapporteur on the Situation of Human Rights

---

59   ECOSOC resolution 2000/22 (2000).

60   Two Canadians serve as independent experts on the Forum: Wilton Littlechild, a Cree; and Wayne Lord, a Metis. They were both elected in 2002.

61   The Working Group was established by ECOSOC resolution 1982/34 (1982). Canada was one of the many states to lobby for the term "populations" rather than "peoples," apparently to avoid self-determination claims. The Working Group meets annually in Geneva for one week. Its mandate is to review and encourage human rights protections for indigenous peoples. The Working Group consists of five independent experts and members of the Sub-Commission, and permits broad state and non-state participation at its sessions. Indigenous participation is facilitated by the UN Voluntary Fund for Indigenous Populations. The Working Group's major achievement is the preparation of the text of the UN Draft Declaration on the Rights of Indigenous Peoples 1993.

62   The Draft Declaration has been under review for a full decade now. Negotiations concerning the Declaration have stalled, as indigenous groups generally insist (without avail) that the existing text be adopted without change. The Draft Declaration deals with a number of controversial topics including self-determination, sovereignty over natural resources, and the right to occupied tribal and ancestral lands.

and Fundamental Freedoms of Indigenous People.[63] The Forum held its first meeting in May 2002.

Other important ECOSOC commissions include the Commission on Population and Development, the Commission for Social Development, and the Commission on Sustainable Development.

1) The Commission on Human Rights

Although today the theme of human rights impinges on a number of UN institutions, the Commission on Human Rights continues to serve as the chief standard-setting and decision-making forum for human rights within the UN system. In 1947, when the Commission met for the first time, its sole function was to draft the UDHR. For the next twenty years, it concentrated its efforts on standard-setting, having concluded that it lacked authority to respond to human rights complaints. Then in 1967, ECOSOC authorized the Commission to start dealing with human rights violations.[64] Since then, the Commission has set up an elaborate system of procedures, both country-oriented and thematic, to monitor compliance by states with their human rights obligations and investigate alleged violations.

The Commission on Human Rights meets annually in Geneva for six weeks.[65] It comprises fifty-three states, each elected for a three-year term following the principle of equitable geographical distribution. Most states, as well as a wide range of NGOs, participate at the annual meeting to lobby and present information on situations or issues of concern to them. Only states can sponsor and vote on resolutions, but NGOs often persuade and assist sympathetic states to sponsor resolutions on issues of shared concern.

The Commission's debates and the resolutions it adopts often reflect its political character. North-South divisions, bloc voting, and

---

63   The office of the Special Rapporteur, established by the Commission on Human Rights in April 2001, has a three-year mandate. See UN doc. E/CN.4/RES/2001/57. The Special Rapporteur, Rodolfo Stavenhagen of Mexico, conducts studies, undertakes country visits, and brings relevant violations to the attention of governments.

64   Early human rights initiatives included the establishment in 1967 of a special working group of experts to study the ill-treatment of prisoners and detainees in South Africa, and the creation in 1975 of a special working group to investigate the human rights situation in Chile.

65   The Commission also meets on an *ad hoc* basis in "emergency" situations (for example, in October 2000 concerning the Israeli-Palestinian conflict).

constant targeting of Israel still beset the Commission and impede progress on a wide range of issues.[66] At the end of the Commission's 2002 session, Israel was the only country to be the subject of multiple critical resolutions, and it is the only country for which there exists a country rapporteur with an open-ended (as opposed to one-year) mandate.[67] The following year at the Commission, a resolution critical of Zimbabwe — the site of some of the worst human rights violations at the time — was removed as a subject of debate from the Commission's agenda by means of a so-called "no-action motion" sponsored by a bloc of African states. These sorts of occurrences deeply concern human rights advocates and some governments. According to one expert Canadian commentator, "the annual sessions of the Commission have degenerated into an adversarial exercise, in which progress in the protection and promotion of human rights appears to have become a secondary interest."[68]

Still, the Commission on Human Rights has been very useful at times in expanding the human rights agenda and ushering in innovative procedures for the more effective scrutiny of human rights violations. Some of these procedures are examined below.

a) The Sub-Commission on the Promotion and Protection of Human Rights

The Sub-Commission on the Promotion and Protection of Human Rights is the main subsidiary body of the Commission on Human Rights.[69] The Sub-Commission is composed of twenty-six expert members acting in their personal capacity (that is, not on behalf of any government). The Commission elects each member for a renewable four-year term, taking into account the principle of equitable geographical distribution. The Sub-Commission's principal function is to undertake studies and make

---

66 During the Cold War, things were often much the same except that the predominant divisions were East-West rather than North-South.

67 See M. Dennis, "Human Rights in 2002: The Annual Sessions of the UN Commission on Human Rights and the Economic and Social Council" (2003) 97 AJIL 364 at 384.

68 J. Bauer, "Summary Report — UN Commission on Human Rights 2002 Session (Fifty-eighth)," 30 April 2002, prepared for the Department of Foreign Affairs and International Trade and Rights & Democracy, http://www.hri.ca/uninfo/unchr2002/report.htm.

69 The Commission on Human Rights established the Sub-Commission at its first session in 1947. It was originally entitled the Sub-Commission on Prevention of Discrimination and Protection of Minorities. In 1999, ECOSOC changed its name to the Sub-Commission on the Promotion and Protection of Human Rights.

recommendations to the Commission concerning the prevention of discrimination, and the protection of racial, national, religious, and linguistic minorities. The Sub-Commission holds an annual three-week-long session in Geneva. The session typically draws observers from states, UN and other intergovernmental bodies, and NGOs with consultative status.

The Sub-Commission also has four working groups which meet before each session: the Working Group on Communications, which considers complaints under the "1503 procedure" discussed immediately below; the Working Group on Contemporary Forms of Slavery; the Working Group on Indigenous Populations; and the Working Group on Minorities.

b) The 1503 Procedure

The "1503 procedure" is a confidential Commission on Human Rights procedure for dealing with "consistent patterns of gross and reliably attested violations of human rights."[70] The ostensible objective of the procedure is to use quiet diplomacy to address particularly gross and widespread abuses being committed in a state. In recent years, the procedure has undergone significant reform to address some of its deficiencies.[71] The original procedure was the slowest of all UN human rights mechanisms, invariably taking several years and thousands of human rights complaints before even being brought to the attention of the Commission, by which time the abuses highlighted in the complaint had often become moot.[72]

Under the revised procedure, human rights complaints are reviewed and organized by the Office of the High Commissioner for Human Rights before being brought to the attention of the Sub-Commission on the Promotion and Protection of Human Rights' Working Group on Communications. Where in the view of the Working Group there is evidence of a consistent pattern of gross violations in a country, the matter is referred to the Commission on Human Rights' Working Group on Situations, which may refer the matter to the full Commission by way of a confidential report. Upon referral, the Commission may convene closed meetings to consider the matter, in which

---

70   The procedure was established by ECOSOC in resolution 1503 (XLVIII) (1970).

71   See ECOSOC resolution 2000/3 (2000), which describes the revised procedure.

72   Allegations of genocide against indigenous groups in Paraguay remained under 1503 scrutiny for nine years without any action being taken. Similarly, it took seven years for the Commission on Human Rights to issue a decision on violations committed in military-ruled Uruguay. By the time the decision was finally taken, the government had been removed. J. Donnelly, *International Human Rights* (Ithaca: Cornell University Press, 1998) at 53.

case the state in question is invited to make its own interventions. Ultimately the Commission may discontinue consideration of the matter, keep it under review, appoint an independent expert to monitor and report on it, or begin public consideration of it pursuant to ECOSOC Resolution 1235 (1967).[73]

While all aspects of the 1503 procedure take place in closed session, at the end of deliberations the Chair of the Commission on Human Rights publicly announces which countries are being reviewed under the 1503 procedure. Thus, although the 1503 procedure offers no direct redress to individual victims, it does offer the possibility of public shaming and investigation of the state concerned. States go to great lengths to avoid being placed on the 1503 "black list."

c) Special Procedures

In addition to the 1503 procedure, the Commission on Human Rights administers a variety of "special procedures," sometimes referred to as "extra-conventional mechanisms" (that is, mechanisms not established under a treaty). These special procedures flow from ECOSOC Resolution 1235. There are three types of special procedures:

- working groups of the Commission, composed of experts acting in their personal capacity,
- independent monitors of the Commission, variously designated "special rapporteurs," "special representatives," or "independent experts," and
- independent monitors appointed by the UN Secretary-General.

There are currently four open-ended working groups: the Working Group on Enforced or Involuntary Disappearances (operational since 1980),[74] the Working Group on Arbitrary Detention (operational since 1991), a Working Group on the problems of racial discrimination faced by people of African descent (established in 2002), and a Working Group on the effective implementation of the Durban Declaration and Programme of Action (established in 2002).

---

73   The relevant portion of Resolution 1235 provides that the Commission on Human Rights may "make a thorough study of situations which reveal a consistent pattern of violations of human rights . . . and report, with recommendations thereon, to the Economic and Social Council." Although some states initially argued that the wording of Resolution 1235 suggested apartheid and related policies were to be the focus, today it is undisputed that the Resolution applies to any situation involving gross and systematic human rights violations.

74   Stephen Toope, a Canadian, is a member of the Working Group on Enforced or Involuntary Disappearances.

The mandates of independent monitors typically grant competence to examine, monitor, and publicly report on major human rights themes,[75] or human rights situations in specific countries or territories.[76] Mandates on thematic issues tend to have durations of three years, whereas those on specific countries are only authorized for one year (though they are often renewed). As a rule, country mandates are eliminated when the situation on the ground changes and monitoring is no longer warranted. The question of which countries end up the subject of inquiry by independent monitors is one of the most fiercely-debated aspects of the annual Commission on Human Rights session, since it is seen as a stain on a state's human rights record.

None of the working groups or independent monitors is empowered to order remedies or make findings in individual cases.[77] Their main role is to transmit allegations of violations to governments for their comment, and conduct in-country missions with the consent of the concerned state. Special urgent action procedures have also been established in connection with certain of these mechanisms, for example, the Special Rapporteur on Extrajudicial, Summary, or Arbitrary Executions, and the Working Group on Enforced or Involuntary Disappearances. These procedures allow urgent individual cases to be transmitted through them to the concerned state. States are requested to investigate and report back on the case. Information and co-operation from states is rarely forthcoming.[78]

Because working groups and independent monitors report to the Commission on Human Rights rather than acting as its voice, they are able to conduct their work with relative independence, albeit without

---

75 There have been independent monitors on topics including extrajudicial, summary, or arbitrary executions; the effects of foreign debt on the full enjoyment of economic, social and cultural rights; the independence of judges and lawyers; the question of religious intolerance; the question of torture; violence against women, its causes and consequences; human rights and extreme poverty; structural adjustment policies; the right to development; and internally displaced persons.

76 There have been independent monitors on the human rights situations in countries including Afghanistan, Bosnia and Herzegovina, Burundi, the Democratic Republic of the Congo, Equatorial Guinea, Iraq, Myanmar, Sudan, Cambodia, the Islamic Republic of Iran, Rwanda, Haiti, and Somalia.

77 The only exception is the Working Group on Arbitrary Detention, which formulates "opinions" on individual cases.

78 According to the Working Group on Enforced or Involuntary Disappearances' 2001 annual report, UN doc. E/CN.4/2001/68 at para. 3: "The total number of cases transmitted by the Working Group to Governments since the Group's inception stands at 49,546. The total number of cases being kept under active consideration, as they have not yet been clarified, now stands at 45,998."

pay or adequate technical support. As important as their work can sometimes be, the activities and reports generated by working groups and independent monitors often go unnoticed due to lack of significant media coverage.

Rarely has Canada been investigated or questioned in any aspect by a working group or independent monitor.[79]

2) The Commission on the Status of Women

ECOSOC created the Commission on the Status of Women in 1946 and mandated it to "prepare recommendations and reports to ECOSOC on promoting women's rights in political, economic, social and educational fields" and "make recommendations to ECOSOC on urgent problems."[80] The Commission is composed of forty-five states, each elected by ECOSOC according to criteria of equitable geographical representation.

The Commission meets in regular session once a year. Since 1995, the Commission has focused on enhancing the follow-up process to the Fourth World Conference on Women (1995), by regularly reviewing and reporting on the level of implementation of the Beijing Declaration and Platform for Action that was adopted at the Conference. The Commission's focus has tended to be on standard-setting rather than on responding to specific violations of women's human rights.[81] Since 1984, however, the Commission has operated a procedure to handle complaints relating to violations of women's human rights. The procedure, which is entirely confidential, is similar in many respects to the Commission on Human Rights' 1503 procedure. The UN Division for the Advancement of Women conducts the initial screen of relevant communications, and provides an opportunity for the implicated state to reply to the allegations. Original communications and state replies

---

79 But in the autumn of 2003, Doudou Diene, the UN Special Rapporteur on Contemporary Forms of Racism, Racial Discrimination, Xenophobia, and Related Intolerance, made an official visit to Canada for ten days to examine the state of racism in the country. His report is not available as of this writing.

80 ECOSOC resolution 11 (II) (1946). In accordance with a recommendation made by the Commission on the Status of Women at its first session in 1947, ECOSOC expanded its mandate to include the promotion of women's civil rights. ECOSOC expressly stated that recommendations on "urgent" aspects of women's rights should be aimed at achieving de facto observance of the principle of equality between men and women.

81 The Commission drafted many of the key treaties on women's human rights including the Convention on the Political Rights of Women 1952 [1957] CanTS no. 3 and the CEDAW.

are then forwarded to the Commission's Working Group on Communications, which prepares and submits a report to the full Commission. The Commission may then make recommendations to ECOSOC aimed at identifying and responding to the situations revealed by the communications. No decisions are taken on the merits of any individual case.

C. OFFICE OF THE HIGH COMMISSIONER FOR HUMAN RIGHTS

1) Establishment of the OHCHR

On 25 June 1993, at the Second World Conference on Human Rights, the representatives of 171 states — with pressure and encouragement from hundreds of NGOs — adopted by consensus the Vienna Declaration and Programme of Action 1993. The Declaration was intended to serve as a global agenda for enhancing human rights norms and procedures.[82] Perhaps the most important of the Declaration's recommendations was the creation of the Office of the High Commissioner for Human Rights (OHCHR). The following December, General Assembly Resolution 48/141 established the High Commissioner as the UN official with principal responsibility for human rights activities, albeit "under the direction and authority of the Secretary-General" and "within the framework of the overall competence, authority and decisions of the General Assembly, the Economic and Social Council and the Commission on Human Rights."

The OHCHR is based in Geneva. It is part of the UN Secretariat. Functions of the OHCHR include: providing substantive support to treaty bodies, the Commission on Human Rights, the Sub-Commission on the Promotion and Protection of Human Rights, and related bodies; preparing research and reports; reviewing complaints of human rights violations; providing advisory services and technical assistance to governments; and supporting human rights field presences and missions.

---

82 Among other things, the Declaration proclaimed all human rights to be universal, indivisible, interdependent, and interrelated; reaffirmed the right to development and the "inextricable" relationship between human rights and development; urged universal ratification of human rights treaties; and called for more resources to be provided to UN human rights activities.

2) Role of the High Commissioner

The UN Secretary-General, with the approval of the General Assembly, appoints the High Commissioner for a four-year term. The High Commissioner has the rank of an Under Secretary-General of the UN. The first High Commissioner, José Ayala Lasso, formerly Ecuador's Permanent Representative to the UN, assumed office in the spring of 1994. Mary Robinson, a former President of Ireland, succeeded him in 1997. Sergio Vieira de Mello, a Brazilian with significant prior UN experience, succeeded her in 2002. Vieira de Mello was killed in a bomb attack in Iraq in August 2003 while he was serving as Special Representative of the Secretary-General in Iraq. Louise Arbour, formerly the ICTY's Chief Prosecutor and most recently a justice of the Supreme Court of Canada, was appointed as the new High Commissioner in February 2004 and took up her post in July 2004.

The High Commissioner runs the OHCHR under the authority and direction of the Secretary-General.[83] He or she also engages in dialogue with governments to secure respect for human rights. Commissioners serve in their personal capacity and not on behalf of any particular government or state. At their most influential, they can have something close to the profile of the UN Secretary-General, in effect speaking and acting as the voice and conscience of human rights victims around the world. High Commissioners can also work more discretely, for example, by inquiring about political prisoners to government officials in the course of official visits. The position requires a strong combination of advocacy and diplomacy skills.[84]

3) OHCHR Technical Cooperation

Technical co-operation is one of the key areas of OHCHR human rights activity. The UN Technical Co-operation Programme in the Field of Human Rights helps states build and strengthen domestic human rights mechanisms such as human rights commissions. The Programme also works on the incorporation of human rights standards into domestic laws and policies and the formulation of national plans of action for the promotion and protection of human rights. Technical co-operation takes the form of expert advisory services, training cours-

---

83 GA res. 48/141 (1993).
84 See generally, B. Ramcharan, *The United Nations High Commissioner for Human Rights: The Challenges of International Protection* (The Hague: Martinus Nijhoff, 2004).

es, workshops, fellowships, grants, provision of information and documentation, and assessment of domestic human rights needs. At present, the OHCHR operates dozens of technical co-operation projects, primarily in the developing world.

4) Human Rights Field Presences

The OHCHR maintains or supports a number of field offices and operations responsible for monitoring human rights situations and capacity building in particular countries. The earliest human rights field presences were created prior to the establishment of the OHCHR by UN political departments (for example, El Salvador in 1991) and regional bodies like the OAS (for example, Haiti in 1992). Following its inauguration in 1994, the OHCHR began to establish its own human rights field presences independent of UN peacekeeping, peacemaking, and peacebuilding missions. The first one was established in Rwanda in late 1994 shortly after the genocide there.[85] Since then, human rights field operations have been established by various procedures, including at the initiative of the Security Council (for example, Angola), at the initiative of the UN General Assembly (for example, the civilian mission in Guatemala), at the request of the Commission on Human Rights (for example, the former Yugoslavia), or within the framework of bilateral agreements between the OHCHR and individual states (for example, Colombia). As a rule, the tasks of a UN human rights field operation include monitoring, investigating, and reporting on the human rights situation on the ground, and improving local capacity in human rights protection. Because they are nearer to victims, field operations may constitute the most important and effective human rights activities carried out by the UN.[86] There is, however, an ongoing challenge to ensure greater use of the information and experience gained in the field for purposes of decision-making at UN headquarters. Also, the effectiveness of UN human rights field operations is often hampered by vague mandates and unstable funding arrangements.[87]

---

85   One year prior, the UN Centre for Human Rights, OHCHR's predecessor, established a field office in Cambodia following a request of the Commission on Human Rights.

86   See I. Martin, "Closer to the Victim: United Nations Human Rights Field Operations," in Y. Danieli et al., eds., The Universal Declaration of Human Rights: Fifty Years and Beyond (Amityville, NY: Baywood Publishers, 1999) at c. 8.

87   Ibid.

D. THE SECURITY COUNCIL

The Security Council is the UN body with primary authority for maintaining international peace and security,[88] and the only international institution capable of lawful coercion in response to violations of human rights. It is composed of fifteen members. Five of the members (the Russian Federation, the USA, the UK, France, and China) are permanent and possess unilateral veto powers.[89] The UN General Assembly elects the non-permanent members of the Security Council.[90] Non-permanent members do not have veto powers. The presidency of the Council rotates on a monthly basis among permanent and non-permanent members. Canada was most recently elected a non-permanent member of the UN Security Council from 1999–2000.[91]

The Security Council makes decisions and recommendations. Only its decisions are binding. In Canada, decisions of the Security Council are regarded as treaty commitments, consistent with UN Charter article 41.[92]

Under Chapter VII of the UN Charter, the Security Council is empowered to adopt measures to enforce any decisions it takes concerning threats to or breaches of international peace and security. The use of collective force can only be authorized when peaceful means of settling a dispute have been exhausted, and only after positively determining the existence or occurrence of a "threat to the peace, a breach of the peace, or an act of aggression."[93] Typically, when a dispute or conflict involving significant human rights violations is first brought to the Council's attention, it will urge the peaceful settlement of the matter under Chapter VI, and may itself undertake or recommend the undertaking by the Secretary-General or a designated special envoy of an investigation or mediation mission.[94]

If its efforts fail and conflict occurs or continues, the Council's focus turns to ending the dispute. The Council may first authorize non-coercive measures such as the deployment of peacekeeping forces.

---

88   UN Charter art. 24.
89   During the Cold War, permanent members made frequent use of their veto powers. Since the end of the Cold War, use of the veto has become increasingly rare.
90   UN Charter art. 23.
91   Canada previously served terms as a non-permanent member of the Council in 1948–49, 1958–59, 1967–68, 1977–78, and 1989–90.
92   M. Copithorne, "National Treaty Law and Practice: Canada" in M. Leigh et al., eds., National Treaty Law and Practice (Baltimore: American Society of International Law, 2003) at 10.
93   UN Charter art. 39.
94   Ibid., arts. 33–34.

Peacekeeping generally refers to operations authorized by the Security Council and consented to by the host state(s) in which international and often regional military personnel are charged with the prevention of armed conflict (known as "preventive deployment"), the maintenance of a ceasefire and separation of the warring forces, and/or the protection of humanitarian operations during an armed conflict.[95] Peacekeeping forces are primarily comprised of soldiers, with smaller numbers of military observers and civilian police forces.

The Council may also impose sanctions or embargoes to pressure states to comply with Council resolutions.[96] An interesting example is Security Council Resolution 1343 (2001), which prohibited all UN member states from importing "rough diamonds" from Liberia. The illicit diamond trade was known to be aggravating the civil war in neighbouring Sierra Leone.[97] The Council may also adopt other measures such as the creation of safe areas,[98] the imposition of compensation schemes,[99] the imposition of mandatory weapons inspections

95   Former Prime Minister and Nobel Peace Prize winner, Lester B. Pearson, introduced peacekeeping as a part of UN activities. In 1994, the government of Canada founded the Lester B. Pearson Canadian International Peacekeeping Training Centre in Cornwallis, Nova Scotia. On peacekeeping generally, see J. Hillen, *Blue Helmets: The Strategy of UN Military Operations*, 2d ed. (Dulles, Virginia: Brassey's Inc., 2000). See also the Report of the Panel on UN Peace Operations (often referred to as the "Brahimi Report"), UN doc. A/55/305–S/2000/809.

96   UN Charter art. 41 provides:

   The Security Council may decide what measures not involving the use of armed force are to be employed to give effect to its decisions, and it may call upon the Members of the United Nations to apply such measures. These may include complete or partial interruption of economic relations and of rail, sea, air, postal, telegraphic, radio, and other means of communication, and the severance of diplomatic relations.

97   See also SC res. 1173 (1998) concerning the illicit trade in rough diamonds in Angola. Today the global trade in so-called "conflict diamonds" is being addressed through a formal international regime called the Kimberley Process Certification Scheme. The Scheme has received enthusiastic Security Council support. See, for example, SC res. 1459 (2003).

98   See, for example, SC res. 819 (1993) regarding Srebrenica, which demanded that all parties to the conflict in the former Yugoslavia treat the city as a safe area. See also subsequent Resolution 836 (1993), which authorized NATO to carry out air strikes to assist UN forces in securing the safe area. The safe area policy effectively ended in July 1995 when the Srebrenica massacre occurred.

99   The Security Council established a special fund — the UN Compensation Commission (UNCC) — to pay claims for damages, losses, and injuries incurred by foreign states, foreign nationals, and foreign corporations resulting from Iraq's invasion and brief occupation of Kuwait in the early 1990s. Claims were paid out of the proceeds of Iraqi oil sales. See generally Shelton, *Remedies,* above note 50 at 337–45.

regimes,[100] and the establishment of ad hoc international criminal tribunals to prosecute individuals for the international crimes of genocide, crimes against humanity, and war crimes.[101]

As a last resort, the Council may authorize armed force to respond to armed conflict (for example, Resolution 678 (1990) regarding the Iraq-Kuwait conflict) or to "secure an environment for humanitarian relief operations" (for example, Resolution 794 (1994) regarding Somalia).[102] Though sanctioned by the Security Council, enforcement actions of this kind are entirely under the control of the participating states. The Security Council's job is simply to "make recommendations, or decide what measures shall be taken to maintain or restore international peace and security."[103] While UN Charter article 43 requires that military forces be made available to the Security Council pursuant to agreements between it and UN member states, no such agreements are in place. Without them the Security Council can only recommend, and not order, collective intervention. As for the state that is the subject of intervention, it is not open to it to assert the principle of non-intervention in domestic affairs.[104]

Following the conclusion of a conflict, the Security Council will often authorize the deployment of a "peacebuilding operation." Peacebuilding generally refers to post-conflict operations authorized by the Security Council and consented to by a host government in which international military, police, and civilian personnel are entrusted with

---

100 See, for example, SC res. 687 (1991) establishing the UN Special Commission on Weapons (UNSCOM).

101 See Chapter Seventeen.

102 UN Charter art. 42 provides:

> Should the Security Council consider that measures provided for in art. 41 would be inadequate or have proved to be inadequate, it may take such action by air, sea, or land forces as may be necessary to maintain or restore international peace and security. Such action may include demonstrations, blockade, and other operations by air, sea, or land forces of Members of the United Nations. . . .

103 *Ibid.*, art. 39.

104 Under UN Charter art. 2(7), the Security Council may legally take such measures concerning matters that are within the domestic jurisdiction of a state, since the principle of non-intervention in domestic affairs of states "shall not prejudice the application of enforcement measures under Chapter VII." But note art. 57, which provides a partial exception to this rule:

> Nothing in the present Charter shall impair the inherent right of individual or collective self-defence if an armed attack occurs against a Member of the United Nations, until the Security Council has taken measures necessary to maintain international peace and security. . . .

the consolidation of peace through activities in areas including military security, policing and judicial reform, electoral assistance, and human rights monitoring. Peacebuilding operations, like peacekeeping operations, have frequently been hampered by factors such as unwillingness of UN member states to supply troops, inadequate resources, and weak and unrealistic mandates.

Until the 1990s, the Security Council rarely invoked human rights. This changed with the end of the Cold War. Since then, the Security Council has frequently invoked human rights norms, particularly in response to the many civil wars that have occurred in recent years. The Council has also adopted a number of human rights-related resolutions on issues such as the use of children in armed conflict.[105] Unfortunately, open discussion of human rights by the Council remains constrained in at least two respects. First, the High Commissioner for Human Rights is very rarely invited to address or report to the Security Council. Second, the Council's permanent members have effectively precluded discussion of human rights situations that directly implicate them, including Chechnya (in the case of Russia), Tibet (in the case of China), and Northern Ireland (in the case of the UK). Similarly, permanent members have often blocked adverse actions against key allies (for example, the US in respect of Israel).

In the aftermath of the events of September 11, 2001, the Security Council adopted Resolution 1373 (2001) acting under Chapter VII of the UN Charter. The resolution declared international terrorism a threat to international peace and security, and required all UN member states to take certain measures, including the adoption of counter-terrorism legislation. The Security Council borrowed provisions from various multilateral counter-terrorism treaties, none of which enjoy universal adherence, and made them binding on UN member states.[106] The resolution is remarkable in at least two respects. It marked the first time that a Chapter VII resolution ordered all states to take certain measures without reference to a particular country or conflict. It also

---

105 See, for example, SC res. 1460 (2003) and SC res. 1379 (2001).

106 Resolution 1373 also established the Security Council Counter-Terrorism Committee (CTC), which is probably the most important such body in the world today. The CTC receives assistance from a group of ten experts. The OHCHR and the Human Rights Committee have worked with the CTC in an effort to ensure consideration of the human rights implications of counter-terrorism measures. SC res. 1456 (2003), which requires states to "ensure that any measure taken to combat terrorism comply with all their obligations under international law" and adopt measures "in compliance with international law, in particular international human rights, refugee and humanitarian law," is partly the fruit of that labour.

put the Security Council very much in the position of a legislator, thus arguably stepping outside of its UN Charter mandate.[107] Whether Resolution 1373 heralds the beginning of a new and expanded role for the Security Council, or provides an exception that proves the rule, remains uncertain.

E. THE GENERAL ASSEMBLY

The General Assembly is the main deliberative organ of the UN. Like parliamentary bodies in national governments, the General Assembly is composed of members with one vote each.[108] The difference, of course, is that each member is a sovereign state at international law. The functions and powers of the General Assembly are defined in the UN Charter.[109] The General Assembly meets in regular session yearly, usually beginning each September, and may also meet in special sessions.

The General Assembly's subject matter competence is almost unlimited. UN Charter article 10 allows the Assembly to "discuss any questions or any matters within the scope of the present Charter" and to make recommendations to UN member states on matters arising under the UN Charter. Additionally, UN Charter article 13(1)(b) authorizes the General Assembly to "initiate studies and make recommendations" for the purpose of "assisting in the realization of human rights and fundamental freedoms for all without distinction as to race, sex, language, or religion."[110] The General Assembly's recommendations and resolutions, adopted by majority vote, are not legally binding on states. However, the impact of an Assembly recommendation or resolution may be persuasive in the case of a text adopted unanimously, by consensus, or without dissenting vote.

Under the UN Charter, the General Assembly has significant powers of control over the operation of most UN institutions, many of which have a direct impact on human rights. For example, it partici-

---

107 See E. Rosand, "Security Council Resolution 1373, the Counter-Terrorism Committee, and the Fight Against Terrorism" (2003) 97 AJIL 333 at 333–34.

108 UN Charter art. 18(1).

109 *Ibid.*, arts. 10–17.

110 Most substantive discussions and negotiations in the area of human rights take place not at the General Assembly level, but rather at the committee level, and in particular at the level of the Third Committee which deals with "Social, Humanitarian and Cultural" matters.

pates in the election of judges to the International Court of Justice[111] and non-permanent members to the Security Council.[112] It also decides the budget of all UN bodies.[113] Most relevantly for our purposes, the General Assembly must give final approval to all UN-sponsored human rights treaties.

The General Assembly has played a major role in several international human rights campaigns, particularly those related to apartheid and colonialism. It has established human rights-related bodies of its own, such as the Commission on Human Settlements[114] and the Special Committee to Investigate Israeli Practices Affecting the Human Rights of the Palestinian People and Other Arabs of the Occupied Territories.[115] The General Assembly has also convened and endorsed the results of a number of very significant global conferences on human rights themes.[116]

F. THE INTERNATIONAL COURT OF JUSTICE

The International Court of Justice is the successor to the Permanent Court of International Justice and the principal judicial organ of the UN. It comprises fifteen permanent judges selected by the UN General Assembly and the Security Council.[117] The Court was formally established by the UN Charter and is governed by the ICJ Statute, which is annexed to the UN Charter.

---

111 Statute of the International Court of Justice 1945 (ICJ Statute), [1945] CanTS no. 7, art. 4.
112 UN Charter art. 23(1).
113 *Ibid.*, art. 7.
114 The Commission was established pursuant to GA res. 32/162 (1977). It comprises fifty-eight states and focuses on supervising the implementation of the recommendations made at the two UN global conferences on the subject of human settlements: Habitat I in 1977 and Habitat II in 1996.
115 The Special Committee was established by GA res. 2443 (XXIII) (1968) and has been in operation ever since. The Israeli government has refused to co-operate with the Committee or provide it access to the occupied territories.
116 Examples include the 1968 and 1993 World Conferences on Human Rights in Tehran and Vienna, respectively; the 1994 International Conference on Population Development in Cairo; the 1995 World Conference on Women in Beijing; the 1996 World Summit on Social Development in Copenhagen; and the 2001 World Conference against Racism, Racial Discrimination, Xenophobia, and Related Intolerance in Durban.
117 Only one Canadian has ever served as a permanent judge on the Court: John E. Read. He served from 1946 to 1958.

The Court has two types of jurisdiction: advisory and contentious. Pursuant to ICJ Statute article 65(1), the Court can render an advisory opinion "on any legal question at the request of whatever body may be authorized by or in accordance with the UN Charter to make such a request."[118] Although advisory decisions are not legally binding (hence the term "advisory"), states may expect condemnation if they act in a manner incompatible with advisory opinions directed at them.

The Court's contentious jurisdiction is limited to disputes between states such as Canada that have consented to its jurisdiction.[119] States may also refer contentious cases to the Court by bilateral or special agreement, or pursuant to undertakings in a separate treaty. Non-state actors, whether individuals or groups, do not have standing as parties before the Court.

The Court has rendered little more than one hundred judgments in over fifty years of operation. States appear to prefer to resolve their disputes by diplomatic means. Nevertheless, since 1998, the Court has taken steps to expedite its work on contentious cases by, for example, permitting only one round of written pleadings. Since none of the principal human rights treaties requires adjudication by the Court,[120] it has dealt with few human rights cases. The Court's decisions on cases with human rights components have, however, been very influential and have served to affirm certain fundamental principles. The Court has, for example, highlighted the immoral and illegal character of genocide,[121] indicated that human rights obligations are obligations *erga omnes*,[122] and made important decisions on racial discrimination and the right to self-determination.[123] More recently, it has rendered major

---

118 UN Charter art. 96 empowers the General Assembly and the Security Council to request advisory opinions.

119 The Court has jurisdiction over states that have expressly accepted its "compulsory jurisdiction" under ICJ Statute, above note 111, arts. 34–36. See the Declaration of Acceptance of the Compulsory Jurisdiction of the International Court of Justice 1994 [1994] CanTS no. 41.

120 At best, human rights treaties provide for an optional referral to the Court concerning matters of treaty interpretation. See, for example, CAT art. 33; CERD art. 22; CEDAW art. 29.

121 See *Reservations to the Convention on the Prevention and Punishment of the Crime of Genocide* [1951] ICJ Rep 15 at 29–30. The UN General Assembly requested the opinion.

122 See *Case Concerning the Barcelona Traction Light and Power Co. Ltd.* [1970] ICJ Rep 3 at 32. The case arose out of the bankruptcy in Spain of Barcelona Traction, a company incorporated in Canada.

123 See, for example, *Advisory Opinion on the continued Presence of South Africa in Namibia (S.W. Africa)*, [1971] ICJ Rep 16; *Case Concerning East Timor (Portugal v. Australia)*, [1995] ICJ Rep 90.

judgments on assertions of universal jurisdiction,[124] privileges and immunities for UN officials,[125] and the use of the death penalty.[126] In one of its most controversial human rights-related cases to date, the Court has also been asked to decide on the international legality of Israel's so-called "security fence," built with the ostensible objective of protecting Israelis from Palestinian terrorist attacks.[127]

The International Court of Justice has no police or other body to enforce its judgments. In one infamous case, enforcement proved to be an insurmountable problem in the absence of Security Council support. In *Case Concerning Military and Paramilitary Activities in and*

---

124 See *Case Concerning the Arrest Warrant of 11 April 2000 (DRC v. Belgium)* (2002), 41 ILM 536, in which the Court held that when abroad, sitting foreign ministers and similar government officials enjoy full immunity from criminal jurisdiction, including for war crimes and crimes against humanity. The Court, however, held that the court of one state may — provided it has jurisdiction under international law — try the former foreign minister of another state for any acts committed before or after the minister's period of office, as well as for private acts committed during his time in office. The Court also affirmed that former or incumbent foreign ministers may be tried by international criminal tribunals with jurisdiction over the particular crimes.

125 See *Difference Relating to Immunity from Legal Process of a Special Rapporteur of the Commission on Human Rights* [1999] ICJ Rep 62. In 1998, ECOSOC requested an advisory opinion concerning the applicability of s. 22 of the Convention on the Privileges and Immunities of the United Nations 1946, [1948] CanTS no. 2, to Param Cumaraswamy, who at the time was the UN Special Rapporteur on the independence of judges and lawyers. The Court held that he was entitled to "immunity from legal process of every kind" for his official acts, and thus to immunity from defamation suits brought against him in Malaysia. Although the Court's decision was of an advisory character, s. 30 of the Convention provides that in any dispute between the UN and a state party, an advisory opinion of the International Court of Justice "shall be accepted as decisive by the parties."

126 In *Avena and Other Mexican Nationals (Mexico v. US)* (Provisional Measures), [2003] ICJ Rep 2 at paras. 55 and 59, the Court allowed provisional measures requested by Mexico against the US. The Court held that the US could not execute three Mexican nationals convicted of capital offences in the US, because that would cause irreparable prejudice to any rights of Mexico that the Court might later recognize. The Court ordered the US not to execute the men until it had reached a final judgment. See also the *LaGrand Case (Germany v. US)* (Judgment), [2001] ICJ Rep 3 Both cases are reviewed by W. Aceves in (2003) 97 AJIL 923.

127 Israel and forty-two other states submitted written pleadings to the Court, but Israel refused to plead orally. In February 2004 the Court closed the oral proceedings and took the case under advisement.

against Nicaragua (Nicaragua v. USA),[128] the Court held that US support of the Contras and US armed attacks against Nicaragua constituted violations of international law; specifically, of the obligations not to intervene in the affairs of another state, not to use force against another state, not to violate the sovereignty of another state, and not to encourage the commission of violations of humanitarian law. The Court ordered the US to cease hostilities and make reparation for its breaches, but the US never implemented the judgment and vetoed attempts by Nicaragua to enforce it through the Security Council.[129]

To date Canada has only been a party to three cases before the International Court of Justice. Only one of them, *Legality of Use of Force (Serbia and Montenegro v. Canada)*, concerned human rights-related issues.[130] The *Legality of Use of Force* case was one of ten actions brought by Serbia and Montenegro (formerly the Federal Republic of Yugoslavia) against NATO member states in 1999 accusing them of bombing Yugoslav territory contrary to international law. The cases, of which eight remain, were ordered stayed at the request of the government of Serbia and Montenegro due to "dramatic" and "ongoing" changes in the country which they claimed had put the cases "in a quite different perspective."[131]

G. THE SECRETARY-GENERAL

The UN General Assembly appoints a UN Secretary-General every five years upon the recommendation of the Security Council.[132] Article 97 of the UN Charter describes the Secretary-General as the "chief administrative officer" of the UN. However, much more than an administrator, the Secretary-General is the symbol of the UN in the eyes of the world. The position involves a degree of intrinsic tension due to the UN Charter's definition of the job, which requires the Secretary-Gener-

---

128 [1986] ICJ Rep 14.
129 See generally M. O'Connell, "The Prospects of Enforcing Monetary Judgements: A Study of Nicaragua's Judgement Against the US" (1990) 30 Virginia Journal of International Law 891.
130 [1999] ICJ Rep 10. The other two cases involved maritime law matters.
131 See International Court of Justice Press Release 2002/10 (22 March 2002).
132 The current Secretary-General is Kofi Annan (Ghana). His predecessors were: Boutros Boutros-Ghali (Egypt), Javier Perez de Cuellar (Peru), Kurt Waldheim (Austria), U Thant (Burma), Dag Hammarskjold (Sweden), and Trygve Lie (Norway). So far, there has not been a female Secretary-General.

al to function simultaneously as spokesperson for the international community, servant of UN member states, and head of the UN Secretariat.[133] But overall, this broad set of responsibilities grants the Secretary-General a powerful and unique mandate for action.

The Secretary-General is probably best known for using his "good offices" to help prevent national and international conflicts from arising, escalating, or spreading. Yet the position also entails routine consultations with world leaders and UN personnel.[134] In addition, each year the Secretary-General issues a report appraising the work of the UN and advancing his views of its future priorities. The current Secretary-General, Kofi Annan, has focused significant attention in his annual reports on the promotion and protection of human rights.[135] Annan has also ushered in major reforms to enhance the mainstreaming of human rights within the UN system.[136] In addition, he established the "Global Compact," a challenge to world business leaders to "embrace and enact" nine universally agreed values and principles in the areas of human rights, labour rights, and the environment.[137]

The Secretary-General is supported by the Deputy Secretary-General. Louise Fréchette, a former Deputy Minister of National Defence of Canada, was the first and remains the only Deputy Secretary-General. This is the highest position ever attained within the UN secretariat by a Canadian.

---

133 UN Charter art. 99 empowers the Secretary-General to bring to the attention of the Security Council any matter that, in his opinion, threatens the maintenance of international peace and security. Also, UN Charter art. 98 calls upon him to perform "such other functions" as are assigned by the Security Council, the General Assembly, and the other main UN organs.

134 The confidentiality of such consultations was recently brought into question when it was alleged that the American and British governments had bugged the Secretary-General's office in the run-up to the 2003 invasion of Iraq. See "UN Shrugs Off Bugging Furore," BBC News (http://news.bbc.co.uk), 28 February 2004.

135 See also Boutros-Ghali, Boutros, An Agenda for Peace, UN doc. A/47/277 (1992).

136 Annan authored Renewing the United Nations: A Programme for Reform, UN doc. A/51/950 (1997) in which he stressed that human rights are a core part of the UN mission and should be designated as a "cross-cutting theme" in the four substantive fields of the UN's work programme, namely in peace and security matters, economic and social affairs, development co-operation, and humanitarian affairs. To that end, the OHCHR was made a member of each of the four powerful executive committees that were established by the Secretary-General as part of his Programme for Reform, namely the Executive Committee on Peace and Security, the Executive Committee on Humanitarian Affairs, the Executive Committee on Economic and Social Affairs, and the UN Development Group.

137 See http://www.unglobalcompact.org.

H. OTHER UN AGENCIES, FUNDS, AND PROGRAMS

A number of other UN agencies, funds, and programs carry out significant human rights activities according to their particular mandates and expertise. These include: the UN Development Fund for Women (UNIFEM),[138] the Division for the Advancement of Women (DAW),[139] the United Nations Population Fund (UNFPA),[140] the United Nations Children's Fund (UNICEF),[141] the World Health Organization (WHO),[142] the Joint United Nations Programme on HIV/AIDS (UNAIDS),[143] the UN

---

138 UNIFEM provides financial and technical assistance to projects that advance women's human rights, economic security, and political participation. UNIFEM was created by a UN General Assembly resolution in 1976. See http://www.unifem.org.

139 DAW is a body within the Department of Economic and Social Affairs. Among other things, DAW acts as the secretariat for the Committee on the Elimination of Discrimination against Women. It has also served as the secretariat for all of the world conferences on women, namely those held in Mexico City (1975), Copenhagen (1980), Nairobi (1985), and Beijing (1995). See http://www.un.org/womenwatch/daw.

140 UNFPA is the world's largest fund for the promotion of reproductive health. It provides financial and technical assistance to developing countries. Its primary focus is on family planning, safety in pregnancy and childbirth, the prevention of sexually transmitted diseases, and the elimination of violence against women (including the practice of female genital mutilation). See http://www.unfpa.org.

141 The UN General Assembly established UNICEF in 1946 to meet the emergency needs of children in post-war Europe and China. Later its mandate was expanded to include the needs of children (and women) in all developing countries and emergency situations. Its current priorities include education for all children (especially girls), child vaccination, assistance to children affected by HIV/AIDS, and early childhood programming. In all of its work it takes a "human rights based approach," with a focus on the realization of the rights set out in the CRC and the CEDAW. See http://www.unicef.org.

142 Established in 1948, the WHO is the UN's specialized agency for health issues. It focuses on ensuring the highest possible level of health for human beings, including physical, mental, and social health. The WHO has designated human rights as a cross-cutting issue in its work and actively promotes a "health and human rights" agenda. See http://www.who.int.

143 See http://www.unaids.org. UNAIDS and the OHCHR jointly published the *International Guidelines on HIV/AIDS and Human Rights*, UN doc. HR/PUB/98/1 (1998). Stephen Lewis has been UN Secretary-General Kofi Annan's special envoy for HIV/AIDS in Africa since June 2001. He is a former Canadian ambassador to the UN, and was previously a deputy executive director at UNICEF.

Development Programme (UNDP),[144] the World Food Programme (WFP),[145] and the UN Food and Agriculture Organization (FAO).[146] The OHCHR has organized inter-agency memoranda of understanding regarding the promotion of human rights with many of these agencies in order to ensure effective "mainstreaming" (integration) of human rights in UN programming and procedures.

Since 1978 the UN Educational, Scientific and Cultural Organization (UNESCO) has operated a confidential human rights complaint procedure.[147] The procedure, not based on any particular treaty, allows petitions from victims, NGOs, or persons with reliable knowledge of a human rights violation related to education, science, culture, or information. The specific rights within UNESCO's field of competence include the right to education (UDHR article 26); the right to share in scientific advancement (UDHR article 27); the right to participate freely in cultural life (UDHR article 27); and the right to information, including freedom of opinion and expression (UDHR article 19).[148] Petitions are transmitted to the government concerned and examined by the Committee on Conventions and Recommendations, a permanent committee of the UNESCO Executive Board that is responsible for

---

144 UNDP is the UN's global development arm. It works on a very wide range of issues including democratic development, poverty reduction, crisis prevention and recovery, the environment, technology issues, and HIV/AIDS. It is probably best known for its annual Human Development Report, which ranks every state in areas such as per capita income, literacy, life expectancy, and respect for women's human rights. Canada ranked first in the world each year for most of the 1990s. See http://www.undp.org. More recently, UNDP presented a report to the UN Secretary-General on the role of the private sector in development. The report, entitled "Unleashing Entrepreneurship: Making Business Work for the Poor" (http://www.undp.org/cpsd), was prepared by the UNDP-appointed Commission on the Private Sector and Development. Canadian Prime Minister Paul Martin served as the Commission's co-chair.

145 Established in 1963, the WFP is the world's largest humanitarian agency providing food to the world's poorest persons, including most of the world's refugees and internally displaced persons. See http://www.wfp.org.

146 The FAO was founded in 1945. It is the lead UN agency for agriculture, fisheries, and rural development. Among its primary goals is the promotion of food security, which it defines as "the access of all people at all times to the food they need for an active and healthy life." See http://www.fao.org.

147 Canada is a party to the UNESCO Constitution 1945 [1945] CanTS no. 18. Article 1 of the Constitution states that UNESCO's purpose is to promote inter-state collaboration on issues of education, science, and culture in order to further universal respect for justice, the rule of law and human rights.

148 On cultural human rights generally, see J. Symonides, "Cultural Rights," in J. Symonides, ed. Human Rights: Concept and Standards (Paris: UNESCO, 2000).

implementing the procedure. Rules regarding admissibility and examination on the merits generally parallel those of UN treaty bodies, except that the UNESCO procedure is confidential from start to finish and the emphasis is more on conciliation than adjudication.[149] The fact that the procedure is confidential prevents us from giving examples of cases involving the Canadian government.

Also of note is the Conciliation and Good Offices Commission that operates under the auspices of UNESCO. Its mandate is to assist in the settlement of any disputes that may arise between states parties to the Convention against Discrimination in Education 1960.[150] The Commission consists of eleven expert members elected by the General Conference of UNESCO and serving in their personal capacity.

Two other important UN agencies — the ILO and the UNHCR — are reviewed in Chapter Sixteen. The Commission is responsible for seeking a settlement of any disputes that may arise between states parties to the Convention.

---

149 The full procedure is set out in 104 EX/Decision 3.3 and can be found on
     UNESCO's website at http://www.unesco.org/general/eng/legal/hrights/procedure.shtml.
150 429 UNTS 93. Canada is not a party to the Convention. See also the Protocol
     Instituting a Conciliation and Good Offices Commission 1962, 651 UNTS 362.

CHAPTER 15

REGIONAL HUMAN RIGHTS MECHANISMS

This chapter will review the Inter-American, European, and African multilateral mechanisms for the promotion and protection of human rights. Of these, the Inter-American and European mechanisms are the oldest and by any measure the most developed, particularly the latter.[1] Each regional system is also composed of institutions that pursue economic development, social development, and the maintenance of peace and security. The focus of this chapter, however, is human rights mechanisms.

Not discussed in this chapter are various other regional multilateral mechanisms with peripheral human rights elements, such as the South African Development Community (SADC) and the Economic Community of West African States (ECOWAS).[2] Also not discussed

---

1   While the African system has not been especially effective to date, this may be less a question of defects in design than the absence of political will on the part of African states.

2   Article 4 of the Amended Declaration and Treaty of SADC 1992 requires member states to act in accordance with "human rights, democracy, and the rule of law." Breaches of the Treaty are justiciable before the SADC Tribunal, which is contemplated in the Treaty but not yet established. Similarly, the Treaty of Lagos 1975 establishing ECOWAS is based on various relevant principles including "recognition, promotion and protection of human and people's rights in accordance with the provisions of the African Charter on Human and Peoples' Rights." Breaches of the Treaty are justiciable before the Community Court of Justice, which was established in 1991.

here is the emerging human rights system of the League of Arab States. It has a permanent Permanent Arab Commission on Human Rights, which is similar in mandate to the UN Commission on Human Rights, and a specialized agency on labour rights, the Arab Labour Organization.[3] In addition, the Arab Charter on Human Rights 1994 — which has yet to be ratified by a single member of the League — contains a proposed mechanism for enforcement of human rights. Article 40 authorizes states parties to the Charter to elect a Committee of Experts on Human Rights. The Committee would supervise a state reporting system akin to that under the ICCPR. As for Asia, to date there is no multilateral human rights system for the region.[4]

A. THE INTER-AMERICAN SYSTEM

The OAS is the oldest of all regional organizations. All thirty-five independent states in the Western hemisphere — almost all of them democratically governed — are OAS members.[5] Canada became a Permanent Observer to the OAS in 1972, and has been a full member since 1990. Shortly after becoming a member, Canada took a lead role on various human rights issues within the OAS.[6]

The OAS consists of two main bodies: the General Assembly and Permanent Council. The Assembly meets annually in a regularly scheduled session, but also on an *ad hoc* basis as necessary. It is responsible for setting most OAS policy and is roughly equivalent to the UN General Assembly. The Council is the chief decision-making branch of the organization, especially when the General Assembly is not in session. It is the OAS equivalent to the UN Security Council.[7] Both the OAS General Assembly and Permanent Council have authority to deal with human

---

3   See generally A. Robertson (revised by J. Merrills), *Human Rights in the World*, 3d ed. (Manchester: Manchester University Press, 1992) at 198–200. To date, the Commission has focused overwhelmingly on the situation of Palestinians living in the occupied territories.

4   But see the discussion of ASEAN in Chapter Sixteen.

5   Cuba is a member of the OAS as well, but its government has been excluded from participation since 1962.

6   For example, Canada was active in establishing the Unit for the Promotion of Democracy, currently headed by Canadian Elizabeth Spehar. The Unit is the main body within the OAS General Secretariat focused on democratic consolidation in OAS member states.

7   Canada has twice been Chair of the OAS Permanent Council. Most recently Canada was the chair from 1 October to 31 December 2000.

rights issues.[8] Other relevant specialized organizations of the OAS concerned with human rights include the Pan-American Health Organization, the Inter-American Children's Institute, the Inter-American Commission of Women, and the Inter-American Indigenous Institute.

The primary OAS mechanisms for the promotion and protection of human rights are the Inter-American Commission on Human Rights and the Inter-American Court of Human Rights.[9] The Inter-American Commission on Human Rights has jurisdiction to receive cases based on the AmDR and the ACHR, while the Inter-American Court of Human Rights has jurisdiction to receive cases based exclusively on the ACHR. Unlike the UN system, the OAS does not establish a separate treaty body for each of its human rights treaties, but rather situates them within the existing authority and procedures of the Inter-American Court and Commission, as the case may be.[10] This is a far more efficient arrangement.

1) The Inter-American Commission on Human Rights

The Inter-American Commission on Human Rights was established in 1959 by the OAS Permanent Council, a decade before the ACHR was

---

8   For example, art. 21 of the Inter-American Democratic Charter 2001 explicitly authorizes the OAS General Assembly to suspend member states where democratic rights have been overturned:

When the special session of the General Assembly determines that there has been an unconstitutional interruption of the democratic order of a member state, and that diplomatic initiatives have failed, the special session shall take the decision to suspend said member state from the exercise of its right to participate in the OAS by an affirmative vote of two thirds of the member states in accordance with the Charter of the OAS. The suspension shall take effect immediately. The suspended member state shall continue to fulfill its obligations to the Organization, in particular its human rights obligations.

9   On the Inter-American human rights system generally, see D. Harris & S. Livingstone, eds., *The Inter-American Human Rights System* (New York: Oxford University Press, 1998); T. Buergenthal & D. Shelton, *Protecting Human Rights in the Americas: Cases and Materials*, 4th ed. (Arlington: N. P. Engel, 1995); J. Davidson, *The Inter-American Human Rights System* (Aldershot: Dartmouth, 1997).

10   The one exception is the Inter-American Convention on the Elimination of All Forms of Discrimination Against Persons with Disabilities 1999 OAS doc. AG/RES. 1608. Article 6 of that Convention provides for the establishment of a Committee for the Elimination of All Forms of Discrimination against Persons with Disabilities, composed of one representative appointed by each state party. States parties are required to submit periodic reports for review by the Committee, which then issues concluding observations and recommendations.

adopted. In 1965, OAS member states authorized it to examine communications regarding alleged human rights violations. The Commission functioned as an "autonomous entity" of the OAS until the Protocol of Buenos Aires 1967[11] came into effect in 1970, making it an official OAS Charter organ with responsibility for the promotion and protection of human rights.[12]

Today the Commission, which is based in Washington, D.C., reviews alleged violations of the OAS Charter and the AmDR by OAS member states, and of the ACHR by its states parties. Thus, it has two distinct if overlapping roles: one as a "Charter organ" vis-à-vis all OAS member states and one as a "Convention organ" in respect of ACHR states parties.[13] The Commission has seven members. They are elected by the member states of the OAS and serve in their personal capacity. Commissioners are assisted by a small permanent staff and perform their duties in two annual sessions of three weeks' duration each.

The Commission has played a significant role in the promotion and protection of human rights in the Americas, particularly in the last twenty years. Among other things, it has conducted important on-site investigations and published damning reports on the state of human rights in particular countries.[14] Today most of its work is focused on individual petitions. There have been no inter-state petitions submitted to the Commission thus far. And unlike the UN treaty body system, there is no obligatory state reporting procedure contemplated by the OAS Charter or the ACHR.[15]

a) The Commission as a Charter Organ

The Commission has a number of functions in its capacity as a Charter organ, including assisting in the development of human rights

---

11   119 UNTS 3.

12   See the revised Charter of the Organization of American States 1948 (OAS Charter), [1990] CanTS no. 23, arts. 53(e) and 106.

13   The Commission also has a role in respect of other OAS human rights treaties, as explained below.

14   As of May 2002, the Inter-American Commission on Human Rights had conducted eighty-three visits to more than two dozen OAS member states. The full list of on-site visits (beginning in 1961) can be found on the OAS website (http://www.oas.org). Like UN treaty bodies, the Commission is very reliant on the reports of human rights NGOs.

15   However, ACHR art. 42 requires states parties to transmit to the Commission a copy of the reports they submit annually to the Executive Committees of the Inter-American Economic and Social Council and the Inter-American Council for Education, Science, and Culture.

instruments, providing advice to the OAS Permanent Council and General Assembly, mediating human rights issues in contexts of war or internal tensions, and preparing special resolutions and reports on specific regional issues.[16] It also undertakes country studies and in-country investigations in the event of serious concerns about a general or particular human rights situation in an OAS member state.

The Commission has created its own robust Rules of Procedure to govern in-country missions.[17] Missions are conditional upon receipt of an invitation from the government in question or its prior consent in "serious and urgent cases."[18] In some cases, the Commission may publish a report based on investigations conducted outside the concerned state where that state refuses an in-country mission.[19] Article 54 of the Rules of Procedure compels governments to assist the members of a visiting mission, and to refrain from adverse measures against those who co-operate with it.[20] Article 55 of the Rules allows mission members to travel freely within the host country and to meet anyone, including prisoners. It also requires the host country to co-operate with requests for information and ensure the mission's safety during the investigation.[21] Following the conclusion of an in-country investigation, the mission presents a draft report for confidential comment by the concerned government. If the government fails to respond, the Commission must publish the report; if there is a response then publication of the report is optional.[22]

---

16 See, for example "Report on the Human Rights Situation of the Indigenous People in the Americas," OEA/Ser.L/V/II.108 doc. 62 (2000).

17 The Rules of Procedure of the Inter-American Commission on Human Rights were approved at its 109th special session held from 4–8 December 2000, and amended at its 116th regular period of sessions held from 7–25 October 2002.

18 Rules of Procedure, *ibid.*, art. 40.

19 See, for example, the Commission's report on Cuba, reproduced in *The Organization of American States and Human Rights 1960–1967* (1972) in Part III. After being denied entry to Cuba, the Commission held hearings and interviewed refugees in Miami. The report is based on those hearings and interviews.

20 A similar but more detailed provision can be found in Optional Protocol to the Convention Against Torture and Other Cruel, Inhuman or Degrading Treatment or Punishment 2002 (CAT-OP), (2003) 42 ILM 26, arts. 15 (regarding co-operation with the Sub-Committee on Prevention) and 21 (regarding co-operation with national preventive mechanisms).

21 Compare with CAT-OP, *ibid.*, arts. 14 (regarding the Sub-Committee on Prevention) and 20 (regarding national preventive mechanisms).

22 Rules of Procedure, above note 17, art. 58. Reports are generally forwarded to the OAS General Assembly for a possible hortatory resolution addressed to the concerned government. The General Assembly tends, however, to draft weak and vague resolutions.

To date, Canada has only been the subject of one in-country investigation by the Inter-American Commission on Human Rights.[23]

In its capacity as a Charter organ, the Commission is also authorized to receive individual petitions under article 20 of its Statute.[24] Petitions may be resolved by friendly settlement or decided on the merits. The procedure for handling individual petitions is very similar to the procedure for handling ACHR-based petitions, discussed immediately below. The major difference is that Charter-based petitions may not be referred to the Inter-American Court of Human Rights. The Commission simply publishes its conclusions and recommendations and forwards them to the parties and the OAS General Assembly.[25]

Canada has only been the subject of two Charter-based petitions. Both decisions were on admissibility alone and both involved refugee-related claims.[26] It is not easy to explain the underuse of the Inter-American Commission on Human Rights by Canadian victims. It is especially confounding given that the AmDR guarantees rights not covered by the ICCPR and thus not justiciable by the UN Human Rights Committee.[27]

b) The Commission as a Convention Organ

In its capacity as a Convention organ, the Commission exercises many of the same functions as it does in its capacity as a Charter organ. It participates in the development of human rights instruments, assists

---

23 See "Report on the Situation of Human Rights of Asylum Seekers within the Canadian Refugee System," OEA/Ser.L/V/II.106 doc. 40 rev. (2000). The on-site visit was carried out in October 1997.

24 Statute of the Inter-American Commission on Human Rights, OEA/Ser.L.V/II.82 doc.6 rev.1 at 93 (1992).

25 The General Assembly generally does not enforce the Commission's recommendations. As a result, the Commission has adopted an internal enforcement procedure. Article 46(1) of the Commission's Rules of Procedure, above note 17, provides:

> Once the Commission has published a report on a friendly settlement or on the merits in which it has made recommendations, it may adopt the follow-up measures it deems appropriate, such as requesting information from the parties and holding hearings in order to verify compliance with friendly settlement agreements and its recommendations.

26 *Joseph v. Canada* (1993), Case no. 11.092 (finding the complaint inadmissible); and *Suresh v. Canada* (2002), Case no. 11.661 (finding the complaint admissible).

27 For example, the AmDR includes protections for mothers (art. 7), the right to health (art. 11), the right to education (art. 12), property rights (arts. 13 and 23), rights in respect of culture and science (art. 13), the right to work (art. 14), the right to rest and leisure (art. 15), the right to social security and insurance (art. 16), and the right to asylum (art. 27). None of these rights are covered in the ICCPR. Most of them are covered by the ICESCR, but as we saw in Chapter Fourteen, there is no petition procedure before the Committee on Economic, Social and Cultural Rights.

the OAS Permanent Council and General Assembly, mediates human rights crises, and carries out in-country investigations.

However, ACHR articles 44–51 establish a distinct individual and inter-state complaints procedure before the Commission for states parties to the ACHR. Article 44 permits any individual, group, or recognized NGO to submit an individual complaint to the Commission regarding a violation by any ACHR state party.[28] Article 45 permits a state party to submit a complaint against another state party, provided that both states have accepted the Commission's jurisdiction over inter-state complaints. Articles 46 and 47 provide a standard set of rules of admissibility applicable to individual and inter-state complaints. In contrast to UN treaty body rules of admissibility, ACHR article 46(1)(b) requires a complaint to be filed with the Commission "within a period of six months from the date on which the party alleging violation of his rights was notified of the final judgment" at the domestic level.[29] Provisional measures are available in particularly serious and urgent cases to prevent irreparable harm.[30]

ACHR articles 48–51 govern complaint resolution. The Commission reviews and investigates the facts alleged in an admissible complaint and then holds hearings in which both parties participate. If a friendly settlement is reached, the Commission draws up a report setting out the facts and the solution.[31] Friendly settlements have often provided for multiple remedies, including significant compensatory damages.[32] Where a friendly settlement is not achieved, the Commission may give the respondent state its conclusions and recommendations in private in the form of a preliminary report, permitting the state a brief time to comply or contest.[33] When that time runs out, the Commission may do one of two things: deliver a final report which, in the event of further non-com-

---

28   Until recently, most cases before the Commission were initiated by family members of the victim, since the violations often involved forced disappearance or summary execution.

29   This helps to ensure that the matter in dispute does not continue indefinitely. See also ACHR art. 46(2), which provides that the rule of domestic exhaustion will not apply if (a) there are no domestic remedies to protect against the particular violation, (b) there has been adverse interference with respect to vindication of available remedies, or (c) there have been unwarranted delays in obtaining available domestic remedies.

30   Rules of Procedure, above note 17, art. 25.

31   ACHR art. 49.

32   See, for example, *Pablo Ignacio Livia Robles v. Peru* (2002), Case no. 12.035 Report no. 75/0231 (Friendly Settlement), in which the Commission negotiated a settlement providing for, *inter alia*, state acknowledgment of responsibility, compensation for material and moral damages, and recognition of years of service lost as a result of unfair dismissal.

33   ACHR art. 50.

pliance, the Commission will usually make public; or take the case to the Inter-American Court of Human Rights, provided that it does so within three months of the delivery of its preliminary report and provided that the state has declared its acceptance of the Court's jurisdiction.[34] Individual complainants may not refer cases to the Court; only the Commission or a state party may do so.[35] Where the Commission refers a case to the Court, it must appear before the Court.[36] Its function there is much like a *Ministerio Publico* in a civil law system; the Commission strives to protect the integrity of the legal order and to ensure the proper application of the ACHR, and not to advance the interests of any party.[37]

The conclusions and recommendations of the Commission in contentious cases carry significant weight, but do not bind states in the judicial sense. The Inter-American Court of Human Rights has, however, stated that

> in accordance with the principle of good faith . . . if a State signs and ratifies an international treaty, especially one concerning human rights, such as the American Convention, it has the obligation to make every effort to comply with the recommendations of a protection organ such as the Inter-American Commission. . . .[38]

c)   The Commission and other OAS Human Rights Treaties

The Inter-American Commission on Human Rights also plays an important supervisory role concerning other OAS human rights treaties. For instance, pursuant to article 13 of the Inter-American Convention on the Forced Disappearance of Persons 1994,[39] individuals may submit complaints to the Commission alleging the forced disappearance of persons. The complaints are subject to the same procedures established in the ACHR and in the Commission's and Court's respective statutes, regulations, and rules of procedure.[40] Article 12 of the

---

34   *Ibid.*, art. 51.
35   Individuals do, however, have an independent right to be heard by the Court once it has seized jurisdiction of their case. See art. 43(3) of the Commission's revised Rules of Procedure.
36   ACHR art. 57.
37   See *In the Matter of Viviana Gallardo and others (Costa Rica)* (1981) I/A Court HR Series A no. G 101/81 at para. 22.
38   *Loayza Tamayo Case (Peru)* (1997) I/A Court HR Series C no. 33 at para. 80.
39   (1994) 33 ILM 1429.
40   Note also art. 14 of the Convention, *ibid.*:

> Without prejudice to the provisions of the preceding article, when the Inter-American Commission on Human Rights receives a petition or communication regarding an alleged forced disappearance, its Executive Secretariat shall

Inter-American Convention on the Prevention, Punishment and Eradication of Violence against Women 1994[41] provides much the same.[42] By contrast, individual petitions before the Commission are not possible under the Inter-American Convention to Prevent and Punish Torture 1985,[43] although there is a state reporting obligation and a corresponding supervisory function for the Commission.[44]

The Additional Protocol to the ACHR in the area of Economic, Social, and Cultural Rights 1988 (ACHR-OP1) also requires state parties to submit periodic performance reports.[45] It authorizes the Inter-

---

> urgently and confidentially address the respective government, and shall request that government to provide as soon as possible information as to the whereabouts of the allegedly disappeared person together with any other information it considers pertinent, and such request shall be without prejudice as to the admissibility of the petition.

41   (1994) 33 ILM 1534.

42   Article 12 of the Convention, *ibid.*, provides:

> Any person or group of persons, or any nongovernmental entity legally recognized in one or more member states of the Organization, may lodge petitions with the Inter-American Commission on Human Rights containing denunciations or complaints of violations of Article 7 of this Convention by a State Party, and the Commission shall consider such claims in accordance with the norms and procedures established by the American Convention on Human Rights and the Statutes and Regulations of the Inter-American Commission on Human Rights for lodging and considering petitions.

Note also that art. 10 of the same Convention provides for a reporting obligation to the Inter-American Commission of Women:

> In order to protect the rights of every woman to be free from violence, the States Parties shall include in their national reports to the Inter-American Commission of Women information on measures adopted to prevent and prohibit violence against women, and to assist women affected by violence, as well as on any difficulties they observe in applying those measures, and the factors that contribute to violence against women.

43   OAS TS no. 67.

44   Article 17 of the Convention, *ibid.*, provides:

> The States Parties undertake to inform the Inter-American Commission on Human Rights of any legislative, judicial, administrative, or other measures they adopt in application of this Convention. In keeping with its duties and responsibilities, the Inter-American Commission on Human Rights will endeavor in its annual report to analyze the existing situation in the member states of the Organization of American States in regard to the prevention and elimination of torture.

45   OAS TS no. 69. Article 19(1)–(2) of the ACHR-OP1 requires states parties to submit periodic reports to the Secretary-General of the OAS, who must transmit them to the Inter-American Economic and Social Council and the Inter-American Council for Education, with a copy to the Inter-American Commission on Human Rights.

American Commission on Human Rights to make observations and recommendations on those reports and on state performance general-ly.[46] ACHR-OP1 article 19(6) authorizes the Commission (and when applicable, the Court) to process individual petitions, but only with respect to the right to unionize (article 8(1)(a)) and the right to education (article 13). These petitions are handled according to the same procedures applicable to complaints under the ACHR.

To date, Canada is not party to any of these treaties and hence is not subject to such procedures.

d) Special Rapporteurs of the Commission

In 1994, the Commission established the permanent office of the Rapporteurship on the Rights of Women. The Rapporteurship publishes thematic studies, assists in developing the Commission's jurisprudence concerning the rights of women, and examines issues affecting women's rights in specific countries through in-country missions and reports. In 2002, the Rapporteurship conducted its first independent in-country mission, for the purpose of investigating the situation in Ciudad Juárez, Mexico where hundreds of women have been killed or disappeared in recent years.[47]

In 1998, the Commission created the permanent office of the Special Rapporteur for Freedom of Expression. The Special Rapporteur provides legal assistance to the Commission and to OAS member states, carries out promotion and protection activities concerning freedom of expression, conducts visits to member states, and publishes thematic, country, and annual reports.

---

46 Article 19(7), *ibid.*, provides:

> [T]he Inter-American Commission on Human Rights may formulate such observations and recommendations as it deems pertinent concerning the status of the economic, social and cultural rights established in the present Protocol in all or some of the States Parties, which it may include in its Annual Report to the General Assembly or in a special report, whichever it considers more appropriate.

But note art. 19(8):

> The Council and the Inter-American Commission on Human Rights, in discharging the functions conferred upon them in this article, shall take into account the progressive nature of the observance of the rights subject to protection by this Protocol.

47 The visit was undertaken as a result of multiple NGO requests, and following the invitation of the Mexican government. The mission report, "The Situation of the Rights of Women in Ciudad Juárez, Mexico: The Right to be Free from Violence and Discrimination," can be found on the OAS website (http://www.oas.org).

2) The Inter-American Court of Human Rights

The Inter-American Court of Human Rights was established in 1979 under the ACHR.[48] Today, it has its own Statute[49] and Rules of Procedure.[50] The Court is composed of seven judges elected by ACHR states parties. It is based in San Jose, Costa Rica. Nationals of any OAS member state may sit on the Court, whether or not their state is party to the ACHR. To date, no Canadians have served as judges on the Court.[51] The judges sit on a part-time basis only, as the Court is only in session for approximately ten weeks each year.[52] The Court is assisted by the Inter-American Institute for Human Rights, an autonomous human rights education and research centre based, like the Court, in San Jose.[53]

The Court only has jurisdiction over ACHR states parties that have accepted its compulsory jurisdiction under ACHR articles 48 and 50.[54] Like most supranational tribunals, the Inter-American Court of Human Rights exercises both advisory and contentious jurisdiction. In contrast to the European Court of Human Rights, however, individuals and NGOs may not submit petitions before the Court. Instead, contentious cases may only be initiated by ACHR states parties or by the Inter-American Commission on Human Rights.[55] To date, no ACHR state party has

---

48   On the work of the Court generally, see J. Pasqualucci, *The Practice and Procedure of the Inter-American Court of Human Rights* (Cambridge: Cambridge University Press, 2003).

49   The OAS General Assembly adopted the Court's Statute at its Ninth Regular Session, held in La Paz, Bolivia, October 1979 (Resolution no. 448).

50   The Court's Rules of Procedure were approved by it at its Forty-Ninth Regular Session held from 16–25 November 2000.

51   Retired Supreme Court of Canada Justice Bertha Wilson was nominated in the early 1990s by the Canadian government but lost in the election for the vacant post. Canada was unable to vote, not being a party to the ACHR: W. Schabas, *International Human Rights Law and the Canadian Charter*, 2d ed., (Scarborough: Butterworths, 1996) at 99.

52   The Court does, however, have a small permanent staff to assist with case management throughout the year.

53   The Institute was established in 1980 by agreement between the Republic of Costa Rica and the Inter-American Court of Human Rights. The Institute helps to train people regarding use of the Inter-American human rights system, including the Inter-American Court of Human Rights and the Inter-American Commission on Human Rights.

54   The majority of ACHR states parties have accepted the Court's compulsory jurisdiction.

55   ACHR art. 61(1). Neither the Commission nor states parties can submit a case until the Commission's proceedings have been completed (art. 61(2)). Were it otherwise, states would have an advantage over victims, who until recently had

submitted a case to the Court against another state party. Thus, all of the contentious judgments rendered by the Court so far have been initiated by the Commission. Advisory cases may be initiated by any OAS member state (including non-parties to the ACHR like Canada) or by certain OAS organs.[56] The cases may relate to the ACHR or to "other treaties concerning the protection of human rights in the American states."[57]

ACHR article 63(1) permits the Court broad discretion to impose remedies. It provides:

> If the Court finds that there has been a violation of a right or freedom protected by this Convention, the Court shall rule that the injured party be ensured the enjoyment of his right or freedom that was violated. It shall also rule, if appropriate, that the consequences of the measure or situation that constituted the breach of such right or freedom be remedied and that fair compensation be paid to the injured party.

Among other things, the Court has required states to change legislation to make it compatible with the ACHR. It has ordered a wide variety of non-monetary remedies including orders for restitution of rights or property, acknowledgment of wrongdoing, public investigation, punishment of the perpetrator, medical treatment for the victim, and measures to guarantee non-repetition of the violation.[58] The Court has also ordered payment of specific damages for pecuniary and non-pecuniary injuries. As a rule, the question of damages is handled in a second phase of proceedings following judgment on the merits. Where possible, the Court allows the parties to settle the quantum among themselves, limiting its role to verification of the fairness of any settlement.

---

no standing before the Inter-American Court of Human Rights. See art. 35(4) of the Court's Rules of Procedure:

> When the application has been notified to the alleged victim, his next of kin or his duly accredited representatives, they shall have a period of 30 days to present autonomously to the Court their requests, arguments and evidence.

56 OAS organs must prove a "legitimate institutional interest" in relation to any request. See *Advisory Opinion OC-2/82* (1982) I/A Court HR Series A no. 2 at para. 14.

57 ACHR art. 64(1). The Court has held that "other treaties" means any OAS or international human rights treaty applicable in the concerned state. See, for example, *Advisory Opinion OC-16/99* (1999) I/A Court HR Series A no. 16 at para. 109, where the Court held that provisions of the ICCPR "concerned the protection of human rights in the American states." States can also ensure compatibility of their own domestic laws with OAS human rights obligations by referring laws to the Court for an advisory opinion (ACHR art. 64(2)).

58 See generally D. Shelton, *Remedies in International Human Rights Law* (Oxford: Oxford University Press, 1999) at 295–302 [Shelton, *Remedies*].

In a number of recent cases brought by the Inter-American Commission on Human Rights, states have conceded responsibility for violations of the ACHR and left it to the Court to determine the quantum of damages to be awarded to victims.[59] At any stage of its proceedings, the Court may also order provisional measures.[60]

In making its judgments, the Court is at liberty to reverse the Commission's findings of fact or law. Since there is no appeals chamber, all of the Court's judgments are final and not subject to appeal.[61] The Court is required to inform the OAS General Assembly of cases of non-compliance with its decisions, but there is no mechanism to ensure enforcement of the Court's decisions. As a result, the Court keeps cases open until the state party in question has fully complied with the judgment.[62] During the last ten years, the record of state compliance with adverse judgments has been encouraging.[63]

In contrast to the Commission — which has rendered hundreds of findings in individual cases — the Court has rendered relatively few judgments to date.[64] While the Court's caseload remains quite small, it is growing, due largely to the active human rights NGO movement in Latin America. The most significant contentious judgments rendered by the Court remain its early judgments in the so-called "Honduran Disappearance Cases."[65] These were the first international judgments

---

59   See, for example, *El Caracazo Case (Venezuela)* (1999) I/A Court HR Series C no. 58. The Court has on occasion established trust funds and overseen the making of compensation payments. For example, in *Aloeboetoe et al. Case (Suriname)* (1993) I/A Court HR Series C no. 15, the Court established and appointed the members of a foundation with a mandate to act as trustee of the funds. See Shelton, *Remedies, ibid.* at 192.

60   ACHR art. 63(2).

61   *Ibid.,* art. 67.

62   Shelton, *Remedies,* above note 58, at 13.

63   See "Enhancing Canada's Role in the OAS: Canadian Adherence to the American Convention on Human Rights," Report of the Senate Standing Committee on Human Rights, May 2003 (http://www.gibvanert.com/using/pdfs/senate_achr.pdf) at 38.

64   As of 1 January 2003, the Court had rendered ninety-seven judgments concerning thirty-eight separate contentious cases, seventeen advisory opinions, and more than one hundred orders for provisional measures. Source: http://www.oas.org.

65   The cases are:
   a) the *Velásquez Rodríguez Case,* including (i) *Preliminary Objections* (1987) I/A Court HR Series C no. 1, (ii) *Judgment* (1988) I/A Court HR Series C no. 4, (iii) *Compensatory Damages* (1989) I/A Court HR Series C no. 7, and (iv) *Interpretation of the Compensatory Damages Judgment* (1990) I/A Court HR Series C no. 9;
   b) the *Godínez Cruz Case,* including (i) *Preliminary Objections* (1987) I/A Court HR Series C no. 3, (ii) *Judgment* (1989) I/A Court HR Series C no. 5, (iii) *Compen-*

dealing with forced disappearance and led to groundbreaking rulings on the nature of state obligations.[66] Since then, the Court has rendered major judgments on issues such as *habeus corpus* guarantees in states of emergency,[67] the death penalty,[68] and the abduction, torture, and murder of street children by police officers.[69]

While the jurisprudence of the Court is somewhat underdeveloped in comparison to that of the European Court of Human Rights, it has greater expertise in human rights matters that have arisen more frequently in OAS member states than in Europe, such as forced disappearances and amnesty laws. It has also developed a much richer jurisprudence of remedies. Today, as democratic practices consolidate throughout the Americas, the Court's docket is starting to focus on less extreme types of violations ranging from wrongful dismissal of judges to film censorship.

B. EUROPEAN SYSTEMS

There are three relevant intergovernmental systems that deal with human rights in Europe: the Council of Europe, the EU, and the Organization for Security and Co-operation in Europe (OSCE).

1) The Council of Europe

The Council of Europe human rights system is the oldest, most developed, and arguably most effective of all supranational human rights systems. Established in 1953, the Council of Europe is an international organization based in Strasbourg, France and composed of forty-five member states. All Council of Europe member states are parties to the

---

satory Damages (1989), I/A Court HR Series C no. 8, and (iv) *Interpretation of the Compensatory Damages Judgment* (1990) I/A Court HR Series C no. 10; and
c) the *Fairén Garbi and Solís Corrales Case*, including (i) *Preliminary Objections* (1987) I/A Court HR Series C no. 2, and (ii) *Judgment* (1989) I/A Court HR Series C no. 6.

66 See the discussion in Chapter Twelve.

67 *Advisory Opinion OC-9/87* (1987) I/A Court HR Series A no. 9. The opinion was requested by the Inter-American Commission on Human Rights.

68 *Advisory Opinion OC-3/83* (1983) I/A Court HR Series A no. 3.

69 "The Street Children Case" (Villagrán Morales et al. v. Guatemala), including (i) *Preliminary Objections* (1997), I/A Court HR Series C no. 32, (ii) *Judgment* (1999), I/A Court HR Series C no. 63, and (iii) *Reparations* (2001), I/A Court HR Series C no. 77.

ECHR. Today accession to the ECHR is a condition of membership of the Council.[70] The Council of Europe comprises two main bodies: the Committee of Ministers and the Parliamentary Assembly. The Committee of Ministers is the Council's primary decision-making body. It is composed of the foreign affairs ministers of all Council of Europe member states or their permanent diplomatic representatives in Strasbourg. The Parliamentary Assembly is composed of parliamentary representatives of all Council member states, each elected or appointed by national parliaments. The Canadian government has maintained observer status before the Committee of Ministers since May 1996, and before the Parliamentary Assembly since May 1997.[71] Both the Parliamentary Assembly and the Committee of Ministers play a role in the enforcement of human rights. However, the primary mechanism for the promotion and protection of human rights within the Council of Europe system is the European Court of Human Rights.

a) The European Court of Human Rights
Until November 1998, the Council of Europe human rights system maintained a human rights commission and court; today there is only a court.[72] The European Court of Human Rights is currently the only supranational human rights tribunal in the world that permits individuals to make direct claims against member states. In contrast to the Inter-American Court, the jurisdiction of the European Court is compulsory for all ECHR states parties. The Court's one hundred judges are elected for renewable six-year terms from a list of nominees submitted by ECHR states parties. Nominees do not need to be nationals of a Council of Europe member state.[73] Unlike the Inter-American Court, the European Court of Human Rights sits on a permanent rather than part-time basis. The Court is divided into a trial chamber ("Chambers") and an appeals chamber ("Grand Chamber"). The Court has jurisdic-

---

70 Non-member states of the Council of Europe, such as Canada, may not accede to the ECHR.

71 Only a handful of other states have observer status to either of these bodies, including the US, Mexico, Israel, Japan, and the Vatican.

72 See ECHR Protocol No. 11 (1994) ETS No. 155, which replaced the European Commission and Court of Human Rights with the new European Court of Human Rights. When it existed, the European Commission of Human Rights received inter-state and individual petitions. See generally N. Bratza & M. O'Boyle, "The Legacy of the Commission to the New Court under the Eleventh Protocol," in M. de Salvia & M. Villiger, eds., *The Birth of European Human Rights Law: Essays in Honour of Carl Aage Norgaard* (Baden-Baden: Nomos, 1998).

73 R. St. J. Macdonald, a Canadian, served for many years as a judge on the former European Court of Human Rights following his nomination by Liechtenstein.

tion over all aspects of a case, including admissibility, fact-finding, and decisions on the merits. Like other supranational courts, it exercises both contentious and advisory jurisdiction. By most accounts, its jurisprudence has had a powerful influence on European states.[74]

Both individuals and states have the right to bring contentious cases before the Court. In inter-state cases the applicant state does not need to have a relationship to the actual victim of the violation to bring the case. The only admissibility requirement for such cases is exhaustion of domestic remedies.[75] States parties rarely invoke the inter-state complaint mechanism.[76]

In petitions brought by private parties against states,[77] ECHR article 34 provides that the Court may receive petitions from "any person, non-governmental organization or group of individuals," including legal persons, claiming to be a victim of a violation by an ECHR state party. An individual need not file claims against the state of his or her nationality; claims can be made against any ECHR state party. Thus, a national of state A can file an application against state B if the latter was the state responsible for the alleged violation. The admissibility requirements for bringing a case before the Court are virtually the same as those for UN treaty bodies.[78]

Once a claim is deemed admissible, it is the responsibility of the Court to "pursue the examination of the case," including if necessary by investigation.[79] If a friendly settlement is reached, the Court must issue a decision setting out the facts and the solution reached in order to facilitate the Committee of Ministers' enforcement of the settlement.[80] Fail-

---

74 See generally R. Blackburn, ed., *The European Convention on Human Rights: The Impact of the European Convention on Human Rights on Human Rights in the Legal and Political Systems of Member States* (London: Mansell, 1996).

75 See ECHR art. 35. In *Akdivar v. Turkey* (1996), 23 EHRR 413 at para. 69, the Court held that in the context of human rights proceedings the rule of exhaustion of domestic remedies must be enforced "with some degree of flexibility and without excessive formalism."

76 During the time of the European Commission of Human Rights, ECHR states parties had the option of denying their nationals a right of private petition before the Court. The inter-state proceedings were therefore the only way to hold some states to account within the ECHR system. Today, however, the right of private petition is no longer optional for ECHR states parties. See generally S. Prebensen, "Inter-State Complaints under Treaty Provisions: The Experience Under the European Convention on Human Rights" (1999) 20 Human Rights Law Journal 44.

77 There is no right of petition of one private individual against another.

78 See ECHR art. 35.

79 *Ibid.*, art. 38(1).

80 *Ibid.*, art. 39.

ing a friendly settlement, a hearing may be held. The hearing must be held in public, other than in "exceptional circumstances."[81] Decisions of Chambers may be appealed to the Grand Chamber at its discretion within three months of judgment, but only if the case involves "a serious question affecting the interpretation or application of the Convention or the protocols thereto, or a serious issue of general importance" (article 43(2)).

While there is no rule of *stare decisis* (binding precedent) applicable to the judgments of the European Court of Human Rights,[82] the Court nevertheless tends to follow its own case law. The largest share of cases has involved claims arising under ECHR articles 5 (right to liberty and security of the person) and 6 (right to a fair hearing). Upon a finding of violation, the Court may afford "just satisfaction" (article 41) to the injured party. This may include a declaration or finding of breach (a moral remedy) or compensation for pecuniary and non-pecuniary harm (a material remedy). The Court cannot reverse national judicial decisions or annul national laws but it can declare a national law in conflict with the ECHR and call for the adoption of new legislation. In deciding whether there has been a violation at all, the Court allows states parties a "margin of appreciation" (that is, a degree of deference to local standards and approaches).[83]

Concerning its advisory jurisdiction, only the Committee of Ministers may request advisory opinions from the Court. Such opinions may not deal with

> any question relating to the content or scope of the rights or freedoms defined in Section I of the Convention and the protocols thereto, or with any other question which the European Court of Human Rights or the Committee of Ministers might have to consider in consequence of any such proceedings as could be instituted in accordance with the Convention.[84]

Although the Court lacks a formal mechanism for enforcement of its decisions, to date the record of compliance with its judgments has been exemplary.[85] In the event of non-compliance with a judgment of

---

81 *Ibid.*, art. 40(1).
82 Like the International Court of Justice, the decisions of the European Court of Human Rights are only binding on the parties to the litigation.
83 See the discussion of this concept in Chapter Two.
84 ECHR art. 47(1)–(2).
85 See generally R. Blackburn & J. Polakiewicz, *Fundamental Rights in Europe: The European Convention on Human Rights and its Member States, 1950–2000* (Oxford: Oxford University Press, 2001).

the Court, the matter goes onto the agenda of the Committee of Ministers within six months. The Parliamentary Assembly assists with the enforcement of judgments via its Assembly Monitoring Committee, which may adopt adverse resolutions and remove a state delegation's credentials.

The current challenge for the Court is dealing with the backlog of cases that resulted from the enormous expansion in its caseload following the adoption of ECHR Protocol 11 which, as noted above, replaced the prior commission and court with the new permanent European Court of Human Rights.[86] The Court receives more than 30,000 petitions every year, almost half of which indicate a *prima facie* case. Although the Court manages to render hundreds of final judgments each year, and thousands of decisions on admissibility, the situation is not sustainable. As a consequence, the Committee of Ministers established a Steering Committee for Human Rights to propose changes. It recommended urgent reforms that were quickly endorsed by the Committee of Ministers.[87]

b) The European Committee of Social Rights

Because it only examines cases involving violations of the ECHR and its protocols, the European Court of Human Rights does not have jurisdiction over violations of economic and social rights. Instead, the EurSC, the primary Council of Europe treaty dealing with economic, social and cultural rights, established a separate supervisory body, the European Committee of Social Rights.[88] It consists of thirteen independent experts elected by the Committee of Ministers for renewable terms of six years.[89]

---

86 The Court's caseload expanded by 900% between 1998 and 2000 alone. See "Effectiveness of European Human Rights Court in grave danger, Evaluation Group Chairman warns," Council of Europe Press Release, 10 October 2001.

87 See the Committee of Ministers' "Declaration on Guaranteeing the long-term effectiveness of the European Court of Human Rights," adopted at its 112th session on 15 May 2003. The Declaration calls for an amending protocol to the ECHR and other relevant human rights instruments to implement the recommended reforms. The Steering Committee's final report was adopted on 4 April 2003, and is registered as CM doc. 2003/55.

88 The fact that Council of Europe member states were not prepared to make economic and social rights justiciable before the European Court of Human Rights is further evidence of the hierarchy between civil and political rights on the one hand, and economic and social rights on the other.

89 On the work of the Committee generally, see D. Harris, "Lessons from the Reporting System of the European Social Charter," in P. Alston & J. Crawford, eds., *The Future of UN Human Rights Treaty Monitoring* (Cambridge: Cambridge University Press, 2000).

The Committee oversees a state party reporting procedure and, since the entry into force of the Additional Protocol Providing for a System of Collective Complaints 1995,[90] a "collective complaints" procedure. Every two years, states parties to the EurSC and its protocols must submit a report on their performance. The Committee then publishes its own "conclusions."[91] If the concerned state fails to address any matter covered in the Committee's conclusions, the Committee of Ministers may issue a "recommendation" to that state calling upon it to do so. The Committee of Ministers' work is prepared by a "Governmental Committee" comprising representatives of the states parties to the EurSC and its protocols, assisted by observers representing European employers' and workers' organizations.

In the collective complaints procedure, certain organizations — notably eligible NGOs and employers' and workers' organizations — are permitted to file complaints with the Committee.[92] Once a complaint has been deemed admissible, there follows an exchange of memorials between the parties, followed by a possible public hearing. Decisions on the merits are communicated to the parties and to the Committee of Ministers, which may ultimately recommend specific measures to remedy any proven violation. The Parliamentary Assembly also receives the decision and makes it public.

c) Other Council of Europe Mechanisms

Since May 1999, the Council of Europe has had a Commissioner for Human Rights.[93] The Commissioner is elected by the Parliamentary Assembly for a non-renewable six-year term.[94] The Commissioner's responsibilities are largely promotional in nature and aimed especially at the prevention of violations.[95] While the Commissioner has authority to conduct investigations, he cannot respond to petitions from individuals or groups. Investigations are generally carried out by means of

---

90   ETS no. 158.
91   Under EurSC art. 26, an ILO representative participates in the Committee's deliberations.
92   Article 1 of the 1995 Protocol, above note 90.
93   http://www.coe.int/T/E/Commissioner_H.R.
94   Alvaro Gil-Robles was appointed the first Commissioner. His term will expire in 2005.
95   The Committee of Ministers established the mandate of the Commissioner for Human Rights by Resolution 99/50 (1999). The Resolution authorizes the Commissioner to carry out human rights education, identify examples of non-compliance among Council of Europe member states, and generally promote greater human rights observance.

official visits to Council of Europe member states, whether by invitation or at the Commissioner's own initiative. Following a visit, the Commissioner prepares a report containing conclusions and recommendations. The report is submitted to the Committee of Ministers and the Parliamentary Assembly and ultimately made public.

The European Commission against Racism and Intolerance, in operation since 1993, is responsible for examining and making recommendations concerning laws and policies of Council of Europe member states with a view to reducing racism and intolerance. The Commission conducts detailed studies of country situations. It then confidentially forwards the studies for comment to the concerned member state, before ultimately submitting a final report to it through the Committee of Ministers. The Commission completes about a dozen country reports each year.

The European Commission for Democracy through Law (better known as the Venice Commission) is composed of independent constitutional experts elected for four-year renewable terms. The Commission's initial purpose was to provide constitutional assistance to newly-democratic states of the former Soviet Union and Eastern Europe. Its focus was on the consolidation of democracy, human rights, and the rule of law in those states, with a special emphasis on minority rights. The Commission's revised statute has continued and expanded that mandate.[96] Canada has observer status before the Commission.

In addition to the three aforementioned commissions, there are several treaty-specific mechanisms within the Council of Europe human rights system.

There is a committee of experts responsible for supervising adherence to the European Charter for Regional or Minority Languages 1992.[97] States parties are required to submit periodic reports to the

---

96 Revised Statute of the European Commission for Democracy through Law 2002, adopted by the Committee of Ministers on 21 February 2002 at the 784th meeting of the Ministers' Deputies. Article 1 provides:

> The European Commission for Democracy through Law shall be an independent consultative body which co-operates with the member states of the Council of Europe, as well as with interested non-member states and interested international organisations and bodies. Its own specific field of action shall be the guarantees offered by law in the service of democracy. It shall fulfil the following objectives: strengthening the understanding of the legal systems of the participating states, notably with a view to bringing these systems closer; promoting the rule of law and democracy; examining the problems raised by the working of democratic institutions and their reinforcement and development.

97 ETS no. 148.

committee. National groups or associations may also provide information or comments on state performance. Following a country review, the committee provides a report to the Committee of Ministers, which may then make recommendations to the concerned state.

The Framework Convention for the Protection of National Minorities 1995[98] establishes a similar oversight procedure. States parties to the Framework Convention are required to file periodic reports to the Committee of Ministers, which is assisted by a special Advisory Committee.[99] This committee then prepares its views on the country reports and forwards them to the Committee of Ministers. The latter then issues its conclusions and recommendations. The Committee of Ministers makes all of the state reports and its own conclusions and recommendations public.

The European Committee for the Prevention of Torture and Inhuman or Degrading Treatment or Punishment is responsible for ensuring compliance with the European Convention for the Prevention of Torture and Inhuman or Degrading Treatment or Punishment 1987.[100] The Committee is composed of independent experts, and has authority to conduct in-country investigations, visit detention centres, and make recommendations to states.[101] Although it generally operates on a confidential basis, the Committee will make a matter public in cases of non-co-operation or refusal to implement its recommendations.

Finally, the Convention for the Protection of Human Rights and Dignity of the Human Being with regard to the Application of Biology and Medicine 1997[102] designated the Steering Committee on Bioethics, a body previously established by the Committee of Ministers, to oversee implementation of the Convention. Any of the Steering Committeee on Bioethics, the Committee of Ministers, or states parties may request the European Court of Human Rights to give an advisory opinion on legal issues related to the interpretation of the Convention.

---

98 ETS no. 157.
99 Framework Convention, *ibid.*, arts. 25–26.
100 See generally M. Evans & R. Morgan, *Preventing Torture: A Study of the European Convention for the Prevention of Torture and Inhuman or Degrading Treatment or Punishment* (New York: Oxford University Press, 1998).
101 But note art. 17(3), which precludes the Committee from visiting places "which representatives or delegates of Protecting Powers or the International Committee of the Red Cross effectively visit on a regular basis . . . ."
102 ETS no. 164.

2) The European Union and the European Court of Justice

The European Union (EU) is composed of five main institutions: the European Parliament, the Council of Ministers, the European Commission, the Court of Auditors, and the European Court of Justice. There is also a European Ombudsman to handle complaints regarding EU institutions and a European Initiative for Democracy and Human Rights to promote and fund human rights and democratic programs in foreign states.

The European Court of Justice, which sits in Luxembourg, is the highest judicial body within the EU on questions of EU law. The Court is divided into a Chamber and Grand Chamber, each exercising contentious and advisory jurisdiction. Individuals may bring actions against EU member states or against EU institutions for violations of EU law. EU law contains a number of human rights-like entitlements including freedom of movement, non-discrimination, and voting rights. These have been the subject of much jurisprudence.[103]

The European Court of Justice has consistently held that EU law includes fundamental rights within the "general principles of law" that are part of its subject-matter jurisdiction. The Court relies on the ECHR in determining the content of those rights.[104]

3) The Organization for Security and Cooperation in Europe[105]

The OSCE is not, strictly speaking, a European organization. Although it is dominated by European states and works closely with the Council of Europe, Canada and a few other non-European states have been members since its establishment under the Helsinki Final Act 1975.[106]

---

103 See, for example, *Groener v. Minister for Education*, [1989] ECR 3967, in which the European Court of Justice dealt with the question of language-based discrimination. See also *Al-Jubail Fertilizer Co. v. Council*, [1991] ECR I-3187, in which the Court found an implicit obligation to ensure a fair hearing.

104 See *Hauer v. Land Rheinland-Pfalz*, [1979] ECR 3727. On the EU and human rights generally, see P. Alston, ed., *The EU and Human Rights* (Oxford: Oxford University Press, 1999); N. Neuwahl & A. Rosas, eds. *The European Union and Human Rights* (The Hague: Martinus Nijhoff, 1995).

105 The OSCE was originally called the Conference on Security and Co-operation in Europe. In 1994, it adopted its current name.

106 (1975) 14 ILM 1292.

Despite the end of the Cold War (its original reason for being), the OSCE remains an important human rights institution.[107]

The contemporary "OSCE process" consists of regular intergovernmental conferences among participating states. At these conferences the human rights performance of OSCE members is assessed, and new human rights norms are introduced in a so-called "concluding document" adopted by consensus at the conference's end. There is also what is known as the "Human Rights Dimension Mechanism," a procedure consisting of inter-state negotiations, mediation, and fact-finding generally on human rights matters. The procedure operates as follows: one state makes a claim against another state; a diplomatic exchange follows; if no resolution is achieved, the matter moves to the OSCE general agenda for follow-up efforts; if these efforts fail, then an independent investigator can be appointed to investigate alleged violations.

A key OSCE human rights mechanism is the Office for Democratic Institutions and Human Rights. The Office's mandate — to strengthen democracy and human rights in OSCE member states — is defined in the Helsinki Document 1992.[108] The Office is based in Warsaw and comprises over one hundred staff members. It focuses particular attention on assisting the Roma and Sinti communities of Europe.[109]

There is also an OSCE High Commissioner for National Minorities, who responds to allegations of violations against minorities. Established in 1992, the High Commissioner mediates between minority groups and OSCE member states. The objective is to provide for early warning and prompt action to protect minority groups.[110]

In 1997, the OSCE created the Vienna-based office of the Representative on Freedom of the Media to focus on "obstruction of media activities and unfavourable working conditions for journalists."[111] The Representative acts as an advocate on freedom of expression and the right to a free press, providing early warning on violations. It publishes selected country assessments each year, and reports directly to the OSCE Permanent Council.[112]

---

107 The OSCE played a significant role in the transition from communism to democracy in the former Soviet bloc. See D. Thomas, *The Helsinki Effect: International Norms, Human Rights, and the Demise of Communism* (Princeton: Princeton University Press, 2001). Remarkably, the OSCE did not even have a permanent secretariat until 1990.

108 See http://www.htmh.hu/dokumentumok/helsinki.htm.

109 See http://www.osce.org/odihr.

110 See http://www.osce.org/hcnm.

111 See the Mandate of the OSCE Representative on Freedom of the Media (5 November 1997), PC Journal No. 137, Decision No. 193, para. 2.

112 See generally http://www.osce.org/fom.

C. THE AFRICAN UNION

In July 2002, the Organization of African Unity (OAU) became the African Union (AU), a change that was intended to symbolize a new and more EU-like approach for the organization.[113] Unlike the OAU, the new AU allows for so-called "peer reviews" of a member state's record, as well as sanctions and intervention in case of widespread atrocities.[114] The AU is still in formation. Ultimately it will be composed of a Commission (a permanent secretariat), a Pan-African Parliament, an Assembly of Heads of States and Government, an Executive Council of Ministers of Foreign Affairs, and a Court of Justice. Most of these bodies will be established and defined under separate protocols. Few such protocols have been adopted to date.

1) The Future African Court on Human and Peoples' Rights

In 1998, the Protocol to the African Charter on Human and Peoples' Rights on the Establishment of an African Court on Human and Peoples' Rights 1998 was adopted.[115] The Protocol requires fifteen ratifications before it can come into force.[116] The models for the proposed African Court are the European Court of Human Rights and the Inter-American Court of Human Rights. The Court will be composed of eleven judges serving for a maximum of two six-year terms.[117] It will exercise contentious and advisory jurisdiction. In contentious cases, only the African Commission on Human and Peoples' Rights, states parties, and "African Intergovernmental Organizations" will have the right to submit cases.[118] NGOs with observer status before the Commission will also be able to submit cases, provided their state has made an appropriate enabling declaration upon becoming a party to the Protocol.[119] The Court will be able to make declaratory judgments and order compensa-

---

113 See C. Packer & D. Rukare, "The New African Union and its Constitutive Act" (2002) 96 AJIL 365 at 367.

114 Constitutive Act of the African Union 2000, art. 4(h).

115 The Protocol was adopted at its 19th Ordinary Session on 9 July 1998. For a critical assessment of the planned Court, see M. Mutua, "The African Human Rights Court: A Two-Legged Stool?" (1999) 21 Human Rights Quarterly 342.

116 Article 34(3). There are currently five states parties to the Protocol.

117 The Protocol calls for fair gender representation in the nomination and election of judges (art. 12(2)).

118 Article 5(1).

119 Articles 5(3) and 34(6).

tion and reparation.[120] It will also be authorized to issue provisional measures in cases of "extreme gravity and urgency."[121] Judgments will be binding and final since there will be no appeals chamber.[122] The AU Council of Ministers will enforce the Court's judgments.[123] In advisory cases, only AU organs, AU member states, and African organizations recognized by the AU will have the authority to request such opinions.[124] The African Court will be able to render advisory opinions

> on any legal matter relating to the [AfrCHPR] or any other relevant human rights instruments, provided that the subject matter of the opinion is not related to a matter being examined by the [African Commission on Human and Peoples' Rights].[125]

The Court's relationship to the African Commission on Human and Peoples' Rights will be much like the relationship between the Inter-American Commission on Human Rights and the Inter-American Court of Human Rights.

2) The African Commission on Human and Peoples' Rights

In the absence of the Court, the African Commission on Human and Peoples' Rights remains the principal human rights body in the AU system.[126] Established in 1987 and based in Banjul, The Gambia, the Commission is composed of eleven members elected to six-year terms and serving in their personal capacities. Like its counterpart in the Americas, the African Commission has adopted its own Rules of Procedure.[127] It is in session only twice a year and lacks sufficient funding and staff.[128]

---

120 Article 27(1).
121 Article 27(2).
122 Article 28(2).
123 Article 31.
124 Article 4(1).
125 Article 4(1).
126 On the African Commission on Human and Peoples' Rights generally, see M. Evans & R. Murray, eds., *The African Charter on Human and Peoples' Rights: The System in Practice, 1986–2000* (Cambridge: Cambridge University Press, 2002). Note that some Canadian NGOs, including Human Rights Internet and Rights & Democracy, have observer status before the Commission.
127 The Commission adopted its most current Rules on 6 October 1995.
128 See Fifteenth Annual Activity Report of the African Commission on Human and Peoples' Rights (2001–2002). The Report notes at paras. 49–56 that the Commission continues to solicit international financial assistance to make up for the "limited resources allocated by the OAU."

The Commission has a very broad promotional mandate. Article 45(1)(a) of the African Charter on Human and Peoples' Rights 1981 (AfrCHPR) includes the following among the functions of the Commission:

> to collect documents, undertake studies and researches on African problems in the field of human and peoples' rights, organize seminars, symposia and conferences, disseminate information, encourage national and local institutions concerned with human and peoples' rights, and should the case arise, give its views or make recommendations to Governments. . . .

In fulfilment of this promotional mandate, the Commission grants "affiliated status" to national human rights commissions or institutions that conform to the Principles relating to the Status of National Institutions (also known as the Paris Principles) adopted in 1993 by the UN General Assembly.[129] Affiliated status entitles national institutions to be invited to sessions of the Commission, to participate without voting rights in Commission deliberations, and to submit proposals which may be put to vote at the request of any Commission member.[130]

The Commission also has jurisdiction to review bi-annual reports submitted by states (AfrCHPR article 62). The examination of reports takes place in a public forum, and only the Commission can put questions to the state. The procedure, which is modelled on the UN treaty body reporting process, suffers from chronic delays in the submission of reports and grudging co-operation by states. About half of all states parties to the AfrCHPR have failed to submit any report at all since 1991 when the procedure was established.[131]

The Commission has jurisdiction to handle both inter-state complaints (AfrCHPR articles 47–54) and individual complaints (AfrCHPR articles 55–56). The inter-state procedure has been invoked only once.[132] Like its regional equivalents, the African inter-state complaints procedure begins when one state delivers a complaint to another state,

---

129 UN doc. A/RES/48/134 (1993).

130 See the Commission's Resolution on Granting Observer Status to National Human Rights Institutions in Africa, adopted on 31 October 1998 in Banjul.

131 See the Commission's website (http://www.achpr.org/Status_of_States_Reports_33rd_OS__Eng_.doc).

132 See *Democratic Republic of Congo v. Burundi, Rwanda and Uganda* (1999), Comm. no. 227/99. In 2002, the Commission planned to hold an "Extra-Ordinary Session" to seek to resolve the matter, but it was not possible due to lack of funds. See Fifteenth Annual Activity Report of the African Commission on Human and Peoples' Rights (2001–2002) at paras. 42–43.

with a copy to the AU Secretary-General and the Commission. If the matter is not resolved within three months, then the Commission may privately investigate the matter and receive further submissions from each state, before ultimately preparing a report for delivery to the states involved and to the AU Assembly.[133]

The Commission's individual complaints procedure differs from its UN and Inter-American equivalents. On paper, it does not resemble an individual petition procedure at all, but rather something more like the Commission on Human Rights' 1503 Procedure described in Chapter Fourteen. Article 58(1) of the AfrCHPR provides that the Commission can only act upon "special cases which reveal the existence of a series of serious or massive violations of human and peoples' rights," suggesting that a single human rights violation is not enough to trigger the Commission's jurisdiction. In practice the Commission has tended to ignore this language. It has relied on AfrCHPR article 55(2) to justify its consideration of petitions that do not meet the "special case" test.[134]

The Commission can receive communications from individuals and from NGOs with observer status. The Commission will examine complaints regarding violations of any AfrCHPR right. Its rules of admissibility resemble those of UN treaty bodies and other regional equivalents.[135] Upon certifying a complaint as admissible, the Commission will seek an amicable resolution of the matter, failing which it will provide a report of its findings and recommendations to the AU Assembly. There is a requirement of confidentiality throughout the proceedings up until the time the Commission completes its conclusions and recommendations. Officially, decisions of the Commission are to remain confidential until the AU Assembly decides otherwise.[136] However, the Commission now regularly publishes its findings. To date, the Commission has rendered a handful of significant decisions. These have concerned issues such as the

---

133 Although the Commission's report is supposed to be confidential, Rule 77 of the Commission's Rules of Procedure provides that the Chairman must publish the report following its delivery to the AU Assembly unless the latter affirmatively requests otherwise.

134 AfrCHPR art. 55(2) provides: "A communication shall be considered by the Commission if a simple majority of its members so decide."

135 But note that the AfrCHPR establishes more victim-friendly criteria in respect of the rule on prior exhaustion of domestic remedies. AfrCHPR art. 50 provides that all domestic remedies must have been exhausted "unless it is obvious to the Commission that the procedure of achieving these remedies would be unduly prolonged."

136 AfrCHPR art. 59.

criteria for a fair trial,[137] the right to self-determination,[138] and the right to a generally satisfactory environment.[139]

The Commission can also issue something close to advisory opinions on AfrCHPR norms. Specifically, AfrCHPR article 45(3) lists as one of the Commission's functions to "[i]nterpret all the provisions of the present Charter at the request of a State party, an institution of the OAU or an African Organization recognized by the OAU . . . ."

The Commission also has a unique quasi-legislative function. Article 45(1)(b) authorizes it to "formulate and lay down, principles and rules aimed at solving legal problems relating to human and peoples' rights and fundamental freedoms upon which African Governments may base their legislation."

Under AfrCHPR articles 60 and 61, the Commission is permitted to rely on a uniquely broad range of sources in carrying out its tasks, including all significant human rights instruments adopted by the UN and by the AU and, as "subsidiary measures," any relevant African human rights practices.

---

137 See, for example, *Forum of Conscience v. Sierra Leone* (2000), Comm. no. 223/98. The complaint was submitted by a Sierra Leonean NGO on behalf of twenty-four soldiers who were sentenced to death by a court martial and later executed for their alleged roles in a coup d'etat. The complaint alleged, and the Commission agreed, that (i) the Court Martial that tried and convicted the victims breached AfrCHPR art. 7(1) because it allowed no right of appeal against conviction or sentence, and (ii) the execution constituted arbitrary deprivation of life within the meaning of AfrCHPR art. 4.

138 See, for example, *Katangese Peoples' Congress v. Zaire* (1995), Comm. no. 75/92. The complainant sought recognition of the Katangese Peoples' Congress as a liberation movement, but failed to allege any violations. Nevertheless, the Commission noted at para. 4 that

> self-determination may be exercised in any of the following ways: independence, self-government, local government, federalism, confederalism, unitarism or any other form of relations that accords with the wishes of the people but fully cognisant of other recognised principles such as sovereignty and territorial integrity.

139 *Social and Economic Rights Action Center/Center for Economic and Social Rights v. Nigeria* (2002), Comm. no. 155/96. The complaint was filed by two NGOs on behalf of the people of Ogoniland, Nigeria. The Commission held that environmental degradation is a violation of the AfrCHPR, and also one that leads to the violation of other rights. Nigeria was found in breach of AfrCHPR arts. 2, 4, 14, 16, 18(1), 21, and 24. See generally D. Shelton, "Decision Regarding Comm. 155/96 (*Social and Economic Rights Action Center/Center for Economic and Social Rights v. Nigeria*)" (2002) 96 AJIL 937.

Overall, the African Commission on Human and Peoples' Rights — and the AU human rights system as a whole — is notably weaker than its UN and regional equivalents. Yet the Commission is gradually becoming more effective. Among other things, it has begun to undertake fact-finding missions to countries in which there are systematic violations, and to appoint special rapporteurs on key topics including prisons and conditions of detention, arbitrary and summary executions, and the rights of women.

3) The Committee of Experts on the Rights and Welfare of the Child

Article 32 of the African Charter on the Rights and Welfare of the Child 1990[140] establishes an African Committee of Experts on the Rights and Welfare of the Child. The Committee, which has only recently begun work, consists of eleven independent expert members elected by states parties. States parties are required to provide reports to the Committee every three years concerning their implementation of the treaty (article 43). Individuals, groups, and recognized NGOs may submit confidential communications to the Committee for its consideration (article 44), and the Committee may investigate using "appropriate" methods (article 45).

---

140 OAU doc. CAB/LEG/24.9/49 (1990).

CHAPTER 16

OTHER MULTILATERAL MECHANISMS

The UN and regional human rights mechanisms described in Chapters Fourteen and Fifteen are not the only multilateral human rights mechanisms of note. We consider the others in this chapter. Many predate the UN, including the International Committee of the Red Cross and the Commonwealth. Others are of more recent vintage, such as the Francophonie and the NAFTA-related Commission for Labour Cooperation. Still others are part of the UN network of institutions, focusing on separate, if related, areas of international law. These include the International Labour Organization (ILO) and the Office of the UN High Commissioner for Refugees. All of these bodies complement the work of the mechanisms discussed in prior chapters.

A. INTERNATIONAL LABOUR LAW MECHANISMS

The ILO operates a range of unique mechanisms for the protection of labour rights. The labour protection mechanisms established under the North American Agreement on Labour Cooperation 1993 (NAALC)[1] are also of relevance to Canada. Each is examined below.[2]

---

1   [1994] CanTS no. 4.
2   Not discussed here is the Administrative Tribunal of the ILO. It has been in operation since 1949 and is responsible for appeals by UN employees regarding workplace violations such as discrimination and sexual harassment.

1) ILO Mechanisms

The ILO is a Geneva-based[3] specialized agency of the UN for the promotion and protection of international labour rights and standards.[4] There are currently 177 member states, including Canada. The ILO consists of three main bodies: the International Labour Conference, the Governing Body, and the International Labour Office. The International Labour Conference is composed of all ILO member states and holds an annual meeting in Geneva each June to adopt new international labour norms and discuss the major international labour concerns of the day. The Governing Body takes decisions on core ILO policy, elects the ILO Director-General every five years, and prepares the programme and the budget for subsequent adoption by the Conference.[5] The International Labour Office is the ILO's permanent secretariat consisting of almost 2,000 employees. Each of these bodies incorporates the unique ILO tripartite structure, which features direct representation and participation by governments, national employers' organizations, and national workers' organizations.[6] The ILO also operates dozens of field presences or "multi-disciplinary advisory teams" in the developing world to advise governments and civil society on the implementation of ILO standards.

All ILO member states must submit reports to the International Labour Office every two years regarding the measures they have taken to give effect to the treaties to which they are party.[7] The Governing Body may also request ILO member states to report periodically on law and practice concerning ILO conventions to which they are not a party. Member states must send copies of these reports to their domestic work-

---

3   During the Second World War, the ILO temporarily relocated to McGill University in Montreal before ultimately returning to Geneva in 1948.

4   On the ILO, labour rights, and human rights generally, see H. B. de la Cruz *et al.*, *The International Labor Organization: The International Standards System and Basic Human Rights* (Boulder, Colorado: Westview Press, 1999).

5   The Governing Body is composed of twenty-eight member states, ten of which are permanent and unelected and the rest elected for three-year terms. The ten permanent seats are held by "states of chief industrial importance." Canada is one.

6   In the case of Canada, because labour matters fall under both federal and provincial jurisdictions, provincial governmental officials are usually included in official Canadian ILO delegations. Regarding employer and worker representation, the main Canadian participants are the Canadian Employers Council, the Canadian Labour Congress, and the Confédération des syndicats nationaux.

7   Article 22 of the ILO Constitution 1946 [1946] CanTS no. 48. The ILO Constitution has undergone numerous amendments, the most recent being in 1997.

ers' and employers' organizations.[8] The submitted reports are reviewed by the Committee of Experts on the Application of Conventions and Recommendations (CEACR), a body composed of twenty elected experts who meet annually for the purpose of examining state reports.[9] The CEACR may follow up state reports with direct requests to governments and to national employers' and workers' organizations to clarify general concerns and request changes in domestic law and practice. If there are very serious concerns about rights violations, the CEACR can issue observations to the state in question. These are published in an annual report to the Conference and submitted to the Governing Body.

The ILO Conference Committee on the Application of Conventions and Recommendations (CCACR) — a standing tripartite committee of the ILO Conference — can follow up on the observations made by the CEACR. It can ask the concerned government to appear before it and answer questions.[10] The CCACR may also raise individual

---

8   ILO Constitution, *ibid.*, art. 23.

9   The CEACR reports on Canada's performance can be found on the ILO website at http://www.ilo.org/ilolex/cgi-lex/countrylist.pl?country=Canada. In its most recent report, the CEACR focused on provincial laws and policies that deny freedom of association to certain categories of workers, particularly those in essential services. CEACR, *Observation Concerning Convention No. 87: Canada* (2003).

10   CCACR reports on Canada's performance can be found on the ILO website. In its most recent report, *Examination of individual case concerning Convention No. 87: Canada* (1999), the CCACR noted the following in its summary:

> [T]he Committee observed that for a number of years the Committee of Experts and the Committee on Freedom of Association had been making comments on a number of issues relating to the application of the Convention. These issues included the excessive restrictions on the right of workers' organizations to formulate their programmes without undue interference from the public authorities resulting from federal and/or provincial legislation. The Committee further noted that labour relations legislation in some Provinces (Alberta, New Brunswick, Ontario) excluded a number of workers from their coverage, including workers in agriculture and horticulture or domestic workers, thereby denying them the protection provided with regard to the right to organize and to negotiate collectively. The present Committee, like the Committee of Experts, stressed that the guarantees provided under the Convention applied to all workers without distinction whatsoever, and that all workers should enjoy the right to establish and join organizations of their own choosing to further and defend their occupational interests. The Committee further stressed that workers' organizations should enjoy the right to formulate their programmes without interference from the public authorities. The Committee expressed the firm hope that the Government would supply a detailed report to the Committee of Experts on the concrete measures taken to bring its legislation and practice into full conformity with the Convention.

cases for debate during the annual Conference. The CCACR must ultimately submit a final report to the Conference. There is a high rate of state reporting under these procedures. Compliance with recommendations of the CEACR and the CCACR is generally very high.[11]

The ILO also operates several complaint procedures. Pursuant to article 24 of the ILO Constitution, employers' and workers' organizations can submit complaints to the Governing Body alleging that a member state has breached its obligations under any ILO convention to which it is a party or under any of the ILO "fundamental conventions" (whether or not it is a party).[12] The Governing Body may then appoint a special tripartite committee to assess the substance of the complaint. The committee ultimately submits a report to the Governing Body, which may publish the complaint, the government's response, and its own analysis.

A second procedure deals with inter-state complaints. Pursuant to article 26 of the ILO Constitution, ILO member states may submit complaints to the International Labour Office regarding alleged violations by another ILO member state concerning an ILO convention to which each is party.[13] The Governing Body may then appoint an independent Commission of Inquiry to examine the matter, a procedure that usually involves hearings in Geneva as well as in-country investigation. The Commission of Inquiry will ultimately prepare a report containing conclusions and recommendations, which is to be submitted to the Governing Body and published.[14] The government in question may accept the recommendations or appeal the matter to the International Court of Justice, whose decision is final. Decisions of a Commission of Inquiry are not subject to appeal by an ILO body.[15] Article 26 procedures are invoked only in cases of persistent and serious violations of international labour standards or repeated refusal by an ILO member state to comply with recommendations of any of the ILO's supervisory mechanisms.

---

11 J. Donnelly, *Universal Human Rights in Theory and Practice*, 2d ed. (Ithaca: Cornell University Press, 2003) at 146–47.
12 See the discussion of the ILO's fundamental conventions in Chapter Seven.
13 Article 26 complaints may also be submitted by the Governing Body itself or by any delegate to the ILO Conference.
14 See, for example, the July 1998 Report of the Commission of Inquiry appointed under ILO Constitution art. 26 to examine the observance by Myanmar of the Forced Labour Convention (No. 29) 1930. Available at http://www.ilo.org/public/english/standards/relm/gb/docs/gb273/myanmar.htm.
15 ILO Constitution, above note 7, arts. 26–29 and 31–34.

Because of the particular importance attached by the ILO to the right of freedom of association, two supervisory bodies exist to ensure compliance with it. These are the Fact-Finding and Conciliation Commission on Freedom of Association (FFCCFA), a tripartite body established in 1950 and composed of nine independent experts appointed by the Governing Body, and the Committee on Freedom of Association (CFA), a tripartite committee of the ILO Governing Body in operation since 1951.[16] Most ILO complaints are brought before the CFA. The CFA meets three times each year. Since its establishment, it has considered over 1800 cases.

The CFA's procedure for handling freedom of association complaints is as follows. A complaint is submitted to the CFA by an aggrieved party, or referred from UNESCO or the ILO Governing Body. The CFA determines whether the complaint is admissible.[17] If so, it considers the case on its merits. An information-gathering process follows, which generally includes direct communications with the complainant and the respondent state. At any time during the information-gathering stage, the CFA may undertake a "Direct Contact Mission" (a visit) with the consent of the respondent state.[18] In the last stage, the CFA issues conclusions and recommendations. If there is an adverse finding against a state party that relates to an ILO freedom of association convention to which it is party,[19] the matter is followed up by the CCACR before being referred to the FFCCFA. If the adverse finding relates to a freedom of association convention to which the state is not a party, the matter is followed up by the CFA before being referred to the FFCCFA (but in this case, only with the state's approval). FFCCFA decisions can be appealed to the International Court of Justice for a final determination. Canada has been the subject of a substantial number of complaints under these procedures.[20]

---

16   The CFA was established by agreement between the ILO and ECOSOC.

17   Complaints are inadmissible if they are filed by an unrecognized group, unsubstantiated, or excessively vague. They may also, of course, be found inadmissible if they relate to issues outside of the competence of the CFA.

18   The last such mission to Canada was in 1985 in connection with four complaints against Canada.

19   Recall that there are two ILO treaties dealing with freedom of association: the Freedom of Association and Protection of the Right to Organize Convention (No. 87) 1948, [1973] CanTS no. 14, to which Canada is a party, and the Right to Organize and Collective Bargaining Convention (No. 98) 1949, 96 UNTS 257, to which it is not.

20   See B. Burkett et al., "Canada and the ILO: Freedom of Association since 1982" (2003) 10 Canadian Labour and Employment Law Journal 231.

2) North American Agreement on Labour Cooperation Mechanisms

The Commission for Labour Cooperation is the main labour rights institution created under the NAALC. The Commission is not an independent oversight body. Instead, it consists of two intergovernmental bodies: a Ministerial Council and a Secretariat.

The Council is composed of the Canadian Minister of Labour and the US and Mexican Secretaries of Labour. Its role is to supervise the Secretariat and to oversee the general implementation of the NAALC. It also promotes labour cooperation among NAFTA states by means of conferences, workshops, and similar initiatives. In furtherance of its mandate, the Council has established Evaluation Committees of Experts from the three NAALC states parties to review and make recommendations regarding labour law enforcement in specified subject areas. It has also established Arbitral Panels to resolve disputes that arise among the governments concerning NAALC obligations.

The Secretariat, based in Dallas, is composed of a professional staff drawn equally from the three NAFTA states parties. The main roles of the Secretariat are to conduct research, prepare public reports on labour issues, and carry out general administration responsibilities in support of the NAALC.

The NAALC also requires each government to have a National Administrative Office within its Department (or Ministry) of Labour. The National Administrative Offices share information with all NAALC stakeholders and the general public. They are authorized to handle complaints sent by members of the public relating to the enforcement of labour standards in other NAFTA states parties.

NAALC complaint procedures operate in an incremental manner and rely heavily on political engagement between the three countries. The first level of treatment of a complaint occurs at the National Administrative Office stage. Article 16 of the NAALC requires each National Administrative Office to receive communications from any person or organization including unions and NGOs, relating to the general (as opposed to case-specific) enforcement in another state of any of the eleven NAALC labour principles.[21] Following receipt of the

---

21   As described in Chapter Seven, the NAALC divides these principles into three tiers: the first tier deals with freedom of association, collective bargaining, and the right to strike; the second tier deals with forced labour, pay equity, employment discrimination, compensation in case of injury or illness, and protection of migrant labour; and the third tier deals with child labour, minimum wages, and occupational safety.

complaint, the Office informs its counterparts in the other two states and the Secretariat of the Commission for Labour Cooperation. It then decides whether the submission is admissible. A National Administrative Office may also initiate a study of the enforcement of the eleven NAALC principles in another NAFTA state; it need not act only in response to a complaint.

Each National Administrative Office is responsible for the design of its own procedures. In the Canadian procedure, once a communication is determined to be admissible, the Office reviews the matter and decides whether to recommend the second stage in the NAALC procedure, namely Ministerial Consultations as provided for under NAALC article 22.[22] If the Minister of Labour decides to request such consultations, she then seeks to resolve the matter cooperatively with her counterparts in the other states. A Ministerial Consultation may relate to any of the NAALC's eleven labour principles. If the Consultation fails to produce a resolution of the matter, the Minister may request the establishment of an independent Evaluation Committee of Experts to produce a report and recommendations concerning all three states' performances in the particular subject area raised in the Minister's request.[23] However, an Evaluation Committee of Experts may only examine "patterns of practice" concerning tiers two and three of the eleven labour principles. If the Evaluation Committee of Experts discovers a "persistent pattern of failure" to enforce labour laws and regulations, further consultations ensue. If those too are unsuccessful, the Minister may request the establishment of a five-member Arbitral Panel pursuant to NAALC article 29 — but only pertaining to the third tier of the eleven labour principles. The Panel may issue a decision and an "action plan." If the action plan is not implemented, the Panel is empowered to impose an "enforcement assessment" (a monetary fine). The proceeds of that assessment may be used to fund improvements in labour law enforcement in the territory of the state party that was the subject of the complaint.

Overall, the NAALC provides a rather weak structure for the protection of the NAALC's eleven labour principles. The NAALC does not

---

22   The review may include private meetings with the petitioner and other interested parties, public meetings, appointment of an independent examiner, or requests for additional information. Other than for confidential or proprietary information (as defined in NAALC art. 44), personal communications and supporting documents are made available to the public on request.

23   NAALC, above note 1, art. 23. NAALC art. 45 requires states parties to draw on the expertise of the ILO for purposes of establishing rules of procedure for the Evaluation Committees of Experts.

assist in the resolution of individual violations in specific cases. Instead, it aims to encourage the improvement of labour law enforcement generally. It does so by means of a complaint procedure that, by all appearances, suffers from the same under-use as all other inter-state complaint mechanisms designed to resolve rights violations. In a published report on NAALC procedures,[24] the international NGO Human Rights Watch identified numerous problems. It found that:

- important issues that have come to light through complaints have gone unaddressed by the governments;
- complainants' concerns have been ignored;
- some case reports have been devoid of findings of fact;
- interpretation of the NAALC's obligations has been minimal; and
- agreements between governments to address concerns arising in NAALC cases have provided little possibility of resolving the problems identified by complainants.

The report also observed that, as of 2001, not one of the twenty-three complaints filed under the NAALC had resulted in sanctions.[25]

The mechanisms contemplated under the Canada-Chile Agreement on Labour Cooperation 1997 and the Canada-Costa Rica Agreement on Labour Cooperation 2001 resemble those established under the NAALC. The biggest difference is that there are no sanctions available under the Chilean or Costa Rican agreements.

B. INTERNATIONAL REFUGEE PROTECTION MECHANISMS

The main institution responsible for the global protection of refugees is the Office of the UN High Commissioner for Refugees (UNHCR).[26] The UNHCR, based in Geneva, was created in 1950 to supervise the resettlement of refugees displaced during and after the Second World

---

24 Human Rights Watch, *Trading Away Rights: The Unfulfilled Promise of NAFTA's Labor Side Agreement* (2001).
25 For analysis of a specific case concerning Canada, see N. Keresztesi, "Mexican Labour Laws and Practices Come to Canada: A Comment on the First Case Brought to Canada Under the North American Agreement on Labour Cooperation" (2000) 8 Canadian Labour & Employment Law Journal 411.
26 See http://www.unhcr.org. On refugee protection mechanisms generally, see J. Fitzpatrick, ed., *Human Rights Protection for Refugees, Asylum-Seekers, and Internally Displaced Persons: A Guide to International Mechanisms and Procedures* (Ardsley, NY: Transnational Publishers, 2001).

War.[27] Today it is one of the largest of the UN's humanitarian agencies, with a staff of over 5,000 serving in more than 120 countries worldwide. The High Commissioner for Refugees is the head of the UNHCR. The UN General Assembly elects her. An Executive Committee comprised of sixty-four member states, including Canada, approves the UNCHR's budget, guidelines, and programs. The Executive Committee meets annually in Geneva. There it takes decisions on international refugee protection. Its "Conclusions on International Protection," adopted by consensus at the annual meeting, are not law but bear significant influence on the application of refugee protection standards. A Standing Committee carries out the work of the Executive Committee during most of the year.

The UNHCR does not enforce implementation of the UN Convention Relating to the Status of Refugees 1951[28] or the Protocol Relating to the Status of Refugees 1967.[29] Instead, its role is to assist states parties in implementing their obligations. In the case of non-states parties, it is the UNHCR itself that tends to make refugee status determinations.[30] Applications for refugee status are ordinarily made on an individual basis. But sometimes during a mass exodus it is not possible to make individual determinations. In such circumstances, the UNHCR encourages the host government to make a group determination or grant temporary protection. Many refugees prefer to repatriate to their home state once conditions improve. But for some, neither repatriation nor remaining in the country of asylum is an option. In such cases, the concerned person may request resettlement in a third country and the UNHCR will provide assistance.

In addition to assuring basic legal protection for refugees, the UNHCR provides direct material assistance in humanitarian operations involving large-scale population flows. It also helps protect and assist stateless persons and internally displaced persons. The UNHCR works closely with other UN agencies, funds, and programs such as UNICEF, the World Food Programme, the World Health Organization, and the United Nations Development Programme. In the context of armed conflicts, the UNHCR also works with the International Committee of the

---

27　See Statute of the Office of the United Nations High Commissioner for Refugees 1950 [1969] CanTS no. 7.

28　[1969] CanTS no. 6.

29　[1969] CanTS no. 29.

30　At least one author has been very critical of UNHCR refugee determination procedures, arguing that they fail to meet international human rights standards. See M. Alexander, "Refugee Status Determination Conducted by the UNHCR" (1999) 11 International Journal of Refugee Law 251.

Red Cross. Cooperation among these agencies is facilitated by the fact that most of the world's refugees live in specially established, if minimally adequate, settlements or camps accommodating hundreds and often thousands of people at a time.

Another UN refugee protection agency is the United Nations Relief and Works Agency for Palestine Refugees in the Near East (UNRWA).[31] It was established in 1949 for the exclusive protection of Palestinian refugees.

Yet another refugee protection body is the International Organization for Migration.[32] It was established in 1951 as an independent intergovernmental organization to resettle European displaced persons, refugees, and migrants. Its mandate has grown to encompass a variety of migration management activities throughout the world including assistance to refugees and internally displaced persons.

C. INTERNATIONAL HUMANITARIAN LAW MECHANISMS

1) The International Committee of the Red Cross

The International Committee of the Red Cross (ICRC) is a private humanitarian institution incorporated under Swiss law for the purposes of protecting and assisting victims of war and internal violence.[33] Since its establishment in 1863, the ICRC has expanded into the "International Red Cross and Red Crescent Movement." The Movement is composed of the ICRC, national societies from 178 countries, and the International Federation of national societies. Though all members of the Movement abide by a common set of fundamental principles, they are not linked in a centralized hierarchy.

The ICRC is a non-governmental body but it does not consider itself an NGO in the traditional sense — nor should it. It has a unique status under international law, in particular under international humanitarian law treaties. It also does not conduct typical NGO activities such as advocacy and campaigning. Instead, neutrality, confiden-

---

31   See http://www.un.org/unrwa.
32   See http://www.iom.int. Canada is a member of the IOM.
33   See http://www.icrc.org. The ICRC was originally established as the International Committee for Relief of Wounded Soldiers, but changed its name to the ICRC in 1880.

tiality, and impartiality are its cardinal principles. These principles are also prerequisites for working directly within zones of conflict.

While protecting victims and coordinating international relief efforts are the ICRC's main tasks, it also does other work. It sometimes serves as an intermediary between parties to an armed conflict.[34] It conducts international humanitarian law education and training programs worldwide. It runs the Central Tracing Agency, a unique global body that assists in locating missing persons, reuniting families, and transmitting correspondence between family members separated by armed conflict.[35] It also conducts confidential inspections of national detention centres. Generally the ICRC will not publish the results of these inspections, but it will consider publishing them if a state attempts to distort its findings or fails to take action on its recommendations.[36]

2) Other International Humanitarian Law Mechanisms

The Geneva Conventions contemplate the establishment of a unique supervisory mechanism known as the "Protecting Powers."[37] Each state party involved in an international conflict can designate a neutral country, or alternatively designate the ICRC, to serve as its Protecting Power. The role of a Protecting Power is to verify the humane treatment of prisoners detained in a conflict. In contemporary practice, Protecting Powers are rarely named and the ICRC performs the role instead.

In a similar vein, article 90 of the GC Protocol 1 envisages a mechanism known as the International Fact-Finding Commission. Article 90(2)(a) provides:

> The High Contracting Parties may at the time of signing, ratifying or acceding to the Protocol, or at any other subsequent time, declare that they recognize *ipso facto* and without special agreement, in relation to any other High Contracting Party accepting the same obliga-

---

34   Common Article 3 provides: "An impartial humanitarian body, such as the International Committee of the Red Cross, may offer its services to the Parties to the conflict."

35   The Agency transmits over one million messages annually, and operates a central register containing over 60 million personal descriptions.

36   See, for example, "Guantanamo Detentions Blasted," BBC News (http://news.bbc.co.uk), 10 October 2003.

37   The Protecting Power mechanism can be traced back to the 1870 Franco-Prussian War. A. Robertson (revised by J. Merrills), *Human Rights in the World*, 3d ed. (Manchester: Manchester University Press, 1992) at 274. It was also included in the Geneva Convention relative to the Treatment of Prisoners of War 1929 [1933] CanTS no. 5, [1942] CanTS no. 6.

tion, the competence of the [Commission] to enquire into allegations by such other Party, as authorized by this Article.[38]

Although the first elections for the Commission were held in 1991, the Commission has never been asked to carry out a fact-finding mission by parties to any international conflict.

Finally, modern international criminal tribunals and UN peace-making and peacekeeping missions play an increasingly important role in the enforcement of international humanitarian law.[39]

D. OTHER RELEVANT MULTILATERAL MECHANISMS

Three other multilateral mechanisms with existing or emerging human rights components are of note because of Canada's participation in them. They are: the Commonwealth, the Francophonie, and ASEAN.[40]

1) The Commonwealth

The Commonwealth, established in 1931 and based in London, is a multilateral organization consisting of fifty-four member states drawn from the former British empire.[41] Canada is one of its founding members. Human rights are among the core principles enunciated in the Commonwealth's Harare Declaration 1991.[42]

---

38   Canada made a declaration under art. 90 on 20 November 1990:

>   The Government of Canada declares that it recognizes ipso facto and without special agreement, in relation to any other High Contracting Party accepting the same obligation, the competence of the Commission to enquire, as authorized by Article 90 of Protocol I, into allegations by such other Party that it has been the victim of violations amounting to a grave breach or other serious violation of the Geneva Conventions of 1949 or Protocol I.

39   On the role of international criminal tribunals, see Chapter Seventeen. On the role of UN peace operations, see M. Hoffman, "Peace Enforcement Actions and Humanitarian Law: Emerging Rules for Interventional Armed Conflict" (2000) 82 International Revue of the Red Cross 193.

40   Canada is also a member of the Asia Pacific Economic Cooperation (APEC), the North Atlantic Treaty Organization (NATO), and the Arctic Council. Although there are human rights issues that arise within these organizations, none of them has or is developing an explicit human rights dimension.

41   See http://www.commonwealth.org.

42   See http://www.thecommonwealth.org/gender/htm/commonwealth/about/declares/harare.htm.

The Commonwealth played an important, if belated, role in the fight against apartheid in South Africa. More recently it played a significant role in restoring democracy in a range of countries including Nigeria and Sierra Leone. Acting through its Ministerial Action Group (CMAG) — composed of eight ministers of foreign affairs from different member states — the Commonwealth has periodically investigated "serious and persistent violations" of human rights in member states.[43] In addition to sending investigative missions, the Commonwealth has occasionally suspended and expelled member states with bad human rights records, Zimbabwe being the most recent example.[44]

2) Organisation internationale de la Francophonie

The Francophonie, established in 1986 and based in Paris, is a multilateral organization consisting of fifty-six member states.[45] Canada is a founding member. The Charter of the Francophonie was adopted in 1996 and lists democratic development, human rights, and the rule of law among its core objectives.[46]

The subject of human rights now occupies a prominent place on the organization's regular agenda. On 3 November 2000, its member states adopted the Bamako Declaration on democracy, good governance, and human rights.[47] The Declaration provides enforcement mechanisms and guidelines for dealing with crises of democracy or serious violations of human rights by member states.[48] Thus far, no

---

43 The CMAG was established to implement measures set out in the "Millbrook Action Programme," which was adopted at the 1995 Commonwealth Heads of Government Meeting. Canada was a member of CMAG between 1995–2002.

44 "Zimbabwe row mars summit finale," BBC News (http://news.bbc.co.uk), 8 December 2003. Zimbabwe was re-admitted in March 2004.

45 See http://www.francophonie.org.

46 Article 1 provides in its relevant part:

La Francophonie, consciente des liens que crée entre ses membres le partage de la langue française et souhaitant les utiliser au service de la paix, de la coopération et du développement, a pour objectifs d'aider : à l'instauration et au développement de la démocratie, à la prévention des conflits et au soutien à l'État de droit et aux droits de l'homme. . . .

47 See http://www.francophonie.org/documents/word/declarations/Declaration_de_bamako.rtf

48 For example, Bamako Declaration, ibid., art. 3, provides for the immediate suspension of a country in the event of a military coup d'état against a democratically elected government. ("En cas de coup d'Etat militaire contre un régime issu d'élections démocratiques, la suspension est décidée.")

sanctions have been applied to any member state on the basis of its human rights record.

3) Association of Southeast Asian Nations

The Association of Southeast Asian Nations (ASEAN), founded in 1967, is a multilateral organization consisting of ten member states from Southeast Asia.[49] Canada has been a "dialogue partner" of ASEAN since the late 1970s. Thus far ASEAN has not developed a human rights system. Since 1996, however, a "Working Group for an ASEAN Human Rights Mechanism" has been active in developing proposals for such a system.[50] While it is not clear that ASEAN member states are ready for a robust human rights mechanism, ASEAN recently issued its first public criticism of a member state on a human rights issue.[51] Also, at its Ninth ASEAN summit in October 2003, ASEAN member states for the first time expressly committed themselves to democratic governance.[52]

---

49   See http://www.aseansec.org.

50   Among other things, the Working Group has noted that a human rights mechanism would be consistent with the ASEAN Declaration of 8 August 1967, which includes among the Association's aims and purposes "to promote regional peace and stability through abiding respect for justice and the rule of law in the relationship among countries in the region and adherence to the principles of the United Nations Charter."

51   In June 2003, ASEAN called for the release from prison of Aung San Suu Kyi, Burma's democratically elected leader. It was, however, only a declaration; no sanctions were threatened. BBC News (http://news.bbc.co.uk), "ASEAN Calls for Suu Kyi Release," 17 June 2003.

52   The agreement adopted at the end of the conference, entitled the Bali Concord II (http://www.aseansec.org/15159.htm), provides in its relevant part: "The ASEAN Security Community is envisaged to bring ASEAN's political and security cooperation to a higher plane to ensure that countries in the region live at peace with one another and with the world at large in a just, democratic and harmonious environment."

CHAPTER 17

INTERNATIONAL AND MIXED CRIMINAL TRIBUNALS

In this chapter we review the structure and mandate of the international criminal tribunals now in operation. We also examine the three "mixed" criminal tribunals that have been established in recent years in Kosovo, Timor-Leste, and Sierra Leone. These various tribunals constitute the leading edge in accountability concerning especially serious violations of international human rights and humanitarian standards. They reflect a paradigm shift in the international community, away from diplomacy and toward legality. Despite limitations and imperfections, international and mixed criminal tribunals have changed the face of international justice.

A. *AD HOC* INTERNATIONAL CRIMINAL TRIBUNALS

The International Criminal Tribunal for the former Yugoslavia (ICTY) and the International Criminal Tribunal for Rwanda (ICTR) are the only two contemporary *ad hoc* (that is, special purpose) international criminal tribunals currently in existence.[1] We pay particular attention

---

1   In February 2004, Human Rights Watch published a comprehensive digest that organizes all of the judgments of the ICTY and ICTR by topic. The digest, entitled *Genocide, War Crimes and Crimes Against Humanity: Topical Digests of the Case Law of the ICTR and the ICTY*, is available on the organization's website (http://www.hrw.org).

to the ICTY, which was the precursor to and model for the ICTR. Most of the successes and challenges of the ICTY recounted below apply in like manner, if in a different context, to the ICTR.

Both tribunals, but especially the ICTY, have had a profound impact on the development of international criminal law and procedure. In demonstrating that fair trials at the international level are possible, these tribunals helped inspire states to establish the International Criminal Court. Their cost and remote locations also influenced the development of mixed criminal tribunals, which are more economical and more directly linked to the strengthening of domestic justice systems.

1) The International Criminal Tribunal for the former Yugoslavia

In 1993, in an unprecedented action made possible by the end of the Cold War, the UN Security Council established the ICTY.[2] It was the first international war crimes tribunal since Nuremberg and Tokyo.[3] Responding to the deaths of hundreds of thousands of civilians in the former Yugoslavia, the Security Council declared the war there a "threat to international peace and security" under Chapter VII of the UN Charter.[4]

Unlike the Nuremberg tribunal, the ICTY is internationally representative in its composition and therefore less vulnerable to criticisms of "victor's justice." It is composed of a staff of judges, prosecutors,

---

2   The ICTY's website is http://www.icty.org. On the ICTY generally, see R. Kerr, *The International Criminal Tribunal for the Former Yugoslavia: An Exercise in Law, Politics and Diplomacy* (Oxford: Oxford University Press, 2004); J. Ackerman & E. O'Sullivan, *Practice and Procedure of the International Criminal Tribunal for the Former Yugoslavia* (The Hague: Kluwer, 2000).

3   The international legal basis of the ICTY was challenged in the trial of the first defendant. The ICTY Appeals Chamber, unsurprisingly, found that it had been lawfully established by the Security Council. *Prosecutor v. Tadic* (1995), Case no. IT-94-1-AR72, Judgment on Interlocutory Appeal, ICTY Appeals Chamber.

4   Two Security Council resolutions preceded the ICTY's establishment: SC res. 771 (1992) (which declared persons responsible for grave breaches of the Geneva Conventions individually responsible, and urged the collection of information on such breaches) and SC res. 780 (1992) (which requested the Secretary-General to establish a Commission of Experts, which ultimately reported that widespread grave breaches had been committed in the territory of the former Yugoslavia). Subsequently the Council adopted SC res. 808 (1993), which called for an international criminal tribunal and requested the Secretary-General to submit a report on it. Finally, the Council adopted SC res. 827 (1993), which approved the Secretary-General's report and created the ICTY.

defence counsel, and personnel from around the world. The Tribunal is divided into three units: the Judges Chambers, the Office of the Prosecutor, and the Registry. The Judges Chambers consist of sixteen permanent judges and a maximum at any one time of nine *ad litem* (temporary) judges drawn from a pool of twenty-seven. The permanent judges are divided into three trial chambers composed of three judges each, and one appeals chamber composed of seven judges, two of whom are also judges at the ICTR. The UN General Assembly elects the ICTY's judges for four-year renewable terms based on a list of candidates submitted by the Security Council.[5] The UN General Assembly also elects *ad litem* judges.[6] The Office of the Prosecutor is run by the Chief Prosecutor, who is appointed directly by the UN Security Council for a four-year term.[7] The Registry performs a variety of functions, including the provision of victim and witness support, judicial support, defence counsel to indigent defenders, and public information. The chief Registrar is appointed directly by the UN Secretary-General after consultation with the ICTY President.

The ICTY is located in The Hague and receives the bulk of its funding from UN member states through assessed contributions. It has jurisdiction over crimes committed in the former Yugoslavia since 1991. Under its Statute,[8] the Tribunal is responsible for investigating and prosecuting individuals suspected of committing four types of crime: grave breaches of the Geneva Conventions (article 2), violations of the laws and customs of war (article 3), genocide (article 4), and crimes against humanity (article 5). In anticipation of any claims that parts of the ICTY Statute violate the principle of *nullem crimen sine lege*,[9] the UN Secretary-General asserted that the Hague Convention (IV) respecting the Laws and Customs of War on Land 1907, the IMT Charter, the Genocide Convention and the Geneva Conventions had "beyond doubt" become part of customary international law.[10] The

---

5   Jules Deschênes, a Canadian, was a former permanent judge on the ICTY.
6   Sharon Williams, a Canadian, recently served as an *ad litem* judge on the ICTY.
7   The current Chief Prosecutor is Carla Del Ponte, Switzerland's former attorney general and chief federal prosecutor. She succeeded Louise Arbour, a Canadian who served as ICTY's Chief Prosecutor from 1996 to 1999. As noted in Chapter Fourteen, Arbour was appointed the UN High Commissioner for Human Rights in 2004.
8   UN doc. S/Res./827 (1993), as amended.
9   The principle holds that no one may be held criminally responsible for an act that did not constitute a criminal offence at the time when it was committed. The principle is enshrined in various international instruments including UDHR art. 11(2), ICCPR art. 15, ACHR art. 9, and ECHR art. 7.
10 See Report of the Secretary-General pursuant to paragraph 2 of Security Council Resolution 808, UN doc. S/25704 (1993) at para. 35.

ICTY's Rules of Procedure, which were drafted by the judges and represent a unique blend of the civil and common law traditions, have influenced all subsequent international and mixed tribunals.[11]

The ICTY has primacy over the domestic courts of the former Yugoslavia and every other country in the world. It is empowered, as a consequence, to request that domestic courts halt proceedings against individuals subject to its jurisdiction and transfer them and all related evidence to it. Individuals prosecuted by the ICTY may not be prosecuted subsequently for the same acts before domestic courts, but individuals already prosecuted by domestic courts may, in limited circumstances, be prosecuted by the ICTY.[12] The ICTY is empowered to convict accused persons and sentence them to terms of imprisonment. The Tribunal also has jurisdiction to order the transfer to victims of money and other property collected through fines or forfeiture, but thus far it has not done so.

The ICTY has no control over the territory of the former Yugoslavia and lacks a police force of its own to arrest those it indicts. It must rely on state cooperation — obligatory under Resolution 827 of the Security Council and article 25 of the ICTY Statute — to arrest suspects and gather evidence. This situation may be contrasted with that of the Nuremberg and Tokyo tribunals. Those tribunals were established during the Allied Powers' occupation of Germany and Japan. Many of the accused were already in custody when the war ended, and the tribunals had the Allied armies at their disposal to gather evidence.

Due to prosecutorial preferences and a lack of state cooperation in the ICTY's early years (when it was in no position to refuse defendants), much of the Prosecutor's efforts were expended on low or mid-level perpetrators. Although the Tribunal issued a considerable number of public indictments, none of the accused persons was arrested and none surrendered voluntarily. As a result, the ICTY devised a unique procedure to hear evidence in such cases.[13] The so-called "Rule 61 procedure" allowed ICTY prosecutors to present an indictment together with all its evidence before a Trial Chamber of the ICTY, all in the absence of the accused. If the Trial Chamber was satisfied that there were reasonable

---

11   See generally R. May & M. Wierda, *International Criminal Evidence* (Ardsley, NY: Transnational Publishers, 2003).

12   The ICTY may re-try a case when the characterization of the act by a domestic court does not match its characterization under the ICTY Statute, or when a domestic trial fails to meet minimum conditions of impartiality and fairness. But at sentencing the ICTY must take into account any prior sentence imposed at the domestic level.

13   The ICTY is not authorized to conduct trials *in absentia*.

grounds for believing that the accused committed the crimes charged, it would issue an international arrest warrant for transmission to all UN member states, making the suspect an international fugitive and enabling the freezing of his assets. If a state where the accused resided failed or refused to cooperate, the Tribunal could report this to the Security Council for further action. If the accused was later arrested, his trial would start afresh before a new Trial Chamber, and the Rule 61 findings would play no part in deciding his guilt or innocence.

In the course of 1997, the Tribunal's docket started to fill, in part through surrenders but also by means of arrests carried out by the NATO-led Implementation Force (IFOR) and its successor the Stabilisation Force (SFOR).[14] In the following years IFOR and SFOR seized some high-profile indicted persons.[15] Still, the Tribunal faced resistance from states in gathering documentary evidence, which can be critical to proving cases.[16] Changes of governments in the former Yugoslavia have led to improved state cooperation in the making of arrests and the transfer of evidence. Arguably the pinnacle of cooperation was the handing over by Federal Republic of Yugoslavia (FRY) authorities of former President Slobodan Milosevic in 2001. He had been publicly indicted in 1999.[17]

As a result of these and other developments, the ICTY's caseload increased considerably. In early 1997, there were fewer than ten

---

14   In 1995, IFOR had made it a policy to arrest indicted persons only if they happened to come into contact with them. By 1998, primarily in response to pressure from Western governments and the ICTY, some SFOR troop providers (in particular the US and the UK) became more proactive in making arrests.

15   A reversal in the Prosecutor's policy of initially issuing only public, rather than sealed indictments, facilitated other high-level arrests. Sealed indictments are kept confidential until the indicted person is arrested. This enables the conduct of surprise operations.

16   See, for example, *Prosecutor v. Blaskic* (1997), Case no. IT-95-14-AR108bis, Judgment, ICTY Appeals Chamber. In this case a subpoena was issued against the Croatian government ordering it to disclose certain documents. The Croatian government appealed, challenging the power of the ICTY to issue such an order to a sovereign state. The ICTY Appeals Chamber upheld Croatia's challenge in part, noting that non-compliance with a subpoena is usually punished with criminal sanctions, and states cannot be the subject of such sanctions. However, it found that the ICTY was able to issue binding orders to sovereign states, and that in cases of non-compliance, the ICTY was authorized to refer the matter to the UN Security Council.

17   The Milosevic handover was mainly prompted by the FRY's need of ongoing US and IMF economic assistance, which had been conditioned on his handover. The US government still makes the country's effective cooperation with the Tribunal a condition of economic assistance.

accused persons in its custody; as of October 2002, there were over fifty either in custody or on provisional release.[18] Partly as a result of these new circumstances, the ICTY has had to find ways to expedite its trials. Individual trials by the ICTY have taken, on average, over one hundred sitting days. Some trials have taken two years or longer to complete just at the Trial Chamber level. This is due in large measure to the difficult factual and legal issues that the Tribunal is called upon to resolve, as well as the practice of calling large numbers of live witnesses each of which is examined in accordance with rigorous standards of due process. The ICTY's Rules of Procedure have undergone numerous revisions aimed at reducing delays. Recently the Tribunal has had to become more liberal in granting provisional release to accused persons due primarily to the length of trials.

Since being established, the ICTY has rendered a number of significant decisions. In an early case it decided that duress is not a complete defence against a war crime or a crime against humanity.[19] It conducted the first-ever international trial in which a policy of rape was treated as a war crime and a crime against humanity.[20] It has ruled that crimes against humanity do not require a war nexus,[21] and that the scope of superior responsibility includes both civilian and military leaders and can rest on *de jure* or *de facto* authority.[22] In recent years the Tribunal has brought to trial former FRY President Slobodan Milosevic and other senior political figures in the former Yugoslavia alleged to be architects of the worst crimes.[23]

Yet concerns have been expressed about the public perception of the ICTY in parts of the former Yugoslavia and the degree to which it has been able to contribute to regional reconciliation, as its Statute directs. In places such as Serbia and the Republika Srpska, trust was never likely to be high, given the role of NATO member states in forming the Tribunal, and given the nature and quantity of alleged viola-

---

18   See http://www.icty.org. Pre-trial detention is the rule, and provisional release the exception, in the practice of international and mixed criminal tribunals.

19   *Prosecutor v. Erdemovic* (1997), Case no. IT-96-22-A, Sentencing Appeal, ICTY Appeals Chamber.

20   *Prosecutor v. Kunarac et al.* (2001), Case no. IT-96-23-T & IT-96-23/1-T, Judgment, ICTY Trial Chamber.

21   *Prosecutor v. Tadic* (1997), Case no. IT-94-1-T, Judgment, ICTY Trial Chamber.

22   *"Celibici Judgment" (Prosecutor v. Zejnil Delalic et al.)* (1998), Case no. IT-96-21-T, Judgment, ICTY Trial Chamber.

23   ICTY Statute, above note 8, art. 7(2) provides that "the official position of any accused person, whether as Head of State or Government or as a responsible government official, shall not relieve such person of criminal responsibility nor mitigate punishment."

tions committed by Serb forces and the necessary focus on them.[24] Some decisions taken by the Tribunal and the Prosecutor, no matter how meritorious, appear to have reinforced distrust.[25] In addition, it may be inevitable that a court situated in a foreign country and conducting its proceedings mostly in English and French (with translation into Bosnian-Serbian-Croatian) will be poorly perceived. An effective outreach programme from the start might have helped to build trust, and fortunately one has since been put in place.

Another concern relates to the cost of operating the Tribunal. Its annual budget has averaged in excess of US$100 million in recent years, and it employs approximately 1,300 staff.[26] Despite this, the Tribunal concludes only a handful of cases each year. Although the importance of the Tribunal cannot be measured in numbers alone, the stark differential between input and output invites criticism.

Still, the ICTY plays a critical role in the former Yugoslavia. Indeed, until very recently, domestic courts were mostly unwilling or unable to confront the perpetrators in their midst. But the ICTY is only temporary. The Tribunal will wind down its investigations by the end of 2004, and complete all first instance trials by 2008 and appeals by 2010.[27] The present challenge, therefore, is to finish investigations and trials and hand over remaining cases to domestic authorities. It is noteworthy that there are plans underway to create a special War Crimes Chamber within the State Court of Bosnia and Herzegovina (BiH). It will hear ICTY transfer cases[28] as well as a limited number of "Rules of the Road" cases, that is,

---

24   According to a comprehensive survey based on 10,000 face-to-face interviews conducted during January and February 2002, trust in the ICTY ranges from 83% (Kosovo) and 51% (Bosnian Federation), to 24% (Montenegro), 21% (Croatia), 6% (Serbia), and 4% (Republika Srpska) respectively. See International IDEA, *South East Europe Public Agenda Survey* (2002). Available at: http://www.idea.int/press/pr20020404.htm.

25   For example, the ICTY Prosecutor decided not to continue with an investigation into NATO's bombing of the FRY in 1999, stating "although NATO had made some mistakes, it had not deliberately targeted civilians." See UN Security Council Press Release, SC/6870, 2 June 2000. Several law professors from Osgoode Law Faculty were among those who petitioned the ICTY Prosecutor to investigate NATO's conduct. See M. Mandel, "Politics and Human Rights in International Criminal Law: Our Case Against NATO and the Lessons to Be Learned from It" (2001) 25 Fordham International Law Journal 95.

26   http://www.un.org/icty/glance/index.htm.

27   ICTY, *Ninth Annual Report* (2002).

28   These consist of so-called Rule 11 *bis* cases, where the indictment has already been issued and confirmed, and cases still under investigation in which no indictment has been issued.

cases initiated by BiH authorities rather than arriving by ICTY referral.[29] The Chamber is scheduled to begin hearing cases in early 2005. The Chamber will comprise international and domestic judges and prosecutors. Increased use of plea-bargaining procedures at the ICTY can also be expected. Though controversial, such procedures will, if properly handled, encourage guilty pleas and avoid expensive and time-consuming trials.[30]

2) The International Criminal Tribunal for Rwanda

In 1994, Hutu extremists in Rwanda murdered up to one million Tutsis and moderate Hutus in a genocide that lasted little more than three months. The international community failed to halt the genocide, despite many prior warnings about it.[31] Many reasons have been given for the international failure to intervene, including French and US resistance in the Security Council, the lack of any strong geopolitical interest on the part of developed countries, and unconcern or inactivity on the part of the UN bureaucracy.[32]

Eventually the Security Council declared the situation in Rwanda a threat to international peace and security under Chapter VII of the UN

---

29   Further to the Rome Agreement of 18 February 1996 (commonly referred to as the "Rules of the Road"), the Office of the ICTY Prosecutor established a procedure whereby it reviews domestic case files and gives them a marking as to whether or not domestic authorities can try the cases. Over the past eight years, the Tribunal has permitted local authorities to try hundreds of individuals under the system, but in practice most have not gone forward.

30   See, for example, N. Coumbs, "International Decisions: *Prosecutor v. Plavsic*" (2003), 97 ASIL 929. Plavsic, a former President of the Republika Srpska, was the first Bosnian Serb to plead guilty at the ICTY. She struck a deal with the ICTY prosecutor to drop two charges of genocide and six out of seven charges of crimes against humanity in exchange for a guilty plea. Following a sentencing hearing that saw the defence and prosecution jointly present two witnesses (Drs. Madeline Albright and Alex Boraine), Plavsic was sentenced to eleven years' imprisonment. Many victims condemned the sentence as too lenient,

31   Retired Canadian General Romeo Dallaire — at the time head of UN forces in Rwanda — famously failed to persuade the UN Security Council to send more troops in time to stop the impending genocide.

32   See generally International Panel of Eminent Personalities to Investigate the 1994 Genocide in Rwanda and Surrounding Events, *The Preventable Genocide* (2000). The Panel was established by the OAU. Canadians Stephen Lewis and Gerald Caplan were member and author, respectively. See also: M. Barnett, *Eyewitness to a Genocide* (Ithaca: Cornell University Press, 2002); and R. Dallaire, *Shake Hands With the Devil — The Failure of Humanity in Rwanda* (Toronto: Random House, 2003).

Charter.[33] In November 1994, the Security Council adopted Resolution 955 establishing the ICTR.[34] The ICTR Statute[35] closely resembles that of the ICTY, and the ICTR has modeled its Rules of Procedure and Evidence on those used by the ICTY.

The Tribunal's Trial Chamber (composed of nine permanent judges and one *ad litem* judge) and Registry are located in Arusha, Tanzania. The Prosecutor's Office is shared between Kigali, Rwanda and Arusha.[36] The ICTR shares the same Hague-based Appeals Chamber as the ICTY.[37]

The ICTR has rendered a number of important decisions, though far fewer than the ICTY. Perhaps the most cited case is *Prosecutor v. Jean Paul Akayesu*,[38] in which the ICTR found that acts of sexual violence, including rape, can rise to the level of a crime against humanity or genocide.[39] The ICTR has also conducted important group trials including the recent "media case" in which the Tribunal examined the role of a radio station and newspaper in fomenting the genocide.[40] Regrettably, the vast majority of people in Rwanda — an impoverished and largely rural country — has been unable to view or learn much about the ICTR proceedings.

The ICTR and ICTY have many similarities but important differences too. Like the ICTY, the ICTR receives most of its funding from

---

33 The Security Council first adopted SC res. 935 (1994) in which it asked the Secretary-General to establish a commission of inquiry to investigate the events in Rwanda. The commission's conclusions included a finding of "overwhelming evidence of genocide." See Final Report of the Commission of Experts established pursuant to Security Council resolution 935 (1994), UN doc. S/1994/1405 (1994).

34 The ICTR's website is http://www.ictr.org. On the ICTR generally, see V. Morris & M. Scharf, *The International Criminal Tribunal for Rwanda* (Ardsley, NY: Transnational Publishers, 1998).

35 UN doc. S/Res./955 (1994), as amended.

36 In August 2003, Gambian judge, Hassan Jallow, was appointed as the ICTR's Chief Prosecutor. He is based in Kigali, Rwanda. Previously the ICTR shared the same Hague-based Chief Prosecutor as the ICTY.

37 The Appeals Chamber judges travel to Arusha when necessary to hear appeals from judgments of the ICTR Trial Chamber. Interlocutory appeals are often decided in The Hague.

38 (1998) Case no. ICTR-96-4-T, Judgment, ICTR Trial Chamber.

39 See also *Prosecutor v. Kambanda* (1998), Case no. ICTR-97-23-S, Judgment, ICTR Trial Chamber. The judgment itself is of less interest than the fact that it was made against the former Prime Minister of Rwanda, Jean Kambanda, who pleaded guilty to six counts of genocide and crimes against humanity. The Appeals Chamber turned down his recent request for a re-trial. Kambanda was the first head of government ever to be convicted of genocide.

40 The trial lasted three years and all three accused were convicted and sentenced to terms ranging from 35 years to life. See C. MacKinnon, "*Prosecutor v. Nahimana, Barayagwiza and Ngeze*" (2004) 98 AJIL 325.

UN member states through their assessed contributions, has jurisdiction only over natural persons, and enjoys primacy over the domestic courts of any country. Unlike the ICTY, the ICTR was established in response to a purely internal conflict. Accordingly, the ICTR Statute covers genocide (article 2), crimes against humanity (article 3), and violations of Common Article 3 and the GC Protocol II (article 4), but does not cover grave breaches of the Geneva Conventions, which only occur in international armed conflicts. Another difference is that the ICTR, unlike the ICTY, has jurisdiction over crimes committed in the territory of conflict (Rwanda) as well as over crimes committed by Rwandans in neighbouring countries.

Many African and European states have arrested and transferred indicted persons to the ICTR.[41] The Rwandan government has, however, resisted cooperation with the ICTR. It considers it inefficient and costly.[42] It also believes that the ICTR was inspired less by a desire for justice than a need to atone for the failure to prevent the genocide in the first place. At the nadir of the Rwandan government's relationship with the ICTR, cooperation with the ICTR was formally suspended. This occurred following the acquittal of Jean-Bosco Barayagwiza by the ICTR Trial Chamber on grounds of excessive pre-trial detention. The Rwandan government thereafter denied an entry visa to the ICTR Prosecutor and prohibited witnesses from travelling to Arusha to testify in any ICTR trials. The ICTR Prosecutor subsequently filed a motion to reconsider the acquittal, purportedly due to "new facts."[43]

In lieu of cooperation, the Rwandan government has preferred to carry out its own investigations and prosecutions. Despite a dearth of human and financial resources, the domestic courts in Rwanda have

---

41 Kenya, Cameroon, Belgium, and Tanzania have arrested and transferred the bulk of suspects, but many other states have been co-operative as well. See Coalition for International Justice, "ICTR Indictees" (http://www.cij.org). These arrests have been critical since, in contrast to the ICTY (which has benefited from a relatively large number of surrenders), there have been few surrenders to the ICTR.

42 The ICTR's annual budget has averaged in excess of US$80 million in recent years. Despite a staff of approximately 800, it has concluded few trials to date. There have been no indictments for international crimes committed by any members of the Rwandan Patriotic Front (RPF) — formerly the Rwandan Patriotic Army and currently Rwanda's ruling party. RPF members are believed to have committed war crimes in Rwanda in 1994.

43 For a detailed summary of what transpired, see A. Danner, "Enhancing the Legitimacy and Accountability of Prosecutorial Discretion at the International Criminal Court" (2003) 97 AJIL 510 at 530–31 [Danner, "Enhancing the Legitimacy"]. More recently cooperation was suspended when the ICTR reportedly opened investigations into some RPF members.

managed to convict approximately 6,500 *genocidaires* to date; of these, more than 600 have received death sentences, 23 of which have been carried out.[44] But with as many as 110,000 suspects in detention without trial for nearly a decade, and no realistic possibility of ever trying all of those in detention, the bulk of cases are being handled by a new village-level system called *gacaca* that is loosely based on an indigenous model of justice.[45] There are over 10,000 *gacaca* "tribunals" across Rwanda, which are being administered by some 250,000 elected *gacaca* "judges." The *Gacaca Law* claims as its objectives the revelation of truth about the genocide, the punishment of those who perpetrated it, the acceleration of prosecutions for those currently accused of genocide, the participation of the population as a means to eradicate the culture of impunity, the development among Rwandan citizens of the tools needed to manage conflict peacefully, and the promotion of national reconciliation.[46] The law is a response to the political impossibility of simply releasing tens of thousands of alleged *genocidaires*, the practical impossibility of trying all those responsible, and the unfairness of keeping people in detention for years without trial. But *gacaca* is controversial. Concern has been expressed about its failure to guarantee minimum fair trial standards.[47]

B. THE INTERNATIONAL CRIMINAL COURT

The International Criminal Court, seated in The Hague, is the world's first and only permanent international criminal court.[48] Since 1948, when the UN General Assembly originally asked the International Law

---

44   "Mass Genocide Verdict Delivered," BBC News (http://news.bbc.co.uk), 1 August 2003. The cases have been conducted mostly as group trials for defendants accused of participating in the same crimes.

45   *Gacaca* was established under the *Loi Organique N° 40/2000 du 26/01/2001 portant création des Juridictions gacaca et organisation des poursuites des infractions constitutives du crime de génocide ou de crimes contre l'humanité commises entre le 1er octobre 1990 et le 31 décembre 1994 (Gacaca Law)*.

46   *Gacaca Law* preamble.

47   See, for example, Amnesty International, *Gacaca: A Question of Justice* (2002).

48   The Court's website is http://www.icc-cpi.int. On the International Criminal Court generally, see W. Schabas, *An Introduction to the International Criminal Court* (Cambridge: Cambridge University Press, 2001); L. Sadat, *The International Criminal Court and the Transformation of International Law: Justice for the New Millenium* (Ardsley, NY: Transnational Publishers, 2002); and A. Cassese et al., eds., *The Rome Statute of the International Criminal Court: A Commentary* (Oxford: Oxford University Press, 2002).

Commission to study the possibility of creating such a court, the idea had remained a distant aspiration. Then in 1994, the Commission submitted to the General Assembly a draft statute for a permanent court covering various international crimes.[49] The draft statute was amended and debated in succeeding years. In the summer of 1998, the General Assembly convened a Diplomatic Conference of Plenipotentiaries in Rome to finalize a text for adoption. To almost everyone's surprise, the Rome Statute of the International Court 1998 (Rome Statute)[50] was adopted. The Canadian government, and in particular former Foreign Affairs Minister Lloyd Axworthy, played a lead role in the adoption of the Rome Statute. Even more pivotal was the role of NGOs who created a highly effective global coalition that partnered with various small and medium-sized states to ensure its adoption.[51]

Currently, there are ninety-two state parties to the Rome Statute. Another forty-eight states have signed but not ratified it. Ratification of the treaty proceeded far more rapidly than expected. Yet many of the world's most populous and powerful states have not ratified the Rome Statute, including the US, China, India, and Russia. The US government has been very opposed to the Court in recent years, despite having played a significant role in devising it. Under threat of withdrawal of economic or military assistance, the US has pressured many states parties to the Rome Statute to enter into bilateral "Article 98 agreements." These agreements preclude the surrender or transfer to the Court of a national of either signatory.[52]

The Rome Statute is supplemented by other important instruments. In 2000, the Preparatory Commission for the Court finalized the Elements of Crimes (ICC Elements),[53] which will assist the Court in interpreting the crimes listed in the Rome Statute. The Preparatory

---

49   Report of the International Law Commission on the work of its forty-sixth session, UN doc. A/49/10 (1994).

50   [2002] CanTS no. 13.

51   See Human Rights Watch, *World Report* (1999); see also the website of the (NGO) Coalition for the International Criminal Court (http://www.iccnow.org).

52   For a detailed analysis and critique of these agreements, see Amnesty International, *International Criminal Court: US Efforts to Obtain Impunity for Genocide, Crimes against Humanity and War Crimes* (2002). More than forty states have now signed such agreements with the US. See also the *American Service-Members' Protection Act* 2002, Supplemental Appropriations Act for Further Recovery from and Response to Terrorist Attacks on the United States, Pub. L. No. 107-206, ss. 2001–15, 116 Stat. 820 (2002), which among other things permits the revocation of US military assistance to certain states parties to the Rome Statute if they refuse to enter an Article 98 agreement.

53   UN doc. PCNICC/2000/1/Add.2 (2000).

Commission also adopted the Rules of Procedure and Evidence (ICC Rules),[54] which drew directly from the rules and practice of the ICTY and the ICTR. Other important instruments relating to the administration of the Court include the Agreement on the Privileges and Immunities of the International Criminal Court 2002, the Relationship Agreement between the International Criminal Court and the UN 2002, and the International Criminal Court Financial Regulations and Rules 2002.

The Court itself is composed of eighteen permanent judges elected for terms of three, six, or nine years by the states parties to the Rome Statute. Philippe Kirsch, a Canadian, is President of the Court.[55] Seven of the eighteen judges are women, far more than on any other international or mixed criminal tribunal.[56] The Rome Statute also established a Prosecutor's Office. The Prosecutor is Luis Moreno Ocampo, a prominent attorney and former prosecutor from Argentina. More than 200 complaints had been registered with the Court prior to his appointment.[57]

Like the ICTY and the ICTR, the International Criminal Court only has jurisdiction to try natural persons (Rome Statute article 25(1)).[58] The Court's subject matter jurisdiction is limited to three types of international crime: genocide (article 6), crimes against humanity (article 7), and war crimes (article 8).[59] The crimes are subject neither to limitation periods (article 29) nor to state immunities (article 27(2)).[60] Possible defences to these crimes, all of which are carefully delimited in the Rome Statute, include mental incapacity (article 31(1)(a)), intoxication (article 31(1)(b)), self-defence (article 31(1)(c)), duress (article 31(1)(d)), mistake of fact (article 32(1)), mistake of law (article 32(2)), and obedience to superior orders (article 33).[61]

---

54 UN doc. PCNICC/2000/1/Add.1 (2000).
55 Judge Kirsch previously served as Chairman of the Preparatory Commission for the International Criminal Court from 1999 to 2002.
56 Rome Statute, above note 50, art. 8(a)(iii) requires states parties to seek to achieve a "fair representation of female and male judges."
57 BBC News (http://news.bbc.co.uk), "Profile: Luis Moreno Ocampo," 21 April 2003.
58 But note art. 26: "The Court shall have no jurisdiction over any person who was under the age of 18 at the time of the alleged commission of a crime."
59 The Court will also have jurisdiction over the crime of aggression (art. 5(1)(d)), but only after a provision is adopted defining the crime and setting out the conditions under which the Court may exercise jurisdiction with respect to the crime (art. 5(2)). This has not yet occurred and may never occur.
60 State or sovereign immunity is also rejected in the ICTY Statute, above note 23 (art. 7(2)), and the ICTR Statute, above note 35 (art. 6(2)).
61 All of these defences are generally invoked to refute the *mens rea* (mental element) of a crime, and are without prejudice to the right of an accused to refute the *actus reus* (the criminal act itself).

The International Criminal Court does not have retroactive jurisdiction and therefore it will not be able to try crimes committed before 1 July 2002, when the Rome Statute came into force.[62] The Rome Statute provides that the Court only has jurisdiction over individuals who are nationals of a state party or who committed enumerated crimes on the territory of a state party. A state that is not a party to the Rome Statute may also accept the jurisdiction of the Court in a particular case (article 12(2)–(3)).[63] In addition, the Security Council may refer a case to the Court whether or not the individual in question is a national of a state party or committed crimes on the territory of a state party (article 13).

States parties are required to cooperate with the Court with regard to arrests, sharing of evidence and other matters pursuant to properly executed requests by the Court. There are, however, exceptions to the general obligation to cooperate and weak powers of enforcement in cases of non-cooperation. For example, state parties may refuse requests for assistance from the Prosecutor where they concern evidence or documents that relate to national security (article 93(4)). In the event of non-cooperation by a state party, the Court may refer the matter to the Assembly of States Parties, or in the case of a Security Council referral, to the Security Council.

Persons convicted under the Rome Statute are subject to a maximum sentence of life in prison. They may also be fined and required to forfeit any proceeds, property, and assets they derived from the crime (article 77). Sentences of imprisonment are served in states that have indicated their willingness to accept sentenced persons (article 103). In addition to sentencing the accused, the Court may order the transfer of money and other property collected through fines or forfeiture to a Trust Fund to be established by the states parties for the benefit of victims of the crimes within the Court's jurisdiction and their families (article 79).[64] The Court

---

62   Rome Statute, above note 50, art. 11(1) provides: "The Court has jurisdiction only with respect to crimes committed after the entry into force of this Statute." Rome Statute art. 24(1) provides: "No person shall be criminally responsible under this Statute for conduct prior to the entry into force of the Statute."

63   The fact that a state is not party to the Rome Statute does not, therefore, shield a war criminal in that state from the Court for crimes he committed after 1 July 2002 and before the date of ratification or accession. A successor government in that state could authorize the Court to act in the particular case by simply making an art. 12(3) declaration, provided the declaration is made prior to becoming a party to the Rome Statute.

64   In Canada's case, funds obtained from the disposal of forfeited assets related to Rome Statute crimes will be paid into the Crimes Against Humanity Fund, established under the *Crimes Against Humanity and War Crimes Act*, SC 2000 c. 24. Canada may then deliver the obtained funds to the International Criminal Court, to its Trust Fund, or to victims directly.

can also make an order against a convicted person for restitution, compensation, or rehabilitation of victims (article 79). Both the Prosecutor and the convicted person are entitled to file appeals in respect of decisions of acquittal or conviction, and against sentence (article 81).[65]

One of the most distinctive and important features of the International Criminal Court is its relation to national courts. The Rome Statute is premised on the principle of complementarity. This means that the International Criminal Court will only act when states are unable or unwilling genuinely to investigate or prosecute cases at the domestic level. Specifically, Rome Statute article 17(1) provides that a case will be inadmissible before the International Criminal Court where

a) the case is being investigated or prosecuted by a State which has jurisdiction over it, unless the State is unwilling or unable genuinely to carry out the investigation or prosecution;
b) the case has been investigated by a State which has jurisdiction over it and the State has decided not to prosecute the person concerned, unless the decision resulted from the unwillingness or inability of the State genuinely to prosecute;
c) the person concerned has already been tried for conduct which is the subject of the complaint, and a trial by the Court is not permitted under article 20, paragraph 3;[66] or
d) the case is not of sufficient gravity to justify further action by the Court.

In this respect the International Criminal Court differs from the ICTY and ICTR, which have primacy over all cases within their subject matter jurisdiction whether or not there are investigations or prosecutions at the domestic level.

The Rome Statute sets out specific factors to determine unwillingness and inability in any particular case. On unwillingness, article 17(2) requires the Court to consider whether one or more of the following factors is present:

a) the proceedings were or are being undertaken or the national decision was made for the purpose of shielding the person concerned from criminal responsibility for crimes within the jurisdiction of the Court referred to in article 5;

---

65 The grounds are procedural error, error of fact, and error of law. The convicted person may also appeal based on "any other ground that affects the fairness or reliability of the proceedings or decision" (art. 81(1)(b)(iv)). Appeals may also be made against other decisions of the Court including decisions concerning jurisdiction or admissibility. See generally art. 82.
66 See the discussion of Rome Statute art. 20(3) below.

b) there has been an unjustified delay in the proceedings which in the circumstances is inconsistent with an intent to bring the person concerned to justice; or

c) the proceedings were not or are not being conducted independently or impartially, and they were or are being conducted in a manner which, in the circumstances, is inconsistent with an intent to bring the person concerned to justice.

On inability, article 17(3) requires the Court to consider

> whether, due to a total or substantial collapse or unavailability of its national judicial system, the State is unable to obtain the accused or the necessary evidence and testimony or otherwise unable to carry out its proceedings.

Rome Statute article 20(3) reinforces article 17 by providing an exception to the principle of *ne bis in idem* (double jeopardy), allowing the Court jurisdiction to hear cases previously tried at the domestic level if the domestic trials were a sham.[67]

Proceedings before the International Criminal Court may be initiated by the Prosecutor (article 53), a state party to the Rome Statute (article 14), or the Security Council (article 13). Article 53 gives the Prosecutor the discretion to initiate a prosecution if, among other things, a case is or would be admissible under article 17 and would likely serve the interests of justice. In the event of a decision not to investigate or prosecute, the Prosecutor's exercise of discretion may be subject to review by the Court's Pre-Trial Chamber (article 53(3)). Also, pursuant to a resolution under Chapter VII of the UN Charter, the Security Council has the power to request a deferral of investigation or prosecution for a period of up to twelve months, which period may be renewed under the same conditions (article 16).[68]

---

67   Article 20(3) provides:

> No person who has been tried by another court for conduct also proscribed under articles 6, 7 or 8 shall be tried by the Court with respect to the same conduct unless the proceedings in the other court: (a) Were for the purpose of shielding the person concerned from criminal responsibility for crimes within the jurisdiction of the Court; or (b) Otherwise were not conducted independently or impartially in accordance with the norms of due process recognized by international law and were conducted in a manner which, in the circumstances, was inconsistent with an intent to bring the person concerned to justice.

68   See SC res. 1487 (2003), which renews a prior Chapter VII resolution prohibiting the Court from exercising jurisdiction for a one-year period over nationals of states not party to the Rome Statute in respect of any military or peace operation

For the moment it is impossible to predict how broadly or narrowly articles 17, 20, or 53 will be interpreted. The publication of prosecutorial guidelines would help guide states parties and also help assuage the concerns of non-state parties, many of whom consider the Office of the Prosecutor — an office entrusted with the power to investigate and prosecute sitting heads of state if necessary — too independent and unaccountable.[69]

Considering its lack of retroactive jurisdiction and other barriers to jurisdiction and admissibility, it is possible that the Court will lie relatively dormant for the first few years of its life. Yet the indirect impact of the Rome Statute on domestic accountability efforts may be quite substantial. One of the great virtues of the Rome Statute is that it encourages states parties to codify, investigate, and try the international crimes it defines. This is critical, because even after the Court becomes more fully operational, it will likely be unable to handle any greater number of cases than the ICTY or ICTR. Domestic courts will remain, necessarily, the forum of primary resort.

C. MIXED CRIMINAL TRIBUNALS

Mixed criminal tribunals (sometimes called "hybrid" or "internationalized" criminal tribunals) represent the latest trend in international criminal justice. The appellation "mixed" stems from two features of these tribunals: jurisdiction to apply a combination of domestic and international law, and a judicial and prosecutorial staff drawn from a domestic and international pool of candidates. Mixed tribunals are located in the state where the violations actually took place, rather than in a foreign state. This enables greater access to evidence and witnesses, and may also have positive effects on the local justice system. It also keeps costs down. The Sierra Leone Special Court is budgeted to cost a mere fifth of the ICTY on an annual basis.[70]

---

established or authorized by the UN. As this book went to press, Resolution 1487 expired and was not renewed. See "Analysis: US drops immunity request" BBC News, (http://news.bbc.co.uk), 24 June 2004.

69   See Danner, "Enhancing the Legitimacy," above note 43.

70   See UN Press Briefing on Sierra Leone Special Court, 20 March 2002. According to the briefing, the Security Council had made it clear that it did not want another ICTY or ICTR for various reasons, including "their budgets and the speed at which they operated." Although the Special Court's budget is expected to increase significantly as it moves out of the start-up phase, it will never approach the budgets of the ICTY or ICTR.

Unlike the ICTY and the ICTR, existing mixed tribunals do not possess Chapter VII powers (though future mixed tribunals could). They therefore lack a direct relationship with the UN Security Council for purposes of compelling states to cooperate in the transfer of suspects and evidence. But their location on-site lessens the need for this sort of support.

There are currently three mixed tribunals in operation, namely those of Kosovo ("Regulation 64" panels), Timor-Leste ("Serious Crime Panels") and Sierra Leone (the "Special Court"). Each is reviewed below. There will also soon be established a mixed criminal tribunal in Cambodia. Between 1975 and 1979, the Khmer Rouge, a brutal Maoist regime that killed more than one million people, ruled Cambodia. No Khmer Rouge leader has ever been fairly tried,[71] and its overall leader, Pol Pot, is already dead. After five years of negotiation, the UN and the Cambodian government recently agreed on the establishment of the tribunal.[72] The so-called "Extraordinary Chambers" will be based in Phnom Penh, Cambodia, and will try remaining "senior leaders" of the Khmer Rouge and "those who were most responsible" for the crimes of genocide, crimes against humanity, and war crimes. The tribunal will have a majority of Cambodian judges and a minority of international judges, and will work alongside Cambodian and international co-prosecutors.[73]

1) Kosovo

Following the NATO-led intervention in Kosovo in 1999, the UN Interim Administration Mission in Kosovo (UNMIK) faced the challenge of re-building a devastated local justice system that had been dominated by Serbian judges and lawyers. While the ICTY was expected to deal with the worst instances of international crime committed in Kosovo,

---

71   During its occupation of Cambodia, the Vietnamese conducted a show trial of Khmer Rouge leaders in *absentia*. S. Ratner & J. Abrams, *Accountability for Human Rights Atrocities in International Law*, 2d ed. (Oxford: Oxford University Press) at 277.

72   The agreement was reached in March 2003 and later approved by the UN General Assembly. It is, however, subject to final approval by the Cambodian National Assembly.

73   Human rights NGOs such as Amnesty International and Human Rights Watch have criticized the proposed tribunal for Cambodia. They have expressed concerns about various issues including the lack of victim and witness protections and the susceptibility of the proposed tribunal to government interference and manipulation. See Human Rights Watch, *Serious Flaws: Why the UN General Assembly Should Require Changes to the Draft Khmer Rouge Tribunal Agreement* (2003).

there remained a great many who would need to be tried within Kosovo proper. UNMIK chose to issue regulations permitting foreign judges to serve alongside domestic judges on existing Kosovar courts, and foreign lawyers to join forces with local lawyers to prosecute as well as defend individual cases. The arrangement is intended to be temporary, pending improvements in the capacity and reputation of the Kosovar judiciary. The applicable law is a hybrid of international law and the law in force in Kosovo prior to 22 March 1989.[74]

In the initial phase of operation, the foreign judges comprised a minority on any individual trial panel. UNMIK subsequently issued a new regulation permitting defendants in highly sensitive cases (or their lawyers, prosecutors, or the Department of Justice) to petition UNMIK to hold the trial before three judges, at least two of whom would be international.[75] These so-called "Regulation 64 panels" have held more than two dozen war crimes trials. They will likely remain in place for many years to come, pending a final determination on the status of Kosovo, which remains a dependency under UN administration and authority.[76]

2) Timor-Leste

During a quarter-century of Indonesian occupation (1975–99), almost one-third of the population of East Timor (now Timor-Leste) was killed. In September 1999, immediately after the release of results of a UN-sponsored referendum on independence, Indonesian forces and local militias launched a final attack on Timorese civilians resulting in the death of hundreds of people, the displacement of hundreds of thousands more, and the destruction of most of the island's infrastructure. Order was finally restored forcibly by INTERFET, an Australian-led multinational force on which Canada served. On 25 October 1999, the UN Security Council, using its Chapter VII authority to restore peace and security, adopted Resolution 1272 establishing the UN Transitional Administration in East Timor (UNTAET). The UN Secretary-General was given authority under the resolution to appoint a UN administrator to exercise all legislative and executive authority, includ-

---

74 UNMIK Resolution 1999/24 and UNMIK Resolution 1999/25. Local Kosovar law is only applicable to the extent it conforms to international human rights norms.

75 Regulation 2000/64. In all other cases the trial is conducted before a panel of Kosovar judges and a single international judge.

76 See generally W. Betts et al., "The Post-Conflict Transitional Administration of Kosovo and the Lessons Learned in Efforts to Establish a Judiciary and the Rule of Law" (2001) 22 Michigan Journal of International Law 371 at 381.

ing the administration of justice — at least until the date of the island's independence.[77]

Under UNTAET administration, "Special Panels" within the Dili District court were established. They were vested with exclusive jurisdiction over "serious criminal offences," defined in various UNTAET regulations to include genocide, war crimes, and crimes against humanity, as well as murder, sexual offences, and torture.[78] The Panels, and the appeals chamber, each comprise two international judges and one East Timorese judge (although a panel of five judges, composed of three international and two East Timorese judges, may be established in appeal cases of especial importance). The Panels are supported by a Serious Crimes Unit (SCU), which is responsible for investigating and prosecuting crimes within the Panels' jurisdiction. The majority of the SCU's staff is international, but many East Timorese are being trained as investigators and prosecutors to carry out this work. The Special Panels are also supported by a legal aid service, which provides defence counsel to accused persons. The Panels are complemented by the work of the East Timor Commission for Reception, Truth, and Reconciliation (CRTR), a truth commission established to support justice, reconciliation, and reconstruction efforts within the country.[79] To date, the Special Panels have only heard cases involving serious criminal offences committed in 1999. The Serious Crimes Unit can, however, investigate and bring charges for crimes committed prior to 1999 as long as they fall within its general subject-matter jurisdiction. Despite a large number of indictments against Indonesian suspects, to date

---

77   Timor-Leste became an independent, sovereign state on 20 May 2002.

78   Under UN Regulations 2000/11 (para. 10.2) and 2000/15 (para. 2.3), the Special Panels of the District Court in Dili have exclusive jurisdiction over cases of rape and murder committed between 1 January 1999 and 25 October 1999. Other district courts are vested with jurisdiction over cases of rape and murder committed outside that time frame.

79   The CRTR receives confessions from perpetrators of human rights violations. Prior to accepting any confession, the CRTR must inform the confessant that a copy will be sent to the Office of the General Prosecutor (OGP). The OGP then has 14 days to make a decision regarding whether the confession discloses serious criminal offences and whether the individual will be prosecuted for those offences. If the OGP declines the option of prosecution, the Commission may initiate a "community reconciliation process" for the confessant, which involves a public hearing and the arrangement of a "community reconciliation agreement" between him and a "community of reception." The agreements generally require the confessant to perform acts of community service and express his contrition.

Indonesia has refused to extradite any of those indicted by the Special Panels.[80]

3) Sierra Leone

In the 1990s, Sierra Leone experienced a period of civil war marked by the use of child soldiers, sexual enslavement, and systematic acts of physical mutilation. Rampant corruption, widespread poverty, and a dysfunctional judicial system compounded the situation. In June 2000, Sierra Leonean President Ahmad Tejan Kabbah requested UN assistance in establishing a forum to try persons suspected of committing international crimes during the civil war. In response, the UN Security Council passed Resolution 1315 (2000), which requested the Secretary-General to enter into negotiations with the government on the establishment of a "Special Court" for Sierra Leone. A draft agreement and draft statute for the Court were eventually agreed upon by the UN and the government of Sierra Leone, and by 2002 the Court became operational.[81] Its initial three-year budget is approximately US$75 million, and is based entirely on voluntary contributions from UN member states.[82] Canada chairs the non-judicial Management Committee of the Special Court.[83]

Based in Freetown, Sierra Leone, the Special Court consists of a Trial Chamber and an Appeals Chamber. The Court is composed of eight judges — five appointed by the UN Secretary-General (three of whom serve on the Appeals Chamber) and three appointed by the gov-

---

80　See generally the website of the Judicial System Monitoring Programme: http://www.jsmp.minihub.org/trials.htm. It is an NGO based in Timor-Leste that monitors the trials daily.

81　The Court's website is http://www.sc-sl.org/.

82　Canada is contributing $2.25 million over three years to the Court, a portion of which will be used to hire Canadian experts to work there. DFAIT press release, "Canadian Appointed to Sierra Leone Special Court," 25 July 2002.

83　Article 7 of the Agreement between the UN and the Government of Sierra Leone on the Establishment of a Special Court for Sierra Leone 2002 sets out the Committee's role and composition:

> It is the understanding of the Parties that interested States will establish a management committee to assist the Secretary-General in obtaining adequate funding, and provide advice and policy direction on all non-judicial aspects of the operation of the Court, including questions of efficiency, and to perform other functions as agreed by interested States. The management committee shall consist of important contributors to the Special Court. The Government of Sierra Leone and the Secretary-General will also participate in the management committee.

ernment of Sierra Leone (two of whom serve on the Appeals Chamber). Two of the judges are Sierra Leoneans and the remaining six are foreign nationals.[84] The prosecutors and investigators are also a mix of nationals and foreigners. The Special Court has jurisdiction over crimes committed by any natural person in the territory of Sierra Leone after 30 November 1996, the date of the failed Abidjan Peace Agreement.[85] Thus, the Court can also indict citizens of other states provided their crimes were committed in the territory of Sierra Leone, though there is no duty on foreign states to cooperate with the Court.[86] The Special Court's statute authorizes it to try persons who bear "the greatest responsibility" for the following crimes: crimes against humanity, violations of Common Article 3, and other serious violations of international humanitarian or Sierra Leonean law.[87]

Unlike the mixed tribunals in Timor-Leste and Kosovo, the Special Court operates outside of the domestic judicial system rather than being grafted onto it. And while there is a parallel truth commission in operation in Sierra Leone, just as there is in Timor-Leste, in this case the commission is legally and operationally independent of the Court.[88]

---

84   Brigadier-General Pierre G. Boutet, a longtime judge in the Canadian Armed Forces, is a judge in the Special Court's Trial Chamber.

85   This limitation in the Court's temporal jurisdiction was controversial, since many atrocities were committed during the early part of the civil war between 1991 and 1996.

86   In June 2003, the Special Court issued a warrant for the arrest of (then incumbent) President Charles Taylor of Liberia. Taylor is accused of having armed and trained Sierra Leone's rebels. He was granted asylum in Nigeria, which has so far resisted calls to transfer him to the Court. "Arrest Warrant for Liberian Leader," BBC News (http://news.bbc.co.uk), 4 June 2003.

87   For domestic crimes that the Court is empowered to try (for example, "abuse of girls" and "wanton destruction of property"), the *de facto* start date of the Court's jurisdiction is 7 July 1999. That was the date the Sierra Leone government and rebels signed the Lomé Peace Accord. It granted a blanket amnesty for all crimes committed during the conflict. At the signing of the accord, the UN Secretary-General's special representative placed a last-minute reservation stipulating that the UN considered the amnesty inapplicable to "international crimes of genocide, crimes against humanity and war crimes." See Report of the Secretary General on the Establishment of a Special Court for Sierra Leone, UN doc. S/2000/915 (2000) at paras. 22–24. Because of the UN reservation, the Special Court is able to try international crimes committed during the period otherwise covered by the amnesty.

88   Although there initially appeared to be a need for a formal information sharing arrangement between the truth commission and the Special Court, in the end both bodies chose to conduct independent investigations. See W. Schabas, "The Relationship Between Truth Commissions and International Courts: The Case of Sierra Leone" (2003) 25 Human Rights Quarterly 1035. Schabas, a Canadian, serves as a commissioner on the Sierra Leone Truth and Reconciliation Commission.

**Table 17.1: A Comparison of Selected International and Mixed
Criminal Tribunals (as of February 2004)**

	ICTY	ICTR	International Criminal Court	Sierra Leone Special Court
Location	The Hague, Netherlands	Arusha, Tanzania (Trial Chamber), Kigali, Rwanda (Office of the Prosecutor), and The Hague (Appeals Chamber)	The Hague, Netherlands (but the Court can sit elsewhere)	Freetown, Sierra Leone
How established	By the UN Security Council acting under Chapter VII	By the UN Security Council acting under Chapter VII	By treaty (Rome Statute)	By mutual agreement between the UN and the government of Sierra Leone
Period of operation	1993–	1995–	2002–	2002–
Duration of existence	Temporary	Temporary	Permanent	Temporary
Subject-matter jurisdiction	Grave breaches of the Geneva Conventions 1949, violations of the laws and customs of war, genocide, and crimes against humanity	Violations of Common Article 3 or the GC Protocol II, crimes against humanity, genocide	Crimes against humanity, war crimes, genocide	Crimes against humanity, violations of Common Article 3 and the GC Protocol II, other serious violations of humanitarian law, and serious crimes under Sierra Leonean law
Temporal jurisdiction	Crimes committed since 1 January 1991 (no end date)	Crimes committed in 1994	Crimes committed after 1 July 2002 (and possibly later, depending on nature and date of ratification)	Crimes committed after 30 November 1996
Territorial jurisdiction	Crimes committed on the territory of former Yugoslavia	Crimes committed on the territory of Rwanda (by anyone) or in neighbouring countries (by Rwandans)	See personal jurisdiction below.	Crimes committed on the territory of Sierra Leone

	ICTY	ICTR	International Criminal Court	Sierra Leone Special Court
Personal jurisdiction	Natural persons of any state.	Natural persons of any state.	Natural persons. Nationals of a state party, nationals of a non-state party (where crimes were committed on the territory of a state party, or where the state makes a declaration under Rome Statute art. 12(3) or where the Security Council refers the case to the Court)	Natural persons of any state. Persons "who bear the greatest responsibility for serious violations of international humanitarian law and Sierra Leonean law."
Relation to national courts	Primacy over domestic courts of any country in the world. Jurisdiction is concurrent not exclusive.	Primacy over domestic courts of any country in the world. Jurisdiction is concurrent not exclusive.	No primacy. Not concurrent either. Court only has jurisdiction where state is unwilling or unable genuinely to investigate or prosecute a case.	Primacy over Sierra Leonean courts. Jurisdiction is concurrent not exclusive.
Appeals structure	Separate appeals chamber (shares with ICTR)	Separate appeals chamber (shares with ICTY)	Separate appeals chamber	Separate appeals chamber
Annual Budget	US$100 million (ca.) (2002)	US$80 million (ca.) (2002)	US$50 million (ca.) (for first year of operation)	US$18 million (ca.) (for first year of operation)
Primary Source of funds	UN assessed contributions	UN assessed contributions	Contributions by states parties	Voluntary contributions, by Canada, the US, the UK, and the Netherlands
Number and nationality of judges	16 permanent judges, 9 *ad litem* (all from diverse countries)	9 permanent judges, 1 *ad litem* judge (all from diverse countries)	18 permanent judges (all from states parties)	8 permanent judges (6 foreign nationals, 2 Sierra Leoneans)
Number and nationality of staff	1,300 (ca.) (from diverse countries)	800 (ca.) (from diverse countries)	In process of recruitment	Approx. 300 (about half of whom will be Sierra Leoneans)
Number of completed cases	50	19	None	None

CHAPTER 18

FOREIGN CRIMINAL AND CIVIL PROCEEDINGS

With increasing frequency, courts outside the state where gross and systematic human rights violations occur are conducting criminal trials against those responsible — even where the crime in question involves foreigners and foreign elements.[1] Criminal trials by foreign courts have been particularly significant in cases where the judicial system in the state of commission is unable or unwilling to punish the offender, and where there is no international tribunal with jurisdiction. Some states also allow victims of extra-territorial human rights violations to seek and obtain civil redress before their courts. It is only in the US, however, that civil redress is available for extra-territorial human rights violations committed by foreign nationals against other foreign nationals.

The availability of criminal and civil proceedings before foreign courts is circumscribed not only by a state's domestic law but also by various rules of jurisdiction under international law. We begin by explaining these rules, before turning to consider the use of foreign courts to remedy human rights violations.

---

1 Subject to applicable rules of private international law, a foreign court may be able to try an international crime using domestic criminal laws (for example, to try forced disappearance as kidnapping). The focus of this chapter, however, is on trials for international crimes as such. See S. Ratner & J. Abrams, *Accountability for Human Rights Atrocities in International Law*, 2d ed. (Oxford: Oxford University Press, 2001) at 181–12 [Ratner, *Accountability*] regarding the use of ordinary criminal laws to try cases of gross human rights violations.

A. JURISDICTION

1) Prescriptive Jurisdiction

It is a widely acknowledged rule of international law that states (and therefore their courts) are generally prohibited from interfering in the domestic affairs of other states. Yet events or offences occurring in one state may have a range of connecting factors to another state. Consequently, there exist a number of international principles regarding what is known as "prescriptive jurisdiction" — a state's jurisdiction or power to prescribe conduct. These principles are found not only in the domestic law of individual states, but also in international treaty and customary law.[2]

There are five principles of prescriptive jurisdiction. A foreign court must be acting under at least one. The first and most important is the *territorial principle*, which provides that a court will generally have jurisdiction over all aspects of a case involving an offence committed within its national territory. A French court, for example, will generally have jurisdiction over a murder that was committed in France, even if the perpetrator and victim were non-nationals.[3]

If, however, an offence is committed outside of French territory, a French court (or any other foreign court) might establish jurisdiction on the basis of one or more of the following four principles:

a) the *nationality principle*, whereby a French court purports to exercise jurisdiction over an offence committed outside France based solely on the fact that the alleged offender is a French national,

b) the *passive personality principle*, whereby a French court purports to exercise jurisdiction over an offence committed outside France based solely on the fact that the victim is a French national,

c) the *protective principle*, whereby a French court purports to exercise jurisdiction over an offence committed outside France by and against persons who are not French nationals based on the fact that the offence was considered to have had a detrimental effect on the security interests of France, or

d) the *universality principle*, whereby a French court purports to exercise jurisdiction over an offence committed outside France by and

---

2   For more on prescriptive jurisdiction, see J. Currie, *Public International Law* (Toronto: Irwin Law, 2001) [Currie, *International Law*] at 297–310.

3   See, for example, CAT art. 5(1)(a). It requires states parties to exercise jurisdiction over instances of torture when committed "in any territory under its jurisdiction or on board a ship or aircraft registered in that State."

against persons who are not French nationals based on the fact that the offence is considered by the international community to be of universal, and not simply French, concern.

The nationality principle, like the territorial principle, is accepted across the vast majority of domestic legal systems. The other three principles, but especially the protective principle, are less widely accepted.

2) Enforcement Jurisdiction

A foreign court having prescriptive jurisdiction over a case will need to be able to enforce its orders against persons and property. The rules of enforcement jurisdiction govern whether and how that is done. The most important rule of enforcement jurisdiction is that states, through their courts, exercise near-plenary enforcement jurisdiction in regard to persons and property located within their territorial boundaries. This means, for example, that France may generally investigate, arrest, and prosecute a non-national residing in France for crimes committed there. If, however, the individual resides outside of France, then it must legally obtain custody of him. In criminal matters, this is usually effected by way of extradition; in civil matters, this is usually effected by service of process.[4]

3) Jurisdictional Immunities

Even if a foreign court possesses prescriptive jurisdiction and can enforce its orders, it still may not be able to exercise its jurisdiction because of state or diplomatic immunity.

The function of state (or sovereign) immunity is to shield certain organs or officials of a state from most exercises of prescriptive or enforcement jurisdiction by another state or its courts. Canada's *State Immunity Act* defines "foreign state" to include

a) any sovereign or other head of the foreign state or of any political subdivision of the foreign state while acting as such in a public capacity,
b) any government of the foreign state or of any political subdivision of the foreign state, including any of its departments, and any agency of the foreign state, and

---

4   For more on enforcement jurisdiction, see Currie, *International Law*, above note 2 at 293–96.

c) any political subdivision of the foreign state.[5]

Other jurisdictions such as the US and the UK employ similar definitions.

While the rules of state immunity may seem almost absolute, they are in fact limited. For example, the customary international law doctrine of restrictive state immunity provides that a state is immune from the jurisdiction of foreign courts for its sovereign or public acts (*jure imperii*) but not for acts of a private or commercial character (*jure gestionis*). Another limitation on the scope of state immunity turns on the distinction between immunity *ratione personae* (personal jurisdiction) and immunity *ratione materiae* (subject-matter jurisdiction). Under this distinction, a state official might find himself unable to rely on state immunity, not because he lacks the status of a state official, but because the acts complained of cannot be described as state acts; the official enjoys immunity *ratione personae*, but not immunity *ratione materiae*.[6] To date, human rights litigants have faced enormous difficulty in overcoming state immunity defences.[7]

Diplomatic and related immunities may also limit the exercise of prescriptive and enforcement jurisdiction. The Vienna Convention on

---

5   RSC 1985 c. S-18. Compare against the International Law Commission's Draft Articles on Jurisdictional Immunities of States and Their Property (1991) 30 ILM 1554. The Commission defines "state" at art. 1(b) to mean:

   i)   the State and its various organs of government;
   ii)   constituent units of a federal State;
   iii) political subdivisions of the State which are entitled to perform acts in the exercise of the sovereign authority of the State;
   iv)   agencies or instrumentalities of the State and other entities, to the extent that they are entitled to perform acts in the exercise of the sovereign authority of the State;
   v)   representatives of the State acting in that capacity.

6   See, for example, *In re: Estate of Ferdinand Marcos Human Rights Litigation*, 25 F. 3d 1467 (9th Cir. 1994) at 1470–72 [*Marcos*], in which a US court held that official status does not provide immunity for gross violations of human rights because they can never be properly characterized as official acts. See also the opinion of Lord Browne-Wilkinson in *R. v. Bow Street Metropolitan Stipendiary Magistrate and others, ex parte Pinochet Ugarte (No. 2)*, [1999] 2 WLR 272 (H.L.) [*Bow Street*].

7   Recently, some litigants have asserted a so-called "normative hierarchy theory." The theory operates as follows: state immunity is not a peremptory international legal norm; some human rights are peremptory norms; in case of conflict between peremptory human rights norms and non-peremptory state immunity, the former trump because they outrank the latter in the hierarchy of international legal sources. For a critical appraisal of the theory, see L. Caplan, "State Immunity, Human Rights and *Jus Cogens*: A Critique of the Normative Hierarchy Theory" (2003) 97 AJIL 741.

Diplomatic Relations 1961[8] provides broad immunities and privileges to diplomatic personnel and property attached to embassies and high commissions. Under the Convention, the host state owes a general duty of protection to diplomats. They and their family members are entitled to be free from physical restraint or interference[9] and from any local legal process.[10] A similarly broad set of immunities and privileges applies to consular officials[11] and UN officials.[12]

While these immunities and privileges create conditions for abuse, a host state can always revoke an individual's diplomatic status (that is, declare her *persona non grata*) or bring an international claim against the sending state. For its part, the sending state retains the right to waive the diplomatic immunity of the individual in question.

B. HUMAN RIGHTS-RELATED FOREIGN CRIMINAL PROCEEDINGS

States are generally not required to make their courts available for criminal actions in respect of extra-territorial human rights offences. This rule may, however, be displaced by treaty. Some treaties create a state obligation to prosecute and punish extra-territorial offences.[13] Others create an obligation to "extradite or prosecute."[14] States are also free to exceed what is strictly required by treaty. For example, the Genocide Convention only requires states parties to punish acts of genocide when they are carried out on national territory. Yet a number of states permit the prosecution of extra-territorial acts of genocide.[15]

---

8   [1966] CanTS no. 29.

9   *Ibid.*, art. 29. This is known as the principle of "inviolability."

10   *Ibid.*, art. 37. Art. 38 limits a diplomat's immunity to "official acts performed in the exercise of his functions," and art. 41 requires a diplomat to "respect the laws and regulations of the receiving State."

11   Vienna Convention on Consular Relations 1963 [1974] CanTS no. 25.

12   Convention on the Privileges and Immunities of the United Nations 1946 [1948] CanTS no. 2.

13   See, for example, Genocide Convention art. 6; Hague Convention for the Protection of Cultural Property in the Event of Armed Conflict 1954, 249 UNTS 240, art. 28.

14   See, for example, CRC-OP-SC art. 5; GC4 art. 146; GC Protocol I art. 85(1).

15   For example, Canada permits prosecutions for genocide, crimes against humanity, and war crimes committed outside Canada if the accused is a Canadian citizen or someone employed by Canada in a civilian or military capacity, or is a citizen of an enemy state or employed by an enemy state. Canada also permits prosecutions for these crimes if the victim was a Canadian or a citizen of an

Where a state is required or permitted to try an extra-territorial human rights offence, it must have custody of the defendant. Although there remain some legal systems that permit criminal trials in *abstentia* — mostly European civil law systems — these remain somewhat controversial.[16] Where the defendant is not already on the territory of the prosecuting state, custody of the defendant is typically acquired by way of extradition. Many states are party to bilateral extradition treaties and, as just noted, states may also be bound to extradite persons pursuant to multilateral treaties. Extradition treaties tend to limit the availability of extradition to those crimes listed in the treaty and constituting a crime in both the sending and receiving state.[17] Another typical provision in extradition treaties is the rule of specialty, which requires that the receiving state try the accused only for the crime that formed the express basis of the extradition request.[18] Consistent with the rule against double jeopardy, bilateral extradition treaties also tend to bar extradition where the person sought has already been acquitted or convicted in the sending state for the same offence for which extradition is requested.[19] In many treaties the running of limitation periods for certain offences may serve as a bar to extradition as well.[20]

State may also gain custody of wanted persons in the absence of a treaty. Extradition may occur on the basis of principles of reciprocity and comity. States may also obtain custody of an accused by means of

---

allied state, or if the alleged offender is present in Canada: *Crimes Against Humanity and War Crimes Act* SC 2000 c. 24 s. 8.

16 Note that ICCPR art. 14(3)(d) entitles everyone to "defend himself in person."

17 See, for example, art. 2(1) of the Canada-South Africa Extradition Treaty 2001 [2001] CanTS no. 20. This is known as the rule of "dual criminality."

18 See, for example, *ibid.*, art. 17.

19 See, for example, *ibid.*, art. 3(5). But see Principle 9(1) of the Princeton Principles on Universal Jurisdiction 2001:

> In the exercise of universal jurisdiction, a state or its judicial organs shall ensure that a person who is subject to criminal proceedings shall not be exposed to multiple prosecutions or punishment for the same criminal conduct where the prior criminal proceedings or other accountability proceedings have been conducted in good faith and in accordance with international norms and standards. Sham prosecutions or derisory punishment resulting from a conviction or other accountability proceedings shall not be recognized as falling within the scope of this Principle.

20 See, for example, the Canada-South Africa Extradition Treaty, *ibid.*, art. 3(3). But see Principle 6 of the Princeton Principles on Universal Jurisdiction 2001: "Statutes of limitations or other forms of prescription shall not apply to serious crimes under international law as specified in Principle 2(1)."

deportation, or by simply arresting him as he passes through on a visit (as occurred with General Pinochet in the UK). Such arrests may be carried out pursuant to a domestic or international arrest warrant.[21] States have occasionally abducted accused persons from within the borders of foreign states, but such actions violate international law.[22] Foreign courts will also generally need access to property and evidence related to the crime. As a rule, such access is obtained by means of formal requests for judicial assistance, whether by means of letters rogatory or under the terms of a bilateral or multilateral treaty for mutual legal assistance.[23]

Upon obtaining custody of the defendant, the foreign court must justify its seizure of jurisdiction on the basis of one of the five principles of prescriptive jurisdiction. In the human rights context the most common, and controversial, basis of jurisdiction is the universality principle.[24] Most treaties are silent on the question of universal jurisdiction: they neither prohibit nor require it. Other treaties, such as the CAT (article 7(1)) and the Geneva Conventions (for example, GC4 article 147), require it. For international crimes that are primarily based on custom, international law generally takes a permissive approach to invocations of the universality principle.[25]

The watershed universal jurisdiction event in the post-Cold War era was the UK arrest, and subsequent hearings, concerning former

---

21 International arrest warrants are authorized by means of Interpol "red notices." The basis for a red notice is the arrest warrant or court order issued by judicial authorities in the state seeking the arrest.

22 Perhaps the most famous example was Israel's abduction of Adolf Eichmann from Argentina in 1960, which was condemned but tolerated by the international community. See the decision of the Israeli Supreme Court in *Attorney General of Israel v. Eichmann* (1962), 36 ILR 277.

23 For example, CAT art. 9 provides:

> (1) States Parties shall afford one another the greatest measure of assistance in connection with criminal proceedings brought in respect of any of the offences referred to in article 4, including the supply of all evidence at their disposal necessary for the proceedings.
>
> (2) States Parties shall carry out their obligations under paragraph 1 of this article in conformity with any treaties on mutual judicial assistance that may exist between them.

See also the Inter-American Convention on Mutual Assistance in Criminal Matters 1992 [1996] OAS TS no. 75. Canada ratified the Convention on 3 June 1996. It is not yet listed in the CanTS.

24 See generally L. Reydams, *Universal Jurisdiction: International and Municipal Legal Perspectives* (Oxford: Oxford University Press, 2003).

25 Ratner, *Accountability*, above note 1 at 162.

Chilean President, General Augusto Pinochet. In 1996, lawyers acting on behalf of Argentine and Chilean victims who had been unable to pursue their claims domestically, filed criminal complaints in Spain against Pinochet.[26] Spanish courts allowed the complaints to proceed, relying on the principle of universal jurisdiction enshrined in Spanish legislation. In October 1998, Pinochet travelled to the UK. A Spanish judge investigating one of the cases, Baltasar Garzón, requested the UK authorities to arrest and extradite him. The UK arrested him.

Pinochet challenged the arrest on the basis that he enjoyed immunity from arrest and extradition as a former head of state. But the House of Lords twice rejected his claim of immunity. In its first judgment, subsequently vacated,[27] the Lords held that international crimes such as torture and crimes against humanity are not functions of a head of state and thus not covered by head of state immunity. In the second decision, the Lords held that Pinochet could not claim immunity for acts of torture that had been committed after the dates that the UK and Chile had ratified the CAT.[28] Subsequently, a British magistrate held that Pinochet could be extradited to Spain on charges of torture and conspiracy to commit torture. But in March 2000, after medical tests determined that he lacked the mental capacity to stand trial, Pinochet was released and returned to Chile.[29]

---

26   In civil law countries such as Spain, victims are often permitted to file a complaint directly before an investigating judge, who may or sometimes must open an investigation concerning the subject matter of the complaint.

27   *R. v. Bow Street Metropolitan Stipendiary Magistrate and others, ex parte Pinochet Ugarte (No. 1)*, [1998] 3 WLR 1456 (HL). The wife of one of the Law Lords hearing the case had previously served on the board of Amnesty International, an *amicus curiae* (friend of the court) in the case. This was the basis for vacating the judgment.

28   *Bow Street*, above note 6.

29   Upon his return to Chile, Pinochet was again brought to trial. There too the Chilean Supreme Court ultimately found him unfit to stand trial on grounds of mental health. Next a Chilean judge, spurred by victims' groups, attempted to have Pinochet stripped of his immunity. But the Chilean Supreme Court rejected the application. "Pinochet immunity challenge fails," BBC News (http://news.bbc.co.uk), 22 October 2003. These setbacks notwithstanding, the effect of the Pinochet case on Chilean truth and justice efforts appears to have been salutary. The Pinochet case spurred many criminal suits in Chilean courts against Pinochet and others, and precipitated an important series of roundtable discussions on human rights involving the military, human rights lawyers, and others. See generally J. Zalaquett, "The Pinochet Case: International and Domestic Repercussions" in A. Henkin, ed., *The Legacy of Abuse* (New York: Aspen Institute and NYU School of Law, 2002).

Outside of Chile, the Pinochet precedent stimulated a torrent of new and unrelated universal jurisdiction cases. Many new cases arose in Europe. Primarily these concerned victims of the genocides in Rwanda and the former Yugoslavia. Investigating judges in Spain also invoked the universality principle to indict past and present military officials responsible for atrocities in Latin America during the 1970s and 1980s. But the largest number, and greatest variety, of universal jurisdiction cases arose in Belgium. Until recently, it had the most permissive domestic criminal provisions on universal jurisdiction. Cases were filed in Belgium against, among others: Mauritanian President Maaouya ould Sid'Ahmed Taya; former Iraqi President Saddam Hussein; Israeli Prime Minister Ariel Sharon; Ivory Coast President Laurent Gbagbo; Rwandan President Paul Kagame; Cuban President Fidel Castro; Central African Republic President Ange-Felix Patassé; Republic of Congo President Denis Sassou Nguesso; Palestinian Authority President Yassir Arafat; former Chadian President Hissène Habré; former Iranian president Hashemi Rafsanjani; and former US President George Bush Sr. The cases in Belgium provoked harsh criticism in some quarters, and even direct threats of reprisal by a few foreign governments.[30] Inevitably, the universal jurisdiction provisions of Belgium's legislation were curtailed. The revised law applies only to cases in which the perpetrator or victim is a Belgian national or a long-term resident of Belgium. The Belgian federal prosecutor must approve all cases with no direct connection to Belgium and then decide whether the case can go forward. Previously there were no such restrictions.[31] Many viewed these reforms as a setback to the cause of universal jurisdiction, but they could also be viewed as refinements that will better serve the cause of international justice over the long term.[32]

---

30 Perhaps the two most notorious examples relate to Israel and the US. When the Belgian Supreme Court held that Israeli Prime Minister Ariel Sharon could be prosecuted after leaving office, Israel recalled its ambassador. When US Secretary of State Colin Powell and former US President George Bush Sr. were named as defendants in an action, the US government threatened to remove NATO headquarters from Brussels. "Belgium drops war crimes cases," BBC News (http://news.bbc.co.uk), 24 September 2003.

31 "Belgium amends war crimes law," BBC News (http://news.bbc.co.uk), 1 August 2003.

32 For a comprehensive overview of the history of the Belgian legislation, see S. Ratner, "Belgium's War Crimes Statute: A Postmortem" (2003) 97 AJIL 888. The author aptly concludes (at 888): "The life and death of Belgium's universal jurisdiction law is a textbook case of the intersection of law and power in the international arena."

The emergence of universal jurisdiction cases around the world in recent years is generally viewed as a positive development. Yet various law and policy concerns have also been expressed.[33] For example, it is commonplace to note that foreign court cases against incumbent dictators and tyrants could increase their incentive to stay in power and limit options like offering sanctuary as a means to encourage democractic transition. Due to the decentralized and *ad hoc* character of universal jurisdiction efforts, there is also concern that arrest warrants issued by unaccountable foreign prosecutors or magistrates could adversely affect otherwise benign national political arrangements.[34] There is concern too about the impact of universal jurisdiction on the conduct of diplomacy inasmuch as foreign indictments against ministers and heads of state could curtail their travel. More generally, concerns persist about the appropriateness of having courts resolve matters that took place wholly within the territory of a foreign state and that concerned mostly or only the citizens of that state. These are valid concerns. But they are concerns that cannot, perhaps, be fully overcome. To a large extent they inhere in the exercise of the universality principle.

C. HUMAN RIGHTS-RELATED FOREIGN CIVIL PROCEEDINGS

Generally, universal jurisdiction relates to criminal matters. But one state, the US, allows human rights-related civil suits on the basis of the universality principle. The two relevant statutes are the *Alien Tort Claims Act*[35] and the *Torture Victim Protection Act*.[36] They have no equivalent in any other country. Both statutes have been relied upon by victims of human rights violations around the world. They have turned the US into the civil suit equivalent of Belgium.[37]

---

33 See generally "Symposium: Universal Jurisdiction: Myths, Realities, and Prospects" (2001) 35 New England Law Review 241.

34 The scenario that is commonly evoked relates to South Africa, where the delicate transition out of white rule might have been upset had there been foreign court cases against senior members of the apartheid-era governments.

35 1 Stat. 73 at 77 (1789) (codified at 28 USC § 1350 (2000)).

36 28 USC § 1350 (2000).

37 In civil law countries, victims commonly seek civil relief in the course of filing criminal complaints. But these are not civil suits. Rather, they are requests for civil relief connected to judicial proceedings of a criminal nature. We do not, therefore, examine them in this section. We also do not examine other US statutes such as the *Antiterrorism and Effective Death Penalty Act* 1996, Pub. L.,

1) The *Alien Tort Claims Act*

The *Alien Tort Claims Act* was enacted as part of the *Judiciary Act* 1789,[38] which purported to set out the scope of federal court jurisdiction over the main subjects of international law at the time. Section 9 of the latter Act provides,

> The district courts shall have original jurisdiction of any civil action by an alien for a tort only, committed in violation of the law of nations or a treaty of the United States.[39]

For almost 200 years this section — known today as the *Alien Tort Claims Act* — remained a rarely-invoked basis of US federal court jurisdiction.

This all changed in 1980 as a result of the landmark *Filártiga v. Peña-Irala* decision.[40] In that case, a civil suit was brought under the *Alien Tort Claims Act* by the family of a seventeen-year-old Paraguayan who had been tortured to death in his country by a police official who subsequently emigrated to the US. In finding for the plaintiff, the court hearing the case made several important pronouncements. It held that whenever an alleged torturer (including an alien) is properly served by an alien plaintiff within the US, the federal courts have subject-matter jurisdiction over the matter.[41] It also held that federal courts must interpret customary international law (that is, the "law of nations") not as it was in 1789, but as it exists today.[42] In addition, the court found that modern international law permits individuals to assert claims against their own state for violations committed by it against them,[43] and that torture committed by public officials constitutes an international tort (that is, a compensable international offence).[44]

No. 104-132, s. 221, 11 Stat. 1214 at 1241. The Act permits civil suits against foreign states for monetary damages causing personal injury or death by, among other things, torture or extrajudicial killing. The victim must have been a US national at the time of the injury, and the foreign state must have been designated a sponsor of terrorism by the US Secretary of State. See, e.g., *Cicippio v. Islamic Republic of Iran*, 18 F. Supp. 2d 62 (D.D.C. 1998).

38   1 Stat. 73.
39   The reasons why the US Congress originally promulgated this law remain in dispute among legal scholars.
40   630 F. 2d 876 (2d Circ. 1980) [*Filártiga*].
41   *Ibid.* at 878.
42   *Ibid.* at 881.
43   *Ibid.* at 884. But note that the *Alien Tort Claims Act* is limited to aliens within the US, and American citizens cannot sue the US government under the Act.
44   *Filártiga, ibid.* at 884.

Later cases have affirmed *Filártiga* with some reservations.[45] A three-part test has emerged since *Filártiga* for determining what categories of acts constitute international torts. The test provides that to constitute an international tort an act must be universally accepted, definable (that is, specific), and obligatory.[46] Thus far in applying the test, US federal courts have affirmed that the following acts constitute international torts: torture;[47] extrajudicial killings;[48] prolonged arbitrary detention;[49] genocide;[50] forced disappearances;[51] and centuries-old violations such as piracy and slavery.[52] Other torts (for example, cruel, inhuman or degrading treatment) have received mixed approval by federal courts as to their international legal status. Others still (for example, fraud) have been rejected, albeit by lower courts only.[53] US case law under the *Alien Tort Claims Act* may be on the verge of further

---

45 The one major exception to the generally favourable line of cases is *Tel-Oren v. Libyan Arab Republic*, 726 F. 2d (D.C. Cir. 1984) at 774, 798–823 [*Tel-Oren*], and particularly the opinion of Bork J., who rejected most of the *Filártiga* principles. He held that the *Alien Tort Claims Act* could have application only to those violations of the law of nations recognized at the time Congress passed the statute in 1789 — namely, violations of safe conduct, infringements of the rights of ambassadors, and piracy. The main thrust of the Bork J.'s arguments has not been affirmed by any subsequent federal court. It has, however, received support among some legal commentators. See, for example, C. Bradley & J. Goldsmith, "The Current Illegitimacy of Human Rights Litigation" (1997) 66 Fordham Law Review 319.

46 *Marcos*, above note 6 at 1475–76 (citing *Filártiga*), and *Xuncax v. Gramajo*, 886 F. Supp. 162 (D. Mass. 1995) at 184 [*Xuncax*]. See also R. Goodman & D. Jinks, "Symposium: Human Rights on the Eve of the Next Century: UN Human Rights Standards & US Law: *Filartiga*'s Firm Footing: International Human Rights and Federal Common Law" (1997) 66 Fordham Law Review 463 at 497.

47 *Filártiga*, above note 40 at 881, and *Marcos, ibid.* at 1472.

48 *Forti v. Suarez-Mason I*, 672 F. Supp. 1531 (N.D. Cal. 1987) at 1539 [*Forti I*], and *Xuncax*, above note 46 at 185.

49 *Forti I, ibid.* at 1541, and *Hilao v. Estate of Marcos*, 103 F .3d 789 (9th Cir. 1996) at 795.

50 *Kadic v. Karadzic*, 70 F. 3d 232 (2d Cir. 1995) at 242 [*Kadic*], in which the international tort of genocide was found to apply to both state and non-state actors.

51 *Forti v. Suarez-Mason II*, 694 F. Supp. 707 (N.D. Cal. 1988) at 710.

52 *Tel-Oren*, above note 45 at 794, and *Kadic*, above note 50 at 240. Regarding all of these crimes, see American Law Institute, *Restatement Third, Foreign Relations Law of the United States* § 702 (1987).

53 See generally Goodman & Jinks, above note 46 at 506–11. See also B. Stephens & M. Ratner, *International Human Rights Litigation in US Courts* (New York: Transnational Publishers Inc., 1996) at 63–94 [Stephens, *Litigation in US*].

developments. As we write, the US Supreme Court has reserved judgment in *Alvarez-Machain v. US*.[54]

Since defendants often fail to appear in cases brought under the *Alien Tort Claims Act*, most are decided by default judgment.[55] In the cases in which litigation has been successful, multi-million dollar judgments have frequently been awarded.[56] Generally, however, the recovery of judgments has been unsuccessful because defendants either have no significant assets in the US, or transfer assets out of the country while the litigation is pending. The problem is exacerbated by difficulties in locating and freezing assets after the start of legal attachment proceedings, the uncertainty of convincing foreign courts to enforce US judgments against their citizens, and the failure to reach the deeper pockets of culpable governments.[57]

2) The *Torture Victim Protection Act*

In March 1992, both Houses of the US Congress voted overwhelmingly in favour of the enactment of the *Torture Victim Protection Act*, and the President signed it into law. By all appearances, its passage was partly intended to complement the *Alien Tort Claims Act* and the principles laid down in *Filártiga* and later cases.[58]

The *Torture Victim Protection Act* authorizes federal civil suits against individuals who "under actual or apparent authority, or color of law, of any foreign nation" torture or summarily execute another person. According to section 2(a), to be a plaintiff in a torture claim one must be a victim, and to be a plaintiff in an extrajudicial killing claim

---

54 334 F. 3d 604 (2003). The case will involve the first in-depth review of the *Alien Tort Claims Act*.

55 The non-appearance of defendants is, however, less common now than in the past.

56 The high damage awards can be explained by the extreme nature of the violations (for example, genocide, torture, forced disappearance) and the fact that there is no cap on the quantum of awardable punitive damages.

57 Although pre-judgment attachment of a defendant's assets will avoid most such problems, this may be either too expensive or simply impossible as a matter of law. In most US states, plaintiffs must post an enormous pre-judgment bond before assets will be frozen. Moreover, foreign courts are often reluctant to freeze assets while litigation is pending. See generally Stephens, *Litigation in US*, above note 53 at 168–69, 218–24.

58 The evidence for this assertion can be found in at least three documents drawn from the legislative record of the *Torture Victim Protection Act*, all of which are contained in Appendix B to Stephens, *Litigation in US*, *ibid.*: the House of Representatives' report on the Act; the Senate's report on the Act; and the signing statement of former President Bush.

one must be a legal representative of the victim's estate or a person who may be a claimant in an action for wrongful death. Section 2(b) provides that plaintiffs must have exhausted all domestic remedies in the state where the alleged tort occurred.[59]

The *Torture Victim Protection Act* differs from the *Alien Tort Claims Act* in important ways. First, the *Torture Victim Protection Act* permits US citizens to claim under it, while the *Alien Tort Claims Act* may only be invoked by foreign nationals. Second, the range of human rights violations covered by the *Torture Victim Protection Act* is limited to torture and extrajudicial killing. Third, the *Torture Victim Protection Act* sets out a ten-year limitation period; by contrast, the *Alien Torts Claims Act* contains no limitation provision.

The *Torture Victim Protection Act* has been used as a basis for jurisdiction in a wide variety of cases of torture and summary execution. Thus far, the treatment of these cases by US courts is similar to the treatment afforded in *Alien Tort Claims Act* cases on similar legal issues.

3) The Future of Foreign Civil Proceedings for Human Rights Violations

On the basis of the US experience, there appear to be several potential benefits of permitting foreign civil suits against human rights violators. Civil suits can provide a measure of psychological relief for individual victims and their communities, and of legal accountability for perpetrators. They may also help create an official record regarding specific violations, and may help deter ongoing or future violations. Also, the initiation of such suits does not preclude the pursuit of simultaneous criminal proceedings (or vice versa), while at the same time offering more flexible evidentiary standards. Finally, these lawsuits can have the benefit of depriving international criminals of the ability to safely visit or reside in the US, or to maintain assets there.

Although civil suits for human rights violations have the potential to impair foreign policy imperatives, to date none of the cases brought under the US statutes has had a discernible adverse impact on sensitive relationships with a foreign government.[60] This may start to change,

---

59 The exhaustion requirement has generally been applied to actions under the *Alien Tort Claims Act* as well.

60 This stands to reason. Plaintiffs must prove exhaustion of domestic remedies. They must also persuade the court that the US is the *forum conveniens* (i.e., that the convenience of the parties and the interests of justice are best served by holding the trial in the US and not elsewhere).

however, as more and more cases are brought against private corporations for their alleged complicity in extra-territorial human rights violations.[61] There have been at least twenty-five such cases against companies in the last decade, though most have been dismissed. In one of the more recent cases, a New York federal district court ruled that a Canadian oil company can be sued for genocide in the US on the basis of its alleged complicity with the Sudanese government in military actions against civilians near its oil fields.[62]

To date, no other country has enacted legislation comparable to the *Alien Tort Claims Act* or the *Torture Victim Protection Act*.[63] A UK-based human rights NGO, Redress, has prepared a parliamentary draft bill (the Redress for Torture Bill) for possible enactment in the UK. The bill has been temporarily shelved as a result of the European Court of Human Rights' decision in *Al-Adsani v. United Kingdom*.[64] The Court held by a 9–8 majority that the UK has no obligation to provide a judicial civil remedy for torture alleged to have been committed by a foreign state.[65] The Superior Court of Justice in Ontario in *Bouzari et al v. Republic of Iran* made a similar finding.[66] In that case, Swinton J. held that Canada has no treaty obligation (including under CAT article 14) that would require it to afford a civil remedy for acts of torture carried

---

61 In May 2003, the US Department of Justice filed an *amicus curiae* brief for the defence in a civil case alleging that the oil company Unocal was complicit in forced labour and other violations attributed to the Burmese military during the construction of a gas pipeline. The case, *Doe v. Unocal Corp.*, 963 F. Supp. (C.D. Cal. 1997), was originally filed in 1996 and is scheduled for rehearing by the US Ninth Circuit Court of Appeals. The US Department's brief went well beyond the *Unocal* case and urged a fundamental re-interpretation of the *Alien Tort Claims Act*. Among other things, the brief asserted that the Act could not serve as a basis for filing civil actions, that its Act's reference to "law of nations" excludes human rights treaties, and that abuses committed outside of the US are not covered. See S. Murphy, "Contemporary Practice of the United States: Department of Justice Position in Unocal Case" (2003) 97 AJIL 703.

62 *Presbyterian Church of Sudan, et al. v. Talisman Energy Inc.*, F. Supp. 2d 289 (S.D.N.Y. 2003). Human rights NGOs have long campaigned against Talisman. Less than a month before the US court's ruling, Talisman sold its 25 percent stake in Sudan's Greater Nile Oil Project. "Talisman pulls out of Sudan," BBC News (http://news.bbc.co.uk), 10 March 2003.

63 For a consideration of the complexity of enacting legislation similar to the US statutes, see C. Scott, ed., *Torture as Tort* (Portland: Hart Publishing, 2001).

64 (35763/97), [2001] ECHR 752 (21 November 2001).

65 *Al-Adsani*, ibid., at para. 40. More generally see Redress, *The Impact of Al-Adsani v. the UK* (2002), available at http://www.redress.org/publications/al_adsani_V_uk.pdf.

66 [2002] OJ No. 1624 (SCJ) [*Bouzari*].

out by a foreign state.[67] Swinton J. further held that the possible *jus cogens* character of the prohibition on torture "does not require an interpretation of the *State Immunity Act* that imports a new exception for actions for damages for torture committed outside Canada, nor does it make the Act contrary to s. 7 of the *Charter*."[68]

In light of the understandable reluctance of courts to create new civil actions, plaintiffs might attempt to found their actions on the basis of domestic tort law rather than an alleged international tort law. In US cases, domestic tort law is frequently pleaded as an alternative source of law in the event that the domestic tort's international equivalent is rejected. Thus, plaintiffs in a torture case will often plead the provisions of the CAT as well as the provisions on assault and battery found in statute or common law.[69] This approach will not necessarily overcome defences or challenges on the basis of jurisdictional immunities, expired limitation periods, relevant rules of conflict of laws (for example, the doctrine of *forum non conveniens*), or relevant rules of civil procedure (for example, rules regarding service of process and the freezing of assets). However, the same would generally be true — in the absence of contrary domestic legislation — of actions grounded in international law.

---

67   *Ibid.* at paras. 50–56.
68   *Ibid.* at para. 89. The European Court in *Al-Adsani*, above note 64, made a similar finding at paras. 61–67 of the judgment. *Bouzari* was upheld on appeal (30 June 2004).
69   On pleading domestic torts and their parallels under international law, see the discussion in Chapter Thirteen. See also Stephens, *Litigation in US*, above note 53 at 38. On torture in particular, note that while CAT art. 14(1) requires states parties to ensure that their legal systems provide torture victims with "an enforceable right to fair and adequate compensation," there is no express obligation to do so by creating the right to a civil action for torture. Nor is there any explicit requirement to provide compensation for acts of torture committed abroad.

CHAPTER 19

NON-GOVERNMENTAL
ORGANIZATIONS

In recent years, a wide range of non-state actors, known collectively as "civil society," has made its presence felt on the international stage, particularly in the field of international human rights. The people and organizations that make up civil society include all forms of media, trade unions and similar labour associations, churches and other faith-based institutions, think tanks, professional associations, students, artists, and more. Arguably, however, the leading civil society actors in the human rights field are the world's non-governmental organizations (NGOs). It is difficult to imagine an effective global human rights system in their absence. They are, simply put, critical to the effective global promotion and protection of human rights. In this chapter we review the historic and contemporary roles of human rights NGOs, both internationally and in Canada.

A. HISTORY OF HUMAN RIGHTS NGOS

Human rights NGOs have been active in the world for almost two centuries, even if they did not always conceive of themselves as such. The Anti-Slavery Society for Human Rights was formed in 1838 with the aim of abolishing the slave trade and, ultimately, slavery itself.[1] The Interna-

---

1   Today the organization continues under the name Anti-Slavery International.

tional Committee of the Red Cross (originally called the International Committee for Relief of Wounded Soldiers) was created in 1863 to protect combatants and civilians at risk during wartime.[2] The French League for the Defence of the Rights of Man and the Citizen was established in 1898 and inspired by the promise of the French *Declaration of Rights* 1789.[3] The Congo Reform Association was created in Great Britain in 1909 to publicize the atrocities being committed in the Belgian Congo under King Leopold.[4] And the International Federation of Human Rights was established in Paris in 1922 at the initiative of several European human rights organizations. It continues today under the same name.

Although originally based largely in Europe and North America, NGOs now operate in most countries around the world. The real explosion in NGO growth began in the 1970s following the establishment of the Helsinki Watch committees.[5] That growth continues, and today NGOs active in the field of human rights number in the thousands.[6]

After the Second World War, NGOs played a critical role alongside various faith-based organizations in incorporating human rights into the UN Charter and drafting the UDHR.[7] Yet in the early years of the UN, human rights NGOs were often disenchanted with the organization. The first few decades after the adoption of the UDHR witnessed, among other things, anti-colonial struggles, civil wars and violent dictatorships resulting in the deaths of millions of innocent civilians.[8] With the response of the UN and the world's superpowers subject to the paralysis of Cold War politics, it was largely NGOs that urged observance of human rights standards without concession to *realpolitik*. In good times

---

2   See the discussion in Chapters One and Sixteen.

3   Today the organization is known as the *Ligue des Droits de l'Homme* (League of Human Rights).

4   See A. Hochschild, *King Leopold's Ghost: A Story of Greed, Terror and Heroism in Colonial Africa* (USA: Mariner Books, 1998) at 207–16.

5   Paragraph 55 of the Helsinki Final Act 1975 laid the foundation for NGOs to monitor human rights in the member states of the OSCE (formerly the CSCE). It affirmed "the right of the individual to know and act upon his rights and duties in this field." See W. Korey, *NGOs and the Universal Declaration of Human Rights: A Curious Grapevine* (New York: Palgrave, 1998) at c. 10 [Korey, *NGOs*].

6   According to a UN report on global governance referred to in The Economist, there were over 29,000 international NGOs in 1995. See "Sin of the Secular Missionaries," The Economist, 29 January 2000 at 25–27.

7   Key in this effort was the work of the American Jewish Committee, the Federal (later National) Council of Churches, and the Commission to Study the Organization of Peace. See Korey, *NGOs*, above note 5 at 33–34.

8   See generally A. Neier, *War Crimes: Brutality, Genocide, Terror, and the Struggle for Justice* (New York: Times Books, 1998).

and bad, NGOs remained focused. They continued to participate in the drafting of major human rights instruments, including the ICCPR and the CAT.[9] They also continued to participate in the establishment or strengthening of a multitude of agencies and institutions designed to prevent, deter, and punish human rights violations, including UN treaty bodies and, more recently, international criminal tribunals.[10]

B. HUMAN RIGHTS NGOS TODAY

Contemporary NGOs are marked by great diversity in their size, mandate, structure, and funding base. They range from small, localized entities to large, global institutions. There are NGOs that focus on human rights in their international,[11] regional,[12] and domestic[13] dimensions. Some NGOs concentrate on the entire family of human rights,[14] some on a sub-set of human rights,[15] and some on a particular human right.[16] There are NGOs organized as not-for-profit corporations, trusts, private voluntary organizations, and community-based organizations. There are NGOs structured as decentralized networks, membership-based organizations, and charter-based organizations. Some NGOs manage very large budgets,[17] and some (in fact, most) manage very small budgets. While some NGOs willingly accept funds from

---

9   See Korey, *NGOs*, above note 5 at 266, 309, 402, 505.

10   *Ibid.* at 203, 320, 323.

11   For example, Amnesty International (http://www.amnesty.org), which was formed in 1961 and is based in London. International NGOs like Amnesty International are sometimes referred to as INGOs.

12   For example, the Andean Commission of Jurists (http://www.cajpe.org.pe/), which focuses on human rights in the Andean region of Latin America; but also the Washington Office on Latin America (http://www.wola.org/), which is based in the US but focuses on human rights in Latin America.

13   For example, the Canadian Civil Liberties Association (http://www.ccla.org), which is based in and focused on civil liberties in Canada; but also NGOs like Human Rights in China (http://iso.hrichina.org/iso), which is based in the US but focused on human rights in China.

14   For example, Human Rights Watch (http://www.hrw.org).

15   For example, Center for Economic and Social Rights (http://www.cesr.org).

16   For example, Article 19 (http://www.article19.org), which focuses on freedom of opinion and expression (UDHR art. 19).

17   For example, Amnesty International's secretariat in London operates on an annual budget of more than £20 million. See http://web.amnesty.org/web/aboutai.nsf. Human Rights Watch has an annual operating budget of US $20 million. See http://www.hrw.org/about/faq/.

domestic and/or foreign governments, others prefer not to in order to guarantee their independence.[18] In countries like Canada, it is generally acceptable to receive funds from departments of the national government such as the Canadian International Development Agency and the Department of Foreign Affairs and International Trade. But in more repressive states, the acceptance of funds from the national government would be unthinkable. Instead, NGOs in such countries tend to rely on funds from the agencies of selected foreign governments (for example, the EU, Scandinavia and Canada) and various private sources such as US, European and Canadian foundations.[19]

The activities of modern human rights NGOs run the gamut. There are NGOs that engage in monitoring, investigation, and publication. There are others that provide technical assistance and training, or participate in standard-setting activities such as the drafting and negotiation of domestic human rights laws and multilateral treaties. Advocacy, lobbying, and campaigning in defence of particular causes is at the heart of some NGOs' work, while other NGOs litigate specific cases before domestic, foreign, regional and international courts. Some NGOs organize boycotts and "urgent action" letter-writing campaigns, whereas others conduct human rights education programs. NGOs also carry out less orthodox activities such as writing open letters to the Security Council, and organizing "popular tribunals" for the purpose of hearing cases that may not be justiciable before ordinary courts.[20]

NGOs participate heavily in UN human rights activities. NGO participation at UN human rights conferences and meetings is governed by ECOSOC Resolution 1996/31. It establishes three categories of "consultative status" for NGOs: general status (for large international NGOs

---

18 Amnesty International is an excellent case in point. It accepts no government funds of any kind, and has more than one million members, supporters, and subscribers in over 140 countries.

19 Several US foundations — for example, the John D. and Catherine T. MacArthur Foundation (http://www.macfound.org/), the Ford Foundation (http://www.fordfound.org) and the Open Society Institute (http://www.soros.org) — provide a significant percentage of such funding, in addition to carrying out human rights work in their own right.

20 For example, the Women's International War Crimes Tribunal, a mock court established by women's NGOs from eight countries, held hearings in Tokyo (2000) and The Hague (2001) in which victims testified about Japan's policy of forcing as many as 200,000 Korean and Chinese women to work as sex slaves in Japanese military brothels during the Second World War. See "Japan found 'guilty' of sex slave crimes," BBC News (http://news.bbc.co.uk), 4 December 2001.

with broad mandates), special status (for NGOs with more specialized expertise), and roster (for all other eligible NGOs).[21] Organizations from all three categories are invited to attend UN conferences and meetings of ECOSOC and its subsidiary bodies, and are permitted to receive UN documents and make statements while there. Organizations with general status may propose items for the agenda of meetings of ECOSOC or its subsidiary bodies, and those with general or special status may circulate statements at such meetings. Often, however, effective participation is frustrated in practice. For example, while NGOs with consultative status have the right to make oral statements at UN gatherings, they are only entitled to do so after member states have made their statements. In practice, this often means that few state delegations remain in attendance by the time NGOs are given the floor.[22]

NGOs do not require consultative status to lobby or submit information to treaty bodies or special procedures. They can be, and often are, quite effective outside of official UN events and processes. The NGO contribution has been particularly evident at recent world conferences and summits hosted by the UN, such as the Second World Conference on Human Rights (Vienna, 1993), the Fourth World Conference on Women (Beijing, 1995) and the World Conference Against Racism, Racial Discrimination, Xenophobia and Related Intolerance (Durban, 2001).[23]

Despite their noble aims, NGOs are not without critics. Legitimate questions persist about their accountability. Many NGOs are accountable only to a board of directors, and not to any external stakeholders.[24] There are also questions about the representativeness of NGOs. Many are not based on membership yet purport to serve as the voice of large sectors of the public. Further concerns relate to their level of professionalism.[25] Probably the most common complaint levelled against

---

21 Regional human rights systems have adopted similar rules for NGO participation.
22 With hundreds of NGOs in attendance at most major UN events, however, it is not viable to permit all NGOs to make formal interventions. The challenge is how to encourage NGO participation within limits.
23 On global NGO activism generally, see M. Keck and K. Sikkink, *Activists Across Borders: Networks in International Politics* (Cornell: Cornell University Press, 1998).
24 In this respect, we note the recent establishment of "NGO Watch" (http://www.ngowatch.org) by the Federalist Society for Law and the American Enterprise Institute — a self-described effort to "bring clarity and accountability to the burgeoning world of NGOs."
25 There is, for example, no body responsible for setting international or even regional standards for NGO investigation and reporting. Nor are there any standardized practices concerning confidentiality, standards of proof, and levels of corroboration. This is to be contrasted with professions like journalism and accounting.

NGOs concerns their emphasis on criticism and alleged inability to offer viable solutions to identified problems. Certainly there are examples of such NGOs, but they are surely the exception. Most NGOs, particularly the larger and more established among them, generally offer valuable recommendations alongside their criticisms.

The work of human rights NGOs is sometimes carried out at great personal risk. Domestic NGOs, lacking the profile and clout of international NGOs, may be particularly vulnerable to government repression and intimidation, particularly in authoritarian regimes or during periods of armed conflict.[26] While there has long been a call for an international treaty to protect human rights NGOs (and other "human rights defenders") from persecution and attack, thus far there is only a UN declaration on the subject.[27]

C. AMNESTY INTERNATIONAL AND HUMAN RIGHTS WATCH

Two human rights NGOs deserve special mention. Amnesty International (AI) and Human Rights Watch (HRW) are by far the biggest and best-known human rights NGOs in operation today.[28] These two entities — both multinational, globalized operations — receive by far the greatest coverage among NGOs in international media. In terms of political influence, their voice resonates with almost unmatched force on human rights issues, exceeding any UN or regional human rights body.

Amnesty International was founded in 1961 by British lawyer Peter Benenson with the intent of obtaining amnesties for prisoners of conscience all over the world. Prisoners of conscience refers to people imprisoned for their convictions, their racial or ethnic origin, or their

---

26   See, for example, the *Report of the Special Representative of the Secretary-General on Human Rights Defenders*, UN doc. A/57/182 (2002).

27   See, for example, UN Declaration on the Right and Responsibility of Individuals, Groups and Organs of Society to Promote and Protect Universally Recognized Human Rights and Fundamental Freedoms 1999, GA res. 53/144.

28   Other large and well-known international NGOs include the Committee to Protect Journalists (http://www.cpj.org), the International Commission of Jurists (http://www.icj.org), Physicians for Human Rights (http://www.phrusa.org), the International Federation of Human Rights (http://www.fidh.org), Human Rights First (http://www.humanrightsfirst.org), the International Centre for Transitional Justice (http://www.ictj.org) and the International Centre for the Legal Protection of Human Rights (http://www.interights.org).

faith — provided they have not used or advocated violence. AI began to document prisoners of conscience around the world, establishing an international secretariat in 1963 and quickly expanding. An important part of its work on behalf of prisoners of conscience was (and still is) massive letter-writing campaigns on behalf of individuals and communities at risk. AI's advocacy work has expanded over time beyond prisoners of conscience to encompass the protection of human rights generally. AI was awarded the Nobel Peace Prize in 1977. It currently claims to have over 1.8 million members around the world. It is based in London.

Human Rights Watch was founded in 1978 under the name Helsinki Watch. Its purpose was to monitor the compliance of Soviet bloc countries with the human rights provisions of the Helsinki Accords. Similar "watch committees" were later established to monitor human rights in Central America and Asia. These committees united under the name Human Rights Watch in 1988. Today, HRW is the largest US-based human rights NGO in the world. Its principal activity is the investigation and exposure of human rights abuses throughout the world, often by means of on-the-ground fact-finding missions. The reports and other publications HRW generates are an essential source of independent, current human rights information. HRW also promotes human rights issues through governmental lobbying and publicity campaigns.

AI and HRW have much in common. Both aim to produce reliable, detailed, and authoritative reports that serve to hold abusers accountable by embarrassing them in the eyes of their citizens and of the world. The researchers, investigators and monitors that compile the information for these reports must sometimes put themselves in harm's way, embarking on in-country missions to speak directly to combatants, witnesses, victims, and local groups. Both organizations recognize that the accuracy of their reports is essential to their credibility and a precondition for effectively shaming governments and influencing public opinion. Information is checked and corroborated before being published, and as a rule reports do not get published where there is insufficient evidence to support a claim.[29] Another similarity between the two organizations (and indeed many human rights NGOs) is their reliance on the technology of mass communication. The international impact of AI's and HRW's work is dependent on a free and internationalized press and now the internet. Both organizations make skilful use

---

29   For example, during the genocide in Cambodia, AI was slow to conclude genocide was taking place because it did not believe there was adequate evidence to corroborate the accounts of Cambodian refugees. S. Power, *A Problem From Hell: America and the Age of Genocide* (New York: Basic Books, 2002) at 113.

of these media. Yet another similarity is that Canada has not been spared from scrutiny by either organization.[30]

D. CANADIAN NGOS

Canadian civil society, and in particular Canadian human rights NGOs, play an important role in the promotion and protection of human rights in Canada and internationally. Canadian human rights NGOs and similar organizations tend to rely on financial assistance from the federal and provincial governments for a portion of their operating costs. Indeed, there appears to be a mostly open relationship between government and NGOs. For example, each year the Department of Foreign Affairs and International Trade holds consultations with Canada's main human rights NGOs and aboriginal organizations just prior to the annual session of the Commission on Human Rights in Geneva. As a rule, the government also consults with NGOs in the course of becoming a party to, or reporting under, any major human rights treaty.

Like their international counterparts, Canadian human rights organizations are diverse in their structures and mandates. Some operate as affiliates of larger US, British or international NGOs. This is true of AI-Canada,[31] PEN Canada,[32] and the B'nai Brith Canada League for Human Rights,[33] for example. Yet most are independent organizations. This is the case for Human Rights Internet,[34] the Canadian Human Rights Foundation,[35] and the Canadian Lawyers Association for International Human Rights,[36] to name a few. There is at least one example of a prominent Canadian human rights organization that was created by Parliament, namely Rights & Democracy.[37] In addition, there is a multitude of Canadian organizations that do human rights work in fact if not always in name, such as Oxfam Canada[38] and the Association in Defence of the

---

30   See, for example, Human Rights Watch, *Abusing the Abuser: Police Misconduct, Harm Reduction and HIV/AIDS in Vancouver* (2003). See also Amnesty International, *World Report 2003* (Canada section), which focused on concerns about police accountability and refugee protection.

31   See http://www.amnesty.ca.

32   See http://www.pencanada.ca.

33   See http://www.bnaibrith.ca.

34   See http://www.hri.ca.

35   See http://www.chrf.ca.

36   See http://www.claihr.org.

37   See http://www.ichrdd.ca.

38   See http://www.oxfam.ca.

Wrongly Convicted.[39] There are also organizations in Canada that do important rehabilitation work with victims of gross violations of human rights, such as the Canadian Centre for Victims of Torture.[40] And several Canadian law schools host human rights-related institutes and programs, including the University of Ottawa (Human Rights Research and Education Centre),[41] McGill University (InterAmicus),[42] the University of Alberta (International Ombudsman Institute),[43] the University of Toronto (International Human Rights Program),[44] and the University of British Columbia (International Centre for Criminal Law Reform and Criminal Justice Policy).[45]

There are many important Canadian organizations doing work in the related fields of international labour law, refugee law, humanitarian law, and criminal law as well. These include the Canadian Labour Congress,[46] the Canadian Council for Refugees,[47] national and provincial Red Cross Societies,[48] and the International Criminal Bar.[49]

Finally, many aboriginal organizations in Canada, including the Assembly of First Nations,[50] the Métis National Council,[51] and the Inuit Tapiriit Kanatami[52] use human rights norms in a manner much like NGOs. Indeed, within Canada aboriginal organizations are probably among the most prolific users of international human rights norms and mechanisms.

---

39   See http://www.aidwyc.org.
40   See http://www.icomm.ca/ccvt. According to its website, the Centre has assisted approximately 12,000 torture survivors from 99 different countries since it was established in 1977.
41   See http://www.uottawa.ca/hrrec.
42   See http://interamicus.law.mcgill.ca.
43   See http://www.law.ualberta.ca/centres/ioi.
44   See http://www.law.utoronto.ca.
45   See http://www.icclr.law.ubc.ca. The International Centre for Criminal Law Reform and Criminal Justice Policy is also the subject of a bilateral treaty between the UN and Canada. See the Agreement between the United Nations and the Government of Canada for the Affiliation of the International Centre for Criminal Law Reform and Criminal Justice Policy 1995 [1995] CanTS no. 12.
46   See http://www.clc-ctc.ca.
47   See http://www.web.net/~ccr.
48   See http://www.redcross.ca.
49   See http://www.bpi-icb.org.
50   See http://www.afn.ca.
51   See http://www.metisnation.ca.
52   See http://www.tapirisat.ca.

CONTEMPORARY TRENDS AND ISSUES

International human rights law is constantly evolving. Its major controversies tend to track global political developments. This final chapter examines some of the main contemporary debates and emerging trends in the field and offers some reflections on the challenges particular to Canada's reception of, and participation in, the field of international human rights law.

A. TERRORISM AND HUMAN RIGHTS

Following the massive terrorist attacks of September 11, 2001, governments around the world proclaimed a "war" against terrorism as a central domestic and foreign policy objective. But despite the existence of well over a dozen anti-terrorism treaties, there is still no generally accepted definition of the term "terrorism."[1] The lack of a definition

---

1   The key UN treaties are: the Convention on Offences and Certain Other Acts Committed on Board Aircraft 1963 [1970] CanTS no. 5, the Hague Convention for the Suppression of Unlawful Seizure of Aircraft 1970 [1972] CanTS no. 23, the Convention for the Suppression of Unlawful Acts against the Safety of Civil Aviation 1971 [1973] CanTS no. 6 and the Protocol for the Suppression of Unlawful Acts against the Safety of Civil Aviation 1988 [1993] CanTS no. 8, the Convention on the Prevention and Punishment of Crimes against Internationally Protected Persons, including Diplomatic Agents 1973 [1977] CanTS no. 43, the Convention against the Taking of Hostages 1979 [1986] CanTS no. 45, the

was one reason why terrorism was not included as a crime in the Rome Statute.[2] To some extent the controversy over its definition centres on the familiar adage that one person's terrorist is another person's freedom fighter. But there is also controversy regarding fundamental questions such as who can be responsible for acts of terrorism — private individuals only, or states as well?

Counter-terrorism efforts raise a number of important human rights questions. Indeed, the so-called war on terrorism presents a major new challenge to the human rights movement.[3] Many human rights advocates are concerned that the war against terrorism is nothing more than a war against human rights, and in particular civil rights. This may be a valid concern. The counter-terrorist legislation enacted in many states in the aftermath of September 11th often strained the balance between public security and the protection of individual rights. In the US, Japan, the UK, Australia, and even Canada, the threat of terrorism prompted, or was used to justify, far-reaching legislation unimaginable before the September 11th attacks.[4] There are examples of legislation authorizing, among other things: detentions of indefinite duration of legal and ille-

---

Convention on the Physical Protection of Nuclear Material 1980 [1987] CanTS no. 35, the Convention for the Suppression of Unlawful Acts against the Safety of Maritime Navigation 1988 [1993] CanTS no. 10, the Convention on the Marking of Plastic Explosives for the Purpose of Detection 1991 [1998] CanTS no. 54, the International Convention for the Suppression of Terrorist Bombings 1997 [2002] CanTS no. 8, the International Convention for the Suppression of the Financing of Terrorism 1999 [2002] CanTS no. 9.

2   See "Note by the Secretary-General on the establishment of an international criminal court," UN doc. A/53/387 (1998) at para. 9, which states that the UN Diplomatic Conference of Plenipotentiaries on the Establishment of the International Criminal Court

   regretted that no generally acceptable definition of the crimes of terrorism and drug crimes could be agreed upon for the inclusion, within the jurisdiction of the Court [and recommended that] a Review Conference should consider the crimes of terrorism and drug crimes with a view to arriving at an acceptable definition and their inclusion in the list of crimes within the jurisdiction of the Court.

3   See, for example, M. Ignatieff, "Mission Impossible?" New York Review of Books, 19 December 2002.

4   See generally Amnesty International, World Report (2003) at "2002 In Focus," "Introduction," and "Counter-Terrorism and Human Rights." The report notes: "Exploiting the atmosphere of fear that followed 11 September, many governments ignored, undermined or openly violated fundamental principles of international human rights and humanitarian law." Regarding Canada, the report states that "fears increased that people accused of supporting armed Islamist groups were at risk of being deported to countries where they faced a serious risk of torture."

gal aliens who are "suspected" of terrorist activity; the establishment of secret courts and commissions before which even the most rudimentary guarantees of procedural fairness are absent; vastly extended powers for police and intelligence agencies in terms of spying, arrest, and detention; and criteria for defining the "enemy" that are as broad as they are vague.[5] As a recent UN report noted:

> United Nations human rights experts have stressed that human rights have come under significant pressure worldwide as a result of counter-terrorism measures, at both the national and the international level. Concerns have been raised over pressures on a wide range of rights, including the right to life and to freedom from torture, due-process rights and the right to seek asylum.[6]

It is too early to say whether, in future years, the general public in countries like Canada will look back with wonder at how it could have permitted such extensive erosions of civil liberties and standards of due process. But it is not too early to observe that these laws have sapped some of the moral authority of developed democratic states to condemn atrocities by less democratic states committed on the now-acceptable pretext of fighting terrorism. The fight against terrorism has provided yet another excuse for repressive governments to violate human rights. Human Rights Watch's 2003 *World Report* makes the point well:

> Washington's subordination of human rights to the campaign against terrorism has . . . bred a copycat phenomenon. By waving the anti-terrorism banner, governments such as Uzbekistan seemed to feel that they had license to persecute religious dissenters, while governments such as Russia, Israel, and China seemed to feel freer to intensify repression in Chechnya, the West Bank, and Xinjiang. . . . In sub-Saharan Africa, some of the mimicry took on absurd proportions. Ugandan President Yoweri Museveni shut down the leading independent newspaper for a week in October because it was allegedly promoting terrorism (it had reported a military defeat by the government in its battle against the Lord's Resistance Army rebel group). In June, Liberian President Charles Taylor declared three of his critics — the editor of a local newspaper and two others — to be 'illegal combatants' who would be

---

5   See the discussion of terrorism in Chapter Eleven. See also R. Daniels *et al.*, *The Security of Freedom: Essays on Canada's Anti-Terrorism Bill* (Toronto: University of Toronto Press, 2001); and Human Rights First, *Assessing the New Normal: Liberty and Security for the Post-September 11 United States* (2003).

6   "Report of the Secretary-General on the Protection of Human Rights and Fundamental Freedoms While Countering Terrorism," UN doc. A/58/266 (2003).

tried for terrorism in a military court. Eritrea justified its lengthy detention of the founder of the country's leading newspaper by citing Washington's widespread detentions. Zimbabwean President Robert Mugabe justified the November 2001 arrest of six journalists as terrorists because they wrote stories about political violence in the country. Elsewhere, even former Yugoslav President Slobodan Milosevic defended himself against war-crimes charges by contending that abusive troops under his command had merely been combating terrorism.[7]

Notwithstanding these and other criticisms by human rights groups, it must be acknowledged that terrorism, today as in the past, presents a grave threat to the civilians of target states. Those concerned to protect rights must not be naïve or indifferent to this fact. Questions of public protection and national security are not imaginary. While it is important to resist hasty and uncritical expansions in the powers of intelligence agencies, it is also necessary to acknowledge the role they can serve in a modern democracy. The dangers present in the world today are greater than they have been in the past, not least because of a globalization in crime and weapons that has accompanied the globalization in communications and technology. Human rights advocates must even acknowledge that some aspects of counter-terrorism policies, such as laws on the freezing of funds,[8] may be having a salutary effect in bringing closure to civil wars in places such as Sri Lanka[9] and Northern Ireland.[10]

Still, the danger to human rights presented by the war against terrorism is all too real. If counter-terrorism laws and policies end up tak-

---

7   Human Rights Watch, *World Report* (2003) at "Introduction."

8   See, for example, *Proceeds of Crime (Money Laundering) and Terrorist Financing Act*, RSC 2000 c. 17. The Financial Transactions and Reports Analysis Centre of Canada administers the Act.

9   See, for example, "Q & A: Sri Lanka Peace Talks," BBC News (http://news.bbc.co.uk), 23 April 2003, in which the impact of September 11th ("in refocusing the world on terrorism and cracking down on the financing of terrorist activities") is cited as a factor making possible the December 2001 ceasefire and ensuing peace talks in Sri Lanka. The LTTE, Sri Lanka's Tamil rebel army, received a significant portion of its funds from sympathetic Tamils living outside of Sri Lanka. Governments in Canada, Australia, and elsewhere froze those funds following September 11th. (The LTTE is banned as a terrorist group in many countries.)

10   See, for example, "Terrorism: Questions and Answers (IRA)," Council on Foreign Relations, http://cfrterrorism.org/groups/ira.html. The events of September 11th are cited by the Council on Foreign Relations as a factor pushing forward the peace process in Northern Ireland by creating pressure on the Irish Republican Army (IRA) to give up its weapons and ending residual Irish-American financial support for IRA hardliners.

ing on a Machiavellian logic of ends justifying means, of rights subordinated to security, they will produce an untenable human rights situation. They will come to resemble in practice the national security doctrines of the Cold War era, when almost everything could be justified — in the minds of some, at least — by the fight against communism. Counter-terrorist measures may come to resemble in their logic the very terrorist acts they purport to oppose. In brief, the struggle against terrorism ought to be conceived and waged not in opposition to human rights but in their defence.[11]

B. BUSINESS AND HUMAN RIGHTS

For the most part, international human rights law benefits natural persons (humans) and not legal persons (corporations).[12] Likewise, international human rights law mostly creates responsibilities for states and not for private or non-state actors.[13] In short, the question of corporate behaviour falls largely outside of the ambit of international human rights law. More and more, segments of the international community perceive this as a problem because corporations are sometimes directly implicated in human rights abuses including the use of child labour, the suppression of trade union rights, and the failure to provide healthy and safe working conditions.

---

11   For a balanced approach to the issue, see Inter-American Convention Against Terrorism 2002 art. 15, which provides:

1.   The measures carried out by the states parties under this Convention shall take place with full respect for the rule of law, human rights, and fundamental freedoms.

2.   Nothing in this Convention shall be interpreted as affecting other rights and obligations of states and individuals under international law, in particular the Charter of the United Nations, the Charter of the Organization of American States, international humanitarian law, international human rights law, and international refugee law.

3.   Any person who is taken into custody or regarding whom any other measures are taken or proceedings are carried out pursuant to this Convention shall be guaranteed fair treatment, including the enjoyment of all rights and guarantees in conformity with the law of the state in the territory of which that person is present and applicable provisions of international law.

12   The same is true of international humanitarian law. See Chapter Two.

13   We have noted the exceptions to this rule throughout the book. See, for example, Chapter Eighteen concerning civil suits brought against corporations in the US pursuant to the *Alien Tort Claims Act*.

Recently, the UN Sub-Commission for the Promotion and Protection of Human Rights approved Draft Norms on the Responsibilities of Transnational Corporations and Other Business Enterprises with Regard to Human Rights 2003 (Draft Norms).[14] Its provisions are not binding, but may provide a model for the first multilateral treaty on the subject of corporate responsibility.[15] The Draft Norms articulate how companies can uphold human and labour rights, and provide guidelines for companies operating in conflict zones. They prohibit bribery and activities that injure consumers such as polluting the environment. The Draft Norms contemplate a monitoring and verification mechanism too, and a reparation obligation for corporations in the event of a violation. The Commission on Human Rights will table the Draft Norms for adoption at its annual session in 2004. Many are hopeful that large corporations will already start to adopt and implement the Draft Norms, and that a binding treaty will follow in future years. For now, however, there are no universally binding international human rights standards for corporations.

Fortunately, many corporate actors appear to have a new awareness of the importance and relevance of human rights. Human rights have become impossible to ignore. The number of initiatives and trends linking human rights and the conduct of business, and economic and trade issues more broadly, continues to grow. There are emerging forms of multilateral regulation of labour rights such as the European Committee of Social Rights and the various mechanisms established under the NAALC.[16] There are ongoing debates about fair trade and social and economic rights at the various rounds of WTO trade talks.[17] There is

---

14   UN doc. E/CN.4/Sub.2/2003/12/Rev.2 (2003).

15   Previous UN attempts to draft norms or codes of conduct for corporations have not taken hold. See, for example, Draft UN Code of Conduct on Transnational Corporations 1983 (1984) 23 ILM 626.

16   See Chapters Fifteen and Sixteen, respectively.

17   Cancún, Mexico was the site of the most recent failed trade talks. Most news reports ascribed the failure of the talks to developed countries' refusal to abandon domestic farm subsidies that make it impossible for farmers from developing countries to compete. Approximately 25,000 US cotton farmers receive about US$3 billion annually in subsidies, which is triple the amount the US gives in foreign aid to Africa. See T. Friedman, "Connect the Dots," New York Times, 25 September 2003. See also World Bank, *Global Economic Prospects 2004: Realizing the Development Promise of the Doha Agenda* (2003), which asserted that reducing the developed world's tariffs and agricultural subsidies could raise global income by US$500 billion a year by 2015. Over 60 percent of that new income would go to poor countries and 144 million people would be pulled out of poverty.

the Global Compact initiative of the UN Secretary-General,[18] and the many private attempts to foster corporate responsibility such as the Fair Labor Association[19] and Canadian Business for Social Responsibility.[20] There has also been a proliferation of voluntary corporate codes of conduct dealing with human rights,[21] and a continuing rise in shareholder activism calling for company improvements in human rights matters.[22] The increased focus on questions of good governance, public corruption, and bribery of foreign officials is yet another illustration of the linkage of business and human rights.[23]

Complementing these developments are longstanding voluntary multilateral initiatives, in particular the procedures established under the Organization for Economic Cooperation and Development (OECD) Guidelines for Multinational Enterprises 1976, which were revised in 2000.[24] The OECD Guidelines provide voluntary standards for responsible corporate conduct in areas including human rights. Canada is an "adhering government" to the Guidelines along with all other OECD member states plus three non-OECD members (Argentina, Brazil, Chile). Adherence is monitored at three levels: so-called "national contact points" (generally government departments); the OECD Committee on International Investment and Multinational Enterprises; and the latter's advisory committees of business and labour federations. NGOs have been allowed to participate in the procedures of these bodies.

---

18   See http://www.globalcompact.org.
19   The Fair Labor Association (http://www.fairlabor.org) is a US-based coalition of human rights NGOs, labour rights groups, consumer groups, colleges, universities, and multinational companies.
20   Canadian Business for Social Responsibility (http://www.csbr.ca) is a business-led non-profit organization that promotes corporate social responsibility.
21   A corporate code of conduct is a company's formal statement of business ethics. Examples of codes with references to human rights include those of Jones Apparel Group, Inc. and Spiegel, both of which require their business partners to comply with the host country's child labour law or UN standards, whichever is higher. See ILO Bureau for Workers' Activities, "Corporate Codes of Conduct" (http://www.itcilo.it/english/actrav/telearn/global/ilo/code/main.htm).
22   On shareholder activism generally, see R. Monks, *The Emperor's Nightingale: Restoring the Integrity of the Corporation in the Age of Shareholder Activism* (Oxford: Capstone, 1998).
23   The leading organization on this issue is Transparency International (http://www.transparency.org). See also the OECD Convention on Combating Bribery of Foreign Public Officials in International Business Transactions 1997 [1999] CanTS no. 23; and the Inter-American Convention against Corruption 1996 [2000] CanTS no. 21.
24   See also the ILO's non-binding Tripartite Declaration of Principles Concerning Multinational Enterprises 1977 (1978) 17 ILM 422.

Among other things, the Guidelines provide that multinational enterprises should "[r]espect the human rights of those affected by their activities consistent with the host government's international obligations and commitments." The Guidelines also deal with issues of non-discrimination, forced labour, child labour, and freedom of association and collective bargaining.[25]

Ultimately, however, success in changing the philosophy and approaches of corporations to human rights issues will depend on more than OECD Guidelines, voluntary initiatives, and multilateral supervision. It will depend, at least in part, on persuading corporations that it is in their own self-interest to care about human rights issues. Not all multinational corporations are concerned only with bottom line considerations. In some cases there is a genuine humanitarian impulse at work, often emanating from forward-thinking CEOs. But where such an impulse is absent, as it often is, human rights supporters need to make use of incentive-based arguments to persuade companies to care about human rights.

As it turns out, there is often a real nexus between human rights and corporate self-interest.[26] For example, investing in very repressive countries or war zones may create a significant business risk. Instability caused by severe human rights violations can cause labour strife, restricted access to goods and services, and delays in the transportation of finished products. There are also significant insurance and security costs associated with investment in repressive countries and war zones, as well as the risk of multilateral trade and investment sanctions that could lead to cancellation of orders from importers.[27] Corporate atten-

---

25   For a recent example of the utility of the OECD Guidelines, see the "Final Report of the UN Panel of Experts on the Illegal Exploitation of Natural Resources and Other Forms of Wealth of the Democratic Republic of the Congo," UN doc. S/2003/1027 (2003). The Security Council established the panel in 2001. The panel initially accused eight Canadian companies of violating the OECD Guidelines for Multinational Enterprises but later dropped its allegations against all but one.

26   See generally M. Freeman, "Doing Well By Doing Good: Linking Human Rights With Corporate Self-Interest" (2001) 6 International Business Law Journal 741.

27   See Draft Norms, above note 14, art. 3:

Transnational corporations and other business enterprises shall not engage in nor benefit from war crimes, crimes against humanity, genocide, torture, forced disappearance, forced or compulsory labour, hostage-taking, extrajudicial, summary or arbitrary executions, other violations of humanitarian law and other international crimes against the human person as defined by international law, in particular human rights and humanitarian law.

tion to human rights issues may also help avoid damaging consumer boycotts and shareholder criticism. Human-rights-related negative publicity can do serious harm to a company's public image and brand equity, and consequently to company profitability. By being sensitive to and vocal about human rights issues from the outset, companies are in a better position to speak with public credibility in the event of a boycott, shareholder criticism, or other forms of human rights complaint.

It is also in the self-interest of companies to treat their workers fairly. There is a perception among North American and European workers that most multinational corporations are taking advantage of cheap labour and poor human rights records in the developing world. This perception can provoke calls for both trade sanctions and protectionism, thereby reducing political commitment to free markets — a development that would be undesirable for most multinational corporations. By adopting a human rights approach in their overseas workplaces and promoting greater respect for human rights and labour rights within the host state, companies can help keep borders open and ensure that multilateral sanctions do not limit their ability to conduct business. Providing economic security for workers can also help create a more loyal and honest workforce, thereby reducing costs associated with turnover, corruption, and theft.[28] In addition, reasonable and safe conditions of work can help reduce companies' financial exposure. The failure to provide a safe workplace can lead to injuries and fatalities, which in turn can trigger expensive legal liabilities in some states. Unsafe working conditions can also lead to negative publicity, affecting the company's public image.[29]

None of this is to suggest that corporations should take on human rights obligations equivalent to states. To the contrary, it is in everyone's interest that states retain primary responsibility for respecting and

---

28   See Draft Norms, *ibid.*, art. 8:

> Transnational corporations and other business enterprises shall provide workers with remuneration that ensures an adequate standard of living for them and their families. Such remuneration shall take due account of their needs for adequate living conditions with a view towards progressive improvement.

29   See Draft Norms, *ibid.*, art. 7:

> Transnational corporations and other business enterprises shall provide a safe and healthy working environment as set forth in relevant international instruments and national legislation as well as international human rights and humanitarian law.

ensuring human rights.[30] But most corporations can and should do much more.

C. HUMANITARIAN INTERVENTION

As we saw in Chapter One, the issue of humanitarian intervention long predates the emergence of international human rights law. Yet for most of the Cold War era, the subject generated little discussion. Between 1945 and 1989, there were only a few instances of interventions conceived and carried out with a humanitarian objective. The most-cited examples are India's intervention in East Pakistan (Bangladesh) in 1971,[31] Vietnam's intervention in Cambodia in 1978,[32] and Tanzania's intervention in Uganda in 1979.[33] In each of these cases the intervention was justified as self-defence and not as humanitarian intervention. Therefore even these instances may not properly be characterized as humanitarian interventions, notwithstanding the presence of a humanitarian impulse. Other Cold War era interventions — such as the Belgian intervention in the Congo in 1960, the US intervention in the Dominican Republic in 1965, the French intervention in Central Africa in 1979, the US intervention in Grenada in 1983 or the US intervention in Panama in 1989 — cannot be described as humanitarian interventions without distorting the meaning of the term.

---

30 This is supported by Draft Norms, *ibid.*, art. 1:

> States have the primary responsibility to promote, secure the fulfilment of, respect, ensure respect of and protect human rights recognized in international as well as national law, including ensuring that transnational corporations and other business enterprises respect human rights. Within their respective spheres of activity and influence, transnational corporations and other business enterprises have the obligation to promote, secure the fulfilment of, respect, ensure respect of and protect human rights recognized in international as well as national law, including the rights and interests of indigenous peoples and other vulnerable groups.

31 See, for example, T. Franck & N. Rodley, "After Bangladesh: The Law of Humanitarian Intervention by Military Force" (1973) 67 AJIL 275.

32 See, for example, S. Murphy, *Humanitarian Intervention: The United Nations in an Evolving World Order* (Philadelphia: University of Pennsylvania Press, 1996) at 102–5 [Murphy, *Humanitarian*].

33 See, for example, F. Hassan, "Realpolitik in International Law: After the Tanzanian-Ugandan Conflict 'Humanitarian Intervention' Revisited" (1981) 17 Willamette Law Review 859.

With the end of the Cold War everything changed. Over the last fifteen years, the principle of humanitarian relief as a basis for intervention has been invoked on many occasions and today it is one of the most hotly (even excessively) debated topics of international law.[34] The International Commission on Intervention and State Sovereignty (ICISS) usefully describes the contours of the current debate:

> For some, the international community is not intervening enough; for others it is intervening much too often. For some, the only real issue is in ensuring that coercive interventions are effective; for others, questions about legality, process and the possible misuse of precedent loom much larger. For some, the new interventions herald a new world in which human rights trumps state sovereignty; for others, [they usher] in a world in which big powers ride roughshod over the smaller ones, manipulating the rhetoric of humanitarianism and human rights.[35]

The UN Charter's rules on the use of force are the necessary starting point for examining the question of humanitarian intervention in international law. Under UN Charter article 2(4), the threat or use of force by an individual state against another state is illegal.[36] However, the use of force is legal in individual or collective self-defence, albeit only until the Security Council has taken measures to restore international peace and security.[37] The use of force is also legal when undertaken pursuant to Security Council authorization.[38]

---

34   In the last ten years alone, dozens of books have been published on the topic. Leading publications include: N. Wheeler, *Saving Strangers: Humanitarian Intervention in International Society* (Oxford: Oxford University Press, 2000); J. Holzgrefe & R. Keohane, *Humanitarian Intervention: Ethical, Legal and Political Dilemmas* (Cambridge: Cambridge University Press, 2003); and Murphy, *Humanitarian*, above note 32.

35   The Canadian government established the ICISS in September 2000 in response to an appeal by the UN Secretary-General for new ideas about how to resolve the dilemma of humanitarian intervention. Gareth Evans, President and CEO of the International Crisis Group, and Mohamed Sahnoun, the UN Secretary-General's Special Adviser on Africa, served as co-chairs of the ICISS. The ICISS's mandate was to propose formulas for reconciling humanitarian intervention and state sovereignty. See the ICISS final report: http://www.dfait-maeci.gc.ca/iciss-ciise/report2-en.asp.

36   Article 2(4) provides: "All Members shall refrain in their international relations from the threat or use of force against the territorial integrity or political independence of any state, or in any other manner inconsistent with the Purposes of the United Nations."

37   UN Charter art. 51.

38   *Ibid.*, art. 42.

The scope of the right of self-defence is not clearly defined in the UN Charter. For example, it is not clear whether it extends to protection of nationals living in a foreign country, although today most commentators appear to reject the idea.[39] The meaning of collective, as opposed to individual, self-defence is also uncertain. In particular, it is not clear whether UN Charter article 51 empowers non-victim states to support a victim state in the exercise of its right of self-defence, or whether it only permits multiple victim states collectively to exercise a right of self-defence. The majority of the International Court of Justice in *Case Concerning Military and Paramilitary Activities in and against Nicaragua (Nicaragua v. USA)*[40] took the former view, but there was a strong dissenting judgment by Judge Jennings that was subsequently endorsed by numerous commentators.[41] The extent to which international law permits anticipatory or pre-emptive self-defence is also ambiguous.

What is clear, however, is the distinction between self-defence and humanitarian intervention. Self-defence involves the defence of nationals or national interests. Humanitarian intervention, by contrast, involves the defence of non-nationals. While the scope of the right of self-defence may have some useful bearing on our understanding of humanitarian intervention,[42] it is a mistake to describe any self-defence intervention as a humanitarian intervention. It matters not whether there is a humanitarian impulse present.[43]

Other than self-defence, the only lawful use of force permitted under the UN Charter is pursuant to Security Council authorization. In practice, since the end of the Cold War, the Security Council has often shown itself prepared to act in response to humanitarian crises, particularly when there are widespread human rights violations occurring in a context of civil war or absence of state authority. There have been many fairly uncontroversial interventions of this sort authorized by the

---

39   See generally C. Gray, *Use of Force in International Law* (Oxford: Oxford University Press, 2001) at 108–9, where the author asserts that only four states (Israel, the US, the UK, and Belgium) have invoked this argument.

40   [1986] ICJ Rep 14.

41   *Ibid.* at 139.

42   For example, analysis of the scope of pre-emptive self-defence can inform our understanding of the scope of any right to pre-emptive humanitarian intervention.

43   For example, in October 2001 the US and the UK reported to the Security Council an intention to act in their individual and collective self-defence against Afghanistan. Although there was ostensibly a humanitarian dimension to their intervention (namely, bringing an end to Taliban oppression of the Afghan people, especially women), it cannot properly be described as a humanitarian intervention.

Security Council in the last fifteen years, including in Somalia, Haiti, Rwanda, Liberia, East Timor, and Sierra Leone.[44]

But the Security Council's record on intervention is far from consistent. Like cases have not always been treated in like manner, and this has understandably generated claims of double standards and unfairness.[45] Such inconsistency is often a consequence of the distribution of power within the Security Council. There are five permanent members with veto powers. Any intervention that is implacably opposed by a permanent member — whether in a matter directly implicating it (for example, Tibet/China) or affecting a close ally or vital interest (for example, Serbia/Russia) — can be blocked by veto. It is, therefore, tempting for the UN to intervene in deserving circumstances where Security Council consensus exists, even if it results in dissimilar treatment of similar situations. While the rule that all like cases be treated alike is morally persuasive, taken to an extreme it could lead to a level of inaction that would serve nobody very well.

But what of those conscience-shocking situations where prior Security Council authorization is impossible? What should be the rules for Kosovo-like circumstances? These are what might be called the "tough cases" for which there are no clear-cut positions.[46] Under the

---

44   Perhaps the first relevant resolution was SC res. 688 (1991), which authorized the use of force against Iraq in order to protect its Kurdish minority from atrocities. Most recently, the Security Council authorized an Interim Emergency Multinational Force to take "all necessary measures" to fulfil its mandate of assuring the protection of civilians and internally displaced persons living in the Bunia district of the Democratic Republic of Congo. See SC res. 1484 (2003).

45   Rwanda is the most obvious example. It is a matter of historical record that in April and May 1994, as massacres of Rwandan Tutsis were taking place on a daily basis, certain members of the UN Security Council hesitated to use the "g word" (genocide). The Clinton administration actually forbade its use by US officials. The apparent rationale: acknowledging the fact of genocide would make military intervention obligatory. P. Gourevitch, *We Wish to Inform You That Tomorrow We Will Be Killed With Our Families: Stories from Rwanda* (New York: Picador, 1999) at 152–54.

46   For those in immediate and grave danger, however, the issue is less troubling: rescue must come at any cost. See, for example, Jose Ramos-Horta, "War for Peace? It Worked in My Country," New York Times, 25 February 2003. Ramos-Horta, a Noble Peace Prize winner and currently Timor-Leste's minister of foreign affairs, observes: "It would certainly be a better world if war were not necessary. Yet I also remember the desperation and anger I felt when the rest of the world chose to ignore the tragedy that was drowning my people. We begged a foreign power to free us from oppression, by force if necessary." Regarding the 2003 invasion of Iraq by the "Coalition of the Willing," he states: "[I]f the anti-

strictest reading of the UN Charter, a humanitarian intervention not authorized by the Security Council, and not justified on the basis of collective self-defence, is illegal.[47] Those who wish to justify intervention in Kosovo-like situations must ground their case primarily on moral arguments. Thus, the Independent International Commission on Kosovo famously, and perhaps fairly, described the NATO intervention in Kosovo as "illegal but legitimate."[48]

To enjoy such legitimacy, states that carry out humanitarian interventions must do more than make the moral case for intervention. Consistent with the UN Charter, intervening states must show that their actions are a last resort.[49] Non-coercive measures such as bilateral or multilateral sanctions may have to be exhausted and given a reasonable time to prove their effectiveness before resort to military action is had.[50] It is also widely acknowledged that intervening states must demonstrate a reasonable prospect of success in alleviating the suffering that constitutes the object of the intervention. The level of financial and other support the objects of intervention receive from their professed liberators after the fact is another relevant criterion of legitimacy. Lastly, immediately following the intervention an attempt should be made to obtain after-the-fact ratification of it. This serves to rein-

---

war movement dissuades the United States and its allies from going to war with Iraq, it will have contributed to the peace of the dead."

47   But see A. Klinton, "NATO's Intervention in Kosovo: The Legal Case for Violating Yugoslavia's National Sovereignty in the Absence of Security Council Approval" (2000) 22 Houston Journal of International Law 403.

48   Independent International Commission on Kosovo, *The Kosovo Report: Conflict, International Response, Lessons Learned* (New York: Oxford University Press, 2000) at 4.

49   This principle is affirmed in UN Charter art. 2(3): "All Members shall settle their international disputes by peaceful means in such a manner that international peace and security, and justice, shall not be compromised."

50   Sanctions can take a variety of forms including: travel restrictions, cultural and sporting bans, suspension or expulsion from international organizations, flight bans, arms embargoes, asset freezes, and oil and energy embargoes. But note that some types of sanctions (for example, comprehensive and long-term sanctions) may occasionally produce worse humanitarian consequences than military intervention. In this regard, see ICESCR General Comment no. 8 (1997) at para. 16:

[T]he inhabitants of a given country do not forfeit their basic economic, social and cultural rights by virtue of any determination that their leaders have violated norms relating to international peace and security . . . lawlessness of one kind should not be met by lawlessness of another kind which pays no heed to the fundamental rights that underlie and give legitimacy to any such collective action.

force the international rule of law and avoid diminishing the authority of the Security Council.[51]

Ultimately, we question whether there is any purpose to be served by amending the UN Charter rules on the use of force to facilitate humanitarian intervention. It seems already clear that the sovereignty of states is neither inherent,[52] nor unconditional.[53] By guarding the existing rules on the use of force, humanitarian intervention will remain an exceptional recourse. States that violate the UN Charter will continue to bear the onus of justification, thus reinforcing the very rules from which they seek an exemption.

D. TRANSITIONAL JUSTICE

The field of transitional justice has emerged in recent years as one of the most significant developments and fastest-growing disciplines within the larger field of human rights.[54] Transitional justice is about

---

51   The Security Council effectively endorsed the NATO intervention in Kosovo when it defeated by a vote of 12 to 3 a Russian resolution demanding an immediate end to the NATO action on 27 March 1999. The Council subsequently adopted SC res. 1244 (1999) endorsing the terms imposed on the FRY by NATO as a precondition for ending the air strikes.

52   Contrary to what many states suggest, sovereignty is not an inherent right but instead derives from and is limited by the need for recognition by other states. Donnelly makes this point succinctly: "States often present their sovereignty as a natural right or an inescapable logical feature of their existence. In fact, however, it is a matter of mutual recognition: sovereigns are those who are recognized as sovereign by other sovereigns. . . ." J. Donnelly, *Universal Human Rights in Theory and Practice*, 2d ed. (Ithaca: Cornell University Press, 2003) at 250.

53   UN Secretary-General Kofi Annan introduced the helpful concept of "sovereignty as responsibility." He observed that the sovereignty of any state is not absolute; among other things, it is conditioned on upholding fundamental human rights. K. Annan, "Two Concepts of Sovereignty," The Economist, 18 September 1999.

54   The literature on transitional justice is considerable. See, for example, Aspen Institute, *State Crimes: Punishment or Pardon: Papers and Reports of the Conference, November 4–6, 1988, Wye Centre, Maryland* (Queenstown, Md.: Aspen Institute, 1989); B. Ackerman, *The Future of Liberal Revolution* (New Haven: Yale University Press, 1992); N. Kritz, ed., *Transitional Justice: How Emerging Democracies Reckon with Former Regimes* (Washington, DC: United States Institute for Peace Press, 1995); N. Roht-Arriaza, ed., *Impunity and Human Rights in International Law and Practice* (New York: Oxford University Press, 1995) [Roht-Arriaza, *Impunity*]; A. McAdams, ed., *Transitional Justice and the Rule of Law in New Democracies* (London: University of Notre Dame Press, 1997) [McAdams, *Transitional Justice*]; R.

how societies in transition from war to peace or from authoritarian rule to democracy address legacies of mass human rights abuse. Transitional justice also concerns ways for established democracies to resolve historical injustices.

Most countries recovering from periods of war or repression face the almost certain prospect of flawed justice. Democratic and post-conflict transitions are characterized by seemingly insurmountable moral, legal, and political challenges. In many cases, transitional governments are forced to choose between justice and peace, or justice and democracy. Even where such dilemmas are less prominent, the scale of past abuse and the shortage of financial and human resources almost invariably make ordinary justice impossible. As a result, multiple strategies and mechanisms are required, going well beyond the limited reach of criminal justice.

Transitional justice has come to be associated with four mechanisms in particular: criminal trials; non-judicial fact-finding bodies (especially truth commissions); reparations initiatives; and institutional reform.

Criminal Trials. There are many reasons why criminal trials for gross and systematic human rights violations are essential, particularly those carried out at the domestic level. Criminal trials can contribute to specific and general deterrence and express public denunciation of criminal behaviour. They can provide a direct form of accountability for perpetrators, and justice for victims. Criminal trials can also contribute to greater public confidence in the state's ability and willingness to enforce the law.

Achieving and balancing the varied objectives of criminal justice is not easy. First, there are a number of general challenges that apply to almost all criminal justice systems: delays, high costs, lack of available witnesses and evidence, and the difficulty of proving a case beyond a reasonable doubt. Often there is also inadequate attention to victim needs — little victim counselling, low possibilities of compensation, and minimal direct participation. In addition to these challenges, there are many that are specific to contexts of democratic or post-conflict transition. Scarce financial resources and weak or corrupt justice systems directly limit criminal justice options. So too does the sheer size

---

Rotberg & D. Thompson, eds., *Truth v. Justice* (Princeton: Princeton University Press, 2000); R. Teitel, *Transitional Justice* (New York: Oxford University Press, 2002); A. Henkin, ed., *The Legacy Of Abuse* (New York: The Aspen Institute & NYU School of Law, 2002); M. Freeman, "Transitional Justice: Fundamental Goals and Unavoidable Complications" (2001) 28 Manitoba Law Journal 113.

of the caseload; victims and perpetrators may both number in the hundreds or thousands. Often there is also the risk of jeopardizing a fragile peace or democracy, and the competing and concomitant need to deal with current crime. In many cases there are legal limitations such as amnesty laws, prescription laws, and executive and parliamentary immunities too.

From a transitional justice perspective, domestic prosecutions are generally to be preferred over prosecutions before international or foreign courts. Domestic criminal trials are more likely to strengthen local prosecutorial capacity and be in tune with the changing social and political context of a transition. Domestic proceedings are invariably less expensive to carry out. They allow for better access to victims, witnesses, and evidence, and are generally more accountable and locally credible than foreign courts or international tribunals. It is common wisdom among transitional justice experts that the best examples of domestic prosecutions in a transitional context — measured in terms of fairness and effectiveness — were those that took place following the return to democratic rule in Greece in the 1970s and in Argentina in the 1980s.[55] Other notable examples include the German trials of former Nazis in the 1960s and of East German communists in the 1990s.[56]

In addition to criminal trials, there are a number of *sui generis* mechanisms that share some of the same attributes but that are different from typical courtroom proceedings. Examples of such mechanisms include those falling under the general rubric of restorative justice,[57] and indigenous-inspired procedures such as *gacaca* in Rwanda, discussed in Chapter Seventeen.

Non-Judicial Fact-Finding Bodies. The fact-finding body most closely associated with transitional justice is the truth commission.[58] Truth

---

55 On Greece see, for example, C. Woodhouse, *The Rise and the Fall of the Greek Colonels* (London: Granada, 1985); N. Alivizatos & P. Diamandouros, "Politics and the Judiciary in the Greek Transition to Democracy," in McAdams, *Transitional Justice, ibid.* at 27. On Argentina see, for example, C. Nino, *Radical Evil on Trial* (New Haven: Yale University Press, 1996); J. Malamud-Goti, *Game Without End: State Terrorism and the Politics of Justice* (Norman: University of Oklahoma Press, 1996).

56 On the Nazi trials see, for example, A. Rosenbaum, *Prosecuting Nazi War Criminals* (Boulder: Westview Press, 1993). On the East German communist trials see, for example, A. McAdams, "Communism on Trial: The East German Past and the German Future," in McAdams, *Transitional Justice, ibid.* at 239.

57 See generally B. Galaway & J. Hudson, eds., *Restorative Justice* (Monsey: Criminal Justice Press, 1996).

58 The leading book on truth commissions is P. Hayner, *Unspeakable Truths: Confronting State Terror and Atrocity* (New York: Routledge 2001) [Hayner, *Unspeak-*

commissions are temporary non-judicial fact-finding bodies, usually in operation for one to two years. Typically they are established and empowered by the state, usually at moments of democratic or post-conflict transition. Truth commissions focus on the investigation of patterns as well as specific instances of past human rights abuse. They tend to operate in a victim-centred fashion, and usually conclude their work with the delivery of a final report containing conclusions and recommendations. There have been at least twenty-five truth commissions established around the world since 1974, although they have gone by many different names.[59] The most prominent and influential past commissions are those of Argentina, Chile, El Salvador, South Africa, Guatemala, and Peru.[60] Among the most prominent contemporary truth commissions are those in Timor-Leste, Sierra Leone, Ghana, and Morocco.[61]

While truth commissions may not be appropriate in every situation, they have the potential to assist societies in transition. Under optimal conditions they may help establish the truth about the nature and scale of past human rights violations and serve as a guard against nationalist or revisionist accounts of the past. They may foster the accountability of perpetrators by collecting and preserving evidence and publicly identifying those responsible. They may recommend detailed victim reparations programs and necessary legal and institutional reforms. Truth commissions can also provide a public platform for victims to directly address the nation with their personal stories. They can inform and catalyze public debate about how to deal with the past and how to ensure a better future. They can also cultivate reconciliation and tolerance at the individual, community, and national level.

---

able]. See also M. Freeman & P. Hayner, "Truth-Telling," in *Reconciliation After Violent Conflict: A Handbook* (Stockholm: Institute for Democracy and Electoral Assistance, 2003); and M. Freeman & J. Quinn, "Lessons Learned: Practical Lessons Gleaned from Inside the Truth Commissions of Guatemala and South Africa" (2003) 25 Human Rights Quarterly 1117.

59   For example, there have been: "commissions on the disappeared" in Argentina, Uganda, and Sri Lanka; "truth and justice commissions" in Haiti, Ecuador, and now Paraguay; "truth and reconciliation commissions" in Chile, South Africa, Sierra Leone, Peru, and Serbia and Montenegro; and now a "commission for reception, truth and reconciliation" in Timor Leste.

60   See Hayner, *Unspeakable*, above note 58 at 33–49.

61   For detailed information and useful links regarding these and other contemporary commissions, see the website of the International Center for Transitional Justice (http://www.ictj.org).

Many external factors can limit or thwart the attainment of these potential benefits. These factors include a weak civil society, political instability, victim and witness fears about testifying, a weak or corrupt justice system, and the distraction of ongoing violations. In addition, significant operational constraints may hamper commissions. As a rule, there is insufficient time to carry out the mandate, insufficient funding, and an excessive caseload. The absence of perpetrator co-operation, weak investigative powers, and the inability to provide witness protection are other possible operational constraints.[62]

In addition to truth commissions, there are other fact-finding mechanisms that bear mention and that in some transitional contexts may constitute the only available or most suitable mechanism for inquiry. There are *ad hoc* historical commissions of inquiry.[63] There are *ad hoc* domestic inquiries into past human rights violations, that share some of the main characteristics of truth commissions but are more limited in scope, authority, or independence.[64] There are *ad hoc* inquiries at the international level too.[65] There are also NGO and other civil society projects that have documented violations and patterns of abuse of a previous regime.[66] Finally, there are permanent fact-finding bodies that monitor, investigate, and report on violations of human rights.[67]

---

62 M. Freeman & P. Hayner, "Truth-Telling," above note 58 at 125–29.

63 These are essentially present-day inquiries into state abuse that occurred years or decades prior. Examples include the Canadian Royal Commission on Aboriginal Peoples and the US Commission on Wartime Relocation and Internment of Civilians. See Hayner, *Unspeakable*, above note 58 at 17–19.

64 Examples of such commissions include: the various parliamentary inquiries and congressional investigative committees established by legislatures around the world to look into matters or events of public controversy, the investigations carried out by the Northern Ireland Victims Commissioner in the late 1990s, and the inquiry undertaken by the National Commissioner for the Protection of Human Rights in Honduras in 1993. See Hayner, *Unspeakable*, *ibid.* at 19–20.

65 Examples include the various international commissions of inquiry established by the UN to look into war crimes committed in places such as Yugoslavia (1992), Rwanda (1994), Burundi (1995), and East Timor (1999). A hybrid example under consideration is the Commission to Investigate Illegal Groups and Clandestine Security Apparatuses in Guatemala, which is to be composed of one UN representative, one OAS representative, and one Guatemalan national.

66 Examples include the work of organizations such as SERPAJ in Uruguay in the 1980s (http://www.serpaj.org.uy), and Memorial in Russia during the 1990s (http://www.memo.ru). See Hayner, *Unspeakable*, above note 58 at 21–22.

67 These include domestic bodies such as national and sub-national human rights commissions, as well as international bodies such as UN treaty bodies and analogous regional fact-finding mechanisms under the OAS, Council of Europe, or AU systems of human rights protection. See Chapters Fourteen and Fifteen.

Reparations.[68] In the face of widespread human rights violations, states have the obligation not only to act against perpetrators, but also to act on behalf of victims. Given the unlikelihood of mass prosecutions in transitional contexts, a complementary way to address victims' claims for justice without directly threatening political stability is to try to repair some of the harm suffered. The motivations for reparation measures, whether material or symbolic in nature, are many. Reparation measures can provide recognition to victims, both collectively and individually. They can foster a collective memory of past abuse and social solidarity with victims. They also constitute a concrete response to calls for remedy, and can help promote reconciliation by restoring victims' confidence in the state.[69]

Material forms of reparation present particularly difficult moral, legal, and political challenges — especially government-sponsored victim compensation programs of massive coverage.[70] Such programs involve complex questions of design. Decisions are required about who the victim or beneficiary class will be, and whether to award compensation to individuals for personal suffering or to groups for collective harm suffered. It must also be decided whether to structure material reparation as service packages (for example, special medical, educational, or housing benefits), cash payments, or a combination of both, and what kinds of harm to cover, whether economic, physical, or emotional. Whether compensation should be based on harm, need, or a combination must also be decided. Similarly, program sponsors must consider how to quantify the harm (for example, how much should someone receive for losing an arm vs. being raped), how much compensation to provide (for example, whether or not the amount should be identical for each beneficiary), and how to distribute compensation (for example, if cash payments, whether to provide one lump sum payment or multiple periodic payments, and in either case by what body). Most difficult of all, program sponsors must consider how to fund the program, given that it must usually compete with other social programs under conditions of scarcity.

---

68 We gratefully acknowledge the unpublished work of Pablo de Greiff on this topic.
69 On reparation generally, see G. Ulrich & L. Boserup, eds., *Reparations: Redressing Past Wrongs* (The Hague: Kluwer, 2003).
70 While the focus here will be on national governmental programs, victim compensation can also be awarded by foreign governments (for example, German compensation of Holocaust victims), corporations (for example, Swiss banks' compensation to Holocaust victims), or *sui generis* institutions (for example, the UN Compensation Commission established by the Security Council to compensate certain victims of Iraq's invasion of Kuwait).

Without doubt the most ambitious material reparations program ever implemented is that of Germany in respect of Holocaust survivors. Its size and complexity vastly surpass all other programs.[71] The victim compensation programs established in the 1990s in Chile, and later in Argentina, are the most well-known instances of domestically focused programs established in transitional contexts.[72]

Victim reparation can extend beyond material compensation. In some contexts it may be important for a new government to seek to provide restitution of victims' legal rights or property.[73] It may be important in some places to offer dedicated programs of rehabilitation for victims, including emotional counselling, physical therapy, or medical assistance. A wide range of symbolic reparation measures might also be considered, both for individual victims (for example, personal letters of apology from successor governments, or proper burial for murder victims) and for victimized groups (for example, official acknowledgements of past oppression, dedication of public spaces and street names or the construction of public memorials).

Institutional Reform. Countries emerging from war or tyranny will often need to adopt institutional, legal, and policy reforms to prevent civic or democratic collapse. The range of possible justice reforms is extremely broad.

Often the most immediate and important reform is the removal of corrupt and abusive officials from public sector positions through "vetting" procedures.[74] In its most familiar guise, vetting is the practice of

---

71   It is the longest running program (operating since 1951), the most expensive program (payments to Holocaust survivors exceed US$60 billion to date) and the broadest reaching program (more than 500,000 Holocaust survivors in almost 70 countries have received some form of compensation). See, for example, R. Zweig, *German Reparations and the Jewish World: A History of the Claims Conference* (Boulder: Westview Press, 1987); A. Baker, *Unfinished Business: Compensation and Restitution for Holocaust Survivors* (New York: The American Jewish Committee, 1997).

72   On the Chilean and Argentine reparations programs, see Hayner, *Unspeakable*, above note 58 at 172–78.

73   Examples of restitution might include: assistance to populations that have been forcibly transferred or had land stolen; restoration of persons' liberty, social status, or citizenship rights; or reinstatement of persons in former positions of public employment.

74   The literature on vetting is sparse. See, for example, V. Nanda, "Civil and Political Sanctions as an Accountability Mechanism for Massive Violations of Human Rights" (1998) 26 Denver Journal of International Law and Policy 398; L. Joinet, "Set of Principles for the Protection and Promotion of Human Rights through Action to Combat Impunity," UN doc. E/CN.4/Sub.2/1996/18 (1996) at arts. 48–50. This in contrast to the extensive literature on lustration, described below.

removing individuals responsible for serious misconduct from police and prison services, the army, and other public institutions. The vetting process typically involves a thorough background check of multiple sources of information and evidence. Persons under investigation are made aware of the allegations against them and given an opportunity to reply to them. In this and other respects, vetting may be distinguished from "lustration," a term commonly used in Eastern and Central Europe to refer to laws and policies involving wide-scale dismissal and disqualification based not on individual records, but on party affiliation, political opinion, or association with a hitherto oppressive secret service. Many lustration laws were criticized internationally for having violated fundamental standards of procedural fairness by punishing on the basis of collective not individual guilt, violating the presumption of innocence, imposing bans on elected or appointed positions in violation of the principle of non-discrimination on the basis of political opinion, unfairly limiting rights of appeal before judicial bodies, and relying too heavily on spurious Communist-era records to prove criminal behaviour.[75]

By itself, vetting is an incomplete solution to either punishing or preventing human rights abuse and corruption. Vetting needs to be accompanied by broader, systemic reforms in the justice sector. For example, new institutions may need to be created such as civilian oversight bodies (to monitor the police or military), an ombudsman's office (to receive and investigate complaints about public officials), a national human rights commission, an anti-corruption bureau, and specialized courts. Human rights and anti-corruption training policies and programs may also be established for police, soldiers, judges, prosecutors, and civil servants to convert them from instruments of repression or indifference into instruments of redress and public service. In addition, constitutional, legal, and policy reforms to consolidate democracy, human rights, and the rule of law can be important in such areas as: land tenure; refugee protection; pay equity; judicial appointment, tenure, promotion and discipline; election procedures; media inde-

---

75 See, for example, M. Ellis, "Purging the Past: The Current State of Lustration Laws in the Former Communist Bloc" (1996) 59 Law and Contemporary Problems 181. On lustration generally see T. Garton-Ash, *The File* (New York: Knopf, 1998); K. Smith, "Decommunization after the 'Velvet Revolutions' in East Central Europe," in Roht-Arriaza, *Impunity*, above note 54; H. Schwartz, "Lustration in Eastern Europe" (1994) 1(2) Parker School Journal of Eastern European Law 141; A. Stinchcombe, "Lustration as a Problem of the Social Basis of Constitutionalism" (1995) 20(1) Law & Social Inquiry 245.

pendence; freedom of information; affirmative action; criminal law and procedure; and constitutional governance.[76]

As an academic as well as a professional discipline, further growth in the field of transitional justice seems assured. The interest in and demand for information about transitional justice is growing constantly, as more and more countries seek proven ways to confront the tragedies of their past and chart more peaceful and democratic futures.

E. REFORM OF THE UN HUMAN RIGHTS SYSTEM

As demonstrated in earlier chapters, the UN is active in human rights on several fronts, serving as standard-setter, diplomat, and forum of appeal. Certain competitive advantages continue to make the UN the essential forum for world affairs. It is the most universal institution, comprised of almost every country in the world. It is an institution that allows for extensive and generally equal entry points for participation by its members on all major decisions (the Security Council being the obvious exception). It has a global presence, including a vast network of in-country offices and missions. And it has a broad and comprehensive mandate that spans economic, social, cultural, civil, and political matters.

The UN is not, however, a world government. It is an intergovernmental organization with a mandate that extends no further than its members — all of them sovereign states — allow. As such it is an inherently political body. Politics, and not law, will more often be the driving force behind its actions, including in the area of human rights. All too often states condemn their enemies and support their allies, paying little regard to the actual objective human rights records of either. Indeed, some states have been routinely condemned out of all proportion to the nature and scale of their violations measured against those of other states, while others' human rights records have been largely overlooked.[77]

---

76   Regarding the latter, see M. Freeman "Constitutional Frameworks and Fragile Democracies: Choosing Between Parliamentarism, Presidentialism and Semipresidentialism" (2000) 12 Pace International Law Review 253.

77   The example *par excellence* is Israel, which is routinely condemned in General Assembly and Commission on Human Rights resolutions, while states with far worse human records escape censure. The point is not that Israel does not deserve criticism, but that the nature and quantity of criticism it receives is radically unbalanced.

At the same time, in recent years there has been a noticeable improvement in and expansion of UN mechanisms available for the promotion and protection of human rights. Not only are there three international criminal tribunals, but there has also been a modest increase in the powers of UN treaty bodies.[78] In addition, the Security Council is increasingly responding to human rights crises with a creative sense of purpose that was utterly absent during the Cold War.

Yet the unfortunate fact is that the development of human rights norms by the UN still far exceeds in quality and quantity the mechanisms available for their enforcement. At the international level, we are still a long way from having an independent and universal system of remedial mechanisms comparable to domestic systems. The problem is unavoidable. As both the principal subjects and violators of human rights, states have an inherent disincentive to vest UN bodies with independent or vigorous enforcement powers.

Too often, the practical result of this is that the more accessible and effective the proposed mechanism — in terms of standing for individuals, availability of remedies, binding character of decisions, and scope for enforcement of decisions — the less likely it is that most states will support or participate in it. Conversely, the weaker the mechanism, the greater the support and participation it will tend to enjoy. While this may be less true in regional regimes involving democratic states, such as the OAS and the Council of Europe, it is an undeniable fact at the UN, which comprises a number of undemocratic states that are openly hostile to human rights.

To be fair, states of all stripes have an aversion to independent scrutiny of their human rights records. Developed democratic countries have opposed the creation of strong, independent international bodies for all sorts of reasons. They may, for example, view international bodies as unnecessary (since human rights are alleged to be adequately protected already at the domestic level) or undesirable (since international mechanisms are alleged to be less accountable, representative, and impartial than domestic mechanisms). At the same time, no states — not even those that regularly violate fundamental human rights — deny being legally bound or politically committed to human rights. They understand human rights as international obligations and not as optional policy. And many, if not most, states measure their conduct with due regard to the possible consequences of violations they commit, however minor those consequences may be.

---

78   The powers of various treaty bodies have been expanded by new optional protocols (for example, the CAT-OP and the CEDAW-OP).

Against this challenging backdrop, there remain many possible sites for reform within the UN system. We have already discussed reforms to UN treaty bodies.[79] Many would also like to see reforms at the Security Council, mostly aimed at curbing the power of the veto-wielding permanent members. But Security Council reform is an idea with no support among the permanent members and therefore no real prospect of fulfilment, at least for now. A more viable target of reform is the OHCHR. If the UN human rights system is to develop to its full potential (taking into account inherent institutional constraints), the OHCHR will need to play a central role. The OHCHR has a particularly vital role to play in human rights monitoring, capacity building, and technical co-operation programs. But the OHCHR is hampered by its limited budget, which has never exceeded 2 percent of the total annual UN budget. It is also hampered by its location. Geneva is far away from UN headquarters in New York, where all of the key decision-making takes place. New York is where the Security Council, the UN Secretariat, and the General Assembly meet; it is where UN officials set long-term strategy, respond to crises, and deploy peacekeeping operations; and it is headquarters for many major international NGOs and press outlets. Success on the human rights front requires a large and visible presence there.

Yet even a much-strengthened OHCHR would not diminish the primary role that states must play in the promotion and protection of human rights. The state, and not the UN, remains the most important guarantor of human rights. The UN must remain a forum of last and not first resort regarding human rights protection. As a rule, it should offer protection only when effective domestic protection is unavailable, whether due to incapacity or unwillingness. Like any good human rights organization, the UN must in a sense seek its own obsolescence. The underlying goal must always be to make human rights protection self-sustaining within the state.

F. DOMESTIC RECEPTION OF HUMAN RIGHTS NORMS

International human rights law takes greater interest in the individual — her well-being, her beliefs, her relations with others and with the state — than any other area of international law. Though conceived and

---

79   See Chapter Fourteen.

elaborated internationally, it is as domestic — indeed, as intimate — as law can be. The domestic reception of human rights norms, and of international law in general, should therefore be of great interest to human rights scholars and advocates.

And yet quite the opposite has long been the case. In spite of some notable contributions (especially more recently),[80] the domestic reception of international law has not yet arisen as an acknowledged body of law or an established field of academic study. Reception discourse remains trapped in tedious debates about the theoretical merits of monism and dualism, when it should be seeking to explain to judges and lawyers how they can in fact use international law to resolve cases. Studies of international human rights law usually neglect reception, while works on domestic human rights (especially in Canada) often treat the international dimension only in passing. Human rights, and international law as a whole, are ill-served by both approaches.

The example of Canada is illustrative. The Canadian judiciary and legal profession must be among the most well-versed in the theory and practice of human rights in the world. We enjoy the benefits of strong constitutional rights guarantees, comprehensive anti-discrimination laws, and a legal and political culture that is generally sympathetic to the claims of human rights law. And yet the international dimension of human rights remains unexplored territory for most Canadian judges and lawyers. Theoretical confusion prevails about the interaction between the *Charter* and international law, thus discouraging most judges and lawyers from looking to Canada's treaty obligations except in cursory ways. Compounding this theoretical problem is the unfamiliarity of even rudimentary international law concepts to many practitioners.

If international human rights law is to succeed, it must succeed domestically. Human rights scholars and advocates must therefore do

---

80   Examples include: H. Lauterpacht, "Is International Law a Part of the Law of England?" [1939] Transactions of the Grotius Society 51; R. Macdonald, "The Relationship between Domestic Law and International Law in Canada" in R. Macdonald *et al.*, eds, *Canadian Perspectives on International Law and Organization* (Toronto: University of Toronto Press, 1974) at 88; F. Mann, *Foreign Affairs in English Courts* (Oxford: Clarendon Press, 1986); J. Jackson, "Status of Treaties in Domestic Legal Systems: A Policy Analysis" (1992) 86 AJIL 310. More recently, see: W. Schabas, *International Human Rights Law and the Canadian Charter*, 2d ed (Scarborough: Carswell, 1996); M. Hunt, *Using Human Rights Law in English Courts* (Oxford: Hart Publishing, 1998); C. Heyns & F. Viljoen, *The Impact of the United Nations Treaties on the Domestic Level* (The Hague: Kluwer Law International, 2002); G. van Ert, *Using International Law in Canadian Courts* (The Hague: Kluwer Law International, 2002).

more than simply point to international norms and complain of their non-implementation in domestic law. They must familiarize themselves with the laws governing the reception of international law in the jurisdictions they criticize, and suggest ways to improve domestic compliance through the improvement of reception law. A promising sign that this is beginning to happen, in Canada at least, is a recent initiative by the National Judicial Institute (Canada's judicial education program) on the domestic application of international law. The Institute has designed education modules on the reception of customary and conventional international law in Canada and run seminars on these themes for judges across the country. This commendably practical approach to international law and its reception in domestic law is more likely to advance human rights and other areas of international law than purely academic contributions.

The institution most well-placed to advance the domestic reception of international human rights law in Canada is, of course, the Supreme Court. The Court's track record on international human rights questions is decidedly mixed. In contrast to its American counterpart, the Supreme Court of Canada and most other final courts of appeal in the democratic world compare favourably. But that is not a proper comparison, for the US court has largely turned its back on international law.[81] The Supreme Court of Canada's jurisprudence on the reception of international human rights law throught the *Charter* and other Canadian laws must be measured against the requirements of law itself. Is it clear? Is it predictable? Is it intelligible? Is it in conformity with international requirements? In our view, the answer to these questions is, nearly. Outside of the *Charter* context, Canadian reception rules are well-established (if unfamiliar to most practitioners). As for the *Charter*, in the jurisprudence of Dickson C.J. the Supreme Court of Canada came tantalizingly close to a sophisticated, rigorous approach to the reception of international human rights norms in Canadian law. That approach — if only it had been enunciated more clearly and adopted more enthusiastically — would have been to interpret the *Charter*, like other Canadian laws, according to the rebuttable presumption that it conforms to Canada's obligations under binding rules of international human rights law. Non-binding international norms would have been

---

81   See H. Blackmun, "The Supreme Court and the Law of Nations" (1994–5) 104 Yale LJ 39; see also R. Bader Ginsburg, "Remarks for the American Constitution Society: Looking Beyond Our Borders: The Value of a Comparative Perspective in Constitutional Adjudication" (2 August 2003).

treated as relevant and persuasive for the purposes of *Charter* analysis but not subject to the same presumption. This approach to the *Charter* would not give automatic or direct effect to international human rights law through the *Charter*, for it would always remain open to the government or other litigants to show that the presumption of conformity was rebutted in given instances. Since Dickson C.J.'s departure, the court has strayed from the approach he (somewhat ambiguously) enunciated. Yet even its more disappointing international law judgments have not put the Dickson doctrine out of reach. It is not too late for the court to place its *Charter* jurisprudence on sound international and reception law footing by affirming the presumption of conformity.

G. CONCLUDING THOUGHTS

In Canada, as elsewhere, human rights have become part of our political and legal vocabulary. Media reports every day feature human rights stories. Whether it is horrific accounts of torture and illegal detention, uplifting reports of human rights abusers brought to justice or commonplace stories of discrimination and mistreatment in the workplace, human rights news abounds.

But though we know what human rights are, we are less aware of the scope of Canada's contribution to their realization. We tend at once to underestimate and overestimate Canada's role in the advancement of international human rights. Few Canadians are likely aware that Canadians occupy the two most high-profile human rights positions in the international system, namely the UN High Commissioner for Human Rights (Louise Arbour) and the President of the International Criminal Court (Philippe Kirsch). Many more Canadians are probably familiar with, and justly proud of, Canada's past contributions to UN peacekeeping. But how many of us would be surprised and dismayed to learn that Canada's current troop and personnel contributions pale in comparison to such countries as Bangladesh and Ghana? There are other grounds for concern. Canada's international aid budget is paltry compared to the past. Our foreign policy, like that of most states, is increasingly driven by trade considerations rather than human rights or other concerns. And our domestic human rights record, though very good in most respects, has major weaknesses. For example, the situation of Canada's aboriginal peoples remains, in the words of the current prime minister, shameful. Poverty is another human rights challenge Canada continues to face.

To be sure, Canadians can take some pride in this country's advancement and implementation of international human rights. But we must acknowledge and seize the many opportunities for strengthening our participation in the international human rights system. Canada can certainly do more.

CONCORDANCE OF CANADIAN AND INTERNATIONAL HUMAN RIGHTS INSTRUMENTS

This Appendix provides a table of concordance comparing the rights of the *Charter* and the *Bill of Rights* with selected binding and non-binding international human rights instruments.

Provisions listed in the leftmost column summarize the rights indicated, e.g., "Presumption of innocence" for *Charter* s. 11(d) and similar provisions. Only provisions that closely match the right or freedom given in the leftmost column have been included in the table. This does not exclude the possibility of interpreting a given provision to include some related right or freedom. For example, at the row "Right to counsel" the table indicates that no such provision occurs expressly in the UDHR, yet it is possible to interpret UDHR art. 11(1) as including this right. Similarly, the *Charter* column for the row "Right to examine witnesses" is marked "—" because no such right is explicitly found in the *Charter*, yet such a right has been held to form part of ss. 7 and 11(d).

Right	Canadian instruments		Binding international instruments — See text on bindingness of UDHR and AmDR							Non-binding international instruments		
	Charter	Cdn Bill of Rights	UDHR	ICCPR	ICESCR	CERD	CEDAW	CRC	AmDR	ACHR (including protocols)[1]	ECHR (including protocols) and EurSC[2]	AfrCHPR (including protocol)[3]
Freedom of thought, conscience and religion	2(a)	1(c)	18	18(1)	—	5(d)(vii)	—	14(1)	3	12, 13(1)	9(1)	8
Freedom of opinion and expression	2(b)	1(d), 1(f)	19	19(1), 19(2)	—	5(d)(viii)	—	13(1)	4, 24	13(1)	10(1)	9
Prohibition of war- and hate-speech	—	—	—	20	—	4(a)	—	—	—	13(5)	—	—
Freedom of peaceful assembly	2(c)	1(e)	20	21	—	5(d)(ix)	—	15(1)	21	15	11(1)	11
Freedom of association	2(d)	1(e)	20	22(1)	—	5(d)(ix)	—	15(1)	22	16(1)	11(1)	10(1), 10(2)
Right to vote in genuine, periodic elections	3, 4, 5	—	21(3)	25(b)	—	5(c)	7(a)	—	20	23(b)	—	—
Right of equal access to public service	—	—	21(2)	25(c)	—	5(c)	7(b)	—	—	23(c)	—	13(2)

1   ACHR protocol provisions are indicated thus: P1:3 = First Protocol art. 3. ACHR P1 is the Additional Protocol to the American Convention on Human Rights in the Area of Economic, Social and Cultural Rights 1988. ACHR P2 is the Protocol to the American Convention on Human Rights to Abolish the Death Penalty 1990.

2   ECHR protocol provisions are indicated thus: P7:4 = Seventh Protocol art. 4. ECHR protocol 12 is not yet in force. EurSC is the European Social Charter (revised) 1996.

3   The protocol is the Protocol to the African Charter on Human and Peoples' Rights on the Rights of Women in Africa 2003. Protocol provisions are indicated thus: P:2(1) = Women's Protocol art. 2(1).

Right to participate in government	—	—	21(1)	25(a)	—	5(c)	7(b), 7(c)	—	20	23(a)	—	13(1), P9
Mobility rights	6	—	13	12	—	5(d)(i), 5(d)(ii)	15(4)	—	8	22(1), 22(2)	P4:2, P4:3	12
Right to life	7	1(a)	3	6(1)	—	—	—	6	1	4,	2, P6:1, P6:2	4, P:4(1)
Right to liberty and freedom from slavery	7	1(a)	3, 4	8, 9(1)	—	—	—	—	1	6, 7	4, 5	5, 6
Right to security of person	7	1(a)	3	9(1)	—	5(b)	—	—	1	7(1)	5	4, 6, P:4(1)
Deprivation of life, liberty and security according to law	7	1(a), 2(e)	—	6(1), 9(1)	—	—	—	—	—	7(2), P2:1	—	4
Rights to property	—	1(a)	17	—	—	5(d)(v), 5(d)(vi)	15(2)	—	13, 23	21	P1:1	14
No imprisonment for debt	—	—	—	11	—	—	—	—	25	7(7)	P4:1	—
Rights to privacy and reputation (including protection from search or seizure)	8	—	12	14(1), 17	—	—	—	16, 40(2)(b)(vii)	5, 9, 10	11	8(1)	—
No arbitrary arrest or detention	9	2(a)	9	9(1)	—	—	—	37(b)	25	7(3)	5(1)	6
Right to be informed of reason for arrest or detention	10(a)	2(c)(i)	—	9(2)	—	—	—	40(2)(b)(ii)	—	7(4)	5(2)	—
Prisoners' right to humane treatment	—	—	—	10(1)	—	—	—	37(c)	25	5(2)	—	—
Right to counsel in criminal proceedings	10(b)	2(c)(ii), 2(d)	—	14(3)(a)	—	—	—	37(d)	—	8(2)(d), 8(2)(e)	6(3)(c)	7(1)(c)
Habeas corpus or similar procedure	10(c)	2(c)(iii)	—	9(4)	—	—	—	37(d)	25	7(6)	5(4)	—

Right	Canadian instruments		Binding international instruments — See text on bindingness of UDHR and AmDR							Non-binding international instruments		
	Charter	Cdn Bill of Rights	UDHR	ICCPR	ICESCR	CERD	CEDAW	CRC	AmDR	ACHR (including protocols)	ECHR (including protocols) and EurSC	AfrCHPR (including protocol)
Right to be informed of offence upon charge	11(a)	—	—	9(2)	—	—	—	40(2)(b)(ii)	—	8(2)(b)	6(3)(a)	—
Right to trial within reasonable time	11(b)		—	9(3), 14(3)(c)	—	—	—	40(2)(b)(iii)	25	7(5), 8(1)	5(3)	—
Right to examine witnesses	—	—	—	14(3)(e)	—	—	—	40(2)(b)(iv)	—	8(2)(f)	6(3)(d)	—
Privilege against self-crimination	11(c), 13	2(d)	—	14(3)(g)	—	—	—	40(2)(b)(iv)	—	8(2)(g)	—	7(1)(d)
Presumption of innocence	11(d)	2(f)	11(1)	14(2)	—	—	—	40(2)(b)(i)	26	8(2)	6(2)	7(1)(b)
Right to fair and public hearing	11(d)	2(f)	10	14(1)	—	—	—	40(2)(b)(iii)	18, 26	8(1), 8(5)	6(1)	7(1)
Right to independent and impartial tribunal	11(d)	2(f)	10	14(1)	—	—	—	40(2)(b)(iii)	26	8(1)	6(1)	7(1)(d), 26
Right to bail	11(e)	2(f)	—	9(3)	—	—	—		—	—	5(3)	—
Right to trial by jury	11(f)	—	—	—	—	—	—		—	—	—	—
Protection from retroactive criminal laws	11(g)	—	11(2)	15	—	—	—	40(2)(a)	25, 26	9	7	—
Protection from double jeopardy	11(h)	—	—	14(7)	—	—	—	—	26	8(4)	P7:4	—
Right to benefit of lesser punishment	11(i)	—	11(2)	15(1)	—	—	—	—	—	9	—	—
Right to interpreter	14	2(g)	—	14(3)(a), 14(3)(f)	—	—	—	40(2)(b)(vi)	—	8(2)(a)	6(3)(e)	—

Right												
Protection from torture and cruel, inhuman or degrading treatment or punishment[4]	12	2(b)	5	7	—	—	—	37(a)	2	5(2)	3	5, P4(1)
Equality before the law	15(1)	1(b)	7	14(1), 26	—	5, 5(a)	15(1)	—	2	24	—	3(1), P8
Equal protection of the law	15(1)	1(b)	7	26	—	—	15(2), 15(3)	—	—	24	—	3(2), P8
Protection from discrimination	15(1), 15(2)	1	2, 7	2(1), 26	2(2)	—	2, 11(2)	2	2	1, 24, P1:3	14, P12:1	2, 18(3), 19, P:2(1)
Affirmative action	15(2)	—	—	—	—	2(2)	4(1)	—	—	—	P12: preamble	—
Equality of sexes	15, 28	—	Preamble, 2, 16(1)	3, 23(4)	3	—	Throughout	—	—	—	—	18(3), P:2(1)(a)
Self-determination of peoples	—	—	—	1	1	—	—	—	—	—	—	20(1)
Protection of aboriginal rights and freedoms	25	—	—	—	—	—	—	—	—	—	—	—
Protection of minority rights	27	—	—	27	—	—	—	30	—	—	—	—
Right to legal personality	—	—	6	16	—	—	15(2)	—	17	3	—	5
Right to nationality	—	—	15	24(3)	—	5(d)(iii)	9(1), 9(2)	7(1)	19	20	—	—
Right to adequate standard of living	—	—	25(1)	—	11(1)	—	—	27(1)	—	—	ESC4(1), EurSC30	—
Right to social security and insurance	—	—	22	—	9	5(e)(iv)	11(1)(e)	26	16	P1:9	ESC12, EurSC13, EurSC14	—
Freedom from hunger	—	—	—	—	11(2)	—	—	—	—	P1:12	—	P:15

4   See also the CAT, which is not included in this concordance because it addresses a relatively narrow range of rights

Right	Canadian instruments		Binding international instruments See text on bindingness of UDHR and AmDR							Non-binding international instruments		
	Charter	Cdn Bill of Rights	UDHR	ICCPR	ICESCR	CERD	CEDAW	CRC	AmDR	ACHR (including protocols)	ECHR (including protocols) and EurSC	AfrCHPR (including protocol)
Right to health	—	—	—	—	12	5(e)(iv)	12	24	11	P1:10	ESC11	16, P:14
Right to marry	—	—	16(1), 16(2)	23(2)	—	5(d)(iv)	16	—	6	17(2)	12	—
Protection of family	—	—	16(3)	23(1)	10(1)	—	—	—	6	P1:15	ESC16	18(1), 18(2)
Protection for mothers	—	—	25(2)	—	10(2)	—	11(2)	—	7	P1:15(3)(a)	ESC8	—
Protection for children	—	—	25(2)	23(4), 24	10(3)	—	—	Throughout	7	17(5), 19, P1:16	ESC7, EurSC17	—
Best interests of child	—	—	—	—	—	—	5(b), 16(1)(d)	3(1)	—	17(4)	—	—
Right to education	—	—	26	—	13	5(e)(v)	10	28, 29	12	P1:13	P1:2	17(1), P:12
Right to culture and science	—	—	27	—	15	5(e)(vi)	—	—	13	P1:14, P1:15	—	17(2)
Right to work	—	—	23(1)	—	6(1)	5(e)(i)	11(1)(a)	—	14	P1:6	ESC1	15
Right to favourable working conditions	—	—	23(1)	—	7	5(e)(i)	11(1)(f)	—	—	P1:7	ESC2, EurSC3	—
Right to equal pay for equal work	—	—	23(2)	—	7(a)(i)	5(e)(i)	11(1)(d)	—	—	P1:7(a)	ESC4(3)	P:13(b)
Right to rest and leisure	—	—	24	—	7(d)	—	—	31	15	P1:7(h)	ESC2	—
Right to form trade unions	—	—	23(4)	22(1)	8(1)(a)	5(e)(ii)	—	—	22	P1:8(1)(a)	11(1), EurSC5	—
Right to lawful strike	—	—	—	—	8(d)	—	—	—	—	P1:8(1)(b)	ESC6(4)	—
Right to asylum	—	—	14	—	—	—	—	—	27	22(7)	—	12(3)
Protection from expulsion	—	2(a)	—	13	—	—	—	—	8	22(5), 22(6)	P4:3, P4:4, P7:1	12(4), 12(5)

	1	—	29(2)	12(3), 14(1), 18(3), 19(3), 21, 22(2)	4, 8(1)	—	—	10(2), 13(2), 14(3), 15(2)	28	12(3), 13(4), 15, 16(2), 22(3), 22(4), 30, 32(2), P1:5	6(1), 8(2), 9(2), 10(2), 11(2), P4:2 EurSC31	8, 9, 10(1), 11, 12(2)
Limitation of rights and freedoms												
Derogation from rights and freedoms	33	2	—	4	—	—	—	—	—	27	15, EurSC30	—
Protection of other rights and freedoms	26	5(1)	—	5(2)	5(2)	—	23	41	—	29(b), P1:4, P1:8(2)	53	—
Right to a remedy	24	—	8	2(3)	—	6	—	—	—	25	13	P:25
Right to compensation for unlawful arrest	—	—	—	9(5)	—	—	—	—	—	—	5(5)	—
Right to compensation for wrongful conviction	—	—	—	14(6)	—	—	—	—	—	10	P7:3	—

UNDERSTANDING CANADA TREATY SERIES CITATIONS

The Treaty Section of the Department of Foreign Affairs and International Trade is responsible for the publication of the Canada Treaty Series (CanTS). Most treaties currently in force for Canada, dating back to 1928, are published in the CanTS. The CanTS has recently established a website[1] which includes a partial list of treaties in force for Canada. Other CanTS references may be found in "Treaty Action Taken by Canada," a section within the *Canadian Yearbook of International Law*.

Throughout this book, we use CanTS citations in preference to all others. The advantage of this practice is that the reader knows, upon seeing the CanTS citation, that Canada has become a party to this treaty.

The style we use is as follows:

Convention on the Rights of the Child 1989 [1992] CanTS no. 3

The portion before the CanTS citation is the treaty's name and the year in which it was opened for signature. The figure in square brackets is the annual volume of the CanTS in which the treaty was published. Canada's usual practice is to publish the treaty in the CanTS in the same year as it came into force for Canada. Thus, if the treaty came into force upon signature, Canada will usually publish it in the CanTS that year. If the treaty was already in force when Canada acceded to it,

---

1   See http://www.treaty-accord.gc.ca.

Canada will usually publish it the year it acceded. If the treaty was not in force when Canada ratified it, Canada will delay publication until the treaty comes into force. We stress that this is the usual, not the invariable, practice. The year of publication in CanTS cannot always be taken as the year in which the treaty came into force for Canada.

Although we consider it the preferred form of citation (when available), it is important to bear in mind the limitations of a CanTS citation. The citation alone does not indicate any reservations or declarations Canada has made (though these are published in the CanTS itself). The citation does not indicate whether the treaty remains in force. Nor does it tell you how Canada became a party to the treaty (i.e., by ratification or accession). Note also that many treaties binding on Canada (particularly ones from the colonial era, but also some recent and especially long treaties) are not published in the CanTS. Finally, the CanTS takes no account of the date of a treaty's implementation, if any, into domestic law. It is concerned only with the coming into force of the treaty for Canada for purposes of international law.

SELECTED TREATIES IN FORCE FOR CANADA

We have divided this Appendix into five sections: League of Nations treaties, UN treaties, ILO conventions, OAS treaties, and other treaties. In each section, treaties are listed chronologically according to their date of entry into force for Canada.

League of Nations Treaties

Slavery Convention
Reference: [1928] CanTS no. 5
Date of adoption: 25 September 1926
Date of Canada's ratification/accession: 6 August 1928 (R)
Date of entry into force for Canada: 6 August 1928
Reservations, statements or declarations made by Canada: None

UN Treaties

Charter of the United Nations
Reference: [1945] CanTS no. 7
Date of adoption: 26 June 1945
Date of Canada's ratification/accession: 9 November 1945
Date of entry into force for Canada: 9 November 1945
Reservations, statements or declarations made by Canada: None

Convention on the Prevention and Punishment of the Crime of Genocide
Reference: [1949] CanTS no. 27
Date of adoption: 9 December 1948
Date of Canada's ratification/accession: 3 September 1952 (R)
Date of entry into force for Canada: 2 December 1952
Reservations, statements or declarations made by Canada: None

Protocol Amending the Slavery Convention
Reference: [1953] CanTS no. 26
Date of adoption: 23 October 1953
Date of Canada's ratification/accession: 17 December 1953
(binding signature — no requirement of ratification)
Date of entry into force for Canada: 17 December 1953
Reservations, statements or declarations made by Canada: None

Convention on the Political Rights of Women
Reference: [1957] CanTS no. 3
Date of adoption: 20 December 1952
Date of Canada's ratification/accession: 30 January 1957 (A)
Date of entry into force for Canada: 30 April 1957
Reservations, statements or declarations made by Canada:

Reservation (made upon accession):

> Inasmuch as under the Canadian constitutional system legislative jurisdiction in respect of political rights is divided between the provinces and the Federal Government, the Government of Canada is obliged, in acceding to this Convention, to make a reservation in respect of rights within the legislative jurisdiction of the provinces.

Convention on the Nationality of Married Women
Reference: [1960] CanTS no. 2
Date of adoption: 29 January 1957
Date of Canada's ratification/accession: 21 October 1959 (R)
Date of entry into force for Canada: 19 January 1960
Reservations, statements or declarations made by Canada: None

Supplementary Convention on the Abolition of Slavery, the Slave Trade, and Institutions and Practices Similar to Slavery
Reference: [1963] CanTS no. 7
Date of adoption: 7 September 1956
Date of Canada's ratification/accession: 10 January 1963 (R)
Date of entry into force for Canada: 10 January 1963
Reservations, statements or declarations made by Canada: None

Protocol Relating to the Status of Refugees
Reference: [1969] CanTS no. 29
Date of adoption: 31 January 1967
Date of Canada's ratification/accession: 4 June 1969 (A)
Date of entry into force for Canada: 4 June 1969
Reservations, statements or declarations made by Canada: None

Convention Relating to the Status of Refugees
Reference: [1969] CanTS no. 6
Date of adoption: 28 July 1951
Date of Canada's ratification/accession: 4 June 1969 (A)
Date of entry into force for Canada: 2 September 1969
Reservations, statements or declarations made by Canada:

Reservation (made upon accession):

> Canada interprets the phrase 'lawfully staying' as referring only to refugees admitted for permanent residence: refugees admitted for temporary residence will be accorded the same treatment with respect to the matters dealt with in Articles 23 and 24 as is accorded visitors generally.

Declaration (made on 23 October 1970):

> The Government of Canada declares that for the purposes of its obligations under the Convention relating to the Status of Refugees done at Geneva on July 28, 1951, the words 'events occurring before 1 January 1951' in Article 1, Section B(1) of the said Convention shall be understood as meaning 'events occurring in Europe or elsewhere before 1 January 1951.'

International Convention on the Elimination of All Forms of Racial Discrimination
Reference: [1970] CanTS no. 28
Date of adoption: 21 December 1965
Date of Canada's ratification/accession: 14 October 1970 (R)
Date of entry into force for Canada: 13 November 1970
Reservations, statements or declarations made by Canada: None

International Covenant on Economic, Social and Cultural Rights
Reference: [1976] CanTS no. 46
Date of adoption: 16 December 1966
Date of Canada's ratification/accession: 19 May 1976 (A)
Date of entry into force for Canada: 19 August 1976
Reservations, statements or declarations made by Canada: None

International Covenant on Civil and Political Rights

Reference: [1976] CanTS no. 47
Date of adoption: 16 December 1966
Date of Canada's ratification/accession: 19 May 1976 (A)
Date of entry into force for Canada: 19 August 1976
Reservations, statements or declarations made by Canada:

Declaration (on 29 October 1979):

> Canada recognized the competence of the Human Rights Committee to receive and consider inter-state complaints against it.

Optional Protocol to the International Covenant on Civil and Political Rights

Reference: [1976] CanTS no. 47
Date of adoption: 16 December 1966
Date of Canada's ratification/accession: 19 May 1976 (A)
Date of entry into force for Canada: 19 August 1976
Reservations, statements or declarations made by Canada: None

Convention on the Reduction of Statelessness

Reference: [1978] CanTS no. 32
Date of adoption: 30 August 1961
Date of Canada's ratification/accession: 17 July 1978 (A)
Date of entry into force for Canada: 15 October 1978
Reservations, statements or declarations made by Canada: None

Convention on the Elimination of All Forms of Discrimination Against Women

Reference: [1982] CanTS no. 31
Date of adoption: 18 December 1979
Date of Canada's ratification/accession: 10 December 1981 (R)
Date of entry into force for Canada: 10 January 1982
Reservations, statements or declarations made by Canada:

Statement (made upon ratification):

> The Government of Canada states that the component legislative authorities within Canada have addressed the concept of equal pay referred to in article 11(1)(d) by legislation which requires the establishment of rates of remuneration without discrimination on the basis of sex. The component legislative authorities within Canada will continue to implement the object and purpose of article 11(1)(d) and to that end have developed, and where appropriate will continue to develop, additional legislative and other measures. [*Canada withdrew the statement on 28 May 1992.*]

Convention Against Torture and Other Cruel, Inhuman or Degrading Treatment or Punishment

Reference: [1987] CanTS no. 36
Date of adoption: 10 December 1984
Date of Canada's ratification/accession: 24 June 1987 (R)
Date of entry into force for Canada: 24 July 1987
Reservations, statements or declarations made by Canada:

Declarations (made on 13 November 1989)

> Pursuant to arts. 21 and 22 of the Convention, Canada recognized the competence of the Committee against Torture to receive and consider inter-state and individual complaints against it.

Convention on the Rights of the Child

Reference: [1992] CanTS no. 3
Date of adoption: 20 November 1989
Date of Canada's ratification/accession: 9 December 1991 (R)
Date of entry into force for Canada: 8 January 1992
Reservations, statements or declarations made by Canada:

Reservations (made upon ratification):

> 1. With a view to ensuring full respect for the purposes and intent of Article 20(3) and Article 30 of the Convention, the Government of Canada reserves the right not to apply the provisions of Article 21 to the extent that they may be inconsistent with customary forms of care among aboriginal peoples in Canada.

> 2. The Government of Canada accepts the general principle of Article 37(c) of the Convention, but reserves the right not to detain children separately from adults where this is not appropriate or feasible.

Statement (made upon ratification):

> It is the understanding of the Government of Canada that, in matters relating to aboriginal peoples of Canada, the fulfilment of its responsibilities under Article 4 of the Convention must take into account the provisions of Article 30. In particular, in assessing what measures are appropriate to implement the rights recognized in the Convention for aboriginal children, due regard must be paid to not denying their right, in community with other members of their group, to enjoy their own culture, to profess and practice their own religion and to use their own language.

Optional Protocol to the Convention on the Rights of the Child on involvement of Children in Armed Conflicts
Reference: [2002] CanTS no. 5
Date of adoption: 25 May 2000
Date of Canada's ratification/accession: 7 July 2000 (R)
Date of entry into force for Canada: 12 February 2002
Reservations, statements or declarations made by Canada:

Declaration (made upon ratification):

> Pursuant to article 3, paragraph 2, of the Optional Protocol to the Convention on the Rights of the Child on Involvement of Children in Armed Conflicts, Canada hereby declares:
>
> 1. The Canadian Armed Forces permit voluntary recruitment at the minimum age of 16 years.
> 2. The Canadian Armed Forces have adopted the following safeguards to ensure that recruitment of personnel under the age of 18 years is not forced or coerced:
>   (a) all recruitment of personnel in the Canadian Forces is voluntary. Canada does not practice conscription or any form of forced or obligatory service. In this regard, recruitment campaigns of the Canadian Forces are informational in nature. If an individual wishes to enter the Canadian Forces, he or she fills in an application. If the Canadian Forces offer a particular position to the candidate, the latter is not obliged to accept the position;
>   (b) recruitment of personnel under the age of 18 is done with the informed and written consent of the person's parents or legal guardians. Article 20, paragraph 3, of the National Defence Act states that 'a person under the age of eighteen years shall not be enrolled without the consent of one of the parents or the guardian of that person',
>   (c) personnel under the age of 18 are fully informed of the duties involved in military service. The Canadian Forces provide, among other things, a series of informational brochures and films on the duties involved in military service to those who wish to enter the Canadian Forces; and
>   (d) personnel under the age of 18 must provide reliable proof of age prior to acceptance into national military service. An applicant must provide a legally recognized document, that is an original or a certified copy of their birth certificate or baptismal certificate, to prove his or her age.

Rome Statute of the International Criminal Court
Reference: [2002] CanTS no. 13
Date of adoption: 17 July 1998
Date of Canada's ratification/accession: 7 July 2000 (R)
Date of entry into force for Canada: 1 July 2002
Reservations, statements or declarations made by Canada: None

Optional Protocol to the Convention on the Elimination of Discrimination Against Women
Reference: Not yet listed in CanTS
Date of adoption: 6 October 1999
Date of Canada's ratification/accession: 18 October 2002 (A)
Date of entry into force for Canada:18 January 2003
Reservations, statements or declarations made by Canada: None

ILO Conventions

Abolition of Forced Labour Convention (No. 105)
Reference: [1960] CanTS no. 21
Date of adoption: 25 June 1957
Date of Canada's ratification/accession: 14 July 1959 (R)
Date of entry into force for Canada: 14 July 1960
Reservations, statements or declarations made by Canada: None

Discrimination (Employment and Occupation) Convention (No. 111)
Reference: 362 UNTS 31 (Canada is a state party, but the treaty is not published in CanTS)
Date of adoption: 25 June 1958
Date of Canada's ratification/accession: 26 November 1964 (R)
Date of entry into force for Canada: 26 November 1965
Reservations, statements or declarations made by Canada: None

Freedom of Association and Protection of the Right to Organize Convention (No. 87)
Reference: [1973] CanTS no. 14
Date of adoption: 9 July 1948
Date of Canada's ratification/accession: 23 March 1972 (R)
Date of entry into force for Canada: 23 March 1973
Reservations, statements or declarations made by Canada: None

Equal Remuneration Convention (No. 100)
Reference: [1973] CanTS no. 37
Date of adoption: 29 June 1951
Date of Canada's ratification/accession: 16 November 1972 (R)

Date of entry into force for Canada: 16 November 1973
Reservations, statements or declarations made by Canada: None

Worst Forms of Child Labour Convention (No. 182)
Reference: [2001] CanTS no. 2
Date of adoption: 17 June 1999
Date of Canada's ratification/accession: 6 June 2000 (R)
Date of entry into force for Canada: 19 November 2000
Reservations, statements or declarations made by Canada: None

OAS Treaties

Charter of the Organization of American States (as amended)
Reference: [1990] CanTS no. 23
Date of adoption: 30 April 1948
Date of Canada's ratification/accession: 8 January 1990
Date of entry into force for Canada: 8 January 1990
Reservations, statements or declarations made by Canada: None

Convention on the Nationality of Women
Reference: [1991] CanTS no. 28
Date of adoption: 26 December 1933
Date of Canada's ratification/accession: 23 October 1991 (A)
Date of entry into force for Canada: 23 October 1991
Reservations, statements or declarations made by Canada: None

Convention on the Granting of Civil Rights to Women
Reference: [1991] CanTS no. 30
Date of adoption: 2 May 1948
Date of Canada's ratification/accession: 23 October 1991 (A)
Date of entry into force for Canada: 23 October 1991
Reservations, statements or declarations made by Canada: None

Convention on the Granting of Political Rights to Women
Reference: [1991] CanTS no. 29
Date of adoption: 2 May 1948
Date of Canada's ratification/accession: 23 October 1991 (A)
Date of entry into force for Canada: 23 October 1991
Reservations, statements or declarations made by Canada: None

Other Treaties

Geneva Convention for the Amelioration of the Condition of the Wounded and Sick in Armed Forces in the Field
Reference: [1965] CanTS no. 20
Date of adoption: 12 August 1949
Date of Canada's ratification/accession: 14 May 1965 (R)
Date of entry into force for Canada: 14 November 1965
Reservations, statements or declarations made by Canada: None

Geneva Convention for the Amelioration of the Condition of Wounded, Sick and Shipwrecked Members of Armed Forces at Sea
Reference: [1965] CanTS no. 20
Date of adoption: 12 August 1949
Date of Canada's ratification/accession: 14 May 1965 (R)
Date of entry into force for Canada: 14 November 1965
Reservations, statements or declarations made by Canada: None

Geneva Convention relative to the Treatment of Prisoners of War
Reference: [1965] CanTS no. 20
Date of adoption: 12 August 1949
Date of Canada's ratification/accession: 14 May 1965 (R)
Date of entry into force for Canada: 14 November 1965
Reservations, statements or declarations made by Canada: None

Geneva Convention relative to the Protection of Civilian Persons in Time of War
Reference: [1965] CanTS no. 20
Date of adoption: 12 August 1949
Date of Canada's ratification/accession: 14 May 1965 (R)
Date of entry into force for Canada: 14 November 1965
Reservations, statements or declarations made by Canada: None

Protocol Additional to the Geneva Conventions of 12 August 1949, and relating to the Protection of Victims of International Armed Conflicts (Protocol I)
Reference: [1991] CanTS no. 2
Date of adoption: 8 June 1977
Date of Canada's ratification/accession: 20 November 1990 (R)
Date of entry into force for Canada: 20 May 1991
Reservations, statements or declarations made by Canada:

Reservations (made upon ratification):

Article 11 — Protection of persons (Medical procedures)

The Government of Canada does not intend to be bound by the prohibitions contained in Article 11, sub-paragraph 2 (c), with respect to Canadian nationals or other persons ordinarily resident in Canada who may be interned, detained or otherwise deprived of liberty as a result of a situation referred to in Article 1, so long as the removal of tissue or organs for transplantation is in accordance with Canadian laws and applicable to the population generally and the operation is carried out in accordance with normal Canadian medical practices, standards and ethics.

Article 39 — Emblems of nationality (Enemy uniforms)

The Government of Canada does not intend to be bound by the prohibitions contained in paragraph 2 of Article 39 to make use of military emblems, insignia or uniforms of adverse parties in order to shield, favour, protect or impede military operations.

Statement of understanding (made upon ratification): (Conventional weapons)

It is the understanding of the Government of Canada that the rules introduced by Protocol I were intended to apply exclusively to conventional weapons. In particular, the rules so introduced do not have any effect on and do not regulate or prohibit the use of nuclear weapons.

Article 38 — Recognized emblems (Protective emblems)

It is the understanding of the Government of Canada that, in relation to Article 38, in situations where the Medical Service of the armed forces of a party to an armed conflict is identified by another emblem than the emblems referred to in Article 38 of the First Geneva Convention of August 12, 1949, that other emblem, when notified, should be respected by the adverse party as a protective emblem in the conflict, under analogous conditions to those imposed by the Geneva Conventions of 1949 and the Additional Protocols of 1977 for the use of emblems referred to in Article 38 of the First Geneva Convention and Protocol I. In such situations, misuse of such an emblem should be considered as misuse of emblems referred to in Article 38 of the First Geneva Convention and Protocol I.

Articles 41, 56, 57, 58, 78 and 86 (Meaning of "'feasible")

It is the understanding of the Government of Canada that in relation to Article 41, 56, 57, 58, 78 and 86 the word "feasible" means that which is practicable or practically possible, taking into account all circumstances ruling at the time, including humanitarian and military considerations.

Article 44 — Combatants and prisoners of war (Combatant status)

It is understanding of the Government of Canada that:
(a.) the situation described in the second sentence of paragraph 3 of Article 44 can exist only in occupied territory or in armed conflicts covered by paragraph 4 of Article 1; and (b.) the word "deployment" in paragraph 3 of Article 44 includes any movement towards a place from which an attack is to be launched.

Part IV, Section I — General protection against effects of hostilities (Standard for decision-making)

It is the understanding of the Government of Canada that, in relation to Articles 48, 51 to 60 inclusive, 62 and 67, military commanders and others responsible for planning, deciding upon or executing attacks have to reach decisions on the basis of their assessment of the information reasonably available to them at the relevant time and that such decisions cannot be judged on the basis of information which has subsequently come to light.

Article 52 — General protection of civilian objects (Military objectives)

It is the understanding of the Government of Canada in relation to Article 52 that: (a.) a specific area of land may be a military objective if, because of its location or other reasons specified in the Article as to what constitutes a military objective, its total or partial destruction, capture or neutralization in the circumstances governing at the time offers a definite military advantage; and (b.) the first sentence of paragraph 2 of the Article is not intended to, nor does it, deal with the question of incidental or collateral damage resulting from an attack directed against a military objective.

Article 53 — Protection of cultural objects and of places of workshop (Cultural objects)

It is the understanding of the Government of Canada in relation to Article 53 that: (a.) such protection as is afforded by the Article will be lost during such time as the protected property is used for military purposes; and (b.) the prohibitions contained in sub-paragraphs (a) and (b) of this Article can only be waived when military necessity imperatively requires such a waiver.

Article 51, sub-paragraph 5 (b), 52, paragraph 2, and 57, clause 2 (a) (iii) (Military advantage)

It is the understanding of the Government of Canada in relation to sub-paragraph 5 (b) of Article 51, paragraph 2 of Article 52, and clause 2 (a) (iii) of Article 57 that the military advantage anticipated from an attack is intended to refer to the advantage anticipated from the attack considered as a whole and not from isolated or particular parts of the attack.

Article 62 — General protection (Protection of civil defence personnel)

It is the understanding of the Government of Canada that nothing in Article 62 will prevent Canada from using assigned civil defence personnel or volunteer civil defence workers in Canada in accordance with nationally established priorities regardless of the military situation.

Article 96 — Treaty relations upon entry into force of this Protocol, paragraph 3 (Declaration by national liberation movement)

It is the understanding of the Government of Canada that the making of a unilateral declaration does not, in itself, validate the credentials of the person or persons making such declaration and that States are entitled to satisfy themselves as to whether in fact the makers of such declaration constitute an authority referred to in Article 96. In this respect, the fact that such authority has or has not been recognized as such by an appropriate regional intergovernmental organization is relevant.

Declaration (made upon ratification):

Article 90 — International Fact-Finding Commission

The Government of Canada declares that it recognizes ipso facto and without special agreement, in relation to any other High Contracting Party accepting the same oligation, the competence of the Commission to enquire, as authorized by Article 90 of Protocol I, into allegations by such other Party that it has been the victim of violations amounting to a grave breach or other serious violation of the Geneva Conventions of 1949 or of Protocol I.

Protocol Additional to the Geneva Conventions of 12 August 1949, and relating to the Protection of Victims of Non-International Armed Conflicts (Protocol II)
Same reference, date of adoption, date of ratification and date of entry into force as Protocol I
Reservations, statements or declarations made by Canada:

Statement of understanding (made upon ratification):

> The Government of Canada understands that the undefined terms used in Additional Protocol II which are defined in Additional Protocol I shall, so far as relevant, be construed in the same sense as those definitions. The understandings expressed by the Government of Canada with respect to Additional Protocol I shall, as far as relevant, be applicable to the comparable terms and provisions contained in Additional Protocol II.

North American Agreement on Labour Cooperation
Reference: [1994] CanTS no. 2
Date of adoption: 14 September 1993
Date of Canada's ratification/accession: 14 September 1993
(binding signature — no requirement of ratification)
Date of entry into force for Canada: 1 January 1994
Reservations, statements or declarations made by Canada: None

TABLE OF
INTERNATIONAL
INSTRUMENTS

Treaties (*protocols are listed with the treaties they amend*):

Other Instruments:

TABLE OF STATUTES

Canadian Statutes (including UK statutes about Canada):

Other Jurisdictions:

TABLE OF CASES

Canadian Cases (including Privy Council appeals from Canada):

Other Jurisdictions:

INDEX

References to international instruments, statutes and cases are not reproduced here. Consult the applicable tables at the end of the book.

ABOUT THE AUTHORS

Mark Freeman holds a BA in liberal arts from McGill University, an LLB from the University of Ottawa, and an LLM from Columbia University. He has published extensively on human rights topics and is currently co-authoring a book on procedural fairness and truth commissions (Cambridge University Press, 2005). Based in Toronto, he is an independent consultant on human rights issues affecting states in democratic and post-conflict transition. He has conducted missions to a wide range of countries including Morocco, Kenya, Ghana, the Democratic Republic of Congo, Burundi, Sri Lanka, Colombia, and Serbia and Montenegro. A member of the Law Society of Upper Canada, he will be a visiting professor at the University of Ottawa Faculty of Law in January 2005.

Gibran van Ert holds a BA in history from McGill University, an MA in law from Sidney Sussex College, Cambridge, and an LLM from the University of Toronto. He is a former law clerk to Madam Justice Prowse of the Court of Appeal for British Columbia (2001–2) and to Justices Gonthier and Fish of the Supreme Court of Canada (2003). He is the author of *Using International Law in Canadian Courts* (Kluwer Law International, 2002). He is a member of the Law Society of British Columbia and practises in Vancouver.

MEMBER OF SCABRINI MEDIA

Quebec, Canada
2004